SOCIAL INCLUSION
AND THE LEGAL SYSTEM:
PUBLIC INTEREST LAW
IN IRELAND

SOCIAL INCLUSION
AND THE LEGAL SYSTEM:
PUBLIC INTEREST LAW
IN IRELAND

BY

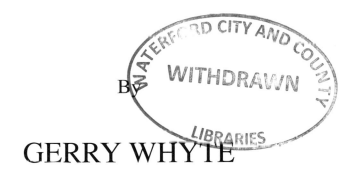

GERRY WHYTE

IPA
INSTITUTE OF PUBLIC
ADMINISTRATION

Published in 2002
by the Institute of Public Administration
57–61 Lansdowne Road
Dublin 4

British Library Cataloguing in Publication Data
A catalogue record for this book
is available from the British Library.

ISBN 1 902448 66 9

Cover design by M&J Graphics, Dublin
Origination by Carole Lynch, Dublin
Printed by Future Print, Dublin

Dedicated to my wife, Mary Bergin, and
to our daughter, Audrey Whyte

The Arthur Cox Foundation

Arthur Cox, solicitor, classical scholar and former President of the Incorporated Law Society of Ireland, was associated with the setting up of many Irish companies, not least the ESB. He was a specialist in company law and was a member of the Company Law Reform Committee which sat from 1951 and reported to the government in 1958, ultimately giving rise to the Companies Act, 1963. When he decided to retire from practice as a solicitor in 1961 a number of his clients, professional colleagues and other friends, in recognition of his outstanding contribution to Ireland and his profession, thought that a fund should be established as a tribute to him which fund would be used to encourage the writing and publication of legal text books. There was a generous response to this appeal.

After his retirement he studied for the priesthood and was ordained in 1963. He went to Zambia to do missionary work. He died there in 1965 as a result of a car accident.

The Foundation was established to honour Arthur Cox and was for many years administered by Mr Justice John Kenny in conjunction with the Law Society. In paying tribute to the memory of Arthur Cox it is appropriate that tribute should also be paid to Mr Justice John Kenny, who died on 25 March, 1987. John Kenny was a close personal friend of Arthur Cox and, like Arthur Cox, graced with distinction his own barristers' profession, as a chancery practitioner, and both the High Court and Supreme Court, as a judge. John Kenny was the encouraging force behind the publication of a number of Irish legal textbooks. Without his quiet drive and enthusiasm there would have been no foundation. To both Arthur Cox and John Kenny we pay tribute.

The Law Society, as the continuing trustee of the Foundation, is pleased to have been able to assist in the publication of this book.

Elma Lynch
President
Law Society of Ireland

December, 2001

Table of Contents

Acknowledgements

In the course of writing this book, I derived great assistance from a number of individuals who agreed to be interviewed about their involvement in public interest law activities, who assisted me in my quest for information or who shared freely with me their technical expertise in relation to different aspects of law and social policy. In that regard, I am very grateful to Frank Brady of the Legal Aid Board, the European Commissioner for Health and Consumer Protection, David Byrne SC, Ian Candy, Mrs Justice Susan Denham, Ronnie Fay of Pavee Point, Brian Gallagher, solicitor, John Hanlon BL, Mr Justice Vivian Lavan, Denis McCullough SC, Gerry Ryan of the National Association for the Mentally Handicapped in Ireland, Marie O'Donoghue, Dr Eoin O'Sullivan of the Department of Social Studies, Trinity College Dublin, Grainne O'Toole of the Irish Traveller Movement, Alan Shatter TD, solicitor, Dr Michael Shevlin of the Education Department, Trinity College Dublin, Dr Patricia Walsh of the Centre for the Study of Developmental Disabilities, National University of Ireland, Dublin and Sheena Walsh McMahon. I am particularly grateful to the following current and past members of the Free Legal Advice Centres Ltd. and the Coolock Community Law Centre Ltd for their assistance with this project and also for their friendship over the years, Éilís Barry BL, Róisín Connolly, solicitor, Mel Cousins BL, Dave Ellis, solicitor, Elisabeth Gallagher-Egan, Iseult O'Malley BL, Síobhan Phelan BL and Peter Ward BL. Three of my colleagues at Trinity College Law School, Professor Yvonne Scannell, Eoin O'Dell and Declan McGrath, provided me with invaluable assistance in relation to different issues covered in this book and to them I express my heartfelt thanks. I owe a debt of a different kind to my other colleagues in the Law School, past and present, for the wonderful working environment they have created and which I have had the great privilege to enjoy for the past twenty years. As will soon become apparent from a perusal of chapter 1, I also owe a considerable intellectual debt to an American colleague and close friend, Professor Michael Perry, for the manner in which he has influenced my thinking on the interaction between law and politics.

Penultimately, I am very grateful to my editor, Tom Turley, for his painstaking work on this book and also to Tony McNamara for seeing this work through to publication. In this context, I would also like to express my gratitude to the trustees of the Arthur Cox Foundation for their generous financial assistance towards the cost of publication.

My final and greatest debt goes to my wife, Mary Bergin, and to our daughter, Audrey, for their love and companionship and for the joy they bring into my life.

While acknowledging my indebtedness to all of the foregoing, the usual disclaimer of responsibility also applies – any errors and omissions are mine alone. I have attempted to describe the state of the law and social policy in Ireland as I understood them to be on 1 March 2001, save that, through the kind indulgence of my publishers, I have been able to add an addendum dealing with the important Supreme Court decisions in *Sinnott v. Minister for Education* and *T.D. v. Minister for Education*, handed down after the main text had gone to the printers.

Gerry Whyte
10 January 2002

Table of Cases

xiii

UNITED KINGDOM

EUROPEAN COURT OF JUSTICE

EUROPEAN COURT OF HUMAN RIGHTS

OTHER JURISDICTIONS

Table of Provisions of the Constitution of Ireland 1937

Table of Statutes

OTHER LEGISLATION

Table of Statutory Instruments and Orders

Table of Legislation of the European Communities

Table of Articles of European Convention on Human Rights

Introduction

Notwithstanding the economic success of the Celtic Tiger, poverty and social exclusion continue to bedevil our society. The structural unemployment of the 1970s and 1980s may be a thing of the past for most people but new problems have taken its place. The exorbitant cost of housing is generating a housing crisis; the State is floundering in its attempts to provide for children who are homeless or otherwise at risk and the influx of asylum-seekers challenges our society to find ways of accommodating different cultures. And, of course, other issues never went away. Travellers continue to endure third world conditions of living; a drug culture ravages our inner cities and we are only beginning to address the needs of people with disabilities.

In an ideal world, the solution to these pressing social problems should emerge from the political system, following a process of deliberation that takes proper account of the needs of all interested parties. Unfortunately, there is reason to believe that the Irish political system does not operate in this way and that it is deaf to the voices of electorally insignificant groups calling for change.[1] It is certainly the case that, during the past twenty years or so, various marginalised groups seeking State support, such as children from dysfunctional families, Travellers, and people with disabilities, have increasingly called on lawyers to assist them in pressing their claims. The most obvious manifestation of this development is the use of what is known as public interest litigation requiring the courts to adjudicate upon claims for increased support from the State. The term "public interest law" was originally coined in the US during the 1970s to describe attempts to use the law and legal services on behalf of the disadvantaged[2] and that is the sense in which this term, and the related term, "public interest litigation", is used in this book. Of course, this is only part of a wider

---

[1] See ch.1, pp. 32 *et seq.*

[2] See Dhavan, "Whose Law? Whose Interest?" in Cooper and Dhavan (eds.) *Public Interest Law* (Basil Blackwell, 1986) at p. 17. The editors of this book define "public interest law" as "the use of litigation and public advocacy (i.e. lobbying by representation or publication) to advance the cause of minority or disadvantaged groups, and individuals, or the public interest" – *op. cit.* at p. 5, though they also accept that the term now embraces the use of the law to promote other sectional interests such as, for example, consumer rights, environmental protection and business interests.

phenomenon of lobby groups relying on the legal system to press their claims and in their time, taxpayers, landlords and farmers, among others, have also had recourse to the courts in defence of sectional interests.[3] In both situations, the courts are being asked to decide cases that can have significant implications for public policy and public expenditure, a position that some judges find quite uncomfortable.

This, however, is not something new. The phenomenon of seeking social and political change through the courts has an older pedigree than is sometimes imagined and Harlow and Rawlings have shown that such litigation was a feature of both the English and US legal systems as early as the late eighteenth century.[4] During the 1960s, however, there was a resurgence of interest among lawyers in the western world in the potential of the legal system to tackle social exclusion. This movement, which embraced strategies such as public advocacy and education in addition to litigation strategy, originated in the United States where, during the first half of the twentieth century, three different historical developments presaged the subsequent emergence in the 1960s of public interest law activities combating social exclusion.[5] The first of these was the establishment of the American Civil Liberties Union in 1920. In seeking to protect civil liberties, this organisation engaged in a variety of different strategies, including litigating, lobbying and educating the public, all of which are now standard strategies of public interest law organisations. The second development was the enactment of the New Deal legislation during the 1930s which involved acceptance of the principle that the State could regulate the market in order to protect public welfare. Finally, also during the 1930s, the National Association for the Advancement of Colored People initiated a comprehensive campaign against the major disabilities encountered by the Afro-American community.[6] An important part of this campaign was a litigation strategy which sought to eliminate racial segregation in education, employment and housing and which scored such notable successes in the courts as *Brown v. Board of Education of Topeka*[7] and *NAACP v. Button.*[8]

---

[3] Thus Barrington J., writing extrajudicially in 1988 on constitutional developments after the 1960s, said, "[C]itizens generally had become more conscious of the Constitution. The civil rights movements in the United States of America and in Northern Ireland made people more concerned with questions of constitutional rights. Significantly the great interest groups in society began to take an interest in the Constitution ... [I]n the past twenty years there have been many cases where interest groups have consciously used the Constitution to redress some grievance of their members. Thus there have been representative actions brought on behalf of farmers, ratepayers, taxpayers, trade unions, bank officials, police officers and many others. This also repeats the American experience and is, perhaps, a healthy phenomenon, as interest groups jostle for power within the context of a society governed by law." Barrington, "The Constitution in the Courts" in Litton, (ed.) *The Constitution of Ireland 1937-1987* (IPA, 1988), 110 at pp. 115-6.

[4] See C. Harlow and R. Rawlings, *Pressure Through Law* (London, 1992), chs. 1 and 2.

[5] For useful accounts of the development of public interest law in the US, see Harlow and Rawlings, ch.2 and Aron, *Liberty and Justice for All: Public Interest Law in the 1980s and beyond* (Westview Press, 1989), ch.1.

[6] For an interesting account of the NAACP's efforts to use the courts to promote its objectives, see Harlow and Rawlings, pp. 81-8.

[7] 347 US 483 (1954); 98 L ed 873.

[8] 371 US 415 (1963); 9 L ed 2d 405. This case had particular significance for litigation strategy in the US in that the Supreme Court invalidated state legislation, directed against the NAACP,

During the 1960s and 1970s, a number of more immediate factors helped to create a climate conducive to the emergence of public interest law activities targeting poverty.[9] First, the Federal Office of Economic Opportunity established a Legal Services Program which was seen as an important aspect of President Johnston's War on Poverty. While there was widespread belief that this programme should contain a legal services component, there was a great deal of controversy about whether legal services should have a law reform orientation or whether it should focus on servicing individual cases. Eventually the proponents of law reform won the debate and this led to the setting up of Law Centres in disadvantaged neighbourhoods throughout the country. While these centres sought to redress substantive inequalities through the use of litigation strategy, including class actions, they also tried to organise their clients around issues of common concern and to engage in political lobbying. Moreover control of the centres was vested in the local communities, from whom members of the management committees were drawn. Using these tactics, the Law Centre movement hoped to break down the social, cultural and psychological barriers that inhibit poor people from availing of legal services.[10] Second, private philanthropic foundations began to fund public interest law activities in relation to civil rights, consumers' rights, protection of the environment and also anti-poverty programmes. Third, law schools and the private bar became involved in these activities through the establishment, respectively, of clinical legal education programmes and programmes of *pro bono* work.

The 1960s were, of course, heady days in the US and not just for public interest lawyers. In contrast, the 1980s witnessed a swing to the right in the politics of the western world generally and the creation of a political environment, particularly in the US, that was very hostile to the use of the law to tackle social disadvantage.[11] Nonetheless the earlier US experience did have an important spin off effect in Ireland in that it led to the fostering of interest in the whole question of access to legal services and this, in turn, was an important catalyst in the development of public interest law

---

prohibiting persons from advising others that their legal rights had been infringed and referring them to particular lawyers and prohibiting the lawyers from taking on such cases. The Court ruled that the activities of the NAACP was a form of political expression and as such protected by the First Amendment to the US Constitution.

9 See Aron, pp. 11-13; Zander, *Legal Services for the Community* (Temple Smith, 1978) at pp. 60-4.

10 Following on the US example, neighbourhood law centres were also established in the UK, Australia, Canada, New Zealand, The Netherlands and Finland. See J. Cooper, *Public Legal Services: A Comparative Study of Policy, Politics and Practice* (1983). One such centre, the Coolock Community Law Centre, was also established in Ireland.

11 See R. Cranston, Legal Foundations of the Welfare State (London, 1985) at pp. 292-3; N. Aron, pp. 14-23; Johnson, "Justice and Reform: A Quarter Century Later" in Regan, Paterson, Goriely, Fleming, The Transformation of Legal Aid: Comparative and Historical Studies (Oxford University Press, 1999) p. 9; Kilwein, "The Decline of the Legal Services Corporation: 'It's ideological, stupid!'" in Regan, Paterson, Goriely, Fleming, p. 41. The last author attributes the decline in the fortunes of the Legal Services Corporation during the 1980s and 1990s to a "thirty year ideological battle waged by radical conservatives opposed to the idea of effective access for the poor to the legal system" – *op. cit.* at p. 43.

activities directed against different aspects of poverty. While such activities relied heavily on the Fabian model for securing reform, i.e. by presenting the case for change through reasoned argument, lobbying and publicity, this emergence of a cadre of public interest lawyers, coupled with the activism of the Ó Dálaigh Supreme Court, inevitably and eventually led to recourse to the courts, from the 1970s onwards, to resolve certain issues of social exclusion.[12]

In the first two parts of this book, I attempt to address a number of important issues raised by this phenomenon of tackling social exclusion through public interest litigation. A very important preliminary question is whether such litigation is legitimate, both from a constitutional and political perspective. Doubts have been expressed about whether, having regard to the constitutional doctrine of separation of powers, the courts can entertain this type of litigation that almost invariably has implications for public spending. Moreover judicial involvement with policy formulation is also open to the charge that it is anti-democratic, given that the judiciary are drawn from an unrepresentative elite and that they are not directly accountable to the electorate. In chapter 1 of this book, I defend the constitutional and political legitimacy of public interest litigation targeting social exclusion. The essence of my argument is that one can infer a commitment to social inclusion from the text of the Constitution and that the most appropriate agency for policing that constitutional norm is the judiciary, given the failure, indeed at times egregious failure, of our political system to attend to the needs of marginalised minorities.

Public interest litigation is qualitatively different from conventional litigation in a number of respects, not the least of which is that it involves the courts in a prospective, ongoing review of State action. In chapter 2, I consider to what extent Irish procedural law is capable of accommodating this qualitatively different type of litigation. My conclusion is that in a number of areas, notably in relation to the rules on standing, the doctrine of mootness, third party interventions and the formulation of remedies, the existing system has the potential to rise to the demands posed by public interest litigation, though further change is required in order to facilitate the taking of group actions. The final chapter in this part of the book looks at some practical difficulties arising from the use of litigation strategy, especially where legal services are provided on a *pro bono* basis as is often the case where litigation involving marginalised groups is concerned.

While such academic comment as there is on public interest litigation in this jurisdiction tends to focus on the constitutional legitimacy of judicial activism, an equally important issue, in my opinion, is whether litigation is actually an effective method of achieving social change. Accordingly, in Part 2 of the book, I attempt to evaluate the use of litigation in obtaining improved State support for four low-income or marginalised groups. These are social welfare claimants, children from

[12] At least two NGOs, the Simon Community and the Irish Traveller Movement, have published material examining the potential for litigation to resolve the social difficulties they encounter – see *Practical Aspects of Bringing a Right to Shelter Case to the Supreme Court* (Simon Community, 1985) and *Traveller Accommodation and the Law: Action for Change through the Courts* (Irish Traveller Movement, 1991).

dysfunctional families and children with mental handicap, Travellers and, finally, a low-income group encountered directly by the judicial system itself, litigants seeking free legal aid. My general conclusion here is that litigation strategy is a limited, but nonetheless, useful mechanism for promoting social inclusion. It certainly enhances the procedural rights of marginalised groups and occasionally is capable, on its own, of achieving some substantive change. However, its principal value arguably lies in the fact that it can require the political system to begin to address issues of social exclusion that would otherwise be ignored. Rather than pre-empting politics, litigation strategy can provoke politics. Ultimately, therefore, it is most effective when used in conjunction with a political campaign designed to elicit a particular response from the executive or legislative branches of government.

It follows that recourse to the courts cannot be regarded as a complete alternative to the use of political campaigning. In the final part of the book, therefore, I examine the role of the law generally in tackling social exclusion, with particular reference to Ireland. This entails an examination of different models of legal aid and an evaluation of both the State and voluntary legal aid sector in Ireland. Again, I come to a relatively modest conclusion, which is that while the legal system is not capable of generating radical change in society, within the paradigm of the capitalist order, the strategic model of legal aid is capable of achieving limited but nonetheless worthwhile social reforms.

****

Social exclusion is not, in my opinion, an inevitable state of nature. Rather it stems from the manner in which we as a society arrange our affairs. In particular, it is affected by decisions taken in relation to public finances – decisions as to who pays taxes and at what rate, what resources are to be exempt from taxation and what services and financial support the State should provide for its citizens.

Given that it is largely a social construct, the existence of social exclusion in our society should be a matter of concern of all citizens. The position defended in this book is that it is also legitimately a matter of concern for members of the judiciary acting in their professional capacity, given their obligation to uphold a Constitution that is committed, *inter alia*, to assuring the dignity and freedom of the individual and to assuring true social order. To those who argue that it is anti-democratic for the judiciary to take on such a role, the short answer is that, as experience has shown, it is always possible for the People to assert the primacy of their views over those emanating from the courts. So one should not overestimate the impact that the judiciary may have on issues of social justice and, by the same token, one must accept that ultimately such matters will have to be resolved through the political process. However where that process persistently ignores the needs of marginalised minorities, the use of public interest litigation as a means of eliciting an appropriate political response to those needs is, in my opinion, entirely legitimate.

"Think of the poorest person you have ever seen and ask if your next act will be of any use to him".

M.K. Gandhi

(1869-1948)

PART 1

PUBLIC INTEREST LITIGATION PROMOTING SOCIAL INCLUSION – THEORETICAL AND PRACTICAL ISSUES

Chapter 1

The Legitimacy of Judicial Activism on behalf of the Disadvantaged

The practice of resorting to the courts to resolve contentious social issues has a longer pedigree than is sometimes realised, dating back to the late eighteenth century at least.[1] In more recent times, this phenomenon was given a significant fillip in this jurisdiction by the judicial discovery of implied fundamental rights in the Constitution in *Ryan v. Attorney General*[2] and since then a variety of interest groups have sought to have their grievances redressed in the context of constitutional litigation. More recently again, there is evidence of a growing tendency for marginalised groups concerned with social exclusion to bring their case before the courts. In particular, the courts have had to consider constitutional claims advanced by Travellers, children from dysfunctional backgrounds and children with severe mental handicap. Typically, the claim is that the plaintiff is entitled, usually under the Constitution, to a social service that the political process has failed to provide. Such claims clearly raise issues concerning the legitimacy of asking the courts to direct the legislature or the executive to provide such services and so in this chapter we address the topic of the legitimacy, both constitutional and political, of judicial activism on behalf of the disadvantaged.

In a carefully reasoned judgment, the constitutional legitimacy of such activism was denied by Costello J. (as he then was) in *O'Reilly v. Limerick Corporation*.[3] The facts of the case, briefly, were that the plaintiffs were members of the Travelling community residing, in conditions of great poverty and deprivation, in caravans on unofficial sites in the city of Limerick. The plaintiffs had no running water or toilet facilities; no hard surface on which to place their caravans; no means for storing their domestic refuse and

---

[1] Thus in the late eighteenth and early nineteenth centuries, abolitionists in both the UK and the US attempted to counteract slavery through the courts – see Harlow and Rawlings, *Pressure Through Law* (London, 1992), chs.1 and 2.
[2] [1965] IR 294.
[3] [1989] ILRM 181.

no service for its collection and, as noted by the judge, they had been described by the city manager in a report to the city council of 4 December 1987 as "living in totally unacceptable conditions without basic facilities". The plaintiffs' legal claim was summarised by Costello J. as follows:

> The plaintiffs' wants are comparatively modest. They do not demand that they be rehoused by the corporation; what they need are serviced halting sites, that is, sites with hard surfaces on which their caravans could be placed, toilet facilities, running water and a regular refuse collection. Their principal claim is for a mandatory injunction directing the corporation to provide such sites, claiming that the corporation have a duty to do so under the Housing Act, 1966. Their second principal claim is that the State should pay them damages for the suffering, inconvenience and mental distress which they have undergone, a claim based on an allegation that the conditions which they have been required to endure amounted to a breach of their constitutional rights.[4]

In the event, Costello J. dismissed this particular claim, essentially on the ground that he had no authority, under the Constitution, to entertain it.[5] As he put it, such a demand "should, to comply with the Constitution, be advanced in Leinster House rather than in the Four Courts".[6] This decision stands full square in opposition to public interest litigation, for if Costello J. is correct, then much of the type of litigation with which public interest lawyers are concerned is precluded by the Constitution. So *O'Reilly* forces us to confront the question – is it ever legitimate for the courts to attempt to protect economically and socially disadvantaged groups against (a) legislative or executive action which is inimical to their interests or, more commonly, (b) legislative or executive inaction which means that the pressing needs of such groups are not addressed by the political process?[7]

While I can appreciate the concerns for the democratic process which underpin Costello J.'s position in *O'Reilly*, and while in consequence I would not advocate that marginalised groups should have recourse to the courts as a first resort for a solution of their problems, nonetheless I defend the legitimacy of judicial activism in elaborating the constitutional rights of marginalised groups in circumstances in which it is apparent that their rights are not adequately protected by the political process. In defending this position, I begin by providing a more detailed account of Costello J.'s reasoning in *O'Reilly* before moving on to consider, in sequence, three possible defences of his position. The first of these is the contention that, as a matter of constitutional law, judges are precluded from engaging in judicial activism on behalf of marginalised groups. The second is the view, rooted in political theory, that democratic politics precludes such a role. Finally, there is the objection that the courts are incapable of performing this function.

---

[4] *Ibid.* at p. 182.
[5] The statutory claims made by the Travellers are considered below in ch. 6.
[6] At p. 195.
[7] As this book is concerned with the use of public interest litigation to promote social inclusion, it is worth emphasising that my concern in this chapter is in evaluating the legitimacy of judicial activism *specifically on behalf of disadvantaged groups*, not judicial activism *per se,* though no doubt some of my arguments may be relevant to that larger issue.

I conclude the chapter by making the case for judicial recognition and enforcement of socio-economic rights in circumstances where the existence of such rights is a necessary condition for ensuring participation in society but where one is also sceptical about the ability of the political process to protect such rights. In this context, I also consider the recent debate on the inclusion of socio-economic rights in the Constitution provoked by the Report of the Constitution Review Group.

Costello J.'s reasoning in *O'Reilly v. Limerick Corporation*

In dismissing the plaintiffs' constitutional claim, Costello J. relied heavily upon the Aristotelian distinction between commutative (or corrective) justice, which is properly the concern of the courts, and distributive justice, which he considered to be exclusively the concern of the Government:

> There is an important distinction to be made between the relationship which arises in dealings between individuals (a term which includes dealings between individuals and servants of the State and public authorities) and the relationship which arises between the individual and those in authority in a political community (which for convenience I will call the Government) when goods held in common for the benefit of the entire community ... fall to be distributed and allocated. Different obligations in justice arise from these different relationships. Distributive justice is concerned with the distribution and allocation of common goods and common burdens. But it cannot be said that any of the goods held in common ... belong exclusively to any member of the political community. An obligation in distributive justice is placed on those administering the common stock of goods, the common resource and the wealth held in common which has been raised by taxation to distribute them and the common wealth fairly and to determine what is due to each individual. But that distribution can only be made by reference to the common good and by those charged with furthering the common good (the Government); it cannot be made by any individual who may claim a share in the common stock and no independent arbitrator, such as a Court, can adjudicate on a claim by an individual that he has been deprived of what is his due. This situation is very different in the case of commutative justice. What is due to an individual from another individual (including a public authority) from a relationship arising from their mutual dealings can be ascertained and is due to him exclusively and the precepts of commutative justice will enable an arbitrator such as a Court to decide what is properly due should the matter be disputed. This distinction explains why the court has jurisdiction to award damages against the State when a servant of the State for whose activity it is vicariously liable commits a wrong and why it may not get jurisdiction in cases where the claim is for damages based on a failure to distribute adequately in the plaintiffs' favour a portion of the community's wealth.[8]

On reviewing the constitutional design for the governing of the State, Costello J. concluded that this distinction accorded well with the constitutional text and continued:

---

[8] [1989] ILRM 181 at p. 194.

What could be involved in the exercise of the [jurisdiction suggested by the plaintiff] would be the imposition by the Court of its view that there had been an unfair distribution of national resources. To arrive at such a conclusion, it would have to make an assessment of the validity of the many competing claims on those resources, the correct priority to be given to them and the financial implications of the plaintiffs' claim. As the present case demonstrates, it may also be required to decide whether a correct allocation of physical resources available for public purposes has been made. In administering this function the Court would not be administering justice as it does when determining an issue relating to commutative justice but it would be engaged in an entirely different exercise, namely, an adjudication on the fairness or otherwise of the manner in which other organs of State had administered public resources. Apart from the fact that members of the judiciary have no special qualification to undertake such a function, the manner in which justice is administered in the Courts, that is on a case by case basis, make them a wholly inappropriate institution for the fulfillment of the suggested role. I cannot construe the Constitution as conferring it on them.[9]

The decision of Costello J. in *O'Reilly* is a very valuable contribution to the debate about the role of the courts in Irish society.[10] As the only attempt to date by an Irish judge to provide guidelines for delimiting the boundary between the judicial and legislative functions,[11] it has very properly been described as "the beginning of an

---

[9] At p. 195.

[10] And was cited with approval by the Supreme Court in *MhicMhathúna v. Attorney General* [1995] 1 IR 484; [1995] 1 ILRM 69.

[11] Of all the cases before the Irish courts in which the doctrine of separation of powers has been implicated, only seven, including *O'Reilly,* involved the rejection of a plaintiff's claim on the ground that the claim should be more properly addressed to the Oireachtas. The remaining six cases are *O'Shaughnessy v. Attorney General,* unreported, High Court, 16 February 1971, in which O'Keeffe P. dismissed a challenge to the Criminal Justice (Legal Aid) Act 1962 because it failed to make provision for civil legal aid; *L. v. L.* [1992] 2 IR 77; [1992] ILRM 115 and the companion case, *N. v. N.* [1992] 2 IR 116, [1992] ILRM 127, in which the Supreme Court dismissed claims that the plaintiffs were entitled to a share in the matrimonial home by virtue of Article 41; *A.D. v. Ireland* [1994] 1 IR 369 in which Carroll J. rejected the plaintiff's claim that she was entitled to compensation from the State because of certain criminal injuries sustained by her; *MhicMhathúna v. Attorney General* [1995] 1 IR 484; [1995] 1 ILRM 69 in which the Supreme Court held, approving *O'Reilly,* that the plaintiff's claim that the tax and welfare codes discriminated unlawfully against married families raised issues of distributive justice which fell within the remit of the legislature and executive, rather than the courts; and *Wright v. Board of Management of Gorey Community School,* unreported, High Court, 28 March 2000, in which O'Sullivan J. declined to accede to the request of the applicant, a minor, that limitations be placed on the reporting of the case. In each of these cases, the court did not go beyond simply stating that recognition of such claims was a matter for the legislature. In three other cases, the courts refused to direct the executive to take a specified course of action. In *The State (C) v. Frawley* [1976] IR 365, Finlay P. held that he could not require the executive to provide a specialised psychiatric unit for prisoners. In *Comerford v. Minister for Education* [1997] 2 ILRM 134, McGuinness J. refused to take up an invitation from counsel to consider and deal with the issue of limitation of expenditure in cases concerning the constitutional rights of children to free primary education on the ground that "for the Court to embark on such an exercise would be a wrongful trespass by the

increased sophistication in the manner by which the judiciary view their relationship with the other branches of government".[12] Nonetheless, I would submit that this decision does not conclusively establish the proposition that Irish judges are constitutionally precluded from enforcing socio-economic rights that promote social inclusion. In the first place, the distinction between distributive and commutative justice is not always as watertight as appears from *O'Reilly*. Claims on commutative justice may have implications for public expenditure[13] and cannot be discounted by the courts simply for that reason. Second, and going to the heart of this dicussion about the role of the judge in relation to issues of social and economic exclusion, one might question whether the Constitution does erect an impenetrable barrier between the courts and issues of distributive justice. For example, Article 42.4 would appear to give parents and children a justiciable right to insist that the State should finance primary education, a right enforced, indeed, by O'Hanlon and Barr JJ. in the case of severely mentally handicapped children in *O'Donoghue v. Minister for Health*[14] and

---

Court into the prerogative of the Executive power." – [1997] 2 ILRM 134 at p. 146. Nonetheless, she did go on to grant a declaration that the respondents had failed in their constitutional duty to provide for a suitable primary education for the applicant. Finally, in its *ex tempore* decision in *Breathnach v. Ireland*, unreported, 3 December 1998, the Supreme Court held that it was not part of its function to enter into a general commission of inquiry into the various actions of various departments of government relating to the prison system.

12 Byrne and Binchy, *Annual Review of Irish Law 1988* (Dublin, 1989) at p. 115.

13 See, e.g. *The State (Healy) v. Donoghue* [1976] IR 325; *Murphy v. Attorney General* [1982] IR 241; *Blake v. Attorney General* [1982] IR 117, cases which either resulted in increased public expenditure or reduced tax yields. Writing in the context of the US Constitution, Eisenberg and Yeazell observed, "When the courts order the government to observe an individual's right, the government must relinquish some existing claim of dominion over that individual. This diminished authority may obscure a corresponding and inevitable financial expense: whatever money the individual might have provided must be raised in some other way, or the government's desired objective must be attained through the exertion of extra effort on its part. When, however, the person asserting the newly recognized right is particularly dependent on the government, recognition of the right may involve a more obvious, direct expenditure of funds: a schoolchild must be given certain educational advantages, a prisoner must receive an additional blanket, an inmate of a mental institution must be furnished with medical care. But whether or not the expenditure is obvious, judicial enforcement of individual rights often necessarily involves the reallocation of funds." – "The Ordinary and the Extraordinary in Institutional Litigation" (1980) 93 *Harv. L. Rev* 465 at p. 507.

14 [1996] 2 IR 20. An appeal against this decision taken by the Minister was settled shortly after argument in the case began before the Supreme Court – see *The Irish Times*, 7 March 1997. Just over eighteen months later, and facing at that time a further 56 High Court actions, the Minister for Education announced the creation of an extra 65 teaching posts and approximately 200 childcare jobs designed to provide a formal system of education and childcare for primary school children with special educational needs – *The Irish Times*, 6 November 1998.

Staying with the constitutional right to free primary education, in *O'Shiel v. Minister for Education and Science* [1999] 2 IR 321; [1999] 2 ILRM 241, the plaintiffs challenged the State's refusal to provide financial support for their primary school. The defendants argued, *inter alia*, that the determination of eligibility for public funding in this context was an issue of policy and not a matter for the courts. Dismissing this argument, Laffoy J. said, [1999] 2 IR 321 at p. 348 and [1999] 2 ILRM 241 at p. 264:

Sinnott v. Minister for Education[15] respectively. Another judge, Kelly J., has instructed the Minister for Justice to provide and maintain high support units for children in care[16] while in *McKenna v. An Taoiseach (No.2)*[17] the Supreme Court reviewed a decision of the Government to spend public funds on a publicity campaign in the divorce referendum. Another possible example here is Article 41.2.2 which obliges the State to endeavour to ensure that mothers are not obliged by economic necessity to work outside the home. While some judges are, admittedly, uncomfortable with this provision,[18] Finlay C.J. accepted, in *L. v. L.,*[19] that it imposed an obligation on the judiciary as well as on the legislature and the executive.

This last objection to Costello J.'s reasoning is the most fundamental. Essentially my argument here is that the Irish Constitution, partly inspired as it is by the Judeo-Christian tradition, does provide, both explicitly and implicitly, for the protection of socio-economic rights and that such rights are judicially enforceable, albeit that going to court should be seen as a last resort, a course of action to be pursued only where the political process has failed to protect the rights in question.[20] Before we get to that point, however, it is necessary to consider the three possible defences of Costello J.'s position in *O'Reilly* referred to above.[21]

Is judicial activism precluded by the Constitution?

The first of these is the suggestion that the Constitution, as a matter of law, precludes judicial activism on behalf of marginalised groups. Two different points have to be addressed here. First, it is sometimes argued that such activism is precluded by virtue of the doctrine of separation of powers.[22] In particular, it is sometimes suggested that judges have no function in filling gaps in social policy left by the legislature or

---

"Unquestionably fixing the parameters of the criteria for recognition of a primary school and consequent eligibility for public funding has budgetary implications. However, in my view, it does not follow that the issue whether the criteria fixed are proper having regard to the provisions of the Constitution is not justiciable. Nor does it follow that the Court would be usurping the function of the Executive if it were to find that any criterion was wrongfully exclusionary against the constitutional interest of a child or his parent and if it were to direct that proper provision in accordance with the State's constitutional obligation be made for the child. As pointed out in Casey in *Constitutional Law in Ireland,* 2nd edition at page 526 the judgments in *Byrne v. Ireland* [1972] IR 241 show that, failing action by other organs of State, it falls to the Courts to secure performance of the State's constitutional obligations."

15 Unreported, High Court, 4 October 2000.
16 See *D.B. v. Minister for Justice* [1999] 1 IR 29; [1999] 1 ILRM 93 and *T.D. v. Minister for Education* [2000] 3 IR 62; [2000] 2 ILRM 321.
17 [1995] 2 IR 10.
18 Barrington J. described it as a duty of imperfect obligation in *Hyland v. Minister for Social Welfare* [1989] IR 624 at p. 639; [1989] ILRM 196 at p. 208.
19 [1992] ILRM 115, at 121.
20 See below, pp. 43 *et seq.*
21 See p. 10.
22 See, for example, the comments of the *Report of the Constitution Review Group* (Pn.2632) at pp. 235-6.

executive. Second, it is sometimes argued that the only legitimate way in which to interpret the Constitution is one in which the judges are prevented from formulating public policy. Debate in the US about methods of constitutional interpretation forms an important backdrop to Irish academic commentary on this issue.[23] I will take each point in turn.

a) Doctrine of separation of powers

The Constitution nowhere explicitly prescribes a separation of powers among the different branches of government. However such a doctrine has been held to be inherent in Article 6.[24] That Article reads:

1. All powers of government, legislative, executive and judicial, derive, under God, from the people, whose right it is to designate the rulers of the State and, in final appeal, to decide all questions of national policy, according to the requirements of the common good.
2. These powers of government are exercisable only by or on the authority of the organs of State established by this Constitution.

Other constitutional provisions, notably Article 15.2.1 ("The sole and exclusive power of making laws for the State is hereby vested in the Oireachtas: no other legislative authority has power to make laws for the State"), Article 28.2 ("The executive power of the State shall, subject to the provisions of this Constitution, be exercised by or on the authority of the Government") and Article 34.1 ("Justice shall be administered in courts established by law by judges appointed in the manner provided by this Constitution, ...")

> do in fact entrench the different arms of government in varying degrees and prescribe their sovereignty in their own areas, without, however, hermetically insulating the different powers from one another in all respects;...[25]

---

23 See Quinn, "Reflections on the Legitimacy of Judicial Activism in the Field of Constitutional Law" (Winter 1991) *DLí* 29; by the same writer, "The Nature and Significance of Critical Legal Studies" (1989) 7 *I.L.T.* 282; Hogan, "Unenumerated Personal Rights: *Ryan's* Case Re-Evaluated" (1990-1992) XXV-XXVII *Ir. Jur.* 95; Humphreys, "Constitutional Interpretation" (1993) 15 *DULJ (n.s.)* 57; by the same writer, "Interpreting Natural Rights" (1993-1995) XXVIII-XXX *Ir. Jur.* 221; and Kavanagh, "The Quest for Legitimacy in Constitutional Interpretation" (1997) XXXII *Ir. Jur.* 195. It is, perhaps, worth sounding a cautionary note about excessive reliance on the US debate for the purpose of illuminating aspects of Irish constitutional law for, as Ely comments, "What has distinguished [the US Constitution], and indeed the United States itself, has been a process of government, not a governing ideology" – *Democracy and Distrust: A Theory of Judicial Review* (Cambridge, 1980) at p. 100. A similar point is made by Ackerman when he contrasts the US Constitution with what he calls "foundationalist" constitutions such as that of the former West Germany – *We the People: Foundations* (Cambridge, 1991), pp. 10-16. Insofar as the Irish Constitution endorses a particular ideology (or ideologies), rather than simply establishing a system of government, the lessons to be learnt from the US experience may be of limited relevance.

24 See the remarks of Finlay C.J. and O'Flaherty J. in *Attorney General v. Hamilton (No.1)* [1993] 2 IR 250 at pp. 267-8 and 299 respectively; [1993] ILRM 81, at pp. 96 and 123-4 respectively. See also *Laurentiu v. Minister for Justice, Equality and Law Reform* [1999] 4 IR 26; [2000] 1 ILRM 1.

25 *Kelly's The Irish Constitution* (3rd ed.) (Hogan and Whyte, eds.) (Dublin, 1994) at p. 40.

However the simple fact remains that the literal text of these provisions does not tell us, one way or another, whether Irish judges may legitimately engage in judicial activism on behalf of disadvantaged groups.[26] To answer that question, one has to supply a set of political values which either precludes or tolerates such a role. The following comment by Sunstein in relation to the interpretation of legal documents generally makes my point.

> Every legal text requires interpreters to draw on background principles that they must supply. It is often true that a text has a plain meaning, or that there is no room for interpretative doubt. But when this is so, it is because there is no disagreement about the appropriate background principles. It is not because there is a preinterpretive "fact" that people can uncover without resort to substantive principles.
>
> Those who deny the existence of such principles are without self-consciousness. They believe that their own views are so self-evident that they do not amount to interpretive principles at all, but instead are just "part" of the text. But interpretive principles are always at work. That is no embarrassment to constitutional law, or indeed to law itself, but instead an inevitable part of the exercise of reason in human affairs. The question is not whether interpretive principles exist, but whether they can be defended in substantive terms.[27]

As a matter of Irish constitutional law, the political values to be used in interpreting the Constitution (and specifically, in our context, the doctrine of separation of powers) must be rooted in the democratic tradition.[28] Thereafter, however, the constitutional text does not explicitly prescribe what understanding of democracy is to prevail nor does it explicitly proscribe an activist role for the judiciary.

---

[26] And neither does the Irish jurisprudence on the doctrine of separation of powers – *O'Reilly v. Limerick Corporation* apart – tell us anything about this point. In the leading book on this area, Professor Gwynn Morgan observes that "the Irish judges have been reluctant to articulate and confront the policy choices presented by the separation of powers. Given the peculiar artificiality of the doctrine – embarnacled by several centuries of political thought; admired without being analysed; and imported to Ireland with little or no debate – though regrettable, this reluctance is hardly surprising." – *The Separation of Powers in the Irish Constitution* (Round Hall/Sweet and Maxwell, 1997) at p. 297. In *Laurentiu v. Minister for Justice, Equality and Law Reform* [1999] 4 IR 26; [2000] 1 ILRM 1, Denham J. accepted that the separation of powers under the Irish Constitution is not clear-cut, saying, at p. 21,

> [T]he general structure of the Constitution follows the doctrine of the separation of powers. A similar approach, though not identical, can be seen in the Constitution of the United States of America. The Irish structure is not a simple or clear-cut separation of powers. There is overlapping and impingement of powers. However, in a general sense there is a functional division of power.

On the doctrine of separation of powers, see also McDermott, "The Separation of Powers and the Doctrine of Non-Justiciability" (2000) XXXV *Ir. Jur. (n.s.)* 280.

[27] *The Partial Constitution* (Cambridge, 1993), pp. 103-4. Substantive principles, in Sunstein's lexicon, are those which require a substantive political justification. He distinguishes them from semantic principles which interpret texts in a simple, dictionary sense – *ibid.*, pp. 101-2.

[28] This requirement that the political values must respect democracy is derived from Article 5 of the Constitution which provides that "Ireland is a sovereign, independent, democratic state".

Consequently one cannot argue that the Constitution unequivocally precludes a model of democratic politics which tolerates judicial activism in pursuit of social justice.[29] However the view that our Constitution sets its face against judicial activism of this nature is so ingrained in some quarters that it is necessary to emphasis this very modest point, namely that a reading of the Constitution which precludes judicial activism depends on the prior adoption of a political value system which prizes such restraint.[30] Consequently, if one does not subscribe to such a value system, one will not be persuaded that judicial activism is necessarily precluded by the Constitution.

Before leaving the doctrine of separation of powers, it is necessary to consider one further related issue, namely whether the review function of the courts is limited to reviewing action already taken by the legislature or executive or whether the courts may also review the *failure* of the legislature or executive to take action on a particular point.

In relation to the executive, the Irish courts now accept that an order of mandamus can lie against the Government.[31] Clearly, however, this will not be appropriate in every case in which the Government fails to take a certain course of action. So, for example, in two recent cases, *Cummins v. D.P.P.*,[32] and *Iordache v. Minister for Justice*,[33] the Supreme Court and High Court held, respectively, that the courts had no jurisdiction to direct the Government to arrange for the enactment of the European Convention on Human Rights into domestic law or to bring proceedings under the Constitution against Romania over that country's alleged noncompliance with the Geneva Convention on the Status of Refugees. In both cases, however, the Constitution explicitly precludes the courts from having any role in such matters inasmuch as Article 29.6 provides that the incorporation of international agreements is a matter for the Oireachtas while Article 29 4 1 entrusts the power of the State in relation to foreign affairs to the executive.[34] Subject to this condition of justiciability,

---

[29] Indeed, I argue below for one understanding of constitutional rights which would demand such activism – see pp. 48-9.

[30] "[T]he line separating law from politics is not all that distinct and ... its very location is a question of politics" – Brest, "Interpretation and Interest" (1982) 34 *Stanford L. Rev* 765, at p. 773. I defer consideration of the impact of different versions of democracy on the judicial role until I examine the second possible defence of Costello J.'s position in *O'Reilly* – see below, pp. 28 *et seq.*

[31] See *The State (King) v. Minister for Justice* [1984] IR 169 and *The State (Sheehan) v. Government of Ireland* [1987] IR 550. In the latter case, Costello J. in the High Court said, at p. 555, that "there was no constitutional reason ... which would prohibit the making of an order of mandamus against the Government" though, on appeal, a majority of the Supreme Court held the statutory discretion conferred on the Government to decide when to bring s.60(1) of the Civil Liability Act 1961 into effect was unreviewable by the courts.

[32] Unreported, *ex tempore* decision of the Supreme Court, 3 December 1998.

[33] Unreported, High Court, 30 January 2001.

[34] As we have just noted, in *The State (Sheehan) v. Government of Ireland* [1987] IR 550, the Supreme Court also held that it could not direct the Government to exercise its discretion to bring a statutory provision (s.60(1) of the Civil Liability Act 1961) into effect. However this case turns on the interpretation of the legislation in question rather than on the constitutional limits to the judicial power. But even here, the remarks of O'Flaherty J. in the subsequent case of *Rooney v. Minister for Agriculture and Food* [1991] 2 IR 539 raise the possibility that the courts might have the power to direct the Government to bring into effect a piece of legislation if there was proof of *mala fides* or abuse of power on the part of the Government.

however, the courts do have jurisdiction to review the failure of the executive to act. In particular, where constitutional rights are affected, the court's constitutional duty to vindicate fundamental rights entitles it to review executive inaction.

Thus in a number of cases commencing in the mid-1990s, the High Court repeatedly castigated the executive branch and its administrative agencies for their failure to protect the constitutional rights of certain categories of children.[35] Initially the judges tended to confine themselves to clarifying the rights of the children and the corresponding duties of the State. More recently, however, in *D.B. v. Minister for Justice*[36] Kelly J. directed the respondent to provide sufficient funding to allow the then Eastern Health Board to build, open and maintain a twenty-four bed high support unit for children in the Dublin area. In response to counsel's argument that the court had no jurisdiction to make such an order (insofar as it involved the court in matters of policy), the judge cited the comments of Hamilton C.J. in *D.G. v. Eastern Health Board*[37] in support of the proposition that "in carrying out its constitutional function of defending and vindicating personal rights, the Court must have available to it any power necessary to do so in an effective way".[38] He also relied on remarks of Finlay C.J. in *Crotty v. An Taoiseach*[39] when rejecting the claim that the court did not have the jurisdiction to interfere with the administrative branch of Government in the manner sought by the applicant.[40] In the event, Kelly J. held that he was not, in fact, interfering with policy in the instant case but rather was acting to ensure that the Minister would implement a policy which he, the Minister, had previously decided upon. At the same time, however, he did remark, *obiter*, that it would be open to the court to become involved in matters of policy if this was required to vindicate personal rights. In deciding to grant the order sought by the applicant in the instant case, Kelly J. took into account the fact that the High Court had already granted declaratory relief concerning the constitutional obligation of the State to provide high support accommodation for children in need of such accommodation; that the necessary steps consequent upon such declarations would have to be taken expeditiously, before the children reached the age of majority, if the declarations were to be of any benefit; that the effect of a failure to provide appropriate facilities would have profound effect on the lives of these chldren and put them at risk of harm; and, finally, that the ministerial response had been "neither proportionate, efficient, timeous or effective".[41]

---

[35] See further below, ch. 5. In one further recent case, *Breathnach v. Ireland* [2000] 3 IR 469, Quirke J. granted a declaration that a failure on the part of the State to provide the applicant, a convicted prisoner, with the necessary machinery to enable him to vote amounted to a breach of the State's obligations under Article 40.1 of the Constitution.

[36] [1999] 1 IR 29; [1999] 1 ILRM 93. See also his decision in *T.D. v. Minister for Education* [2000] 3 IR 62; [2000] 2 ILRM 321.

[37] [1998] 1 ILRM 241.

[38] [1999] 1 IR 29 at p. 40; [1999] 1 ILRM 93 at pp. 101-2.

[39] [1987] IR 713; [1987] ILRM 400.

[40] However it should be noted that *Crotty* was concerned with an instance of governmental action – attempting to ratify the Single European Act without consulting the People – rather than governmental inaction.

[41] [1999] 1 IR 29 at p. 43; [1999] 1 ILRM 93 at p. 104.

The right of children at risk to State support, which was at issue in *D.B.,* is only one of a range of *affirmative* rights conferred by the Irish Constitution. Thus Article 40.3.1 contains a pledge by the State both that it will respect the personal rights of the citizen (seen in this context as "negative liberties") *and* that it will defend and vindicate those rights as far as practicable. The second limb of this provision clearly imposes a duty on the State to take positive action in appropriate circumstances. The State has a similar duty in respect of the right to life of the unborn (Article 40.3.3). In relation to the family and education, the State's duties are, at times, even less qualified than they are under Article 40.3. Thus the State has an unqualified duty to protect both the Family in its constitution and authority (Article 41.1.2) and the institution of Marriage (Article 41.3.1); a duty to "endeavour to ensure" that mothers are not obliged by economic necessity to engage in labour to the neglect of their duties in the home (Article 41.2.2); a duty to ensure that children receive a certain minimum moral, intellectual and social education (Article 42.3.2); an unqualified duty to provide for free primary education (Article 42.4); and a duty, in those exceptional cases in which parents fail, for physical or moral reasons, in their duty towards their children, to endeavour to supply the place of the parents by appropriate means (Article 42.5). Clearly, therefore, the rights guaranteed under the Irish Constitution are not confined to negative liberties but also include a number of affirmative constitutional rights the vindication of which may, as happened in *D.B. v. Minister for Justice*[42] and *T.D. v. Minister for Education,*[43] require the courts to compel the executive to take positive action in appropriate cases.[44]

Moreover any view that the courts should confine themselves to reviewing executive action, ignoring executive inaction, rests on contentious philosophical premises. According to Bandes, the philosophical justification for restricting the focus of the courts to action, rather than inaction, is derived from

> assumptions that individuals are atomistic and motivated by self interest, and that the optimal society is one in which each individual is left alone to do as he wishes so long as he causes no harm to others…
>
> In its political version, … identical assumptions [are made] about the role of government. Its optimal role is noninterference, or at least the smallest amount of interference necessary to permit individuals to exercise the greatest degree of freedom without encroaching on others.[45]

She further contends that both the philosophical and political versions of this argument rest on the strong, unarticulated, premise

> that individuals are on equal footing and can fend for themselves without the assistance of government. That is not to say that all people are equally strong, quick, or intelligent,

---

[42] [1999] 1 IR 29; [1999] 1 ILRM 93.

[43] [2000] 3 IR 62; [2000] 2 ILRM 321.

[44] See also the decision of Barr J. in *Sinnott v. Minister for Education*, unreported, High Court, 4 October 2000.

[45] Susan Bandes, "The Negative Constitution: A Critique" (1990) 80 *Michigan Law Review* 2271 at p. 2314.

but that no structural imbalances or hierarchies exist which might require intervention. If government will simply leave us alone, and we leave each other alone, the resulting order will be just.[46]

For those who do not subscribe to this philosophical position, the proposition that the Constitution might preclude the courts from addressing ills stemming from governmental inaction is simply not self-evident and, indeed, on a reading of the Constitution inspired by different philosophical values, the courts are indeed obliged to fill gaps in State policy if this is necessary to vindicate constitutional rights.[47]

With regard to the review of legislative omissions, the courts have held that their function of reviewing legislation under the Constitution is limited to declaring an Act to be invalid and that they cannot rewrite Acts of the Oireachtas so as to fill perceived legislative *lacunae*. Thus in *Somjee v. Minister for Justice*[48] Keane J. said

> The jurisdiction of this Court in a case where the validity of an Act of the Oireachtas is questioned because of its alleged invalidity having regard to the provisions of the Constitution is limited to declaring the Act in question invalid, if that be the case. The Court has no jurisdiction to substitute for the impugned enactment a form of enactment which it considers desirable or to indicate to the Oireachtas the appropriate form of enactment which should be substituted for the impugned enactment.[49]

---

[46] *Ibid.*, p. 2316.

[47] See below, pp. 48-9. Bandes concludes her article:

Ultimately, the objections to affirmative rights are based on a vision of the Constitution as a negative document which prevents government and citizens alike from harming one another by force. A more appealing vision would recognise that just as we are inextricably bound to each other, we are dependent on government to preserve our liberty by providing certain things we require and expect, and that these things must be singled out for constitutional protection. The identification of the things we require and expect, as a constitutional matter, is crucial. The Court has concerned itself with the elusive and ultimately irrelevant distinction between "freedom from and freedom to." The question that should be asked instead is: what must we have in order to be free?

[48] [1981] ILRM 324. The plaintiff here challenged the constitutionality of the Irish Nationality and Citizenship Act 1956 on the ground that it failed to treat alien men married to Irish citizens in the same way as alien women married to Irish citizens.

[49] At p. 327. This statement was expressly approved by the Supreme Court in the subsequent case of *Mhic Mhathúna v. Ireland* [1995] 1 IR 484, [1995] 1 ILRM 69 (complaint of failure on the part of the State to make comparable provision in the tax and welfare codes for married families with children as is made for one-parent families). For other authorities taking a similar line, see *O'Shaughnessy v. A.G.*, unreported, High Court, 16 February 1971, in which O'Keeffe P. refused to invalidate the Criminal Justice (Legal Aid) Act 1962 because it did not provide for civil legal aid; *Reynolds v. A.G.*, unreported, High Court, 16 February 1973, where Kenny J. held that he had no power to amend the Electoral Acts to provide for the registration of the new electors entitled to vote as a result of the lowering, by constitutional amendment, of the voting age to eighteen; *McGrath v. McDermott* [1988] IR 258; [1988] ILRM 647, where the Supreme Court refused to read Irish taxation legislation in the light of the doctrine of "fiscal nullity"; *Bloomers v. Law Society* [1995] 3 IR 14, in which Laffoy J. held that, having declared part of a statutory instrument regulating exemptions from the Law Society's entrance examination to be invalid, she had no jurisdiction to make an alternative regulation or to indicate to the appropriate law-making body (the Law Society)

In a number of other cases in which new rights were asserted in the absence of any existing statutory framework, the courts similarly held that they had no jurisdiction to entertain such claims.[50]

This approach is open to criticism on the ground that it can leave constitutional rights without proper protection. In this regard, it is important to note that legislative inaction can sometimes be as damaging to constitutional rights as legislative action. Bandes makes this point in relation to State inaction generally, contending that the

> assumption that government can deprive individuals of protected rights only by its actions does not take into account government's pervasive influence through regulatory action and inaction, its displacement of private remedies, and, indeed, its monopoly over some avenues of relief ...
>
> Government can harm by its inaction and its inadequate action, as well as by its direct action. Government can cause harm by failing to promulgate and enforce rules and failing to supervise. It can cause harm by allocating scarce resources in an arbitrary or discriminatory fashion. It can harm by skewing incentives so that its employees find it more opportune to fail to protect or assist. It can harm by displacing private services and failing to ensure adequate replacement services. In short, it can harm by its ostensible omissions as seriously as, and often more efficiently than, by its direct, tangible actions.[51]

This point is equally applicable to legislative inaction and a particularly good example of damage through legislative omission occurs where legislation is underinclusive. In such circumstances, legislative inaction results in damage to the interests of the excluded class. To say that the courts cannot address legislative inaction may then result in a situation in which constitutional duties are not enforced. Consider the recent case of *McMenamin v. Ireland*[52] which, though it did not concern underinclusive legislation, illustrates this potential problem. Here the plaintiff complained of the

---

an alternative form of regulation; *Dornan Research Development Ltd. v. The Labour Court* [1998] ELR 256, in which Geoghegan J. held, *inter alia*, that he could not direct the Oireachtas to amend the Employment Equality Act 1977 to provide for wider rights of appeal; and *Lowth v. Minister for Social Welfare* [1998] 4 IR 321; [1999] 1 ILRM 5, in which the Supreme Court alluded to the difficulty facing the plaintiff in identifying any mechanism for extending deserted wives' payments to deserted husbands. (His complaint was that the State's failure to provide such payments to deserted husbands meant that the relevant statutory provisions were unconstitutional.)

[50] Apart from *O'Reilly v. Limerick Corporation* [1989] ILRM 181, discussed above, pp. 9 *et seq.*, see also *L. v. L.* [1992] 2 IR 77, [1992] ILRM 115 in which the Supreme Court dismissed the respondent's claim that she was entitled to a share in the matrimonial property by virtue of Article 41.2 of the Constitution; *A.D. v. Ireland* [1994] 1 IR 369 in which Carroll J. dismissed the plaintiff's claim that she was entitled to be compensated by the State for criminal injuries she sustained; and *Hynes-O'Sullivan v. O'Driscoll* [1988] IR 436 where Henchy J. in the Supreme Court relied on the doctrine of separation of powers to justify a refusal to extend the defence of privilege in defamation actions. In *Corway v. Independent Newspapers Ltd.* [2000] 1 ILRM 241, the Supreme Court, *per* Barrington J., held that the task of defining crime is a legislative, rather than a judicial, function and that given the uncertain state of the law relating to blasphemy, the Court could not authorise the institution of a criminal prosecution for blasphemy against the respondents.

[51] *Ibid.*, at p. 2283-4 (notes omitted).

[52] [1997] 2 ILRM 177.

failure of the Oireachtas to adjust statutory provision for judicial pensions in the light of changing actuarial factors over a thirty-year period with the result that judicial remuneration was reduced contrary to Article 35.5.[53] While accepting the validity of the plaintiff's complaint and that the resulting situation was unjust and inequitable, the Supreme Court unanimously refused to grant a declaration to that effect, having regard to the doctrine of separation of powers. However each member of the Court then went on essentially to express the hope that those in authority "would do the right thing". But is it sufficient that the discharge of constitutional obligations should ultimately depend on the good will of the authorities? Or can it not be argued that the courts' constitutional duty to vindicate personal rights should inform their understanding of the doctrine of separation of powers rather than, as appears to be the situation at present, the doctrine of separation of powers informing their understanding of the extent of their power to protect constitutional rights?[54]

That said, given the established authorities on this point, it is unlikely that the courts will take it upon themselves to direct the Oireachtas to fill legislative *lacunae*. However it is also clear that they do not have a similar reluctance in relation to executive inaction where the issue can be regarded as justiciable and particularly where constitutional rights are at stake.

I turn now to consider the impact of the debate on methods of constitutional interpretation on this issue of the extent of the judicial role.

b) Constitutional interpretation

In the US, concern about the extent of the judicial role underpins much recent debate about the manner in which the Constitution should be interpreted. In particular, support for what is called the "originalist"[55] approach to constitutional interpretation is often prevalent among those who advocate a restrictive role for the courts, though, as a matter of logic, an originalist approach to constitutional interpretation does not inevitably lead to an endorsement of judicial minimalism.[56] To that extent, a discussion of originalism is logically irrelevant to a consideration of the legitimacy of judicial activism. However, such is the influence of the originalist school that it cannot be

---

[53] In 1961, a reduction of 25% of pension was introduced to finance two new benefits payable in respect of judges, a lump sum gratuity payable on retirement and a death benefit. Actuarial evidence indicated that by 1994, a reduction of 22% would have been sufficient to cover the costs of these benefits.

[54] In this regard, it is interesting to note that the German Constitutional Court developed a jurisdiction to declare a statute to be unconstitutional but not void in circumstances in which the Constitution was breached by a legislative omission – see Rupp-von Brunneck, "The Admonitory Functions of the German Constitutional Court" (1972) 20 *Am. Journal of Comparative Law* 387, especially pp. 393-5. Sherlock also supports the idea that the Irish courts could exercise a declaratory jurisdiction to alert the Oireachtas to legislative failure to protect constitutionally guaranteed rights – see "Self-executing Provisions in EC Law and under the Irish Constitution" (1996) *European Public Law* 103, at p. 116-7.

[55] This term gained currency from an article by Paul Brest of Stanford University, "The Misconceived Quest for the Original Understanding" (1980) 60 *Boston University L. Rev* 204.

[56] See below, pp. 26-8.

ignored in any discussion of the role of the judiciary in a constitutional democracy.

One of the most prominent defenders of this approach to constitutional interpretation is Judge Robert Bork.[57] In his book, *The Tempting of America: The Political Seduction of the Law,*[58] he articulates and defends this theory of constitutional interpretation and also mounts a polemical attack on its opponents who, according to Bork, are largely drawn from the academic world. The justification offered by Bork for preferring originalism to its alternatives is that, in his opinion, it is the only theory of constitutional interpretation which prevents the courts acting as a naked power organ and which therefore possesses democratic legitimacy. Thus it is a theory of interpretation designed to protect the doctrine of separation of powers, as understood by Bork.

Essentially his thesis is that a judge should apply the Constitution according to the principles intended by those who ratified (or, in the Irish context, adopted and enacted) the Constitution. That he does not defend that version of originalism which suggests that the judges must decide a case the way the ratifiers of the Constitution would have decided it in their day is evident from his endorsement of the following description of originalism by John Hart Ely:

> What distinguishes interpretivism[59] from its opposite is its insistence that the work of the political branches is to be invalidated only in accord with an inference whose starting point, whose underlying premise, is fairly discoverable in the Constitution. That the complete inference will not be found there – because the situation is not likely to have been foreseen – is generally common ground.[60]

Bork then continues:

> In short, all that a judge committed to original understanding requires is that the text, structure, and history of the Constitution provide him not with a conclusion but with a major premise. That major premise is a principle or stated value that the ratifiers wanted to protect against hostile legislation or executive action. The judge must then see whether that principle or value is threatened by the statute or action challenged in the case before him. The answer to that question provides his minor premise, and the conclusion follows.[61]

---

[57] A former Solicitor General under President Nixon, Bork was nominated to the US Supreme Court by President Reagan in 1987 only to have his nomination defeated by the Senate Judiciary Committee. For a sympathetic reading of Bork in the Irish context, see Hogan, (1990-2). For another defence of originalism, see *A Matter of Interpretation: Federal Courts and the Law* (Princeton University Press, 1997) by Judge Antonin Scalia of the US Supreme Court.

[58] New York, 1990.

[59] Ely's term for originalism.

[60] Ely, at pp. 1-2. Bork's endorsement is at p. 162 of his own book.

[61] Bork does allow for one qualification to his originalist approach to constitutional interpretation when he concedes that the virtue of stability may protect long-established, non-original judicial decisions. The previous decision on the subject may be clearly incorrect but nevertheless has become so embedded in the life of the nation, so accepted by society, so fundamental to the private and public expectations of individuals and institutions, that the result should not be changed now. Bork, p. 158.

Applying this originalist approach to constitutional interpretation in the Irish context, therefore, if we assume, *arguendo*, that the electorate in 1937 wanted to protect the right to marital privacy, the fact that the same electorate would not have countenanced the use within marriage of contraceptives would not prevent the Supreme Court coming to the conclusion it reached in *McGee v. Attorney General.*[62]

Staying in the Irish context, how would an originalist identify the principles intended by those who adopted and enacted the Constitution? Clearly it is impossible to ascertain the subjective intentions of the 685,105 people who voted in favour of the Constitution in 1937 but equally clearly this is not what is required by originalism. Monaghan, another US originalist, has said:

> Although the intention of the ratifiers, not the Framers, is in principle decisive, the difficulties of ascertaining the intent of the ratifiers leaves little choice but to accept the intent of the Framers as a fair reflection of it.[63]

In the Irish context, one should read "electorate" for "ratifiers"[64] and "Messrs. de Valera, Hearne and Matheson" for "Framers".[65] However, at the same time, the intent of the framers is not conclusive for, as Bork put it:

> What the ratifiers understood themselves to be enacting must be taken to be what the public of that time would have understood the words to mean ... The search is not for a subjective intention. If someone found a letter from George Washington to Martha telling her that what he meant by the power to lay taxes was not what other people meant, that would not change our reading of the Constitution in the slightest ... When lawmakers use words, the law that results is what those words ordinarily mean ... All that counts is how the words used in the Constitution would have been understood at the time. The original understanding is thus manifested in the words used and in secondary materials, such as debates at the conventions, public discussion, newspaper articles, dictionaries in use at the time, and the like.[66]

---

[62] [1974] IR 284 (In *McGee* the Supreme Court invalidated legislation prohibiting the importation of contraceptives).

[63] "Our Perfect Constitution" (1981) 56 *New York University L. Review* 353 at p. 375, n.130.

[64] Unlike the Irish Constitution, the US Constitution was not ratified by the electorate but rather by the legislatures of the thirteen founding states.

[65] According to official records, "the preparation of the original draft [of the Constitution] was done mainly by John Hearne, BL, Legal Adviser of the Department of External Affairs, in consultation with the Parliamentary Draftsman, Matheson, BL, under the personal direction of the President [of the Executive Council, i.e. de Valera]." Quoted in Keogh, "The Irish Constitutional Revolution: An Analysis of the Making of the Constitution" in Litton, ed., *The Constitution of Ireland 1937-1987*, (Dublin, 1987) at p.9.

[66] Bork, p. 144. For an echo of this approach in the Irish context, see the dissenting judgment of Henchy J. in *The People (D.P.P.) v. O'Shea* [1982] IR 384; [1983] ILRM 549. A practical problem with originalism in the Irish context is that here, unlike the US, there is a dearth of documentary evidence as to the intention of the framers of the Irish Constitution (though in recent years the papers of Eamon de Valera have been made available to the public and presumably could be looked to by those wishing to produce an originalist interpretation of the Constitution). This is not fatal to the originalist claim given that originalists do not seek the subjective intention of the framers, but rather their objective intention which is reflected in the historical sources. In the virtual absence of such sources, however, we have to infer this objective intention from our

The Tempting of America was a contribution to a burgeoning debate among the US constitutional community on the most appropriate mode of constitutional interpretation and might be seen as offering some support for the view that the Irish constitutional order precludes judicial activism. It is submitted, however, that this latter proposition can be rebutted by at least two different arguments.

The first of these disputes whether originalism is an appropriate method of interpreting a constitution. A major criticism of Bork is that his thesis is circular – the original understanding of the Constitution is binding because that was the original understanding[67] – and that a proper defence of originalism requires an independent normative theory which Bork does not supply. Thus Ronald Dworkin, for example, argues that an important distinction should be drawn between the framers' *linguistic* intentions – their intentions that the Constitution should contain particular statements – and their *legal* intentions – their intentions about what the law would be in virtue of these statements – and that the fallacy in Bork's originalism is to make the latter intention decisive over the former.[68] As it is not self-evident that legal intention should prevail over linguistic intention, an independent argument is needed to support Bork's thesis. Dworkin identifies this as the argument that since the framers were the people who made the Constitution our fundamental law, their convictions should be respected. However, as he also points out, this argument necessarily draws on normative

---

understanding of public opinion in 1937 – see O'Keeffe P. in *McGee v. A.G.* [1974] IR 284. However, in relation to certain issues arising under the Constitution, it is virtually impossible to ascertain what public opinion was in 1937 as neither the electorate nor its elected representatives ever adverted to such questions. Thus McCarthy J., commenting extra-judicially, said

> ... I would not depend much of the construction of the Constitution on an assumed knowledge of the electorate of 1937 who voted, to a man and to a woman, in accordance with the recommendation of the political party enjoying their support. If the construction of the Constitution were to depend upon establishing the intent of the enacting voters as to each item of that Constitution – as to the minutiae of legal detail, *etc.* – I doubt if the judicial activism that sprang from the High Court and the Supreme Court throughout the last twenty-five years would have had much success. If the construction of the Constitution were to depend upon the intention of the then Dáil, an examination of the debates in that House on the draft Constitution would give little further encouragement as to this being a reliable canon of construction. The deputies at that time, quite a number of those contributing to the debate being lawyers engaged in private practice, appeared to have confined their arguments largely to three topics – the rights of women, freedom of expression in newspapers and radio, *etc.* and, perhaps most surprisingly, the allegedly excessive powers being granted to the President – the thrust of the argument being that Mr de Valera planned to make himself a dictator – the debate reflected more the state of the world at the time than the aspirations of the Nation.

"To do a great right, do a little wrong" (1987) 6 *JISLL* 1, at p. 10. See also Costello J., "The Irish Judge as Law-maker" in Curtin and O'Keeffe eds., *Constitutional Adjudication in European Community and National Law* (Dublin, 1992) 159, at p. 163.

[67] According to Sunstein, this historical claim is itself debatable and he contends that there is evidence that the framers did not believe that their original understanding would control the future – Sunstein, at p. 99.

[68] "Bork's Jurisprudence" (1990) 57 *University of Chicago L. Rev* 657, republished as ch. 14 of Dworkin's book, *Freedom's Law: The Moral Reading of the American Constitution* (Cambridge, 1996).

assumptions about the proper relationship between the framers and contemporary judges and legislators, rather than being based on logical or semantic assumptions. Furthermore, these normative assumptions can only be justified by means of a circular argument, namely, appealing to the intentions of the framers whose authority one is attempting to describe. Finally, he also argues that, even if this argument is made out, it is incomplete, given that in most pertinent cases, "the question at issue is not whether the convictions, expectations and beliefs of those in authority count, but which of these mental states and how". He continues:

> We must assume that the legal intentions of the framers were honorable rather than cynical. They intended to commit the nation to abstract principles of political morality about speech and punishment and equality, for example. They also had a variety of more concrete convictions about the correct application of these abstract principles to particular issues. If contemporary judges think that their concrete convictions were in conflict with their abstract ones, because they did not reach the correct conclusions about the effect of their own principles, then the judges have a choice to make. It is unhelpful to tell them to follow the framers' legal intentions. They need to know which legal intentions – at how general a level of abstraction – and why. So Bork and others who support the original understanding thesis must supply an independent normative theory – *a particular political conception of constitutional democracy*[69] – to answer that need.[70]

In the same vein, Sunstein argues that Bork's claim (that the binding character of the original understanding is settled by the original understanding) "is not an argument at all; it is circular, or a rallying cry".[71] According to Sunstein:

> The view that the original understanding is binding requires a moral or political theory – in terms of, say, a theory of democracy. Acceptance of that view itself rests on a controversial moral foundation. Bork's own approach thus relies on political and moral decisions. These decisions are necessarily external to the Constitution. They need to be defended.[72]

Even if one assumes that the Constitution should be interpreted in an originalist fashion, a second argument is available to rebut the suggestion that this precludes the

---

[69] Emphasis added.

[70] Dworkin (1990), at p. 664; Dworkin (1996), at pp. 293-4.

[71] Sunstein, p. 99.

[72] *Ibid.*, p. 101. See also Humphreys, (1990) 12 *DULJ (n.s.)* 127 at p. 131, where he cites *McGee* and also *The State (Healy) v. Donoghue* [1976] IR 325 in support of the view that "[o]riginalism is now completely discredited as a system of constitutional interpretation except in relation to purely procedural aspects of the Constitution where an originalist approach may provide a degree of enlightenment and fidelity to the text not otherwise attainable". See also the remarks of Budd J. in *Croke v. Smith*, unreported, High Court, 27 and 31 July 1995, at p. 123 wherein he said, citing a passage from the judgment of O'Higgins C.J. in *The State (Healy) v. O'Donoghue* [1976] IR 325 at p. 347, "[T]he Supreme Court has recognised that concepts relating to human rights evolve over the years and in considering rights protected by the Constitution the court, recognising this evolution, should apply contemporary norms rather than an originalist approach of assessing the present situation according to the norms and values existing at the time when the Constitution was enacted in 1937".

courts from engaging in judicial activism. As a number of writers point out,[73] originalism does not necessarily entail a minimalist role for the courts. This is because, as Perry convincingly demonstrates, the historical inquiry may yield up more than one plausible interpretation of the Constitution and even where only one such interpretation is discovered, that interpretation may be relatively indeterminate in the context of the case in which it is sought to be applied. In either of these situations, choices between competing outcomes will have to be made and those choices are very likely to be influenced by the judge's understanding of the proper judicial role. Originalism does not clarify what this role should be and, therefore, cannot be regarded as automatically precluding judicial activism.[74]

In particular, it is difficult to defend the thesis that originalism, in the Irish context, automatically precludes judicial activism for, as Hogan concedes, "the language and structure of Article 40.3 and Article 45 strongly suggest that the rights protected in Article 40.3.1 are not confined to the rights expressly enumerated elsewhere in the Constitution".[75] From this one might plausibly infer that the People in 1937 implicitly approved of the active role subsequently undertaken by the courts from the mid-1960s onwards in identifying implied fundamental rights, though it is probably nearer the mark to say that the potential role of the judiciary was not a major factor in influencing the outcome of the plebiscite on the Constitution.[76] However there is

---

[73] See Ely, ch. 2; Perry, *The Constitution in the Courts: Law or Politics?* (New York, 1994), chs. 4 and 5; Sunstein, p. 103; Dworkin, "Comment" in Scalia, p. 115.

[74] In this context, it is worth noting that Michael Perry is perhaps the only constitutional scholar of note to have switched sides in the debate on originalism. Having been a leading non-originalist for more than fifteen years, in *The Constitution in the Courts: Law or Politics?*, published in 1994, he defends a moderate version of originalism as the most appropriate way of interpreting the US Constitution. Notwithstanding this significant change of view, his defence of judicial activism in the protection of certain fundamental rights remains a constant throughout his work. For a useful account of the development of Perry's views on this area, see Saphire, "Originalism and the Importance of Constitutional Aspirations" (1997) 24 *Hastings Constitutional Law Quarterly* 599.

[75] Hogan (1990-2), p. 114.

[76] A further complicating factor in the Irish context lies in the fact that the Irish Constitution is partly inspired by natural law and given the indeterminate nature of natural law principles, this again points to a constitutive role for the courts in interpreting the Constitution – see the remarks of Walsh J. in *McGee v. A.G.* [1974] IR 284 at pp. 317-8. In recent times there has been a sustained academic debate on the role of natural law in the Irish constitutional order – see Clarke, "The Role of Natural Law in Irish Constitutional Law" (1982) XVII *Ir. Jur. (n.s.)* 187; O'Hanlon "Natural Rights and the Irish Constitution" (1993) 11 *ILT* 8; Murphy, "Democracy, Natural Law and the Irish Constitution" (1993) 11 *ILT* 81; O'Hanlon, "The Judiciary and the Moral Law" (1993) 11 *ILT* 129; Clarke, "The Constitution and Natural Law: A Reply to Mr Justice O'Hanlon" (1993) 11 *ILT* 177; Whyte, "Natural Law and the Constitution" (1996) 14 *ILT* 8; Duncan, "Can Natural Law be Used in Constitutional Interpretation?" in Treacy and Whyte, *Religion, Morality and Public Policy* (1995), at p. 125 and de Blacam, "Justice and Natural Law" (1997) XXXII *Ir. Jur. (n.s.)* 323 – and in *In Re Article 26 and the Regulation of Information (Services outside the State for Termination of Pregnancies) Bill 1995* [1995] 1 IR 1; [1995] 2 ILRM 81, the Supreme Court held that the concept of natural law did not constitute a fetter on the People's power to amend the Constitution. While the Court's reasoning in this case is ultimately unconvincing – see my comment on the decision in "Natural Law and the Constitution" (1996) 14 *ILT* 8 – even if one takes the decision at face value, it does not affect the point that I am making here, given that the decision does not completely preclude any role for natural law in constitutional interpretation.

certainly no evidence that the People intended, by the enactment of the Constitution in 1937, to set their face resolutely against judicial activism.[77]

Nor, as I have argued above, can one say that the constitutional text on the doctrine of separation of powers unequivocally proscribes such activism. In order to reach such a conclusion on the basis of the existing text, one would have to establish that the Constitution unequivocally endorses a model of democratic politics that precludes judicial activism.[78] This leads us on to the second possible defence of Costello J.'s decision in *O'Reilly*, namely, that such a role for the judiciary is incompatible with democratic politics.

Is judicial activism precluded by democratic politics?

A typical reaction to judicial activism is that it is objectionable because it constitutes the imposition of the will of an unelected and unrepresentative oligarchy on the broad mass of society. Thus the late Niall McCarthy, himself a Supreme Court judge, had this to say about the dangers of judicial power:

> The control exercised by the judiciary against the abuse of executive power contains within itself a very real danger – the abuse of judicial power. In the field of unenumerated rights, the judicial power can only be self-restrained. It enjoins upon the judicial power to be alert not to substitute personal preference and, consequently, personal prejudice for the perceived needs of the people and the nation.[79]

A related concern is that judicial activism will undermine the value of legal certainty.

I believe that these concerns are overstated and misplaced in the context of the Irish constitutional order.

To begin with what Bickel called the "counter-majoritarian difficulty",[80] two arguments can be made in defence of judicial activism in this jurisdiction. The first defence of judicial activism as a phenomenon compatible with democratic politics draws heavily on the work of Michael Perry, a US constitutional scholar. Essentially,

---

[77] Article 45 of the Constitution does, admittedly, provide that the principles of social policy contained therein "shall not be cognisable by any Court under any of the provisions of the Constitution". However that strengthens my argument that judicial activism is not precluded by the Constitution for it implies that principles of social policy derived from other provisions of the Constitution are cognisable by the courts. It is also worth noting that the People explicitly strengthened the power of judicial review in the 1937 Constitution, by comparison with the position which obtained under the Constitution of the Irish Free State.

[78] In my treatment of the Constitution thus far, I have confined myself to a rebuttal of the argument that the Constitution precludes judicial activism. In a later section in this chapter – see below, p. 43 *et seq.* – I outline constitutional arguments *in support* of judicial activism on behalf of marginalised groups.

[79] "Observations on the Protection of Fundamental Rights in the Irish Constitution" in Curtin and O'Keeffe (eds)., *Constitutional Adjudication in European Community and National Law* (London, 1992) at p. 181.

[80] *The Least Dangerous Branch: The Supreme Court at the Bar of Politics* (Yale, 1962), pp. 16-23. Bickel is here referring to the power of judicial review of legislation generally.

this defence is that a certain amount of judicial activism, or judicial creativity, is unavoidable because of what Perry calls the "indeterminacy of constitutional morality", i.e. the indeterminacy of constitutional directives. Moreover, given the inability of what Perry calls "ordinary politics" to protect the interests of marginalised groups, the courts remain the only effective guardian of the constitutional rights of the socially excluded.

In his book, *The Constitution in the Courts: Law or Politics?*[81] Perry defends the concept of judicial review as the best available mechanism, at the moment, for protecting those fundamental values which those responsible for drafting and enacting the Constitution wished to put beyond the reach of the ordinary politics of the community. He then moves to consider how the courts should go about the task of interpreting the Constitution when exercising their power of judicial review. In this context, he argues that constitutional adjudication can involve two distinct functions, *constitutional interpretation* and *constitutional specification*. The former seeks to ascertain what principle (directive) a particular provision of the constitutional text represents. This interpretative inquiry is only relevant where the text is initially vague, ambiguous, in some way unclear. Thus, in the Irish context, this step would not have to be taken by a judge dealing with, say, the definition of the national flag in Article 7. However it could be relevant in relation to, say, the guarantee of equality in Article 40.1 insofar as the scope of that guarantee could conceivably range from a mere assurance that, in their dealings with the courts, all citizens will be treated equally to a more radical proposition that society must so organise itself as to ensure that every citizen has the same opportunity to realise his or her potential.

The second function, constitutional specification, is relevant where the principle, ascertained through the interpretative inquiry, is indeterminate in the context of the dispute to be resolved and entails deciding what the norm requires in the context of that dispute. So, for example, the interpretative inquiry might yield the principle that Article 44.2.2 prohibits State endowment of all religions, rather than merely discriminatory endowment of some religions, and yet that principle might be indeterminate in resolving a dispute as to whether the State could pay the salaries of school chaplains.[82] Or, another example, Article 40.3 clearly commits the State to defending and vindicating the personal rights of the individual but is not specific as to the nature of all of the rights so protected.[83]

---

[81] Oxford University Press, 1994.

[82] I consider this particular issue in some detail in "Religion, Education and an Indeterminate Constitution" (1997) *Doctrine and Life* 274.

[83] Perry cautions that specifying a norm should not be confused with applying a norm in a particular context:

> To rule that an ordinance that by its terms governs "automobiles" governs "Honda Accords" is ... to "apply" the ordinance, not to "specify" it. By contrast, to construe a directive that forbids government to prohibit any religious practice absent a compelling justification [as forbidding] government to prohibit the sacramental use of wine at Mass is to "specify" the principle. Whereas the process of applying a determinate directive is essentially deductive, the process of specifying an indeterminate directive is essentially nondeductive. A specification "of a principle for a specific class of cases is not a deduction from it, nor a discovery of some implicit meaning; it is the act of setting a more concrete and categorical requirement in the spirit of the principle..."

Perry (1994), p. 75. (The quotation within this passage is taken from MacCormick, "Reconstruction after Deconstruction: A Response to CLS" (1990) 10 *Oxford J. Legal Studies* 539, 548).

Perry advocates an originalist approach to the interpretative inquiry, whereby the understanding of those involved in drafting and enacting the Constitution – the original understanding – should be deemed authoritative for the purpose of deciding what principles are contained in the Constitution. He defends this position on the simple ground that it is impossible to achieve any consensus on what should replace the original understanding, if that is to be abandoned.[84] In common with Robert Bork, he argues that the specification of an indeterminate norm – deciding what it means in the context of an actual case – is not governed by the views of the framers of the Constitution.[85] He parts company with Bork in his acceptance of the fact that the task of specification is always at least partly constitutive[86] insofar as it involves making choices about which of two or more competing values should be preferred and/or about the extent to which to achieve such values. Thus he accepts that constitutional adjudication can, in appropriate cases, amount to a kind of legislative judgment.

However Perry's support of judicial activism is qualified and nuanced. He is prepared to accept that, in the context of the US Constitution, a minimalist approach by judges to constitutional adjudication is appropriate in determining the vertical distribution of power between federal government and the governments of the states and also in determining most issues arising out of the horizontal distribution of power between the three departments of the federal government. However he argues that the minimalist approach is less appropriate for determining claims that government (either federal or state) is acting in violation of certain constitutional norms regarding a right or liberty of the people. Perry's defence of judicial activism in this context is based on two premises. First, he is sceptical about the ability of "ordinary politics" to specify indeterminate norms relating to certain fundamental rights or liberties because of the value of incumbency to sitting politicans.

> [I]ncumbency is undeniably a fundamental value for most members of the Congress. Members of the Congress are therefore more likely to cater to the interests and views of their constituents – and of their contributors – than they otherwise would. Responsiveness to constituent interests and views is not always a bad thing; it is often, though not always, a good thing. The point is simply that a regime in which incumbency is (inevitably?) a

---

[84] However, as we have noted above, n. 66, the originalist approach to constitutional interpretation encounters practical difficulties in the Irish context.

[85] In support of this position, Perry adopts Bassham's defence of what the latter calls "moderate intentionalism" originalism (as opposed to "strict intentionalism" originalism). In *Original Intent and the Constitution: A Philosophical Study* (1992), Bassham argues that moderate intentionalism originalism "recognises the importance of striking a balance between the values of predictability and stability on the one hand, and those of flexibility and adaptability on the other ... Moderate intentionalism enjoys the significant advantage of being able to respond, as strict intentionalism does not, both to originalism's traditional concern with the values of certainty, stability and judicial restraint, and to the perennial complaint of originalism's critics that the theory is hopelessly at odds with the need to treat the Constitution as a living, flexible document". Cited in Perry (1994), p. 44.

[86] By "constitutive" he means that the decision identifies the person or the community as one sort of person or community rather than another.

fundamental value seems often illsuited ... to a truly deliberative, truly dialogic specification of indeterminate constitutional norms.[87]

Second, and more positively, he believes that the process of adjudication may be superior to the legislative process in specifying certain indeterminate constitutional norms. He cites the following passage from Bickel with approval:

> The courts are concerned with the flesh and blood of an actual case. This tends to modify, perhaps to lengthen, everyone's view. It also provides an extremely salutary proving ground for all abstractions; it is conducive, in a phrase of Holmes, to thinking things, not words, and thus to the evolution of principle by a process that tests as it creates.[88]

A final finesse to Perry's position is that he accepts that a minimalist approach may be appropriate to the specification of certain norms relating to fundamental rights, such as the requirement, arguably contained in section 1 of the Fourteenth Amendment, that every law should regulate for the public good in a reasonable fashion, as a non-minimalist approach in this context would "collapse ... any meaningful distinction between the legislative function and the judicial function".[89] However he stoutly defends a non-minimalist approach to the specification of the principle of equality, on the ground that experience in the US shows that ordinary politics is particularly ill-suited to that task.

In summary, then, Perry contends that, given the indeterminate nature of some constitutional norms, judicial activism is inevitable and even, in the case of norms promoting social inclusion of minorities, desirable, given the inability of ordinary politics to observe such norms adequately. How well do Perry's views apply to our central concern in this chapter which is whether judicial action on behalf of economically and socially disadvantaged groups is constitutionally legitimate? The Constitution certainly contains a number of provisions pertinent to the problem of disadvantage which require both interpretation and specification. For example, could the guarantee of equality in Article 40.1 – "All citizens shall, as human persons, be held equal before the law"[90] – possibly be interpreted to oblige the State to pursue radical policies on redistribution of income? Does Article 41.2.2 – "The State shall ... endeavour to ensure that mothers shall not be obliged by economic necessity to engage in labour to the neglect of their duties in the home" – oblige the State to pay means-tested social welfare to mothers? What are the implications of Article 42.3.2 –

---

[87] Perry (1994), p. 107. Commenting on the failure of a local authority to provide halting sites for Travellers, Flood J. remarked, "The situation would appear to be that sites for travellers... when located by members of the technical staff of the County Council, do not find favour with the elected representatives [of the Council] essentially because they are not prepared to vote for sites for reasons which appear to be unrelated to the suitability of the sites and to be solely related to their geographical and social and future electoral implications". – *Co. Meath VEC v. Joyce* [1994] 2 ILRM 210 at p. 218.

[88] Bickel, p. 26, cited in Perry (1994), p. 109.

[89] Perry (1994), p. 166.

[90] The clause goes on to provide that "This shall not be held to mean that the State shall not in its enactments have due regard to differences of capacity, physical and moral, and of social function".

"The State shall, ... as guardian of the common good, require in view of actual conditions that the children receive a certain minimum education, moral, intellectual and social" – for the rights of children from deprived areas, or severely mentally handicapped children, or children who are out of control? Do the personal rights of the citizen, which the State is obliged, by Article 40.3, to defend and vindicate, encompass socio-economic rights such as a right to shelter, a right to civil legal aid, or a right to a serviced halting site?

My purpose in raising these issues is not to suggest particular answers but rather to show that provisions in the text of the Constitution need to be interpreted and specified (in Perry's sense of that term) if answers are to be found. Perry's thesis calls for an originalist (though not necessarily minimalist) approach to constitutional interpretation, the task of identifying constitutional norms. However, as I have argued above,[91] it is far from clear whether such an approach is possible in the Irish context and one can argue that the Irish judiciary may have to play a constitutive role, even in relation to the task of constitutional interpretation.[92]

In relation to the specification of indeterminate norms, Perry advocates an activist role for the courts in defending fundamental rights promoting inclusion, at least in those circumstances in which one could reasonably be sceptical about the ability of ordinary politics to discharge this important task. In the Irish context, I believe that there is evidence to support a sceptical view of the potential of ordinary politics to protect the interests of disadvantaged groups generally. Thus studies by Maguire,[93] Breen *et al*[94] and Whelan *et al*.[95] led one commentator to observe that "there is little to counter the view that modern Irish society remains a profoundly inegalitarian society".[96] Moreover, research commissioned by the Constitution Review Group revealed that lower socio-economic groups are significantly underrepresented in the Dáil and Seanad,[97] prompting one member of that Review Group to question the ability of the Oireachtas to protect systematically the interests of welfare recipients or low-paid workers.[98] The Review

---

[91] N.66.

[92] Though, as I argue below, pp.36-8, this should not give rise to undue concern, given the relative ease with which the People can correct what they might consider to be judicial aberrancy.

[93] "Ireland" in *Growth to Limits: The Western European Welfare States since World War II*, Vol. 2, P. Flora (ed.), (Berlin, 1986).

[94] Breen, Hannan, Rottman and Whelan, *Understanding Contemporary Ireland: State, Class and Development in the Republic of Ireland* (Gill and Macmillan, 1990).

[95] Whelan, Breen and Whelan, "Industrialisation, Class Formation and Social Mobility in Ireland" in *The Development of Industrial Society in Ireland*, Goldthorpe and Whelan, eds. (Oxford University Press, 1992).

[96] Mair, "The Absence of Class Politics" in Goldthorpe and Whelan (eds.), at p. 401.

[97] 32% of the population between the ages of 21 and 70 belong to the skilled manual, semi-skilled manual and unskilled manual categories, yet only 2% of the membership of the 27th Dáil belonged to the skilled manual category and no member of that Dáil came from either of the other two categories.

[98] See Kathleen Lynch's paper appended to the *Report of the Constitution Review Group* (Pn.2632), at pp. 492-3.

Group itself recommended that the Constitution be amended to facilitate improved participation in the democratic process.[99]

In an insightful account of the nature of Irish democracy, Professor Garvin has written:

> The Irish Republic is a liberal democracy, that is a polity whose rulers are selected regularly by popular election, and is one of under forty such political systems in the world. Furthermore, it is probably one of the most populist of such political systems. By populist I mean a political system in which elites and masses, or political leaders and the general population, to use more conventional terminology, are unusually vulnerable to influence by each other. The Irish population is very close to its leaders, knows them with a directness and intimacy unusual in larger nation-states and the leaders are, in their turn, abnormally open to pressure from their electors and even at times terrorised by them. The characteristic democratic syndrome of majority tyranny, detected by Alexis de Tocqueville a century and a half ago, is alive and well in Ireland.[100]

Later he comments, "Irish government could at one time by aptly characterised as rule-bound bureaucracy tempered by clientelist democracy. The latter may now be prevailing over the former".[101]

---

[99] Constitution Review Group, p. 43. However the subsequent *Second Progress Report of the All-Party Oireachtas Committee on the Constitution* (1997, pn. 3835), dealing with Seanad reform, does not give grounds for optimism on this score. Two and a half pages of the All-Party Committee's ten pages of deliberations on reform of the Seanad were devoted to the issue of the composition of the Seanad. The Committee, which consisted of nine TDs and two senators, recommended that fifteen members of the Seanad should be directly elected by the general electorate from the European Parliament constituencies, commenting, at p. 10, "[T]his schema would encourage the nomination of people who have contributed significantly to various aspects of our society. It could also provide a proving ground for aspirant MEPs". The Committee recommended that a further twenty-eight members be elected by an electorate consisting of people who have been themselves elected by the people, fourteen by the incoming Dáil – "This would provide opportunities for young, aspirant politicians and also facilitate the election of former members of the Dáil who might wish to continue to be involved in national affairs" (p. 11) – and fourteen by members of county councils and county borough councils. Finally, a further six seats would be allocated to representatives of third-level education and the Taoiseach would retain the power of appointing eleven senators. In its deliberations, however, the Committee did not even advert to, let alone dismiss, the recommendation of one member of the Constitution Review Group (Kathleen Lynch) that emigrants, the unemployed and other welfare claimants, the elderly and minority groups such as Travellers and person with disabilities be represented in the Seanad and the observation in a report, commissioned by the All-Party Committee itself and reproduced in the *Second Progress Report*, that "there is ... a case for looking carefully at the capacity of the Seanad to act as a voice for special groups that might otherwise be kept at a distance from Irish political life, such as representatives of the Irish abroad, [and] of marginal groups within Irish society ..." (p. 94).

[100] "Democracy in Ireland: Collective Somnambulance and Public Policy" in (1991) 39 *Administration* 42 at p. 44. Professor Garvin goes on to identify the ideological division which is at the heart of contemporary Irish political culture – a division between what he calls "communalism" and "individualism". This is an important theme on which I comment further below at pp. 50-1.

[101] Garvin, at p. 45.

While Garvin himself does not address the issue of how Irish democracy responds to the demands of marginalised groups, it is submitted that his description of Irish democracy resonates, to some degree, with that of the political system in the US and the UK provided by Galbraith in his book, *The Culture of Contentment*.[102] Galbraith's central thesis is that modern political behaviour in the west is determined by those whom he calls "the contented and the self-approving" who are numerous, very influential and a majority of those who vote.

> Those responding to [the politics of contentment] are a majority of those voting in the United States; they are not ... a majority of the adult population ... [T]he larger justification for not voting is that ... it is an idle exercise for the eligible poverty-ridden citizen. It is rightly perceived that the difference between the two parties on the immediately affecting issues is inconsequential; accordingly, why bother to decide between them? Thus the majority rule of the contented is or has been ensured.
>
> It follows further that presidential and legislative action, or more seriously, inaction, however adverse and alienating the effect on the socially excluded – homelessness, hunger, inadequate education, drug affliction, poverty in general – is under the broad sanction of democracy. A disturbing parallel ... emerges here. Prior to the great revolt of 1989-90 in Eastern Europe, dissatisfaction and alienation were under the broad gloss of socialism; if the people had socialism, they could not be unhappy. The case is now similar in language to the United States: this is the democratic system; systematically it is above error. The fact that a full half of the population does not participate in presidential elections, yet fewer in congressional contests, does not go unnoticed, but it also does not impair the assumption that democracy is controlling and benign.[103]

A recent article by Dr Niamh Hardiman supports a very similar analysis of Irish society.[104] Notwithstanding conscious efforts made during the 1990s to improve the participation of marginalised groups in policy formation[105] and notwithstanding the unprecedented growth in prosperity during the same period, Hardiman argues that the political system has failed to address adequately the issue of social inequality.

---

[102] (Penguin Books, 1993). This is a perceptive (and wry) analysis of the type of politics which Galbraith considers to be dominant in both the US and the UK and of the self-serving and inconsistent economic theory which it generates.

[103] Galbraith, pp. 150-1.

[104] "Inequality and the representation of interests" in Crotty and Schmitt, (eds.), *Ireland and the Politics of Change* (Addison Wesley Longman Ltd., 1998) at p. 122.

[105] Thus since 1997, representatives of womens' organisations, the unemployed, youth, the elderly, people with a disability and environmentalists have been provided with an official channel for expressing their views in the National Economic and Social Forum. Moreover this same "third strand" participated, along with Government and the social partners, in the negotiations leading up to the national pay agreement, "Partnership 2000 for Inclusion, Employment and Competitiveness". In addition, since 1991, a number of Area-Based Partnerships have been formed to promote local community development and these Partnerships usually contain community representatives. In addition to the foregoing initiatives to enhance the involvement of marginalised groups in policy formation, in 1997 the then Government adopted a national anti-poverty strategy – *Sharing in Progress: National Anti-Poverty Strategy* (April 1997).

... [W]e can see that there are many reasons ... why the least advantaged may not be able to influence decision-making effectively. It is difficult for people in disadvantaged situations to become organised: their circumstances make it hard to build up networks of involvement. There are many aspects of social disadvantage, making it difficult to establish common concerns between organisations. These organisations may themselves face challenges as to how representative they really are. The trade union movement may champion some issues on behalf of the disadvantaged. But it also has obligations to its own membership which may at certain points limit how vigorously it can press issues pertaining to social disadvantage.

Even where the disadvantaged acquire a voice with which to lobby government, they do not necessarily gain influence, at least not when their objectives are held to conflict with those of business. The Irish economy is small and very open, and is particularly dependent on retaining and expanding investment in the multinational sector. Business interests do not necessarily oppose government initiatives to reduce social inequalities. But they can bring a powerful influence to bear on the priority which governments accord to redistributive issues, both through direct lobbying, and through what we might think of as the particular structural advantage they enjoy in the Irish economy. The possibility also exists that business interests may influence government priorities indirectly, through the financial donations they make to political parties.

Finally, the prevailing style of setting priorities and deciding upon the distribution of resources within the Irish political system tends to favour those best able to promote their group's interests and claims. Within the established way of doing things, radical policy innovations are not so much resisted as never seriously contemplated.[106]

Dealing specifically with disadvantage and electoral politics, Hardiman cites studies which show strong correlations at the aggregate level between low electoral participation and social deprivation in the Dublin area and that long-term non-voters are

---

[106] Hardiman, p. 134. A similar view was expressed by Professor Fred Powell, writing in 1992, when he said:

What is most striking about the [period inaugurated by the election of President Mary Robinson in November 1992] is the preoccupation with libertarian issues. So far there has been little attention to the plight of the poor and the need for more redistributive social policies. President Robinson has openly identified with the problems of the unemployed and those forced to emigrate; promoted Travellers' rights and presented herself as a voice for the voiceless. It remains to be seen whether she can utilise her period in office (which will span most of the 1990s) to advocate a more egalitarian and caring society. While libertarian issues capture the attention of the media because they impinge upon the interests of the majority, egalitarian concerns receive less publicity – particulary when they address the needs of the underclass. Furthermore, it is highly likely that Centre-Right parties will continue to dominate political decision-making during the 1990s. The era of draconian public expenditure cuts associated with the ideological domination of the New Right in the 1980s may be on the wane but there is little concrete evidence that a more tolerant political climate will benefit the poor. Full citizenship for the socially deprived underclass, which comprise the largest minority group in Irish society, remains to be achieved.

The Politics of Irish Social Policy 1600-1990 (The Edwin Mellen Press, 1992) at p. 332. See also his subsequent article, "Citizenship and Social Exclusion" (1995) 43 *Administration* 22.

far more likely to be socially disadvantaged that regular voters. In contrast, swing voters who "occupy far more of politicians' and party activists' attention ... are far more likely to be urban, middle-class, and articulate about their interests and preferences".[107]

In conclusion, therefore, on this point, it is inevitable that some constitutional norms will be indeterminate (and certainly some norms in the Irish Constitution *are* indeterminate) and that our existing political system will not always be capable of refining or specifying such norms. In particular, there are very good grounds for doubting the ability of this system to specify indeterminate constitutional norms promoting social inclusion. In such circumstances, the judiciary is the only agency available which can specify and defend those norms.

My second defence of judicial activism is specific to the Irish situation and focuses in on what is understood by democratic decision-making. Those who argue that judicial activism negates democratic decision-making invariably assume that the People can only express their will through the proxy system of legislative deliberation[108] or, more rarely, directly through referenda. However my argument here is that the People are not so restricted in the expression of their will. There is a third way. The silence of the People in the face of judicial activism does not have to be interpreted as the silence of impotent rage – it could be regarded as the approving silence of an electorate who are satisfied with the decisions of their judges, or, perhaps more accurately, the disinterested silence of an electorate (or their political representatives) who are not sufficiently antagonised by those decisions to wish to change them.

An interesting characteristic of the Irish Constitution, and one which marks it off quite significantly from its US counterpart, is the relative ease with which it may be amended. Articles 46 and 47 prescribe a three stage process for amendment – a bill proposing an amendment has to be passed by the two Houses of the Oireachtas and then approved by a simple majority of the votes cast at a referendum on the proposal, following which it is signed by the President. On a number of occasions, this process has been used to reverse, modify or otherwise circumvent judicial decisions or comments on different aspects of the Constitution. Perhaps the most spectacular example of this phenomenon, in terms of alacrity, was the Tenth Amendment to the

---

[107] Hardiman, p. 135. See also similar comments by Sinnott in relation to voting patterns in Dublin in *Irish Voters Decide: Voting Behaviour in Elections and Referendums since 1918* (Manchester University Press, 1995) at p. 142.

[108] This equation of democracy with parliamentary sovereignty is itself a fiction given the indifference of some electors and the inability of others to influence parliamentary deliberations between elections. Thus Ackerman says: "During normal politics, *nobody* represents the People in an unproblematic way ... Given the 'softness' of normal public opinion, it is simply impossible to say how the people of today would decide an issue if they mobilized their political energies and hammered out a new constitutional solution. In the very process of mobilized debate and decision, many minds would change, many new directions would be explored before a new constitutional solution was reached. Only a fool would predict the outcome of this hypothetical higher lawmaking process on the basis of the 'soft' opinions expressed during a period of normal political life. We must instead face up to the Publian truth: during normal politics, the People simply do not exist; they can only be represented by 'stand-ins'". Ackerman, at p. 263.

Constitution, approved by the People on 26 May 1987, which permitted the State to ratify the Single European Act. This was in reaction to the Supreme Court decision in *Crotty v. An Taoiseach,*[109] some six weeks earlier, holding that the Government was not entitled to enter into this international agreement. Seven other constitutional amendments were similarly provoked by decisions, actual or anticipated, of the judiciary. Thus the Sixth Amendment to the Constitution, giving express constitutional protection to the adoption process, was enacted in response to judicial misgivings expressed in the course of the hearing of *M. v. An Bord Uchtála;*[110] the ostensible motivation behind the Eighth Amendment to the Constitution in 1983 was to pre-empt any judicial attempt to relax the existing ban on abortion; *In re Article 26 and the Electoral (Amendment) Bill 1983,*[111] dealing with the voting rights of non-citizens, was reversed by the Ninth Amendment to the Constitution in 1984; the Thirteenth and Fourteenth Amendments to the Constitution in 1992 were a reaction to the Supreme Court decisions in *Attorney General (S.P.U.C. (Irl.) Ltd.) v. Open Door Counselling Ltd.*[112] and *Attorney General v. X.;*[113] the Sixteenth Amendment to the Constitution in 1996 reversed the Supreme Court decision in *The People (Attorney General) v. O'Callaghan*[114] on the availability of bail where there was a likelihood of the defendant committing further offences while on bail; and, in the following year, the doctrine of cabinet confidentiality first enunciated by the Supreme Court in *Attorney General v. Hamilton (No.1)*[115] was modified by the Seventeenth Amendment to the Constitution.

These examples suggest that the People (or, perhaps more accurately, the political elite[116]) are quite prepared to take action to control judicial decision-making with which they do not agree. Consequently, it is surely reasonable to infer from the People's passivity in the face of other judicial decisions that these decisions reflect popular sentiment (or perhaps more accurately in relation to some decisions, especially those of a technical nature, do not offend against that sentiment). Thus one can argue that the whole corpus of implied fundamental rights identified by the courts since the 1960s carries with it implicit popular approval insofar as no attempt has ever been made to modify this development by way of constitutional amendment.

One commentator, Adrian Twomey, has advanced two possible objections to this argument.[117] He suggests that an originalist would argue that the Court has no authority

---

109 [1987] IR 713; [1987] ILRM 400.

110 [1977] IR 287.

111 [1984] IR 268; [1984] ILRM 539.

112 [1988] IR 593; [1988] ILRM 19.

113 [1992] 1 IR 1; [1992] ILRM 401. A third proposal to modify the effect of the *X* ruling was rejected by the People in November 1992.

114 [1966] IR 501; (1968) 102 ILTR 45.

115 [1993] 2 IR 250; [1993] ILRM 81.

116 Many, if not most, constitutional amendments originate in decisions taken by the political elite to effect change, rather than in any popular outcry for reform.

117 "Bork's Originalism: Reconciling Judicial Constitutional Interpretation with the Rule of Law" (1996) 14 *ILT* 278, at p. 282, n. 54. (I originally presented this argument in an article entitled "Constitutional Adjudication, Ideology and Access to the Courts" in Whelan (ed.), *Law and Liberty in Ireland* (Oak Tree Press, 1993), at p. 149.)

in the first place to be judicially active, even if the "corrective" power of the People lurks not far behind. This presupposes that originalism offers the only legitimate approach to constitutional interpretation, a position I have already rejected earlier.[118] But in any event, my argument is not designed to challenge the internal logic of the originalist position; rather it addresses the concern motivating that position, the fear that without an originalist approach to constitutional interpretation, the courts will act as a "naked power organ". My argument, quite simply, is that the Irish Constitution provides the People with the means to control judicial activism, control which has been exercised in the past, and, to that extent, fear that the courts can usurp the authority of the People is overstated. The second objection is that "the subsequent correction of the Court by the People would provide little solace to the unsuccessful litigant in the case in question".[119] This objection assumes that the initial decision by the court is "mistaken" and that the court should never, therefore, have arrived at such a conclusion.[120] This is to misunderstand the process with which we are concerned here. My argument is not about correcting mistaken decisions of the courts; it is about defending the legitimacy of those decisions from the charge that they frustrate the democratic will of the People and, for that reason, are illegitimate. The unsuccessful litigant in this scenario is in exactly the same position as the unsuccessful litigant whose case highlights some anomaly in the common law or in legislation which is subsequently corrected by the Oireachtas. The change comes too late for that litigant but it does not follow that the original court decision was "mistaken". In the same way, the fact that subsequent action by the People may ultimately vindicate the position of the unsuccessful litigant is not a ground for impugning the validity of the original judicial decision.

Having addressed the argument that judicial activism is anti-democratic, there is, finally, the related concern that such activism undermines the value of legal certainty. This proposition certainly cannot be denied. However what can be called into question is whether the legal system can ever completely preclude uncertainty. Writing in another context,[121] Brady criticised what he termed the "durable myth" of legal certainty, "the illusion that the law is, or can be made, a comprehensive, eternised set of rules which embrace all possible legal disputes and settle them in advance".[122] This point appears equally apposite in the context of constitutional

---

[118] See above, pp. 25-6.

[119] (1996) 14 *ILT* 278, at p. 282, n. 54.

[120] Twomey describes my argument as a suggestion "that the Irish Supreme Court need be less concerned than its American counterpart about the democratic legitimacy of its decisions simply because a sufficiently vocal majority has the ability to 'correct' the Court's mistakes". – *Ibid.*

[121] That of the innovative use of equitable remedies in the interests of social reform by some members of the English judiciary during the 1960s and 1970s.

[122] "Legal Certainty: The Durable Myth" (1973) VIII *Ir. Jur. (n.s.)* 18, at p. 18. In this article, Brady drew support for his position from a book by US Judge Jerome Frank, *Law and the Modern Mind* (Stevens, 1949) in which that judge derided the view that "law is [to be] dealt with as if it were settled once and for all; its rules are supposed to operate impartially, inflexibly; justice must be uniform and unswerving. In other words, the stress is on generalisations, not on concrete happenings, on averages, not on details. Little allowance can be made for justice in the particular case: thus the law is written and thus it must be applied. Novely and creativeness must not be

adjudication. If complete legal certainty is unattainable, we should really consider whether the attempt to ensure predictability in the law does not carry more costs than benefits. In particular, we may consider that an increase in uncertainty is a price worth paying for the benefits to be gained from a system which is more responsive to the needs of marginalised groups.

Limited capacity of the courts

The final objection to judicial activism promoting social inclusion is that even if such activism is constitutionally and politically legitimate, the courts are simply incapable of performing this function. Unlike the preceding points, this is a pragmatic, rather than principled, objection to judicial activism and, quite simply, it can be met by arguing that if there is a problem here, the answer is not necessarily to preclude judicial activism but rather to improve the ability of the courts to tackle these issues. I do not propose, at this point in the book, to examine whether the Irish courts, as they currently function, are capable of dealing with the type of litigation under consideration here and, if not, what sort of changes might be required.[123] Instead, I propose to take a brief look at the experience of the Indian courts in this regard in order to demonstrate that there are no insurmountable institutional obstacles to public interest litigation.[124]

The development of public interest litigation in India is closely linked to the experiences of the judiciary during the Emergency of 1975-77, in the aftermath of which the judges sought to improve the popular perception of a judicial system tarnished by a number of decisions sustaining the Emergency. However the radical views of two particular Supreme Court judges, Chief Justice Bhagwati and Mr Justice Krishna Iyer,[125] also contributed significantly to this development, leading Baxi to remark that "A striking feature of [public interest litigation in India] is that it is primarily judge-led and even judge-induced".[126]

The same commentator's list of the earlier instances of public interest litigation gives a very good flavour of the nature of this new jurisdiction.

---

permitted. Adaptation of the rules to peculiar individual circumstances is frowned upon. Discretion in the judge must be avoided for fear that it would lead to dangerous arbitrariness. Individualization of controversies, response to the unique human facts of the particular case, would make the law uncertain, unpredictable". – pp. 118-9.

[123] I do examine these issues in more detail below, see ch. 2.

[124] On public interest litigation in India, see U. Baxi, "Taking Suffering Seriously: Social Action Litigation in the Supreme Court of India" in *Judges and the Judicial Power: Essays in Honour of Justice V.R. Krishna Iyer* (London and Bombay, 1985), (eds. R. Dhavan, R. Sudarshan and S. Kurshid) at p. 289; R. Dhavan, "Managing Legal Activism: Reflections on India's Legal Aid Programme" (1986) 15 *Anglo-American Law Review* 281; J. Cassels, "Judicial Activism and Public Interest Litigation in India: Attempting the Impossible?" (1989) 37 *American Journal of Comparative Law* 495; P.P. Craig and S.L. Deshpande, "Rights, Autonomy and Process: Public Interest Litigation in India" (1989) 9 *Oxford Journal of Legal Studies* 356; G.L. Peiris, "Public Interest Litigation in the Indian Subcontinent: Current Dimensions" (1991) 40 *I.C.L.Q.* 66.

[125] Krishna Iyer was briefly a Cabinet Minister in the Communist dominated coalition government in the State of Kerala until its dismissal in 1959.

[126] Baxi, at p. 291.

... [T]he first dramatic opportunity was provided by a Supreme Court advocate ... who filed a writ based on a series of articles in a national daily ... exposing the plight of Bihar undertrial prisoners, most of whom had served long pre-trial detention, indeed to a point that they had as it were, sentences to their credit. In 1980, two professors of law made a letter to the editor of [a national daily] describing the barbaric conditions of detention in the Agra Protective Home for Women the basis for a writ petition under Article 21. This was followed by a similar petition for Delhi Women's Home by a third year law student in Delhi Law Faculty and a social worker. A law teacher on a social science research fellowship successfully brought to completion the trial of four young tribals, who grew up in a sub-jail awaiting trial. Three journalists, after an exposé of a thriving market in which women were bought and sold as chattels, filed a writ demanding prohibition of this practice and immediate relief for their (sic) victims through programmes of compensation and rehabilitation. In the same year, a legal correspondent of *The Statesman* brought to the notice of the court the inhumane conditions of detention of Naxalite prisoners in the Madras jail, challenging in the process the entire edifice of the Prisons Act, 1892. The special correspondent of *The Hindustan Times* also brought to the court a social activist's report on forced importation of seventy-five young children for homosexual relations in Kanpur jail. In early 1982, social workers of the Gandhi Peace Foundation, assisted by the author, filed writ proceedings against the state of Madhya Pradesh for allowing bonded labour to be paid wages of disability: that is, wages in kind of kesari dal, a toxic substance causing incurable lathyrism among the bonded labourers. A newly formed association of law teachers has brought writ proceedings against the same state for inhuman torture of young prisoners in Chattarpur jail.[127]

As Dhavan points out, public interest litigation fell into two distinct categories.[128] Many cases were concerned with specific outrages, such as the torture and ill-treatment of detainees. However other cases raised broader socio-economic problems, such as the plight of rickshawallahs, the issue of bonded labour and environmental protection. In all of these different contexts, however, the essence of the jurisdiction was that it was concerned with gross violations of fundamental rights or infringements of the rule of law caused, either through commission or omission, by the State and its agencies.

Four features of Indian public interest litigation are worthy of note in the present context. The first of these is the manner in which the Indian courts liberalised rules on standing to the point where, in certain circumstances, a third party can take legal action on behalf of an oppressed individual or class. Thus, in *S.P. Gupta v. Union of India*[129] Bhagwati C.J. said,

---

127 *Ibid.*, pp. 295-6. (Footnotes omitted).

128 *Ibid.*, pp. 297-8.

129 (1982) 2 S.C.R. 365; A.I.R. 1982 S.C. 149, (quoted in Peiris at p. 68). This case involved, *inter alia*, a challenge to the validity of a ministerial circular implementing a policy under which only a certain percentage of the judges who sat within a particular area could come from that area and a challenge to governmental policy of making short-term judicial appointments. The petitioners were the Bombay Bar Association and Law Society and the issue of standing arose because the defence argued that the petitioners themselves had not suffered any legal injury.

… [W]here a legal wrong or a legal injury is caused to a person or to a determinate class of persons by reason of violation of any constitutional or legal right or any burden is imposed in contravention of any constitutional or legal provision or without authority of law, or any such legal wrong or legal injury or illegal burden is threatened and such person or determinate class of persons is by reason of poverty, helplessness or disability or socially or economically disadvantaged position, unable to approach the Court for relief, any member of the public can maintain an application for an appropriate direction, order or writ in the High Court under Article 226 [of the Constitution] and, in the case of breach of any fundamental right, in the Supreme Court under Article 32.

Two factors arguably account for this development. The first is peculiar to India and simply reflects the fact that the social and cultural conditions of that country are very different from those of the English common law which spawned the requirements of *locus standi* in the first place. The second, however, has a wider relevance and reflects the view of members of the Indian judiciary that rules of standing designed for private law litigation are not always appropriate for the very different functions of public interest litigation. Peiris summarises this point as follows:

… [T]he view has been expressed with apparent cogency by the Supreme Court of India that the rule of law requires, as its irreducible premise, that the exercise of power by any organ of the State, whether it be the legislature, the executive or any other authority, has increasingly to be effected within the parameters of constitutional constraints and that, if any practice adopted by the State has the appearance of a breach of constitutional limitations, any member of the public has sufficient interest in the subject matter to impugn the practice by means of a writ petition which the Supreme Court, in the exercise of its constitutional jurisdiction, is bound to entertain and adjudicate upon. The thrust of the reasoning of Indian courts is that the restrictive postulates of *locus standi*, designed to attain the objective of depriving, upon the threshold, an "officious intermeddler" of the right to a hearing are generally inapplicable to the category of matters subsumed in the concept of public interest litigation.[130]

Another noteworthy feature of the Indian experience is the emergence of its distinctive "epistolatory jurisdiction", a relaxation of the procedural rules governing the initiation of litigation. The phrase "epistolatory jurisdiction" stems from the fact that actions need not necessarily be commenced by way of formal petition but may be initiated by letter to the court. Indeed, in one case, a judge converted a letter to the

---

[130] Peiris, p. 69. (Footnotes omitted). Baxi, drawing on the judicial reasoning of Mr Justice Bhagwati as he then was, offers the following justifications for this development: "First, the rules of law will be 'substantially impaired' if 'no one can have standing to maintain an action for judicial redress in case of public wrong or public injury'. It is 'absolutely essential that the rule of law must wean people away from the lawless street and *win them for the court of law.*' If breach of public duties was 'allowed' to go unredressed by courts on the ground of standing, it would 'promote disrespect for rule of law.' It will also lead to corruption and encourage inefficiency. It might also create possibilities of the 'political machinery' itself becoming 'a participant in the misuse or abuse of power'. Finally, the newly emergent social and economic rights require a new kind of enforcement." Baxi, n.62.

editor of a newspaper into a public interest law writ.[131] According to Baxi, this procedure was developed by Mr Justice Bhagwati partly to enable him to retain jurisdiction over public interest law cases, though this came at a price, depriving other judges of any exposure to this type of litigation and (Baxi speculates) contributing to a growth of factionalism on the Supreme Court.[132]

Public interest litigation in India has also generated a novel approach to fact-finding by the courts. Undoubtedly the most striking development here is the empanelment, by the courts, of socio-legal commissions of enquiry. Thus in one case concerning the impact of mining and quarrying operations on the environment, the court appointed a committee consisting of geologists, environmental scientists and town and country planners to report on the issue.[133] In another case concerning radiation levels in milk and dairy products, the court sought a report from a committee consisting of members of the Planning Commission, the Economic and Planning Council and the Atomic Energy Centre. An alternative mechanism used for fact-finding is the delegation of this function to the local judiciary. In both situations, the court confers extensive powers of investigation and discovery upon the committee or judge, as the case may be.

Finally, the Indian courts, like their US counterparts, have also taken innovative steps in relation to remedies, particularly in relation to the use of affirmative decrees. These consist of detailed administrative instructions to public bodies to remedy injustices or wrongdoing identified by the court. Given that such orders are detailed and require continuous supervision, they differ radically from traditional private law remedies. However that reflects the radical difference between conventional private law and public interest litigation, the former controlled by two parties and concerned with the past actions of those parties, where remedy and right are closely linked, the latter concerned with public policy and forward looking, where the remedy is intended to correct, rather than to compensate.[134] Indeed the Indian courts have carried the logic of this analysis of public interest litigation to its ultimate conclusion in issuing directions, which are sometimes quite elaborate, to federal and state governments for the laying down of policy.[135]

The purpose of providing this short account of the procedural innovations generated by public interest litigation in India is very modest. I do not contend that these innovations are necessarily appropriate in the rather different social and cultural conditions of Ireland. Nor do I cite the Indian experience as conclusive proof of the efficacy of public interest litigation in remedying social injustice.[136] However what the

---

[131] See Peiris, n. 5.

[132] Baxi, pp. 297-8.

[133] *Rural Litigation and Entitlement Kendra v. State of Uttar Pradesh* [1986] (Supp.) S.C.C. 517.

[134] For further consideration of this difference, see A. Chayes, "The Role of the Judge in Public Law Litigation" (1976) 89 Harvard Law Review 1281, referred to below, pp. 58-60.

[135] See Peiris, pp. 81-84.

[136] Galanter comments that "[p]ublic interest litigation [in India] ... is initiated and controlled by elites and is responsive to their sense of priorities. It carries no accountability to a specific client constituency nor does it imply a sustained commitment to such a constituency. Typically, it is an episodic response to a particular outrage. It does not mobilise the victims nor help them to develop capabilities for sustained effective use of law." – *Law and Society in Modern India*, (Oxford University Press, 1989), p. 291. For similar criticism of public interest litigation in India, see Dhavan (1986).

Indian experience does show is that objections to judicial activism rooted in a perceived inability of the courts to deal with issues of social justice are not necessarily conclusive. If public interest litigation is perceived as constitutionally and politically legitimate, then it should not be beyond the wit of the judiciary to develop appropriate procedural devices and remedies to cope with this very distinctive type of litigation.

The case for judicial enforcement of socio-economic rights

Having dealt with the three main objections to judicial activism, I now go on the offensive to argue the case for the judicial recognition of socio-economic rights under the Irish Constitution in circumstances in which the political process has failed adequately to vindicate those rights.

My argument here builds as follows. First, I point out that the Constitution does recognise two specific socio-economic rights. Then I argue that the Constitution can also be interpreted as protecting implied socio-economic rights which promote social inclusion. Finally, I contend that judicial enforcement of socio-economic rights is not precluded by the Constitution, though I also argue that such enforcement is only appropriate in circumstances in which the rights have clearly been neglected by the political process.

Socio-economic rights address the social and economic conditions necessary to facilitate participation in society and are part of what is known as second-generation rights referring to various aspects of social, cultural and economic activities.[137] Such rights may be either positive or negative, that is, the State may be obliged to take active steps (including the incurring of expenditure) to vindicate them or it may be restrained from interfering with their exercise. However inasmuch as they sometimes require positive State action for their vindication, socio-economic rights cannot be distinguished from civil and political rights, some of which, such as the right to a fair trial, the right to legal representation or the right to vote, are also positive rights.[138]

A perusal of the text of the Constitution quickly reveals a number of provisions which have a bearing on the issue of social inclusion.[139] Chief of these is Article 45

---

[137] See the discussion in de Villiers, "Social and Economic Rights" in *Rights and Constitutionalism: The New South African Legal Order* (van Wyk, Dugard, de Villiers and Davis, eds.) (Clarendon Press, 1996) at pp. 602-3. First generation rights refer to traditional liberal civil and political rights, while third generation rights refer to the right to self-determination, peace, development and a protected environment.

[138] Thus Sadurski argues that "there is nothing about the putative rights to a minimum subsistence which makes them relevantly different from 'the old civil rights' and which, therefore, makes their status *qua* rights questionable". See "Economic Rights and Basic Needs" in *Law, Rights and the Welfare State* (Sampford and Galligan, eds.) (Croom Helm, 1986) at pp. 49-50. See also the discussion in *Re-Righting the Constitution – The Case for New Social And Economic Rights: Housing, Health, Nutrition, Adequate Standard of Living* (Irish Commission for Justice and Peace, 1998) at pp. 13-16 and in Murphy, "Economic Inequality and the Constitution" in Murphy and Twomey (eds.), *Ireland's Evolving Constitution 1937-1997* (Hart Publishing, 1998) at pp. 169-171.

[139] For a very useful discussion, in the context of the Irish Constitution, of social rights (which embrace, but are also somewhat more extensive than, the category of rights under consideration here), see Phelan, "The Concept of Social Rights" (1994) 16 *DULJ (n.s.)* 105.

which explicitly lists a number of directive principles of social policy.[140] One of the constitutional provisions in respect of whose drafting the then Rev John Charles McQuaid[141] was actively involved,[142] Article 45 reflects a

> Catholic social teaching [which] sees the ideal society as one in which all social actors, the state included, are animated by right morality and a sense of justice in all spheres, directing their activity towards God as man's 'final end' and in which as a consequence there are no inherent or essential conflicts, as for example between employer and employee. It is a vision of social peace pervading a society in which all elements fulfil their moral duty. Its function is inspirational and didactic.[143]

The provision of Article 45 most directly relevant to social inclusion is that contained in section 4, sub-section 1:

> The State pledges itself to safeguard with especial care the economic interests of the weaker sections of the community and, where necessary, to contribute to the support of the infirm, the widow, the orphan, and the aged.

The remaining principles in Article 45, though not specifically focussing on social inclusion, also reflect a communitarian vision of society[144] insofar as they identify, as a goal of social policy, the need to promote the common good.[145]

---

[140] In this, the Irish Constitution set a trend which was subsequently followed by Burma in 1947, India in 1950, Nigeria in 1989 and Namibia in 1990.

[141] Then President of Blackrock College, Dublin, later Catholic Archbishop of Dublin.

[142] See Keogh, at p. 20.

[143] Coughlan, "The Constitution and Social Policy" in Litton, at p. 147.

[144] For further discussion of communitarianism and its relationship to social inclusion, see below, pp. 50-1.

[145] Sections 1 to 3 read:

1. The State shall strive to promote the welfare of the whole people by securing and protecting as effectively as it may a social order in which justice and charity shall inform all the institutions of the national life.

2. The State shall, in particular, direct its policy towards securing:-
   i. That the citizens (all of whom, men and women equally, have the right to an adequate means of livelihood) may through their occupations find the means of making reasonable provision for their domestic needs.
   ii. That the ownership and control of the material resources of the community may be so distributed amongst private individuals and the various classes as best to subserve the common good.
   iii. That, especially, the operation of free competition shall not be allowed so to develop as to result in the concentration of the ownership or control of essential commodities in a few individuals to the common detriment.
   iv. That in what pertains to the control of credit the constant and predominant aim shall be the welfare of the people as a whole.
   v. That there may be established on the land in economic security as many families as in the circumstances shall be practicable.

3. 1° The State shall favour and, where necessary, supplement private initiative in industry and commerce.

However the directive principles of social policy are clearly stated, in Article 45,[146] not to be cognisable by any court under any of the provisions of the Constitution and, therefore, do not directly give rise to justiciable socio-economic rights.[147] A number of such rights are, however, envisaged in Articles 41 and 42. Thus, Article 42.4 obliges the State, *inter alia*, to provide for free primary education, from which one can effortlessly infer a right on the part of children to such education.[148] Article 42.5 places a duty on the State to endeavour to supply the place of parents in those exceptional cases in which the parents have, for physical or moral reasons, failed in their duty towards their children. At minimum, it cannot be disputed that this obliges the State to provide shelter, food and clothing to children who have been abandoned by their parents or who are suffering from extreme neglect. Article 41.2.2 recognises a duty on the State "to endeavour to ensure that mothers shall not be obliged by economic necessity to engage in labour to the neglect of their duties in the home". The explicit recognition of such a duty, albeit one of "imperfect obligation",[149] arguably gives rise to a right on the part of mothers to some assistance, albeit unspecified, from the State.[150]

Moving on to the next part of my argument, I contend that the corpus of implied rights protected by the Constitution may embrace socio-economic rights necessary for participation by the individual in society. This argument rests on the view that the Constitution endorses values of social solidarity and social inclusion and that these values can inform our reading of Article 40.3 which protects the unenumerated fundamental rights of the citizen.[151] In support of this position, I would cite the

---

2° The State shall endeavour to secure that private enterprise shall be so conducted as to ensure reasonable efficiency in the production and distribution of goods and as to protect the public against unjust exploitation.

Section. 4. 2° reads:

The State shall endeavour to ensure that the strength and health of workers, men and women, and the tender age of children shall not be abused and that citizens shall not be forced by economic necessity to enter avocations unsuited to their sex, age or strength.

146 The prefatory clause in Article 45 provides:

The principles of social policy set forth in this Article are intended for the general guidance of the Oireachtas. The application of those principles in the making of laws shall be the care of the Oireachtas exclusively, and shall not be cognisable by any Court under any of the provisions of this Constitution.

147 This aspect of Article 45 is discussed further below at p. 50.

148 See *Crowley v. Ireland* [1980] IR 102; *O'Donoghue v. Minister for Health* [1996] 2 IR 20; *G.L. v. Minister for Justice*, unreported, High Court, 24 March 1995; *Comerford v. Minister for Education* [1997] 2 ILRM 134; *Sinnott v. Minister for Education*, unreported, High Court, 4 October 2000.

149 Barrington J.'s description in *Hyland v. Minister for Social Welfare* [1989] IR 624 at p. 639; [1989] ILRM 196 at p. 208.

150 Writing extra-judicially in 1987, Walsh J. expressed astonishment at the fact that "this protective guarantee" had never been invoked in any litigation – "The Constitution and Constitutional Rights" in Litton, p. 86 at p. 98. In fact, a subsequent (and to date only) attempt by a woman to use Article 41.2.2 in the courts to assert new rights failed when, in *L. v. L.* [1992] 2 IR 77; [1992] ILRM 115, the Supreme Court dismissed a claim that this provision entitled a wife to a share in the matrimonial property.

151 See *Ryan v. A.G.* [1965] IR 294.

Preamble to the Constitution which clearly reflects the Christian inspiration of the Constitution[152] and which states the purpose of the Constitution as "seeking to promote the common good, *with due observance of Prudence, Justice and Charity, so that the dignity and freedom of the individual may be assured, true social order attained*, the unity of our country restored, and concord established with other nations".[153] This purpose is also echoed in Article 45.1 which commits the State "to strive to promote the welfare of the whole people by securing and protecting as effectively as it may a social order in which justice and charity shall inform all the institutions of the national life".[154] My contention is that the references to the dignity of the individual, to the attainment of true social order and to the Christian virtues of justice and charity[155] clearly support the argument that a commitment to social justice and social inclusion is an important "preinterpretive" principle[156] informing the Constitution. Moreover, I argue that such a principle in turn supports the proprosition that the Constitution can give rise to positive entitlements, not merely provide protection for negative immunities, and that those entitlements will encompass socio-economic rights necessary to ensure participation in society.

Building this argument, I start with the views of Walsh J. on the significance of the virtues of prudence, justice and charity as expressed by him in *McGee v. Attorney*

---

[152] The opening lines of the Preamble are: "In the Name of the Most Holy Trinity, from Whom is all authority and to Whom, as our final end, all actions both of men and States must be referred".

[153] Emphasis added.

[154] While, as we have already noted, Article 45 states that the principles contained therein "shall not be cognisable by any Court under any of the provisions of the Constitution", some members of the judiciary have taken the view that this applies only in the context of judicial review of legislation and that the courts can take Article 45 into account when deciding whether a claimed constitutional right exists – see *Murtagh Properties Ltd. v. Cleary* [1972] IR 330 (Kenny J.); *A.G. v. Paperlink Ltd.* [1984] ILRM 373 (Costello J.), though see n. 174 below.

[155] Mullally is critical of reliance on the values of "prudence, justice and charity" in identifying rights – which she classifies as a "relativist natural law" approach to the identification of rights – on the grounds that it does not guard against judicial subjectivism and that it does not adequately protect the values of "pluralism and tolerationism" – see "Searching for Foundations in Irish Constitutional Law" (1998) XXXIII *Ir. Jur. (n.s.)* 333 at pp. 343-6. I have already argued above – see pp. 36-8 – that in the Irish context, judicial activism is ultimately subject to "popular override" and that fears of such activism are overstated. In relation to Mullally's second point, this is based on an equation of the values of prudence, justice and charity with Dworkin's "critical cultural morality" or Rawls "public, political culture". This equation is questionable and it is indisputable now that, whatever about the tragedies of the past, the major religious traditions in Ireland recognise the primacy of individual conscience which should afford adequate protection for pluralism and tolerance.

[156] See Sunstein's remarks above, p. 16. Article 40.1 of the Constitution provides for a guarantee of equality before the law. While one possible understanding of the concept of equality is that it is designed to improve the relative position of disadvantaged groups [the so-called "results approach" to equality], it is far from clear that this is how Article 40.1 should be understood and so I do not rely on the guarantee of equality in arguing for the constitutional recognition of socio-economic rights. See further, by the present author, "A Comment on the Constitution Review Group's Proposals on Equality" in Duncan and Byrne (eds.) *Developments in Discrimination Law in Ireland and Europe*, (I.C.E.L., 1997).

General.[157] According to Walsh J. those virtues serve as a lodestar for judges seeking to discern the personal rights implicitly protected by the Constitution and have to be viewed in the light of contemporary ideas and concepts.

> [J]udges must ... as best they can from their training and their experience interpret [the personal rights of the individual] in accordance with their ideas of prudence, justice and charity. It is but natural that from time to time the prevailing ideas of these virtues may be conditioned by the passage of time; no interpretation of the Constitution is intended to be final for all time. It is given in the light of prevailing ideas and concepts.[158]

Earlier in his judgment, he clearly identified the concept of charity with the Christian virtue of charity, saying,

> [T]he great additional virtue introduced by Christianity was that of charity – not the charity which consists of giving to the deserving, for that is justice, but the charity which is also called mercy.[139]

In attempting to understand what is meant by the constitutional value of charity, therefore, it would seem appropriate to consider how this concept is understood in the Judeo-Christian tradition from whence it came. According to *The Oxford Dictionary of the Christian Church,*[160] there are seven corporal works of mercy,[161] namely, feeding the hungry, giving drink to the thirsty, clothing the naked, harbouring the stranger, visiting the sick, ministering to prisoners and burying the dead. Commenting on these works of mercy, McBrien states that

> Although most of these works have to do with a Christian's obligations to the neighbor in need, they also have broader social and political implications today and are to be linked in many cases with the overriding demands of social justice ... But the dimension of mercy reminds Christians that their obligations go beyond even those required by social justice. Perhaps the bridge between social justice and mercy today is the "preferential option for the poor", now enshrined in Catholic social teachings ...[162]

This "preferential option for the poor" commits the Christian to a position of solidarity with the marginalised and excluded, an idea that is central to the Judeo-Christian tradition. Thus the World Council of Churches has affirmed "God's preferential option for the poor and [the Christian duty] to embrace God's action in the struggles of the poor in the liberation of us all",[163] while writing from the Jewish

---

[157] [1974] IR 284.

[158] *Ibid.* at p. 319.

[159] *Ibid.*

[160] Oxford University Press, 1997.

[161] There are also seven spiritual works of mercy but these are not relevant in the present context.

[162] *Catholicism* (3rd ed.) (Geoffrey Chapman, 1994) at p. 942.

[163] See *Justice, Peace, Integrity of Creation: World Convocation, Seoul, Korea, March 6-12, 1990; Final Document* (W.C.C., Central Committee, 25-30 March 1990, Document No. 19). For a very useful account of the development of both Roman Catholic and mainline Protestant social teaching during this century, including the growing emphasis on social inclusion, see Dorr, *The Social Justice Agenda: Justice, Ecology, Power and the Church* (Gill and Macmillan, 1991), pp. 45-82.

tradition, Cohn-Sherbok sees the commitment to promote social justice as an area of common ground between Judaism and Christianity.[164]

Drawing on this tradition which clearly influenced the Constitution, one can, therefore, readily impute a commitment to social inclusion as an important value in the Irish constitutional order. However the religious ancestry of this commitment also enables us to make the further argument that the Constitution protects justiciable socio-economic rights necessary to promote social inclusion. Commenting on the understanding of the nature of rights within the Roman Catholic tradition, Hollenbach states:

> Basic to [the Roman Catholic understanding of rights] is the primacy granted to the idea of rights as positive empowerments over rights as negative immunities. In classical liberalism rights are identified with certain freedoms that are protected against coercion or interference by others. They are defenses against the intrusions that other persons or the government might try to make into the individual's zone of freedom ... The argument for a communitarian understanding of rights questions whether this view of the political rights stressed by classical liberalism does justice to their true importance and meaning.[165]

Thus, in relation to traditional concepts such as freedom of speech or freedom of religion, Hollenbach argues that their real significance is not to protect a zone of privacy for individual pronouncements or beliefs but rather to enable citizens to deliberate with each other about ideas which can shape the nature of society. This understanding of political rights as "positive empowerments for life in community"[166] also

> shows why economic rights are indispensable conditions for any sort of life in common with other human beings.
>
> Like the political rights of classical liberalism, economic rights involve immunities from interference by others. They rule out stealing the last loaf of bread from a person facing starvation. They mean not preventing relief organizations from getting food to a region of an African nation suffering from famine because the inhabitants of that region are political adversaries. They mean not discriminating against blacks or women in ways that prevent them from obtaining the jobs and education they need and are capable of.
>
> These economic rights also have a positive dimension that expresses the fact that all rights are rights to participation in community. First, respect for these rights means that individuals

---

[164] Thus in "A New Agenda for Society" in *The Liberation Debate: Rights at Issue*, Leahy and Sherbok, (eds.) (Routledge, 1996) 213, he states, at p. 217,
> Here we can see the point of intersection between the Jewish faith and Christian liberation theology. For both Jews and liberation theologians, the coming of the kingdom in which God's heavenly rule will be made manifest is a process in which all human beings have a role. It involves the struggle for the reign of justice and righteousness on earth.

[165] "A Communitarian Reconstruction of Human Rights: Contributions from Catholic Tradition" in Douglas and Hollenbach (eds.), *Catholicism and Liberalism: Contributions to American Public Philosophy* (Cambridge University Press, 1994) at p. 141. See also, on this theme, Langan, "Human Rights in Roman Catholicism" in Curran and McCormick (eds.), *Readings in Moral Theology No.5: Official Catholic Social Teaching* (Paulist Press, 1986) at p. 110.

[166] *Ibid.*, p. 144.

and society as a whole have obligations to take the positive steps necessary to assure that all persons obtain the nutrition, housing, and employment necessary if they are to live minimally decent and active lives. Some of these steps will take the form of direct acts of assistance by one person to another. Others will be indirect, such as the creation of the social and economic institutions needed to secure these rights in a stable way for all over time.

Second, these economic rights call for enabling persons to express their agency through positive participation in the life of society ... [R]espect for human agency demands ... that people not only be maintained alive, but alive as active agents of their own well-being through participation in social life, for example, through being able to get a job with adequate pay and decent working conditions.[167]

In essence, therefore, the second part of my argument is that the Constitution, inspired as it is by the Judeo-Christian tradition, can be read as endorsing an understanding of rights which encompass socio-economic rights promoting social justice and participation in society and that those implied rights may be protected by Article 40.3.[168]

This proposition raises one important question which has to be addressed before I move on and that is, to what extent, if at all, is it permissible in a pluralist democracy to rely on a religious tradition in making the argument I advance here? At least two arguments can be advanced to justify reliance on religious values in making the case I argue for here.[169] The first would be to say that, even though it might be politically inappropriate for lawmakers in a pluralist society to rely on religious values in the making of civil laws, it might yet be necessary, as a matter of constitutional interpretation, to interpret the Irish Constitution in the light of a particular religious value.[170] So one might have to agree, as a matter of textual analysis, that the Constitution endorsed a religious view on some issue even though one might prefer that that approach had not been taken.

A second argument, and one on which I prefer to rest my case, is to say that reliance on religious values in formulating constitutional policy in this jurisdiction is permissible

---

[167] *Ibid.*, pp. 145-6.
[168] There does not appear to be anything distinctive about socio-economic rights that would warrant denying them constitutional protection – as we noted above, p. 43, both socio-economic and civil-political rights have positive, as well as negative, dimensions – and, indeed, the Irish courts have already recognised a right to earn a livelihood as one of the implied rights protected by Article 40.3 – see Kelly, *The Irish Constitution* (3rd ed.) (Dublin, 1994) at pp. 761-766.
[169] No doubt there are others. Consider, for example, Michael Perry's argument that the very notion of universal human rights itself is "ineliminably religious" – *The Idea of Human Rights: Four Inquiries* (Oxford University Press, 1998), ch. 1. In "Why Political Reliance on Religiously Grounded Morality is Not Illegitimate in a Liberal Democracy" (2001) 36 *Wake Forest Law Review* 217, Perry defends the use of religious beliefs in formulating public policy in a liberal democracy, developing his views expressed in *Religion in Politics* (Oxford University Press, 1997).
[170] See the analogous argument advanced by Costello J., writing extra-judicially in "The Irish Judge as Lawmaker" (published in *Constitutional Adjudication in European Community and National Law* (Curtin and O'Keeffe, eds., Butterworth (Ireland) Ltd., 1992) wherein he said, at p. 161, in relation to the use of natural law, "A judge may be a legal positivist and have no use for natural law concepts, but if the Constitution (as it does) explicitly recognises the existence of rights anterior to positive law these jurisprudential views must yield to the clear conclusions which are to be drawn from the construction of the constitutional text".

where (a) the text of the Constitution refers to such values *and* (b) the policy formulated is also capable of being supported by *secular* argument.[171] In the present context, therefore, the text of the Constitution arguably compels us to have regard to the Christian tradition in order to understand what is meant by the reference to "Justice and Charity" as it is that tradition which clearly inspired the use of those terms. Moreover, the policy argued for here, that this reference, taken in conjunction with other constitutional references to the dignity of the individual and true social order, commits the Constitution to an endorsement of social inclusion, is clearly defensible on secular terms and so the religious tradition is being used to identify which of a number of competing secular perspectives warrants constitutional protection.

If, contrary to what I have argued for above, one cannot rely on religious tradition in interpreting the Constitution, one can still argue that the constitutional objectives of assuring the dignity and freedom of the individual and of attaining true social order justify a reading of the Constitution that promotes social inclusion and that protects implied socio-economic rights.[172] Protecting the dignity of the individual clearly provides a warrant for tackling the conditions of deprivation endured by some in our society and the constitutional understanding of a "true social order" is an inclusive one, given the reference in Article 45.1 to the role of the social order in promoting the welfare of the "whole people". Moreover if, as Kenny J. held in *Murtagh Properties Ltd. v. Cleary*[173] it is legitimate for the courts to have regard to Article 45 for the purpose of identifying the implied personal rights protected by Article 40.3, then the State's pledge, in Article 45.4.1, "to safeguard with especial care the economic interests of the weaker sections of the community, and, where necessary, to contribute to the support of the infirm, the widow, the orphan, and the aged" again supports the view that Article 40.3 can protect socio-economic rights promoting social inclusion.[174]

At this point in our discussion of the constitutional understanding of personal rights, we may have arrived at the fringes of the contemporary and very large debate between

---

[171] This represents a change in my earlier published views on this question. In "The Role of Religion in the Constitutional Order" in Murphy and Twomey, p. 51, I argued against reliance on religious language in any circumstances as a justification for a policy that is coercive of conscientiously held beliefs. I now contend that reliance on religious argumentation is appropriate to resolve a "tie-break" between competing understandings of the Constitution, each of which is capable of being supported by secular argument.

[172] For a defence of socio-economic rights in the Irish context from a liberal-democratic perspective, see Quinn, "Rethinking the Nature of Economic, Social and Cultural Rights in the Irish Legal Order" in Costello (ed.), *Fundamental Social Rights: Current European Legal Protection & the Challenge of the EU Charter of Fundamental Rights* (Irish Centre for European Law, Dublin, 2001), p. 35.

[173] [1972] IR 330. See also *Nova Media Services v. Minister for Posts and Telegraphs* [1984] ILRM 161 and *A.G. v. Paperlink Ltd.* [1984] ILRM 373 where Costello J. also had regard to Article 45 in identifying implied rights for the purposes of Article 40.3.

[174] It should be noted, however, that in its recent decision in *In re Article 26 and the Planning and Development Bill 1999*, [2000] 2 IR 321; [2001] 1 ILRM 81, the Supreme Court expressly reserved its opinion as to whether *Murtagh Properties Ltd. v. Cleary* [1972] IR 330, *Nova Media Services v. Minister for Posts and Telegraphs* [1984] ILRM 161 and *A.G. v. Paperlink Ltd.* [1984] ILRM 373 were correctly decided in relation to their use of Article 45 – see n.154.

liberal and communitarian understandings of society.[175] Classical liberalism, after all, with its emphasis on liberty as a set of negative immunities protecting the individual from a coercive State, and with a commitment to neutrality in relation to conceptions of good, hardly provides an encouraging environment for judicial activism targeting marginalisation. Communitarianism, on the other hand, with its stress on the individual's life *in community*, would surely support the notion of a right to social inclusion. Both philosophies, moreover, are represented in the Irish Constitution. The constitutional guarantees of personal liberty, freedom of expression, freedom of assembly, freedom of association and freedom of religion are clearly inspired by the liberal tradition, while the provisions relating to the family and to private property are clearly derived from the communitarian tradition of Roman Catholic social teaching. However I suspect that, ultimately, the debate between liberalism and communitarianism may not be of assistance as we contemplate whether the Irish Constitution endorses a commitment to social inclusion. This is because my description of liberalism and communitarianism is wildly generalised; in fact, each of these philosophies is a very broad church, with each faith containing different strands of belief. Thus liberalism ranges from the libertarianism of writers like von Hayek[176] or Nozick, on the one hand, to the welfare state liberalism of Rawls or Dworkin, on the other. Conversely, communitarianism can embrace the democratic socialism of Walzer and the traditional conservatism of Oakeshott. Moreover, communitarianism is notoriously vague as to what is meant by "community". Can Travellers, for example, claim membership of a common community with settled people or are we dealing here with two separate communities? Consequently, wherever the fault-line between liberalism and communitarianism runs, it does not necessarily coincide with the division between those who wish to see the State actively committed to securing social inclusion and those who would deny the State that function.[177]

---

[175] A useful introduction to liberalism and communitarianism is provided by Festenstein – "Contemporary Liberalism" – and Frazer – "Communitarianism" – respectively, both in *New Political Thought: An Introduction,* Lent (ed.) (London, 1998). For a more detailed treatment of this debate, see *Liberalism and Its Critics,* Sandel (ed.) (New York University Press, 1984); *Communitarianism and Individualism,* Avineri and De-Shalit (eds.) (Oxford, 1992); Kymlicka, *Liberalism, Community and Culture* (Oxford, 1989) and *Contemporary Political Philosophy* (Oxford, 1990); and Mulhall and Swift, *Liberals and Communitarians* (2nd ed.) (Blackwell Publishers Ltd., 1996). See also Honohan, "The Common Good and the Politics of Community" in Dunne, Ingram and Litton (eds.) *Questioning Ireland: Debates in Political Philosophy and Public Policy* (I.P.A., 2000) at p. 73.

[176] Arguing that, because no one can have a comprehensive view of society, it is impossible to know what is of value to society and that, therefore, the concept of social justice was an illusion, von Hayek once wrote, with reference to altruism and solidarity, "It is these two instincts, deeply embedded in our purely instinctive or intuitive reactions, which remain the great obstacle to the development of the modern economy" – *Law, Legislation and Liberty, Vol. III,* (London, 1979) at p. 170. *Cp.* Margaret Thatcher's remark, "There is no such thing as Society. There are individual men and women and there are families" – *The Observer,* 27 December 1987.

[177] Though for an interesting attempt to defend public interest litigation in terms of one strand of communitarianism, civic republicanism, see Feldman, "Public Interest Litigation and Constitutional Theory in Comparative Perspective" (1992) 55 *MLR* 44. The dividing-line between those supportive of State action against social exclusion and those opposed *does* coincide with the

In conclusion, therefore, on this point, my argument is, essentially, that a commitment to social inclusion can fairly be read as part of the Irish constitutional order, that such a commitment may be inferred from the religious tradition that inspires part of the constitutional text or, if necessary, from a wholly secular reading of that text and that, insofar as this commitment may then be taken as a "preinterpretive fact" when interpreting the Constitution, there is thus a basis for recognising implied socio-economic rights promoting social inclusion.

I turn now to the final part of my argument in which I seek to establish that judicial enforcement of socio-economic rights is not precluded by the Constitution. The reader might wonder why, given that I have already argued that the Constitution protects socio-economic rights, I feel it necessary to deal separately with the question of the judicial enforcement of such rights. It certainly is legitimate to argue that once the Constitution protects a right, judicial enforcement of that right should follow as a matter of course. However there is a view abroad that it is somehow inappropriate for judges to involve themselves with socio-economic rights. Thus the principal argument listed by the *Report of the Constitution Review Group* against the explicit recognition of socio-economic rights in any reformulation of the Constitution, is that

> these are essentially political matters which, in a democracy, it should be the responsibility of the elected representatives of the people to address and determine. It would be a distortion of democracy to transfer decisions on major issues of policy and practicality from the Government and the Oireachtas, elected to represent the people and do their will, to an unelected judiciary.[178]

In the face of this type of argument, then, I wish to consider whether there is any reason why the socio-economic rights which I argue are explicitly or implicitly protected by the Constitution should not be enforceable by the judiciary.

Three possible arguments present themselves. First, there is the argument that I have just cited from the *Report of the Constitution Review Group*, namely that judicial enforcement of socio-economic rights is a "distortion of democracy". In response to this, I would simply refer the reader to the earlier section of this chapter in which, applying the arguments of Michael Perry, I defend judicial activism as compatible with democracy.[179] A second possible argument might be that, when compared to civil-political rights which are justiciable, socio-economic rights have distinctive characteristics which warrant the view that they are inherently justiciable. However,

---

distinction between a deliberative politics, which challenges, and ultimately seeks to transform, group or sectional preferences through public and rational discussion and a politics which treats those preferences as a given, described by Sunstein as a commitment to "status quo neutrality" – Sunstein, pp. 3-4 – or by Perry as "manipulative, self-serving politics" – *Morality, Politics and Law* (Oxford, 1988), pp. 151-2. For a more detailed examination of this distinction, see Nino, *The Constitution of Deliberative Democracy* (Yale University Press, 1996) at pp. 70-102. For a description of the second type of politics (which he considers to be dominant in both the US and the UK) and of the self-serving and inconsistent economic theory it generates, see Galbraith.

[178] Constitution Review Group, at p. 235.

[179] See above, pp. 28 *et seq.*

as we have already noted,[180] there do not appear to be any such relevant distinctions. Both types of right have positive, as well as negative, dimensions and both may require the expenditure of public money for their vindication. Finally, it might be argued that the prefatory remarks in Article 45 acts as a constitutional barrier to the judicial enforcement of socio-economic rights. If that ever was the intention behind those remarks, then it has to be said that the formula used is singularly ill-suited to achieve this purpose. At the highest, the remarks deny access by the courts to the principles of social policy listed in Article 45;[181] they do not preclude the courts from enforcing socio-economic rights derived from other provisions of the Constitution.

If there are no arguments against the judicial enforcement of socio-economic rights in the Irish Constitution, there appear to be at least two arguments in favour of such enforcement. The first flows from the rejection of the suggestion that relevant distinctions exist between socio-economic rights and civil-political rights. If no such distinctions exist, and if civil-political rights are justiciable, then surely socio-economic rights must be justiciable also. The alternative is to produce a two-tier system of constitutional rights without any apparent justification for the differentiation.[182] The second argument is derived from a concern with the process of law-making in a democracy and builds on an argument developed by Ely who defends a judicial activism designed to ensure that the political process is "open to those of all viewpoints on something approaching an equal basis".[183] Ely justifies this type of judicial activism on the ground, *inter alia,* that it is entirely consistent with representative democracy. Using this approach, he defends judicial action designed to facilitate the representation of minorities and judicial review of impediments to free speech, publication, political association and the right to vote. However he also concedes that "[t]he elaboration of a representation-reinforcing theory of judicial review could go many ways".[184] In the Irish context, this approach would, at a minimum, justify judicial enforcement of the socio-economic right to free primary education derived from Article 42 as it is difficult to imagine how anyone deprived of such an education could participate in any meaningful sense in the democratic process.[185] However, as Michelman points out,[186] this approach can also justify judicial

---

[180] See above, p. 43.

[181] Note that some judges would deny even this, arguing that the courts are precluded from relying on Article 45 only for the purpose of invalidating legislation but that for any other purpose, such as the identification of implied rights, the courts may legitimately take account of the Directive Principles of Social Policy – see cases referred to in Kelly, pp. 1120-2. See also n.154 above.

[182] An alternative way of putting this point would be to say that insofar as the Constitution commits itself, explicitly and implicitly, to the substantive principle of the protection of socio-economic rights, full effect, including judicial enforcement of those rights, should be given to that principle.

[183] Ely, at p. 74. The defence is set out in detail in ch. 4 of Ely's book. Nino takes a similar position – Nino, pp. 199-203.

[184] Ely, p. 181.

[185] Consequently this theory can be used to defend the judicial activism in relation to children's rights discussed in ch. 5.

[186] "Welfare Rights in a Constitutional Democracy" (1979) *Washington University Law Quarterly* 659, at p. 677.

protection of other socio-economic rights such as rights to subsistence, shelter and health care.

In conclusion, therefore, there would appear to be no good arguments against, and some good arguments for, the judicial enforcement of socio-economic rights. However, there are two very important caveats worth emphasising here. To argue that the courts *may* enforce socio-economic rights is not to say that they should be first into the fray. There are good institutional reasons why we should look initially to the legislative and executive branches for protection of such rights. Those branches have access to greater expertise in such matters and have more discretion or powers in relation to the means of protection. Consequently, I would argue that the courts should only be used as a last resort, when it is clear that the political process is incapable of protecting the right in question. Even at that, one can understand why the courts might prefer to limit their involvement in such cases to the granting of declarations. In many cases, this will vindicate the right in question and then return the initiative to the legislative or executive branch to take appropriate action. However, in extreme cases of egregious neglect of socio-economic rights by those two branches of government, such as we have witnessed over the past thirty years or so in relation to children at risk, the courts may have no option but to go beyond the granting of declarations to make orders directing the executive to take specific steps to remedy the situation.[187]

The second caveat that I want to enter at this point is to acknowledge that to argue that the courts may enforce socio-economic rights is not to establish that judicial intervention in this area has necessarily proved to be beneficial. The actual contribution of judicial intervention to the protection of socio-economic rights in Ireland is evaluated in Part II of this book.

Report of the Constitution Review Group

Before closing this chapter, I wish to digress slightly to consider the rejection by a majority of the Constitution Review Group of calls for the explicit inclusion in the Constitution of guarantees of socio-economic rights. The most that the Review Group was prepared to contemplate was the inclusion of rhetorical statements committing the State to, *inter alia*, the abolition of poverty, the promotion of justice and equality of opportunity in Article 45.[188] However a majority of the Group come out very strongly against the recognition of any legally enforceable rights in this context, essentially arguing that this would amount to a "distortion of democracy".[189] Elaborating on this argument, the Report expressed concern that the judges would

---

[187] See, most notably in this regard, the decisions of Kelly J. in *D.B. v. Minister for Justice* [1999] 1 IR 29; [1999] 1 ILRM 93 and *T.D. v. Minister for Education* [2000] 3 IR 62; [2000] 2 ILRM 321.

[188] Constitution Review Group, p. 394. In the event of an extended Preamble being retained (against the recommendation of a majority of the Review Group), the Group agreed that it might list society's aspirations to, *inter alia*, peace, reconciliation, justice, freedom and economic, social and cultural progress and indicate that these would be pursued on the basis of the inherent dignity of the individual and the equality of all – *ibid.*, p. 6.

[189] *Ibid.*, pp. 235-6.

have to rely on their own subjective appraisal of what constituted poverty and that judicial interpretation of a socio-economic right could deprive the Oireachtas and the Government of any power to determine the cost of implementing the right in issue.

At least four criticisms can be made of this reasoning. First, it is arguable that the Review Group's assertion that the recognition of socio-economic rights is a "distortion of democracy" is based on one particular political vision, classical liberal democracy.[190] Thus it will not convince those who do not subscribe to this particular vision of liberalism.[191] (In this context, it is perhaps worth noting in passing that the members of the Constitutional Assembly of the Republic of South Africa saw nothing objectionable in providing constitutional protection for a set of justiciable socio-economic rights designed to combat social exclusion.[192]) Moreover, as the Irish Commission for Justice and Peace points out,[193] it is difficult to see how the insertion of a clause guaranteeing socio-economic rights into the Constitution could distort democracy, given that such a move would require the approval of the People voting directly on the issue in a referendum. The Commission also points out that the Review Group's fear of judicial activism in this context is somewhat inconsistent with the Group's acceptance of the inevitability of subjective judicial appraisal of the guarantee of private property in Article 40.3 and 43 and it further argues that expansive judicial interpretation of socio-economic rights is unlikely, given the social background of the judiciary.[194]

Second, this section of the Review Group report is open to the charge of inconsistency. Listed in the arguments against recognising socio-economic rights is the view that, in any event, judicial vindication of the rights to life and to bodily

---

[190] Commenting on this aspect of the Review Group's report, Tim Murphy observes that, "The problem is essentially one of the majority regarding that which is historically contingent as 'given'" – Murphy, p. 169. Note also Butler and O'Connell's criticism of the Review Group that "they do not debate the different models of representative democracy and the values they serve". – "A Critical Analysis of Ireland's Constitutional Review Group Report" (1998) XXXIII *Ir. Jur. (n.s.)* 237 at p. 244. I attempt to identify the philosophical values underpinning the Review Group's recommendations relating to fundamental rights, including socio-economic rights, in "Discerning the philosophical premises of the Report of the Constitution Review Group: an analysis of the recommendations on Fundamental Rights" (1998) *Contemporary Issues in Irish Law and Politics* 216.

[191] Thus Feldman comments, "[T]here is nothing in democratic liberal theory which necessarily excludes legal protection for positive social and economic rights. People who deprecate attempts to enforce such rights (for example, those on the political Right who consider that the European Social Charter does not deserve to be considered as conferring rights on anyone or imposing duties on governments) are articulating a personal preference for one type of political or economic programme over others. Their claims, when analyzed, do not turn out to have an irrebuttable philosophical foundation." *Civil Liberties and Human Rights in England and Wales* (Oxford, 1993), at p. 17.

[192] The new Constitution of the Republic of South Africa, adopted by the Constitutional Assembly on 8 May 1996, provides for a right to have access to adequate housing (article 26); a right to have access to health care services, sufficient food and water and social security (article 27) and a right to basic education (article 29).

[193] Irish Commission for Justice and Peace, at p. 7.

[194] *Ibid.*, pp. 8 – 9.

integrity offer ultimate protection to anyone who might fall below a minimum level of subsistence so as to suffer from a lack of food, shelter or clothing. If this is so, then it is difficult to see what possible objection there could be to recognising, for example, an explicit right to shelter, enforceable by the courts, as an alternative to requiring the courts to infer such a right from the rights to life and bodily integrity. Moreover, in the section on education, the report calls for explicit recognition of the right of every child to free primary education and for possible extension of this right to cover second level education.[195] Yet the Review Group does not explain why a right to education should receive constitutional protection in this way while other, more basic (and sometimes less expensive) socio-economic rights, such as the right to shelter, are kept outside the constitutional pale.

Third, the Review Group's understanding of the nature of socio-economic rights has been challenged on two fronts – according to the Irish Commission for Justice and Peace, the Group's concern about uncontrollable costs resulting from judicial intervention here "appears to assume that there is no middle way between stating socio-economic rights in a totally open-ended manner, or excluding them from the Constitution altogether".[196] But as the Commission argue, it is possible to frame rights, including socio-economic rights, in a manner which allows considerations of practicability to limit the extent of the State's obligations and the Review Group itself recognises that in relation to the guarantee of the personal and property rights of the individual.[197] The Commission also accuses the Review Group of assuming a dichotomy between civil-political and socio-economic rights, a distinction for which there does not appear to be any justification[198] and which ignores developments in international law.[199]

Finally, the Commission points out that Ireland has, through ratifying a variety of international treaties, made itself subject to the scrutiny of a number of international bodies, including the European Court of Human Rights, in relation to its performance on socio-economic matters and it wonders whether it is not therefore anomalous to deny a similar role to the Irish courts.

In conclusion, therefore, the Review Group's rejection of the proposal to recognise certain socio-economic rights in the Constitution rests on suspect argumentation, the implications of which do not appear to have been fully thought through in relation to all aspects of the Review Group's report, and there does not appear to be anything in the Review Group's reasoning which presents a serious challenge to any of the arguments advanced in this chapter.

---

[195] The Report asks the Oireachtas to give serious consideration to extending the right to free education to cover second level education "as this may be defined by law". However the proposed reformulation of the Constitution in this regard contains a reference to a right to free second-level education which, one imagines, could be used as the basis for judicial review of the efforts of the Oireachtas in this regard – Constitution Review Group, p. 353.

[196] Irish Commission for Justice and Peace, p. 11.

[197] On this point, see also Murphy, p. 172.

[198] See above, p. 43.

[199] Irish Commission for Justice and Peace, pp. 13-16.

O'Reilly v. Limerick Corporation – the sequel

This chapter opened with a consideration of the decision of Costello J. in *O'Reilly v. Limerick Corporation* in which that judge dismissed a claim by Travellers that the State had a constitutional obligation to provide them with serviced halting sites on the ground that, under the Constitution, such a claim had to be addressed to the legislative branch of government rather than to the judiciary. I have sought to rebut three possible defences of Costello J.'s decision. These are the arguments that, first, the Constitution, as a matter of law, precludes judicial activism on behalf of marginalised groups; second, democratic politics precludes such a role; and, third, the courts lack the capacity to undertake such a role. I then argue the case in favour of judicial enforcement of socio-economic rights, contending that such rights are protected under the Irish Constitution, that they do not differ in any relevant respect from civil-political rights which are justiciable, and that the protection of representative democracy justifies judicial protection of such rights (though I also accept that recourse to the courts should only be as a matter of last resort, where it is clear that the political process has failed to protect the right in question).

Six years after he decided *O'Reilly*, Costello J. handed down an *ex tempore* judgment in the case of *O'Brien v. Wicklow UDC*.[200] This case again concerned a claim by Travellers that the State, acting through the local authority, had a duty to provide serviced halting sites for them. Once more, the evidence before the court was that the Travellers were living in appalling conditions which were unfit for human habitation. On this occasion, Costello J. held that such a duty did exist, following Barron J.'s interpretation of the Housing Act 1988 in *University of Limerick v. Ryan*.[201] But then he continued:

> I don't think it is necessary to say whether I am now expressing a different view to the one which I expressed in the case of *O'Reilly and Ors. v. Limerick Corporation*. In that case I was not considering the terms of Section 13 of the [Housing Act 1988]. Even, however, if the view which I am now expressing represents a change of views on my part, then I accept that my views have changed… I accept the argument that the plaintiffs have a constitutional right to bodily integrity which is being infringed by the conditions under which they are living.[202]

O'Reilly v. Limerick Corporation is undoubtedly the most sophisticated judicial attempt to date at analysing the relationship between the judiciary and the other branches of government. The fact that its author should, on a later occasion, courageously admit to a change of view bolsters the case argued for in this chapter, namely, that judicial intervention on behalf of marginalised groups whose pressing needs are studiously ignored by the political process can be defended as both constitutionally and politically legitimate.

---

[200] Unreported, High Court, 10 June 1994.
[201] Unreported, High Court, 21 February 1991.
[202] Unreported, High Court, 10 June 1994, at pp. 3-4.

Chapter 2

The Implications of Public Interest Litigation for Civil Procedures and Remedies

Procedural law, no less than substantive law, does not exist in a value-free zone and rules of procedure are ultimately informed by some perspective or other as to the proper role of the law. In this jurisdiction, procedural rules have traditionally been influenced by the emphasis on individualism at the heart of the common law and this has manifested itself in such areas as the dominant role of the parties to the litigation in controlling the process of litigation, the correspondingly muted role of the judge and the rather limited nature of judicial remedies. Public interest litigation, however, tends to be concerned more with the interests of groups than of individuals and consequently challenges many of the assumptions behind existing procedural rules and practices. In this chapter, I propose to consider the implications for procedural law raised by the pursuit of public interest litigation. I identify a number of issues relating to procedures and remedies that arise from the use of public interest litigation and I consider to what extent the Irish courts have moved to accommodate this qualitatively different form of litigation. We shall see that such development has occurred in relation to the rules on standing and in relation to the types of remedy provided by the court but that following through on the logic of public interest law requires further change in relation to the doctrine of mootness, the use of amicus curiae briefs and mechanisms for enhancing the impact of judicial decisions.

Public Interest Litigation and Conventional Litigation Contrasted

One of the first commentators to identify a difference between public interest litigation and conventional litigation was Abram Chayes. In a seminal article published in 1976, he argued that what he called "public law litigation" could not be accommodated within the traditional conception of adjudication.[1] According to Chayes, the traditional model of litigation has the following characteristics:

(1) The lawsuit is *bipolar*. Litigation is organized as a contest between two individuals or at least two unitary interests, diametrically opposed, to be decided on a winner-takes-all basis.

(2) Litigation is *retrospective*. The controversy is about an identified set of completed events: whether they occurred, and if so, with what consequences for the legal relations of the parties.

(3) *Right and remedy are interdependent*. The scope of the relief is derived more or less logically from the substantive violation under the general theory that the plaintiff will get compensation measured by the harm caused by the defendant's breach of duty – in contract by giving plaintiff the money he would have had absent the breach; in tort by paying the value of the damage caused.

(4) The lawsuit is a *self-contained* episode. The impact of the judgment is confined to the parties. If plaintiff prevails there is a simple compensatory transfer, usually of money, but occasionally the return of a thing or the performance of a definite act. If defendant prevails, a loss lies where it has fallen. In either case, entry of judgment ends the court's involvement.

(5) The process is *party-initiated* and *party-controlled*. The case is organized and the issues defined by exchanges between the parties. Responsibility for fact development is theirs. The trial judge is a neutral arbiter of their interactions who decides questions of law only if they are put in issue by an appropriate move of a party.[2]

Public law litigation, in contrast, shared none of these characteristics. With this type of litigation:

(1) The scope of the lawsuit is not exogenously given but is shaped primarily by the court and the parties.

---

[1] "The Role of the Judge in Public Law Litigation" (1976) 89 *Harvard Law Review* 1281. See also, by the same author, "The Supreme Court 1981 Term – Foreword: Public Law Litigation and the Burger Court" (1982) 96 *Harv. L. Rev.* 4; O. Fiss, "The Supreme Court 1978 Term – Foreword: The Forms of Justice" (1979) 93 *Harv. L. Rev.* 1. The latter commentator refers to "structural reform" litigation which he describes, at p. 2, as litigation "in which a judge, confronting a state bureaucracy over values of constitutional dimension, undertakes to restructure the organization to eliminate a threat to those values posed by the present institutional arrangements". Chayes' "public law litigation" corresponds to Cappelletti and Garth's "second wave" in the effort to improve access to justice – see *Access to Justice, Vol. 1* (Sijthoff, Giuffre, 1975) at pp. 35 to 48 – and may be somewhat broader in its stated object, which is "the vindication of constitutional or statutory policies" – Chayes, p. 1284 – than Fiss' model. (Tobias purports to discern a difference between these two terms – see, "Public Law Litigation and the Federal Rules of Civil Procedure" (1989) 74 *Cornell Law Review* 270 at p. 282.) However given that both models are concerned with the pursuit of important social values through the courts and given that Chayes' description of the judicial decree as "establishing an ongoing affirmative regime of conduct" resonates with Fiss' description of structural reform through the courts, any differences between them are arguably irrelevant in the present context. For an argument that a model of adjudication appropriate for litigation between individual parties is inappropriate for litigation involving bureaucratic organisations, see M. Dan-Cohen, "Bureaucratic Organizations and the Theory of Adjudication" (1985) 85 *Col. L. Rev.* 1.

[2] Chayes, pp. 1282-3.

(2) The party structure is not rigidly bilateral but sprawling and amorphous.

(3) The fact inquiry is not historical and adjudicative but predictive and legislative.

(4) Relief is not conceived as compensation for past wrong in a form logically derived from the substantive liability and confined in its impact to the immediate parties; instead, it is forward looking, fashioned ad hoc on flexible and broadly remedial lines, often having important consequences for many persons including absentees.

(5) The remedy is not imposed but negotiated.

(6) The decree does not terminate judicial involvement in the affair: its administration requires the continuing participation of the court.[3]

(7) The judge is not passive, his function limited to analysis and statement of governing legal rules; he is active, with responsibility not only for credible fact evaluation but for organizing and shaping the litigation to ensure a just and viable outcome.[4]

(8) The subject matter of the lawsuit is not a dispute between private individuals about private rights, but a grievance about the operation of public policy.[5]

Public interest litigation on behalf of the disadvantaged in Irish society contains some, at least, of these latter features. Thus the subject matter of such litigation is usually about the content and/or operation of public policy with the result that the court's decision is likely to affect a significant number of individuals in addition to the particular parties to the litigation; the fact inquiry may be at least partly predictive and legislative, rather than solely historical and adjudicative[6]; and the relief sought may be forward looking, rather than merely designed to compensate for past wrongs.

---

[3] Eisenberg and Yeazell take issue with this aspect of Chayes' analysis, arguing that judicial ordering of the affairs of complex institutions is a feature of much traditional litigation, notably in procedural matters such as default judgments and prejudment remedies and in such substantive areas as probate, trusts and bankruptcy – "The Ordinary and the Extraordinary in Institutional Litigation" (1980) 93 *Harv. L. Rev.* 465.

[4] This feature of public interest litigation undermines an attempt by Peters to defend judicial adjudication as a democratic form of interest representation – see "Adjudication as Representation" (1997) 97 *Col. L. Rev.* 312. According to Peters' theory, for adjudication to function as a democratic form of interest representation, *inter alia*, "the parties must be allowed to take the lead in shaping the litigation through the presentation of proofs and reasoned arguments, and the court's decision must ... actually 'proceed from and be congruent with [the parties'] proofs and arguments'". [p. 375.] However the role of the judge in public interest litigation, as described by Chayes, "implies a reduced role for the litigants – a smaller percentage of actual litigant authorship of the eventual decision". – Peters, at p. 433.

[5] Chayes, p. 1302. This distinction between the traditional conception of litigation and public interest litigation is echoed in the comments of the Indian Supreme Court in a public interest law case, *Dr. P. Nalla Thampy v. Union of India* [1983] 4 S.C.C. 598, (quoted in G.L. Peiris, "Public Interest Litigation in the Indian Subcontinent: Current Dimensions" (1991) 40 *I.C.L.Q.* 66 at p. 71), that, "The *lis* before us is not of the ordinary type where there are two contending parties, a claim is raised by one and denied by the other, issues are struck, evidence is led and the findings follow". According to Peiris, "The Court characterised this type of case as involving, quintessentially, resolve on the petitioner's part 'to voice the grievances of the community'". – *Ibid.*

[6] The distinction between "legislative" and "adjudicative" facts was first drawn by Davis – see "An Approach to Problems of Evidence in the Administrative Process" (1941-2) 55 *Harv. L. Rev.* 364 – and is a distinction between general social and economic facts, on the one hand, and facts which relate to the specific parties to litigation, on the other.

The extent to which contemporary procedural rules and practices of the Irish courts accommodate public interest litigation varies. Clearly there are certain features of these rules and practices which facilitate such litigation. For example, the use of Brandeis briefs,[7] a device used to bring legislative facts to the notice of the court, is now an acceptable feature of forensic practice, primarily in the context of constitutional adjudication.[8] And as we shall see presently, some developments in the rules of standing make it easier to present public interest issues before Irish judges.[9]

However at least some of the procedural rules and practices governing litigation in the Irish courts are informed by the traditional conception of adjudication,[10] with adverse implications for litigation strategy. Yet, if one accepts the constitutional and political legitimacy of public interest litigation,[11] there is no reason why such litigation should be constrained by the use of procedures and remedies inspired by a very different understanding of litigation.[12] In particular, the following issues need to be addressed if the Irish legal system is to accommodate public interest litigation effectively – consideration has to be given to the possibility of allowing the interests of third parties affected by litigation to be presented to the court; the doctrine of

---

[7] The name is derived from the fact that in *Muller v. Oregon* 208 US 412 (1908), counsel for the State of Oregon, Louis Brandeis, filed a detailed brief referring to medical and social science data as part of his defence of the constitutionality of legislation limiting the hours worked by women in laundries. For a brief outline of the history of this case, see Harlow and Rawlings, *Pressure Through Law* (London, 1992), pp. 76-8. Commenting on its impact, the authors say, at p. 77,

> The importance of this innovation for the future of interest-group litigation cannot be overestimated. First, it opened the door to the admission of sociological and other contextual material not normally admissible under legal rules of evidence. This in turn encouraged American courts to take a bolder line on policy-making. Second, when combined with the so-called "amicus brief" ... it provided a convenient way for third parties to participate in court proceedings.

[8] See, e.g., *O'Donovan v. Attorney General* [1961] IR 114; *Ryan v. Attorney General* [1965] IR 294; *Brennan v. Attorney General* [1984] ILRM 355; *O'Reilly v. Minister for the Environment* [1986] IR 143; *O'G. v. A.G.* [1985] ILRM 61; *Norris v. A.G.* [1984] IR 36; *O'Donoghue v. Minister for Health* [1996] 2 IR 20. On the use of Brandeis briefs in Irish constitutional litigation, see a very useful and informative article by Ann Sherlock, "Constitutional Litigation in Ireland" in (1991) 40 *ICLQ* 425.

[9] See pp. 67 *et seq.* below.

[10] Specifically in relation to *locus standi*, see Cane, "The Function of Standing Rules in Administrative Law" (1980) *Public Law* 303, at pp. 327-8.

[11] Of course, for those who do not accept the legitimacy of public interest litigation, much, if not all, of what follows in this chapter would be very objectionable. I engage with their concerns and beliefs in ch. 1 above.

[12] In *Bandhua Mukti Morcha v. Union of India* [1984] 3 S.C.C. 161, the Indian Supreme Court commented, at p. 189, "We have therefore to abandon the *laissez faire* approach in the judicial process ... and forge new tools, devise new methods and adopt new strategies for the purpose of making fundamental rights meaningful for the large masses of people". (Quoted in Cassels, "Judicial Activism and Public Interest Litigation in India: Attempting the Impossible?" (1989) 37 *American Journal of Comparative Law* 495 at p. 501.) See also Sherlock, "Understanding Standing: *Locus Standi* in Irish Constitutional Law" (1987) *Public Law* 245, esp. pp. 267-9, in which she demonstrates the connection between particular perceptions of the power of judicial review and procedural rules such as the doctrine of standing.

mootness needs to be modified so that the settlement of an individual claim will not prevent a judge from resolving an issue that continues to affect similarly situated individuals; and a satisfactory method of extending the benefits of a judicial decision to the wider population affected by the ruling needs to be devised.

In considering the extent to which the legal system is capable of accommodating public interest litigation, I begin by examining three areas where such accommodation arguably is taking place, namely, the rules on *locus standi*, the development of the affirmative judicial decree and the appearance of the pre-emptive costs order, before moving on to consider the issues referred to in the previous paragraph.

Protecting group or public interests through the courts: the rules on standing

The emergence of public interest ligitation raises three issues in relation to the rules on standing.[13] First, do lobby groups have *locus standi* to take proceedings in defence of the interests of their members? Second, to what extent, if at all, can private individuals or groups take legal action in defence of the public interest, that is to say, in cases in which the plaintiff cannot claim to be more affected by the challenged action than any other member of the general public? This last issue shades off into the further question of whether, and if so to what extent, Irish law permits an individual to take legal action on behalf of third parties.

a) Locus standi of association acting in defence of the interests of its membership

In approaching this topic, one should distinguish initially between groups which are still unincorporated associations in law and groups which have been incorporated under the Companies Acts. There would appear to be very few Irish authorities dealing with the right of an unincorporated association or group to take legal action

---

[13] This, of course, assumes that rules of standing, however liberal, should apply to public interest litigation. Not everyone takes that view. In the UK a joint working party from JUSTICE and the Public Law Project argue that in deciding on the admissibility of instances of public interest litigation, the standing of the applicant should be, at most, a secondary consideration.

> "In our view, the key to proper control of litigation of this kind rests in a recognition that in a public interest challenge the court, in deciding whether the application should go ahead, is not primarily concerned with the question of standing at all ... .[I]n a public interest case the court's first concern is to see whether the issue raised is one which ought to be litigated irrespective of the applicant's identity. If it should, the court will then look at the range of other factors, from delay to bad faith, in deciding whether as a matter of discretion the case should go ahead. From first to last the question will be whether the court judges that in all the circumstances the case should in the public interest proceed."

JUSTICE/Public Law Project, *A matter of public interest: Reforming the law and practice on interventions in public interest cases* (London, 1996) at pp. 11-2. For a somewhat critical note on this report, see Schiemann L.J. "Interventions in public interest cases" (1996) *Public Law* 240. For argument in favour of open standing in public interest litigation, see Fisher and Kirk, "Still Standing: An Argument for Open Standing in Australia and England" (1977) 71 *Australian Law Journal* 370.

in its own name on behalf of its membership. However it would appear that, as an unincorporated association does not have a legal identity distinct from that of its membership, it cannot sue in its own right and can only bring its concerns into court by way of a representative action.[14]

The *locus standi* of one particular type of unincorporated association, a trade union registered under the Trade Union Acts 1871-1990,[15] has been considered by the courts on three occasions.[16] In *R.(IUDWC) v. Rathmines UDC*[17] the Supreme Court of Saorstát Éireann unanimously held that such an entity was to be regarded in law as having quasi-corporate status. However, a majority held that the plaintiff union did not have sufficient standing to seek an application for mandamus directing a local authority to enforce legislation enacted for the benefit of the union's members. Speaking for the majority, Murnaghan J. held that the union rule book did not authorise the union to take such legal proceedings but that even if it had, this would not have been sufficient to allow the union to sue as the union, as a legal entity distinct from its membership, had no interest in the subject-matter of the case. According to the judge, the union could not purport to act on behalf of individual members who had such an interest because the principle of individual liberty prevented the merger of the rights of the individual in those of the union.[18]

Murnaghan J.'s concern that the rights of the individual might be overborne by the actions of the assocation arguably carried him too far in his conclusion, for this concern

---

[14] This is probably the basis for the decision of Doyle J. in *The State (King) v. Minister for Justice* [1984] IR 169 that the plaintiffs, who were complaining about the State's failure to maintain Waterford Courthouse, were entitled to relief in their personal capacities as practising solicitors in the area but not in their capacity as members of the unincorporated Waterford Law Society. In *Scarff v. Commissioners of Public Works in Ireland*, unreported, High Court, 15 March 1995, Flood J. indicated that proceedings could not be maintained on behalf of an unincorporated association in the absence of either an application for a representative order or the fiat of the Attorney General.

[15] For detailed discussion of the legal status of such a body, see Kerr and Whyte, *Irish Trade Union Law* (Professional Books Ltd., 1985) at pp. 63-9.

[16] In a fourth case, *Gorman v. Minister for the Environment and Local Government*, unreported, High Court, 7 December 2000, Kelly J. appears to have assumed that a union, the National Taxi Drivers' Union, could take legal proceedings in defence of its members' interests.

[17] [1928] IR 260.

[18] Thus he said, at p. 306:

The individual joining an association or Union remains in the eye of the law the possessor of the rights, and is subject to the duties, of a citizen, and no part of these rights is translated to the entity know (sic) as his Union. Once a trade union is recognised as a legal entity, distinct from the personalities of the individuals who happen to be members, it must be considered quite as distinct from these individuals as is an incorporated company from its shareholders. If any other view were held, what would be the position if the trade union applied for a mandamus against the will of its members affected in the particular area? Is the will of these members to prevail, or are they to be taken to have surrendered their liberty of action to the Union? ... In my view, the doctrine of representation of individuals cannot be applied so as to enable a trade union, which itself has no legal standing, to represent individuals who have. If the individuals who are affected will not for any reason move the Courts to deal with the alleged grievance, the trade union can only resort to such political action as it may think best to induce the appropriate public authority ... to take action.

could have been adequately addressed by requiring that the represented individuals have some degree of control over the conduct of the association.[19] However denying the association the right to sue on behalf of its membership in any circumstances, even where the membership supported such a course of action, closes down an option which might be very important for the vindication of the rights of individuals where, for example, the aggregated resources of the membership would be better able to finance litigation or where it would be desirable to have the particular legal entitlements of the membership determined all at once, rather than through a series of judgments in individual cases. Moreover, one could also conceivably argue that allowing an association to sue on behalf of its membership is an incident of the right of citizens to form associations under Article 40.6.1.iii, a point not considered by the majority in the *IUDWC* case in relation to the equivalent Article 9 of the 1922 Constitution.

In contrast to the majority judgments, the dissenting judgment of Chief Justice Kennedy was more accommodating of the right of a union to take legal action on behalf of its membership. In common with the majority, he held that the union had a distinct legal identity from that of its members but then he went on to hold, having regard to the objects of the union, that it had standing to seek mandamus "to prevent the defeat of some of the very objects for which it existed within the law".[20] Significantly, however, Kennedy C.J. did not see the union as acting in a representative capacity, given that it had a legal identity distinct from those of its members. Rather it had standing in its own right, because of its objectives.

Plaintiff unions were more successful in the remaining two cases under consideration. In *Transport Salaried Staffs' Association v. C.I.É.*,[21] the plaintiff union sought to enforce a statutory duty imposed on the defendants to regulate rates of pay in accordance with agreements made with, *inter alia*, the plaintiff union. Both the High Court (Kenny J.) and the Supreme Court held that the union did have standing to maintain an action for a declaration. According to Walsh J., the union had a sufficiently substantial interest in these proceedings as it was a party to the agreement that it sought to enforce. However this holding would appear to suggest that the union had standing in its own right rather than as representing the interests of its members. A different view was taken by Kelly J. in the last of this trilogy of cases. In *Rafferty v. Bus Éireann*,[22] a legal challenge was made, by way of judicial review, to the introduction of new terms and conditions of employment by the defendant company. One of the three plaintiffs was the National Bus and Rail Union, a registered union representing 600 of the company's employees. One of the company's preliminary objections challenged the *locus standi* of the union on the ground that it was nothing more than the agent of known or ascertainable principals. Dismissing this objection, Kelly J. held that the union was entitled to bring these proceedings in a representative capacity representing all of its members who are in the employment of the company.[23]

---

[19] See Cane, "Standing up for the Public" (1995) *Public Law* 276 at p. 278.
[20] [1928] IR 260 at p. 302.
[21] [1965] IR 180.
[22] [1997] 2 IR 440.
[23] *R. (IUDWC) v. Rathmines UDC* [1928] IR 260 was not cited to the court.

Thus it seems clear that a registered union may bring legal proceedings in defence of its members' interests, suing either in its own right or in a representative capacity on behalf of its members. However registered trade unions are quasi-corporations, with a legal identity separate from that of the membership,[24] so that it does not follow that groups that are clearly unincorporated associations are in the same favourable position.

Consequently, there is no clear authority that unincorporated associations have *locus standi* to represent their members in legal proceedings[25] and some indication that they do not.[26] However it is difficult to see any reason why such standing should be denied in such cases, assuming that the organisation is authorised by its own rules or memorandum of association to take such action.[27] The argument advanced by Murnaghan J. in the *IUDWC* case is arguably mistaken in its assumption that a rejection of the standing of an organisation in this context is necessary in order to protect the liberty of the individual members. In appropriate cases it is arguable that that liberty, and the constitutional right of individuals to form associations, would be more adequately vindicated by permitting the organisation to sue in its own name in defence of the interests of the membership. Moreover, viewing this matter through a constitutional prism, there does not appear to be any reason in principle why the right to sue in this way should be restricted to incorporated bodies, given that freedom of association is not restricted to the formation of incorporated bodies.[28]

However, in the light of the difficulties relating to the *locus standi* of unincorporated associations, it is not surprising that pressure groups sometimes

---

[24] See Kerr and Whyte, pp. 63-6.

[25] Though in *Irish Creamery Milk Suppliers' Association and Ors. v. Government of Ireland* (1979) 3 JISEL 48 – a challenge to the validity of levies imposed by the defendant on certain agricultural products – the court appears to have taken for granted the standing of the plaintiff organisation to represent the interests of its membership. See also *McMenamin v. Ireland* [1996] 3 IR 100, [1997] 2 ILRM 177, in which the plaintiff took proceedings against the State on his own behalf and on behalf of the Association of District Judges. Again his standing to represent his fellow judges was not considered by the court.

[26] See note 14 above. In *Village Residents' Association Ltd. v. An Bord Pleanála*, [2000] 1 IR 65, at p. 72; [2000] 2 ILRM 59, at p. 66, Geoghegan J. observed that, "it is unwieldy and unwise to try and mount litigation in the name of or on behalf of an unincorporated association".

[27] It is perhaps worth noting that in the US, an association has standing to represent the interests of its members when (i) the individual members would have standing to sue in their own right; (ii) the interests the association seeks to protect are germane to its purpose and (iii) the nature of the claim and the relief sought are such that the presence of the individual member is not required – see *Warth v. Seldin* 422 US 490 (1975); *Hunt v. Washington Apple Advertising Commission* 432 US 333 (1977). Closer to home, in the UK, a trade union was held to have standing to seek judicial review of the Chief Adjudication Officer's advice concerning deductions from supplementary benefit payable to its members who were on strike – see *R. v. Chief Adjudication Officer, ex p. Bland*, *The Times*, 6 February 1985.

[28] In this context, it is worth noting that both the UK Law Commission and the JUSTICE/Public Law Project working group have called for recognition of the right of unincorporated associations to bring public interest litigation – see, respectively, *Administrative Law: Judicial Review and Statutory Appeals*, Law Commission No. 226, para. 5.16 to 5.22 and Justice/Public Law Project, p. 10.

incorporate themselves in order to pursue litigation on behalf of their members. In a number of recent cases, the courts have had occasion to consider the standing of limited companies formed by community groups for the protection of their interests. In *Malahide Community Council Ltd. v. Fingal Co. Co.*[29] Lynch J. expressed some doubt, obiter, as to whether the plaintiff company, which was established to provide a framework for individuals and organisations to work together to promote the welfare of the Malahide community, had locus standi to challenge planning decisions made under the Local Government (Planning and Development) Acts 1963 – 1993, given that it did not own any buildings or land which might be affected by such decisions. However that comment runs against the general trend of recognising the standing of such bodies, at least in the context of planning law. In *East Wicklow Conservation Community Ltd. v. Wicklow Co. Co.*[30] the standing of the plaintiff company, which had been formed by local residents to challenge the defendant's decision to locate a landfill site in their neighbourhood, appears to have been taken for granted. But in a series of three other cases, *Lancefort Ltd. v. An Bord Pleanála,*[31] *Blessington Heritage Trust Ltd. v. Wicklow Co. Co.*[32] and *Wicklow Heritage Trust Ltd. v. Wicklow Co. Co.,*[33] the issue of the standing of the plaintiff companies was addressed by the court and resolved in their favour. In a further case, *Lancefort Ltd. v. An Bord Pleanála (No.2),*[34] the Supreme Court accepted that, as a general proposition, a company limited by guarantee having no property or economic interests affected by planning permission might still be entitled to locus standi in proceedings challenging such permission.[35] Delivering the majority judgment, Keane J. (as he then was) said:

> It is, understandably, a matter of concern that companies of this nature can be formed simply to afford residents' associations and other objectors immunity against the costs of legal challenges to the granting of planning permission. Our law, however, recognises the right of persons associating together for non-profit making or charitable activities to incorporate themselves as limited companies and the fact that they have chosen to do so should not of itself deprive them in every case of *locus standi.*[36]

While these cases all arose in the context of planning law, the reasoning of Keane J. is capable of applying to companies formed to protect interests other than those affected by the operation of the planning code and this raises the possibility that limited companies formed to protect the interests of community groups may have

---

[29] [1997] 3 IR 383.

[30] [1997] 2 ILRM 72.

[31] [1997] 2 ILRM 508.

[32] [1999] 4 IR 571. This decision was subsequently cited with approval by Keane J. (as he then was) in *Lancefort Ltd. v. An Bord Pleanála (No.2)* [1999] 2 IR 270; [1998] 2 ILRM 401.

[33] Unreported, High Court, 5 February 1998.

[34] [1999] 2 IR 270; [1998] 2 ILRM 401.

[35] Though in the instant case, a majority held that the plaintiff company had no *locus standi.*

[36] [1999] 2 IR 270 at pp. 317-8; [1998] 2 ILRM 401 at p. 442. In *Village Residents' Association Ltd. v. An Bord Pleanála* [2000] 1 IR 65; [2000] 2 ILRM 59, Geoghegan J. held, following the principles enunciated by Keane J. in *Lancefort*, that a company formed by residents had *locus standi* to challenge a decision of the defendant Board granting planning permission.

standing to protect those interests in legal proceedings.[37] Thus in *Shannon Preservation and Development Company Ltd. v. E.S.B.*[38] O'Sullivan J. held that a company limited by guarantee and formed by six unincorporated fishing clubs had *locus standi* to bring an action complaining of the defendant's alleged breach of its statutory duty to preserve the Shannon fisheries.

The use of company status to litigate community interests does come at a price, however, given that pursuant to s.390 of the Companies Act 1963, the High Court may order a plaintiff company to provide security for costs to the defendant and that course of action was taken by the courts in *Lancefort Ltd. v. An Bord Pleanála,*[39] *Village Residents' Association Ltd. v. An Bord Pleanála (No. 2)*[40] and *Shannon Preservation and Development Company Ltd. v. E.S.B.*[41]

b) Locus standi of private party acting in defence of the public interest

Traditionally, the interests of the public were left to be defended in the courts by the Attorney General either suing directly in his own name or by effectively delegating this role to a member of the public through the so-called "relator action".[42] But, as Cousins points out,

---

[37] In a case which did not concern planning law, *Campaign to Separate Church and State Ltd. and Murphy v. Minister for Education*, [1998] 3 IR 321; [1996] 2 ILRM 241, Costello P. agreed to the unusual course requested by the parties that he deal with the substantive constitutional issues raised by the case – a challenge to the public funding of school chaplains – and that only if he resolved those in favour of the plaintiff company should he then consider the issue of the plaintiff's *locus standi*. As the plaintiff lost on the substantive issue, the question of *locus standi* was not considered by the court nor was it considered by the Supreme Court on appeal – [1998] 3 IR 321; [1998] 2 ILRM 81.

[38] Unreported, High Court, 21 July 2000. See Costello, "Costs Principles and Environmental Judicial Review" (2000) XXXV *Ir. Jur. (n.s.)* 121 at pp. 124-6.

[39] [1998] 2 IR 511. A similar approach has been taken in the UK – see *R. v. Leicester Co. Co. ex parte Blackfordby & Boothcorpe Action Group Ltd.*, unreported, High Court, 15 March 2000; [2000] WL 191261.

[40] [2000] 4 IR 321. In the course of her judgment, Laffoy J. said, at pp. 332-3,
> [W]hen the Court is invited on a challenge to standing to infer that objectors to planning decisions have clothed themselves with limited liability for the less than pure motive of conferring immunity against costs on themselves and the challenge is successfully resisted, on a subsequent attempt to resist an application for security for costs by the company the *bona fides* of the members of the company requires cautious consideration.

As against that again, in this case, Laffoy J. held that Irish courts had the power to grant a pre-emptive costs order directing in advance of the hearing of a case that a litigant should not be liable for the costs of any other party to the proceedings, where the litigation was taken in the public interest and where the litigant had no private interest in the outcome of the case. In the instant case, she refused to grant such an order to the applicant company because, *inter alia*, its members did have a private interest in the outcome of the litigation – see below, p. 90 *et seq*.

[41] Unreported, High Court, 21 July 2000. O'Sullivan J. expressly noted that in holding that the plaintiff company had *locus standi*, he had borne in mind the fact that the defendant Board had made an application for security for costs.

[42] Thus in *Moore v. The Attorney General (No.2)* [1930] IR 471, Kennedy C.J. said, at p. 497, that "the Attorney General is the only legal representative of the public in the courts, and is exclusively

Although the Attorney General has the function of upholding the public interest, he is also the legal adviser to the government. In practice, this can create an impossible situation where a conflict of interest arises between the public interest and the Attorney's role as legal adviser to the government. The result is that the Attorney General plays no role in enforcing the collective rights of individuals (sic) against government activity or inactivity, neither in his own name nor by allowing a relator action. In a very limited number of cases the Attorney General may have a role to play where the defendant is a private body or even a local authority.[43]

However recent developments point towards a liberalisation of the law on standing which may give individuals greater scope for defending the public interest through the courts.

Where the public interest is protected by a duty imposed by the Constitution, it is now clear, in the light of the Supreme Court decision in *Crotty v. An Taoiseach,*[44] that a citizen has *locus standi* to take legal proceedings in defence of that interest where the legal duty involved is owed to the public in general, rather than to any section of the public.[45]

---

entitled to assert or defend public interests". See also the House of Lords decision in *Gouriet v. Union of Post Office Workers* [1977] 3 WLR 300. See generally Hogan and Morgan, *op. cit.*, pp. 758-764; Casey, *The Irish Law Officers: Roles and Responsibilities of the Attorney General and the Director of Public Prosecutions* (Round Hall/Sweet and Maxwell, 1996), ch. 6 and Kelly, *The Irish Constitution* (3rd ed., Hogan and Whyte, eds., 1994) at pp. 316-321. In two cases decided on the same day, the Supreme Court clarified certain aspects of the Attorney General's role in this regard. In *TDI Metro Ltd. v. Delap (No. 1)* [2000] 4 IR 337; [2001] 1 ILRM 321, the Supreme Court held that the Attorney General was not entitled as of right to intervene in proceedings in defence of the public interest but rather that he could apply to the court for permission to be joined as a party and that this was a matter for the court to decide at its discretion. In *McG. v. D.W.* [2000] 2 ILRM 451 the Supreme Court held that where High Court proceedings have concluded, there is no jurisdiction to re-open the case so as to enable the Attorney General to be joined as a notice party for the purpose of defending the public interest. In the subsequent case of *Attorney General v. Lee*, unreported, Supreme Court, 23 October 2000, the Supreme Court held that the Attorney General's power to bring legal proceedings in defence of the public interest was only to be exercised in exceptional circumstances.

[43] "The Protection of Collective Rights Before the Irish Courts" (1996) 14 *ILT* 110 and 134, at p. 110. (Footnotes omitted). A similar view was expressed by McCarthy J. in his dissenting judgment in *The State (Sheehan) v. Government of Ireland* [1987] IR 550, in which the plaintiff, who had been injured as a result of a local authority's failure to maintain a public footpath, sought a writ of *mandamus* directing the Government to bring into force a statutory provision which provided for the liability of local authorities in such circumstances. Dealing with the issue of the plaintiff's *locus standi*, McCarthy J. said, "In theory, the Attorney General could assert the public right and seek the relief claimed; in practice this has no reality. The Attorney General is the legal advisor to the Government and, presumably, has advised the Government that it is not under the legal obligation for which the prosecutor contends." – pp. 562-3. See also Cappelletti and Garth, who comment, at p. 37, "The sad fact is that in both common law and civil law countries the governmental institutions which, by virtue of their tradition, should protect the public interest, are by their nature unable to do so".

[44] [1987] IR 713; [1987] ILRM 400.

[45] Such litigants may also be able to avoid any liability for the costs incurred by their opponents by applying for a pre-emptive costs order prior to the substantive hearing of the case – see *Village Residents' Association Ltd. v. An Bord Pleanála (No. 2)* [2000] 4 IR 321, discussed below, pp. 91-2.

Thus in *Crotty*, the plaintiff sought an injunction to restrain the Government from ratifying an international treaty on the grounds that such ratification could only take place after the People had been consulted through a referendum. The Supreme Court, speaking through Finlay C.J., pointed out that if the treaty came into force, it would affect every citizen and therefore the plaintiff had *locus standi* "notwithstanding his failure to prove the threat of any special injury or prejudice to him, as distinct from any other citizen, arising from this Act".[46] A similar approach was adopted in the subsequent cases of *McGimpsey v. Ireland,*[47] *O'Malley v. An Taoiseach,*[48] *McKenna v. An Taoiseach (No. 2),*[49] *Riordan v. An Tánaiste,*[50] and *Riordan v. An Taoiseach,*[51] in each of which the plaintiff did not have to show a peculiar prejudice or injury because each case involved alleged breaches of constitutional norms affecting all citizens equally.[52]

---

[46] [1987] IR 713 at p. 766; [1987] ILRM 400 at p. 443.

[47] [1990] 1 IR 110; [1990] ILRM 440. This raised a challenge to the Anglo-Irish Agreement on the ground that it violated Arts. 2 and 3 of the Constitution.

[48] [1990] ILRM 461. Here the plaintiff sought an injunction restraining the Taoiseach from advising the President to dissolve Dáil Éireann until the Dáil constituencies had been revised in the light of changes in population distribution.

[49] [1995] 2 IR 10. This case involved a challenge to the constitutionality of the use by the Government of public funding to secure a particular outcome in a constitutional referendum.

[50] [1995] 3 IR 62, [1998] 1 ILRM 494. Here the plaintiff argued that there was a constitutional prohibition on the Taoiseach and the Tánaiste being simultaneously absent from the State. In *Riordan v. An Taoiseach*, unreported, High Court, 14 November 1997, Costello P. had held that the same plaintiff had no *locus standi* to challenge the validity of the appointment of the Chairperson of the Commission of Nursing. However this decision is now presumably overtaken by the more recent Supreme Court case.

[51] Unreported, Supreme Court, 20 May 1999. In this case, the plaintiff challenged the constitutionality of the procedures adopted for amending Arts.2 and 3 of the Constitution in 1998.

[52] In earlier examples of this genre, such as *O'Donovan v. A.G.* [1961] IR 114, *Ryan v. A.G.* [1965] IR 294 and *McMahon v. A.G.* [1972] IR 69, the issue of *locus standi* was not explicitly addressed by the courts. However in *East Donegal Co-Operative Ltd. v. A.G.* [1970] IR 317 and *The State (Lynch) v. Cooney* [1982] IR 337, Walsh J. indicated that, in exceptional circumstances, an *actio popul);* might exist in Irish constitutional law. UK authority also demonstrates some judicial openness to the legitimacy of such an action in appropriate cases. Thus, in *Inland Revenue Commissioners v. National Federation of Self-Employed and Small Businesses Ltd.* [1982] AC 617, Lord Diplock said, at p. 630:

> It would, in my view, be a grave lacuna in our system of public law if a pressure group, like the federation, or even a single public spirited taxpayer, were prevented by outdated technical rules of locus standi from bringing the matter to the attention of the court to vindicate the rule of law and get the unlawful conduct stopped. The Attorney General, although he occasionally applies for prerogative orders against public authorities that do not form part of central government, in practice never does so against government departments. It is not, in my view, a sufficient answer to say that judicial review of the actions of officers or departments of central government is unnecessary because they are accountable to Parliament for the way in which they carry out their functions. They are accountable to Parliament for what they do so far as regards efficiency and policy, and of that Parliament is the only judge; they are responsible to a court of justice for the lawfulness of what they do, and of that the court is the only judge.

See also the High Court decision in *R. v. Secretary of State for Foreign and Commonwealth Affairs, ex p. World Development Movement* [1995] 1 All ER 611 in which the plaintiff organisation was held to have standing to challenge a decision of the UK Foreign Secretary to provide overseas aid to a hydroelectric project in Malaysia. See also the comments of Keane J. in *Iarnród Éireann v. Ireland* [1996] 3 IR 321 at p. 351-2; [1995] 2 ILRM 161 at p. 189.

Recent judicial decisions have also relaxed the requirements of standing where the public interest is protected *by statute*. Prior to the adoption of the Constitution, the position with regard to the enforcement of statutory duties through civil actions (actions for breach of statutory duty) was that a private individual could only sue to enforce a public duty where two conditions were satisfied. First, the duty had to be owed to a particular class and not to the public generally and, second, the particular legislation had to manifest an intention that the individual could sue.[53] There is some evidence now that the second of these conditions has been relaxed somewhat, and also that the liberalisation of the rules of standing in relation to applications for judicial review may provide a viable alternative for anyone wishing to enforce a statutory norm for the benefit of the public generally, thereby, on both counts, enhancing the ability of an individual to take legal action in defence of the public interest.

The earliest developments in this regard occurred in relation to the second condition relating to legislative intention. In *Irish Permanent Building Society v. Caldwell and ors.*,[54] Keane J. had expressed the view (albeit tentatively) that the common law limitations on the right of a private citizen to assert a public right were not affected by the Constitution. However two years later, at a later stage of the same proceedings, the first indication was given that the Attorney General no longer had exclusive jurisdiction to sue for breach of statutory duty in circumstances where the legislation in question did not confer any right of enforcement on private parties. In *Irish Permanent Building Society and Bolger v. Cauldwell and ors*[55] the plaintiffs challenged the validity of the registration of the second defendant as a building society under the Building Societies Act 1976. In defence, it was argued, *inter alia*, that the plaintiffs had no *locus standi* to bring the proceedings as, on the authority of *Moore and ors. v. The Attorney General (No. 2)*,[56] only the Attorney General was entitled to assert or defend public interests in legal proceedings. Dismissing this argument, Barrington J. held that the plaintiffs did have a real grievance arising out of the alleged breach of the 1976 Act, that they had a substantial interest in the outcome of the proceedings, and consequently that they had *locus standi* to maintain the action. However in an interesting dictum, Barrington J. cast doubt on the proposition that the right of a private citizen to sue for breach of statutory duty depended on the intention of the legislature when enacting the legislation in question. Distinguishing British authorities which supported the proposition, he said,

> The British Parliament is a Sovereign Legislature and the rights of the individual plaintiffs are to be ascertained by finding out what was the intention of Parliament in the particular case. If Parliament intended to provide a remedy for the individual plaintiff in the courts then he has a remedy. If it did not intend to provide a remedy then he has not. But in our

---

[53] *McKenna v. Stephen and Hull & Co. Ltd.* [1923] 2 IR 112; *Moore v. Attorney General (No. 2)* [1930] IR 471.

[54] [1979] ILRM 273 at p. 276. See also *Siney v. Dublin Corporation* [1980] IR 412 and the decision of Keane J. in *Wall v. Feely*, unreported, High Court, 26 January 1984.

[55] [1981] ILRM 242.

[56] [1930] IR 471.

jurisdiction the citizen would appear to be entitled to a remedy, by virtue of the provisions of Article 40.3, if he has or may suffer damage as a result of a breach of the law in circumstances which amount to an injustice.[57]

The dictum is open to the interpretation that the citizen has a constitutional right under Article 40.3 not to be subject to injustice as a result of a breach of statutory duty, in which case the right to sue for breach of statutory duty is potentially very expansive.[58] But even if such an open-ended constitutional right does not exist, subsequent decisions have confirmed that, in certain circumstances, infringement of acknowledged *constitutional* rights may afford *locus standi* to sue for breach of statutory duty. In *Parsons v. Kavanagh*[59] O'Hanlon J. held that the plaintiff's constitutional right to earn her livelihood carried with it "the entitlement to be protected against any unlawful activity on the part of another person or persons which materially impairs or infringes that right".[60] In the instant case, therefore, the plaintiff was allowed to maintain her action seeking an injunction to restrain the defendants, her competitors, from operating a passenger transport service without the requisite licence under the Road Transport Acts 1932 and 1933. While this decision was subsequently endorsed by the Supreme Court in *Lovett v. Gogan*,[61] a case with similar facts to *Parsons v. Kavanagh*, the judgment of Finlay C.J. would appear to qualify the principle enunciated by O'Hanlon J. by restricting the plaintiff's entitlement to an injunction to cases in which it can be shown that this is the *only* way of protecting the plaintiff from a threatened invasion of constitutional rights.[62]

---

[57] [1981] ILRM 242 at p. 254.

[58] See further discussion below, at p. 75 *et seq.*, about the extent of the right to sue for breach of statutory duty.

[59] [1990] ILRM 560.

[60] At p. 566. See also *MMDS Television Ltd. v. The South East Community Deflector Association Ltd.*, unreported, High Court, 8 April 1997.

[61] [1995] 1 ILRM 12.

[62] Thus in *O'Connor and ors. v. Williams and ors.* [1996] 2 ILRM 382, Barron J. refused to grant an injunction to restrain the defendants from operating their business in breach of statutory regulations on the ground that, the sanctions imposed by the regulations being substantial, the criminal law was sufficiently strong to prevent the damage being caused to the plaintiffs. This finesse of *Parsons v. Kavanagh* would appear to have been missed by Murphy J. in *The Incorporated Law Society of Ireland v. Carroll* [1995] 3 IR 145 where he accepts, *obiter*, that an individual has a right to maintain civil proceedings in respect of a criminal wrong where a constitutional right is in jeopardy.
It is also worth noting that both Murphy J. in this case and O'Hanlon J. in *Parsons v. Kavanagh* agreed with the view expressed by Costello J. in *A.G. v. Paperlink Ltd.* [1984] ILRM 373 that the High Court has a reserved power to ensure obedience to legislation whenever it is just and convenient so to do. This proposition, first enunciated by Lord Denning M.R. in *A.G. v. Chaudry* [1971] 1 WLR 1614 at 1624, differs from the proposition under consideration in that it is not restricted to cases of interference, or possible interference, with a constitutional right. In *Parsons v. Kavanagh*, O'Hanlon J. indicated that the exercise of this non-constitutional jurisdiction would be appropriate where the existing sanctions for breach of the legislation were inadequate. However, as we have just noted, the Supreme Court in *Lovett v. Gogan* [1995] 1 ILRM 12 would appear to have imposed the same restriction on the exercise of the court's jurisdiction to prevent interference with constitutional rights.

Against the background of these authorities, the decision of the Supreme Court in *The Incorporated Law Society of Ireland v. Carroll and ors.*[63] might, on one view, be regarded as striking a rather discordant note. The plaintiff society sought declarations that the defendants had contravened provisions of the Solicitors Act 1954 and injunctions restraining further contraventions. In the High Court, Murphy J. held that the plaintiff had no *locus standi* to maintain civil proceedings in respect of criminal wrongdoing though he did accept that a person whose constitutional right was in jeopardy had a right to maintain civil proceedings in respect of a criminal wrong and also that in exceptional cases, the High Court had a jurisdiction to ensure obedience to the law whenever it was just and convenient to do so.[64] In the instant case, however, no constitutional rights were asserted, nor did he consider the case to be an exceptional one justifying the intervention of the High Court given that, *inter alia*, a criminal prosecution under the legislation would be just as efficious in enforcing the law as the grant of an injunction.

On appeal, a unanimous Supreme Court upheld Murphy J.'s ruling on *locus standi*, though in the process of doing so, the Court might be regarded, at least on one view, as having taken Irish law on the enforcement of public rights back to the 1930s. Thus Blayney J, with whom Hamilton C.J. and Denham J. concurred, cited *Moore v. The Attorney General (No.2)*[65] in favour of the unqualified proposition that "[when] what is in issue is the enforcement of a public right, the only party who can bring civil proceedings to enforce it is the Attorney General".[66] On one view of this judgment, such a comment would appear to sweep away the exceptions to the Attorney General's jurisdiction to enforce public rights recognised by the Irish courts during the past twenty years or so. However, the Supreme Court makes no reference to cases like *Parsons v. Kavanagh* or *Lovett v. Gogan* and the summary of the argument presented on appeal would appear to indicate that what was at issue before the Court was the extent of the High Court's common law jurisdiction to ensure obedience to the law whenever that was just and convenient so to do. Thus, a better reading of this decision is that it rejects the view that the High Court has an inherent common law jurisdiction to enforce statutory duties but that it has no bearing whatsoever on cases in which constitutional rights are potentially at risk.

To summarise briefly, then, it would appear that, even where legislation fails to provide for the right of individuals to sue to enforce its provisions, a private individual

---

[63] [1995] 3 IR 145.

[64] The proposition that the High Court had a reserved power, not derived from the Constitution, to ensure obedience to legislation whenever it is just and convenient so to do was also accepted by O'Hanlon J. in *Parsons v. Kavanagh* [1990] ILRM 560 and by Costello J. in *A.G. v. Paperlink Ltd.* [1984] ILRM 373 and both O'Hanlon and Murphy JJ. appear to agree that in appropriate cases this would provide standing for private individuals to seek to restrain breaches of statutory duties.

[65] [1930] IR 471.

[66] [1995] 3 IR 145 at p. 174. At p. 175, referring to *A.G. v. Paperlink Ltd.* [1984] ILRM 373, Blayney J. said, "There was no suggestion [in that case] that anyone other than the Attorney General could seek an injunction in the public interest to restrain an offence being committed in breach of a statute ... " See also a similar statement by the same judge in *Society for the Protection of the Unborn Child (Ireland) Ltd. v. Grogan (No.5)* [1998] 4 IR 343 at p. 370.

may enforce statutory duties imposed for the benefit of the general public in circumstances where his or her constitutional rights have been affected or threatened by non-enforcement of such duties and where permitting the right to sue is the only means by which those constitutional rights can be effectively vindicated. In the context of attempts to tackle poverty and social exclusion, one immediately thinks of how the vindication of such constitutional rights as the right to life or bodily integrity through such legislation as the Health Acts 1947-1996, the Housing Acts 1966-1998 or the Social Welfare Acts 1993-2000 might offer potential areas for the exercise of this jurisdiction.

I now turn to consider the second condition which traditionally restricted the scope of the action for breach of statutory duty, namely that the plaintiff must show that the duty is owed to a particular class and not to the public generally. As we have already noted,[67] it is now well settled that an individual can take legal action against public bodies to prevent an infringement of a *constitutional* norm in circumstances in which the constitutional duty involved is owed to the public generally. However it is now arguable, in the light of recent litigation in the area of planning law, that an application for judicial review may be taken in relation to a breach of *statutory* norms by a public body where no particular person is more affected by the breach than anyone else. If so, then it may be that the Attorney General's right to sue on behalf of the public interest is simply concurrent with that of any member of the general public.

The starting point for our discussion of this point is the general rule of standing enunciated by the Supreme Court in *Cahill v. Sutton.*[68] In that case the plaintiff's cause of action for breach of contract was clearly statute-barred by s.11(2)(b) of the Statute of Limitations 1957 and she sought to overcome this hurdle by challenging the constitutionality of this provision on the ground that it failed to relax the limitation period in the case of a person who was unaware of material facts entitling that person to sue and who therefore did not initiate legal proceedings in good time. The difficulty with this argument in the context of the plaintiff's case, however, was that at all material times she was aware of the facts entitling her to sue. Her constitutional argument, therefore, was based on a hypothetical situation and the sole issue with which the Supreme Court concerned itself was whether she had *locus standi* to present such a case. Delivering the leading judgment of a unanimous Court, Henchy J. held against the plaintiff and in a celebrated passage set out the requirements of standing in cases challenging the constitutionality of legislation.

---

[67] See pp. 68-9.

[68] [1980] IR 269. Even though this case concerned a challenge to the constitutionality of legislation, Hogan and Morgan opine that the test is the same where one challenges the constitutionality of executive or administrative action or where one seeks judicial review of an administrative action with no constitutional issue – see *Administrative Law in Ireland* (3rd ed. 1998) at p. 741 and the cases cited in n. 272 therein. Note, however, that both Finlay C.J. and Walsh J. assume in *The Society for the Protection of Unborn Children (Ireland) Ltd. v. Coogan* [1989] IR 734; [1990] ILRM 70 that the requirements of standing are stricter in cases involving a challenge to the constitutionality of legislation. A similar position was adopted by McGuinness J. in *Lancefort Ltd. v. An Bord Pleanála*, unreported, High Court, 12 March 1998. (This issue did not have to be addressed by the Supreme Court on appeal as the challenge to the constitutionality of the Local Government (Planning and Development) Act 1976 was not pursued before that court.)

> If a citizen comes forward in court with a claim that a particular law has been enacted in disregard of a constitutional requirement, he has little reason to complain if in the normal course of things he is required ... to show that the impact of the impugned law on his personal situation discloses an injury or prejudice which he has either suffered or is in imminent danger of suffering.
>
> This rule, however, being but a rule of practice must, like all such rules, be subject to expansion, exception or qualification when the justice of the case so requires. Since the paramount consideration in the exercise of the jurisdiction of the Courts to review legislation in the light of the Constitution is to ensure that persons entitled to the benefit of a constitutional right will not be prejudiced through being wrongfully deprived of it, there will be cases where the want of the normal *locus standi* on the part of the person questioning the constitutionality of the statute may be overlooked if, in the circumstances of the case, there is a transcendent need to assert against the statute the constitutional provision that has been invoked. For example, while the challenger may lack the personal standing normally required, those prejudicially affected by the impugned statute may not be in a position to assert adequately, or in time, their constitutional rights. In such a case the court might decide to ignore the want of normal personal standing on the part of the litigant before it. Likewise, the absence of a prejudice or injury peculiar to the challenger might be overlooked, in the discretion of the court, if the impugned provision is directed at or operable against a grouping which includes the challenger, or with whom the challenger may be said to have a common interest – particularly in cases where, because of the nature of the subject-matter, it is difficult to segregate those affected from those not affected by the challenged provision.[69]

A striking feature of this passage is the potential scope of the qualifications to the normal requirements of standing and before the decade had elapsed, there were concrete illustrations of both examples of such qualifications listed by Henchy J. In *The Society for the Protection of Unborn Children (Ireland) Ltd. v. Coogan,*[70] the Supreme Court, by a majority, held that the plaintiff had *locus standi* in what was a distinctive version of the first example cited by Henchy J., namely a case in which the challenger sought to be permitted to bring suit on behalf of those prejudicially affected because they were not in a position to assert adequately their constitutional rights.[71] (The extent of a *ius tertii* in Irish law is considered in more detail in the next section.) The cases of *Crotty v. An Taoiseach,*[72] *McGimpsey v. Ireland,*[73] *O'Malley v. An Taoiseach,*[74] *McKenna v. An Taoiseach (No. 2),*[75] *Riordan v. An Tánaiste,*[76] and

---

[69] [1980] IR at pp. 284-5.
[70] [1989] IR 734; [1990] ILRM 70; [1990] 1 CMLR 689. See Humphreys and O'Dowd, "Locus Standi to Enforce the Constitution: Society for the Protection of Unborn Children (Ireland) Ltd. v. Coogan" (1990) 8 *ILT* 14.
[71] The case is distinctive because it involved the taking of legal action on behalf of the unborn who, by definition, are not in a position to assert their own constitutional rights.
[72] [1987] IR 713; [1987] ILRM 400.
[73] [1990] 1 IR 110; [1990] ILRM 440.
[74] [1990] ILRM 461.
[75] [1995] 2 IR 10.
[76] [1995] 3 IR 62; [1998] 1 ILRM 494.

Riordan v. An Taoiseach[77] meanwhile, can all be classified as examples of those cases in which the plaintiff does not have to show a peculiar prejudice or injury because "it is difficult to segregate those affected from those not affected by the challenged" action as each case involved alleged breaches of constitutional norms affecting all citizens equally. Thus "there has been a development from the concept of *locus standi* as victim related (the plaintiff proving a detriment actual or apprehended) to a jurisprudence where public interest parties have been adjudged to have standing".[78]

Recent decisions of the High and Supreme Courts in *Lancefort Ltd. v. An Bord Pleanála*[79] raise the possibility that a similar development is taking place in relation to breaches of *statutory* norms which affect all citizens equally through the relaxation of the requirements of standing for bringing applications for judicial review and that this circumvents, to some extent, the second condition restricting the scope of the action for breach of statutory duty.[80] *Lancefort* involved an application seeking leave to apply for judicial review of a decision of An Bord Pleanála affecting listed buildings in a citycentre location in Dublin. Order 84, rule 20(4) of the Rules of the Superior Courts 1986 provides that in respect of an application for judicial review,

> The Court shall not grant leave unless it considers that the applicant has a sufficient interest in the matter to which the application relates.[81]

In the instant case, the application was brought by a company limited by guarantee which, according to the evidence of one of the founders of the company, was established to fulfil "predominantly an active public interest role similar to that of bodies such as Cork Environmental Alliance Limited which co-ordinates public

---

[77] Unreported, Supreme Court, 20 May 1999.

[78] Denham J. in *Lancefort Ltd. v. An Bord Pleanála (No. 2)*, [1999] 2 IR 270 at pp. 286-7; [1998] 2 ILRM 401 at p. 415. See also the comments of Kearns J. in *Murphy v. Wicklow Co. Co.*, unreported, High Court, 19 March 1999, relating to *locus standi* in environmental matters, especially at pp. 23-29.

[79] [1997] 2 ILRM 508 (Morris J.); unreported, High Court, 12 March 1998 (McGuinness J.); [1999] 2 IR 270; [1998] 2 ILRM 401 (Supreme Court).

[80] In a UK case, the plaintiff organisation was allowed to sue in respect of a breach of statutory norms which affected the general public as a whole – see *R. v. Inspectorate of Pollution, ex p. Greenpeace Ltd. (No.2)* [1994] 4 All ER 329. See also Lewis, *Judicial Remedies in Public Law* (London, 1992), pp. 273-4. *Greenpeace* was recently cited with approval by Kearns J. in *Murphy v. Wicklow Co. Co.*, unreported, High Court, 19 March 1999 at pp. 27-9.

[81] This formula is identical to that used in the UK, the interpretation of which by the House of Lords in *IRC v. National Federation of Self-Employed and Small Businesses Ltd.* [1982] AC 617 led to a liberalisation of the rules of standing in that jurisdiction. In this case, the plaintiff association was held to have standing to challenge a tax amnesty negotiated between the Revenue authorities and certain part-time workers (though the substantive claim ultimately failed). Commenting on this case, Hogan and Morgan suggested that it "appears to merge the hitherto distinct concepts of standing and merits by creating a two-stage process. At the leave stage, it is only the hopeless or meddlesome applicants who may be rejected on this ground. At the substantive hearing, the issue of standing has to be considered in the light of the nature of the powers and duties of the public authority and the character of the alleged illegality." – Hogan and Morgan, p. 742. Despite the authors' prediction that the Irish courts would not follow "this rather surprising English authority", this is precisely what the Supreme Court appears to have done in *Lancefort Ltd. v. An Bord Pleanála (No. 2)* [1999] 2 IR 270; [1998] 2 ILRM 401.

efforts for environmental protection in the Cork area and the Sierra Club in the United States of America".[82] The grounds for seeking review were based on, *inter alia,* alleged breaches of statutory duty and on the alleged unconstitutionality of one of the defendant's powers.

The *locus standi* of the company to bring this application was considered initially by Morris J. (as he then was) in the context of an application for leave to apply for judicial review. He began by noting that the people involved in establishing the company were "genuinely and honestly concerned and have devoted significant efforts in the past for the protection of listed and historical buildings and have a legitimate concern for the historical building heritage of Dublin and throughout the country".[83] In response to the obiter dicta of Lynch J. in *Malahide Community Council Ltd. v. Fingal Co. Co. and ors.*[84] questioning the *locus standi* of a limited company to bring proceedings challenging decisions made under the planning code (on the ground that in the absence of economic interest, an artificial legal body cannot be adversely affected by such decisions), Morris J. invoked both *The Society for the Protection of Unborn Children (Ireland) Ltd. v. Coogan*[85] and *Cahill v. Sutton*[86] in support of the proposition that "circumstances may exist and can arise where the Court would permit the right [to sue] to be invoked on behalf of other parties". He continued:

> In the present case a decision has been taken by a number of conscientious concerned persons to seek the protection of the Court through a limited company. It is required that these proceedings be commenced within a period of two months from the date of the delivery of the decision. To rule that the company has no locus standi would have the effect of depriving these persons of access to the Courts. I am of the view that they have demonstrated their bona fide interest in these proceedings by the work and effort which they have given in the past to this project and I am satisfied of their commitment. I think that it would be improper to rely upon the rule of locus standi to deprive them of the opportunity of access to the Court and I believe that there are, in the words of Mr Justice Henchy [in *Cahill v. Sutton*] weighty countervailing considerations justifying the departure from the rule.[87]

---

[82] [1999] 2 IR 270 at p. 277-8; [1998] 2 ILRM 401 at p. 407. As far as I am aware, this would appear to be the first litigation in an Irish court taken by a self-avowed public interest organisation.

[83] [1997] 2 ILRM 508 at p. 513. For comments on this case, see Simons, *"Locus Standi* to Challenge Planning Decisions" (1998) 5 *Irish Planning and Environmental Law Journal* 96 and Dignam, "Lancefort and *Locus Standi"* (1997) 3 *Bar Review* 65.

[84] [1997] 3 IR 383.

[85] [1989] IR 734; [1990] ILRM 70.

[86] [1980] IR 269.

[87] [1997] 2 ILRM 508 at pp. 515-6. Followed, if somewhat reluctantly on the facts of the case, in *Cobh Fishermen's Association Ltd. v. The Minister for the Marine and Natural Resources,* unreported, High Court, 29 August 1997. *Cp.* the decision of MacKenzie J. in the Albert Court of Queen's Bench in *Western Canada Wilderness Committee v. Alberta* (1994) 108 DLR (4th) 495 in which he held that the applicant, an environmental organisation, had standing to challenge the validity of a timber rights agreement entered into between the State and a private company. The judge noted, at pp. 498-9, that "[t]he applicant was incorporated for the purpose of (a) educating the public concerning Canada's wilderness heritage and reasons for preserving representative

Accordingly, he held that the applicant company did have *locus standi* to apply for judicial review. Insofar as the applicant's case rested on alleged breaches of statutory norms (and Morris J. held that in respect of one of these arguments, the applicant had made out a substantial case), it seems clear that the judge accepted that a civic-minded party could sue in respect of breach of a statutory norm which had an impact on the community at large, even though the party suing was not peculiarly affected by the breach. [88]

When the actual application for judicial review came before the High Court, McGuinness J. concurred with the views of Morris J. on the company's standing to apply for judicial review though she also noted that, traditionally, the courts had taken a more flexible approach to matters of standing in planning cases, thus raising the possibility that *Lancefort* may not be applicable to non-planning cases. [89] On appeal, however, the Supreme Court, while denying *locus standi* in the instant case, appears to have liberalised the law on standing to apply for judicial review generally. [90]

---

areas for future generations; (b) conducting research concerning wilderness values; and (c) obtaining and distributing information on areas in western Canada which have the potential for protective wilderness status. That being the case, the applicant is not a busybody wasting the court's time, but has a genuine interest in the above issues. At this time there is no other reasonable and effective manner to bring the issues mentioned before the court." In *Mathias Colomb Band of Indians v. Saskatchewan Power Corp.* (1994) 111 *D.L.R.* (4th) 83, the Manitoba Court of Appeal agreed with the trial judge that the approach to standing was more liberal in Canada than in the UK and approved his statement of legal principle that "standing will be granted in a suit [seeking] a declaration that legislation is invalid, or challenging an exercise of administrative authority, if there is a serious issue; if the plaintiff has a genuine interest as a citizen in the validity of the legislation or the administrative action; and if there is no other reasonable and effective manner in which the issue may be brought before the court". – p. 89.

[88] As Hogan and Morgan point out, *op. cit.*, p. 762, McCarthy J. in *A.G. (McGarry) v. Sligo Co. Co.* [1991] 1 IR 99 showed himself open to this proposition with his suggestion, at p. 114, that it might not have been necessary for the plaintiffs to initiate relator proceedings in respect of that part of their case which involved certain public rights. In this context, the authors also cite (in the second edition of their book at pp. 629-30), the view of Costello J., expressed in interlocutory proceedings in *Martin v. Dublin Corporation*, unreported, High Court, 14 November 1977, that the plaintiff would be able to establish at the trial of the action that the general approach of the courts to the question of standing in constitutional cases should be followed in cases where a citizen claimed that a public body was not carrying out the law.

[89] Unreported, High Court, 12 March 1998. She held, however, that the test for standing to bring judicial review proceedings was not the same as the test for standing to challenge the constitutionality of legislation and that the company did not satisfy this latter test which required, as a general rule, that the plaintiff's interests must have been, or be likely to be, adversely affected by the legislation in question.

[90] [1999] 2 IR 270; [1998] 2 ILRM 401. The plaintiff company had dropped its constitutional challenge to the Local Government (Planning and Development) Act 1976 and consequently the Supreme Court did not have to deal with the issue of standing in this context. In what may be a reaction to this judicial liberalising of the law on standing, s.50(4)(b) of the Planning and Development Act 2000 seeks to restrict the right to seek judicial review of decisions of An Bord Pleanála to persons "with a substantial interest in the matter which is the subject of the application [for judicial review]".

Delivering the judgment of the majority,[91] Keane J. (as he then was) began by describing the competing public values at issue here in language which, with its emphasis on the rule of law, could easily be used to defend public interest litigation.

> The authorities reflect a tension between two principles which the courts have sought to uphold; ensuring, on the one hand, that the enactment of invalid legislation or the adoption of unlawful practices by public bodies do not escape scrutiny by the courts because of the absence of indisputably qualified objectors and, on the other hand, that the critically important remedies provided by the law in these areas are not abused.
>
> In the latter area, the courts have dwelt on occasions on the dangers of giving free rein to cranks and busy bodies. But it is to be borne in mind that the citizen who is subsequently seen to have performed a valuable service in, for example, bringing proceedings to challenge the constitutionality of legislation, while exposing himself or herself to an order for costs, may at the outset be regarded by many of his or her fellow citizens as a meddlesome busybody. The need for a reasonably generous approach to the question of standing is particularly obvious in cases where the challenge relates to an enactment of the Oireachtas or an act of the executive which is of such a nature as to affect all the citizens equally ... But it is also the case that a severely restrictive approach to locus standi where the decision of a public body is challenged would defeat the public interest in ensuring that such bodies obey the law.[92]

He went on to point out that, while as a general rule it is necessary to prove standing, the requirements of standing had been relaxed over the years so that now one only had to show that one had a "sufficient interest" in the matter, rather than that one was a "person aggrieved". Citing *The State (Lynch) v. Cooney*[93] he said that whether or not a plaintiff had such an interest could only be determined by reference to the circumstances of the particular case and in what is arguably a significant development of Irish law on standing, Keane J. appears to take the view that, in determining *locus standi*, one should have regard to the strength of the case advanced by the plaintiff, at least in situations in which no other litigant would emerge if standing was denied.[94] In the instant case, he concluded that if there had been any irregularity in the manner in which the Board discharged its functions, "it could not possibly be regarded as constituting an abuse of power or a default in procedure sufficiently grave to justify

---

[91] Hamilton C.J. and Barrington J. concurred and Lynch J. delivered a separate, concurring judgment. Denham J. dissented, holding that the applicant company had raised a sufficiently important issue to warrant having *locus standi*.

[92] [1999] 2 IR 270 at pp. 308-9; [1998] 2 ILRM 401 at p. 434.

[93] [1982] IR 337.

[94] Though see the views of Kearns J. in *Murphy v. Wicklow Co. Co.*, unreported, High Court, 19 March 1999, cited below, n. 95, on this point. Keane J. also ruled that, at least in applications for judicial review of decisions by planning authorities or An Bord Pleanála, the question of standing should be resolved at the stage of applying for leave to bring judicial review proceedings. In *Murphy*, Kearns J. argues that this point is only of relevance to planning cases as in non-planning cases there is no obligation on an applicant for judicial review to make such application on notice to the respondent.

affording *locus standi* to a body such as the applicant".[95]

While the public interest organisation here was denied standing on the facts of the case, the reasoning of Keane J. clearly supports the view that, in appropriate circumstances, i.e. where no other qualified litigant is likely to emerge and where the abuse complained of is sufficiently grave, a public interest organisation could take legal proceedings in respect of any breach of the planning code which adversely affected the public interest. But perhaps more significantly for present purposes, Keane J.'s remarks on standing arguably apply to applications for judicial review generally and are not confined to issues of planning law.[96] Consequently *Lancefort* may be regarded as further liberalising Irish law on standing to permit a public interest litigant to maintain, in appropriate circumstances, an application for judicial review in respect of a breach of *statutory* norms even though s/he is not more particularly affected by the breach than any other member of the public.[97]

In summary, therefore, these developments would appear to circumvent the second condition that traditionally restricted the scope of the action for breach of statutory

---

[95] [1999] 2 IR 270 at p. 316; [1998] 2 ILMR 401 at p. 440. Commenting on the case made by the applicant, Keane J. noted that the precise claim here, that the permission was invalid because of the failure of the Board to consider whether an EIS was required, could have been brought to the attention of all concerned at any time prior to the granting of permission but was not. Moreover it had not been shown how the assessment of the development carried out by the Board failed to elicit data relevant to an assessment of the effects on the environment of the development. In *Murphy v. Wicklow Co. Co.*, unreported, High Court, 19 March 1999, Kearns J. distinguished *Lancefort Ltd* on the ground, *inter alia*, that in *Murphy*, five different points had been raised in challenge to the authority's policy whereas only one point had been raised in *Lancefort*. He said, at p. 22 of his judgment:

> In a multi-point case such as the instant one, I cannot believe that the decision in *Lancefort* is to be interpreted as requiring the Court to explore the merits of each individual point before arriving at any conclusion as to whether or not an Applicant has *locus standi*. If that were the case, how could time and expense be avoided in the case of a crank or meddlesome litigant if the merits of his case on perhaps a dozen different points had first to be dissected before arriving at any conclusion as to whether or not he had *locus standi*. Accordingly it seems to me that the thrust of the decision in *Lancefort* goes to a case where a single point only is raised and where considerations of *locus standi* and the merits of that one point are inextricably woven together.

[96] Though note that in *Brady v. Cavan Co. Co.* [1999] 4 IR 99; [2000] 1 ILRM 81, a majority of the Supreme Court reserved its opinion as to whether *mandamus* lay at the suit of a member of the public to compel a local authority to perform its duty to maintain roads under the Local Government (Ireland) Act 1898 and in his dissenting opinion, Murphy J. restricted standing in an action for breach of statutory duty to those persons affected by the breach.

[97] Further evidence of this liberalising trend may arguably be seen in the decision of Kearns J. in *Murphy v. Wicklow Co. Co.*, unreported, High Court, 19 March 1999, in which the judge upheld the *locus standi* of the applicant, an eco-warrior, to seek judicial review of the respondent's decision to upgrade a road through an area of great ecological importance. While stressing that this was an exceptional case because of the "unique environmental and statutory mantle" of the area in question (pp. 31-2), Kearns J. did offer support for the view expressed by Denham J. in *Lancefort* that environmental litigation was analogous to litigation for the protection of the Constitution and that the rules of *locus standi* in such cases should take account of the public interest affected – see pp. 23-30. The issue of standing did not have to be decided by the Supreme Court in the subsequent appeal – see *Murphy v Wicklow Co. Co.*, unreported, Supreme Court, 28 January 2000.

duty, namely, that the duty must have been owed to a particular class and not to the public generally. Taken in conjunction with the relaxation of the other pre-condition to the taking of an action for breach of statutory duty,[98] it seems clear that the opportunities for individuals to take legal proceedings in defence of the public interest have been significantly enhanced.

However these developments appear to be restricted to cases in which the public interest generally is implicated and in which it is unlikely that any other party could bring legal proceedings.[99] In relation to public interest litigation targeting social exclusion, one also needs to consider whether, in appropriate circumstances, a civic minded plaintiff could take legal action on behalf of *a section* of the public affected by a breach of a constitutional or statutory norm, even though the plaintiff is not peculiarly prejudiced, given that the claims advanced here would, by definition, concern sectional interests, rather than the interest of the public as a whole.

Acceptance of the right of a civic minded litigant to bring proceedings on behalf of third parties could significantly facilitate those who wish to use litigation to tackle social exclusion, though such a strategy is not without its risks. In particular, this would align the Irish courts with courts in other jurisdictions such as the UK, Canada and Australia where campaigning organisations have been allowed to take legal action on behalf of those for whom they campaign, even though the beneficiaries of the litigation are not members of the organisation taking the action.[100] Essentially, what we are talking about here is to what extent Irish law recognises a *jus tertii* allowing one party to advance the legal claim of another, a topic to which I now turn.[101]

c) Extent of jus tertii in Irish law

Until comparatively recently, it would appear that the law recognised only one situation in which a person could advance legal arguments on behalf of another person who was not party to the litigation, namely, in applications for *habeas*

---

[98] As to which, see above, pp 70-3.

[99] See Keane J.'s comment, at [1999] 2 IR 270 at p. 312; [1998] 2 ILRM 401 at p. 437, *a propos Inland Revenue Commissioners v. National Federation of Self-Employed and Small Businesses Ltd.* [1981] 2 All ER 93 and *R. v. Secretary of State for Foreign and Commonwealth Affairs, ex parte World Development Movement Ltd.* [1995] 1 All ER 611 that these were cases in which "it was unlikely that any other responsible challenger would emerge if standing was denied to the applicants".

[100] In relation to the UK, see Lewis, pp. 275-7, Hough, "'Standing' for Pressure Groups and the Representative Plaintiff" (1991) *Denning Law Journal* 77 and Cane (1995); in relation to Canada, see Bryden, "Public Interest Intervention in the Courts" (1987) 66 *Canadian Bar Review* 490 at pp. 493-4; and in relation to Australia, see Fisher and Kirk.

[101] Strictly speaking, the concept of *jus tertii* limits the type of arguments which can be advanced by a person with *locus standi* to those which are raised by the facts of the person's own case. So, for example, in *Norris v. A.G.*, [1984] IR 36, the plaintiff, a homosexual, had *locus standi* to challenge the constitutional validity of legislation criminalising homosexual behaviour but as he was not married, he could not contend that such legislation infringed a right to marital privacy. However, as Hogan and Morgan point out, Irish courts do not always adhere to this distinction between *jus tertii* and *locus standi* but rather are inclined to treat of the two together as part of the concept of *locus standi* – Hogan and Morgan, p. 755.

corpus.[102] However two Supreme Court cases during the 1980s suggest that there may be a right of broader, though admittedly uncertain, ambit to seek the assistance of the courts on behalf of a third party. The first of these two cases is *Cahill v. Sutton*[103] which is perhaps a little surprising, given that in his leading judgment, Henchy J. expressed some opposition to such a development.[104] Thus he argued:

> While a cogent theoretical argument might be made for allowing any citizen, regardless of personal interest or injury, to being proceedings to have a particular statutory provision declared unconstitutional, there are countervailing considerations which make such an approach generally undesirable and not in the public interest. To allow one litigant to present and argue what is essentially another person's case would not be conducive to the administration of justice as a general rule.[[105]] Without concrete personal circumstances pointing to a wrong suffered or threatened, a case tends to lack the force and urgency of reality. There is also the risk that the person whose case has been put forward unsuccessfully by another may be left with the grievance that his claim was wrongly or inadequately presented ...
>
> ... There is also the hazard that, if the Courts were to accord citizens unrestricted access, regardless of qualification, for the purpose of getting legislative provisions invalidated on constitutional grounds, this important jurisdiction would be subject to abuse. For the litigious person, the crank, the obstructionist, the meddlesome, the perverse, the officious man of straw and many others, the temptation to litigate the constitutionality of a law, rather than to observe it, would prove irresistible on occasion.
>
> In particular, the working interrelationship that must be presumed to exist between Parliament and the Judiciary in the democratic scheme of things postulated by the Constitution would not be served if no threshold qualification were ever required for an attack in the Courts on the manner in which the Legislature has exercised its law-making powers. Without such a qualification, the Courts might be thought to encourage those who have opposed a particular Bill on its way through Parliament to ignore or devalue its elevation into an Act of Parliament by continuing their opposition to it by means of an action to have it invalidated on constitutional grounds.[106]

However none of the first three considerations, which are essentially arguments of prudence, justifies a refusal to allow one person to present legal argument on behalf of another. The personal circumstances of the absent party can be presented to the court in order to supply "the force and urgency of reality" while the ability with which

---

[102] See Article 40.4.2 of the Constitution.

[103] [1980] IR 269.

[104] As we have already seen, pp. 73-4 above, the Supreme Court decided that the plaintiff in that case could not advance legal argument on behalf of a *hypothetical* third party. The present discussion, however, is concerned with whether there is a right to present legal argument on behalf of an *actual* third party.

[105] Here he makes a footnote reference to a passage in *Application of Woods* [1970] IR 154 adverting to the right of one person to seek a writ of habeas corpus on behalf of another.

[106] *Ibid.,* pp. 283-4.

a case is presented has more to do with the competence and skill of the legal team than with the personal situation of the litigant.[107] Moreover not everyone wishing to present legal argument on behalf of a third party can be classified as a crank or meddlesome busybody.

Nor is the argument based on separation of powers necessarily conclusive as one could fairly argue that there is some merit in allowing civic-minded litigants to call in aid the judicial power in order to ensure that constitutionally defective legislation is not allowed to remain for long on the statute books. A corollary of Henchy J.'s objection on this point is that members of the public would be subject to unconstitutional legislation until such time as an aggrieved party had the incentive and the means to present a constitutional challenge.[108]

In fact, Henchy J. himself did not prescribe an absolute ban on the presentation of a *jus tertii*. Describing the rule on standing as a "rule of practice [which] must, like all such rules, be subject to expansion, exception or qualification when the justice of the case so requires",[109] he instanced as one such qualification a situation where "those prejudicially affected by the impugned statute may not be in a position to assert adequately, or in time, their constitutional rights. In such a case the court might decide to ignore the want of normal personal standing on the part of the litigant before it."[110]

In *The Society for the Protection of Unborn Children (Ireland) Ltd. v. Coogan and ors*[111] the Supreme Court had to confront directly the extent to which Irish law recognises a *jus tertii*, albeit in relation to a very particular type of constitutional claim. The plaintiff company, whose primary object was to protect the life of the unborn, sought injunctions restraining the defendants from publishing information about abortion services abroad. Before the Supreme Court, the defendants objected to the plaintiff's *locus standi*. A majority of the Court, however, held that the plaintiff could maintain the action.[112] Given the particular constitutional interest at stake here, namely, the right to life of the unborn, the majority could have restricted their decision on the issue of the plaintiff's right to present argument on behalf of a third party to cases in which the third party was an unborn child. However what is striking about

---

[107] "Another justification for threshold standing is that it screens out parties who would not adequately represent the interests of other aggrieved persons. Rules of standing, however, simply fail to accomplish this task. One plaintiff can be granted standing although he is an inadequate representative of the interests of his class, while another, fully qualified representative is eliminated at the threshold for lack of standing. The courts have not standards for determining which persons or organizations are most representative of the universe of affected interests." – K. Parker and R. Stone, "Standing and Public Law Remedies" (1978) 78 *Col. L. Rev* 771 at p. 775.

[108] A point argued by Humphreys and O'Dowd, p. 14.

[109] [1980] IR 269 at p. 285.

[110] *Ibid.*

[111] [1989] IR 734; [1990] ILRM 70; [1990] 1 CMLR 689.

[112] Finlay C.J., Walsh, Griffin and Hederman JJ. were in the majority; McCarthy J. dissented. The latter's dissent was subsequently cited with approval by the Supreme Court in *The Incorporated Law Society of Ireland v. Carroll and ors.*, [1995] 3 IR 145, though I argue above – at p. 72 – that this decision should not be taken to apply to cases involving constitutional rights.

the two leading judgments in the majority, delivered by Finlay C.J. and Walsh J.,[113] is that their language is not circumscribed in this way.

In his judgment, Finlay C.J. distinguished cases of judicial review of legislation from the present case, where the remedy sought is

> the prevention or prohibition of [an alleged] threatened breach of the Constitution by the defendants.
>
> In such a case ... .the test [for standing] is that of a *bona fide* concern and interest, interest being used in the sense of proximity or an objective interest. To ascertain whether such *bona fide* concern and interest exists in a particular case, it is of special importance to consider the nature of the constitutional right to be protected.[114]

In relation to a threat to the right to life of the unborn, the Chief Justice pointed out that there could never be a victim or potential victim who could sue. Turning to the position of the plaintiff society, he said,

> ... [T]here can be no question of the plaintiff being an officious or meddlesome intervenient in this matter. I would accept the contention that it could not acquire a *locus standi* to seek this injunction merely by reason of the terms of its articles and memorandum of association. The part, however, that the plaintiff has taken in the proceedings to which I have referred, which were successfully brought to conclusion by the Attorney General at its relation, and the particular right which it seeks to protect with its importance to the whole nature of our society, constitute sufficient grounds for holding that it is a person with a *bona fide* concern and interest and accordingly has the necessary legal standing to bring the action.[115]

Walsh J.'s judgment is in similar vein. Once more there is an acceptance of liberal grounds of standing for seeking judicial intervention in defence of the public interest which could, conceivably, encompass the assertion of a *jus tertii*. Thus he commented:

> The citizens' right of access to the courts in the appropriate case will include not only access in defence of their own personal and direct rights which are being threatened by the executive, or by their fellow citizens, but also the right to seek to restrain the acts of the executive or other persons from breaching the constraints imposed by the Constitution if the public interest requires that such breaches or attempted breaches should be restrained.
>
> In a case such as this the essential question is has the plaintiff a *bona fide* interest to invoke the protection of the courts to vindicate the constitutional right in question.[116]

---

[113] Hederman J. concurred with both judgments, while Griffin J. agreed with the Chief Justice but deferred for future consideration the issue of the nature and extent of the right of the Attorney General and private individuals to bring proceedings for the protection of rights, constitutional and otherwise, and the issue of the extent or limits of the decision in *Cahill v. Sutton* and how, if at all, it should be qualified.

[114] [1989] IR 734 at p. 742; [1990] ILRM 70 at p. 73.

[115] [1989] IR 734 at p. 742; [1990] ILRM 70 at p. 73-4.

[116] [1989] IR 734 at p. 744; [1990] ILRM 70 at pp. 75-6.

Moreover he opined that cases involving a challenge to the constitutionality of legislation are not significantly different in this respect from cases involving a claim for the direct applicability of a constitutional provision without legislative intervention. Thus, after citing *East Donegal Co-Operative Livestock Mart Ltd. v. Attorney General*,[117] *O'Brien v. Keogh*[118] and *Cahill v. Sutton*,[119] he said:

> It is quite clear from these and other decisions that even in cases where it is sought to invalidate a legislative provision the Court will, where the circumstances warrant it, permit a person whose personal interest is not directly or indirectly presently or in the future threatened to maintain proceedings if the circumstances are such that the public interest warrants it. In this context the public interest must be taken in the widest sense.
>
> *A fortiori* in a case such as the present where it is sought to restrain, on the basis of a well-founded belief, a threatened breach of the Constitution there can be circumstances where the Court will be justified in permitting such an action to proceed. Examples of this are to be found in the decisions of this Court in *Crotty v. An Taoiseach* [1987] IR 713 and in *Boland v. An Taoiseach* [1974] IR 338. *In the last analysis it is a question reserved exclusively to the courts to decide whether or not in a given case a plaintiff who is not personally affected either individually or as a member of a group directly by the activities complained of may be permitted to maintain an action and to obtain an order restraining or restricting those activities complained of.*[120]

One hesitates to make bricks without straw and one is conscious that judicial decisions must be read in the context of the facts of the case. Yet at the same time, it is striking that, in the context of our present discussion, these judgments recognising the plaintiff's right to raise a *jus tertii* in defence of a constitutional norm do not explicitly restrict that right to cases involving unborn children which would be a very obvious and understandable restriction on such a right. This raises the possibility, which is supported by the earlier dicta of Henchy J. in *Cahill v. Sutton*,[121] that the *jus tertii* recognised by Irish law allowing an appropriate party, acting in a *bona fide* manner, to present legal argument defending the constitutional rights of a third party who is not in a position to take such action, is not restricted to defence of the unborn or to applications for *habeas corpus*. Further judicial guidance is needed to confirm whether this broader version of the *jus tertii* is recognised by Irish law and, if so, what its ambit might be.[122] Going on the basis of *Coogan* and comparative decisions on this

---

117 [1970] IR 317.
118 [1972] IR 144.
119 [1980] IR 269.
120 [1989] IR 734 at p. 746-7; [1990] ILRM 70 at pp. 78-9. (Emphasis added.)
121 [1980] IR 269.
122 In *Society for the Protection of the Unborn Child (Ireland) Ltd. v. Grogan (No.5)* [1998] 4 IR 343 Barrington J. arguably exhibited a more tolerant approach to the *ius tertii*, at least in constitutional cases, when, responding to the fact that *A.G. (Society for the Protection of the Unborn Child (Ireland) Ltd.) v. Open Door Counselling Ltd.* [1988] IR 593; [1989] ILRM 19 had been decided without reference to the facts of any specific case and to the difficulties which arose as a consequence, he observed, at p. 378, "It is true ... that there is nothing like a hard concrete

point, important factors in favour of recognising standing would be the established interest of the plaintiff in the area[123] and the absence, in practice, of other possible applicants.

It remains to be seen whether, if such a broader version of the *jus tertii* exists, it could be exploited to permit a person to sue on behalf of disadvantaged individuals in Irish society.[124] One possible context for its use might be in relation to the constitutional rights of homeless people. It is not inconceivable that the right to bodily integrity might oblige the State to provide basic shelter facilities for people who would otherwise end up sleeping on the streets and an organisation like the Simon Community would presumably be regarded as having a *bona fide* interest and concern in this matter. Of course if this *jus tertii* could be asserted in respect of *statutory* rights (as is the case in the UK) in addition to constitutional rights, then the operation of the social welfare and housing codes offer further potential for its use on behalf of disadvantaged groups by welfare rights groups or tenants' organisations. At the same time, the Irish courts have resolutely set their face against permitting a person to present arguments on behalf of a *hypothetical* third party and so any challenge to the State's policy here would have to be rooted in the particular circumstances of an actual person. Given that, and given that actions concerning other disadvantaged groups, such as welfare claimants and Travellers, for example, have come before the courts without the use of any *jus tertii*, one should not underestimate the difficulty of persuading a judge that no other applicant, other than the pressure group, was available to take the action.

Moreover it also remains to be seen whether, if such a right existed, its use in relation to disadvantaged groups would necessarily be seen as desirable from the

---

case for illustrating the implications and limitations of a principle of constitutional law and that we all have a better understanding of the relevant constitutional provision as a result of the decision in *Attorney General v. X* [1992] 1 IR 1. But to my mind this rather raises the problem of whether it is wise to limit debate in constitutional law cases in the manner contemplated in *Cahill v. Sutton*."

[123] So, for example, in the UK, the Court of Appeal allowed the Child Poverty Action Group to present a case in *R. v. Secretary of State for Social Services, ex p. Child Poverty Action Group* [1990] 2 QB 540, [1989] 1 All ER 1047 after noting that the interest group had played a prominent role in giving advice, guidance and assistance to social security claimants who were affected by the decision being challenged. Fisher and Kirk document a similar approach on the part of the Australian judiciary – Fisher and Kirk, at pp. 376-7.

[124] The *jus tertii* is a commonplace feature in Indian public interest litigation – see above, pp. 40-1 – though of course the scale of poverty and illiteracy is far greater in that country and so it may be easier to justify this relaxation of the normal requirements of standing. However it is interesting to note that in the UK there is some acceptance of the right of pressure groups to being legal actions on behalf of those for whom such groups campaign, even though the beneficiaries of the litigation are not members of the plaintiff group. See, in particular, the remarks of Woolf J. (now Woolf LCJ) in *R. v. Secretary of State for Social Services, ex p. Child Poverty Action Group and the Greater London Council, The Times,* 16 August 1984; *R. v. Secretary of State for Social Services, ex p. Child Poverty Action Group* [1990] 2 Q.B. 540, [1989] 1 All ER 1047 and *R. v. Social Fund Inspector*, unreported, High Court, 20 February 1990. See further, Hough; Cane (1995) and Harlow and Rawlings, pp. 148-151.

perspective of such groups. Litigation strategy carries the risk of reinforcing the dependancy of poor people on middle-class professionals and, indeed, of being more responsive to the agenda of the professionals than to that of the client. This risk would be greatly exacerbated where disadvantaged individuals are not even nominally in control of the litigation as named parties but rather simply supply the factual circumstances to allow a campaigning organisation take legal action on their behalf. At the very least, this factor suggests that a very cautious approach should be taken to the possible use of the *jus tertii* in litigation tackling social exclusion.[125]

Concluding generally on the issue of *locus standi*, it is clear that recent developments in Irish law in this area do a considerable way towards accommodating public interest litigation. Similar developments appear to be taking place in relation to the matter of remedies, to which I now turn.

Remedies

> The centerpiece of the emerging public law model is the decree. It differs in almost every relevant characteristic from relief in the traditional model of adjudication, not the least in that it *is* the centerpiece. The decree seeks to adjust future behaviour, not to compensate for past wrong. It is deliberately fashioned rather than logically deduced from the nature of the legal harm suffered. It provides for a complex, on-going regime of performance rather than a simple, one-shot, one-way transfer. Finally, it prolongs and deepens, rather than terminates, the court's involvement with the dispute.[126]

---

[125] Another factor justifying a cautious approach to the *jus tertii* is the possible impact any litigation might have on the privacy of the third party – see Fisher and Kirk, at p. 374.

[126] Chayes, p. 1298. Fiss describes the differing role played by the remedy in the two types of adjudication thus, "The focus in the dispute-resolution model is the incident, the transaction or occurrence, and the remedial phase is largely episodic. The remedy is designed to correct or prevent a discrete event, and the judicial function usually exhausts itself when judgment is announced and the amount of damages calculated or the decree aimed at some discrete event is issued. Under these assumptions, the lawsuit has ... a beginning, a middle, and an end. In some cases involving a recalcitrant defendant, there may be more to the remedial phase – for example, seizure and sale of assets or a contempt proceeding. But these struggles with the recalcitrant defendant are the exception, and in any event they are not considered an integral part of the first proceeding. They often involve a collateral proceeding handled by different personnel, the sheriff or a master, to enforce the remedy given in the initial proceeding.

The remedial phase in structural litigation is far from episodic. It has a beginning, maybe a middle, but no end – well, almost no end. It involves a long, continuous relationship between the judge and the institution; it is concerned not with the enforcement of a remedy already given, but with the giving or shaping of the remedy itself. The task is not to declare who is right or who is wrong, not to calculate the amount of damages or to formulate a decree designed to stop some discrete act. The task is to remove the condition that threatens the constitutional values. In some instances, where deinstitutinalization is conceivable ... closing the institution may be a viable option. For the most part ... that option is not available. Then the remedy involves the court in nothing less than the reorganization of an ongoing institution, so as to remove the threat it poses to constitutional values. The court's jurisdiction will last as long as the threat persists." – Fiss, pp. 27-8.

One of the most controversial aspects of public interest litigation in the US has been the development of more detailed and intrusive judicial decrees, requiring ongoing supervision by the courts and entailing a greater degree of judicial discretion, for remedying constitutional defects in the operation of such institutions as schools, prisons and mental hospitals. Buckholz *et al.*[127] describe five different approaches which US courts take to the formulation of remedies in institutional reform litigation. The judges may limit their role to the evaluation of the defendant's proposals, essentially placing the onus on the defendant to formulate the remedy.[128] A significant advantage of such an approach is that remedies fashioned by defendants tend to have the greatest prospect of success. Alternatively, the court may impose its own remedy. This is deemed to be most appropriate where the litigation identifies simple institutional conditions that can be reformed quite easily. Another option is for the court to select a remedy from suggestions made by all of the parties. In this scenario, the court will invite all the parties to submit their ideas, plans and supporting information and will then either select one plan from those submitted or devise a composite plan from the various proposals. A fourth approach to remedy formulation is to refer the matter to an expert special master. Such officers are frequently chosen because of their expertise in specialised disciplines or public administration and they are not necessarily lawyers. Finally, the court might limit its role to approving a settlement negotiated by the parties outside the courtroom. This approach has the obvious advantage that the participation of the parties in the process significantly enhances the chance of producing a successful remedy.

Whichever approach is adopted, almost invariably in institutional litigation the remedy which issues will be an affirmative decree which "seeks to realize affirmative goals by requiring a comprehensive pattern of reform by the defendant".[129] This affirmative nature of the remedy inevitably leads to continued judicial involvement in the process of reform, even after formulation of the decree. Thus a court may find itself having to revise substantive aspects of the original decree in order to remedy defects and ambiguities which become apparent during the implementation process or to deal with issues which arise because of changed law or circumstances. Additionally, a wide variety of techniques are available to the court for resolving disputes which arise about implementation of the decree, for monitoring compliance and for supervising the defendant's actions. In addition to conventional administrative techniques which depend on action taken by the parties, the US courts have also developed a range of techniques which can be activated by the court itself. These include the setting of hearing dates to consider compliance reports and the appointment of court appointed

---

[127] Buckholz *et al.*, "The Remedial Process in Institutional Reform Litigation" (1978) 78 *Colum. L. Rev* 784 at pp. 796-812. As will soon become apparent, I have drawn heavily on this article in describing the US experience with regard to remedies in institutional reform litigation. See also the note entitled "Implementation Problems in Institutional Reform Litigation" (1977) 91 *Harv. L. Rev.* 428 and Fletcher, "The Discretionary Constitution: Institutional Remedies and Judicial Legitimacy" (1982) 91 *Yale Law Journal* 635.

[128] Buckholz *et al.* call this "remedial abstention".

[129] *Ibid.*, at p. 813.

agents, classified by Buckholz *et al.* as masters, monitors, mediators, administrators and receivers,[130] to administer the remedy. The master's role at this stage of the process is primarily to formulate a further plan for implementing the decree. A monitor's role is to report on the defendant's compliance with the decree and on the achievement of the decree's goals. A mediator is principally responsible for handing disputes over the decree's meaning, compliance standards and the pace of compliance. The administrator has been described as "the most innovative and unusual of the devices utilized by the courts for remedy implementation".[131] This officer supplements the normal management of the defendant organisation and acts, in an executive capacity and at his own instance, to implement the remedy. In cases in which no co-operation is forthcoming from officers of the defendant organisation, the court may decide to replace those officers either completely or temporarily by appointing a receiver to run the organisation.

In the very recent past, Irish courts, too, have occasionally been called upon to review systemic constitutional defects in the operation of public institutions[132] and while some judges have been content to issue declarations of rights in the expectation that the State would take whatever steps were necessary to vindicate those rights,[133] there is emerging evidence that some members of the Irish judiciary are prepared to fashion more intrusive remedies to correct the behaviour of such institutions. The most dramatic examples of this are the decisions of Kelly J. in *D.B. v. Minister for Justice*[134]

---

[130] *Ibid.* at pp. 826 *et seq.*

[131] *Ibid.*, p. 831.

[132] The best example of this is a series of cases during the 1990s seeking to clarify the extent of the State's legal obligations towards children with learning difficulties and children at risk – see ch. 5. In addition, during the 1970s and early 1980s, there were a number of cases, none successful, challenging the constitutionality of the conditions of detention of convicted prisoners – see Kelly, pp. 818-23, and, more recently, *Brennan v. Governor of Portlaoise Prison* [1999] 1 ILRM 190.

[133] Thus in a series of cases concerning the State's constitutional obligations towards children lacking stable family support, Geoghegan J. adjourned each case after granting declarations sought by the plaintiffs in order to provide the State with an opportunity to respond to the particular case before the court – see *P.S. v. Eastern Health Board*, unreported, High Court, 27 July 1994; *F.N. v. Minister for Education* [1995] 1 IR 409, [1995] 2 ILRM 297; *D.T. v. Eastern Health Board*, unreported, High Court, 24 March 1995 and *G.L. v. Minister for Justice*, unreported, High Court, 24 March 1995. See also the similar approach of Costello J. (as he then was) in *D.D. v. Eastern Health Board*, unreported, High Court, 3 May 1995.

[134] [1999] 1 IR 29; [1999] 1 ILRM 93. In *O'Donoghue v. Minister for Health and ors* [1996] 2 IR 20, the plaintiff, suing through his mother, sought an order of mandamus directing the respondents to provide for free primary education for him, a declaration that in failing to provide for such education for him, the State had deprived him of his constitutional rights, and an award of damages. O'Hanlon J. awarded the plaintiff his damages and also granted him a declaration, saying, at p. 71, "In a case like the present one, it should normally be sufficient to grant declaratory relief in the expectation that the institutions of the State would respond by taking whatever action was appropriate to vindicate the constitutional rights of the successful Applicant". The judge did not make any order of mandamus, though he did give the applicant liberty to apply to the court again in the future for such an order should that become necessary. See also the similar views of McGuinness J. in *Comerford v. Minister for Education* [1997] 2 ILRM 134. In *Sinnott v. Ireland*, unreported, High Court, 4 October 2000, Barr J. awarded the plaintiffs, a mother and her autistic son, damages of £255,000 arising out of the failure of the State to provide for the primary education of the son.

and *T.D. v. Minister for Education*[135] in which he directed the defendants to do all things necessary to facilitate the building, opening and maintenance of high support units for disturbed children. Defending this approach, Kelly J. remarked, in *D.B.*:

> The granting of this injunction means that the Minister is no longer at large concerning the approach to be adopted to solving this problem. The developments proposed will now have to be completed and within the time-scale specified. If there is to be any future change of policy or if the times indicated cannot be met, application will have to be made to this Court on the part of the Minister for a variation of the injunction. This will mean that not merely will the Court have to be informed of all these developments (something sadly lacking to date) but objectively justifiable reasons will have to be furnished to it as to why the injunction should be varied. A variation will not be granted lightly. This will afford to the Court an opportunity of much greater involvement than it has been possible to have in the past. It will mean for these minors that the Court, having declared their entitlements, will now see to their implementation in a direct way.[136]

Persistent delay on the part of the authorities in addressing adequately the plight of these children eventually led to Kelly J. threatening the Ministers of Education, Health and Justice with contempt of court if they failed to provide secure accommodation for one particularly disturbed teenager, a move which provoked quite a hostile reaction from the political establishment.[137]

While no other judges have taken this particular course of action, Kelly J. is not alone among the judiciary in formulating precise steps for executive agencies to take in redressing systemic defects. Thus, in the earlier case of *O'Brien v. Wicklow UDC*[138] Costello J. directed local authorities to provide three additional halting sites for Travellers and, in relation to two existing sites, to provide hardcore for their surface, to connect them to the electricity supply and to drain them and to supply Portaloos while in *Co. Meath VEC v. Joyce*[139] Flood J. ordered the local authority to assess the demand for halting sites within its area and to acquire and prepare, within twelve months of his order, sufficient sites to meet this demand. In October 2001, Barr J. awarded £255,000 to a mother and her autistic son for, *inter alia*, breach of constitutional rights arising out of the State's failure to provide the son with appropriate primary education. More significantly in the present context, he provided that the court would review developments two and a half years after the date of judgment and also threatened the authorities with an award of punitive damages if the State failed to honour its constitutional obligations to the plaintiffs.[140] More recently, Ó Caoimh J. is reported to have required Donegal Co. Co. to provide two halting sites for Travellers within three months of the date of the court hearing.[141]

---

135 [2000] 3 IR 62; [2000] 2 ILRM 321.
136 [1999] 1 IR 29 at p. 45; [1999] 1 ILRM 93 at pp. 105-6.
137 See pp. 195-6 below.
138 *Ex tempore* decision, unreported, High Court, 10 June 1994.
139 [1994] 2 ILRM 210.
140 *Sinnott v. Minister for Education*, unreported, High Court, 4 October 2000. See below, pp. 205 *et seq*.
141 See *The Irish Times*, 2 March 2001. This matter is due to come before the courts in May 2001 when Ó Caoimh J. will review the progress made by the council in meeting its obligations under the Housing (Traveller Accommodation) Act 1998.

While these orders may appear to be very detailed and intrusive, it has to be borne in mind that public interest litigation is qualitatively different to conventional litigation and therefore requires innovative remedies. Moreover, the conceptual framework for such a development is arguably already provided by the Constitution insofar as the protection of constitutional rights is concerned. In *The State (Quinn) v. Ryan*[142] Ó Dálaigh C.J. said:

> It was not the intention of the Constitution in guaranteeing the fundamental rights of the citizen that these rights should be set at naught or circumvented. The intention was that rights of substance were being assured to the individual and that the Courts were custodians of these rights. As a necessary corollary, it follows that no one can with impunity set these rights at naught or circumvent them, and that the courts' powers in this regard are as ample as the defence of the Constitution requires.[143]

Therefore, to the extent to which the courts are dealing with constitutional rights, they have the power to fashion new, intrusive remedies where such a course of action is necessary in order to vindicate the constitutional right in issue and increasingly some judges appear to be prepared to exercise such power.

Pre-Emptive Costs Order

The third area in which Irish legal system appears to be accommodating itself to some forms of public interest litigation relates to the issue of costs and specifically to the possibility of a litigant obtaining an order at a preliminary stage in the proceedings directing that s/he not be held liable for the costs of any other parties to the proceedings, the so-called pre-emptive costs order. The jurisdiction of the High Court to grant such an order was considered in the UK in *R. v. Lord Chancellor, ex p. CPAG*.[144] In this case, Dyson J. considered applications for pre-emptive cost orders from the Child Poverty Action Group (in relation to legal proceedings challenging a decision of the Lord Chancellor to refuse to extend legal aid to some cases before social security tribunals) and Amnesty International UK and The Redress Trust (in relation to legal proceedings challenging a decision of the Director of Public Prosecutions not to prosecute two individuals for possession of an electra-shock baton without a licence).

---

142 [1965] IR 70.
143 At p. 122. See also *Byrne v. Ireland* [1972] IR 241, in which Walsh J. said, at p. 281, "Where the People by the Constitution create rights against the State or impose duties upon the State, a remedy to enforce these must be deemed to be also available". In *D.G. v. Eastern Health Board* [1997] 3 IR 511; [1998] 1 ILRM 241, Hamilton C.J. said, at p. 249, "If the Courts are under an obligation to defend and vindicate the personal rights of the citizen, it inevitably follows that the Courts have the jurisdiction to do all things necessary to vindicate such rights". In *D.B. v. Minister for Justice* [1999] 1 IR 29; [1999] 1 ILRM 93, Kelly J. held that, in carrying out its constitutional function of defending and vindicating personal rights, "the Court must have available to it any power necessary to do so in an effective way" – [1999] 1 IR 29 at p. 40; [1999] 1 ILRM 93 at pp. 101-2.
144 [1999] 1 WLR 347; 1998] 2 All ER 755. See also *R. v. Hammersmith and Fulham LBC, ex p. CPRE London Branch* [2000] Env. L.R. 544.

Dyson J. held that in exercising such a jurisdiction, a distinction had to be made between ordinary private law litigation, on the one hand, and what he called "public interest challenges", on the other hand and that it was difficult to imagine a case of ordinary litigation in which it would be possible for the court to grant a pre-emptive costs order. Such an order could, however, be made in relation to public interest challenges, which he described as follows:

> The essential characteristics of a public law challenge are that it raises public law issues which are of general importance, where the applicant has no private interest in the outcome of the case. It is obvious that many, indeed most judicial review challenges, do not fall into the category of public interest challenges so defined. This is because, even if they do raise issues of general importance, they are cases in which the applicant is seeking to protect some private interest of his or her own.[145]

He subsequently held that pre-emptive costs orders should only be made where certain conditions were satisfied.

> I conclude, therefore, that the necessary conditions for the making of a pre-emptive costs order in public interest challenge cases are that the court is satisfied that the issues raised are truly ones of general public importance, and that it has a sufficient appreciation of the merits of the claim that it can conclude that it is in the public interest to make the order. Unless the Court can be so satisfied by short argument, it is unlikely to make the order in any event. Otherwise, there is a real risk that such applications would lead, in effect, to dress rehearsals of the substantive applications, which in my view would be undesirable. These necessary conditions are not, however, sufficient for the making of an order. The Court must also have regard to the financial resources of the applicant and respondent, and the amount of costs likely to be in issue. It will be more likely to make an order where the respondent clearly has a superior capacity to bear the costs of the proceedings than the applicant, and where it is satisfied that, unless the order is made, the applicant will probably discontinue the proceedings, and will be acting reasonably in so doing.[146]

In the instant case, he held that these conditions were not established in relation to either application.

The jurisdiction to grant pre-emptive costs orders has recently been considered by the Irish High Court. In *Village Residents' Association Ltd. v. An Bord Pleanála (No. 2)*,[147] Laffoy J. was asked to grant a pre-emptive costs order to the plaintiff company in relation to legal proceedings instituted by it challenging a planning decision of the defendant Board. She held that the High Court did have such a jurisdiction by virtue of O.99, r.5 of the Rules of the Superior Courts 1986 which provides that costs may be dealt with by the court at any stage in the proceedings. Order 99, r.1(1) provided that the costs of and incidental to every proceeding in the Superior Courts should be in the discretion of those Courts. She also accepted as a broad proposition that it would be

---

[145] *Ibid.*, at p. 762.
[146] *Ibid.*, at p. 766.
[147] [2000] 4 IR 321. See Costello, pp. 134-6.

difficult to envisage granting such an order in ordinary private law litigation.

> As a broad proposition the principles enunciated by Dyson J – confining the possibility
> of making such orders to cases involving public interest challenges, as Dyson J explained
> the concept of a public interest challenge, and requiring that the issues raised on the
> challenge be of general public importance and that at the stage at which it is asked to
> make the order the Court should have a sufficient appreciation of the merits of the claim
> to conclude that it is in the public interest to make the order – would seem to meet the
> fundamental rubric that the interests of justice should require that the order be made.[148]

The instant case failed to meet any of the criteria laid down by Dyson J. The challenge
was not a public interest challenge inasmuch as members of the company clearly had
a private interest in the outcome of the case nor did the case raise an issue of general
public importance. Moreover the judge was not satisfied that she had sufficient
appreciation of the merits of the application to conclude that it would be in the public
interest to make a pre-emptive costs order. Finally, the applicant also sought a pre-
emptive costs order against a private company that was party to the litigation and
Laffoy J. held that it would fly in the face of justice to penalise that company in
relation to costs.

Although the application in *Village Residents* failed, the significance of the case in
the present context is that Laffoy J. accepted that, in appropriate circumstances, certain
public interest litigants could apply for a pre-emptive costs order and the case is yet
another example of the judicial system accommodating certain forms of public interest
litigation. That said, it has to be conceded that pre-emptive costs orders will probably
be restricted to *Crotty*-type litigants raising issues that affect all citizens equally and
that public interest litigants targeting social exclusion will not benefit given that such
litigants almost invariably have a private interest in the outcome of the case.

Thus far we have covered developments in Irish adjectival law that facilitate public
interest litigation. However if such litigation is to be embraced wholeheartedly by the
Irish legal system, further changes are needed in at least three specific areas. Irish law
needs to be able to take into account the interests of third parties affected by litigation;
it needs to modify the doctrine of mootness to prevent that doctrine being used to
thwart test cases; and it needs to develop mechanisms for enhancing the impact of
judicial decisions. I turn now to consider each of these issues.

Taking account of the interests of those affected by litigation[149]

As we have already noted,[150] one of the characteristics of public interest litigation is that
it is likely to affect a significant number of people in addition to those who initiate or
who defend the litigation. Thus, for example, an action taken by residents challenging

---

[148] *Ibid.*, at p. 330.
[149] In writing this section I have benefited considerably from having read a research paper, "Amicus
Curiae/Public Interest Brief Feasibility Study" prepared for the Free Legal Advice Centres Ltd.
in 1997 by Matthew A. Miller, a law student from Washington State University.
[150] See above, p. 60.

the validity of a decision of a local authority to locate a halting site for Travellers in their area has very obvious implications for Travellers even though they are not party to the litigation. This raises the question of whether, and if so, how, the interests of those affected by litigation should be taken into account by the court.[151] Three arguments can be advanced in support of the view that the court should take such interests into account. First, there is the argument which informs the principle of constitutional justice that those who are affected by a decision should be allowed to present their views to the decision-maker. In *Glover v. BLN Ltd.*[152] Walsh J. observed that

> the dictates of constitutional justice require that statutes, regulations or agreements setting up machinery for taking decisions which may affect rights or impose liabilities should be construed as providing for fair procedures.[153]

Clearly Walsh J.'s remarks do not embrace judicial decisions and yet one could argue that the logic of his argument – that where interests are affected, the decision-making process must adhere to fair procedures – fairly raises a presumption that, absent countervailing considerations, all those affected by a judicial decision should be given an opportunity to present their views.[154] Are there any countervailing considerations which would warrant treating the judicial process differently from other decision-making processes in this context? In the course of defending public interest interventions in the judicial process, Bryden identifies three types of argument which could be advanced to justify such differentiation.[155] The first is an argument of principle, rooted in a view of the proper function of the judicial system and of the role of the judge in the litigation process.

> There is a tendency in English law to think of the judge as a neutral arbiter weighing the arguments presented by counsel in order to arrive at the resolution of a dispute. The active participants in this process are counsel, who may choose to advance or refrain from advancing such arguments as they see fit. In this type of legal framework it is considered

---

[151] Note the comments of the Chief Justice of Ontario, Mr Justice Dubin, in *Peel (Regional Municipality) v. Great Atlantic & Pacific Co. of Canada Ltd.* (1990) 46 Admin. L.R. 1, quoted by Anderson J. in *Adler v. Ontario* (1992) 88 D.L.R. (4th) 632 at 637: "In constitutional cases, including cases under the Charter of Rights and Freedoms ... the judgment has a great impact on others who are not immediate parties to the proceedings and for that reason, there has been a relaxation of the rules heretofore governing the disposition of applications for leave to intervene and has increased (sic) the desirability of permitting some such interventions".

[152] [1973] IR 388.

[153] *Ibid.* at p. 425.

[154] Harlow and Rawlings argue that if the courts are prepared to adopt relaxed rules of standing permitting group representation, then they should also adopt a more tolerant approach to the representation of the interests of those affected by a judicial decision because to do otherwise will "confer a considerable advantage on the attacker because it may well be easier to initiate legal action in the name of a group than to interpose at a later stage of the action. In practice this may mean that the group permitted to enter may not be the only, or even the most, representative." – Harlow and Rawlings, p. 312. A similar argument is advanced by Bryden, "Public Interest Intervention in the Courts" (1987) 66 *Canadian Bar Review* 490, at pp. 511-2.

[155] Bryden, pp. 513-521.

inappropriate for judges to base their decisions on arguments that were not advanced by counsel; it is considered equally inappropriate for judges to do independent legal research or to make reference to authorities not cited by counsel.[156]

But as Bryden himself argues, this model ignores the law-making functions of the judiciary and for those who accept the legitimacy of such functions, the argument cited above is simply not a conclusive reason for rejecting the use of devices which would facilitate a wider input of views into the process of litigation. To re-iterate Chayes' thesis, public interest litigation is significantly different from the traditional model of litigation and there is no principled reason why the former should be constrained by procedural rules designed for the latter.[157]

The second argument listed by Bryden is the contention that broadening the list of interests who can present argument to the court will add to the court's burden and ultimately amounts to a waste of resources, in particular, the court's time. As against that, one can argue that it is possible to regulate intervention by outside parties so that it does not overwhelm the court[158] but that even if such intervention does impose some additional burden on the court, then that is a price worth paying for the benefits which are derived from such intervention, such as an improved quality of decision-making and legitimation of the court's decision.

The final argument identified by Bryden is the criticism that those who choose to intervene in litigation may not be representative of the public interest or of the interests of those they claim to be protecting and that the court may thus be presented with an unreliable picture of the concerns of those likely to be affected by its decision. However, on the basis of such (albeit limited) experience that the Irish courts have had in dealing with the *locus standi* of public interest groups, the courts have had very little difficulty in formulating criteria for identifying those who can advance credible arguments on behalf of their constituency.[159] Thus the respective courts in both *The Society for the Protection of Unborn Children (Ireland) v. Coogan*[160] and *Lancefort Ltd. v. An Bord Pleanála*[161] were able to satisfy themselves of the *bona fide* character of the plaintiffs by having regard to their track record, their previous commitment to the interests of those on whose behalf they were litigating. Consequently one can have some confidence in the ability of the Irish courts to filter out interventions that are unrepresentative or lacking in credibility.

Returning to the justification for public interest interventions, in addition to the principled argument that those affected by a decision should be entitled to represent their views to the decision-maker, there are two policy arguments in favour of allowing such public interest intervention in the courts, both adumbrated by Bryden.[162]

---

156 *Ibid.*, p. 513.
157 See above, pp. 58-62.
158 See further below, pp. 99-100.
159 See above, pp. 67-80.
160 [1989] IR 734; [1990] ILRM 70.
161 [1997] 2 ILRM 508.
162 Bryden, pp. 507-510.

The first of these is that permitting such intervention will lead to better judicial decision-making by presenting the court with arguments on legal principles not raised or fully developed by the litigants or on the legislative facts affected by the principles implicated in a case.

> … [P]ublic interest groups sometimes have been able to bring to the attention of the court background information … that has revealed in a particularly telling manner the impact that a legal doctrine has on the people the group represents. Thus in the [US] lawsuits that eventually resulted in the ending of judicial enforcement of racially restrictive housing covenants, a variety of organizations that submitted *amicus curiae* briefs were able to provide especially persuasive accounts of the pernicious effects of discrimination in the provision of housing. On other occasions *amicus curiae* submissions have raised legal issues or ideas that have not been developed by the parties, and these ideas have influenced the way in which judges have formulated their decisions. For example, the *amicus* briefs of the American Civil Liberties Union supporting the notion of a constitutional right to privacy are considered to have had a substantial impact on the development of that doctrine.[163]

Second, Bryden argues that public interest intervention helps to legitimise judicial decisions by creating a moral obligation on the intervenors to respect the outcome of the litigation and by vindicating the human dignity and self-respect of such intervenors through the process of participation.

> … [T]he willingness of courts to listen to intervenors is a reflection of the value that judges attach to people. Our commitment to a right to a hearing and public participation in governmental decision-making is derived not only from the belief that we improve the accuracy of decisions when we allow people to present their side of the story, but also from our sense that participation is necessary to preserve human dignity and self-respect … .[A] willingness to take part in these [i.e. judicial and election] processes is generally thought to imply a willingness to abide by the result. If public interest intervenors are shut out from the courts' decision-making processes, their legal obligation to accept such decisions will doubtless remain but their moral obligation to do so will be subtly undermined.[164]

Having outlined the reasons for permitting those affected by litigation to represent their views to the courts, I turn now to consider how this might be achieved. First, it is important to note that interest groups may be affected by litigation in one of two different ways. They may be affected directly, where the outcome of the litigation directly and immediately impacts on their interests, or indirectly, where legal principles developed in the course of the litigation have potential application to their own situation, albeit in a different context to that of the litigation in hand. An example of the first situation arises where Travellers on a halting site are affected by litigation taken by residents against the local authority challenging the validity of the decision

---

[163] *Ibid.*, pp. 507-8. (Footnotes omitted.)
[164] *Ibid.*, pp. 509-510. (Footnotes omitted.)

to establish the halting site. The case of *O'Reilly v. Limerick Corporation*[165] offers us a good example of the second situation. There the claim of a group of Traveller families that the State should provide them with certain facilities raised the issue of whether the court could, under the doctrine of separation of powers, entertain such a claim. Clearly the outcome of this court's reasoning on this point has major implications for other groups seeking financial assistance from the State, even though they are not directly affected by the court's actual decision in relation to Travellers.

The significance of this distinction lies primarily in the fact that parties in the first situation could be protected by being made parties to the original litigation, pursuant to O.15, r.13 of the Rules of the Superior Courts, 1986[166] whereas this option is not available to parties in the second situation. That rule provides, in relevant part:

> The Court may at any stage of the proceedings, either upon or without the application of either party, and on such terms as may appear to the Court to be just, order ... that the names of any parties, whether plaintiffs or defendants, who ought to have been joined, or whose presence before the Court may be necessary in order to enable the Court effectually and completely to adjudicate upon and settle all the questions involved in the cause or matter, be added.[167]

This provision, and its predecessors, would appear to have received no detailed analysis from the courts.[168] However in *Campaign to Separate Church and State Ltd. v. Minister for Education*[169] Costello P. noted that the Master had joined as additional defendants to the action four parties who would suffer substantial financial loss if the plaintiffs succeeded and who, therefore, had "a material interest in the outcome of the proceedings".[170] If having a material interest in the outcome of the proceedings is the criterion for deciding to admit additional parties as defendants or plaintiffs to an action, then groups in the first category outlined above would appear to be adequately protected by the terms of O.15, r.13.

---

[165] [1989] ILRM 181. See p. 9 *et seq.* above.

[166] Re-enacting O.15, r.13 of the Rules of the Superior Courts, 1962.

[167] See also the similar provision in O.84, r.22(6) relating to applications for judicial review. The Rules of the Superior Courts also recognise a right to intervene in three specific types of case – probate proceedings (see O.12, r.14), admiralty cases (O.64, r.14) and matrimonial causes (O.70, rules 19 and 59).

[168] In *Cupples v. Strahan* (1892) L.R. IR. 120, the former Irish Court of Appeal held that a minor, entitled in remainder to land of which his deceased mother had been a tenant for life, should be joined as a plaintiff to proceedings to restrain the flooding of the land. In *Steele v. Gt. Northern Railway Co.* (1890) 26 L.R. (Ir.) 96, the Court of Appeal held that there was no statutory basis for adding the parents of the deceased as plaintiffs to an action brought by his widow arising out of his death. In *International Trading Group Ltd. v. Dublin Corp.* [1974] IR 373, Kenny J. held that the court would not make an order adding a person as a defendant in an action where the plaintiff seeks this order merely for the purpose of obtaining discovery of documents from the proposed defendant. In *Fusco v. O'Dea* [1994] 2 IR 93, Lynch J. held that it was neither appropriate not necessary to join the Government of the UK as a party to proceedings seeking discovery of documents in connection with the plaintiff's proposed extradition.

[169] [1998] 3 IR 321; [1996] 2 ILRM 241. This issue was not addressed by the Supreme Court on appeal – [1998] 3 IR 321; [1998] 2 ILRM 81.

[170] [1998] 3 IR 321 at p. 325; [1996] 2 ILRM 241 at p. 243.

One further provision permitting intervention in litigation should also be noted. Order 84, rule 26(1) of the Rules of the Superior Courts 1986 provides:

> On the hearing of any motion or summons [seeking judicial review], any person who desires to be heard in opposition to the motion or summons, and appears to the Court to be a proper person to be heard, shall be heard, notwithstanding that he has not been served with notice of the motion or the summons.[171]

This provision is limited in that it applies only to applications for judicial review and, moreover, allows intervention only in opposition to the application. However presumably it could be used by some intervenors in order to gain access to litigation whose outcome was likely to affect their interests.

For those who are not affected directly by the outcome of litigation, but who may nonetheless be affected by the reasoning used by the court, neither O.15, r.13 nor O.84, r.26(1) offer any protection. However one could argue that the courts have an inherent jurisdiction to permit such parties to intervene in the litigation, either as parties to the litigation[172] or as *amici curiae*, as that term is understood in the US.

At common law, the *amicus curiae* operated almost invariably as an impartial assistant to the court, someone who, without having any interest in the action, provided information on a point of law or fact for the benefit of the judge.[173] In one exceptional type of case, the *amicus* could act in a partisan manner and that was where he sought to alert the court to the existence of collusion between the parties to the action.[174]

The device of the *amicus curiae* features rather infrequently in Irish case law. In two *habeas corpus* applications raising issues other than the validity of legislation,[175] where the Attorney General acted in a partisan way in opposing the applications, he was nonetheless described by the law reporter as acting as an *amicus curiae*. An example of an *amicus curiae* acting as impartial assistant may be seen in *The People (Attorney General) v. Tyrrell*[176] where the Attorney General was invited by the Court

---

[171] It is also worth noting that O.84, r.22(2) of the Rules of the Superior Courts 1986 requires an applicant for judicial review to serve the proceedings "on all persons directly affected". In *Spin Communications v. IRTC*, unreported, Supreme Court, *ex tempore*, 14 April 2000, the Supreme Court held that this would include any person vitally interested in the outcome of the proceedings.

[172] In *Re Canadian Labour Congress v. Bhindi* (1985) 17 D.L.R. (4th) 193, the Court of Appeal of British Columbia held that it had an inherent jurisdiction to add public interest intervenors as full parties to litigation.

[173] See, e.g., *Shallow v. Shallow* [1978] 2 All ER 483, a matrimonial case in which counsel for the Attorney General, acting as *amicus curiae*, introduced the Court of Appeal to the intricacies of the State supplementary benefit scheme. In *Quinn's Supermarket Ltd. v. A.G.* [1972] IR 1, the Chief Rabbi of Ireland, acting at the request of the Supreme Court, gave evidence of Jewish religious practice – see [1972] IR 1 at p. 16.

[174] In this context, it is interesting to note that in *O'R. v. B.* [1995] 2 ILRM 57, Kinlen J. expressed the view that in nullity suits in which one of the parties to the marriage was not before the court, it would be eminently desirable to have an *amicus curiae* appointed at public expense to argue in favour of the existence of the marriage. This view was subsequently endorsed by Budd J. in *McG. v. F.*, unreported, High Court, 20 January 2000.

[175] *Application of Woods* [1970] IR 154; *Application of McLoughlin* [1970] IR 197.

[176] [1970] IR 294. See also *In re D* [1987] IR 449; [1988] ILRM 251, a wardship case in which, at the request of the Supreme Court, the Registrar of Wards of Court was appointed as *amicus curiae*.

of Criminal Appeal to provide it with assistance in interpreting s.4(3) of the Criminal Justice (Legal Aid) Act 1962 and this perception of the *amicus curiae* as a disinterested participant may also help to explain a remark of Murnaghan J. in *Byrne v. Ireland*[177] that he had the benefit of counsel's argument, "first as appearing on behalf of the Attorney General, but also as *amicus curiae*".[178]

However in a number of jurisdictions, notably the US[179] and Canada[180] and, to a much lesser extent, Australia[181] and the UK,[182] the concept of the *amicus curiae* has changed significantly from this notion of a disinterested bystander and *amici curiae* are now permitted to act in a partisan way, as advocates for interests affected by the litigation.

Significantly, in each of these four jurisdictions, the courts invoked their *inherent* jurisdiction in order to facilitate public interest intervention in litigation, whether by joining the intervenor as a full party to the proceedings or by permitting it to act as an *amicus curiae*, albeit in a partisan manner. Thus in the US, the change in the *amicus curiae* from disinterested bystander to partisan advocate occurred during the nineteenth century, at a time when there was no legislative regulation of the practice. A similar change appears to be taking place in Australia since the 1980s, again in the absence of legislative regulation.[183] In the UK, the JUSTICE/Public Law Project report cited Mr Justice Popplewell as holding, in *R. v. Minister of Agriculture, Fisheries and Food, ex. p. Anastasiou (Pissouri)*,[184] that the court in judicial review proceedings has an inherent jurisdiction to permit persons to be heard in order to ensure that all those affected by a decision in the case have an opportunity to present

---

[177] [1972] IR 241. The remark occurs at p. 256.

[178] In the recent case of *Brady v. Cavan Co. Co.* [1999] 4 IR 99; [2000] 1 ILRM 81, the Attorney General is also described as having appeared before the Supreme Court in an *amicus curiae* role – see p. 88.

[179] See Krislov, "The *Amicus Curiae* Brief: From Friendship to Advocacy" (1963) 72 *Yale Law Journal* 694; Angell, "The *Amicus Curiae*: American Development of English Institutions" (1967) 16 *International and Comparative Law Quarterly* 1017.

[180] See Bryden.

[181] See Re, "The *Amicus Curiae* Brief: Access to the Courts for Public Interest Associations" (1984) 14 *Melbourne University Law Review* 522.

[182] See Harlow and Rawlings, at p. 194 and the cases cited therein; JUSTICE/Public Law Project, pp. 16-17.

[183] See Re. In *Commonwealth of Australia v. Tasmania* (1984-5) 158 CLR 1, the High Court of Australia indicated, at p. 51, that it was prepared to treat the intervention of an environmental pressure group in a case concerning the power of a state agency to build a dam as an intervention by an *amicus curiae*. Miller cites a more recent case, *Breen v. Williams* (1994) NSW Lexis 13703, 23 December 1994, as evidence of continuing willingness on the part of the Australian judiciary to entertain *amicus* briefs, though only in the form of written briefs at appellate level – Miller, p. 15. In *Wik Peoples v. Queensland* (1996) 187 CLR 1, leave was given by the High Court of Australia to a number of parties to intervene in an appeal relating to the land rights of Aboriginal peoples. The Commonwealth indicated that while it did not object to the grant of leave, it did not regard it as a precedent for other cases where intervention might not be appropriate. Inasmuch as no statutory authority for granting leave to intervene is cited by the court, the court would appear to have been exercising its inherent jurisdiction.

[184] 1994 COD 329.

their case.[185] Similarly, in *Re Canadian Labour Congress and Bhindi*[186] the Court of Appeal for British Columbia exercised its inherent jurisdiction in order to join the Canadian Labour Congress, a public interest intervenor, as a full party to litigation.[187] This raises the possibility that an Irish court, exercising its inherent jurisdiction, could permit such interventions, either by joining the public interest intervenor as a full party to the action or by permitting it to submit an *amicus curiae* brief, representing a partisan interest.

The possible development of the role of the *amicus curiae* raises a number of practical issues to which I would like to suggest possible solutions. To begin with, an important distinction exists between an *amicus curiae* and a party to the litigation in relation to the extent of their participation in the litigation. Unlike a party to litigation, the *amicus curiae* does not have the right to demand service of papers, to file pleadings, to settle the case out of court, to cross-examine witnesses, to appeal against the decision or to apply for a rehearing. On the other hand, the *amicus* is not bound by the decision. Subject to the court's power to compel full participation in litigation as a party thereto, it would seem appropriate to leave it to any potential intervenor to decide whether s/he should seek to be joined as a full party or merely seek to intervene as an *amicus curiae*.

With regard to the question of who should be allowed to intervene as an *amicus curiae*, it is submitted that intervention should be permitted in the case of *bona fide* parties who can show that their interests or the interests of the general public would be materially affected by the outcome of the case (in which eventuality, such parties would also have the option of being joined as full parties to the litigation) or by legal argumentation put to the court (in which case intervention might only be as *amicus curiae*). In all cases the permission of the court would have to be obtained before a

---

[185] JUSTICE/Public Law Project, pp. 16-7.

[186] (1985) 17 D.L.R. (4th) 193.

[187] See also *Morgentaler v. Attorney General of New Brunswick* (1994) 116 D.L.R. (4th) 750 where Stevenson J. of the New Brunswick Court of Queen's Bench briefly adverts, at p. 753, to the court's inherent jurisdiction to allow interventions. In *Peel (Regional Municipality) v. Great Atlantic & Pacific Co. of Canada Ltd.* (1990) 46 Admin. L.R. 1, the Chief Justice of Ontario, Mr Justice Dubin said, at p. 4, that "in determining whether an application for intervention should be granted ... the matters to be considered are the nature of the case, the issues which arise and the likelihood of the applicant being able to make a useful contribution to the resolution of the appeal without causing injustice to the immediate parties". More recently, in *Attorney General for Ontario v. Dieleman* (1994) 108 DLR (4th) 458, Adams J. of the Ontario Court (General Division) observed, at p. 464, that "where intervener status is granted to a public interest group, either as a party or as a friend of the court, at least one of the following criteria is usually met: (a) the intervener has a real, substantial and identifiable interest in the subject-matter of the proceedings; (b) the intervener has an important perspective distinct from the immediate parties; or (c) the intervener is a well-recognised group with a special expertise and with a broad identifiable membership base." In 1987, the Supreme Court of Canada introduced a new system for dealing with public interest interventions before that court. Rule 18(1) of the Rules of the Supreme Court of Canada now provides: "Any person interested in an appeal or a reference may, by leave of a judge, intervene therein upon such terms and conditions, and with such rights and privileges, as the judge may determine".

party could act as an *amicus curiae* and the court could legitimately refuse such permission so as to avoid duplication of argument. Of course, the court could also act pro-actively in this regard, requesting appropriate parties to submit *amicus* briefs.

The interest of the parties to the litigation in keeping legal costs to a minimum would require that interventions as *amicus curiae* be restricted to the issues raised by those parties. Thus intervenors seeking to raise additional issues would seek either to be joined as additional parties pursuant to O.15, r.13 or O.84, r.26(1) or to initiate fresh litigation themselves. Clearly the *amicus curiae* would be allowed to present legal argument to the court and this is most straightforward where the interests of the *amicus* are quite distinct from those of the litigants. However where the *amicus* wishes to support one party to the litigation, the simple endorsement of legal argument already presented by that party could be problematic, however, not only because of the potential waste of the judge's time, but also because it smacks of lobbying. In that regard, Krislov comments:

> Where there is relatively adequate representation of the basic points of view, the *amicus curiae* ... may perform a valuable subsidiary role by introducing subtle variations of the basic argument, or emotive and even questionable arguments that might result in a successful verdict, but are too risky to be embraced by the principal litigant ... .[I]t may very well be advantageous to label the new as unofficial so that, if it should be rejected, a minimum of disapprobation attaches to the official cause. Arguments that might anger the Justices, doctrines that have not yet been legally accepted, and emotive presentations that have little legal standing can best be utilized in most instances by the amicus rather than by the principals.[188]

Where the *amicus* is likely to be materially affected by the outcome of the case, there seems to be little objection to him or her presenting arguments on the facts of the case, in addition to legal argument. However where the concern of the *amicus* is solely with the legal doctrine being developed by the court, it would seem inappropriate to permit him or her to intervene in relation to the facts of the dispute. The interest of efficiency (and the example of comparative practice) suggest that the most appropriate method of intervention would be by way of written brief rather than oral submission. In this regard, the recent increasing emphasis placed by the Irish judiciary on the submission of written legal briefs would facilitate public interest interventions as it would enable the courts to process the interventions in an expeditious manner and would also reduce the expense of intervention to the cost of preparing the written brief.

This leads on to one final practical issue concerning the use of *amicus briefs* – the matter of costs. In the US, each party pays his or her own costs and so the *amicus* simply carries the cost of his or her own intervention. For those jurisdictions, such as our own, where costs follow the event, one could argue that insofar as intervention added to the costs of the successful party, the *amicus* should be liable to pay such costs. However this belies the difficulty in apportioning responsibility for the

---

[188] Krislov, pp. 711-2.

winner's costs as between the unsuccessful party and the unsuccessful *amicus*. Moreover if one wishes to encourage the use of *amicus* briefs, the US approach to costs is much more attractive than that followed here.[189] A useful compromise based on the Canadian experience is suggested by JUSTICE/Public Law Project where they recommend that the matter of costs be entrusted to the discretion of the court.[190]

Doctrine of mootness – the case for modification

A further issue raised by the potentially far-reaching impact of public interest litigation on people other than the actual litigants is whether it is appropriate for such litigation to be subject to the doctrine of mootness so that the settlement of an individual claim prevents the courts from resolving an issue which continues to affect similarly situated third parties.[191] In the context of the traditional model of litigation, where the impact of the judgment is confined to the parties, the rule whereby the courts will not adjudicate on moot points is easily defended as a prudent use of scarce judicial resources. However where the litigation is capable of clarifying the legal rights of many individuals who are not party to the litigation, a prudent use of scarce judicial resources might actually be better served by allowing the court to clarify those rights, even though the point might now be moot in relation to the particular litigants by virtue of an agreed settlement.

Consider the case of *O'Connell v. Ireland*[192] (though it does not involve an agreed settlement) in which the applicant, a welfare claimant, sought to challenge the constitutionality of the obligation placed on litigants to pay stamp duty. This issue arose out of legal proceedings which the applicant brought against the State concerning the operation of the Disabled Person's Maintenance Allowance scheme.[193] When he was asked to pay stamp duty of £53 in relation to these proceedings, the applicant commenced separate proceedings challenging the validity of this duty in which he contended that it was an unconstitutional fetter on his right of access to the courts. In the event, the applicant was able to borrow the money to pay this stamp

---

[189] For that reason, Re suggests that the Australian courts should follow the US example in relation to the costs to be borne by the *amicus curiae* – Re, p. 530. Moreover there does not seem to be any reason in principle why the *amicus curiae* should not obtain legal aid in the preparation of the brief.

[190] JUSTICE/Public Law Project, p. 29.

[191] A statement of the doctrine of mootness may be found in *Murphy v. Roche* [1987] IR 106, where Finlay C.J. said, at p. 110: "There can be no doubt that this Court has decided on a number of occasions that it must decline, either in constitutional issues or in other issues of law, to decide any question which is in the form of a moot and the decision of which is not necessary for the determination of the rights of the parties before it". He went on to state, however, that this principle "must, of course, be subject in any individual case to the overriding consideration of doing justice between the parties". See also *Brady v. Donegal Co. Co.* [1989] ILRM 282; *McDaid v. Sheehy* [1991] 1 IR 1.

[192] Unreported, High Court, 31 July 1997.

[193] See the decision of Barron J. on this claim in *O'Connell v. Ireland* [1996] 2 IR 522; [1996] 1 ILRM 187.

duty and as he was ultimately successful in his primary claim, he recovered all of his out of pocket expenses from the State. Consequently he was not, in fact, denied access to the courts and so Geoghegan J. declined to entertain his secondary claim on the ground, *inter alia,* that it was moot. However this left unresolved the question of the constitutionality of the obligation to pay stamp duty, a matter of some significance for other indigent litigants and in respect of which there was already evidence of some judicial unease.[194]

As I have already indicated, a case can also be rendered moot if the plaintiff's claim is conceded by the defendant in a settlement, thereby preventing the establishment of potentially expensive precedents.[195] Thus in one case of which I am aware, an attempt to challenge certain restrictions on the payment of the former prescribed relative's allowance was thwarted when, on the evening before the case was due to start in the High Court, legal representatives for the State conceded that the claimant was entitled to the allowance.[196] In such a situation, the plaintiff is precluded by the doctrine of mootness from putting the legal issues before the court, even though the litigation may have been partly motivated by the desire to establish a precedent for similarly situated individuals.

In both of these situations, the doctrine of mootness operates to prevent the courts clarifying the legal position of similarly situated third parties, raising the possibility that such individuals would themselves initiate further litigation, in which case one could question whether the doctrine ultimately protects scarce judicial resources. Moreover, the effect of the doctrine in the second situation is to allow State agencies to continue to pursue policies that fail to accord fully with the law.

In the light of these criticisms, it is interesting to note that the US courts have relaxed the doctrine of mootness in a number of ways.[197] In particular, a case is not deemed

---

[194] See Kelly, at p. 389 and the cases cited therein. But see now *Murphy v. Minister for Justice* [2001] 2 ILRM 144.

[195] See Hodge, "A Test Case Strategy" in *Welfare Law and Policy*, Partington and Jowell, eds., (London, 1979), at p. 258.

[196] In order to produce a moot, however, it would appear that the defendants have to concede the plaintiff's *entitlement* to the relief sought. In *O'Donoghue v. Minister for Health* [1996] 2 IR 20, the plaintiff, who was severely mentally handicapped, sought, *inter alia*, an order of mandamus directing the defendants to provide for his free primary education. Counsel for the defendants argued, *inter alia*, that the provision of certain educational facilities for the plaintiff rendered his constitutional claim moot. This was rejected by O'Hanlon J. who said, at pp. 68-9, "I am of opinion that it is not sufficient for the Respondents to grant as a matter of grace and concession, educational benefits which the Applicant is entitled to claim as of right. Were this to foreclose any further action by the Applicant in pursuance of his claim, he would be left in a position where the benefits thus conferred could be withdrawn or varied at any time at the discretion of the Respondents, leaving the Applicant in the position of having to start afresh in seeking to establish his legal entitlement in the matter. I think it is important for all parties to have a determination at this stage of their respective rights and duties."

In the US the defendant's voluntary cessation of a challenged practice does not deprive the federal courts of jurisdiction to determine the legality of the practice – *City of Mesquite v. Aladdin's Castle Inc.,* 455 US 283 (1982).

[197] See Tribe, *American Constitutional Law* (2nd ed., 1988), pp. 82-93; Nowak and Rotunda, *Constitutional Law* (4th ed., 1991), pp. 60-8.

moot if it is "capable of repetition, yet evading review" either for the original litigant or for others in the class which s/he represents.[198] The doctrine has also been qualified by the Irish courts, albeit in more restricted circumstances. In *Condon v. Minister for Labour*[199] the Supreme Court held that the expiry of temporary legislation alleged to be unconstitutional could not prevent the courts from reviewing its constitutionality where there was a possibility that similar legislation could be enacted in the future. In *M.F. v. Superintendent, Ballymun Garda Station*,[200] O'Flaherty J. indicated that the doctrine could be modified in relation to cases concerning the protection of children's rights,[201] so as to enable the courts to give decisions which would be as helpful as possible to all those concerned with the welfare of children. However there does not appear to be any reason why a similar approach could not be taken in relation to other categories of case, in particular ones in which parties other than the litigant were likely to be affected by repetition of the impugned decisions, such as, for example, particular classes of welfare claimants, local authority tenants, medical card holders, etc.[202] Indeed, one could argue that the value of ensuring compliance with the law justifies the courts in going behind a settlement in order to rule authoritatively on the legal issues raised which, notwithstanding the settlement, would continue to affect the legal rights of many people who were not party to the litigation. Thus the State, defending a policy of doubtful legal validity, would not be able to divert the issue from the courts simply by offering the particular plaintiff a settlement but would, if that plaintiff so chose, have to defend the policy in open court.

In conclusion, the wider impact of public interest litigation suggests that there are grounds for modifying the application of the doctrine of mootness to such litigation. Far from carefully shepherding scarce judicial resources, a strict application of the doctrine to such litigation may simply result in further litigation being initiated by those who were not party to the original proceedings. Moreover such an approach may also enable the State to continue to pursue policies of doubtful legal validity.[203]

Enhancing the impact of public interest litigation

As we have already noted, because public interest litigation taken on behalf of disadvantaged individuals or groups is almost invariably concerned with the content

---

[198] *Southern Pacific Terminal Co. v. ICC* 219 US 498 (1911).

[199] [1981] IR 62. In his judgment, Kenny J. explicitly approved of the US authorities on this point. In *Ó Cléirigh v. Minister for Agriculture, Food and Forestry* [1998] 4 IR 15; [1998] 2 ILRM 263, the Supreme Court held that the plaintiff could challenge the constitutionality of legislation providing for the abolition of his office even though the relevant section had not yet been commenced.

[200] [1991] 1 IR 189; [1990] ILRM 767.

[201] Which he considered to be in a "special, and possibly, unique category" – [1991] 1 IR 189 at p. 200; [1990] ILRM 767 at p. 772.

[202] In the US, an action commenced by a plaintiff on behalf of a class will be allowed to continue even though the issue has become moot in respect of the particular plaintiff – *Sosna v. Iowa* 419 US 393 (1975); *Franks v. Bowman Transportation Company* 424 US 747 (1976).

[203] Before closing on this point, it is worth noting that in the US the public interest in deciding an issue can prevent a case from being moot -*Wirtz v. Glass Bottle Blowers Ass'n, Local 153* 389 US 463, 88 S. Ct. 643, 19 L.Ed.2d 705 (1968).

and/or operation of public policy, the court's decision potentially affects many people apart from the particular parties to the case. Notwithstanding this characteristic of such litigation, however, the Irish legal system does not currently offer any expeditious manner for extending the benefits of a judicial ruling, other than one declaring a legislative or administrative act to be unconstitutional[204] or dealing with beneficial interests in a trust or estate,[205] to those who are not party to the original litigation but whose factual situation is on all fours with that of the successful litigant. In the absence of a legislative or administrative decision to apply such a ruling to this extended class, members of that class must themselves bring legal proceedings and invoke the doctrine of precedent in order to avail of the benefits of the original court ruling.

Order 15, rule 9 of the Rules of the Superior Courts 1986 does, admittedly, provide a mechanism, the representative action, whereby large numbers of people may be joined as parties to a particular piece of litigation in certain limited circumstances.[206] This provision reads:

> Where there are numerous persons having the same interest in one cause or matter, one or more of such persons may sue or be sued, or may be authorised by the Court to defend, in such cause or matter, on behalf, or for the benefit, of all persons so interested.

However two pre-conditions for the use of the representative action limit its utility somewhat.[207] First, the traditional view was that a representative action could only be employed where the interests of the prospective litigants were the same – a similarity

---

204 In such cases, the impugned act would cease to be effective in all situations from, at the latest, the date of the judgment. As to the circumstances in which such a judicial ruling may have retrospective effect for non-parties to the litigation, see Kelly, pp. 497-487. See also the Supreme Court decision in *McDonnell v. Ireland* [1998] 1 IR 134.

205 O.15, r.8 and r.10 of the Rules of the Superior Courts 1986.

206 Representative actions do not appear to be very common in the Irish system and apart from the two cases of *Madigan v. A.G.* [1986] ILRM 136 and *Greene v. Minister for Agriculture* [1990] 2 IR 17; [1990] ILRM 364 discussed below, the only other examples of representative actions which I have unearthed are *Brennan v. A.G.* [1984] ILRM 355 which was a representative action taken on behalf of an unincorporated association set up to challenge rateable valuation system, *McGrane v. Louth Co. Co.*, unreported, High Court, 9 December 1983, in which the plaintiff unsuccessfully sought a *quia timet* injunction on behalf of an unincorporated association to restrain the defendant council from committing a nuisance, *Murphy v. Roche (No. 2)* [1987] IR 656, in which a club member unsuccessfully attempted to sue his fellow members by way of representative action arising out of injuries he sustained as a result of a fall in the club premises; *McMenamin v. Ireland* [1996] 3 IR 100, [1997] 2 ILRM 177, in which the plaintiff took proceedings against the State on his own behalf and on behalf of the Association of District Judges and *Rafferty v. Bus Éireann* [1997] 2 IR 424, in which a plaintiff union was held to be entitled to sue on behalf of its members in a representative capacity. In each of these cases, with the exception of *Rafferty*, the standing of the plaintiff to represent the larger group was assumed by the court.

207 A further drawback to the representative action is that, by virtue of s.28(9)(a)(ix) of the Civil Legal Aid Act 1995, legal aid is not available for such proceedings. For a recent, comprehensive account of the limitations of the representative action in English law, see Seymour, "Representative Procedures and the Future of Multi-Party Actions" (1999) 62 *MLR* 564.

of interests would not suffice.[208] This led to some suggestions that one could not bring a representative action sounding in tort[209] nor a representative action seeking damages.[210] In the UK, there is now some evidence of a somewhat more flexible approach on the part of the courts to this requirement. Thus in *Prudential Assurance Co. Ltd. v. Newman Industries (No.1)*[211] Vinelott J. held that a representative action seeking damages for tort could proceed where (1) permitting such an action would not confer a right of action on a member of the class represented who would not otherwise have been able to assert such a right in separate proceedings or bar a defence which might otherwise have been available to the defendant in such a separate action; (2) the class possesses a common interest, i.e., there must be a common ingredient in the cause of action of each member of the class; and (3) the court is persuaded that it is in the benefit of the class to permit the action to proceed. More recently, in *Irish Shipping Ltd. v. Commercial Union Assurance Co. plc.*[212] the Court of Appeal held that a representative action could be taken against 77 insurance companies, all subject to separate but identical contracts, even though some of the issues raised would not affect all 77 equally. It remains to be seen whether the Irish courts are prepared to follow this lead, thereby enhancing the role of the representative action.

Second, each member of the class must authorise the taking or defending of proceedings on their behalf. Thus in *Madigan v. Attorney General*[213] O'Hanlon J. refused to grant a representative order allowing the plaintiff to sue on behalf of "all persons who are assessable persons" under the impugned tax legislation. No evidence was adduced to show that any persons had authorised the plaintiff to act on their behalf. Moreover the judge took the view that this was not an appropriate case in which to make a representative order as he had no knowledge of the number of persons wishing to challenge the validity of the statute or of those who had instituted

---

208 See *Hardie & Lane Ltd. v. Chilton* [1928] 1 K.B. 663 where the plaintiffs were not entitled to sue the defendants in a representative capacity for all members of the Motor Trade Association as that body had a shifting membership with some members coming in and some leaving and consequently the defendants did not have a common interest with the persons to be represented. See also *Adam and ors. v. Minister for Justice, Equality and Law Reform*, unreported, High Court, 16 October 2000, in which O'Donovan J. commented, at p. 3, that as "the respective interests of the several applicants herein vary considerably, I think that it was wholly inappropriate that their respective claims herein should have been included in the one set of proceedings."

209 In *Moore v. Attorney General (No. 2)* [1930] IR 471, Kennedy C.J. stated, at p. 499, that "no such thing is possible as an action of tort against representative defendants". Moreover, O.6, r.10 of the Circuit Court Rules 1950 provides for representative actions "save in actions founded on tort." On the other hand, in *McGrane v. Louth County Council*, unreported, High Court, 9 December 1983, the High Court did entertain a representative action in which the plaintiffs sought a *quia timet* injunction to restrain the defendant from committing a nuisance, though no reference was made to the suitability of the representative action for this type of case.

210 See the comments of Fletcher-Moulton L.J. in *Markt & Co. Ltd. v. Knight SS Co. Ltd.* [1910] 2 KB 1021 at 1035.

211 [1981] Ch. 299.

212 [1991] 2 QB 663.

213 [1986] ILRM 136.

their own proceedings independently of the plaintiff or of those who were content with the status quo. However, in the later case of *Greene v. Minister for Agriculture*[214] a more relaxed approach to this requirement appears to have been taken by Murphy J. Here the plaintiffs challenged the constitutionality of administrative schemes designed to provide compensatory payments to persons farming in disadvantaged areas. The statement of claim asserted that the plaintiffs brought the action "on behalf of themselves and on behalf of all farmers in such areas, and in particular those farmers who are listed in the schedule thereto ... " In place of the aforementioned schedule, solicitors for the plaintiffs had supplied the defendants with a list of 1390 farmers who, it was contended, were plaintiffs in the action. The people on the list had not signed, nor were they asked to sign, any specific authorisation in respect of the proceedings. Nor had the plaintiffs named in the statement of claim applied for the making of a representative order to cover the persons named on the list. However the latter had, apparently, subscribed to a fighting fund to finance the litigation and on that basis, Murphy J. indicated, *obiter*, that they had authorised the proceedings on their behalf and in their name.

It remains to be seen whether this slightly more flexible approach will be regarded by other judges as an acceptable way of authorising the taking of a representative action. In the meantime, however, to be absolutely certain of satisfying this requirement, the legal team mounting the action has to take instructions from each member of the class and obviously the greater the size of the class, the more onerous this requirement becomes.[215]

Given the limited utility of the representative action as a means of extending the benefits of a judicial ruling to significant numbers of people, public interest lawyers on this side of the Atlantic have tended to look wistfully at a procedural device which has played an important role in civil rights litigation in the US, the class action.[216] A

---

[214] [1990] 2 IR 17; [1990] ILRM 364.

[215] This was certainly the experience of FLAC when it instituted the largest representative action taken in this State on behalf of more than 1,700 married women claiming social welfare arrears under EC Directive 79/7/EEC.

[216] Rule 23(b) of the Federal Rules of Civil Procedure of the Federal Courts of the USA provides: "An action may be maintained as a class action if the prerequisites of subdivision (a) are satisfied, and in addition :
(1) the prosecution of separate actions by or against individual members of the class would create a risk of
  (A) inconsistent or varying adjudications with respect to individual members of the class which would establish incompatible standards of conduct for the party opposing the class, or
  (B) adjudications with respect to individual members of the class which would as a practical matter be dispositive of the interests of the other members not parties to the adjudications or substantially impair or impede their ability to protect their interests; or
(2) the party opposing the class has acted or refused to act on grounds generally applicable to the class, thereby making appropriate final injunctive relief or corresponding declaratory relief with respect to the class as a whole; or
(3) the court finds that the questions of law or fact common to the members of the class predominate over any questions affecting only individual members, and that a class action is superior to other available methods for the fair and efficient adjudication of the controversy ..."

useful description of the class action, including a summary of its advantages, is provided by Prosser:

> [A class action enables] a party, in certain conditions, to sue on behalf of a class affected in the same way as the individual party. Although there must be a common grievance, not all members of the class need to be identified individually. All members of the class are treated as parties to the case, and after notifying them, if necessary through a general notice rather than an individual notification, the onus is on them to opt out of the class ...
>
> ... The chief advantages of the procedure are that it enables an authoritative resolution of an issue to be made and hence avoids piecemeal and perhaps inconsistent decisions in a number of cases concerning the same issue. It may prevent ... the 'buying off' of potential test cases [through offers of settlement] as it would be impossible to buy off the whole class without effecting a policy change and thereby, in effect, conceding the case. Finally, the decision will apply to the whole of the class, so in the case of a successful challenge there will be a clear cut liability towards them all.[217]

However the class action is not without its difficulties. In particular, there is always concern that a conflict of interest may arise between the interests of the class representative and the interests of absent class members.[218] Moreover the cost of notifying class members of the existence of the litigation can, in some cases, be prohibitive.[219] In addition, the use of a class action may, in some circumstances, oversimplify the legal relationships between the members of the class *inter se* and between the members of the class and the opposing party and, indeed, one should not underestimate the difficulty in identifying an appropriate class.[220] Concern has also been expressed about the extent to which the judiciary have to become involved in the management of class actions. Not only does the judge have to decide whether to

---

By virtue of the preceding subdivision (A), a class action of any of the types listed in Rule 23(b) will only be allowed to proceed in the federal courts where all of the following questions are answered in the affirmative – (1) Is there an identifiable class? (2) Are those purporting to represent that class members of it? (3) Is the class so large that joinder of all members as parties is impracticable? (4) Are there questions of law or fact common to all the class members? (5) Are the claims or defences of the representatives of the class typical of those of other class members? (6) Will the representatives adequately represent and protect the interests of the absent class members? – see Friedenthal, Kane and Miller, *Civil Procedure* (2nd ed., 1993), at pp. 725-6. These authors treat generally of the class action at pp. 721-759. See also James, Hazard and Leubsdorf, *Civil Procedure* (Little Brown and Co., 1992), pp. 555-573 and the extensive note in (1976) 89 *Harv. L. Rev* 1318. For an historical account of the development of the class action, see Yeazell, *From Medieval Group Litigation to the Modern Class Action* (Yale University Press, 1987).

[217] Prosser, *Test Cases for the Poor,* (London, 1983), p. 11.

[218] See note in (1982) 91 *Yale Law Journal* 590.

[219] By virtue of Rule 23(c)(2), notice to absent members is obligatory in cases taken under Rule 23(b)(3), i.e. typically, class actions for damages. Here notice must be "the best notice practicable under the circumstances, including individual notice to all members who can be identified through reasonable effort". In all other cases, the court has a discretion to order that notice be given "for the protection of the members of the class or otherwise for the fair conduct of the action" – Rule 23(d)(2). In such cases, the manner and scope of the notice are left to the court's discretion.

[220] See Buckholz *et al.*, at pp. 887-901.

certify the litigation as a class action, s/he is also empowered to determine the course of proceedings by prescribing measures to prevent undue repetition and confusion in the presentation of evidence or argument, to communicate directly with class members, to impose conditions upon the class representative (e.g. by redefining the class) and to devise special orders regarding damages.[221] Particular criticism has been reserved for the class damage action under Rule 23(b)(3) whereby numerous relatively small claims against one defendant can be aggregated into a large class action, leading to charges of a form of legalised blackmail.[222]

In the light of these difficulties, one might well be wary of any proposal to introduce the concept of the class action into Irish law. Certainly, for public interest lawyers concerned with disadvantaged clients, the difficulties attaching to the class action enhance the attractiveness of one alternative method of extending the impact of a judicial decision beyond the actual parties to the case, advocated by Cousins.[223] Applicable only to cases in which the class of beneficiaries can be identified from files held by a public body, such as, for example, social welfare claims, this approach requires a public body found to be in breach of its legal obligations to review all cases in which such unlawful behaviour occurred and, where appropriate, to compensate the individuals affected. As Cousins points out, this argument was accepted by Woolf J. (as he then was) in *R. v. Secretary of State for Social Services, ex parte C.P.A.G. and the G.L.C.*[224] Here it was common ground that the then Department of Health and Social Security had wrongfully deducted an average of £25 each from the benefit of some 16,000 to 20,000 claimants. While the DHSS were prepared to review the files of current claimants to see if they were entitled to a backpayment, they refused to review the files of those persons who had ceased to claim the benefit in question, conducting instead two publicity campaigns which generated very few claims. In the High Court, Woolf J. held that the DHSS had a continuing duty to identify the claimants affected. He said:

> On purely financial and administrative convenience grounds a strong case can be made for saying that, if the claimants who have been deprived do not come forward, then the Department should not go to the expense and considerable inconvenience of tracing the claimants when this could result in current claimants being prejudiced. However ... claimants have the right to receive the appropriate amount of supplementary benefit and, if it had not been for the regrettable adminstrative lapses, without any further action on their part, they would have received the additional amounts to which they were entitled. The amount may not be large but, so far as those who need to seek supplementary benefit are concerned, the amount cannot be regarded as *de minimis*. To exercise a discretion in

---

[221] On this point, see Friedenthal, Kane and Miller, pp. 743-749.
[222] See Berry, "Ending Substance's Indenture to Procedure: The Imperative for Comprehensive Revision of the Class Damage Action" (1980) 80 *Colum. L. Rev* 299. For a defence of the class action, see Miller, "Of Frankenstein Monsters and Shining Knights: Myth, Reality and the 'Class Action Problem'" (1979) 92 *Harv. L. Rev* 664.
[223] Cousins (1996), pp. 135-6.
[224] Unreported, High Court of England and Wales, 30 July 1984. See also Smith, "How Good are Test Cases?" in Cooper and Dhavan, *Public Interest Law* (Basil Blackwell, 1986), at pp. 278-80.

favour of the respondents would be, in effect, to acquiesce in the Department relying upon the consequences of its own default to justify it not having to remedy that fault.[225]

On appeal, however, the Court of Appeal held that there was no statutory duty on the DHSS officials to review cases of which they had never been notified.[226] This issue has never yet been considered by an Irish court. However it is interesting to note that, following a number of successful claims for arrears of welfare taken by welfare claimants against the then Department of Social Welfare pursuant to Directive 79/7/EEC on the progressive implementation of the principle of equal treatment of men and women in matters of social security, the Department did eventually undertake to review its own files to try to identify the other welfare claimants affected by its unlawful actions, in addition to running an extensive advertising campaign seeking to make potential claimants aware of their entitlements.[227] Given the fact that most litigation on behalf of disadvantaged individuals and groups in this jurisdiction is likely to be taken against public bodies, acceptance of this duty to review files would seem to be a very effective way of disseminating the benefits of a judicial ruling among the wider population in those cases in which the class of beneficiaries can be identified from the files reviewed.

Conclusion

Public interest litigation is qualitatively different from conventional litigation – the aim of public interest litigation is generally to improve the operation and/or content of social policies which affect significant numbers of people, in contrast to conventional litigation which tends to concentrate on vindicating the rights of individuals. Much of our procedural law is informed by the individualism that is at the heart of the common law. And yet we have seen how in certain respects, such as in relation to the doctrine of standing and the judicial development of remedies, Irish law is already developing an ability to accommodate public interest litigation. However much remains to be done if such litigation is to develop to its full potential. In particular, third parties need to be given better access to litigation through such devices as the *amicus curiae* brief, the doctrine of mootness needs to be modified so that it cannot be used to prevent the courts taking seisin of issues which, though moot as far as the immediate parties to the litigation are concerned, continue to affect many others and, finally, more effective methods of extending the benefits of judicial decisions to those who are not directly party to the litigation need to be devised. Once the constitutional and political legitimacy of public interest litigation is conceded, there is no reason for not adapting our procedural laws appropriately.

---

[225] As quoted by Smith, p. 279.

[226] *The Times*, 16 August 1985.

[227] A similar undertaking was given by the Department in relation to claimants affected by an Appeals Officer's decision that Deserted Wife's Benefit came within the scope of EC Regulation 1408/71 so that social insurance contributions paid in another EC country could be taken into account in order to qualify for the benefit – see *FLAC NEWS* (Oct-Dec.1993), Vol. 4, No.1, p. 2.

Chapter 3

Practical Issues Relating to the Use of Litigation Strategy[1]

"[U]nder the conditions of modern government, litigation may well be the sole practicable avenue open to a minority to petition for redress of grievances."[2]

Introduction

Having argued for the legitimacy, both constitutional and political, of public interest litigation and having analysed the extent to which the rules of practice and procedure accommodate this type of litigation, I turn now to examine a number of issues arising in relation to litigation strategy targeting social exclusion.[3] After some comments on

---

[1] I prefer the term "litigation strategy" to "test case strategy" as the latter term arguably has connotations of the plaintiff as a stalking horse for others and while litigation obviously can have implications for individuals who are not party to it, it is important to remember that at the heart of most litigation strategy is a plaintiff who is seeking a remedy for his or her own grievance and for whom the further implications of the case for others may be of little or no relevance. One reservation about use of the word "strategy" is that it may imply that identification of an issue requiring resolution preceded identification of a case raising the issue, whereas in a significant number of cases, the sequence of events is the other way round.

[2] *Per* Brennan J. of the US Supreme Court in *NAACP v. Button* 371 US 415 (1963) at p. 430; 9 L ed 2d 405 at p. 416.

[3] Harlow and Rawlings have conclusively demonstrated that litigation strategy was a part of the legal systems of England and the US from at least the late eighteenth century – see *Pressure Through Law* (Routledge, 1992), chs.1-2 – and an interesting Irish connection with this early use of the law to effect change may be seen in the life of the United Irishman, William Sampson, about whom Walsh writes in "Redefining Radicalism: A Historical Perspective" (1991) 59 *George Washington Law Review* 636. However litigation strategy targeting socio-economic, as opposed to civil or political, issues is of more recent vintage, originating in the US during the 1960s.

the matter of definition, I outline the preconditions for the use of such litigation strategy. I then examine a number of legal issues arising in relation to *pro bono* litigation strategy before concluding with a brief description of the procedural framework within which the strategy must operate.[4]

Before proceeding further, however, it is important to put this strategy into context and here two points are worth noting. First, not every social issue can be tackled through litigation strategy, whether because of the nature of the issue or because of the failure or inability of lawyers to take the case. Thus some social issues, such as, for example, the failure of the State to provide adequate care for children at risk because of a shortage of child care workers or grievances about the adequacy of social welfare payments or the extent of State support for large families, are simply not susceptible to judicial resolution because of the absence of an applicable legal principle. Even if an issue is susceptible to judicial resolution, lawyers or organisations acting on a *pro bono* basis may find the cost of running long-term litigation that turns on complex factual matters prohibitively expensive. Clearly, therefore, there are limits to the use that can be made of litigation strategy.

Second, litigation strategy is not the only strategy available to lawyers. Two other important strategies exist, namely, public advocacy[5] and empowerment.[6] The former

---

Evaluations of such strategy in the UK are generally very guarded, with commentators highlighting the differences in the constitutional regime, procedures, remedies and judicial attitudes between the US and UK legal systems. See Prosser, T., *Test Cases for the Poor* (London, 1983); Hodge, H. "A Test Case Strategy" in *Welfare Law and Policy,* Partington M., and Jowell J. (eds.), (London, 1979); Smith, R., "How Good are Test Cases?" in Cooper, J. and Dhavan, R., *Public Interest Law* (Oxford, 1986). For a more optimistic account of the use of test cases in defence of civil and political rights in the UK, see Cohen, B., and Staunton, S., "In Pursuit of a Legal Strategy: The National Council for Civil Liberties" in Cooper, J. and Dhavan, R., especially pp. 296-9. For an interesting account of how litigation strategy succeeded in abolishing discrimination against married women in the Irish tax code, see Scannell, "The Taxation of Married Women: *Murphy v. Attorney General* (1982)" in O'Dell, (ed.), *Leading Cases of the Twentieth Century* (Round Hall Ltd., 2000) at p. 327.

4 In Part 2 of this book, I examine the use of litigation strategy to tackle different aspects of social exclusion in Ireland and in chapter 8 thereof I draw certain conclusions about the advantages and disadvantages of litigation strategy.

5 Or what Cranston calls "the Fabian model of effecting social change – seeking to influence government policy by the soundness of ... information and arguments and using the media in an attempt to create a groundswell of public opinion in favour of particular reforms". – *Legal Foundations of the Welfare State* (London, 1985), p. 279. Handler comments, in respect of the US experience, "Law reformers ... have strengths and weaknesses that may or may not serve the best interests of their clients. They favor litigation, especially the big cases, and in some situations, this can be very useful for the social-reform groups. But when problems are long-term, or complex, or require extensive changes in field-level discretion, more effective change may be brought about through lobbying." *Social Movements and the Legal System: A Theory of Law Reform and Social Change* (Academic Press, 1978), p. 32.

6 This represents a different model of effecting social change, what Cranston calls "the community politics model" – Cranston, p. 280. Notwithstanding the different underlying assumptions behind the Fabian and community politics models – on which, see Cranston, pp. 280-1 – public interest lawyers in Ireland in fact pursue both strategies.

entails the gathering and analysing of information and direct lobbying of decision-makers; the latter is generally promoted through the dissemination of information to the general public and, less frequently, through the use of community-based management structures in law centres and by organising clients to act on their common interests.[7] Indeed, one could argue that litigation strategy, pursued in isolation from these other strategies, is actually/potentially inimical to the interests of the poor.[8] Thus Wexler observed,

> Two major touchstones of traditional legal practice – the solving of legal problems and the one-to-one relationship between attorney and client – are either not relevant to poor people or harmful to them. Traditional practice hurts poor people by isolating them from each other, and fails to meet their need for a lawyer by completely misunderstanding that need. Poor people have few individual legal problems in the traditional sense; their problems are the product of poverty, and are common to all poor people. The lawyer for poor individuals is likely, whether he wins cases or not, to leave his clients precisely where he found them, except that they will have developed a dependency on his skills to smooth out the roughest spots in their lives.[9]

Nonetheless, litigation strategy remains the distinctive contribution of lawyers to movements for social reform and so is the focus of examination in this chapter.

Definition

The difficulty in defining litigation strategy can be seen from the first draft of the Civil Legal Aid Bill 1995, s.28(4)(c) of which sought to exclude "test cases" from the scope of the State's civil legal aid scheme. Paragraph (c) originally referred to

> proceedings ... [which] are not solely in the interests of the applicant or a member of the applicant's family or other person for whom the applicant has responsibility but constitute what is commonly referred to as a test case.

That provision eventually emerged from the legislative process as s.28(9)(a)(viii) of the 1995 Act which excludes from the scheme

> a matter the proceedings as respects which, in the opinion of the Board, are brought or to be brought by the applicant as a member of and by arrangement with a group of persons for the purpose of establishing a precedent in the determination of a point of law, or any other question, in which the members of the group have an interest.

---

[7] See further, ch. 9.

[8] Indeed Groenendijk argues that lawyers who concentrate on test cases in the courts without systematic activities elsewhere are in essence "traditional", rather than "public interest", lawyers – "Litigation, Politics and Publicity: Public Interest Law or How to Share the Burden of Change" (1985) 14 *Anglo-American Law Review* 337 at p. 338.

[9] S. Wexler, "Practicing Law for Poor People" (1970) 79 *Yale Law Journal* 1049 at p. 1053.

However even this formula cannot be regarded as a comprehensive definition of litigation strategy for it applies only to actions taken on behalf of a group and would not cover litigation taken by individuals which are, nonetheless, "commonly referred to as [test cases]".[10] In my opinion, the key characteristic of litigation strategy in the context of an anti-poverty policy lies not in the number of plaintiffs involved, or whether one plaintiff is acting with the support of an organised group, or even, indeed, whether the person adopting the strategy is a plaintiff in the action.[11] Rather it lies in the effect of the decision. Thus I would define a case as constituting litigation strategy in this context if it seeks either (a) to establish authoritatively a new legal principle, or establish the application of an existing one, of which policymakers and/or administrators have to take account or (b) to highlight the existing state of the law.[12] This covers cases taken on behalf of groups and cases taken on behalf of individuals and also cases taken *against* groups or individuals. It also encompasses cases which affect thousands of individuals and cases which affect comparatively small numbers.[13]

Legal issues arising in relation to pro bono litigation strategy

A number of factors have to be taken into account before one can consider pursuing litigation strategy. For a start, if one is hoping to obtain a judicial ruling of which policymakers and/or administrators have to take account, there must already be in existence a legal principle, express or implied, which supports the claim and so, as we have already noted, not every social problem is susceptible to judicial resolution.[14] Even where such a principle exists, a litigant still has to comply with procedural requirements relating to *locus standi*[15] and limitation periods.[16] Access to legal services is also important as it increases the likelihood of identifying a legal dimension to the problem in hand but, given the extent to which legal services are, for the most part, market driven, marginalised individuals and groups can experience difficulty in this regard.[17]

Perhaps most obviously of all, litigation strategy can only be pursued where one has found a suitable litigant. In identifying a suitable litigant for litigation strategy,

---

[10] Such as, e.g., *The State (Kershaw) v. Eastern Health Board* [1985] ILRM 235.

[11] As the experience of the Travelling Community has shown, litigation strategy can also be pursued by defendants to legal actions – see ch. 6, below.

[12] In fact, I am not aware of any cases to date which fall into the second limb of this definition but one cannot rule out the possibility that litigation strategy might be employed solely to publicise the plight of a marginalised group.

[13] Such as, e.g. *The State (Kenny) v. Minister for Social Welfare*, unreported, High Court, 15 December 1986, dealing with the welfare entitlements of women with recognised foreign divorces who subsequently had children outside of wedlock.

[14] Of course if a case is being taken solely to generate publicity about the existing state of the law, then this condition does not apply.

[15] As to which, see above, ch. 2.

[16] In what is probably the most common form of litigation strategy targeting poverty-related issues, the application for judicial review, proceedings must be initiated within six months of the relevant decision where *certiorari* is sought and within three months in all other cases, though the High Court may extend these time limits for good reason – O.84, r.21 of the R.S.C. 1986.

[17] I consider how this difficulty can be overcome in ch. 9 below.

solicitors have to be careful that they do not engage in what is known as "touting", defined by article 3 of the Solicitors (Advertising) Regulations 1988[18] as

> a direct approach by or on behalf of a solicitor to a person, who is not an established client, with the intention of soliciting business from that person.

Article 4 of the 1988 regulations prohibits solicitors from engaging in such activity so that unless the likely plaintiff is already an established client of a legal practice, the solicitor concerned cannot proactively seek out a suitable litigant in order to pursue litigation strategy.[19]

Two further issues arise where, as is inevitably the case with public interest litigation targeting different aspects of social exclusion, the litigant is unable to afford the cost of the legal services which have to be provided free of charge. First, does such an arrangement constitute an offence or a tort under the old doctrines of maintenance and champerty?[20] Second, how is liability for costs affected by the fact that litigation is taken on a *pro bono* basis?

It is quite clear that providing legal services free of charge, without more, is not champertous.[21] Champerty consists of an agreement to recover property or assist in the recovery of property *in return for a share of the property recovered*. This precludes lawyers from charging what is known in the US as a contingency fee[22] but it does not apply to an agreement to provide legal services free of charge. Nor is it very likely that such an agreement constitutes maintenance. Maintenance, according to Costello J., is "the giving of assistance or encouragement to one of the parties to an action by a person who has neither an interest in the action nor any other motive recognised by law as justifying his interference".[23] The key question here is whether, in law, the motive of

---

18 S.I. No.344 of 1988.

19 Article 5 of the Solicitors (Advertising) Regulations 1996 [S.I. No.351 of 1996] further provides, *inter alia*, that advertising by solicitors cannot comprise or include unsolicited approaches to any person with a view to obtaining instructions in any legal matter.

20 Arrangements which fall foul of these doctrines are also unenforceable as contrary to public policy.

21 The doctrine of champerty would appear to have been considered in only three cases by the Irish courts since Independence – see *McElroy v. Flynn* [1991] ILRM 294, *Fraser v. Buckle* [1996] 1 IR 1; [1996] 2 ILRM 34 and *O'Keeffe v. Scales* [1998] 1 ILRM 393. The first two of these concerned heir-locator contracts, while in *O'Keeffe* the defendant sought a motion to dismiss the plaintiffs' action against her on the ground that it was commenced and/or continued by reason of an arrangement between the plaintiffs and their solicitor which amounted to maintenance and/or champerty.

22 See also s.68(2) of the Solicitors (Amendment) Act 1994 which provides: "A solicitor shall not act for a client in connection with any contentious business (not being in connection with proceedings seeking only to recover a debt or liquidated demand) on the basis that all or any part of the charges to the client are to be calculated as a specified percentage or proportion of any damages or other moneys that may be or may become payable to the client, and any charges made in contravention of this subsection shall be unenforceable in any action taken against that client to recover such charges".

23 *Fraser v. Buckle* [1994] 1 IR 1 at p. 13. Moreover the maintained action must have failed – see the decision of the House of Lords in *Neville v. London Express Newspapers* [1919] AC 286.

a lawyer in assisting an indigent litigant justifies what would otherwise constitute maintenance. While there does not appear to be any Irish authority directly on this point, the position in the UK has developed to permit the maintenance of actions in the public interest and it is very likely that Irish courts would follow suit. Thus, in *Martell v. Consett Iron Co.*[24] the Court of Appeal allowed a national organisation concerned with the prevention of pollution to support the plaintiffs, who were members of the organisation, by means of an indemnity in respect of costs. Moreover, according to Harlow and Rawlings, a common law defence of "charitable purpose" covered

> the desire 'to assist a poor man to obtain justice that would otherwise be beyond his reach'. For similar reasons, professional lawyers were generally exempt from proceedings for maintenance and champerty and were allowed ... to give their services gratuitously.[25]

In *O'Keeffe v. Scales,*[26] Lynch J., delivering the unanimous decision of the Supreme Court, said that the doctrines of champerty and maintenance should not be extended to deprive people of their constitutional right of access to the courts to litigate reasonably stateable claims. He also doubted whether those doctrines could be used as a defence to an action where the plaintiff did not rely on a champertous agreement to establish his claim.[27] Given this approach on the part of the Supreme Court to the doctrines of champerty and maintenance, it seems very unlikely that they could be invoked to block public interest litigation taken on behalf of indigent litigants unable to pay the fees of their legal team.

Turning to the matter of liability for costs in *pro bono* litigation, three developments in the UK have given rise to some concern in this jurisdiction about possible adverse consequences for solicitors who take *pro bono* cases[28] The first development is the suggestion that a solicitor who acts for an unsuccessful indigent party in *pro bono* litigation could be held personally liable for the costs of his successful opponent. In *Mainwaring v. Goldtech Investments Ltd.*[29] the plaintiffs had obtained an order for costs against the defendant company which, however, had no assets. The plaintiffs

---

[24] [1955] Ch. 363.
[25] Harlow and Rawlings, p. 49. In *Neville v London Express Newspaper Ltd.* [1919] A.C. 368, Lord Haldane said, at p. 389:"Such an interest [*justifying the maintenance of an action*] is held to be possessed when in litigation a master assists his servant, or a servant his master, or help is given to an heir, or a hear relative, or to a poor man out of charity, to maintain a right which he might otherwise lose."
[26] [1998] 1 ILRM 393.
[27] In such circumstances, the doctrines could only be used as the basis for a separate cause of action seeking damages.
[28] More positively, the decision of Dyson J. in *R. v. Lord Chancellor, ex p. CPAG* [1999] 1 WLR 347; [1998] 2 All ER 755 was cited by Laffoy J. in *Village Residents' Association Ltd. v. An Bord Pleanála (No. 2)* [2000] 4 IR 321 in holding that the High Court had a jurisdiction to grant a pre-emptive costs order to certain public interest litigants directing that they should not be held liable for the costs of their opponents. She held, however, that this jurisdiction was not applicable where the private interests of the litigants were at stake and so it would appear to apply only to *Crotty*-type litigation where the litigant sues on behalf of the general public interest.
[29] *The Times*, 19 February 1991.

then applied for their costs to be paid by the defendant's solicitors. While this application failed on its facts, the Court of Appeal was prepared to assume that it would be objectionable and improper for a solicitor to conduct litigation in the knowledge that there was no real likelihood of ever being reimbursed for costs and expenses unless the litigation was successful. The application here was based on O.62, r.11 of the Rules of the Supreme Court, the Irish equivalent to which is O.99, r.7 of the Rules of the Superior Courts 1986 and which provides in relevant part:

> If in any case it shall appear to the Court that costs have been improperly or without any reasonable cause incurred ... the Court may call on the solicitor of the person by whom such costs have been so incurred to show cause why such costs should not be disallowed as between the solicitor and his client and also (if the circumstances of the case shall require) why the solicitor should not repay to his client any costs which the client may have been ordered to pay any other person ...

If Irish courts were to share the perspective of the Court of Appeal in *Mainwaring*, then, on the face of it, solicitors acting for indigent litigants on a "no foal, no fee" basis might face personal liability, under O.99, r.7, for the costs of the opposing side in the event of their client losing the action.

However it is difficult to see why a solicitor, acting *bona fide* on behalf of an indigent litigant, should be regarded as incurring costs "improperly or without any reasonable cause" simply because the client is not in a position to finance the litigation. Failure to assist an indigent client with a stateable case[30] could ultimately lead to infringement of that client's rights and acting to prevent such an outcome is clearly justifiable in policy terms.[31] Moreover, where a case raises a question of considerable public importance, Irish courts have exercised their discretion, on occasion, to refuse to impose liability for the winner's costs on the losing party[32] and

---

[30] Of course, if the *pro bono* litigation was frivolous or vexatious, then the costs of such might be regarded as "improperly or without any reasonable cause incurred", thereby giving rise to possible liability on the part of the solicitor involved

[31] In this context, it is interesting to note that O.90, r.6 of the R.S.C. 1986 provides that no costs shall be allowed in respect of any appeals on a point of law taken to the High Court against decisions of an appeals officer or the Chief Appeals Officer under the Social Welfare Acts 1993-2000, unless the Court makes a special order allowing such costs. One could argue that this displacement of the normal rule that costs follow the event – O.99, r.1(3)-(4) – even where the litigant is unsuccessful recognises the social value in allowing indigent clients the opportunity to have the courts clarify their legal position.

[32] Indeed in *T.F. v. Ireland*, unreported, Supreme Court, 27 July 1995, the Supreme Court awarded the costs of the plaintiff's unsuccessful appeal against the Attorney General because the case raised an issue of considerable public importance – the validity of certain provisions of the Judicial Separation and Family Law Reform Act 1989. (In the High Court, where the plaintiff had also been unsuccessful, the trial judge refused to make any order as to costs. A similar approach was adopted by Keane J. in relation to an unsuccessful High Court challenge by Patricia McKenna to the partisan funding by the Government of the constitutional referendum on divorce – see the transcript of his judgment delivered on 31 October 1995.) *Cp. Lancefort Ltd. v. An Bord Pleanála*, unreported, Supreme Court, 2 December 1999, in which the Supreme Court, *per* Hamilton C.J., classified the plaintiff company's argument seeking to recover the costs of proceedings that the company had lost as unreasonable, given that the other parties to the proceedings had offered to bear their own costs.

it would seem invidious to refuse to apply this practice to cases of indigent litigants. Finally, it is arguable that litigation strategy can be a form of political expression constitutionally protected by Article 40.6.1.i of the Constitution. In *NAACP v. Button*,[33] Brennan J., delivering the majority opinion of the US Supreme Court, said:

> In the context of [the] objectives [of the National Association for the Advancement of Colored People], litigation is not a technique of resolving private differences; it is a means for achieving the lawful objectives of equality of treatment by all government, federal, state and local, for the members of the Negro community in this country. It is thus a form of political expression.[34]

This argument can also be made in relation to public interest litigation in the Irish context, in which case O.99, r.7 will have to be interpreted by the courts in such a way as to facilitate, rather than impede, such litigation.

Accordingly there does not appear to be a good case, *pace* the comments of the Court of Appeal in *Mainwaring*, for imposing a personal liability, pursuant to O.99, r.7,[35] on solicitors who act *pro bono* for unsuccessful indigent clients.

The second development giving cause for concern occurred in *British Waterways Board v. Norman*.[36] Here the tenant of one of the Board's residential properties took an action against the Board in which she argued that the property's state of disrepair was such as to constitute a statutory nuisance. Her solicitors considered her case to be so strong that they never discussed the matter of their costs with their client, acting on the assumption that they would recover their costs from the Board when the action succeeded. Thus the solicitors were acting on the basis of what is called a 'no foal, no fee' arrangement, whereby the legal team agree that if the case is successful, costs will be recovered from the losing side and if the case is lost, the unsuccessful client will not have to pay the costs of his or her team. When the magistrates' court ordered the Board to pay the plaintiff's legal costs, the Board appealed that order to the divisional court of the Queen's Bench on the ground that Mrs Norman had no liability for costs to her solicitors and that, therefore, it had no liability to her. The appeal was successful, the court holding that the "no foal, no fee" arrangement pursuant to which the case had been taken amounted to a contract in law in the instant case and that as Mrs Norman could not have been sued for costs by her solicitors had the action failed, the solicitors could not recover such costs from the Board simply because the action had been successful.

---

[33] 371 US 415 (1963); 9 L ed 2d 405.

[34] 371 US 415 (1963) at p. 429; 9 L ed 2d 405 at p. 416.

[35] A possible alternative basis for such liability might exist if the courts decide that their general power to award costs under O.99, r.1(1) includes the power to award costs against non-parties. Such a power was recognised by the House of Lords in *Aiden Shipping Co. Ltd. v. Interbulk Ltd.* [1986] AC 965 though there is some evidence of subsequent judicial unease with this development – see *Symphony Group plc v. Hodgson* [1993] 4 All ER 143 and *Shah v. Karanjia* [1993] 4 All ER 792. The Irish courts do not appear to have ruled on this point yet. Even if they were to accept that they had such a power, one presumes that it would not be exercised against the solicitor of an unsuccessful indigent litigant whose case raised an issue of considerable public importance.

[36] [1993] 26 HLR 232; *The Times*, 11 November 1993.

Such a development clearly renders the "no foal, no fee" arrangement extremely unattractive from the point of view of the solicitor who is asked to mount speculative action on behalf of an indigent client and could result in the effective withdrawal of legal protection for indigent clients whose cases fall just outside the scope of the Civil Legal Aid and Advice Scheme. It has been suggested, however, that one way of avoiding such an outcome would be for solicitors to make such clients aware, in advance, of their liability for costs irrespective of the outcome of the litigation.[37] Such a practice clearly protects the solicitor's right to be paid his/her fees and yet if the litigation was subsequently unsuccessful, the solicitor might decide not to enforce such a right.[38]

The third development questions the very validity of the "no foal, no fee" arrangement itself which is often the basis upon which lawyers engage in public interest litigation on behalf of indigent clients.[39] In *Geraghty & Co. Ltd. v. Awwad*,[40] the English Court of Appeal held that this type of conditional fee was against public policy and contrary to the common law. The validity of this type of arrangement does not appear to have been considered by the Irish courts nor is it directly provided for by legislation. Insofar as s.68(2) of the Solicitors (Amendment) Act 1994 prohibited the US type contingency fee whereby the successful client pays his or her lawyer a proportion of the damages awarded but remained silent about the "no foal, no fee" arrangement, this might be taken as a tacit endorsement by the Oireachtas of the latter arrangement. However this legislative *omerta* would be to no avail if the Irish courts were to adopt the same view of the common law as that taken in *Geraghty*. One significant difference between the two jurisdictions that could have a bearing on this question is, of course, the existence here of a constitutional right of access to the courts and, as we have already seen, this was relied upon by Lynch J. in *O'Keeffe v. Scales*[41] to oppose any extension of the doctrines of champerty and maintenance. Such an approach might also persuade the Irish courts to refuse to follow the decision of the Court of Appeal in *Geraghty*. Certainly, if *Geraghty* was to be followed in this jurisdiction, this would have quite a serious effect on the ability of individuals of modest means to litigate claims and it would also increase the difficulties encountered by low-income groups seeking to mount public interest litigation.

---

[37] See note by D. Hartley in the UK *Law Society Gazette*, 19 January 1994, at p. 40.

[38] At the end of his judgment in the *British Waterways* case, Tuckey J. said, [1993] 26 HLR 232 at p. 243,

> If... it is made clear that the client is liable for costs irrespective of the outcome of proceedings, there can be no objection to the solicitor agreeing that such liabilty need not be discharged until the outcome of those proceedings, if any, is known. At that stage, provided it has not formed the basis of the agreement with the client, it would be open to the solicitors, if the circumstances warranted it, to decide not to enforce their right to be paid, in the event that some or all of their costs were unrecovered from the other party to the proceedings.

[39] Though solicitors are generally prohibited from advertising their services on this basis – see article 5 of the Solicitors (Advertising) Regulations 1996 [S.I. No.351 of 1996].

[40] Unreported, Court of Appeal, 25 November 1999.

[41] [1998] 1 ILRM 393.

[42] See, e.g., s.271 of the Social Welfare (Consolidation) Act 1993.

Procedural framework

The procedural framework within which a test case is mounted can vary from case to case. If the litigant wishes to challenge a decision of a public body, s/he may be able to avail of a statutory right of appeal to the courts.[42] Alternatively, the litigant may seek to have the decision reviewed by the High Court on the grounds that the body has exceeded its jurisdiction, or has failed to discharge a statutory duty, or has acted in breach of natural justice, or that its decision contains an error on the face of the record. An advantage of this type of proceeding is that it is relatively swift and cases can be determined within a matter of months.

If either of these options is not available, the litigant will have to issue a plenary summons seeking a declaration as to his/her rights and/or damages and/or an injunction where appropriate. A problem here is that it may take considerable time, perhaps as long as two years, before such actions are finally determined. This may be particularly serious in the context of litigation strategy on behalf of poor people where one may be arguing for the provision of basic forms of State support. Indeed, in extreme cases, for example, the individual who suffers from poor health because of an absence of shelter facilities, such delay could literally prove to be fatal.[43] In cases concerning children, time can also be of the essence, given the importance of appropriate support for children during their formative years and also the fact that the litigant may not be able to rely on certain constitutional provisions, such as Article 42.5, once s/he reaches a certain age. In some cases, the litigant may seek an injunction restraining the authorities from implementing a particular policy. An interim injunction of limited duration can be obtained on an *ex parte* basis. On its expiry, the court, after hearing both sides, may grant an interlocutory injunction which lasts until the trial of the action, if it is satisfied that there is a serious issue to be tried and that the balance of convenience favours the granting of the injunction. It is open to both sides to agree that the interlocutory hearing be treated as the full trial of the action, in which case the issue may be finally determined within a matter of months. If no such agreement is forthcoming, however, it may take up to two years for the action to come on for full hearing.

Finally, it is worth noting that defendants to legal proceedings may sometimes be able to turn those proceedings to their own advantage. Thus, for example, Travelling families in the Navan area who were served with a interim injunction directing them to leave unofficial halting sites were able to use those proceedings to challenge the failure of the local authority to provide them with official halting sites.[44]

---

[43] Thus it is that the Simon Community, at p. 5 of their publication, *Practical Aspects of Bringing a Right to Shelter Case to the Supreme Court* (Dublin, 1985), suggest that any person chosen to bring such a case must be of reasonably good health so as to minimise the danger of his or her demise before the action is tried.

[44] See *Co. Meath V.E.C. v. Joyce* [1994] 2 ILRM 210.

Having completed our examination of the legitimacy of public interest litigation promoting social inclusion and of the various procedural and tactical issues that arise in relation to such litigation, it is time now to move to consider the efficacy of such litigation in the Irish context. In the next part of the book, I examine the impact of judicial decisions in the areas of social welfare, children's rights, Travellers' rights and access to the courts, seeking to evaluate the merits of litigation strategy as a mechanism for tackling social exclusion.

PART 2

The Efficacy of Public Interest Litigation in Promoting Social Inclusion

Chapter 4

Judicial Treatment of Social Welfare Issues

In this chapter, I consider whether litigation has resulted in a significant improvement in the position of social welfare claimants. I examine litigation on the social welfare code under four different headings – (a) procedures; (b) entitlement to welfare payments, (c) control provisions and (d) miscellaneous.

Two preliminary points are worth noting. First, while social welfare cases still only account for a small percentage of all cases decided by the courts, the period after 1980 witnessed a significant increase, relatively speaking, in the number of such cases going before the courts. Thus, before that date, the Digests of Cases record nine cases taken in relation to the Social Welfare Acts 1952-1980 whereas after that date, there are more than forty cases dealing with various aspects of the welfare code. While this may be partly attributable to a general increase in litigation during this time, it is also due, in part at least, to the activity of the Free Legal Advice Centres Ltd. (FLAC) which established a number of welfare rights clinics during the 1980s and which arranged for a number of its clients to pursue legal challenges against the Department of Social Welfare, as it then was,[1] through the courts. Second, the period since 1980 has also witnessed, at least on the part of some members of the judiciary, a greater willingness to review decisions of deciding and appeals officers. In relation to judicial review,[2] while in *The State (Power) v. Moran,*[3] Gannon J. held to the traditional view that the absence of probative evidence supporting the decision of an appeals officer was not an error which could be corrected by the courts, in *Foley v. Moulton*[4] the same judge noted that there was evidence reasonably capable of supporting the appeals officer's decision, from which one might infer that the absence of such evidence

---

[1] Now the Department of Social, Community and Family Affairs.
[2] For an account of recent judicial developments in relation to jurisdictional review, see Hogan and Morgan, *Administrative Law in Ireland* (3rd ed.) (Dublin, 1998) at pp. 412-430, and specifically in relation to social welfare appeals, at pp. 281-2.
[3] [1976-7] ILRM 20.
[4] [1989] ILRM 169.

might have resulted in the judicial quashing of the decision.[5] In *Murphy v. Minister for Social Welfare*[6] Blayney J. quashed an appeals officer's decision on the ground that the wrong test had been applied, leading Hogan and Morgan to observe that the case "provides further evidence that the courts are now more willing to scrutinise decisions of deciding and appeals officers in judicial review application".[7]

The courts take a broadly similar approach to cases coming before them pursuant to s.271 of the Social Welfare (Consolidation) Act 1993 which provides for a statutory right of appeal from decisions of an appeals officer or Chief Appeals Officer to the High Court. Thus, in *Henry Denny & Sons Ltd. v. Minister for Social Welfare,*[8] the Supreme Court, *per* Keane J., held that the High Court could set aside the findings of an appeals officer if they were based on an incorrect interpretation of documents or on a mistaken view of the law or, in the case of findings of primary facts, if they were incapable of being supported by the evidence.

That said, a striking feature of the cases in which the courts have set aside decisions of the welfare authorities is that they very rarely involve a rejection by the court of the authorities' interpretation of welfare policy as embodied in the legislation; more usually, a decision is invalidated because of its conflict with a higher norm, such as the constitutional guarantee of fair procedures or, in the case of decisions based on circulars or statutory instruments, with a conflicting higher norm contained in the parent Act or, finally (and occasionally), in the case of a statutory norm, with a conflicting higher norm derived from the Constitution or European law. This suggests that judicial deference to the views of specialists in their area of specialisation, (here the content of welfare policy) is a factor which cannot be discounted in this context.

Social Welfare Procedures

Given the law's concerns about proper procedures, it is perhaps understandable that the impact of the Irish judiciary on the welfare code has been most pronounced in the area of processing claims and appeals. Judicial application of the principles of natural and constitutional justice has significantly improved the legal position of the welfare claimant who wishes to challenge a departmental decision affecting his or her rights under the welfare code.

---

[5] A similar inference might be taken from the decision of Murphy J. in *Corcoran v. Minister for Social Welfare* [1991] 2 IR 175; [1992] ILRM 133, wherein he held that the inferences drawn by the deciding officer from the personal circumstances of the applicant could not be regarded as unreasonable.

[6] [1987] IR 295.

[7] Hogan and Morgan, at pp. 281-2. As against that, the same authors go on to point out, *ibid.*, that the decisions of Costello P. in *Galvin v. Chief Appeals Officer* [1997] 3 IR 240 (holding that incorrect inferences not based on evidence constituted errors within jurisdiction which could not be quashed) and the comments of Hamilton C.J. in *Henry Denny & Sons (Ireland) Ltd. v. Minister for Social Welfare* [1998] 1 IR 34; [1998] ELR 36 (upholding an appeals officer's decision on the insurability of a supermarket demonstrator) indicate that the courts are sometimes still reluctant to interfere with the decisions of deciding and appeals officers.

[8] [1998] 1 IR 34; [1998] ELR 36.

Independence of appeals system

The first judicial decision in this area firmly protects the welfare adjudicative process against ministerial interference. In *McLoughlin v. Minister for Social Welfare*[9] an appeals officer had ruled that the applicant was in insurable employment. In coming to that conclusion, the appeals officer considered himself bound by a direction from the Minister for Finance to that effect. Commenting on this, O'Daly J. (with whom the other members of the Supreme Court agreed), said:

> Such a belief [that a public servant had no option but to act on the direction of a Minister of State] on [the appeals officer's] part was an abdication by him from his duty as an appeals officer. That duty is laid upon him by the Oireachtas and he is required to perform it as between the parties to that appeal before him freely and fairly as becomes anyone who is called upon to decide upon matters of right or obligation ... Appeals officers under the Social Welfare Act, 1952, and equally deciding officers are, and are required to be, free and unrestricted in discharging their functions under the Act.[10]

In *Kiely v. Minister for Social Welfare (No.2)*[11] the Supreme Court again re-asserted the duty on appeals officers to act impartially when deciding appeals. In this case, the appellant's witnesses were required to give evidence on oath and to submit themselves to cross-examination, while her legal representative was denied an opportunity of cross examining the author of a medical report relied on by the Department. According to Henchy J., such a lack of mutuality in the treatment of the parties to the appeal violated natural justice. He said:

> Natural justice is not observed if the scales of justice are tilted against one side all through the proceedings. *Audi alteram partem* means that both sides must be fairly heard. That is not done if one party is allowed to send in his evidence in writing, free from the truth-eliciting processes of a confrontation which are inherent in an oral hearing, while his opponent is compelled to run the gauntlet of oral examination and cross-examination. The dispensation of justice, in order to achieve its ends, must be even-handed in form as well as in content...Where essential facts are in controversy, a hearing which is required to be oral and confrontational for one side but which is allowed to be based on written and, therefore, effectively unquestionable evidence on the other side has neither the semblance nor the substance of a fair hearing.[12]

Appellant's right to be heard

That fundamental element of natural justice, the individual's right to be heard, has also had a significant impact on the operation of the social welfare appeals system.

---

[9] [1958] IR 1.

[10] *Ibid.* at p. 27.

[11] [1977] IR 267.

[12] *Ibid.* at pp. 281-2. It is perhaps also worth noting that in *The Minister for Social, Community and Family Affairs v. Scanlon* [2001] 1 IR 64; [2001] 2 ILRM 342, the Supreme Court held that though deciding officers and appeals officers are obliged to act judicially, they are not exercising judicial functions that, under the Constitution, should be reserved to the judiciary.

At an earlier stage of the *Kiely* litigation,[13] the High Court established, as an aspect of the right to be heard, the very important right of the claimant in a welfare appeal to have access to the evidence relied upon by the deciding officer in coming to his or her conclusion. During the course of an appeal against a deciding officer's refusal to pay her occupational injuries death benefit as a result of her husband's death, Mrs Kiely was denied the opportunity to provide evidence rebutting the conclusions of a medical report adverse to her claim which had been relied upon by the deciding officer. In the High Court, Kenny J. held that this amounted to a violation of the concept of natural or constitutional justice, citing with approval the following comments of Diplock L.J. in *R. v. Deputy Industrial Injuries Commissioner – ex parte Moore*[14]:

> Where … there is a hearing … the second rule [of natural justice] requires the deputy commissioner (a) to consider such "evidence" relevant to the question to be decided as any person entitled to be represented wishes to put before him; (b) to inform every person represented of any "evidence" which the deputy commissioner proposes to take into consideration, whether such "evidence" be proferred by another person represented at the hearing, or is discovered by the deputy commissioner as a result of his own investigation; (c) to allow each person represented to comment upon any such "evidence" and, where the evidence is given orally by witnesses, to put questions to those witnesses: and (d) to allow each person represented to address argument to him on the whole of the case.[15]

As a result of judicial intervention, therefore, claimants pursuing an appeal have a constitutional right of access to any evidence relied upon by the deciding official in coming to his or her conclusion. At a time when the information given by the Department to welfare claimants about decisions affecting them was very prefunctory, this right was a very valuable weapon in the armoury of anyone taking a welfare appeal and, notwithstanding the fact that deciding officers are now required to furnish unsuccessful claimants with a written memorandum of the decision,[16] it remains as an important safeguard of a claimant's right to due process.

and right to an oral hearing

Judicial intervention has also improved a claimant's chances of obtaining an oral hearing of an appeal. Under the relevant regulations,[17] the appeals officer may, at his

---

[13] *Kiely v. Minister for Social Welfare* [1971] IR 21. For a comment on both of these cases, see Clark, "The Case of the Tenacious Widow" (1978) *Gazette of the Incorporated Law Society of Ireland* 79.

[14] [1965] 1 QB 456 at 490.

[15] See also *Duffy v. Eastern Health Board,* unreported, High Court, *ex tempore,* 14 March 1988 where failure on the part of the Board to provide the applicant's legal advisers with material from the file necessary for the preparation of her appeal was held to amount to a breach of natural justice.

[16] See the Social Welfare (Consolidated Payments Provisions) (Amendment) (Miscellaneous Provisions) Regulations 1999 [S.I. No.139 of 1999].

[17] See formerly article 8 of the Social Welfare (Insurance Appeals) Regulations 1952 [S.I. No.376 of 1952], article 15 of the Social Welfare (Assistance Decisions and Appeals) Regulations 1953 [S.I. No.9 of 1953] and now article 11 of the Social Welfare (Appeals) Regulations 1990 [S.I. No.344 of 1990] which provides, in relevant part, "where the appeals officer is of the opinion that the case is of such a nature that it can properly be determined without an oral hearing, he may determine the appeal summarily".

or her discretion, decide to deal with an appeal without an oral hearing if the appeals officer is of opinion that the case is of such a nature that it can properly be so determined. In *Kiely v. Minister for Social Welfare (No.2)*[18] the Supreme Court set very clear limits to the extent of this discretion, saying (*per* Henchy J.):

> [A]n oral hearing is mandatory unless the case is of such a nature that it can be determined without an oral hearing, that is to say, summarily. An appeal is of such a nature that it can be determined summarily if the determination of the claim can fairly be made on a consideration of the documentary evidence. If, however, there are unresolved conflicts in the documentary evidence as to any matter which is essential to a ruling of the claim, the intention of the Regulations is that those conflicts shall be resolved by an oral hearing.[19]

Research in the UK indicates that where a claimant is afforded an oral hearing of his or her appeal, the chances of a successful outcome increase.[20] While no comparable research has been carried out in this jurisdiction, there is no reason to believe that the situation is any different here. At an oral hearing, misunderstandings or assumptions that underpin decisions of the welfare authorities come to light more easily and can be corrected by the claimant. Thus by clarifying when a claimant is *entitled* to such a hearing, *Kiely* affords additional protection to social welfare claimants.

and pre-termination procedures

Judicial consideration of the right to be heard has also had a particular impact on Departmental procedures relating to disqualification for receipt of welfare.

In *The State (Hoolahan) v. Minister for Social Welfare*[21] the Department sought to disqualify the claimant for receipt of deserted wife's benefit and to recover such benefit as had been paid to her during the previous three years and nine months. The ground on which the Department sought to disqualify the claimant was that she was cohabiting[22] and in response to this, the claimant's lawyer sought a detailed statement from the Department outlining its case on this point. The Department furnished such a statement and in reply, the claimant's lawyer argued that the evidence did not point to a sufficiently permanent arrangement to constitute cohabitation. He concluded his letter with the words, "I look forward to having your comments at your earliest convenience". However the Department proceeded to disqualify the claimant without

---

[18] [1977] IR 267.

[19] *Ibid.* at p. 278. In a more recent case, *Galvin v. Chief Appeals Officer* [1997] 3 IR 240, Costello P. ruled that where a factual dispute arose which threw doubt on the accuracy of Departmental records of insurance contributions and the dispute related to particular years in respect of which the fallibility of these records had already been called into question, the matter had to be resolved by oral hearing.

[20] See Lister, "Supplementary Benefits Appeals Tribunals: An Urgent Case for Reform" in Adler and Bradley (eds.), *Justice, Discretion and Poverty: Supplementary Benefit Appeals Tribunal in Britain* (Professional Books Ltd., 1975).

[21] Unreported, High Court, 23 July 1986.

[22] By virtue of the Social Welfare (Deserted Wife's Benefit) Regulations 1973 [S.I. No. 202 of 1973], cohabitation disentitled claimants for receipt of deserted wife's benefit.

reverting back to her lawyer. Moreover it also sought to recover that benefit which it alleged had been wrongfully paid to her.

The claimant obtained an order of the High Court quashing this decision. According to Barron J., in determining the claimant's eligibility for benefit the deciding officer had to act judicially. This meant that he had to make known to her the basis upon which he sought to disqualify her and the basis on which he sought a refund of welfare. Furthermore he also had to give her an opportunity to deal with these contentions and to make such further arguments on her own behalf as she wished, though the judge did allow that it would be perfectly proper for these procedures to be carried out by letter as occurred in this case.[23] In this particular case, Barron J. held that the procedures adopted by the Department were flawed in a number of respects. In particular, the judge noted that the deciding officer had relied upon an allegation of fact to rebut the claimant's case without giving her lawyer an opportunity to answer it. (This referred to the Department's finding that any lack of permanence in the relationship, on the basis of which the claimant argued that the cohabitation rule did not apply, was caused, not by any indifference towards each other on the part of the claimant and her partner, but rather to the fact that his employment necessitated absences from home.) Thus the decision to disqualify was invalid. The Department's decision to seek a refund was also marred by procedural defects. Barron J. held that the relevant legislation[24] required the Department to establish that the original decision awarding payment was given by reason of a fraudulent misrepresentation on the part of the claimant.[25] The Department had made no such allegation against the claimant who consequently was given no opportunity to meet such a case. Therefore the decision to seek a refund was also invalid.

Failure to observe correct pre-termination procedures has resulted in the judicial quashing of a number of other welfare decisions. Thus in *McConnell v. Eastern Health Board*,[26] Hamilton J. set aside a decision of the Board reducing the claimant's Disabled Person's Maintenance Allowance because it had not afforded the claimant's legal

---

[23] This is a disappointing aspect of this case, for it makes the exercise of the right to be heard contingent on a level of literacy which does not exist among some, if not many, social welfare claimants. *Cp.* the US Supreme Court decision in *Goldberg v. Kelly* 397 US 254, 90 S. Ct. 1011, 25 L. Ed. 2d 287 (1970) in which that Court held that welfare claimants were entitled to a *pre-termination hearing* under the Due Process Clause of the Fourteenth Amendment and wherein Brennan J., delivering the opinion of the Court, said, at [397 US 254 at p. 269, 25 L. Ed. 2d 287 at pp. 299-300], "Written submissions are an unrealistic option for most [welfare] recipients, who lack the educational attainment necessary to write effectively and who cannot obtain professional assistance. Moreover, written submissions doe not afford the flexibility of oral presentations; they do not permit the recipient to mould his argument to the issues the decision maker appears to regard as important. Particularly where credibility and veracity are at issue, as they must be in many termination proceedings, written submissions are a wholly unsatisfactory basis for decision."

[24] S.300(5)(a) of the Social Welfare (Consolidation) Act 1981.

[25] Though see now s.278 of the Social Welfare (Consolidation) Act 1993, (originally s.31 of the Social Welfare Act 1993) and the Social Welfare (Code of Practice on Recovery of Overpayments) Regulations 1996 [S.I. No.227 of 1996] which allow for the recovery of overpaid welfare even in the absence of fraud on the part of the claimant. See further below, pp. 167-170.

[26] Unreported, High Court, 1 June 1983.

representatives an adequate opportunity of making representations on behalf of his client. In *O'Connell v. Southern Health Board*,[27] a decision to discontinue the claimant's welfare payment after she was awarded damages in a personal injuries claim was quashed because, *inter alia*, she had not been given any opportunity to present evidence relating to her income; in *Boland v. Eastern Health Board*[28] a decision to disqualify the claimant for receipt of supplementary welfare allowance was set aside because the claimant had not been made aware of the case against her; and in *Thompson v. Minister for Social Welfare*[29] a failure to afford a welfare claimant an opportunity to present his case to the official dealing with the claim resulted in the invalidation of a deciding officer's decision, notwithstanding the fact that he had been given an opportunity to present his case to other Departmental officials. In one further case dealing with a threatened termination of welfare, Lardner J. granted an interlocutory injunction restraining the Eastern Health Board from withdrawing the claimant's supplementary welfare allowance pending a full hearing of the case by the High Court on the ground that, as the claimant had no other source of income, the balance of convenience lay in favour of continuing the allowance – *Boland v. Eastern Health Board*.[30]

Miscellaneous

A number of other judicial decisions deal with miscellaneous aspects of the decision-making process within the social welfare system.

In *Kingham v. Minister for Social Welfare*[31] Lynch J. had to consider, *inter alia*, the extent of the right of appeal to the High Court from decisions of an appeals officer under s.299(b) of the Social Welfare (Consolidation) Act 1981.[32] An interesting characteristic of this right of appeal is that, by virtue of O.90, r.6 of the Rules of the Superior Courts 1986, the normal rule in relation to costs, namely, that the losing party pays the costs of both sides, does not apply. Instead O.90, r.6 provides:

> No costs shall be allowed of any proceedings under this Order unless the Court shall by special order allow such costs.

The right of appeal provided for by s.299(b) related only to questions of law and the section further provided that it did not apply to questions of law to which s.298(6) of the 1981 Act applied. That sub-section, in turn, had provided that the decision of a deciding officer on, *inter alia*, every question arising in relation to a claim for benefit is to be final and conclusive. On one view of these provisions, therefore, as Lynch J. noted, they "could be construed to exclude from appeal the vast majority of questions that might arise under the provisions of the 1981 Act..."[33]

---

[27] Unreported, High Court, *ex tempore*, 12 February 1988.
[28] Unreported, High Court, *ex tempore*, 10 May 1989.
[29] [1989] IR 618.
[30] Unreported, High Court, 9 May 1988.
[31] Unreported, High Court, 25 November 1985.
[32] Re-enacted, with some modification, in s.271 of the Social Welfare (Consolidation) Act 1993.
[33] At p. 3 of his judgment.

However Lynch J. rejected this interpretation, stating that the exclusion had to be construed narrowly so as not to oust the jurisdiction of the High Court save where such ouster is clear. He went on to hold:

> The question raised on this appeal is as to the true construction of the statutes and regulations insofar as they relate to qualification for old age (contributory) pension. It would be strange if the High Court were not to be allowed to assist in resolving such a question although in a wide sense it could be said to be a question arising in relation to a claim for benefit. I think that I have jurisdiction to deal with the question of the true construction of the statutes and regulations relating to the necessary qualifications for old age (contributory) pension and to refer the matter back to the Minister and the Department for reconsideration in the light of such construction if such construction so warrants.[34]

This decision thus broadens the scope of the claimant's statutory right of appeal to the High Court, with its attendant protection in the matter of costs in the event of the appeal failing.

The role of assessors in the welfare appeals system came in for judicial scrutiny in two cases in which the courts clarified the role of the assessor and upheld the right of an appellant to have the assessor present at the appeal. By virtue of s.44(11) of the Social Welfare Act 1952, the Minster was empowered to appoint any person whom he considered suitable to sit as an assessor with an appeals officer when any question which appeared to him to require the assistance of assessors was heard.[35] In *Kiely v. Minister for Social Welfare (No. 2)*[36] a medical assessor had taken part in the appeal hearing with the appeals officer. He cross-examined the appellant's witnesses during the hearing and then subsequently sent a letter to the appeals officer setting out reasons for rejecting the appeal. In the Supreme Court, Henchy J. held, *inter alia*, that an assessor was not entitled to present the case for the deciding officer, having regard to article 10(3) of the Social Welfare (Insurance Appeals) Regulations 1952.[37] Nor should an assessor become a witness by supplying evidence. The function of the medical assessor, rather, was to act as a "medical dictionary … available for consultation by the appeals officer".[38] Thus the appeals officer's decision was fatally flawed because of, *inter alia*, the assessor's interventions in the case.

In the subsequent case of *Thompson v. Minister for Social Welfare*[39] the applicant had appealed against a decision to withdraw his unemployment assistance and he had specifically stated on the notice of appeal that he did not consent to the appeal

---

[34] At p. 4 of his judgment.

[35] S.255(a) of the Social Welfare (Consolidation) Act 1993 now confers this power on the Chief Appeals Officer.

[36] [1977] IR 267.

[37] Which provides: "An assessor shall not while sitting as an assessor with an appeals officer take any part in the proceedings otherwise than in his capacity as such assessor and he shall not sit as an assessor when any question in which he has a personal interest is heard".

[38] [1977] IR 267 at p. 284.

[39] [1989] IR 618.

proceeding in the absence of assessors.[40] Notwithstanding such statement, the appeals officer sat alone without assessors. In the High Court, O'Hanlon J. concluded that this breach of the statutory obligation invalidated the appeals officer's decision.

While all of the aforementioned cases in this section have been decided in a manner favourable to welfare claimants, at least one High Court case dealing with the process of decision-making under the Social Welfare Acts has gone in the opposite direction. In *Corcoran v. Minister for Social Welfare*[41] a deciding officer had decided to terminate the claimant's unemployment assistance on the ground that he did not satisfy the means-test for this payment. The claimant's solicitors wrote to the Department requesting permission to attend any appeal hearing on his behalf but this letter was not received in time and so the appeal went ahead in their absence. At this appeal, the deciding officer's decision was upheld. At a further appeal, at which the solicitors were present, an appeals officer also refused to restore the claimant's unemployment assistance.

In the High Court, Murphy J. dismissed an application to have the decisions quashed. He took the view that the decision to disqualify was not unreasonable and therefore, having regard to *The State (Keegan) v. Stardust Victims' Compensation Tribunal*,[42] it could not be set aside. The claimant had additionally argued that he was entitled to legal representation at the appeal hearings but this was also rejected by the court. Murphy J. noted that the relevant regulations[43] did not provide for a right to legal representation at social welfare appeals and he rejected the proposition that there was a general right to be legally represented at hearings of this nature.

For the sake of completeness, it is worth noting four further High Court decisions dealing with aspects of the decision-making process in the social welfare code. They all deal with very specific points and do not add much to our discussion about the impact of judicial decisions on the position of welfare claimants except, perhaps, insofar as the first two both illustrate the ease with which the Department can sometimes effectively reverse unwelcome judicial decisions. In *Lundy v. Minister for Social Welfare*[44] Keane J. pointed out that s.300(1) of the Social Welfare (Consolidation) Act 1981 empowered a deciding officer to revise an earlier decision of another deciding officer but it did not empower such an officer to revise an earlier decision of an appeals officer. This defect was quickly remedied by s.31 of the Social Welfare Act 1993.[45] In the course of his ruling, Keane J. also held that the power to revise decisions was not a power of a judicial nature such that it could only be exercised by judges appointed under the Constitution.

---

[40] Article 17 of the Social Welfare (Assistance Decisions and Appeals) Regulations 1953 [S.I. No.9 of 1952] provided for the presence of assessors at appeals involving unemployment assistance claims (other than claims for a qualification certificate).

[41] [1991] 2 IR 175; [1992] ILRM 133.

[42] [1986] IR 642; [1987] ILRM 202.

[43] The Social Welfare (Assistance Decisions and Appeals) Regulations 1953, [S.I. No.9 of 1953].

[44] [1993] 3 IR 406. See also the companion case of *O'Connor v. Minister for Social Welfare*, unreported, High Court, 30 April 1993.

[45] Re-enacted in s.248 of the Social Welfare (Consolidation) Act 1993.

In *O'Sullivan v. Minister for Social Welfare*[46] Barron J. held that, in deciding whether to award costs under s.298(11) of the Social Welfare (Consolidation) Act 1981, an appeals officer could not fetter his discretion by deciding instead to award the standard fee of £30 agreed between the Appeal Office and the Law Society as expenses for a solicitor's attendance at a welfare appeal. However s.34 of the Social Welfare Act 1996 subsequently restricted the appeals officer's discretion to an award of expenses only, where expenses are referrable only to the lawyer's attendance at the appeal hearing.

In *Murphy v. Minister for Social Welfare*[47] Blayney J. held, *inter alia*, that the jurisdiction of a deciding officer was restricted to the specific question submitted to him for decision and that he could not address any other issue on his own initiative. Thus, where the claimant had requested a decision from the deciding officer as to the appropriate rate of social insurance contribution payable by the claimant, the deciding officer did not have the power to decide whether or not the claimant's employment was insurable.[48]

Finally, in *Power v. Minister for Social Welfare*[49] the same judge, in the course of a judgment dealing with the insurability of the claimant's employment, noted, *obiter*, that a statutory authority cannot extend its statutory powers by creating an estoppel, so that a representation made to the claimant by the then Department of Labour could not oblige the welfare authorities to grant him a pension.

Briefly reviewing the impact of judicial decisions on the decision-making processes within the social welfare code, it is quite clear that, on balance, judicial intervention has generally worked to the benefit of welfare claimants. In particular, the courts have established that the claimant is entitled to have access to relevant material on his/her file for the purpose of preparing an appeal; that claimants who are facing withdrawal of welfare are entitled to hear the reasons for such a course of action and to have an opportunity to respond to such arguments; that claimants are entitled to an oral hearing of their appeal in appropriate circumstances; and that in determining claims, deciding and appeals officers are independent of the Department. As against that, it must be accepted that judicial interpretation of the provisions of the welfare code on the recovery of overpaid welfare eventually resulted in legislative amendments to the code extending the powers of the authorities in this regard and that the High Court itself has confirmed that a welfare appellant is not entitled to legal representation at the hearing of the appeal. But on balance, however, it would appear that the gains outweigh the losses from the claimant's perspective.

At the same time, this does not necessarily provide grounds for portraying the courts as radical defenders of the interests of welfare claimants. The law, traditionally, has a preoccupation with proper procedures and it could plausibly be argued that the

---

[46] Unreported, High Court, 9 May 1995.
[47] [1987] IR 295; [1987] 6 JISLL 199.
[48] *Quaere* whether this decision is, in fact, correct. S.247 of the Social Welfare (Consolidation) Act 1993 (formerly s.111 of the Social Welfare (Consolidation) Act 1981) confers an extensive statutory jurisdiction on deciding officers without indicating that this jurisdiction can be restricted by interested parties formulating questions in a particular way.
[49] [1987] IR 307; [1987] 6 JISLL 209.

foregoing case-law reflects that preoccupation, rather than any particular concern about the plight of welfare claimants as such. To determine whether public interest litigation is capable of securing significant improvements in the position of social welfare claimants *per se*, we need to consider how the courts have dealt with substantive issues of social welfare law.

Entitlement to welfare payments

Given the obvious relevance of the welfare code to people on low income, a very direct way of using the courts to target social exclusion is to improve access to welfare income for disadvantaged individuals and groups. This can be done either by construing the conditions of eligibility for a payment so as to broaden the category of persons eligible, by establishing that existing claimants are entitled to a higher rate of welfare, or by narrowing, or invalidating entirely, the grounds of disqualification for receipt of the payment.[50] Success in each type of case results in increased welfare expenditure.[51] For this to have a bearing on social exclusion, it is necessary, of course, that the individuals and classes affected be disadvantaged. Thus claims made in respect of social assistance, i.e. means-tested, schemes and claims made on behalf of claimants who cannot legitimately participate in the labour market while at the same time receiving social welfare, i.e. principally the unemployed and certain categories of persons who are incapable of working due to illness or disability, are likely, if successful, to have more impact in tackling social exclusion than other claims made under the social welfare code.[52]

Cases in this section can be classified into three different groups – those that were successful, either wholly or partially, in improving access to welfare payments, those that were unsuccessful in court; and, finally, those that were successful in court but whose precedential value for other claimants was nullified by subsequent legislation.

i) Cases improving access to welfare payments

Claims taken before Irish courts for improved access to welfare payments have been wholly or partially successful in five different contexts, all of which concerned access to means-tested payments.[53]

---

[50] In some cases, challenging the grounds of disqualification simply results in an existing claimant remaining in receipt of welfare but in other cases it allows new claimants to qualify, claimants who would hitherto have been barred by the disqualification.

[51] Of course, success in this context does not consist simply in winning before the courts, it necessarily entails that official policy should change in accordance with the judicial decision.

[52] This is not to suggest, however, that claimants of social insurance payments or claimants such as old age pensioners, widows, widowers, etc. are all comfortably off. Many are not, but some are, whereas in relation to the categories of claimant referred to in the main text, one can fairly assume that, by definition, they will all be on low incomes.

[53] Though the implementation of Directive 79/7/EEC on the progressive implementation of the principle of equality for men and women in matters of social security – see below, p. 141 *et seq.* – also affected social insurance schemes.

a) Fuel vouchers for short-term welfare claimants. The earliest of these claims occurred in relation to what was then called the National Fuel Voucher scheme. Under this scheme, fuel vouchers to the value of £5 p.w. were paid to certain categories of social welfare claimants for the thirty weeks between October and April. A Departmental circular purported to exclude short-term welfare claimants, i.e. claimants of unemployment benefit, unemployment assistance or disability benefit, from the scope of the scheme. While this distinction obviously had financial implications for the scheme, in that it restricted the numbers eligible for a voucher, it made no sense when viewed as part of an anti-poverty strategy. This is because short-term welfare claimants received lower rates of social welfare than long-term welfare claimants and, moreover, could not legitimately supplement their welfare income by working, unlike many of those eligible for fuel vouchers.[54]

The scheme was, nonetheless, formally part of an anti-poverty strategy as its statutory basis, at that time, was s.200 of the Social Welfare (Consolidation) Act 1981,[55] which entitled any person in the State whose means fell below a specified limit to supplementary welfare allowance.[56] The payment of additional supplements over and above this basic entitlement was provided for by s.209(1) which read:

> Where the weekly amount of supplementary welfare allowance, if any, payable to a person pursuant to section 207, and any other income, including any payment under this Act or under any other statute, of that person, is not sufficient to meet his needs, then -
>
> (a) in any case where that person is in receipt of supplementary welfare allowance, the weekly amount of such allowance payable to that person may, subject to this section, be increased, or
>
> (b) in any other case, a weekly payment of supplementary welfare allowance may be made, subject to this section, to supplement that person's other income.

Subsection 2 authorised the Minister to prescribe, by way of regulations, the circumstances under which a payment might be made to any person pursuant to sub-section 1 and the amount of such payments made either generally or in relation to a particular class of persons. The relevant regulations were the Social Welfare (Supplementary Welfare Allowances) Regulations 1977 [S.I. No.168 of 1977], article 6, sub-articles 3 and 6 of which provided respectively, in relevant part:

---

[54] At this time, the Department of Social Welfare directly administered another fuel voucher scheme known as the Urban Fuel Scheme in 17 specified cities and towns. However the coverage of this scheme was also limited and the following categories of welfare claimant failed to come within the scope of *either* scheme – claimants of unemployment benefit, disability benefit, single people claiming unemployment assistance and anyone claiming unemployment assistance in an area not covered by the Urban Fuel Scheme.

[55] See now s.171 of the Social Welfare (Consolidation) Act 1993.

[56] The section read:

Subject to this chapter, every person in the State whose means are insufficient to meet his needs and the needs of any adult or child dependant of his shall be entitled to supplementary welfare allowance.

(3) Where a person to whom Section 11(1)(b) of the Act[57] applies has income which is not sufficient to meet his needs, a weekly payment of an allowance may, subject to the provisions of sub-Article 6 of this Article be made to him of such amount as, when taken together with his other income, is determined by the Health Board to be appropriate to meet such needs.

(6) ... [A]n allowance under sub-Article 3 of this Article shall not without the consent of the Minister exceed £5.00 per week.

Rita Kershaw, an unemployed woman with a dependant child, was refused a fuel voucher because she came within the terms of the Departmental circular excluding short-term welfare claimants from the scope of the scheme and, with the assistance of FLAC, she mounted a legal challenge to the validity of this restriction – *The State (Kershaw) v. Eastern Health Board.*[58]

Finlay J.'s examination of the statutory basis for the scheme led him to two important conclusions. First, where a person's means are insufficient to meet his needs and those of his dependants, he has a statutory right to supplementary welfare allowance, which right is governed, in cases like the instant case, by s.209 and article 6 of the 1977 Regulations. A major implication of this finding was that, notwithstanding the use of the word "may" in s.209, claimants whose means did not meet their needs and who were not already in receipt of supplementary welfare allowance, *viz.*, those persons referred to in s.209(1)(b), were *entitled* to the additions to basic supplementary welfare allowance authorised by s.209. From the point of view of the prosecutor's legal team, this was an unexpected bonus as these additions covered other expenses in addition to heating, such as rent and special dietary needs, and hitherto it had been generally assumed that such payments were entirely at the discretion of the Health Boards. Finlay J.'s second conclusion was that the Minister's function with regard to cases coming within s.209 was limited to the exercise by him of a discretion whether to consent to the making of a payment in excess of £5 per week pursuant to s.209. Consequently, in so far as the Minister had issued a circular which purported to fetter the discretion of the Health Board officials to grant supplementary welfare allowance in the form of fuel vouchers to short-term welfare claimants, he had acted *ultra vires*.

The Departmental response to this decision was not long in coming. By virtue of the Social Welfare (Supplementary Welfare Allowance) (Amendment) Regulations 1985 [S.I. No.49 of 1985], as amended by the Social Welfare (Supplementary Welfare Allowance) (Amendment No.2) Regulations 1985 [S.I. No.334 of 1985], the distinction between long-term and short-term welfare claimants for the purpose of eligibility for fuel vouchers under the National Fuel Scheme was restored. However the validity of these regulations was, in turn, successfully challenged before the Supreme Court in *The State (McLoughlin) v. Eastern Health Board.*[59] The Court

---

[57] This refers to s.11(1)(b) of the Social Welfare (Supplementary Welfare Allowances) Act 1975 which was subsequently re-enacted by s.209(1)(b) of the 1981 Act and is now contained in s.179(1)(b) of the Social Welfare (Consolidation) Act 1993.

[58] [1985] ILRM 235.

[59] [1986] IR 416.

agreed with Barron J. in the High Court that the regulations were *ultra vires* inasmuch as they attempted to alter the general obligations imposed by s.209. Finlay C.J., with whom Henchy, Griffin and Hederman JJ. concurred, also took the opportunity to affirm what he had previously said in *Kershaw* about the effect of s.209, saying:

> I find no reason to alter the view which I expressed in *The State (Kershaw) v. Eastern Health Board* [1985] ILRM 235 that the combined effect of sections 199, 200 and 209 of the Act of 1981 is to give a vested right to any person in the State whose means are insufficient to meet their needs, as both are defined and provided for in sections 207 and 208 of the Act, to a supplementary allowance consisting of either an increase in the existing supplementary allowance or, in the case of a person not in receipt of any supplementary allowance, an allowance granted to be in addition to their means otherwise arising.[60]

Thus, not only had the litigation succeeded in establishing that short-term welfare claimants were entitled to fuel vouchers under the National Fuel Scheme, there was now a basis for welfare claimants to argue that, in appropriate circumstances, they were *entitled* to supplementary welfare allowance additions, payable under s.209.

However the fruits of this victory in the courts were only partially retained by welfare claimants. The Department eventually conceded that claimants on long-term unemployment assistance were entitled to fuel vouchers under the National Fuel Scheme but it continued to deny the vouchers to claimants of unemployment benefit and disability benefit. Morever it funded this expansion of the National Fuel Scheme by reducing the amount of money paid to each claimant from £150 to £130 p.a.[61] Thus claimants on long-term unemployment assistance gained at the expense of other long-term welfare claimants, though it has to be said that this represented a more equitable division of welfare income and a better targetting of resources. As for the Supreme Court's interpretation of s.209, this never took root among welfare activists or claimants; the welfare authorities continued to operate as though payments under s.209 were at their discretion in all cases and eventually, in 1992,[62] the legislation was amended to bring the law into line with practice, thus nullifying this aspect of the rulings in *Kershaw* and *McLoughlin*.

b) Welfare for claimants whose marital status is affected by foreign divorce. On two occasions, the courts have ruled in favour of welfare claimants whose marital status was affected by a foreign divorce.

In *The State (Kenny) v. Minister for Social Welfare*,[63] the claimant succeeded in improving access to another welfare payment, unmarried mother's allowance,[64] by persuading the High Court to strike down an anomaly in that scheme which disentitled mothers with foreign divorces recognisable in this country. She had been married briefly to a British citizen but that marriage had been dissolved by a Scottish court. In

---

[60] *Ibid.* at p. 423.
[61] See *Department of Social Welfare Report, 1987-88* (Pl.6838) at p. 17.
[62] See s.47 of the Social Welfare Act 1992.
[63] [1986] IR 693.
[64] Now subsumed under the one-parent family payment.

the meantime, she had returned to Ireland and had become pregnant by another man. She gave birth to a daughter in December 1983 and when her relationship with the father ended, she applied for unmarried mother's allowance.

The relevant statutory provision at the time was s.197 of the Social Welfare (Consolidation) Act 1981, sub-section 1 of which provided:

> A social assistance allowance shall, subject to regulations, be paid to a woman -
>
> (a) who is unmarried,
>
> (b) who has at least one qualified child residing with her, and
>
> (c) who satisfied the conditions as to means specified for the purposes of this subsection by regulations.

Section 197(4) empowered the Minister to specify by regulation, *inter alia*, the circumstances in which a woman would be regarded as being an unmarried mother. The relevant regulations were the Social Welfare (Social Assistance Allowance) Regulations 1973 [S.I. No.190 of 1973], article 4 of which provided, in relevant part:

> A woman is to be regarded ... as being an unmarried mother if, not being or having been a married woman, she is the mother of a child who has not been adopted.

Under these provisions, the claimant was refused unmarried mother's allowance, she "having been a married woman".

In his judgment, Egan J. pointed out that under chs. 4 and 5 of Part III of the 1981 Act, which included s.197, four classes of mothers were entitled to social assistance payments paid at the same rate, *viz.*, deserted wives, prisoners' wives, unmarried mothers and widows. It appeared to the judge, therefore, that the only class of mother excluded was the mother who was once married but whose marriage was subsequently dissolved.[65] Citing *Cassidy v. Minister for Industry and Commerce*[66] in which Henchy J. stated that a necessary implication in a statutory delegation of a power to issue subordinate legislation was that the power be exercised reasonably and not in an oppressive or unjust manner, Egan J. concluded that the exclusion of mothers such as the claimant in the instant case from the same welfare schemes to which the other classes of mothers were entitled was "oppressive and unjust" and consequently article 4 was invalid.

As the Department took no steps to redraft the regulations on this point, the net outcome of the case, therefore, was to extend slightly the category of claimant entitled to unmarried mother's allowance. However it is likely that this result was tolerated by the Department because it affected relatively few people and consequently would have occasioned a very limited increase in the social welfare budget.

---

[65] In fact, Egan J.'s reasoning on this point was flawed. In the first place, three of the schemes to which the judge referred, namely, deserted wife's allowance, prisoner's wife's allowance and widow's non-contributory pension, were designed to support women in their capacity as *wives* or *widows*, rather than as *mothers* and in many cases women could claim these payments without having to prove motherhood. Second, one other category of mother, separated mothers, was excluded from this type of welfare provision at this time.

[66] [1978] IR 297.

In *Clancy v. Minister for Social Welfare*[67] the social welfare code, specifically the widow's (contributory) pension, provided the context for a detailed discussion by Budd J. of the rules for the recognition of foreign divorces. The plaintiff had been refused a widow's (contributory) pension on the ground that she was not legally married to her late husband. He had previously been married to another woman and had been divorced by this woman in England. The husband had, at all times, an Irish domicile and so the Department of Social Welfare refused to recognise the validity of this divorce on the ground that it did not satisfy the common law requirement that it be obtained in the country of the common domicile of both spouses. Accordingly, the Department also refused to recognise the plaintiff's marriage and so held that she was not entitled to the widow's (contributory) pension.

In the course of an extensive review of the authorities, Budd J. agreed with Barr J. in *M. (C.) v. M. (T.)*[68] that the rule of dependent domicile, whereby the wife's domicile was determined by that of her husband, did not survive the enactment of the Constitution. He then went on to hold that, in the light of this changed situation, the court should recognise a divorce granted in a jurisdiction in which either of the spouses was domiciled at the date of the service of the divorce proceedings. In the instant case, it followed that the plaintiff was lawfully married to her husband and that she was entitled to the widow's (contributory) pension on his death.

c) Disabled Person's Maintenance Allowance for married claimants. Attempts to reduce the amount of disabled person's maintenance allowance [hereafter DPMA] payable to married claimants were successfully resisted, at least partially, in two High Court cases. In *J.H. v. Eastern Health Board*[69] the claimant, a married woman, successfully used the Constitution to challenge a decision of the Health Board restricting the amount of DPMA to which she was entitled. She had been in receipt of DPMA of £7.33 per week, a means-tested payment, since March 1986. Prior to 19 November 1986, her husband was also able to claim an adult dependant allowance of £12.80 per week in respect of his wife as part of his entitlement to unemployment assistance. After that date, the definition of adult dependant for welfare purposes was changed as part of a package of measures implementing Directive 79/7/EEC on the progressive implementation of the principle of equal treatment for men and women in matters of social security[70] and because the claimant was in receipt of DPMA of £7.33 p.w. in her own name, she was no longer regarded as an adult dependant of her husband. Consequently he lost his entitlement to the adult dependant allowance of £12.80. Notwithstanding this change in the family circumstances, the Health Board initially refused to increase the claimant's means-tested allowance. Then they proposed to grant it to her on the basis that she would claim in respect of herself, her husband and their two children, the implication being that he would no longer be

---

[67] Unreported, High Court, 18 February 1994.
[68] [1988] ILRM 456.
[69] [1988] IR 747.
[70] For more detail on these changes, see below, p. 142.

entitled to any unemployment assistance. The motivation behind this move, apparently, was to prevent married couples where both parties were in receipt of social welfare from obtaining an increase in their welfare payments on foot of the re-definition of adult dependant.[71] In the High Court, however, Keane J. took the view that the husband's welfare entitlements would not have been taken into account for the purpose of calculating the wife's entitlements if the couple were unmarried and cohabiting. Accordingly he held that, by discriminating against married couples, the Health Board had applied the relevant regulations[72] in an unconstitutional manner.

Some three years later, an attempt was made to nullify the impact of *J.H.* The statutory basis for DPMA, s.69 of the Health Act 1970, was amended by s.46 of the Social Welfare Act 1991 to provide that cohabiting couples were to be treated in the same way as married couples for the purpose of the scheme, thereby avoiding the constitutional difficulties identified in *J.H.*[73] In addition, the Minister for Health also promulgated articles 6 and 7 of the Disabled Persons (Maintenance Allowance) Regulations 1991,[74] the effect of which was that where a couple, either married or unmarried, were both in receipt of social welfare and one or both were in receipt of DPMA, the combined income of the couple would be the same as that paid to a single claimant with an adult dependant, this to be achieved by reducing the amount of DPMA payable to the claimant or claimants as the case may be.[75] However article 6 of the 1991 Regulations was subsequently declared to be *ultra vires* by Barron J. in *O'Connell v. Ireland*[76] on the ground that the Minister had no power under s.72 of the Health Act 1970 to remove, reduce or otherwise alter obligations imposed on the Health Boards by the Act. In *O'Connell*, both parties had been in receipt of DPMA and so the court did not have to consider the position of a couple where one party is in receipt of DPMA and the other is in receipt of some other form of welfare payment. Article 7 of the Disabled Persons (Maintenance Allowance) Regulations 1996[77] subsequently provided that in such cases, the total amount of welfare payable to the couple cannot exceed the amount payable to a claimant of DPMA or of another form of welfare payment with an adult dependant. When DPMA was subsequently replaced by disability allowance, s.191E of the Social Welfare (Consolidation) Act 1993 (inserted by s.13 of the Social Welfare Act 1996) maintained this limitation on the

---

[71] Section 12 of the Social Welfare (No.2) Act 1985 reflected the same policy in relation to schemes administered by the Department of Social Welfare. See further below, p. 142.

[72] The Disabled Persons (Maintenance Allowance) Regulations 1984 [S.I. No.71 of 1984].

[73] This paralleled developments following on from the Supreme Court decision in *Hyland v. Minister for Social Welfare* [1989] IR 624; [1990] ILRM 213. See below, p. 162.

[74] S. I. No.200 of 1991.

[75] Within a few weeks of the introduction of this change, however, a decision was taken to defer its implementation until such time as the amount of DPMA actually received by a married or cohabiting claimant in 1991 became equivalent to the reduced amount of DPMA payable pursuant to the 1991 regulations, this result to be achieved by withholding the annual increases from the married or cohabiting claimant – see article 8 of the Disabled Persons (Maintenance Allowance) Regulations 1992 [S.I. No. 212 of 1992].

[76] [1996] 2 IR 522; [1996] 1 ILRM 187.

[77] S.I. No.165 of 1996.

amount of disability allowance payable to a claimant whose partner is in receipt of some other form of welfare.

This outcome, therefore, achieves the result desired by the Health Board in *J.H.*[78] though no attempt has been made to nullify Barron J.'s decision in *O'Connell.* Insofar as *O'Connell* is still good law, therefore, this represents a partially successful attempt to improve access to welfare payments, though once again, the class of potential beneficiaries, i.e. couples where both parties are in receipt of disability allowance, is likely to be quite small.

d) Operation of overlapping benefits regulations. In *McHugh v. A.B. (Deciding Officer),*[79] the Supreme Court was asked to rule on an aspect of the Social Welfare (Overlapping Benefits) Regulations which determine whether, and if so, to what extent, a welfare claimant may receive more than one welfare payment simultaneously.[80] The focus in the instant case was on article 4 of the Social Welfare (Overlapping Benefits) (Amendment) Regulations 1974 as amended by article 5 of the Social Welfare (Overlapping Benefits) (Amendment) Regulations 1987 which, *inter alia*, prohibited claimants of unmarried mother's allowance from simultaneously receiving disability benefit. In contrast, such claimants were permitted to claim half of the normal rate of unemployment benefit at the same time as their unmarried mother's allowance. In the Supreme Court, McCarthy J., delivering the leading judgment, accepted that the Minister had power to delimit the plaintiff's claim to disability benefit. However this power had to be exercised reasonably, having regard to the Supreme Court decision in *Cassidy v. Minister for Industry and Commerce*[81] and the judge could find no logic in the differing treatments of unemployment benefit and disability benefit under article 4. As the regulation was "demonstrably lacking in logic and unfair", it was therefore ultra vires. Unlike its earlier decision in *Harvey v. Minister for Social Welfare,*[82] on this occasion the Supreme Court did not deny that the Minister had the power to reduce welfare in the instant case; rather it focused on the manner in which that power was exercised. However as Cousins has observed:

> The power of the Courts to strike down a regulation for unreasonableness has been used sparingly in the past and it would perhaps be unwise to predict that the Courts will rigorously scrutinise the Overlapping Benefits Regulations in the future.[83]

---

[78] Note, however, that s.22 of the Social Welfare Act 1997 removes the limitation in the case of a couple, one of whom is in receipt of Disability Allowance and the other of whom is in receipt of either the old age (non-contributory) pension or invalidity pension.

[79] [1994] 2 IR 139.

[80] Another aspect of these Regulations have previously been declared invalid in *Harvey v. Minister for Social Welfare* [1990] 2 IR 232; [1990] ILRM 185, but this ruling was nullified by subsequent legislation and is considered below, pp. 162-4.

[81] [1978] IR 297.

[82] [1990] 2 IR 232; [1990] ILRM 185. See below, pp. 162-4.

[83] See note in (1992) 14 DULJ 193 at p. 199.

e) Equality for married women. Unquestionably the most significant example of the courts being used to improve access to welfare income for low income individuals occurred in relation to the implementation of Directive 79/7/EEC on the progressive implementation of the principle of equal treatment of men and women in matters of social security.[84] The third in a series of EC directives addressing the issue of sex discrimination, this Directive prohibited discrimination between men and women on grounds of sex, either directly or indirectly by reference, in particular, to marital or family status, in relation to work-related social security schemes.[85]

This Directive posed a serious problem for the Irish welfare authorities because traditionally the household model used for determination of welfare entitlements was that of the male breadwinner with the stay-at-home wife. This patriarchal household model was reflected in a number of discriminatory rules in the welfare code. Thus, a married woman living with her husband was not entitled to unemployment assistance (a means-tested payment). Furthermore, she was automatically regarded as her husband's dependant for the purpose of his welfare entitlements, irrespective of her actual economic status, whereas a husband was treated as the adult dependant of his wife only where he was unable to support himself by virtue of some physical or mental disability. Even when a wife working outside the home could claim insurance benefits in her own name, based on her own social insurance contributions, she received lower rates of unemployment, disability, disablement and injury benefit, invalidity pension and unemployability supplement than a man and, in the case of unemployment benefit, for a shorter period of time (maximum 12 months as opposed to 15 months in the case of a man.) Moreover, she could not claim any dependency increase in respect of her husband or her children unless her husband was, because of a physical or mental disability, incapable of supporting himself.

The Directive was adopted in 1978 and the member states of the EC were required to comply with its terms by 23 December 1984. Despite having six years' notice of this deadline for implementation, however, Ireland failed to implement the Directive in time and even when the State eventually began to implement the Directive, the initial implementing measures contained two significant legal defects, outlined below. This resulted in a number of legal actions being taken against the State, three of which went ultimately to the Court of Justice, before a final attempt was made to implement the Directive in 1995.

Implementation of Directive 79/7/EEC took place over four stages between 1986 and 1995. The first stage occurred in May 1986, when reduced rates of welfare for

---

[84] See generally Whyte (ed.), *Sex Equality, Community Rights and Irish Social Welfare Law* (ICEL, 1988), Cousins, *The Irish Social Welfare System: Law and Social Policy* (Round Hall Press Ltd., 1995), chs. 6 and 7, and Whyte, "Gender and Equality in the Irish Social Welfare System" in Quinn (ed.), *Irish Human Rights Yearbook 1995* at p. 50.

[85] Family payments, therefore, were not covered by the Directive. This limitation in the scope of the Directive reflected the fact that the Directive had its roots in Directive 76/207/EEC on equal treatment of men and women in employment and vocational training – see Hoskyns and Luckhaus, "The European Community Directive on Equal Treatment in Social Security" (1989) 17 *Policy and Politics* 321.

married women were abolished and the maximum duration of payment of unemployment benefit to married women was increased to 15 months.[86] These reforms were achieved through a process of "levelling-up", i.e. by extending to married women the benefits previously accorded to men.

The second stage followed six months later, when a sex-neutral definition of "adult dependant" was introduced, governing entitlement to both adult dependant and child dependant allowances, and married women became eligible for unemployment assistance.[87] On this occasion, however, equality was achieved through a process of "levelling down", i.e. by reducing the entitlements of men. In the first place, "adult dependant" was defined more narrowly as a person earning less than a prescribed sum per week[88] and not in receipt of welfare (other than disablement benefit, orphan's death benefit or orphan's pension or allowance) in his or her own right. This change was very controversial because it resulted in a significant reduction, in some cases by as much as £50 per week, in the level of welfare payments to many families, where the husband lost his adult dependant allowance and half of the child dependency allowance. In order to soften the blow for such families, a system of transitional weekly payments was introduced, which remained in place until 1992.[89] Second, a limitation was placed on the amount of unemployment assistance payable to a married person living with a spouse on welfare so that the total amount of welfare received by that household would not exceed the amount payable to the spouse claiming for an adult dependant. The effect of this "cap" was to reduce the amount of unemployment assistance to a level lower than that payable to a single claimant and because the limitation did not apply to cohabiting couples, this gave rise to constitutional difficulties which were eventually litigated in *Hyland v. Minister for Social Welfare.*[90]

The measures adopted over these two stages suffered from two significant legal defects. First, the measures implemented in the first stage were not made retrospective to 23 December 1984. Thus between that date and May 1986, married women continued to receive lower basic rates of certain welfare payments than men (and in the case of unemployment benefit, for a shorter period of time). Moreover their entitlement to adult and child dependency allowances was much more restricted than that of men. Second, the new transitional payments introduced in November 1986 applied, by definition, only to households where the husband had been in receipt of a prescribed

---

[86] See s.2 of the Social Welfare Act 1986; s.6 of the Social Welfare (No.2) Act 1985 and the Social Welfare (No.2) Act 1985 (Section 6) (Commencement) Order 1986 [S.I. No.173 of 1986].

[87] See Social Welfare (No.2) Act 1985 (Commencement) Order, 1986 [S.I. No.365 of 1986], Social Welfare (Normal Residence) Regulations 1986 [S.I. No.367 of 1986], Social Welfare (Overlapping Benefits) (Amendment) Regulations 1986 [S.I. No.368 of 1986] and Social Welfare (Adult Dependants) Regulations 1986 [S.I. No.369 of 1986]

[88] Originally £50 per week. S.15 of the Social Welfare Act 1995 now provides for a system of tapered increases for adult dependants, (now referred to as "qualified adults" – see s.28 of the Social Welfare Act 1997).

[89] See Social Welfare (Preservation of Rights) (No.2) Regulations 1986 [S.I. No.422 of 1986], as amended. These regulations eventually lapsed in 1992 – see the Social Welfare (Preservation of Rights) (Amendment) Regulations 1992 [S.I. No.43 of 1992].

[90] [1989] IR 624; [1990] ILRM 213. See further below, p. 162.

social welfare payment on the relevant date prescribed in the regulations. A household where the wife had been in receipt of such a payment on the relevant day did not qualify and this clearly constituted a new form of direct discrimination against such women. These defects led to the institution of several different sets of legal proceedings against the State, of which four came on for judgment and of which three were referred to the European Court of Justice under article 177 of the Treaty of Rome. In *Cotter and McDermott v. Minister for Social Welfare,* two married women sought arrears of unemployment benefit dating back to 23 December 1984 to compensate them for the fact that married women had received lower personal rates of unemployment benefit than men during that time. When this issue came before Hamilton P. (as he then was), he submitted two questions to the European Court of Justice for a preliminary ruling, essentially asking whether the Directive had direct effect in Ireland since 23 December 1984 so that it could be invoked by the claimants even in the absence of implementing national legislation. The Court of Justice subsequently ruled that the principle of equal treatment in the Directive could be relied upon by welfare claimants even in the absence of implementing national legislation and that where it was sought to apply the principle of equal treatment retrospectively, i.e. in respect of a period which had already elapsed, this could be achieved only through a process of "levelling up" whereby the benefits previously provided to the privileged group were extended to the disadvantaged group.[91] In anticipation of this ruling, the two women had instituted fresh proceedings in which they made additional claims under the Directive. In addition to the arrears of unemployment benefit already claimed, Ms Cotter[92] sought to be paid adult dependency and child dependency allowances in respect of her husband and children for specified periods between December 1984 and November 1986, pay-related benefit, unemployment assistance in respect of specified periods between 23 December 1984 and November 1986 and transitional payments since November 1986. When the Court of Justice decision came back to the High Court in July 1987 for a decision as to its application to the facts of the case, the opportunity was taken to hear argument on these additional claims as well and Hamilton P. eventually delivered judgment in June 1988.[93]

From the claimants' perspective, the judgment was very disappointing. Hamilton P. held that Ms Cotter was entitled to arrears of unemployment benefit and pay-related benefit but he dismissed each of the remaining claims. With regard to her claim for child dependency allowances for the period between December 1984 and November 1986, the judge held that the preference in the relevant regulations[94] given to fathers

---

[91] *McDermott and Cotter v. Minister for Social Welfare,* Case 286/85, [1987] ECR 1453; [1987] ILRM 324. The Court followed its earlier rulings in *Drake v. Chief Adjudication Officer,* Case 150/85, [1986] ECR 1995; [1987] QB 166; [1986] CMLR 43; [1986] 3 All ER 65, and *The Netherlands v. FNV,* Case 71/85, [1986] ECR 3855; [1987] 3 CMLR 767. As far as *prospective* application of the principle of equal treatment was concerned, welfare authorities had the option of levelling up or levelling down.

[92] Ms McDermott also instituted proceedings at the same time claiming comparable relief but the legal principles here were ultimately discussed by Hamilton P. exclusively in relation to the facts of Ms Cotter's case.

[93] [1990] 2 CMLR 141.

[94] Article 5 of the Social Welfare (Normal Residence) Regulations 1974 [S.I. No.211 of 1974].

and step-fathers over mothers and step-mothers for receipt of such allowances was a reasonable attempt to deal with a situation in which otherwise two people might have been able to claim a dependency allowance in respect of the same child. What this reasoning failed to take into account, however, was that Directive 79/7/EEC did not provide for any defence of reasonableness to a claim of direct discrimination.

In relation to her claim for a transitional payment, Hamilton P. held that she did not qualify for such a payment as her husband was not an adult dependant as defined in the Social Welfare (Adult Dependant) Regulations 1986. However, once more there was a serious flaw in the judge's reasoning for while it was correct to say that entitlement to a transitional payment depended on whether one's spouse was an adult dependant, the correct definition of adult dependant for this purpose was not the reformed definition contained in the Social Welfare (Adult Dependant) Regulations 1986 but rather the original, sexist definition contained in s.2 of the Social Welfare (Consolidation) Act 1981 read in the light of the principle of equal treatment enshrined in Directive 79/7/EEC.[95] That definition, it will be recalled, automatically treated a wife as a dependant of her husband, (unless he was incapable of supporting himself by reason of some physical or mental disability.) Reading that definition in the light of Directive 79/7/EEC broadened the category of adult dependant to include all spouses automatically, and not just wives.[96] Consequently Ms Cotter did satisfy the requirement for eligibility for a transitional payment.[97]

---

[95] Article 5 of the Social Welfare (Preservation of Rights)(No.2) Regulations 1986 [S.I. No.422 of 1986] read, in relevant part, and with emphasis added:

> Articles 5, 6, 7 and 8 of these Regulations shall apply to persons who were entitled to or were in receipt of any [welfare payment], pursuant to the Act, in respect of any day in the week ending on the day *immediately preceding* the day on which the Regulations have effect for the purpose of payment of [the welfare payment], the weekly rate of which was increased in respect of an adult dependant and on the relevant effective date, the weekly rate of entitlement ceased to include such increase by reason of [the introduction of the reformed definition of adult dependant].

[96] By the time of this judgment, the Court of Justice had already held, in both *The Netherlands v. FNV,* Case 71/85, [1986] ECR 3855; [1987] 3 CMLR 767 and *McDermott and Cotter v. Minister for Social Welfare,* Case 286/85, [1987] ECR 1453; [1987] ILRM 324, that *retrospective* implementation of the principle of equal treatment could be achieved only by a process of extending the benefit to the disadvantaged party, i.e. through a process of "levelling up". Hence the broadening of the category of adult dependant to include all spouses automatically.

[97] In this context, it is also worth noting that, in a case decided the previous year, the Court of Justice had held that, not only must the member States have repealed any national provisions inconsistent with the Directive by 23 December 1984, they could not continue the effect of such provisions beyond that deadline – *Clarke v. Chief Adjudication Officer*, Case 384/85, [1987] ECR 2865; [1987] 3 CMLR 277. The background to this case was that the UK had replaced a welfare scheme discriminating in favour of men, the non-contributory invalidity pension, with a new scheme, severe disablement allowance (SDA), which contained no such discrimination. However as a transitional measure, entitlement to SDA was extended to those men who had previously been in receipt of NCIP. According to the Court, this was contrary to the Directive as entitlement to SDA had to be on the same terms for both men and women. The same principle was also applied in the subsequent cases of *Johnson v. Chief Adjudication Officer*, Case 31/90, [1991] ECR I-3723, *Verholen v. Sociale Verzekeringsbank*, Case 89/90, [1991] ECR I-3757, *Dik v. College van Burgemeester en Wethouders,* Case 80/87, [1988] ECR 1601; [1989] 2 CMLR 936 and *De Weerd, née Roks v. Bestuur van de Bedrijsvereniging voor de Gezondheid,* Case 343/92, [1994] ECR I -57.

Ms Cotter's claim for adult dependant allowances with both unemployment benefit and unemployment assistance during the period December 1984 to November 1986 was also dismissed by Hamilton P. The judge accepted that, in not qualifying for such allowances under the *ancien regime*, Ms Cotter had been discriminated against on the basis of her sex. However he denied her any relief by (erroneously) limiting the retrospective effect of the earlier ruling of the Court of Justice in the case. Citing remarks of Henchy J. in *Murphy v. Attorney General*[98] and the judgment of the Court of Justice in *Defrenne v. SABENA*,[99] Hamilton P. argued that, given that Ms Cotter's husband was at all relevant periods engaged in full-time employment:

> it would be unjust and inequitable to pay to the applicant an adult dependant increase when the adult concerned, her husband, was not financially dependant on her and it would be unjust and inequitable to require the people of Ireland to pay her such increase.[100]

This ruling was erroneous if only because the Court of Justice had previously ruled, in *Barra v. Belgium*,[101] that it was only in exceptional cases that the retrospective effect of its judgments could be limited and, moreover, that such limitation had to be laid down in the very judgment in question. No such limitation was contained in the Court's ruling in *McDermott and Cotter*[102] and therefore there was no defence to her claim under the Directive for adult dependant allowances.

Finally, Hamilton P. also dismissed the claim for unemployment assistance on the ground that, as this was a means-tested payment, the Department had been prejudiced by the delay in making a claim because it had not had an opportunity to consider Ms Cotter's entitlement to assistance during the period in question. In the event, however, this claim for unemployment assistance was subsequently conceded by the Department as well all other claims for such assistance taken by married women in respect of the period December 1984 to November 1986.

Given the significant amount of public monies involved in these claims, it is perhaps understandable why Hamilton P. might have taken a cautious approach in this case and his judgment is a good illustration of the conservative approach adopted by some judges when dealing with cases involving fiscal matters. However the errors in his reasoning were so obvious that his judgment in *Cotter* could not be sustained and in the very next case to come before the High Court on these issues, a completely different approach was taken.

---

[98] [1982] IR 241.

[99] Case 149/77, [1978] ECR 1365; [1978] 3 CMLR 312.

[100] [1990] 2 CMLR 141 at p. 158.

[101] Case 309/85, [1988] ECR 355; [1988] 2 CMLR 409.

[102] In fairness to Hamilton P., the decision in *Barra* had not been published prior to the delivery of his judgment in *Cotter and McDermott*. On the other hand, one could argue that the principle in *Murphy* and *Defrenne* was never applicable in *Cotter* in the first place because in those two cases, the respective courts delivered judgments which could fairly be described as unexpected and the respective defendants could reasonably argue that they had no prior intimation that their earlier policies were flawed, whereas in *Cotter*, the State had been on notice since December 1978 that it had to reform the rules relating to the granting of adult dependant allowances to social welfare claimants.

In *Carberry v. Minister for Social Welfare,*[103] the applicant advanced the same claims as had been made in *Cotter and McDermott*, though on this occasion, in respect of disability benefit rather than unemployment benefit and assistance. The Department conceded her entitlement to arrears of disability benefit as compensation for the fact that married women had received a lower personal rate of such benefit than men between 23 December 1984 and May 1986, contrary to Directive 79/7/EEC. However it disputed her entitlement to dependency allowances and to transitional payments.

In relation to the claim for dependency allowances, Barron J. noted that if the position of the applicant and her husband had been reversed during the period 23 December 1984 and 17 November 1986,[104] he would have been able to claim a dependency allowance in respect of her. It followed from the principle of equality that she was therefore entitled to an increase of her benefit in respect of him. This conclusion led inevitably to the second part of his decision which was that the applicant was also entitled to transitional payments, as a man in her position would have received such payments. Barron J. also held, following *Barra v. Belgium,*[105] that the applicant was entitled to make retrospective claims to cover a period before she had instituted legal proceedings.

Thus, in contrast to Hamilton P. in *Cotter v. McDermott*, Barron J. in *Carberry* readily acceded to claims which had very significant financial implications for the State.

Two more Irish cases were referred to the Court of Justice during this phase of the implementation of Directive 79/7/EEC. When the applicants in *Cotter and McDermott v. Minister for Social Welfare* appealed against Hamilton P.'s decision to the Supreme Court, the respondent argued for a novel application of the principle of unjust enrichment[106] to defeat the claim for dependency allowances and transitional payments. Uncertain as to whether this defence was compatible with Directive 79/7/EEC, the Supreme Court referred the following two questions to the Court of Justice for a preliminary ruling:

1.   Is the ruling of the Court of Justice in Case 286/85, *Norah McDermott and Ann Cotter v. Minister for Social Welfare and Attorney General* [1987] ECR 1453, whereby the Court of Justice answered the second question referred to it pursuant to Article 177 EEC by the High Court in its interpretation of the provisions of Article 4(1) of Council Directive 79/7/EEC of 19 December 1978 as follows:

In the absence of measures implementing Article 4(1) of the directive, women are entitled to have the same rules applied to them as are applied to men who are in the

---

103   Unreported, High Court, 28 April 1989.
104   When the rules governing the payment of dependancy allowances with disability benefit were eventually changed.
105   Case 309/85, [1988] ECR 355; [1988] 2 CMLR 409.
106   For an argument that a conventional application of the principle of unjust enrichment could, in the circumstances of this case, have worked only to the benefit of the applicants and not the State, see the note by Eoin O'Dell and the present writer in (1991) 20 *ILJ* 304 at pp. 311-2.

same situation since, where the directive has not been implemented, those rules remain the only valid point of reference

to be understood as meaning that married women are entitled to increases in Social Welfare benefits in respect of

a) a husband as dependant, and

b) a child as dependant

even where it is proved that no actual dependency existed or even if as a result double payments of such increases in respect of dependants would occur?

2. In a claim by women for compensatory payments in respect of discrimination alleged to have been suffered by reason of the failure to apply to them the rules applicable to men in the same situation, is Council Directive 79/7/EEC to be interpreted as meaning that a national court or tribunal may not apply rules of national law such as to restrict or refuse such compensation in circumstances where the granting of such compensation would offend against the principle prohibiting unjust enrichment?

Thus the matter of dependency allowances was addressed by question 1, while question 2 focussed on the payment of transitional payments. Furthermore, a close reading of question 1 reveals the presence of two distinct issues, namely, first, whether the Directive required the payment of dependency allowances even where it was shown that no actual dependency existed and, second, whether the Directive required the payment of such allowances even if that resulted in the State having to pay twice over in respect of the same dependency situation.

In its preliminary ruling on these questions,[107] the Court of Justice pointed out that, on the application of the Directive to situations of notional dependency, the text of article 4(1) itself encompassed increases in respect of spouses who were not dependants.[108] As for payments in respect of dependants other than spouses, in particular children, the Court held that the Directive did not require proof of actual dependency as a prior condition for the application of the principle of equal treatment to such payments. Furthermore the Court, reaffirming its ruling in *Cotter and McDermott*, held that, in the absence of measures implementing Article 4(1) of the Directive, women were entitled to have the same rules applied to them as were applied to men in a similar situation. In the instant case, married men automatically received dependency allowances without having to establish a relationship of actual dependency, prior to the reforms of November 1986, and consequently women were entitled to those increases under the same terms.

The Court also rejected the argument that dependency allowances were not payable if that resulted in unjust enrichment, holding that "to permit reliance on that [argument] would enable the national authorities to use their own unlawful conduct as a ground for depriving Article 4(1) of the directive of its full effect".[109]

---

107 *Cotter and McDermott v. Minister for Social Welfare (No.2)* Case C-377/89; [1991] ECR I 1155.

108 Article 4(1) provides, in relevant part: "The principle of equal treatment means that there shall be no discrimination whatsover on ground of sex ... in particular as concerns ... the calculation of benefits including increases due in respect of a spouse and for dependants..."

109 [1991] ECR I-1155 at p. 1185 [para. 21].

The Court interpreted the second question as requiring it to consider the effect of the anomalies which arose as a result of the introduction, in November 1986, of transitional payments for men who suffered a reduction in welfare income as a result of the implementation of the Directive. The Court held that as the Directive did not provide for any derogation from the principle of equal treatment laid down in article 4(1), any such benefit payable to the husband after the Directive acquired direct effect also had to be paid to the wife. Citing *Dik v. College van Burgemeester en Wethouders,*[110] the Court held that the transitional measures had to respect the rights conferred on individuals by article 4(1) and that, since any unjust enrichment would flow from the Government's prior unlawful conduct, the Government could not rely on such a principle of national law to defeat the appellants' claims.

Thus in relation to the appellants' claims for both dependency allowances and transitional payments, the Court of Justice refused to offer any safe haven to a State seeking to escape the consequences of its failure to comply fully with EC law.

A similar approach was taken by the Court of Justice in the second of these two references, *Emmott v. Minister for Social Welfare.*[111] Mrs Emmott, a married woman with two dependant children, had been in receipt of disability benefit since December 1983. Soon after the Court of Justice handed down its decision in *Cotter and McDermott* in March 1987, Mrs Emmott entered into correspondence with the Department seeking the same amount of welfare as that paid to a married man in similar circumstances to her own. In June 1987, the Department replied saying that, as this issue was still the subject of litigation before the High Court, no decision could be taken in relation to her claim. In July 1988, Mrs Emmott was given permission by the High Court to challenge, by way of judicial review, the Department's failure to pay her the amount of welfare she claimed. At the subsequent hearing, the Department argued that the claim was statute-barred. Order 84, rule 21(1) of the Rules of the Superior Courts 1986 provided that:

> An application for leave to apply for judicial review shall be made promptly and in any event within three months from the date when grounds for the application first arose, or six months where the relief sought is *certiorari*, unless the Court considers that there is good reason for extending the period within which the application shall be made.

Costello J. referred a question to the Court of Justice for a preliminary ruling under article 177 of the Treaty of Rome in which he asked whether the Court's earlier ruling in *Cotter and McDermott* precluded the national authorities from relying on national procedural rules, in particular rules relating to time-limits, in defending claims for arrears of welfare taken pursuant to the Directive. The Court of Justice subsequently ruled that until such time as the Directive was properly transposed into Irish law, the welfare authorities could not rely on time-limits to defeat claims taken under the Directive. Moreover the earlier rulings of the Court that the principle of equal treatment in the Directive could be relied upon by welfare claimants in the absence of

---

110 Case 80/89; [1988] ECR 1601.
111 Case 208/90; [1991] ECR I – 4269; [1991] 3 CMLR 894.

implementing legislation did not amount to proper transposition of the Directive for this purpose.[112]

Thus the cumulative effect of the rulings of the Court of Justice in the three Irish references on Directive 79/7/EEC was that, in sporting parlance, the State was being told it could run, but it could not hide – the entitlement of married women to welfare arrears arising out of the defective attempt to implement Directive 79/7/EEC in 1986 would have to be addressed. Accordingly, in the third stage of the implementation process, the then Minister for Social Welfare, Charlie McCreevy, TD, promulgated the European Communities (Social Welfare) Regulations[113] in June 1992. These Regulations provided for the payment of the arrears (referred to as "household supplement") on a phased basis over three years starting in 1992. However they, too, were legally defective in at least two respects.

As already noted, in both *The Netherlands v. FNV*[114] and *McDermott and Cotter v. Minister for Social Welfare*[115] the Court of Justice held that in applying the principle of equal treatment to a period which had already elapsed, the authorities were obliged to "level up", i.e. to extend to the disadvantaged group the rules which had been applied to the privileged group. In the present context, this meant that in respect of the period between December 1984 and November 1986, married women were entitled to the benefit of the same rules as had applied to married men during that period. However in determining entitlement to arrears of dependancy allowance, the 1992 Regulations provided for the application to the period between December 1984 and November 1986 of the new (and more restrictive) definition of "adult dependant" provided for in the Social Welfare (Adult Dependants) Regulations 1986.[116] It followed that married women were not being treated in exactly the same way as married men in respect of this period – the men had the benefit of the older, sexist definition during this time – and consequently the principle of equal treatment was infringed. A similar problem existed with regard to the calculation of arrears of unemployment assistance, where both the reformed means test for that payment, together with the limitation on the amount of such assistance payable to married

---

[112] However in Case 338/91, *Steenhorst-Neerings v. Bestuur van de Bedrijfsvereniging voor Detailhandel, Ambachten en Huisvrouwen*, [1993] ECR I-5475; (1995) 3 CMLR 323, the Court subsequently drew a distinction between a procedural rule precluding the initiation of judicial proceedings alleging infringement of the Directive and a rule restricting the backpayment of claims for benefits, holding that the latter is not precluded by the Directive as it serves to ensure sound administration and also reflects the need to preserve financial balance in a scheme in which claims submitted by insured persons in the course of a year must in principle be covered by contributions collected during that same year. This distinction undermines to a certain extent the *Emmott* decision which had been described as a "very strong decision in favour of the enforcement of individual rights where directives had not been properly implemented in national law" – Cousins, "Equal Treatment and Social Security" (1994) *ELRev* 123. See also *Johnson v. Chief Adjudication Officer (No.2)*, Case 410/92, [1994] ECR I 5483; [1995] 1 CMLR 725.

[113] S.I. No.152 of 1992.

[114] Case 71/85, [1986] ECR 3855; [1987] 3 CMLR 767.

[115] [1987] ECR 1453; [1987] ILRM 324.

[116] S.I. No. 369 of 1986.

claimants, both of which were introduced in November 1986, were applied retrospectively to the arrears claim. Again neither provision applied to male claimants of unemployment assistance during the period December 1984 to November 1986.

A second problem existed with regard to the payment of transitional payments to which, according to the Court of Justice in *Cotter and McDermott v. Minister for Social Welfare (No.2)*,[117] married women were also entitled. This matter was simply not addressed at all in the Regulations.[118]

Once more, it fell to the courts to tackle these defects in the implementing measure. In *Tate v. Minister for Social Welfare*,[119] the plaintiffs were all married women living with their husbands and either unemployed and not in receipt of welfare or in receipt of unemployment, disability or invalidity payments between 23 December 1984 and 21 November 1986. They claimed that they were entitled to receive the same welfare and have the same rules applied to them that were paid and applied to married men in the same situation from 23 December 1984. Carroll J. held that the payment of transitional payments between November 1986 and July 1992 to households headed by males constituted a breach of the Directive and also that, having regard to *Marshall v. Southampton and South West Hampshire Area Health Authority (No.2)*,[120] the amount of arrears payable to any claimant had to be adjusted in line with the Consumer Price Index in order fully to compensate for delay. She also held that the failure of the State to comply fully with the Directive was neither a breach of constitutional rights, a breach of statutory duty nor a breach of duty of care but was rather a wrong under Community law which approximated to a breach of constitutional duty. The word "tort" in the Statute of Limitations was sufficiently wide to cover this breach of the State's obligations under Community law so that the limitation period of six years in s.11(2) of the Statute was applicable. The 1992 Regulations created a new cause of action insofar as they failed fully to implement the Directive with regard to entitlement to dependancy allowances and arrears of unemployment assistance with the result that, as far as these claims were concerned, the time limit started to run from June 1992. However, insofar as the Regulations never addressed the issue of transitional payments at all, there was no new cause of action here. Moreover, having regard to the effect, in practice, of s.11(2) in cases of continuing breach of duty (i.e. it limited the amount of arrears payable but did not preclude the initiation of any action), that section could be relied on by the State in the light of *Steenhorst-Neerings v. Bestuur van de Bedrijfsveriniging voor Detailhandel, Ambachten en Huisvrouwen*.[121] Carroll J. also

---

117 Case C-377/89, [1991] ECR I – 1155; [1990] 2 CMLR 10.
118 The Regulations also made no provision for the loss in the value of the benefits in the eight years or more since 1984, a problem exacerbated by the fact that the Regulations deferred complete satisfaction of the claims for arrears until July 1994 in some cases. In practice, however, it appears that settlements agreed by the Department did include the payment of interest. It is perhaps ironic, then, that in 1997, the Court of Justice ruled that Directive 79/7/EEC does not require the payment of interest on arrears of social security payable pursuant to the Directive – *R. v. Secretary of State for Social Security, ex parte Sutton*, Case 66/95, [1997] ECR I-2163.
119 [1995] 1 IR 418; [1995] ILRM 507.
120 Case 271/91, [1993] ECR I-4369; [1993] CMLR 293.
121 Case 338/91, [1993] ECR I-5475; (1995) 3 CMLR 323.

found that there was no evidence to support the claim that the State was estopped from relying on the Statute of Limitations. Finally, she held that it was not necessary to declare the 1992 Regulations to be null and void but that the State could not rely on any portion thereof which had the effect of not fully recognising the plaintiffs' rights under the Directive.

In the aftermath of this decision, the then Minister for Social Welfare, Proinsias de Rossa, TD, announced that compensation of up to £265m would be paid to 70,000 married women, thereby effectively bringing the long-drawn saga over the implementation of Directive 79/7/EEC in Ireland to a close.

In the context of this book, the most significant point to note about this saga is the central role of the courts, especially the Court of Justice but also Barron and Carroll JJ. in the Irish High Court, in ensuring proper implementation of Directive 79/7/EEC, notwithstanding the very significant cost to the State. Not only did the litigation strategy successfully clarify the rights of married women under the Directive, eventually leading to full implementation of the Directive, it also served to make the beneficiaries of the Directive aware of their entitlements through the media coverage of each case. The arid provisions of a legal document concerning a technical area of the law were translated into a human reality to which many could relate in the experiences of Ann Cotter, Norah McDermott and the other claimants who pursued the State through the courts.

The money secured for welfare claimants as a result of this litigation was very significant – £265m. – but on this point, the litigation on Directive 79/7/EEC is the exception which proves the rule. In each of the other areas reviewed in this section, the increase in public funds allocated to welfare claimants as a result of judicial decisions was negligible or, in the case of the provision of fuel vouchers, non-existent. The litigation on Directive 79/7/EEC was exceptional in this regard because the Irish courts were asked to enforce an explicit and relatively determinate Community norm against recalcitrant national authorities that were clearly in default. However, as a general proposition, one cannot argue that successful social welfare litigation has led to any significant increase in the social welfare budget, though clearly it has produced some improvements for specific and limited categories of claimants.

A striking feature of these successful cases is that they almost invariably involved an argument that the norm relied upon by the authorities was invalid, having regard to a higher norm. Thus as we have just noted, the decisions on Directive 79/7/EEC involved the application to Irish legislation of a higher EC norm; in the two fuel voucher cases, *Kershaw* and *McLoughlin*, a circular and a statutory instrument were both respectively held to be *ultra vires* the authorities having regard to the parent Act; in one of the two cases concerning the entitlements of married claimants to DPMA, *J.H.*, the authorities' interpretation of a statutory instrument was held to be contrary to the Constitution, while in the other, *O'Connell*, a statutory instrument was held to be *ultra vires* the parent Act; and in two other cases, *McHugh* and *Kenny*, statutory instruments were held to be *ultra vires* the Minister because they were unreasonable. The last two cases are the closest one gets to a situation in which the courts are prepared to substitute their judgment for that of the welfare authorities on the merits of welfare policy and this suggests that judicial deference to the views of the authorities on substantive issues of social welfare policy is a significant factor in social welfare litigation. [122]

Of course, not every attempt to use the courts to improve access to welfare income has been successful. In a number of cases, the courts themselves have ruled against the claim while in others, a favourable judicial ruling is subsequently nullified by legislation. I turn now to consider these cases in order to see what one could infer from them about the likely success of promoting the interests of welfare claimants through litigation.

ii) Cases unsuccessful in court

At least eight cases fall into the first of these two categories. In relation to three of these, the case was arguably very weak to begin with and it is difficult to see how the court in each case could have come to any conclusion other than that actually reached. Thus, in *Kearns v. Minister for Social Welfare*[123] McMahon J. upheld the disqualification of the claimants for receipt of unemployment benefit on the ground that their unemployment was due to a stoppage of work consequent on a trade dispute. Section 35(1) of the Social Welfare (Consolidation) Act 1981 provided, in relevant part:

> A person who has lost employment by reason of a stoppage of work which was due to a trade dispute at the factory, workshop, farm or other premises or place at which he was employed shall be disqualified for receiving unemployment benefit so long as the stoppage of work continues.[124]

"Trade dispute" was defined in sub-section 6 as "any dispute between employers and employees, or between employees and employees, which is connected with the employment or non-employment or the terms of employment or conditions of employment of any persons…".

In the instant case, a disagreement arose between the employer and the employees' union about procedures for selecting workers for redundancy following on the closure

---

[122] In the UK, Lord Denning M.R. stated, in *R. v. Preston SBAT, ex parte Moore*, [1975] 2 AER 807 (at p. 813); [1975] 1 WLR 624 (at p. 631): "It is plain that Parliament intended that the Supplementary Benefit Act 1966 should be administered with as little technicality as possible. It should not become the happy hunting-ground for lawyers. The courts should hesitate long before interfering by certiorari with the decisions of the appeal tribunals." Speaking in similar vein, Hamilton CJ said, in *Henry Denny & Sons Ltd. v. Minister for Social Welfare*, [1998] 1 IR 34 [at p. 37]; [1998] ELR 36 [at p. 50] that courts "should be slow to interfere with the decisions of expert administrative tribunals".

[123] Unreported, High Court, 10 February 1982.

[124] Sections 142 and 203 of the 1981 Act and the Social Welfare (Family Income Supplement) Regulations 1984 [S.I. No.278 of 1984] provided for a similar disqualification, *mutatis mutandis*, in relation to unemployment assistance, supplementary welfare allowance and family income supplement respectively. The provisions of the 1981 Act have since been re-enacted in ss.47(1)-(2), 125(1)-(2) and 174 of the Social Welfare (Consolidation) Act 1993. For a detailed examination of this trade dispute disqualification, see Kerr and Whyte, *Irish Trade Union Law* (Professional Books Ltd., 1985), ch. 13; Clark, "Towards the 'Just' Strike" (1985) 48 *MLR* 659; and Ewing, *The Right to Strike* (Clarendon Press, 1991), ch. 7.

of one of the employer's meat processing plants and this eventually led to the dismissal of all of the employees. Even though no industrial action had been taken or threatened by the union, the employees were subsequently refused unemployment benefit because employment had been lost by reason of a stoppage of work (the dismissals) due to a trade dispute over the redundancy procedures, a view subsequently endorsed by McMahon J. in the High Court. Given the facts of this case, it is difficult to see how the judge could have come to any other conclusion.

However, while this case was unsuccessful in the courts, it is worth noting that the law on this topic was subsequently changed in a manner favourable to the claimants. The claimants were fortunate that many of them resided in a marginal Dáil constituency during a period of political instability and so they were able to extract a commitment to reform which was delivered on by the enactment of the Social Welfare (No.2) Act 1982, providing for the establishment of a Social Welfare Tribunal empowered to restore unemployment benefit or assistance to persons affected by the trade dispute disqualification if it could be shown that such persons were unreasonably deprived of employment.[125]

The second case in this trilogy is *Kingham v. Minister for Social Welfare*[126] in which the claimant sought to establish his entitlement to a contributory old age pension. By virtue of s.79 of the 1981 Act and the Social Welfare (Old Age (Contributory) Pensions) Regulations 1960,[127] as amended by the Social Welfare (Old Age and Widows' and Orphans' (Contributory) Pensions and Retirement Pension) (Amendment) Regulations 1973,[128] a claimant had to have paid 156 social insurance contributions *and* have a yearly average of at least 20 contributions paid or credited since s/he entered into insurance in order to be eligible for the contributory old age pension. This latter condition gave rise to a very anomalous and unjust result in the case of non-manual employees who entered insurance during the 1950s. Until 1974, such workers were excluded from the category of compulsory insurable employees if they earned above a certain income limit.[129] Thus a number of employees, having entered insurance at the beginning of their working careers, found that with salary increases and promotion, they ceased to be compulsorily insured. In 1974, this upper income limit in respect of compulsory insurance was abolished and these employees re-entered the insurance system. At the same time, many other white-collar and mangerial staff became insurable for the first time. When it came to claiming the contributory old age pension, however, it transpired that the latter category of person was usually entitled to the maximum pension, as their yearly average contribution record since 1974 was generally very good, whereas many of those who paid contributions during the 1950s (and in doing so actually contributed more to the Social Insurance Fund than their wealthier colleagues) failed to qualify for a pension

---

125 After an initial flurry of activity during the 1980s, no case has been taken to this Tribunal since *O'Connor v. Irish Press Newspapers Ltd.* [1995] ELR 152.
126 Unreported, High Court, 25 November 1985.
127 S.I. No.274 of 1960.
128 S.I. No.189 of 1973.
129 Though they had the option to retain some social insurance cover as voluntary contributors.

at all as their yearly average contribution record since first entering insurance was very low, given the interruption of their insurance record until 1974.[130] Mr Kingham found himself denied a pension on this basis and he appealed against this decision to the High Court.

We have already referred to Lynch J.'s decision on the jurisdictional issue raised in this case.[131] On the substantive issue, Kingham's lawyers advanced a very technical argument, the net effect of which would have been to oblige the Department to take into account contributions made by the appellant prior to 5 January 1953, which contributions would have taken him over the required yearly average of 20 contributions, thereby entitling him to a pension. The difficulty facing the appellant was that article 6(2)(a) of the Social Welfare (Old Age (Contributory) Pension) (Transitional) Regulations 1960[132] provided that in calculating a claimant's yearly average contribution record, one had to have regard to the period commencing 5 January 1953 where the claimant had been insured prior to the coming into operation of the Social Welfare Act 1952. At the time those regulations were promulgated, the contribution year for a man was defined as the calendar year. Subsequently, s.4 of the Social Welfare (Amendment) Act 1978 changed this to the financial year used for income tax purposes. Section 78(3) of the 1981 Act, in turn, provided that, in calculating a claimant's yearly average, one had to have regard to a period commencing "at the beginning of the contribution year in which his entry into insurance occurred". Counsel for the appellant argued that this provision impliedly amended the 1960 Regulations so as to oblige the Department to have regard to contributions made by the appellant since 6 April 1952, rather than 5 January 1953. Lynch J. felt unable to accede to this argument. While recognising that the merits of the case were all with the appellant, and stating that he reached his conclusion "with considerable regret", he held that the 1960 Regulations were quite clear as to the manner in which the average yearly contributions were to be calculated and that there was no clear intention that the legislature intended to amend these regulations when enacting s.78(3) of the 1981 Act.

Again it is difficult to fault the judge's interpretation of the legislation here and the outcome here reflects the hopelessness of case, from a legal perspective, rather than any judicial antipathy to increased welfare expenditure. Indeed one might infer from Lynch's expression of regret that, had he been able to, he would have ruled in favour of the claimant. Once more, however, the Oireachtas stepped in to amend the law in favour of claimants like Mr Kingham by providing for the payment of reduced rates of old age pension in such cases.[133]

---

[130] The value of this loss was exacerbated by virtue of the fact that a number of free social services, such as free telephone rental, free TV license and electricity allowance, were provided to, *inter alia*, contributory old age pensioners.

[131] See above, pp. 129-130.

[132] S.I. No.255 of 1960.

[133] See s.30 of the Social Welfare Act 1988 as amended by s.25 of the Social Welfare Act 1989. See now s.84(12) of the Social Welfare (Consolidation) Act 1993. It is perhaps worth noting that the Ombudsman was also bringing pressure to bear on the Department to sort out this anomaly – see *Annual Report of the Ombudsman 1984* (Pl.2909) at pp. 18-20 and *Annual Report of the Ombudsman 1985* (Pl.3748), pp. 6-7.

Finally, in *Healy v. Minister for Social Welfare*,[134] the plaintiffs claimed to be entitled to Family Income Supplement while being employed on a Social Employment Scheme. Article 22 of the Social Welfare (Family Income Supplement) Regulations 1991 [S.I. No.279 of 1991] provided, *inter alia*, that persons employed under a Social Employment Scheme were disqualified for receiving Family Income Supplement. The plaintiffs argued that this specific disqualification was *ultra vires* the power of the Minister. The 1991 Regulations also provided, in article 7, that in order to qualify for Family Income Supplement, a claimant had to show, *inter alia*, that he was engaged in remunerative employment which is expected to continue for a period of a minimum of six months and that he is so engaged for not less than 20 hours a week, or he together with his spouse are engaged in such employment for an aggregate of not less than 20 hours a week.

Having ruled that this substantive condition was a valid exercise of the ministerial power to promulgate delegated legislation, Carroll J. held that the plaintiffs were not entitled to Family Income Supplement as under the Social Employment Scheme, they had worked 40 hours every alternate week, rather than at least 20 hours each week. Consequently the court did not have to consider their claim that article 22 was *ultra vires*. Again, it is difficult to see how the Court could have come to any conclusion in this case other than that actually reached by Carroll J.

The remaining five cases are not so clear cut and might offer some support for the view that the courts are reluctant to challenge the decisions of officials with expertise in the area of social welfare. In the first two of these cases, challenges were made to the interpretation of welfare policy by the welfare authorities. The remaining three concern challenges to the constitutionality of two different aspects of the welfare code.

In *Foley v. Moulton*[135] an attempt was made to restrict the application of the so-called "cohabitation rule". This rule disqualified claimants for receipt of certain specified family payments[136] if they were living with another person as man and wife. In the instant case, the claimant challenged a decision of an appeals officer disqualifying her for receipt of a widow's (contributory) pension because of cohabitation. She conceded that she had a sexual relationship with her boyfriend and that they both lived in her house but she argued that, as she received no financial

---

134 [1999] 1 ILRM 72.

135 [1989] ILRM 169. See note by the present author in (1989) 11 *DULJ (n.s.)* 187.

136 At the time of this decision and for a number of years thereafter, virtually all of these payments were payable only to women. With the virtual elimination of gender discrimination from welfare payments for families as a result of the introduction of the one parent family payment in 1996 – see s.17 of the Social Welfare Act 1996 – and the widow's and widower's (non-contributory) pension in 1997 – see s.19 of the Social Welfare Act 1997 – this aspect of the cohabitation rule is now also applicable to men. (Since 1989, the cohabitation rule has also had a bearing on the amount of welfare payable to claimants, since married and cohabiting claimants are subject to particular statutory provisions governing the amount of unemployment assistance and disability allowance they may receive – see ss.122 and 191E (the latter inserted by s.13 of the Social Welfare Act 1996) of the Social Welfare (Consolidation) Act 1993. This aspect of the cohabitation rule has applied to both male and female claimants since its introduction in 1989.)

assistance from him,[137] the cohabitation rule was inapplicable. This argument was based on the fact that, at that time, the welfare system automatically regarded women as dependent on men so that where a woman did not have the support of a man because of bereavement, desertion, the imprisonment of the man or because the woman was unmarried and either a lone parent or approaching old age, dependency was automatically inferred and the State provided financial support.[138] In that context, it could be argued that such financial support should only be withdrawn where the claimant subsequently enters into a relationship in which she received, or could receive, financial support.[139]

Such an argument had found favour with the Divisional Court in Ontario in *Re Proc and the Minister of Community and Social Services*[140] but not with Gannon J. in the Irish High Court. He preferred a literal interpretation of the relevant statutory provision, s.92(3) of the Social Welfare (Consolidation) Act 1981,[141] stating:

> The meaning of sub-s.(3) of s.92 seems to me to be clear and unambiguous and provides for a factual situation or circumstance. I do not think there is anything about the wording of the subsection which warrants importing into it an intention or purpose of a legislative nature by reference to other statutes or a supposed policy of legislation…I do not think it is any function of the Court to enquire into the purposes or motives of legislation, or to endeavour by construction to give the legislation a desirable effect or any effect other than that expressed in the statutes, save only where the terms of the legislation are otherwise incomprehensible.[142]

He went on to endorse the remarks of Lord Goddard C.J. in *Thomas v. Thomas*[143] wherein that judge said of cohabitation that it

> does not necessarily depend upon whether there is sexual intercourse between husband and wife. "Cohabitation" means living together as husband and wife and …consists in the husband acting as a husband towards the wife and the wife acting as a wife towards the husband, the wife rendering housewifely duties towards her husband and the husband cherishing and supporting his wife as a husband should.[144]

Thus the High Court implicitly affirmed the approach of the welfare authorities to the interpretation of the cohabitation rule, whereby the social, sexual and financial aspects of the relationship are all taken into account for the purpose of deciding whether the couple are, in fact, cohabiting.

---

[137] He was already supporting a child of his by a previous relationship and he had a drink problem.
[138] Gender discrimination has since been virtually eliminated from the code by virtue of Directive 79/7/EEC – see above, pp. 141 *et seq.* – and reform of welfare provision for families – see n.136 above.
[139] See Mossman, "The Baxter Case: De Facto Marriage and Social Welfare Policy" (1977) 2 *UNSW Law Journal* 1.
[140] (1975) 53 DLR (3d) 512.
[141] Which reads: "A widow shall be disqualified for receiving a widow's (contributory) pension if and so long as she and any person are cohabiting as man and wife".
[142] [1989] ILRM 169 at p. 175.
[143] [1948] 2 KB 294.
[144] At p. 297.

Inasmuch as *Proc* offered Gannon J. the option of coming to a conclusion which supported the claimant in *Foley*, one cannot say that the arguments before the court[145] ineluctably led to the outcome in the case. Consequently, it could be argued that the decision here reflected a tendency on the part of the judiciary to defer to the views of specialists in the field.

The same may also be said of the next case in this category, *Murphy v. Eastern Health Board*,[146] in which O'Hanlon J. refused to quash a decision of the Board rejecting the applicant's claim for supplementary welfare allowance. The applicant had previous resigned from employment in order to look after her elderly parents, both of whom were very ill. Because of these domestic responsibilities, she was ineligible for unemployment assistance and so she applied for supplementary welfare allowance. At that time, s.206 of the Social Welfare (Consolidation) Act 1981 provided, in relevant part:

> A health board may ... determine that a person shall not be entitled to supplementary welfare allowance unless – (a) he is registered for employment in such manner as the Minister may prescribe.[147]

The respondent Board initially refused to give the applicant any supplementary welfare allowance for a period of approximately three years because she was not signing on as available for employment and then subsequently awarded her an allowance at a rate less than the maximum weekly rate of supplementary welfare allowance. She sought an order of *certiorari* quashing these decisions. Refusing the application, O'Hanlon J. is reported to have said that s.206 left the Board with no option but to reject her application. However this is a questionable interpretation of the legislation. Section 206 conferred a *discretion* on the Board to attach certain conditions to the payment of supplementary welfare allowance – it did not impose an *obligation* to attach such conditions. Such a discretion must be exercised reasonably and one would have thought that the Board's decision in this case, which left the applicant without any independent source of income for approximately three years, was unreasonable under the circumstances. Thus one might well regard this decision as also being unduly deferential to the position of the welfare authorities.

The three remaining cases in this quintet raised complaints of various forms of unconstitutional discrimination in the welfare code. As such, these cases target legislative policy on welfare, as opposed to bureaucratic interpretation of such policy. In *MhicMhathúna v. Attorney General*,[148] which concerned an allegation of unlawful discrimination based on marital status, the plaintiffs complained that aspects of the

---

145 A more compelling justification for this decision, though not one used by Gannon J., is the argument that the Department's interpretation of the cohabitation rule vindicates the constitutional guarantee of the institution of marriage in Article 41.3.1 by ensuring that married couples are not treated less favourably than cohabiting couples – see *Murphy v. Attorney General* [1982] IR 241.

146 An *ex tempore* decision reported in *The Irish Independent*, 4 August, 1988.

147 Since re-enacted by s.176(a) of the Social Welfare (Consolidation) Act 1993.

148 [1995] 1 IR 484; [1995] 1 ILRM 69.

tax and welfare codes were unconstitutional, having regard to the guarantee of equality in Article 40.1 and the constitutional status of the family based on marriage in Article 41.3, because they treated married families less favourably than one-parent households. Thus the latter enjoyed the benefit of tax free allowances for children and of welfare payments such as the unmarried mother's allowance which were not provided to married couples. Dismissing this claim, the Supreme Court offered four reasons for its decision. First, citing *Somjee v. Minister for Justice,*[149] the Court pointed out that its function in hearing a challenge to the constitutionality of legislation was restricted to deciding whether or not the impugned legislation was unconstitutional and that it had no power to direct the legislature to enact new and different provisions. In the instant case, the plaintiffs had stated that they had no desire to reduce or remove payments made to any other category of parent but rather sought to have state assistance for married parents improved. Second, the Court held, following *Madigan v. Attorney General,*[150] that, in reviewing the constitutionality of tax legislation, it had to confine itself solely to the question of whether the legislation adversely affected constitutional rights, obligations or guarantees and that it could not enter into any debate on the merits of taxation policy. Third, the Court noted that the claim in the instant case raised questions about the application by the Oireachtas of resources available as between different objects and persons or categories of persons and it cited, with approval, Costello J.'s decision in *O'Reilly v. Limerick Corporation*[151] in which he held that the courts had no jurisdiction to entertain such questions. Finally, the Court dismissed the plaintiffs' complaint of unlawful discrimination on the ground that there were abundant grounds for distinguishing between the needs and requirements of single parents and those of married parents living together and that once such justification for disparity arose, the court could not interfere by seeking to assess what the extent of the disparity should be. Moreover, as far as Article 41.3.1 was concerned, while the complete removal by the State of financial support for the family could constitute a breach of this provision, the complaint here was about the *measure* of support provided, not about its total removal, and determining the appropriate amount of support to provide was a matter for the executive and legislature, not the courts.

The Supreme Court essentially took a conservative view of its power of judicial review but, as I argued elsewhere in this book,[152] such a position rests on contentious philosophical premises[153] and cannot be regarded as self-evidently correct. In

---

149   [1981] ILRM 324.
150   [1986] ILRM 136.
151   [1989] ILRM 181.
152   See ch. 1, esp. pp. 17-22.
153   Thus Bandes criticises judicial refusal to review executive inaction as resting on the political assumption that "the optimal role [of government] is non-interference, or at least the smallest amount of interference necessary to permit individuals to exercise the greatest degree of freedom without encroaching on others". – See "The Negative Constitution: A Critique" (1990) 80 *Michigan Law Review* 2271 at p. 2314. At pp. 43 *et seq.*, I advance a view of the Constitution which would legitimate judicial activity in the face of legislative and executive inaction in the area of socio-economic rights.

particular, one might well question whether the court's refusal to assert any jurisdiction to review the extent of any disparity of treatment between single parent households and households with married parents is not excessively deferential to the Oireachtas and out of line with contemporary jurisprudence employing the doctrine of proportionality in the review of legislation. In any event, one can characterise *MhicMhathúna* as a judicial decision which is very deferential to legislative policy on welfare. A similar judicial attitude can be discerned in the remaining two cases here, both of which concerned gender discrimination against men in the welfare code.

In *Dennehy v. Minister for Social Welfare*[154] a deserted husband with two sons argued that the failure of the State to pay him a form of social security payable to deserted wives in similar circumstances amounted to invidious discrimination and was therefore contrary to the constitutional guarantee of equality in Article 40.1.[155] Holding against him, Barron J. referred to Article 41.2 of the Constitution which provides:

> The State shall, therefore, endeavour to ensure that mothers shall not be obliged by economic necessity to engage in labour to the neglect of their duties in the home.

Having regard to this provision, the judge reasoned that it was not

> unreasonable, unjust or arbitrary for the Oireachtas to protect financially deserted wives who are mothers who have dependent children residing with them or to recognise that mothers who have had to care for children will have lost out in the labour market and so are likely to need similar protection when similarly deserted.[156]

One of the difficulties with this reasoning is that the group protected by Article 41.2, namely, mothers, was not synonymous with the group privileged under the social welfare code, namely, deserted wives, some of whom, those over 40 years of age, did not have to be mothers in order to qualify for deserted wives' payments.[157] Moreover Article 41.2 referred to the position of mothers generally whereas the complaint here focussed on the legislative treatment of *deserted* spouses.

Mr Dennehy having died shortly before judgment was delivered in his case, it was not possible to pursue an appeal against Barron J.'s decision. However in *Lowth v. Minister for Social Welfare*[158] the Supreme Court was given the opportunity of considering this issue. In this case, the plaintiffs, a deserted husband and his two children, again complained that legislative discrimination in favour of deserted wives was contrary to the constitutional guarantee of equality. In the High Court, Costello J. dismissed the claim on the ground that, under Article 40.1, inequality of treatment is permitted if based on differences of capacity or social function. In the instant case, statistics had been furnished to the court indicating that fewer married women than married men participated in the labour force and also that the average industrial

---

154 Unreported, High Court, 26 July 1984.
155 As we have already noted – see note 136 above – such gender discrimination has since been virtually eliminated from the welfare code.
156 At p. 19 of his judgment.
157 See ss.100 and 195 of the Social Welfare (Consolidation) Act 1981.
158 [1998] 4 IR 321; [1999] 1 ILRM 5.

earnings of women were lower than those of men. The judge held that, in the light of these facts, the Oireachtas could reasonably conclude that deserted wives required greater income support than deserted husbands. In addition, Costello J. also relied on the reasoning of Barron J. in *Dennehy*.

On appeal to the Supreme Court, the plaintiffs challenged Costello J.'s reliance on the aforementioned statistics, arguing that as they referred to the position of men and women generally in the labour force, they could not justify any discrimination between a *deserted father* and a *deserted mother*, neither of whom are able to participate in the labour force because of their family circumstances consequent on the desertion. The Supreme Court rejected this argument, emphasising the very heavy burden of proof which rests on a plaintiff challenging fiscal legislation and noting that the plaintiffs had failed to produce any statistics relating to the percentage of deserted husbands and deserted wives in employment. The Court went on to re-affirm its previously stated position that Article 40.1 only forbids invidious discrimination[159] and the alternative formula of Kenny J. in *Murphy v. Attorney General*[160] that an inequality will not be set aside as repugnant to the Constitution if any state of facts exists which may reasonably justify it. In the instant case, the Court held that there were ample grounds for the Oireachtas to conclude that deserted wives were in general likely to have greater needs than deserted husbands so as to justify the discrimination complained of.

The placing of such a heavy burden of proof on a plaintiff challenging fiscal legislation arguably reflects an institutional bias on the part of the Court in favour of legislative policy on social welfare, albeit a bias which the Court would argue is derived from the doctrine of separation of powers. However, it is interesting to note that, in the context of gender discrimination, a very different approach is taken by the US Supreme Court.[161] In the US, classifications based on gender are permitted only if the state can point to a substantial relationship between the classification and an important interest of government. Thus the burden of proof rests on the State to justify the classification, unlike the approach adopted in *Lowth* where the plaintiffs were required to prove the absence of such justification. Moreover the standard of review is more demanding than that applied in *Lowth* – instead of merely having to show the existence of facts which could reasonably justify the discrimination, the State has to prove the existence of a relationship between the classification and an important interest of government.[162]

---

159 See *O'Brien v. Keogh* [1972] IR 144.
160 [1982] IR 241.
161 In "The Supreme Court and the Equality Clause" (1998) *The Bar Review* 116, Hogan argues that the Supreme Court decision in *Lowth* represents a misapplication of principles borrowed from US jurisprudence.
162 There is some evidence, albeit slight at present, that the Irish courts could yet adopt a similar approach to our constitutional guarantee of equality. In the earlier case of *In re Article 26 and the Employment Equality Bill 1996* [1997] 2 IR 321, the Supreme Court said, *per* Hamilton C.J., at p. 347:

Reviewing these unsuccessful cases, it is interesting to note that a significant number of them involved either a direct challenge to the authorities' interpretation of the relevant law grounding the social welfare policy[163] or had very significant implications for the shaping of such policy.[164] This again suggests that the courts are reluctant to challenge the views of the authorities on the merits of welfare policy.

However, while many of the cases in this section arguably reflect an institutional bias on the part of the courts in favour of legislative policy on welfare and, to a lesser extent, in favour of welfare authorities in the interpretation of such policy, it is submitted that one cannot generalise from these cases to say that public interest litigation on behalf of welfare claimants is inevitably futile. Those cases which support such a proposition are matched by a larger number of cases in which welfare claimants have triumphed in court (even if some of these victories were nullified by subsequent legislative action). Whatever instinctive tendency the courts might have to defer to the views of the welfare authorities, that tendency does not prevail where social welfare policy is clearly in conflict with a higher legal norm.[165]

iii) Cases successful in court but nullified by subsequent legislation

Each of the cases considered in the previous section failed, for whatever reason, before the court. However, in assessing the impact of judicial decisions on the development of the social welfare code, one also has to take into the reckoning those cases in which the litigants obtained a favourable judgment but where the effect of that judgment as a precedent for others was subsequently nullified by legislation. There would appear to be four such cases involving claims for improved access to welfare payments.

We have already noted how, in *The State (McLoughlin) v. Eastern Health Board*,[166] the Supreme Court interpreted s.209 of the Social Welfare (Consolidation) Act 1981 as conferring an *entitlement* to supplementary welfare allowance additions in appropriate circumstances – the generally held view up to that time having been that s.209 conferred a *discretion* on the welfare authorities to grant such an addition.

The forms of discrimination which are, presumptively at least, prescribed by Article 40.1 are not particularised: manifestly they would extend to classifications based on sex, race, language, religious or political opinions.

This comment arguably points towards a two-fold test in relation to equality jurisprudence – classifications presumed to be contrary to Article 40.1 and those presumed to be compatible. In the former case, one would expect the State to have to carry the burden of proof of justifying the classification whereas in the latter case, the task of establishing that a particular classification was unconstitutional would rest with the plaintiff.

163 *Kearns v. Minister for Social Welfare*, unreported, High Court, 10 February 1982, *Kingham v. Minister for Social Welfare*, unreported, High Court, 25 November 1985 and *Foley v. Moulton* [1989] ILRM 169 fall into this category.

164 *MhicMhathúna v. Attorney General* [1995] 1 IR 484, [1995] 1 ILRM 69, *Dennehy v. Minister for Social Welfare*, unreported, High Court, 26 July 1984 and *Lowth v. Minister for Social Welfare* [1998] 4 IR 321; [1999] 1 ILRM 5 fall into this category.

165 See above, pp. 151-2.

166 [1986] IR 416. See above, pp. 135-6.

However s.209 was eventually amended by s.47 of the Social Welfare Act 1992 so as to give the authorities a discretion to grant weekly or monthly additions.

In *Hyland v. Minister for Social Welfare*[167] the Supreme Court declared s.12(4) of the Social Welfare (No. 2) Act 1985 to be unconstitutional. In an attempt to contain the amount of welfare expenditure occasioned by allowing married women access to unemployment assistance, as required by Directive 79/7/EEC, the Oireachtas had essentially provided in s.12 that where a married couple were both entitled to social welfare, with one or both entitled to unemployment assistance, the combined income of the household should be the same as that payable to a welfare claimant with an adult dependant, with each spouse entitled to claim half of this combined income in his/her own name. In contrast, a cohabiting couple in similar circumstances were not subject to this restriction and so could each claim a full personal rate of welfare. In the circumstances of the *Hyland* case, where the plaintiffs, a married couple, were both unemployed, this meant that they received approximately £11 per week less than their cohabiting counterparts. In the High Court, Barrington J. held that this arrangement amounted to an unconstitutional attack on the family, contrary to Article 41.3.1. On appeal, the Minister argued that Barrington J. gave insufficient regard to counterbalancing welfare and other benefits provided only to married couples. He also sought to distinguish earlier authorities[168] dealing with similar discrimination in the tax code on the grounds that (a) the benefits here were different in extent and in their non-quantifiable nature from the benefits in tax concessions, (b) the progressive nature of the burden in tax cases was missing here, and (c) different considerations should apply to welfare legislation than to tax laws. The Minister also contended that the presumption of constitutionality was especially strong in relation to fiscal legislation and that no clearcut attack on the married family was indicated by s.12(4). The Supreme Court dismissed these arguments, re-iterating its earlier views that discrimination against married couples in one situation cannot be compensated for or justified by advantages and privileges provided for in other contexts and that the progressive nature of the tax burden was not a relevant difference between the earlier cases on the tax code and the instant case. The Court also rejected the contention that the difference in objectives between taxation and social welfare statutes affected the issue and it declared s.12(4) to be unconstitutional. However the victory thus secured by the Hylands for married welfare claimants was very short lived as, within four weeks of the Supreme Court decision, the Oireachtas had enacted the Social Welfare (No.2) Act 1989 which abolished the discriminatory treatment experienced by married couples by extending the restriction in the original s.12 to cohabiting couples, *i.e.* by a process of levelling down.

The third case, *Harvey v. Minister for Social Welfare,*[169] involved a challenge to the operation of the Social Welfare (Overlapping Benefits) Regulations which reduce or withdraw entirely a welfare payment where the claimant is entitled to two or more

---

167 [1989] IR 624; [1990] ILRM 213.
168 *Murphy v. A.G.* [1982] IR 241 and *Muckley v. A.G.* [1985] IR 472; [1986] ILRM 364.
169 [1990] 2 IR 232 ; [1990] ILRM 185. See note by Cousins in (1992) 14 *DULJ (n.s.)* 193.

such payments simultaneously. The claimant had been in receipt of both the widow's (non-contributory) pension and the blind pension until she reached pensionable age, when the blind pension was withdrawn. This was because article 38 of the Social Welfare (Overlapping Benefits) Regulations 1953[170] provided that a claimant could not simultaneously claim, *inter alia*, the widow's (non-contributory) pension and the old age (non-contributory) pension. The Department considered that when the claimant reached 66, her blind pension converted into an old age (non-contributory) pension and so it was withdrawn.

The claimant advanced a number of arguments before the Supreme Court challenging this decision. First, it was contended that s.75 of the Social Welfare Act 1970, pursuant to which article 38 had been promulgated, was unconstitutional on the ground that it empowered the Minister to make regulations which were in direct contradiction to the expressed intention and unambiguous effect of s.7 of the Social Welfare Act 1979 (which essentially provided that attainment of pensionable age should not be a ground for disqualification for, *inter alia*, widow's (non-contributory) pension) and that consequently s.75 authorised the carrying out of a legislative function by a body other than the Oireachtas, contrary to Article 15.2 of the Constitution. This argument was rejected by the Court as it simply concluded, implicitly invoking the presumption of constitutionality, that s.75 did not necessarily require the Minister to infringe Article 15.2. The claimant's second argument was that article 38 was inapplicable as the blind pension was not an old age (non-contributory) pension. This contention was rejected by the Court who, after citing the relevant legislative provisions, agreed with Blayney J.'s conclusion in the High Court that the blind pension was merely the old age pension payable at an earlier age to a person who suffers from blindness. A third argument that article 38 did not apply to claimants who were already *in receipt* of both pensions (as opposed to claimants who had an *entitlement* to both) was dismissed on the ground that there was no justification for distinguishing between these two situations. The contention that article 38 was invalid because it was unreasonable also received equally short shrift. In a clear indication of the reluctance of the Court to entertain such an argument, the Chief Justice pointed out that it is for the Oireachtas, rather than the courts, to determine the social policy of the State. In any event, the Court could see nothing unreasonable in terminating a pension, which is related to incapacity to work, upon the claimant reaching an age at which the Oireachtas deems that she will no longer be able to work by reason of age.

The claimant's last argument, however, proved successful. The Court accepted that, in the instant case, the Minister did not have the power to reduce the claimant's welfare entitlements as statutory provisions allowed her to hold both pensions simultaneously.[171] Article 38 directly contravened these provisions and, as such,

---

170 Inserted by article 4 of the Social Welfare (Overlapping Benefits) (Amendment) Regulations 1979 [S.I. No. 118 of 1979].

171 In his judgment, Finlay C.J. pointed out that s.7 of the 1979 Act provided that reaching 66, the qualifying age for the old age (non-contributory) pension, should not be a ground for disqualifying a claimant for receipt of, *inter alia*, the widow's (non-contributory) pension. Moreover rule 1(4) of the Third Schedule to the Social Welfare (Consolidation) Act 1981

amounted to an unconstitutional exercise of the Minister's powers under s.75, contrary to Article 15.2 of the Constitution.

Given the limited nature of this decision – the ruling of invalidity could only apply where statutory provisions entitled a claimant to remain in receipt of two or more welfare payments simultaneously – it was never likely that *Harvey* would have had major implications for welfare expenditure. In any event, the Department took no chances. In anticipation of the Supreme Court ruling, it had previously arranged for the re-enactment of the substance of article 38 of the 1953 Regulations as s.27 of the Social Welfare Act 1989, thus avoiding any difficulties with Article 15.2 of the Constitution or with the *vires* of the Minister. Success in the courts was thus nullified by legislation. Two years later, the Oireachtas attempted to copperfasten this situation by enacting s.43 of the Social Welfare Act 1991 which prohibited the payment of overlapping benefits in most cases subject to the Minister's power to permit such payment by regulation. It remains to be seen whether s.43 will prevent further challenges to Departmental decisions in this area or whether it infringes Article 15.2 of the Constitution by conferring a discretion on the Minister without, at the same time, indicating what principles or policies are to be taken into account in the exercise of this discretion.[172] At the very least, the Minister's power to permit overlapping benefits must be exercised in a reasonable fashion and failure to do so will result in judicial censure.[173]

The final case in this group concerned access to unemployment payments by dockers. In *Louth v. Minister for Social Welfare*[174] the plaintiffs were dockers in Drogheda who operated a co-operative system of work whereby they pooled all earnings from their work and divided the income equally among themselves. Those dockers not selected to unload a ship on any particular day claimed unemployment benefit for that day. Both a deciding officer and an appeals officer had ruled that the men, when not working on the docks, were not unemployed for the purpose of claiming unemployment benefit. In the High Court, the Minister sought to defend this decision on the grounds that the plaintiffs were not employees, but rather independent contractors and, in the alternative, that if they were employees, they were in

---

prohibited, for the purpose of means-testing for either the widow's or old age (non-contributory) pensions, the taking into consideration of the payment of welfare pensions or allowances. In *McHugh v A.B. (Deciding Officer)* [1994] IR 139, however, he subsequently resiled in part from this position, stating that the provisions of rule 1(4) had to be seen as general provisions which could not displace the particular provisions in the Social Welfare (Overlapping Benefits) Regulations, having regard to the rule of statutory interpretation, *generalia specialibus non derogant.*

172   See *Cityview Press Ltd. v. An Chomhairle Oiliúna* [1980] IR 381 in which the Supreme Court held that a delegation of parliamentary power to do more than merely give effect to principles and policies contained in the parent Act would be contrary to Article 15.2

173   See *McHugh v. A.B. (Deciding Officer)* [1994] IR 139, discussed above, p. 140. Even though this decision related to the pre-1991 regime for overlapping benefits, the principle enunciated therein – that delegated legislative power must be exercised in a reasonable fashion – clearly applies to s.43 of the 1991 Act.

174   [1993] 1 IR 339; [1992] ILRM 586.

continuous employment and could not be considered to be unemployed. According to Barron J., the plaintiffs were employed by the stevedores and the fact that they were employed in rotation and that they pooled their earnings did not affect the basic nature of their employment. Had they not agreed to pool their earnings, it would not have been suggested that they were in continuous employment. However the agreement to pool earnings was reached by the dockers *inter se* and formed no part of their arrangement with the stevedores. Consequently they were to be regarded as working pursuant to separate contracts of services and so could claim unemployment payments for days on which they did not work.

Some five years later, however, the conditions of eligibility for unemployment benefit and assistance were altered in a manner which would appear to preclude claimants such as those in *Louth* from qualifying for such payments. Section 30 of the Social Welfare Act 1997, *inter alia*, empowered the Minister to make regulations specifying the circumstances in which a person is to be regarded as being available for and genuinely seeking employment, two substantive conditions of eligibility for unemployment benefit and unemployment assistance.[175] Pursuant to this power, the Minister promulgated the Social Welfare (Consolidated Payments Provisions) (Amendment) (No.4) (Availability and Genuinely Seeking Employment) Regulations 1998 [S.I. No 137 of 1998], article 3 of which provided, *inter alia*, that "a person shall, for the purposes of Chapter 9 of Part II and Chapter 2 of Part III, be regarded as being available for employment, if he or she can show to the satisfaction of the Minister, that he or she is willing and able, at once, to take up an offer of suitable full-time employment". Article 3 also provided that a person should be regarded as genuinely seeking employment if s/he could show, to the satisfaction of the Minister, that s/he had, taken reasonable steps which offered the best prospects of obtaining employment. Given that the claimants in *Louth* regularly suffered short periods of intermittent unemployment from their work, they could not hold themselves out as being available to take up an offer of full-time employment unless they were willing to forsake their occupation as dockers and so it would seem that the High Court decision in this case has been effectively neutralised by subsequent legislation.

These cases illustrate the very obvious point that success in the courts is a necessary, but not sufficient, condition for establishing the merits of public interest litigation. For public interest litigation to be fully successful, it is necessary that the official policy should change to comply with the judicial decision handed down. However unless a judicial decision is rooted in either the Constitution or EU law,[176] the authorities will always have the option of nullifying it by way of amending legislation.

---

175 See s.42(4)(ii) and (iii) and s.120(1)(d) and (e) of the Social Welfare (Consolidation) Act 1993 respectively.

176 And if the decision is rooted in an equality norm in either the Constitution or EU law, the authorities may also be able, at least in some circumstances, to nullify it through the simple expedient of "levelling down" – see *Hyland v. Minister for Social Welfare* [1989] IR 624; [1990] ILRM 213.

Control provisions

I turn now to consider those judicial decisions dealing with the control provisions of the social welfare code. These control provisions fall into two categories – those dealing with the Department's civil powers to police the welfare code and those dealing with criminal prosecutions taken under the welfare code.

Civil powers

The courts have considered three different aspects of the Department's civil control powers – the power of social welfare officers to carry out investigations; the power to disqualify for receipt of welfare and the power to recover overpaid welfare.

power to investigate. In *Minister for Social Welfare v. Bracken*[177] four welfare inspectors had entered the defendant's business premises without permission and started to interview people found on the premises. When challenged by the defendant, each official produced their respective identity cards but they did not caution the defendant prior to questioning him. He then ordered each official to leave the premises as a result of which he was charged with wilfully delaying and obstructing the inspectors contrary to s.114(4)(a) of the Social Welfare (Consolidation) Act 1981. The District Justice stated a case for the High Court on the following questions of law:

a) Was it a requirement on the inspectors to apply for permission from the defendant before entering the premises?
b) Were the identity cards proferred adequate proof of the inspectors' authority?
c) Should the inspectors have cautioned the defendant as a condition precedent to any evidence being given of what the defendant said and did during the incident?

In relation to the first question, Lavan J. held, following *Director of Public Prosecutions v. McCreesh,*[178] that express statutory authority would be required to permit entry onto private property without the owner's permission and that s.114 did not contain any such provision, so that the inspectors should have applied for permission from the defendant before entering his premises.[179] The judge went on to say, however, that an occupier could not refuse entry, without proper cause, for the purposes of illegally frustrating an inquiry under the welfare code.

Answering the second question, the judge ruled that the production of the identity cards would constitute adequate proof of the inspectors' authority provided that the defendant had a reasonable time to satisfy himself, by taking proper and adequate steps, that the inspectors had been duly appointed by the Minister. Given that, on the evidence stated in the case stated, the inspectors were trespassers, a conviction on the

---

[177] [1994] 2 IR 523.
[178] [1992] 2 IR 239.
[179] Section 294F(3) of the Social Welfare (Consolidation) Act 1981, inserted by s.27 of the Social Welfare Act 1993, subsequently empowered inspectors to enter at all reasonable times any premises or place liable to inspection under the Act "without prior notification". See now s.212 (3)(a) of the Social Welfare (Consolidation) Act 1993.

charges laid could not be sustained and so Lavan J. held that he did not have to answer the third question.

power to disqualify. We have already considered judicial supervision of the Department's power to disqualify claimants for receipt of welfare in some detail above[180] and it is sufficient here to recall that the courts have insisted that the welfare authorities make a claimant aware of the case for disqualification and afford him or her the opportunity to respond to such case before exercising the power to disqualify.

power to recover overpaid welfare. Closely linked to the power to disqualify is the power of the welfare authorities to recover overpaid welfare. This power has been considered by the courts on two occasions. In *The State (Hoolahan) v. Minister for Social Welfare*[181] Barron J. held that s.300(5)(a) of the Social Welfare (Consolidation) Act 1981, pursuant to which the Department sought to recover deserted wife's benefit paid to a claimant who the Department subsequently believed was not entitled to such benefit, required the welfare authorities to establish that the original decision awarding payment was given by reason of a fraudulent misrepresentation on the part of the claimant.[182] The Department not having put any such allegation to the claimant, she consequently was given no opportunity to meet such a case and so the decision to seek recovery of overpaid benefit was invalid.

Some five years later, the Department began a process of amending the social welfare code so as to enhance its powers to recover overpaid welfare. First, s.35 of the Social Welfare Act 1991 amended s.300 of the 1981 Act by inserting a new paragraph – para.(aa) – in sub-s.5 which empowered the relevant welfare officials to backdate a revised decision based on new evidence or facts to such date as the official should determine, having regard to the new evidence or facts.[183] Then s.31(1) of the Social Welfare Act 1993 substituted new provisions for s.300, adding, *inter alia*, a provision [s.300B(c)] allowing the relevant welfare officials to backdate a revised decision, in any case not already covered by provisions corresponding to the former s.300(5)(a) and (aa), to any date considered appropriate by the official, having regard to the circumstances of the case and providing, in s.300D(4), for the repayment of overpaid welfare to the Social Insurance Fund, the Minister or a health board, as the case may be.[184]

---

180 See pp. 127-9.
181 Unreported, High Court, 23 July 1986.
182 S.300(5) provided, in relevant part: "A revised decision given by a deciding officer or an appeals officer shall take effect as follows – (a) where any benefit ... will, by virtue of the revised decision, be disallowed or reduced ... and the revised decision is given owing to the original decision having been given ... by reason of any statement or representation ... which was to the knowledge of the person making it false or misleading in a material respect ... it shall take effect as from the date on which the original decision took effect ..."
183 S.40 of the Social Welfare Act 1992 subsequently clarified that s.300(5)(aa) should apply to new facts or evidence relating to periods prior to and subsequent to the commencement of the paragraph.
184 Section 31(1) also empowered designated welfare officials to defer, suspend, reduce or cancel, in accordance with a prescribed code of practice, any amount of welfare due to be repaid by a welfare claimant to the welfare authorities.

The Social Welfare Acts 1981 to 1993 were then consolidated by the Social Welfare (Consolidation) Act 1993, s.249 of which deals with the effect of revised decisions and provides as follows:

A revised decision given by a deciding officer shall take effect as follows –

(a) where any benefit, assistance, child benefit or family income supplement will, by virtue of the revised decision be disallowed or reduced and the revised decision is given owing to the original decision having been given, or having continued in effect, by reason of any statement or representation (whether written or verbal) which was to the knowledge of the person making it false or misleading in a material respect or by reason of the wilful concealment of any material fact, it shall take effect as from the date on which the original decision took effect, but the original decision may, in the discretion of the deciding officer, continue to apply to any period covered by the original decision to which such false or misleading statement or representation or such wilful concealment of any material fact does not relate;

(b) where any benefit, assistance, child benefit or family income supplement will, by virtue of the revised decision, be disallowed or reduced and the revised decision is given in the light of new evidence or new facts (relating to periods prior to and subsequent to the commencement of this Act) which have been brought to the notice of the deciding officer since the original decision was given, it shall take effect from such date as the deciding officer shall determine having regard to the new facts or new evidence;

(c) in any other case, it shall take effect as from the date considered appropriate by the deciding officer having regard to the circumstances of the case.[185]

Section 300D(4) of the 1981 Act, as inserted by s.31(1) of the 1993 Act, providing for a liability to repay overpaid welfare and various mechanisms for such repayment, was re-enacted by s.278 of the 1993 Consolidation Act.

More recently, s.31 of the Social Welfare Act 1997 provides that where a person is convicted of an offence under s.32 of the Larceny Act 1916, by virtue of having received any social welfare payment by way of personation, the amount involved may be recovered from any social welfare payment to which the person is or becomes entitled, while s.20 of the Social Welfare Act 1998 empowers the Department to recover overpaid welfare by obliging claimants to repay such monies on demand, without recourse to court proceedings.

These extended powers of the welfare authorities to recover overpaid welfare were recently considered by the Supreme Court in *Minister for Social, Community and Family Affairs v. Scanlon.*[186] The defendant had been in receipt of disability benefit

---

[185] Ss.264 and 269 of the Social Welfare (Consolidation) Act 1993 make identical provision, *mutatis mutandis*, in respect of revised decisions of, respectively, appeals officers and health board officials dealing with claims for supplementary welfare allowance. The power of welfare officials to defer, suspend, reduce or cancel any welfare due to be repaid by a claimant was re-enacted by s.282 of the 1993 Act, pursuant to which the Minister subsequently promulgated the Social Welfare (Code of Practice on Recovery of Overpayments) Regulations 1996 [S.I. No.227 of 1996].

[186] [2001] 1 IR 64; [2001] 2 ILRM 342.

from September 1985 until May 1994. In June 1994, the original decision to award disability benefit was revised and the benefit disallowed on the ground that the original decision was induced by fraud on the part of the claimant. Following an appeal, the appeals officer ruled that the benefit should be refunded, not on the basis that the claimant knowingly made a fraudulent claim, but rather because there was new evidence indicating that he had worked while claiming benefit. The Minister subsequently instituted legal proceedings against the defendant seeking to recover £43,088.25.

Applying the above-mentioned statutory provisions to the facts of this case, Laffoy J. in the High Court[187] concluded that, following *The State (Hoolahan) v. Minister for Social Welfare*,[188] overpaid welfare could only be recovered by the Department in respect of the period between 1985 and the coming into effect of the Social Welfare Act 1991 where the claimant had knowingly made a fraudulent claim. In the period between the coming into operation of the 1991 Act and the coming into operation of the Social Welfare Act 1993, a revised decision not based on fraud on the part of the claimant could take effect from such date as the welfare official might determine. According to the judge, this gave rise to two issues – first, could the official backdate such a revised decision to a date prior to the commencement of the 1991 Act so as to render recoverable benefit paid prior to such commencement and, second, was there a liability to repay and a statutory mechanism for recovering welfare disallowed on account of new evidence during the period between the coming into operation of the 1991 and 1993 Acts? Finally, in the period after the commencement of the 1993 Act, it was clear, having regard to s.278 of the 1993 Consolidation Act,[189] that welfare disallowed because of fraud on the part of the claimant or because of the emergence of new evidence could be recoverable from such date as the welfare authorities decided. However this gave rise to a further issue as to whether such a decision could be backdated to a date prior to the commencement of the 1993 Act.

On the question of the retrospective application of statutory provisions, Laffoy J. held, following the Supreme Court decision in *Hamilton v. Hamilton*,[190] that the introduction of a statutory requirement to repay welfare paid to a claimant at a time when no such requirement existed when the welfare was received amounted to a retrospective application of legislation. However s.300(5)(aa) of the Social Welfare (Consolidation) Act 1981, as inserted by s.35 of the 1991 Act, did not disclose a clear and unequivocal intention on the part of the legislature that it was to have retrospective effect and so it had to be construed as having prospective effect only. The judge took a similar view of s.300D(4) of the 1981 Act, as inserted by s.31(1) of the 1993 Act, providing for a liability to repay overpaid welfare in non-fraudulent cases and mechanisms for the recovery of such overpayment. Consequently she ruled that, as a matter of law, benefit paid to the defendant prior to the commencement of

---

[187] *Ibid.*
[188] Unreported, High Court, 23 July 1986.
[189] Re-enacting s.300D(4) of the 1981 Act as inserted by s.31(1) of the Social Welfare Act 1993.
[190] [1982] IR 467.

the Social Welfare Act 1993 was not repayable pursuant to a revised decision based on new evidence.[191]

On appeal, however, the Supreme Court took a less restrictive interpretation of the legislation. Delivering the judgment of the Court, Fennelly J. accepted that, in relation to interpreting legislation with potential retrospective effect , one had to consider this in the light of both the Constitution and common law principles. In the instant case, he held that a retrospective reading of s.300(5)(aa) did not affect any constitutional right as the defendant's right to receive benefit and to retain benefit wrongly paid was statutory in origin and did not constitute a property right for the purposes of the Constitution.[192] Turning to the common law approach to the retrospective application of legislation, he held that this approach had two essential elements – first, it was designed to guard against injustice by preventing the unfair imposition of new burdens in respect of past actions; second, the presumption against retrospective effect was a rule of construction, not of law and so could be displaced by the clear words of the statute. In the instant case, Fennelly J. disagreed with the High Court judge in relation to the impact of s.40 of the Social Welfare Act 1992 which provided that s.300(5)(aa) was to apply to new facts or evidence relating to periods prior to and subsequent to the commencement of that paragraph. According to Fennelly J., this provision was clear and unambiguous in enabling decisions made pursuant to s.300(5)(aa) to have retrospective effect. It followed, further, from this that s.300D(4), which provided mechanisms for the recovery of overpayment in non-fraudulent cases, also had retrospective effect. Finally, he also disagreed with the trial judge's ruling that it was necessary for the Department to serve a fresh demand for payment following on the appeals officer's decision, taking the view that s.300H of the 1981 Act[193] implies that the Minister's claim for repayment can proceed on foot of the claim based on the original decision of the deciding officer, including the demand made on foot thereof.

A common thread running through these various cases on the civil powers of the Department is that, with the exception of the Supreme Court decision in *Scanlon*, the court in each case construed the powers narrowly, a position which is consistent with the general approach of the courts to the interpretation of legislation, such as tax or

---

[191] Nor were the welfare authorities able to recover benefit paid to the defendant between April 1993 and May 1994 as there was no evidence before the court of any demand for such repayment following on the decision of the appeals officer and consequently the liability of the defendant under s.278 of the 1993 Consolidation Act had not been made out.

[192] He also rejected the contention that deciding and appeals officers were exercising judicial functions that, under the Constitution, should properly have been reserved to the judiciary.

[193] Now s.283(b) of the Social Welfare (Consolidation) Act 1993. This provides in relevant part:
    In any proceedings ... for the recovery of any sums due to the Minister or the Social Insurance Fund, a decision on any question relevant to the proceedings given in accordance with this Act shall, unless an appeal or reference in respect of the decision is pending or the prescribed time for appealing against the decision has not expired, be conclusive for the purpose of those proceedings and ... where any such appeal or reference is pending ... the court dealing with the case shall adjourn the proceedings until such time as a final decision on the question has been obtained.

penal legislation, which trench on individual rights. To that extent, welfare claimants derive a benefit from judicial monitoring of the control provisions of the welfare code.

Penal provisions

The Irish superior courts[194] have considered the penal provisions of the welfare code on four occasions but, given the technical nature of the issues presented by most of these cases, the judicial impact on this aspect of the welfare code has not been of much significance to welfare claimants generally.

In *Minister for Social Welfare v. Johnston,*[195] Davitt P. in the High Court held that article 11(4) of the Social Welfare (Collection of Contributions) Regulations 1952, which required an employer to stamp and return an arrears card recording the employee's contribution record, created only one complete offence so that a District Justice was correct in dismissing two summonses relating to the same arrears card where an employer had failed both to stamp the card and to return it to a Departmental inspector.[196] In *Minister for Social Welfare v. Lally,*[197] the same judge held that s.53(3) of the Social Welfare Act 1952, dealing with the time-limits for initiating criminal proceedings under the 1952 Act, was an enabling section only which did not introduce a new code of limitations for social welfare offences and that, having regard to s 10(4) of the Petty Sessions Act 1851, proceedings were commenced by the making of a complaint or the laying of an information, not by the issue of the summons charging the offence. In *The State (Wilson) v. Neilan,*[198] Carroll J held, *inter alia,* that the offence of making a false and misleading statement for the purpose of obtaining unemployment benefit, contrary to s.115(1) of the Social Welfare (Consolidation) Act 1981, required the statement to be made to someone empowered under the 1981 Act to decide if benefit would be given. Accordingly, where a false claim for benefit had been presented to the local Garda station for transfer on to an Employment Exchange, the offence was only constituted when the claim was received in the Employment Exchange and the offence was properly prosecuted in the District Court for the area in which the Exchange was located. She went on to hold, following *Charlton v. Ireland*[199] and *The State (Rollinson) v. Kelly,*[200] that in determining whether an offence is or is not a minor offence, each offence must be looked at separately and a minor offence cannot change into a non-minor offence simply because the accused is charged with a number of similar offences. Carroll J. also rejected the argument that there was no offence of making a statement which was false and misleading in a material respect, pointing out that there was an offence under s.115(1)(b)(i) of knowingly making a false statement and that this was the offence with which the

---

194 Prosecutions under the social welfare code are usually taken in the District or Circuit Courts but the decisions of these courts are rarely reported.
195 [1960] IR 185.
196 This system of recording insurance contributions was abolished in 1974.
197 [1964] IR 360.
198 [1985] IR 89; [1987] ILRM 118
199 [1984] ILRM 39.
200 [1984] IR 248; [1984] ILRM 625.

prosecutor had been charged. Finally, as we have just noted, in *Minister for Social Welfare v. Bracken*[201] Lavan J. held that the permission of the occupier was required before inspectors could enter onto private property and where no such permission had been sought, the defendant could not be convicted of wilfully obstructing an inspector in the exercise of his duty, contrary to s.114(4)(a) of the Social Welfare (Consolidation) Act 1981, where he had ordered welfare inspectors to leave his premises prior to the conclusion of their investigations.

Miscellaneous

Finally, in the interest of providing a comprehensive account of judicial involvement with the Irish welfare code, it is necessary to refer briefly to a number of miscellaneous decisions which do not come under any of the preceding headings. These decisions address, in the main, technical aspects of the code and have relatively little impact on welfare claimants generally. Thus in *In re Castlemahon Poultry Products Ltd.*[202] the Supreme Court held that the Revenue authorities' claim for an employer's contribution in respect of social insurance on arrears of wages only got priority over all other debts in a winding up where the wages to which the arrears related had actually been paid. This decision was legislatively reversed by s.36(1) of the Social Welfare Act 1991 which provided, *inter alia*, that the Revenue authorities' claim for an amount due in respect of social insurance contributions on remuneration which should have been paid prior to a winding up would get priority over other debts. However in *In re Coombe Importers Ltd.*[203] Shanley J. held that that provision did not apply to a situation in which the employees did receive remuneration from their employer without deductions for social insurance contributions being made. Moreover that provision could not be invoked retrospectively so as to impair or affect rights existing in parties with an interest in the winding-up of a company which was wound up prior to the enactment of s.36(1).

In *Hearne v. Ó Cionna*[204] the court was asked to consider the liability of the defendants for tax and social insurance contributions due in respect of persons alleged to be their employees. The defendants contended that the employees in question were employed by a limited company for whom the defendants had merely acted as paymasters. O'Hanlon J. ruled that, having regard to the special definition of "employer" in s.124 of the Income Tax Act 1967, the defendants were liable for the tax due in respect of the employees but that, in the absence of a similar definition in the welfare code, it was open to the defendants to argue that the limited company was responsible for the collection and payment of the social insurance contributions. In *Ó Síocháin v. Neenan*[205] the Supreme Court held that an increase in respect of qualified children paid with the Widow's (Contributory) Pension was, for income tax

201 [1994] 2 IR 523.
202 [1987] ILRM 222.
203 [1999] 1 IR 492.
204 Unreported, High Court, 14 June 1988.
205 [1999] 1 IR 533; [1998] 2 ILRM 444.

purposes, the income of the widow. In *Doran v. Dublin Plant Hire Ltd.*[206] Barron J. held that s.306A of the Social Welfare (Consolidation) Act 1981[207] did not provide for the deduction of disability benefit from damages arising out of an occupational accident not involving a mechanically propelled vehicle while in *O'Loughlin v. Teeling*[208] MacKenzie J. held that that section did not require the court to deduct the amount of disability benefit which would have been payable had the plaintiff remained in receipt of such benefit from the date of the hearing to the expiry of the five year period after the accident, but only such benefit as the plaintiff had actually received and was "likely" to receive in the future.

One topic that merits a little closer attention is that of the insurability of individuals under the welfare code. The courts have been asked on eleven occasions to rule on the insurance status of individuals under the welfare code and in a surprisingly high proportion of these cases, the courts have held that the individuals were either not insurable or that they were subject to modified insurance, with a consequent restriction on their welfare entitlements. Thus, in *McLoughlin v. Minister for Social Welfare,*[209] the Supreme Court held that a temporary assistant solicitor employed in Chief State Solicitor's office was not employed in the civil service of the Government within the meaning of para.3(a) of Part I of the First Schedule to the Social Welfare Act 1952 so as to be subject to compulsory insurance while in both *Sr. Dolores v. Minister for Social Welfare*[210] and *National Maternity Hospital v. Minister for Social Welfare*[211] the courts held that student nurses were not employed under a contract of apprenticeship and so were not insurable. In both *Director of Public Prosecutions v. McLoughlin*[212] and *Minister for Social Welfare v. Griffiths*[213] Costello and Blayney JJ. respectively held that the relationship between share fishermen and the skipper of a boat was that of partnership, rather than employer-employee, with the result that the share fishermen were not subject to compulsory insurance.

All of these decisions were nullified or modified by legislation, *McLoughlin*, *Sr. Dolores* and the *National Maternity Hospital* cases by s.14 of the Social Welfare (Miscellaneous Provisions) Act 1960, which extended compulsory social insurance to the relevant categories of worker, and *McLoughlin* and *Griffiths* by the Social Welfare (No.2) Act 1993 which provided for an optional system of social insurance for share fishermen. However other decisions dealing with very limited number of workers have been allowed to stand. Thus in *General Medical Services (Payments) Board v. Minister for Social Welfare*[214] an employee of the plaintiff board was held to be employed in the service of a public authority and so only liable to pay a special rate

---

[206] Unreported, High Court, 25 April 1989.
[207] Now s.237 of the Social Welfare (Consolidation) Act 1993.
[208] [1988] ILRM 617.
[209] [1958] IR 1.
[210] [1962] IR 77; 97 ILTR 103.
[211] [1960] IR 74.
[212] [1986] IR 355; [1986] ILRM 493.
[213] [1992] 1 IR 103; [1992] ILRM 667.
[214] [1976-7] ILRM 210.

of social insurance contribution pursuant to article 5(1)(c) of the Social Welfare (Modification of Insurance) Regulations 1956,[215] with a consequent restriction on his welfare entitlements. Similarly in *Murphy v. Minister for Social Welfare*[216] and *Power v. Minister for Social Welfare*[217] Blayney J. held that ordinary members of the Labour Court were employed in the civil service of the State and accordingly were insurable under the welfare code. However as they were not employed under a contract of service, they were not insurable for the purposes of the old age (contributory) pension. In *McAuliffe v. Minister for Social Welfare*,[218] a person working for a wholesale distributor of newspapers was held to be employed as an independent contractor rather than as an employee and so only insurable as a self-employed person.[219]

On the other side of the fence, in *FÁS v. Abbott*,[220] the Supreme Court held that contracts of employment which had infringed a statutory prohibition against FÁS entering into contracts for the appointment of staff without the consent of the Ministers for Labour and Finance were nonetheless still subject to compulsory social insurance, while in *Henry Denny & Sons (Ireland) Ltd. v. Minister for Social Welfare*[221] the Supreme Court held that a demonstrator in a supermarket was an employee of the company whose product she was promoting.

The fact that in a preponderance of these cases the courts held that the individual concerned was not subject to compulsory social insurance, or was subject to a modified regime of social insurance, might suggest to some an aversion on the part of the courts to the concept of compulsory social insurance. However these cases turn, for the most part, on whether the individuals concerned were employees, self-employed or office-holders, an issue which, notoriously, depends on the particular circumstances of each case. Accordingly, it is probably not wise to impute to the courts any general attitude towards social insurance simply on the grounds of a tally of the cases.

Conclusion

In reviewing Irish jurisprudence on social welfare law, one can classify most of the judicial decisions into four groups. First, there are those decisions which ultimately led to an improvement in the welfare code for welfare claimants. The most significant impact here has been in the areas of adjudicative procedures and the elimination of gender discrimination pursuant to Directive 79/7/EEC, though judicial intervention has also benefited welfare claimants in relation to control provisions, fuel voucher

---

[215] See now article 7 of the Social Welfare (Modification of Insurance) Regulations 1991 [S.I. No.94 of 1991].

[216] [1987] IR 295.

[217] [1987] IR 307.

[218] [1995] 2 IR 238; [1995] 1 ILRM 189.

[219] Compulsory insurance for the self-employed was introduced in 1988 – see the Social Welfare Act 1988, s.11.

[220] Unreported, Supreme Court, 23 May 1995.

[221] [1998] 1 IR 34; [1998] ELR 36.

policy, the payment of DPMA and disability allowance to married claimants and the operation of the overlapping benefits regulations.[222]

Second, there are those cases that were successful in court but where subsequent legislation restored the *status quo ante*. These are the *Hyland*[223] case concerning the entitlement of married claimants to unemployment payments; *The State (McLoughlin) v. Eastern Health Board*[224] concerning entitlement to weekly additions under the supplementary welfare allowance scheme; *Harvey v. Minister for Social Welfare*[225] concerning the operation of the overlapping benefits regulations; *Louth v. Minister for Social Welfare*[226] concerning the welfare entitlements of dockers and, finally, *Lundy v. Minister for Social Welfare*[227] and *O'Sullivan v. Minister for Social Welfare*[228] dealing with aspects of the adjudicative system.

Penultimately, two cases were lost in court but nevertheless contributed to a debate which eventually led to political change which was of benefit to claimants. These are *Kearns v. Minister for Social Welfare*[229] concerning the welfare entitlements of workers affected by industrial action and *Kingham v. Minister for Social Welfare*[230] concerning the welfare entitlements of workers who entered insurance during the 1950s.

Finally there are those cases which were lost in court and which confirmed the *status quo*, such as *Foley v. Moulton*[231] concerning the operation of the cohabitation rule and *Healy v. Minister for Social Welfare*[232] concerning entitlements under the Family Income Supplement scheme.

Thus the effect of litigation on the position of social welfare claimants has varied. In some contexts it has improved access to welfare income and strengthened procedures to the benefit of claimants while in other cases it has confirmed departmental policy and even, on one occasion, (*Hyland*), has resulted in a disimprovement in the entitlements of welfare claimants. Litigation, therefore, is clearly not a foolproof way of protecting the interests of welfare claimants.

It is possible, however, to identify some indicia of probable success. A striking feature of cases successful before the courts is that they are almost invariably based on the court's view that the authorities relied on the wrong legal norm, such as a circular or statutory instrument which was at variance with the parent Act, or legislation which was at variance with an EU norm. Conversely, courts hardly ever

---

[222] Prior to the reform of welfare provision for one parent families, judicial intervention also secured improved welfare entitlements for mothers whose previous marriages had been dissolved by a recognised foreign divorce decree – *The State (Kenny) v. Minister for Social Welfare* [1986] IR 693.

[223] [1989] IR 624; [1990] ILRM 213.

[224] [1986] IR 416.

[225] [1990] 2 IR 232; [1990] ILRM 185.

[226] [1993] 1 IR 339; [1992] ILRM 586.

[227] [1993] 3 IR 406.

[228] Unreported, High Court, 9 May 1995.

[229] Unreported, High Court, 10 February 1982.

[230] Unreported, High Court, 25 November 1985.

[231] [1989] ILRM 169.

[232] [1999] 1 ILRM 72.

reject the authorities' interpretation of welfare policy and will only do so if they can be persuaded that that interpretation is clearly unreasonable.[233]

Of course success in the courts is only part of the story for in order to achieve enduring reform, one has to ensure that legislative policy and administrative practice comes into line with the judicial decision. This is most likely to be achieved where the judicial decision is rooted in a constitutional norm or a norm derived from EU law that cannot easily be amended subsequently by legislative authorities. (In this context, one should also remember that judicial decisions based on the concept of equality can often by neutralised subsequently through the simple expedient of "levelling-down" i.e. by reducing the entitlements of the privileged group to the same level as those of the less-privileged group.) In all other cases, however, a win in the courts is always susceptible to being reversed by subsequent legislation. Looking at the Irish experience, it would seem that where a case identifies an anomaly the correction of which would entail relatively little expenditure, the judicial decision stands some chance of enduring but that in all other cases, the welfare authorities will strive to restore the *status quo ante*.

In conclusion, therefore, public interest litigation is effective in protecting the procedural rights of welfare claimants and occasionally effective in removing anomalies from the system but generally does not improve access to welfare income for disadvantaged individuals or groups in any significant way.

---

[233] See *The State (Kenny) v. Minister for Social Welfare* [1986] IR 693 and *McHugh v. A.B. (Deciding Officer)* [1994] IR 139 in which the courts invalidated provisions of the welfare code on the ground of unreasonableness.

Chapter 5

Litigation and Children's Rights

Introduction

During the 1990s, a growing number of cases came before the Irish courts in which the litigants sought to improve the level of State provision for children. Two distinct categories of children and of State services were involved. The majority of these cases were taken on behalf of homeless children or children from dysfunctional families in need of accommodation and/or education. However the courts were also asked to detail the State's obligation to provide for the education of autistic children and children with other learning disabilities. In both categories, litigation strategy was consciously pursued in an attempt to compel what was perceived as an indifferent political system to devote more resources to these particular marginalised groups.

Homeless children: background to the litigation

During the 1980s and early 1990s, a fairly extensive range of studies into homelessness among young people[1] had been generated and a number of organisations, such as the National Campaign for the Homeless, Streetwise National Coalition and Focus Point, campaigned vigorously around this issue. Notwithstanding such efforts, however, the State failed to make any adequate provision for young homeless children and a number of Government Departments – Justice, Education,

---

[1] See, e.g. National Campaign for the Homeless, *Ireland's Young Homeless* (Dublin, 1985); S. Kennedy, (ed.) *Streetwise – Homelessness among the Young in Ireland and Abroad* (Dublin, 1987); McCarthy and Conlon, *A National Survey on Young People out of home in Ireland* (Streetwise National Coalition, 1988); Focus Point and the Eastern Health Board, *Forgotten Children – Research on Young People who are Homeless in Dublin* (Dublin, 1989); B. Harvey and M. Menton, "Ireland's Young Homeless" *Children and Youth Service Review*, (1989), Vol. 11, p. 31; C. Keane and G. Crowley, *On my own – Report on Youth Homelessness in Limerick City* (Mid-Western Health Board and Limerick Social Services Centre, 1990); E. O'Sullivan and J. Pinkerton, (eds.), *Focus on Children – Blueprint for Action* (Dublin, 1994).

Health and Social Welfare – effectively played pass the parcel with the problem. Then in 1991, the antiquated Children Act 1908 was replaced by the Child Care Act 1991 which, for the first time, made specific legislative provision for homeless children. Section 5 of the Act now provided:

> Where it appears to a health board that a child in its area is homeless, the board shall enquire into the child's circumstances, and if the board is satisfied that there is no accommodation available to him which he can reasonably occupy, then, unless the child is received into the care of the board under the provisions of this Act, the board shall take such steps as are reasonable to make available suitable accommodation for him.

Moreover the 1991 Act extended the definition of "child" to include people up to the age of 18.[2]

However the response of many health boards to this new statutory obligation was less than satisfactory. According to O'Sullivan,

> The majority of the Health Boards did not have an infrastructure in place to allow [them] to meet the new demands of the Act, in particular the influx of a new category of children, the 16-18 year olds, for whom previously they had no responsibility ... Increasingly the boards started to place homeless children in Bed and Breakfast ... accommodation when faced with children [that] the existing hostels could not or would not accommodate.[3]

When traditional lobbying methods by an alliance of organisations working with homeless children failed to stop this practice, a number of individuals came together to form what ultimately became known as the Children's Legal Centre. In the context of this book, one of the more significant objectives of the Centre was "to initiate and pursue legal action on behalf or in association with children and young people to secure their rights under legislation".[4] Their hope now was that such action, invoking the recently enacted Child Care Act 1991, could be used to test the extent of the State's obligations towards homeless children. In addition to the 1991 Act, the Constitution also offered potential support for the claims made by these children against the State. Article 42.5, in particular, provides:

> In exceptional cases, where the parents for physical or moral reasons fail in their duty towards their children, the State as guardian of the common good, by appropriate means shall endeavour to supply the place of the parents, but always with due regard for the natural and imprescriptible rights of the child.

Moreover, by virtue of Article 42.4, the State was obliged to provide for free primary

---

[2] The Children Act 1908 had only covered children up to the age of 16.

[3] "Dimensions of Campaigning for Homeless Children in the Republic of Ireland", paper delivered to the Third International FEANTSA Congress in Madrid, 1995. Health Boards also resorted to the use of hospital beds to accommodate homeless children under the age of 12. According to one magazine, 135 such children were admitted to Temple St Children's Hospital over a two year period beginning in June 1995, between them spending over 3,000 bed nights in wards – see *Magill*, March 1999, p. 39.

[4] See Children's Legal Centre, *Annual Report 1995-6,* p. 2.

education for children while, in common with adults, children have personal rights, both express and implied, which are protected by Article 40.3.

The constitutional powers and obligations of the State in respect of children at risk had initially been considered by the courts in the context of litigation taken by *parents* arising out of *action* by the State in taking their children into care.[5] In the series of cases under consideration here, however, (many of which were supported by the Children's Legal Centre) the courts were now asked to consider the effect of the Child Care Act 1991 and the Constitution in cases taken by *children* arising out of the State's *failure to act*. Understandably, the claims almost invariably focused on the issue of accommodation, though as we shall see, two cases[6] were concerned with the provision of primary education. The State's initial response to this new tactic was to settle each case on an *ad hoc* basis, thereby avoiding the creation of any judicial precedent. Inevitably, however, cases arose in respect of which the State agencies were unable to put suitable arrangements in place and so the State's obligations towards homeless children eventually came under judicial scrutiny.

Two points worth noting emerge from this attempt to use the courts to effect social reform. First, it arguably demonstrates one limitation of litigation strategy, namely, that the judicial response is invariably limited to the specific problem presented by the particular case and has great difficulty in taking on board a broader perspective on the issue. Thus, the children with whom the Children's Law Centre came into contact were those who were in trouble with the law or who were refused places in youth shelters or hostels because of their unruly nature and consequently the cases taken by the Centre inevitably focussed on the needs of this particularly disturbed group of children, rather than on the needs of homeless children generally. Second, the sustained involvement of the courts over a period of years and the State's failure to respond in a meaningful way to the plight of these children during that time has prompted at least one member of the judiciary into a vigorous assertion of judicial power which has important implications for all types of public interest litigation.

Litigation – accommodation

Judicial engagement with the State's policy towards homeless children began in July 1994, when Geoghegan J. handed down his decision in *P.S. v. Eastern Health Board*.[7] This case was taken on behalf of a 14 year old boy in respect of whom it was argued that the Eastern Health Board had failed to promote his welfare as required by s.3 of the Child Care Act[8] and to provide suitable accommodation as required by s.5. The boy in question had lived away from home for many years and had spent some time

---

[5] See cases discussed in Hogan and Whyte (eds.), *Kelly The Irish Constitution* (3rd ed., 1994) at pp. 1043-1050 and Casey, *Constitutional Law in Ireland* (3rd ed., 2000) at pp. 633-8.

[6] See below, pp. 186-8.

[7] Unreported, High Court, 27 July 1994. See Ward, "Homeless Children and the Child Care Act 1991" (1995) *ILT (n.s.)* 19.

[8] Section 3(1) provides that "It shall be a function of every health board to promote the welfare of children in its area who are not receiving adequate care and protection".

sleeping rough on the streets. Eventually the Health Board placed him and another boy in accommodation in Rathmines where they were supervised by a nurse. Evidence before the court indicated that this arrangement exacerbated the applicant's isolation and unfocused lifestyle. According to the senior social worker of the Mater Child Guidance Clinic, the boy needed a placement in a residential setting with secure options to it, an educational programme to respond to his abilities and a consistent therapeutic relationship that might be guaranteed as far as possible over the following four years.

Geoghegan J. concluded that the Health Board had not in breach of s.5 from the moment P.S. was placed in the house in Rathmines and that past breaches of the section by the Board were not the legitimate subject matter of judicial review as the purpose of the section was to ensure that accommodation would be provided, not that compensation could be claimed for a failure to provided accommodation. At the same time, while the house in Rathmines was suitable as emergency or temporary accommodation, the judge held that continued use of the house into the future was not acceptable:

> The stage has now been reached when it can no longer be regarded as reasonable accommodation for the Applicant and there is a statutory duty under section 5 to find a suitable alternative.[9]

In that regard, however, the judge identified an important *lacuna* in the 1991 Act – it made no provision for statutory powers of detention.[10] So the Board's statutory obligations extended to doing everything that was necessary, short of detention. While s.5 dealt only with accommodation and not with other aspects of care such as substitute parental training or education, those factors could not be discounted in determining whether accommodation was suitable. In any event, once the child was in the care of the Health Board, as here, s.3(2)(b)(i) required the Board to have regard to the welfare of the child as the first and paramount consideration and "this means that it must do everything in its power, but within the limitations ... already identified, to give a satisfactory upbringing to the child".[11] In the instant case, the court confined itself to granting a declaration that the accommodation in Rathmines was no longer suitable having regard to the Board's statutory responsibilities under both ss.3 and 5 of the 1991 Act and the case was adjourned so that proper plans could be drawn up to meet the applicant's needs. Geoghegan J. did go on to state that the Board should not permit two boys who are a bad influence on each other to be under the same roof. He had earlier offered the view that the Board's facilities should include closely supervised residential care involving a number of children together, with good sporting and educational facilities and possibly back-up psychiatric facilities, and that there should be a strict policy of immediate prosecution of boys committing criminal offences.

---

[9] At p. 7 of his judgment.

[10] Geoghegan J. commented, *obiter*, that legislation providing for such powers of detention would not necessarily be unconstitutional – p. 10 of his judgment.

[11] *Ibid.*, p. 16.

While *P.S.* was concerned solely with the statutory obligations of the Health Boards towards children at risk, it did indicate that the Eastern Health Board practice failed to discharge even those obligations. At the same time, Geoghegan J. took a very restrained position on the matter of remedies, confining himself to the granting of a declaration and ruling out the possibility of an award of damages for breach of s.5 of the 1991 Act. By adjourning the case, the judge passed responsibility for fashioning the ultimate solution to P.S.'s situation back to the bureaucrats. Thus the court operated in a negative manner only, striking down existing arrangements and requiring the Board to confront the boy's situation once more.

In *F.N. v. Minister for Education*[12] the constitutional obligations of the State towards homeless children were addressed by the Court – Geoghegan J. once again – for the first time. F.N. had been in care since he was five months old. His mother was now dead and his father was unknown. He had lived with foster parents until he was eleven when he was placed in a residential home. This placement was unsuccessful and he was then placed in an assessment centre for one month before being accommodated in a hostel for homeless boys in Tallaght. Evidence from a consultant psychiatrist indicated that F.N. suffered from hyperkinetic conduct disorder and that he required a period of time in a secure unit which could contain him safely while confronting his behaviour.

The pertinent provisions of the Child Care Act 1991 not having been brought into effect at that time, the case was governed by the antiquated provisions of the Children Act 1908. Accordingly, the only statutory remedy available to the court was to send F.N. to an industrial school pursuant to s.58(4) of the 1908 Act. However there were only two such schools in the country at that time and by virtue of s.62(1) of the Act a child could only be sent to such a school if the school manager was willing to receive him or her. In the instant case, both managers refused to accept F.N. and so effectively there was no remedy available under s.58(4). A place was available for the applicant in a Health Board institution for housing more difficult children and the court was satisfied with this as a temporary solution only. However Geoghegan J. rejected the State's argument that it had no constitutional obligation to provide services beyond what was then provided so as to cater for the special needs of the applicant. He held that, in the light of the principles enunciated in *G. v. An Bord Uchtála,*[13] *In re Article 26 and the Adoption (No.2) Bill 1987,*[14] and *M.F. v. Superintendent Ballymun Garda Station,*[15] where there was a child with very special needs which could not be provided by the parents or guardian, there was a constitutional obligation on the State pursuant to Article 42.5 to cater for those needs in order to vindicate the constitutional rights of the child. While he was prepared to accept that the State's duties in this regard were not absolute, the limits of the State's obligations had not been reached in the instant case.

---

12 [1995] 1 IR 409; [1995] 2 ILRM 297.
13 [1980] IR 32.
14 [1989] IR 656; [1989] ILRM 266.
15 [1991] 1 IR 189; [1990] ILRM 767.

[I]t would seem to me that on the balance of probabilities the provision of such necessary accommodation, arrangements and services by the State as might meet the necessary requirements of this Applicant is not so impractical or so prohibitively expensive as would come within any notional limit on the State's constitutional obligations. There may be differences of opinion among the experts as to the level of staffing arrangements which would be required, even on a temporary basis, for the proper care of F.N., but I am not convinced at present that even the more extreme view taken by Doctor Byrne as to staff ratio is prohibitively expensive ... I would have thought that in considering questions of expense and practicality, the State would have regard not merely to the immediate cost but to a possible long term saving of cost if the special treatment of recalcitrant children led in the long term to a reduction of crime and drug abuse. But these are obviously to some extent areas of policy. I advert to them merely to indicate why it is not self-evident to me that the more elaborate requirements suggested by Doctor Byrne fall outside the ambit of any constitutional duty owed by the State.

In summary I take the view that the State is under a constitutional obligation towards the Applicant to establish as soon as reasonably practicable, either by use of Section 58(4) of the 1908 Act or otherwise, suitable arrangements of containment with treatment for the Applicant.[16]

Accepting the temporary solution offered by the Health Board, the judge did not make any immediate declaration or order in the case but rather ordered that the case should stand adjourned.

F.N. is an important case inasmuch as it contains the first judicial statement of the principle that failure on the part of the State to provide for the needs of vulnerable children may constitute a breach of the State's constitutional obligations under Article 42.5. However once more the judge passed responsibility for devising the ultimate solution to F.N.'s situation back to the administrative authorities, rather than taking a more active role in the matter.

On the same day that he delivered his decision in *F.N.*, Geoghegan J. also handed down a judgment in the case of *D.T. v. Eastern Health Board*.[17] Here he had to consider the plight of a 12 year old girl with suicidal tendencies and of such unruly disposition that it was accepted that she needed to be cared for in some kind of suitable confinement. However, as he had just pointed out in *F.N.*, the Child Care Act 1991 did not contain any powers of civil detention. Nor was there any remedy under s.58(4) of the Children Act 1908 as there was no longer any certified industrial school for girls. In these circumstances, the court had to fall back on the Constitution.

I am satisfied for the reasons which I indicated in the N. case that the State owes a constitutional duty to the Applicant, D.T., to cater for her needs. But the situation in her case was so extreme that I acceded to a Health Board request that I make an Order authorising the Garda Síochána to take her into detention and bring her to Oberstown House where she could be kept in confinement and receive suitable care. I took the view

---

16 [1995] 1 IR 409 at p. 416; [1995] 2 ILRM 297 at p. 303.
17 Unreported, High Court, 24 March 1995.

that the problem was so extreme that even though there was no express statutory power enabling me to make that interim Order, I was satisfied, having regard to the principles enunciated in Mr Justice O'Flaherty's judgment in the Supreme Court in *M.F. v. Superintendent Ballymun Garda Station*, [1991] 1 IR 189 at 205, that since such an Order was necessary to vindicate the constitutional rights of the child, the Constitution empowered me to make it. Oberstown House is essentially an assessment centre and there can be no question of her being allowed to remain there for any length of time. However the Director of Oberstown House has agreed to retain her until 10 April 1995. After that date there will be a place for her in Glen House. I may have to consider whether I should make a further Confinement Order in relation to her care in Glen House but I am reluctant to do so at present ... [I]t would only be in extreme circumstances that a Court would consider making a Confinement Order pursuant to the Constitution in circumstances where there was no express statutory power to do so. As in the case of F.N., I will give the State a reasonable opportunity to provide suitable arrangements for the upbringing of D.T. as far as practicable. This is a case where conceivably all potential schemes might fail and the question of limits on the constitutional duty might arise. But that stage has not been reached yet. I will make no declaration or order for the time being but will adjourn the case.[18]

This was the first occasion on which the Constitution was used to authorise protective detention. Given the constitutional base of this power – that it is a remedy for vindicating the constitutional rights of the child – and in the absence at that time of any statutory alternative, the courts inevitably had to be involved in the process of determining whether protective detention was appropriate in any given case. However, once again, Geoghegan J. indicated that the State's duty in this context is not absolute and, once again, by adjourning the case he deferred to the Health Board on the issue of determining what arrangements should ultimately be put in place.

A similar approach was adopted by Costello J. (as he then was) in *D.D. v. Eastern Health Board*.[19] This case concerned an 11 year old boy, D.D., who was in urgent need of special care. Proceedings were taken on his behalf seeking an interlocutory injunction directing the respondents to provide him with care, accommodation and education pending an application for judicial review. On this occasion, the State accepted that, in the light of *F.N.*, it was in breach of its constitutional duty to D.D. to make suitable arrangements to meet his special needs. Evidence before the court indicated that D.D. needed to be kept in a "containing centre" for two years. However the Eastern Health Board had no such secure facility and the only other option available was to place him in Oberstown House which included a reformatory school and a remand centre. However in the opinion of the Director of Oberstown House, that centre was unsuitable because it normally accommodated older boys who stayed for a short time while awaiting sentence, often in respect of serious offences.

The court was informed that proposals had been agreed between the Health Board and the Department of Health for the provision of Special Care Units and that pending

[18] *Ibid.*, at pp. 2-3.
[19] Unreported, High Court, 3 May 1995.

the implementation of these proposals, the Board intended to apply to the Minister to have premises called "Trudder House" approved as a reformatory for purposes of s.58(4) of the Children Act 1908. The issue before the court was what order it could make pending the creation of an approved unit at Trudder House. Costello J. was quite satified that the court could confer legal authority on the Board to detain D.D. in a secure unit but this did not solve the practical problems arising from his behaviour. The judge was reluctant to order D.D.'s detention in the remand centre at Oberstown House because he was not satisfied that that regime was suitable for D.D. and he also accepted that detention there would pose a risk to his moral and physical welfare because of his age. Moreover if the court ordered D.D.'s detention in the remand centre, this would reduce the places available to those children Oberstown was designed to assist. Consequently Costello J. confined himself to ordering that the Health Board should care for and accommodate D.D. in a unit or institution managed by it and under a regime established in accordance with psychiatric or other medical advice until further order; that it should provide suitable education and therapeutic care for him and that it might fulfil its obligations by arranging for the boy's accommodation in a unit or institution managed by another agency or organisation.

D.D. implicitly confirmed Geoghegan J.'s view in *D.T.* that the courts had a constitutional power to order the protective detention of children at risk but once again the problem was sent back to the administrative authorities for resolution of the finer details.[20]

The plight of these children at risk eventually came before the Supreme Court in the case of *D.G. v. Eastern Health Board*[21] in which a majority of the court upheld the decision of Kelly J. in the High Court ordering the temporary protective detention of a teenager with a personality disorder in St Patrick's Institution for young offenders.

In the High Court, Mr Justice Kelly had concluded that the youth was not mentally ill; that he had a serious personality disorder; that he was a danger to both himself and to others; that he had a history of criminal activity and violence, including arson; that he had, in the past, absconded from non-secure institutions and that he had failed to cooperate with Health Board officials. The youth had been residing with Fr Peter McVerry at Ballymun but following an assault by another resident of this hostel, the youth had been hospitalised for a week before being sent by the High Court to Kilnacrot Abbey in June 1997. The authorities at the Abbey indicated to the Court that they could not accommodate the youth after 7 July due to lack of space and against that background, the case came back to the High Court once more. It was agreed by the parties to the case that the High Court had only four options. These were to do nothing; to direct the Kilnacrot authorities to keep the youth; to order that he be detained in the Central Mental Hospital or to order his detention in St Patrick's Institution. After reviewing the situation, Mr Justice Kelly ordered that the youth be detained in St Patrick's Institution for a period of three weeks until his case could be

---

[20] It would appear that in the aftermath of *F.N.* and *D.D.*, two secure units were opened by the Eastern Health Board but these quickly filled up and so litigation in relation to other children continued.

[21] [1997] 3 IR 511; [1998] 1 ILRM 241.

reviewed again. During that time the youth was to be subject to the normal discipline of the prison, though visiting restrictions were to be dispensed with so far as was possible consonant with the good running of the prison in order to allow Health Board officials access to the youth. In addition, he was to have a full psychiatric assessment made on him by the psychiatric staff in the clinic attached to the prison.

Counsel for the youth appealed unsuccessfully against that decision to the Supreme Court. The jurisdiction of the High Court to order the protective detention, in appropriate circumstances, of children in civil institutions was conceded by counsel for the appellant and assumed for the purposes of the case by the Supreme Court. Consequently an authoritative decision of that Court on the existence of this jurisdication is still awaited.[22] But on the assumption that it exists, a majority of the Court, (Denham J. dissenting[23]), held that the jurisdiction extended to ordering protective detention in a penal institution. According to Hamilton C.J., with whom O'Flaherty and Keane JJ. agreed, the constitutional rights of the applicant involved his right to liberty and his rights, as enunciated by O'Higgins C.J. in *G. v. An Bord Uchtála*,[24] "to be fed and to live, to be reared and educated, to have the opportunity of working and of realising his or her full personality and dignity as a human being." In the instant case, there was clearly a conflict between the applicant's right to liberty and the order, made in the interests of his welfare, authorising his detention in St Patrick's Institution. However there was ample evidence to support the trial judge's decision to give precedence to the applicant's welfare over his liberty. At the same time, the Chief Justice cautioned that such a jurisdiction

> should be exercised only in extreme and rare occasions, when the court is satisfied that it is required for a short period in the interests of the welfare of the child and there is, at the time, no other suitable facility.[25]

He went on to state that this decision did not relieve the Health Board of its statutory obligations in regard to the youth and that it should continue its efforts to make suitable alternative arrangements for him.

D.G. vividly illustrated the bankruptcy of State policy towards homeless children inasmuch as the penal system, itself subject to overcrowding, had to be pressed in aid,

---

[22] Insofar as such a jurisdiction might be derived from the High Court's obligation to vindicate the constitutional rights of the individual, it might also, one presumes, be exercisable in relation to certain categories of adult. Such a development would certainly represent a significant extension of the court's traditionally narrow jurisdiction to order that a person be detained for his or her own protection, on which, see Kelly, at p. 870.

[23] Denham J. pointed out that the case raised the question of whether the High Court has an inherent jurisdiction to detain a child in a *penal* institution when that child has neither been convicted of an offence nor charged with an offence, not whether the High Court has an inherent jurisdiction to order the detention of children in child care institutions to protect their welfare. She held that detention in a penal institution infringed his right to liberty, to moral welfare, to equality, to person and good name, to bodily integrity and to social welfare and so could not be authorised by the court in the instant case.

[24] [1980] IR 32 at p. 56.

[25] [1997] 3 IR 511 at p. 524; [1998] 1 ILRM 241 at p. 251.

albeit temporarily, in order to provide accommodation for a child at risk.[26] Nor was this the only case in which the penal system was used for such a purpose for on at least three other occasions, troubled teenagers were held in St Patrick's Institution because of the absence of any other suitable accommodation.[27] Faced with having to take such extreme measures because of the State's failure to act, Kelly J. eventually took dramatic action in order to resolve the situation, as we shall see presently. However before considering this development, it is necessary to consider two remaining cases taken on behalf of children at risk in which the focus of the claim was on the educational needs of the children, rather than on the issue of accommodation.

Litigation – education

The first of these, *G.L. v. Minister for Justice,*[28] was decided on the same day as *F.N.* and *D.T.* and concerned a very disturbed thirteen year old with a criminal conviction who urgently needed residential care with suitable education in a structured environment. In this case accommodation was available but what was at issue was whether such accommodation was suitable, having regard to the needs of the applicant, in particular, his constitutional right to be educated. Notwithstanding the views of certain witnesses, the evidence established that the applicant had been getting on well in Trinity House, a reformatory for boys who were generally much older than him. Geoghegan J. suspended judgment as to whether the applicant needed a more long term placement in a residential setting with a high staff to child ratio, as recommended by a consultant child psychiatrist. On the question of his right to be educated, the judge accepted the views of O'Hanlon J. in *O'Donoghue v. Minister for Health,*[29] outlining the extent of the constitutional duties of the State in relation to elementary education.

> [T]hat being so, I could not accept that on the basis of the principle which was applied in *The State (O) v. Frawley* [1976] IR 365, there is no constitutional obligation to meet the educational requirements of this child. I am satisfied that there is and I am equally satisfied that the Applicant has made out a prima facie case that the State is not in a position to meet his educational requirements at present but having regard to the genuine efforts which the State is making to meet those requirements within the facilities available, I am ... prepared to suspend judgment for the time being and I am therefore postponing the question of whether I will make any declaratory or other relief.[30]

---

26 The European Court of Human Rights subsequently declared a complaint lodged by D.G. under the European Convention on Human Rights to be admissible – see *D.G. v. Ireland,* Application 39474/98, decision of the Court, 9 November 2000. The youth in question was subsequently detained in a psychiatric unit and in November 2000, the High Court ordered that he be moved into a structured community setting – *The Irish Times*, 2 November 2000.

27 See *The Irish Times*, 11 May 1999, 16 October 1999, 20 January 2001 and 31 January 2001.

28 Unreported, High Court, 24 March 1995.

29 [1996] 2 IR 20. See further below, pp. 199-204.

30 Unreported, High Court, 24 March 1995, at p. 4 of his judgement.

Once again Geoghegan J. was content to establish that the applicant had constitutional rights – on this occasion a right to education – which were not being vindicated by the State and then to leave it to the authorities to work out the precise detail of how to remedy the situation.

The second case, *Comerford v. Minister for Education*,[31] concerned an eleven year old boy from a dysfunctional family which had broken up. All of the children of this family were in care and this particular child was out of control and disruptive in school. He was diagnosed as suffering from attention deficit disorder when he was 10 years old and the consultant psychiatrist recommended, *inter alia*, that he be placed in a very small classroom with a high teacher/pupil ratio. At the time of the hearing, he had been allocated a long term care placement in Goldenbridge, a residential home under the aegis of the Health Board so that what was at issue in the case, therefore, was not accommodation but rather how the applicant's right to primary education could be vindicated.

McGuinness J. began by citing with approval the remarks of O'Higgins C.J. in *G. v. An Bord Uchtála*[32] about the constitutional rights of children and also his remarks in *Crowley v. Ireland*[33] about the State's duty to provide for free primary education. She also endorsed the views of O'Hanlon and Geoghegan JJ. in *O'Donoghue v. Minister for Health*[34] and *F.N. v. Minister for Education*[35] respectively on the State's obligation to provide for free basic elementary education for all children. In the instant case, however, she accepted that health boards have no specific statutory duty either to provide education or to provide for education and therefore concluded that the Eastern Health Board, a notice party to the proceedings, had fully carried out its constitutional duty to the applicant under Article 42.5 by providing him with a long term secure placement in Goldenbridge.

Turning to the position of the Minister for Education and the State, she noted that cases of this kind had considerable funding implications for the State and, invoking the doctrine of the separation of powers, she declined the invitation from counsel for the Health Board to deal with the issue of limitation of expenditure in these cases, or the balancing of expenditure as between different priorities by the organs of the State.

> In principle I consider that for the Court to embark upon such an exercise would be a wrongful trespass by the Court into the prerogative of the Executive power. It is for the Executive to make its own decisions in regard to the raising of finance and the prioritising of expenditure.[36]

However, while she was conscious of the difficult budgetary implications of these cases, this did not preclude her from clarifying the applicant's constitutional rights.

---

[31] [1997] 2 ILRM 134.
[32] [1980] IR 32.
[33] [1980] IR 102.
[34] [1996] 2 IR 20.
[35] [1995] 1 IR 409; [1995] 2 ILRM 297. This presumably should have been a reference to *G.L. v. Minister for Justice*, unreported, High Court, 24 March 1995.
[36] [1997] 2 ILRM 134 at p. 146.

On the facts of this case, McGuinness J. concluded that the educational deprivation of the applicant was due to the actions of his parents as well as to any default on the part of the respondents. However once he had been diagnosed as suffering from attention deficit disorder, the respondents had failed in their constitutional duty to provide for a suitable primary education for him because of their failure to fulfil the psychiatrist's recommendations in that regard. In common with all of the other cases in this area, the judge restricted relief to the granting of a declaration "in the expectation that the institutions of the State will respond by taking the appropriate actions to vindicate the constitutional rights of the applicant".[37]

Pausing to take stock of the situation which had developed by 1998, a number of points emerge. First, during the preceding four years, various High Court judges had made it clear that the State was failing to vindicate the statutory and constitutional rights of a group of vulnerable children. Second, most of the cases coming before the courts during this time concerned children with very serious problems in respect of which the provision of secure accommodation had been identified as an important element in any care regime. Responding to these particular cases, the High Court had established that, in appropriate cases, judges could order the protective detention of such children in order to vindicate their constitutional rights. Third, a characteristic of cases decided during this period was the reluctance of the courts to get involved in determining the detail of the solutions required. Instead the courts preferred to grant declarations and/or to adjourn cases with liberty to re-enter so as to afford the administrators an opportunity to fashion an appropriate response to each case. However the State singularly failed to tackle this issue, thereby provoking one judge, Kelly J.,[38] into taking strong action against the executive branch of government.

Judicial response to executive inertia – developing affirmative judicial decrees and threatening the executive with contempt of court.

In three landmark judgments since July 1998, Kelly J. has taken public interest litigation in this area to its logical conclusion by detailing the steps required of the authorities and by threatening them with contempt of court for failure to comply with court rulings.

In *D.B. v. Minister for Justice*[39] he was asked by the applicant to order the defendant Minister to do all things necessary to facilitate the building, opening and maintenance of a high support unit for troubled children in care in Dublin. The applicant in this

---

[37] [1997] 2 ILRM 134 at pp. 147-8.

[38] Mr Justice Peter Kelly had been involved in a number of these cases since his appointment to the bench in April 1996. As we have already noted, he was the High Court judge in *D.G. v. Eastern Health Board*, [1997] 3 IR 511; [1998] 1 ILRM 241, and 10 days before he handed down his decision in *D.B.*, he reluctantly ordered that a 15 year old drug addict who was "very vulnerable" and "out of control" be sent home because there was no suitable State facility to which he could be sent – *The Irish Times*, 18 July 1998.

[39] [1999] 1 IR 29; [1999] 1 ILRM 93. See Ruane, "The Separation of Powers – Grant of Mandatory Orders to enforce Constitutional Rights" (2000) 5 *Bar Review* 416.

case had already succeeded in having the court exercise its original jurisdiction by giving directions as to his custody, care and control by the Eastern Health Board but now sought an order directing the Minister for Health to provide sufficient funding to allow the Board to build, open and maintain a 24 bed high support unit. He also sought an order compelling the Minister to do all things necessary to facilitate the building, opening and maintenance of that unit.

Reviewing the adequacy of the State's response to the situation of these children, Kelly J. pointed out that, after one year on the bench, he had become so concerned at the lack of progress being made in cases of this nature that in April 1997 he directed a hearing take place so that he might be acquainted with developments. At this hearing, it emerged that proposals for the provision of residential places for young offenders and children in care outlined to Geoghegan J. in the immediate aftermath of *F.N.* in March 1995 had been substantially departed from without the court ever being told. Evidence also emerged of unseemly and wasteful wrangles going on for months between various departments as to who would have responsibility for the care of the children in question and apart from the provision of eighteen places in Newtown House and Killinarden, it would appear that no further practical results had been achieved since the decision of Geoghegan J. in *F.N.*

Against that background, counsel for the applicant asked the Court to enforce the constitutional rights of the applicant, pointing out that these rights were limited by time as they could be enjoyed by a citizen only whilst a minor. In the instant case, the breach had gone on for three years and four months and the effect of the breach was one which, as a matter of high probability, would affect the applicants into their future life, possibly having fatal consequences for some of them,[40] given their suicidal tendencies. On the basis that damages could not be an effective relief in this type of case, the judge was invited to grant injunctive relief directing the Minister to provide the facilities required. In response, the State relied on the doctrine of separation of powers, arguing that the granting of such relief would involve the court in matters of policy.

Citing remarks of Hamilton C.J. in *D.G. v. Eastern Health Board*,[41] Kelly J. said that the court's jurisdiction in such cases stems from its obligation to vindicate and defend constitutional rights and that the court must have available to it any power necessary to defend and vindicate such rights in an effective way, regardless of the status of the respondent. He rejected the argument that the court did not have jurisdiction to interfere with the administrative branch of government, citing the view of Finlay C.J. in *Crotty v. An Taoiseach*[42] that the court had a right and duty to interfere with the activities of the executive in order to protect or secure the constitutional rights of individual litigants where such rights have been or are being invaded, or are

---

[40] This argument proved to be tragically prophetic in the case of at least one child who managed to escape from a residential institution and who died from a suspected drugs overdose three weeks later in a Dublin city bed and breakfast – *The Irish Times*, 25 August 2000. On 27 February 2001, Kelly J. commenced an unprecedented High Court inquiry into the circumstances surrounding her death.

[41] [1997] 3 IR 511; [1998] 1 ILRM 241.

[42] [1987] IR 713; [1987] ILRM 400.

threatened with invasion, by those activities.[43] At the same time, he accepted that this jurisdiction was not to be exercised lightly because of the doctrine of separation of powers and the respect which each branch of government should have for the other.[44] However here the State's obligations had been clarified well over three years previously and were not going to be addressed for at least another two and a half years at the earliest.

In a significant *obiter*, Kelly J. also stated that he was unconvinced by the argument that the court was not entitled to become involved in matters of policy, arguing that,

> If such an intervention were required in order for this Court to carry out its duties under the Constitution in securing, vindicating and enforcing constitutional rights then, in my view, it would be open to it to so do.[45]

In the instant case, however, he did not have to decide this point as he did not consider that any order he might make would involve the court in questions of policy, subsequently offering the view that the order he proposed to make "will merely ensure that the Minister who has already decided on the policy lives up to his word and carries it into effect".[46]

In deciding, in the instant case, to grant relief to the applicant, Kelly J. took account of the following factors. First, the High Court had already granted declaratory relief concerning the obligations of the State in cases of this type and in so doing had shown due respect to the administrative branch of Government by going no further than the making a declaration, "thereby affording an opportunity to the Minister to take the necessary steps to put matters right. But it expected those steps to be taken as soon as reasonably practicable."[47] Second, given that the rights in question were those of minors, if the declaration was to be of any benefit, the necessary action had to be taken expeditiously, before the children involved reached the age of majority. Third, the effect of a failure to take appropriate action had a profound effect on the lives of these children and certainly put them at risk of harm up "to and including the loss of their very lives".[48] Finally, the judge had due regard to the efforts made on the part of the Minister to address the difficulties to date. Nonetheless he concluded:

> It is no exaggeration to characterise what has gone on as a scandal. I have had evidence of inter-departmental wrangles over demarcation lines going on for months, seemingly endless delays in drafting and redrafting legislation, policy that appears to be made only

---

[43] A potentially significant difference between *Crotty* and *D.B.* is that the former case concerned executive action – the purported ratification of the Single European Act – whereas *D.B.* arose out of executive *inaction* in relation to the plight of homeless children in need of secure accommodation. Kelly J. did not address this point. However see above, ch. 1 at pp. 17 *et seq.*

[44] He cited as a good example of this restraint the Supreme Court decision in *McMenamin v. Ireland* [1996] 3 IR 100; [1997] 2 ILRM 177.

[45] [1999] 1 IR 29 at p. 42; [1999] 1 ILRM 93 at p. 103. See also his comment to the same effect in *T.D. v. Minister for Education* [2000] 3 IR 62, at p. 83; [2000] 2 ILRM 321 at p. 341.

[46] [1999] 1 IR 29 at p. 45; [1999] 1 ILRM 93 at p. 105.

[47] [1999] 1 IR 29 at p. 42; [1999] 1 ILRM 93 at p. 103.

[48] [1999] 1 IR 29 at p. 43; [1999] 1 ILRM 93 at p. 104.

to be reversed and a waste of public resources on, for example, going through an entire planning process for the Portrane development only for the Minister to change his mind, thereby necessitating the whole process being gone through again.

The addressing of the rights of the young people that I have to deal with appears to be bogged down in a bureaucratic and administrative quagmire.[49]

Kelly J. had invited the State to furnish an undertaking to the court that certain facilities would be completed and put into operation within a time specified by the Minister's officials but no such undertaking was provided. Accordingly, the judge decided that

the time has now come for this Court to take the next step required of it under the Constitution so as to ensure that the rights of troubled minors who require placement of the type envisaged are met.[50]

Therefore he granted an order directing the Minister to provide resources and to take all steps necessary to ensure a 24-bed high support unit for troubled children would be built and opened at Portrane within 3 years, commenting that

I am not dictating or even entering into questions of policy. The Order that I propose making will merely ensure that the Minister who has already decided on the policy lives up to his word and carries it into effect.[51]

One of the significant implications of this order was that, as Kelly J. himself made clear, it paved the way for closer judicial supervision of executive action in this area in the future.

The granting of this injunction means that the Minister is no longer at large concerning the approach to be adopted to solving this problem. The developments proposed will now have to be completed and within the time-scale specified. If there is to be any future change of policy or if the times indicated cannot be met, application will have to be made to this Court on the part of the Minister for a variation of the injunction. This will mean that not merely will the Court have to be informed of all of these developments ... but objectively justifiable reasons will have to be furnished to it as to why the injunction should be varied ... This will afford to the Court an opportunity of much greater involvement than it has been possible to have in the past. It will mean for these minors that the Court, having declared their entitlements, will now see to their implementation in a direct way.[52]

He continued:

It is regrettable that this course has to be adopted. I am, however, satisfied that the court could not keep faith, either with its own obligations under the Constitution or with the minors with whose welfare it is concerned, unless intervention is made now.

---

[49] [1999] 1 IR 29 at pp. 43-4; [1999] 1 ILRM 93 at p. 104.
[50] [1999] 1 IR 29 at p. 44; [1999] 1 ILRM 93 at p. 105.
[51] [1999] 1 IR 29 at p. 45; [1999] 1 ILRM 93 at p. 105. The State did not appeal against Kelly J.'s decision.
[52] [1999] 1 IR 29 at p. 45; [1999] 1 ILRM 93 at pp. 105-6.

In the first quarter of 1999, the Department of Health and Children produced new proposals for meeting the needs of these vulnerable children, winning praise from Kelly J. for its efforts at a High Court hearing on 14 April 1999.[53] It now proposed to create an additional 120 high support places by the end of 2000, bringing the total of such places in the State to approximately 170. In addition, a new Social Services Inspectorate was established to inspect all health board residential care and to consider the appropriateness of individual placements.[54] By December 1999, however, the timetable for the provision of these units had fallen behind schedule, leading to renewed criticism from Kelly J.[55] In a second landmark judgment, *T.D. v. Minister for Education*,[56] he catalogued various delays in providing appropriate facilities in different locations throughout the country, pointing out that some of the delay related to matters wholly within the control of the relevant State authorities.[57] This application was taken by a number of children in the Eastern Health Board area, seeking a series of injunctions directing the Minister to provide specified secure and high support units in a number of prescribed locations and by a specified time. The number of units, their location and the date by which they were to be provided had previously been specified in court by officials from the Department so that the application merely sought to compel the Minister to comply with the latest plans his Department had put before the court.

After reviewing the evidence, Kelly J. concluded that the Department had not made the progress that could reasonably be expected of it, pointing out that none of the timescales previously given in court could now be met and that delay in many cases was the result of manifest inefficiency. He then turned to consider various defences raised by the Minister. The first of these was that the injunctions sought

---

[53] See *The Irish Times*, 15 April 1999.

[54] The State also attempted to supply a legislative basis for the power of protective detention of vulnerable children in Part IX of the Children Bill 1996 but that Bill lapsed with the change of government in 1997. Proposals for the protective detention of children are now contained in Part 3 of the Children Act 2001. The provision of a legislative basis for this power is important as some doubts had been raised about the jurisdiction of the lower courts to order protective detention of children – see G. Durcan, "Secure Accommodation in the Child Care System: The Legal Background" in *Secure Accommodation in Child Care* (Children's Legal Centre, 1997) at p. 9, in which he argued that the High Court was unlikely to accept that the obligation on every court to uphold the constitutional rights of an individual was sufficient to give a court of local and limited jurisdiction the power to order the detention of a person. On the other hand, it could be argued that if the constitutional obligations of such courts are insufficient to ground such a power, it is difficult to see how legislation could improve the situation as such legislation would then, presumably, be unconstitutional.

[55] See *The Irish Times*, 17 and 22 December 1999 and 20 January 2000. The Health Boards have also experienced difficulty in recruiting staff for these special care units and in November 1999, only 80 candidates, some with very basic qualifications, applied for 50 vacancies in the proposed centre at Ballydowd, forcing the Eastern Regional Health Authority to readvertise the posts – see *The Irish Times*, 17 April 2000, 9 June 2000, 11 October 2000 and 20 December 2000.

[56] [2000] 3 IR 62; [2000] 2 ILRM 321.

[57] In particular, a delay in converting a former army barracks into high support units was due partly to what Kelly J. described as "Gilbertian" bureaucratic haggling between various government departments and to a failure to apply for planning permission.

were insufficiently specific. Kelly J. rejected this argument on the grounds that the injunctions merely required the State to carry out what it had already agreed would be done so that there could not be any difficulty on the part of the Minister knowing precisely what was required of him and that a similar injunction had been granted in *D.B.*[58] The State also challenged the *locus standi* of the applicants to seek the relief sought on the ground that no direct benefit would accrue to them, apparently on the basis that the injunctions sought the provision of facilities on a nationwide basis, rather than in respect of individual cases. However the testimony of a divisional inspector from the Department indicated, *inter alia*, that all of the plaintiffs would be expected to avail of the facilities in respect of which the injunctions were sought and that some of them had suffered damage by virtue of the unavailability of appropriate facilities. Accordingly, the judge concluded that they had sufficient *locus standi* to maintain the action. Finally it was argued that the court was precluded from granting the injunctions sought by virtue of the doctrine of separation of powers, as the granting of the injunctions would involve the court in the determination of policy. Not surprisingly, this argument fared no better before Kelly J. in this case than it had in *D.B.*, the judge essentially re-iterating his reasoning in the earlier case on the point.

In deciding to grant the injunctions sought, the judge noted that, with only one exception, the State had failed to abide by its own timetable for the provision of appropriate facilities, that exception being the facilities which were the subject of the order in *D.B.*[59] Moreover the delay was not always due to matters outside the control of the State or its agencies and this fact, coupled with the refusal of the Minister to give an undertaking to the court that the facilities would be provided on time, led Kelly J. to conclude that it was now time for the courts to intervene to ensure that the rights of the children in question were protected. Accordingly he granted injunctions requiring the Minister to complete the proposed developments within the time-scales specified in evidence before the court. He concluded:

> It is a matter of considerable regret that I am forced to take this step, particularly in the light of the history of all this litigation over the last number of years. However, I cannot, for the reasons stated, resile from enforcing the rights of these children in need in the manner sought. To refuse to do so would be to continue to allow their entitlements to be subjected to a real risk of even more delay by the administrative branch of Government. I cannot and will not permit that to happen. Even as things stand, it will be fully seven years since the decision in *F.N.* before these facilities are in operation. These children and others like them are at an important stage in their development. Much can be done for them. Their future lives as adults can be influenced for good but only if the appropriate

---

[58] [1999] 1 IR 29; [1999] 1 ILRM 93.

[59] However even here it subsequently emerged that one of these facilities would not be fully operational on time. The use of defective glass and easily replicated locks, together with staffing difficulties, meant that there were only two children in the 24-bed unit in October 2000 and it was estimated that there would only be eight beds available by Christmas 2000 – see *The Irish Times*, 11 October 2000.

facilities are available. They have a right to them. They ought to have been provided long before now. It is a scandal that they have not. A great deal of time has been lost. This Court can allow no more. The injunctions sought are granted.[60]

Meanwhile, the courts continued to be confronted by dozens of cases of which the following, culled from media reports, are just a representative sample. In May 1999, the only options available to Kelly J. in relation to a vulnerable 15 year old boy were detention in St Patrick's Institution or the Central Mental Hospital until an overcrowded remand centre agreed to take him.[61] Two months later, a 12 year old troubled and mildly mentally handicapped child who was having violent sexual fantasies about women had to remain at a State remand centre as there was nowhere else for him to go.[62] The following month the High Court ordered that a 14 year old homeless boy who was said to be out of control should be arrested and placed in a secure educational institution[63] and in December 1999, a troubled 14 year old girl was sent to a State detention centre in the absence of a suitable treatment facility.[64] In March 2000, Kelly J. felt compelled to detain in the Central Mental Hospital an extremely disturbed 17 year old teenager who was not mentally ill but who was a serious risk to herself and others and in the course of his judgment, he criticised the Oireachtas for failing to enact the Children Bill 1999.[65] Two months later, the same judge had to order the detention of a disturbed 15 year old girl in a remand centre along with convicted offenders,[66] the detention of a 16 year old girl traumatised by sex abuse in a locked adult psychiatric unit[67] and the detention of a 14 year old girl in the adult psychiatric ward of a general hospital.[68] In *D.H. v. Ireland*,[69] he refused to order the detention of the aforementioned sixteen year old teenager in the Central Mental Hospital because of the opposition, on medical, ethical and moral grounds, of a psychiatrist to this course of action and also because that facility was full. He also refused to issue a

---

[60] [2000] 3 IR 62 at p. 85; [2000] 2 ILRM 321 at p. 343. The State has since lodged an appeal to the Supreme Court against this decision, a move subsequently characterised by Kelly J. as "a colossal waste of taxpayers' money", adding that the money involved would be better spent on providing the facilities required – *The Irish Times*, 28 July 2000. See further, pp. 357 *et seq.*

[61] See *The Irish Times*, 11 May 1999.

[62] *The Irish Times*, 24 July 1999. This boy was eventually sent to a special therapeutic centre in Scotland – see *The Irish Times*,, 25 July and 1 August 2000.

[63] *The Irish Times*, 21 August 1999.

[64] *The Irish Times*, 22 December 1999.

[65] *The Irish Times*, 11 and 30 March and 10 May 2000. This Bill was eventually enacted as the Children Act 2001. The Supreme Court subsequently refused to hear an appeal against Kelly J.'s order for detention made on 29 March on the ground that it was rendered moot by the later order for detention made on 9 May 2000 – see *The Irish Times*, 11 May 2000. In December, 2000, Kelly J. made a further order directing that the teenager remain at the Central Mental Hospital until January 2001, after she had absconded and then voluntarily returned to the hospital – *The Irish Times*, 8 December 2000.

[66] *The Irish Times*, 4 May and 29 June 2000. On the latter occasion, Kelly J. again repeated his criticism of the Oireachtas for its failure to enact the Children Bill 1999.

[67] *The Irish Times*, 10, 17 and 18 May 2000.

[68] *The Irish Times*, 18 May 2000.

[69] Unreported, High Court, 23 May 2000.

mandatory order directing that the teenager be detained in a locked ward of an adult psychiatric hospital[70] but agreed to make a permissive order allowing the relevant health board to detain the girl for her own welfare at any facility that had the approval of a named child psychiatrist. Accepting that this was likely to be in the aforementioned adult psychiatric ward, he made a mandatory order compelling the health board and the Minister for Health and Children to refurbish premises on the grounds of the hospital within a period of three months so that it could be used as a place of detention for troubled children such as the girl in the instant case. In July 2000, Kelly J. refused to order the continued detention of a 14 year old boy, a victim of sexual abuse, in a State remand centre and a place was found for him in a unit in London.[71] The following October, a 13-year old boy sentenced to two years' detention at a remand centre had to be held initially for five days at a Garda Station and subsequently at an assessment centre which was not secure because the remand centre was full.[72] The following month, Kelly J. had to order that a 12 year old boy in need of a place in a secure unit with therapeutic facilities be detained in an assessment centre which was not secure, having been told that no secure place would be available until Easter 2001 at the earliest.[73]

On one of these occasions, Kelly J. went to the lengths of threatening to hold the Ministers for Health, Justice and Education in contempt of court if they failed to provide a secure place for the young girl, *D.H.*, who had succeeded in absconding from the therapeutic unit that had been provided for her by the State. This girl was extremely disturbed, having been sexually abused at the age of ten, and had subsequently engaged in prostitution and substance abuse. She had twice tried to hang herself and on one occasion had tried to set herself on fire. In the course of an application by the health board for a direction that the girl's identity be revealed to the public so as to facilitate her safe return to a care environment, (which, incidentally, was refused), Kelly J. ordered the Ministers for Health, Justice and Education and the health board immediately to find a safe and secure place for the girl which would be available if and when she returned into State custody and, in an unprecedented step, warned them that they would be held in contempt if they did not comply.[74] The following day, he rejected the State's request that his order be made against Ireland and not against the Ministers named, pointing out that such an amended order could not be enforced. According to newspaper reports,[75] the judge said that despite other orders he had made, the needs of children were still not being met and he was not going to allow the rights of children to continue to be long-fingered, hence his order.

---

[70] Commenting, at p. 16 of his judgment, "Quite frankly a Minister for Health and Children who asks the Court to make this order should not merely be embarrassed but ashamed to do so".

[71] *The Irish Times,* 27 and 28 July 2000.

[72] *The Irish Times,* 13 October 2000. The media subsequently reported two further cases of children, one of whom was facing criminal charges, being detained in Garda stations because of the absence of suitable alternative accommodation – see *The Irish Times,* 17 and 21 November 2000.

[73] *The Irish Times,* 30 November 2000.

[74] *The Irish Times,* 19 October 2000.

[75] *The Irish Times,* 20 October 2000.

In the event, the authorities complied with this order and so the threat to hold the Ministers in contempt of court was lifted.[76]

One cannot overestimate the significance of these decisions of Kelly J. in the development of public interest law in Ireland. In the first place, in *D.B. v. Minister for Justice*[77] and *T.D. v. Minister for Education*,[78] the judge unequivocally asserts the power and duty of the courts to vindicate the constitutional rights of a marginal group even to the point of directing the executive to allocate resources towards that end. Thus, in contrast to Costello J. in *O'Reilly v. Limerick Corporation*[79] who arguably read the constitutional rights of the plaintiffs in that case in the light of the doctrine of separation of powers, Kelly J. reads the doctrine of separation of powers in the light of the constitutional rights of the applicant. While these decisions may have raised eyebrows in certain quarters, I believe that such a judicial vindication of the rights of children at risk to secure accommodation is both constitutionally and politically legitimate, especially in a situation in which the political system failed to protect that vulnerable group.[80] In the instant cases, children at risk had an affirmative right to State protection that can readily be inferred from Article 42.5[81] and the State had singularly failed to vindicate that right. Judicial restraint in such circumstances would, far from respecting the Constitution, arguably amount to an emasculation of the terms of Article 42.5.

These cases are also very significant for public interest law in this jurisdiction because of their implications for the development of judicial remedies. In the first place, these would appear to be the first occasions on which an Irish judge instructed the executive[82] as to *how* public money should be spent, not merely that it should be spent. Second, Kelly J. clearly signalled that the granting of an order would not terminate judicial involvement but that the court would exercise an ongoing, supervisory jurisdiction in order to ensure that the authorities complied with its directions. This last feature is characteristic of the affirmative decree which has been developed by judges in the US in the context of public interest litigation. Recall Chayes' comment:

> The centerpiece of the emerging public law model is the decree. It differs in almost every relevant characteristic from relief in the traditional model of adjudication, not the least in

---

[76] *The Irish Times*, 21 October 2000. Later that weekend, D.H. returned to State care from which she would appear to have benefitted significantly – see *The Irish Times*, 23 January 2001. At a subsequent hearing concerning this girl, her counsel raised the possibility that, in the light of the decision in *Sinnott v. Minister for Education*, High Court, 4 October 2000 (see p. 205 *et seq.* below), the State's obligation to provide for her needs might not cease at the age of 18 – *The Irish Times*, 28 November 2000.

[77] [1999] 1 IR 29; [1999] 1 ILRM 93.

[78] [2000] 3 IR 62; [2000] 2 ILRM 321.

[79] [1989] ILRM 181.

[80] See the arguments developed in ch. 1.

[81] In common with other children, they also have a right to free primary education the vindication of which could, in their particular circumstances, also possibly justify the order made by Kelly J.

[82] In two earlier cases, two High Court judges directed local authorities to spend public monies in providing specified facilities for Travellers – see *O'Brien v. Wicklow UDC*, an *ex tempore* decision of Costello J. (as he then was) on 10 June 1994, and *Co. Meath VEC v. Joyce* [1994] 2 ILRM 210.

that it *is* the centerpiece. The decree seeks to adjust future behaviour, not to compensate for past wrong. It is deliberately fasioned rather than logically deduced from the nature of the legal harm suffered. It provides for a complex, on-going regime of performance rather than a simple, one-shot, one-way transfer. Finally, it prolongs and deepens, rather than terminates, the court's involvement with the dispute.[83]

Finally, the threat to cite various Ministers for contempt of court if they fail to comply with the court order appears to be the only sanction available to a court confronted by a failure on the part of successive administrations to respond in a timely and appropriate fashion to previous court orders.[84] Thus, far from being an aberration, Kelly J.'s decisions arguably represent the logical outcome of the constitutional recognition of affirmative socio-economic rights.[85] In the face of egregious neglect by the State of such rights, the alternatives are to accept a more active judicial role in the enforcement of such rights or to resign oneself to their emasculation.[86]

---

[83] "The Role of the Judge in Public Law Litigation" (1976) 89 *Harvard Law Review* 1281 at p. 1298. See further, ch. 2. In a subsequent *ex tempore* judgment in the case of *T.D. v. Minister for Education and ors.*, unreported, High Court, 4 December 1998, Kelly J. stated that he was "not content, having regard to the history of tardiness, to simply let the Health Boards and the Department work matters out as between themselves in their own time. The Court will have to monitor very closely the progress being made and, if necessary, intervene by Order or injunction." He went on to express the hope that such action would not be necessary and that ultimately applications of this nature would become a thing of the past when proper facilities were provided. However in the instant case he directed that the court be informed of a) the outcome of the senior managers' group meetings in the near future; b) the Health Board requirements for high support places in each of their catchment areas; c) the steps being taken to provide appropriate facilities; d) an estimate of the time involved for the provision of such facilities; e) information concerning whatever overall plan or strategy has been devised to deal with the problem; and f) any other relevant matter.

[84] In this context, it is worth noting that on two occasions, *Application of MacArthur* [1983] ILRM 355 and *Desmond v. Glackin (No.1)* [1993] 3 IR 1; [1992] ILRM 490 it appears to have been assumed by the courts that members of the executive are subject to the law of criminal contempt as applications to have serving Ministers attached for criminal contempt of court arising out of comments made in relation to pending legal proceedings were considered on their merits. (I am grateful to my colleague, Eoin O'Dell, for bringing this point to my attention.) Note also that in *M. v. Home Office* [1994] 1 AC 377, the House of Lords held that Government Departments and Ministers could be held to be in contempt of court if they failed to obey a court order

[85] In this context, it is perhaps worth recalling the comments of Ó Dalaigh C.J. in *The State (Quinn) v. Ryan* [1965] IR 70 when he said, at p. 122:

It was not the intention of the Constitution in guaranteeing the fundamental rights of the citizen that these rights should be set at naught or circumvented. The intention was that rights of substance were being assured to the individual and that the Courts were custodians of these rights. As a necessary corollary, it follows that no one can with impunity set these rights at naught or circumvent them, and that the courts' powers in this regard are as ample as the defence of the Constitution requires. Anyone who sets himself such a course is guilty of contempt of the Courts and is punishable accordingly.

[86] In the context of this discussion of the relationship between the courts and the administrators, it is perhaps worth noting, in passing, that in *Eastern Health Board v. McDonnell* [1999] 2 ILRM 382, McCracken J. held that s.47 of the Child Care Act 1991 conferred on the District Court a very wide jurisdiction to impose conditions on Health Boards with regard to the care regime of a child who is the subject of a care order under the Act.

By coincidence of timing, in October 2000, Kelly J. was not the only High Court to signal some frustration at the State's protracted failure to vindicate the constitutional rights of vulnerable children and in the postscript to his judgment in *Sinnott v. Minister for Education*,[87] Barr J. hinted that a failure by the State to attend to the educational needs of autistic children could result in the imposition of punitive damages. This is the second type of public interest litigation involving children's rights and to which I now turn.

Securing elementary education for children with severe or profound learning disability

During the 1990s, a spate of cases, two of which went to judgment, were initiated by parents of autistic children and children with other learning disabilities directing the State to provide improved facilities for the education of such children. Three factors would seem to account for the arrival of this issue before the courts. First, there was the dramatic development, during the latter half of the last century, of appropriate educational courses for persons with learning disability and a shift in emphasis away from medical care to support systems involving the combined efforts of physicians, psychologists, teachers and other workers. Second, there was the development, during that same period, of the State's role in the provision of education for children generally and specifically for children with learning disability. By virtue of Article 42.4 of the Constitution, the State was constitutionally obliged to provide for free primary education generally and in 1953 the State started to discharge this obligation specifically in relation to children with moderate learning disability by recognising special schools for this group.[88] Indeed, Ireland was very pioneering in its approach to the education of such children. However, and this is the third factor accounting for the involvement of the judiciary in this area, it failed to keep up with developments in other jurisdictions where educational systems were subsequently extended to cover children with severe and profound learning disability.[89] Notwithstanding the publication of an official Report in 1983 calling for the provision of education and training for people suffering from severe and profound learning disability,[90] the State

---

[87] Unreported, High Court, 4 October 2000.

[88] This was followed up during the 1960s by the establishment of a network of schools for children with mild and moderate learning disability, pursuant to the recommendations contained in the *Report of the Commission of Inquiry on Mental Handicap 1965*.

[89] Thus the Education for All Handicapped Children Act 1970 and the Public Law 1975 made education compulsory for children with profound learning disability in England and Wales and the US respectively.

[90] *The Education and Training of Severely and Profoundly Mentally Handicapped Children in Ireland* (Pl.1969), an official report published in 1983 (commonly called "The Blue Report"), recommended, *inter alia*, that all centres of severely and profoundly mentally handicapped children should have an education and training programme running in a designated space separate from the living quarters of the children and that specific times should be set aside for such a programme. It also recommended that each child should have access to an education and training programme embracing self-help and daily living skills, expressive skills and leisure skills,

made very little provision for the education of children in these categories.[91]

O'Donoghue v. Minister for Health

This sorry state of affairs was graphically illustrated by the plight of Paul O'Donoghue, the plaintiff in the first of two cases in which the High Court pronounced on the constitutional obligations of the State towards children with learning disability. In 1985, Paul had contracted Reye's Syndrome as a small baby, as a result of which he was left severely mentally handicapped. Between that time and late 1991, when legal proceedings were initiated, State support for his education and training was limited to the provision of physiotherapy and occupational therapy for one hour every fortnight from November 1987 onwards, a two-hour period of conductive education every week from November 1988 onwards, and, from late 1990 onwards, funding for his attendance twice-weekly for two and a half hours in the afternoon at the Spastic Clinic pre-school, (though his mother had to pay the necessary transport costs). In contrast, private funding paid for four trips for Paul to the Peto Institute for Conductive Education in Budapest for assessment and treatment, for attendance at Montessori schools for a few hours a week from 1988 onwards, for daily classes in Conductive Education during the latter half of 1990[92] and for weekly classes and music therapy thereafter. In addition, Paul's mother also used the Peto methods of instruction at home and also took him swimming on a weekly basis.

Somewhat understandably, Marie O'Donoghue considered that the level of educational facilities provided for her son by the State was totally inadequate and so, in late 1991, she instituted legal proceedings against the Ministers for Health and Education[93] seeking an order from the High Court directing the defendants to provide for free primary education for Paul and also a declaration that in failing to provide for

---

designed with his or her particular learning needs in mind and subject to review from time to time and that teachers, paid and supervised by the Department of Education, should be made available to severely and profoundly handicapped children. In 1990, the *Report of a Review Group on Mental Handicap Services* endorsed the need for education of handicapped children and recommended that more places be made available for children in all four categories of handicap, mild, moderate, severe and profound. More recently again, the *Report of the Special Education Review Committee,* published in 1993, called for, *inter alia*, a pupil-teacher ratio of 6 to 1, and a pupil-care staff ratio of 3 to 1, in the case of children with severe or profound learning difficulty; appropriate basic training for staff working with such children; the use, and regular review, of individualised education and training programmes for each child with severe or profound learning difficulty; the establishment of a curriculum development project for pupils with severe or profound learning difficulty; and the provision of assistance to parents in implementing in their homes the education and training programmes provided for their children.

[91] Following on the "Blue Report", a pilot scheme for the education of children with this degree of handicap was introduced and by July 1992, there were 16 "Blue" teachers, looking after 192 pupils out of total of about 1600. The *Report of the Special Education Review Committee* in 1993 called for the extension of this scheme to all children with severe and profound learning difficulty – p. 131.

[92] For which Paul's mother, together with two other parents, paid for a Hungarian teacher to come to Cork to help establish the course.

[93] In response to which the State offered Paul day care facilities at the Cope Foundation from May 1992 until September 1992 and thereafter a full-time place, together with necessary transport costs.

such eduation, the State had deprived him of constitutional rights under Articles 40 and 42 of the Constitution.

In defending these proceedings, the State essentially advanced three arguments. First, it was argued that the applicant, by reason of being profoundly mentally and physically disabled, was ineducable and that all that could be done for him to make his life more tolerable was to attempt to train him in the basics of bodily function and movement. Second, the State argued that the constitutional guarantee of free primary education in Article 42.4 referred only to the conventional type of primary education exemplified in the curriculum of the National Schools and that such training as could be given to the applicant could not be regarded as "primary education" within the meaning of that expression as used in Article 42.4. Finally, the State contended that the applicant's claims were now moot, given that he had been given a place in the Cope Foundation and had achieved the essential relief sought to be achieved on his behalf in the proceedings.

After reviewing the extensive evidence, both oral and documentary, and the legal authorities put before the court, O'Hanlon J. came to the following conclusions.[94] First, he held that the applicant was educable. In *Ryan v. Attorney General*[95] the Supreme Court defined education as "the teaching and training of a child to make the best possible use of his inherent and potential capacities, physical, mental and moral". In the light of this definition and having regard to the dramatic advances made in seeking to alleviate the lot of the people with learning disability through education, to the evidence of the witnesses in the case, to comparative developments in other jurisdictions and to the findings and recommendations in the 1983 report, *The Education and Training of Severely and Profoundly Mentally Handicapped Children in Ireland*[96] and in the *Report of the Review Group on Mental Handicap Services,*[97] the judge rejected the contention that the applicant was ineducable.

He then turned to consider whether such education as could be provided for the applicant at his present stage of development could be regarded as "primary education" within the meaning of that phrase as used in Article 42.4. After examining the dictionary definitions of some of the terms used in that Article, and in particular, the definition of the Irish phrase, "bun-oideachas", O'Hanlon J. stated:

> [T]here is a constitutional obligation imposed on the State ... to provide for free basic elementary education of all children and ... this involves giving each child such advice, instruction and teaching as will enable him or her to make the best possible use of his or her inherent and potential capacities, physical, mental and moral, however limited these capacities may be. Or, to borrow the language of the United Nations Convention and Resolution of the General Assembly "such education as will be conducive to the child's achieving the fullest possible social integration and individual development; such

---

[94] *O'Donoghue v. Minister for Health and ors.* [1996] 2 IR 20. See Ring, "A Right to an Education" (1997) 2 *Bar Review* 219.
[95] [1965] IR 294.
[96] Prl.1969, (the so-called "Blue Report").
[97] Government of Ireland, 1991.

education as will enable the child to develop his or her capabilities and skills to the maximum and will hasten the process of social integration and reintegration."[98]

He continued:

> This process will work differently for each child, according to the child's own natural gifts, or lack thereof. In the case of a child who is deaf, dumb, blind or otherwise physically or mentally handicapped, a completely different programme of education has to be adopted and a completely different rate of progress has to be taken for granted, than would be regarded as appropriate for a child suffering from no such handicap. [99]

While the State had discharged its constitutional obligations in this regard in relation to most categories of children with disability, it had not done so in relation to those suffering from severe and profound learning disability. According to O'Hanlon J., however, the State's constitutional obligations also extended to this group.

> Admittedly it is only in the last few decades that research into the problems of the severely and profoundly physically and mentally handicapped has led to positive findings that education in a formal setting, involving schools and teachers, educational equipment of many kinds, and integration as far as possible in the conventional school environment, can be of real benefit to children thus handicapped. But once that has been established – and my conclusion is that it has been established on a world-wide basis for many years past – then it appears to me that it gives rise to a constitutional obligation on the part of the State to respond to such findings by providing for free primary education for this group of children in as full and positive a manner as it has done for all other children in the community.[100]

Nor was it open to the State to argue that such education as could be provided for children suffering from severe and profound learning disability did not fall within the scope of "primary education" as used in Article 42.4, given what had already taken place in relation to education for children with mild and moderate learning disability. Special schools, integrated into the ordinary National School system, had been established for children in these categories and a special curriculum was drawn up, very different in content from that used in other National Schools. In this curriculum, emphasis was placed on personal and social development, rather than on academic subjects of the conventional kind and a comparison of this curriculum with a curriculum for children suffering from severe and profound learning disability produced in evidence revealed that both were dealing with the same problem and differing only in degree – "the task of schools and teachers provided for the severely or profoundly mentally handicapped being that much more difficult than that which arises when seeking to educate pupils with mild or moderate mental handicap".

The judge continued:

> I believe that it has now come to be accepted that trained teachers and the school environment can make a major contribution to this process which cannot – with the best

---

[98] [1996] 2 IR 20 at p. 65.
[99] *Ibid.*
[100] *Ibid.* at p. 65-6.

will in the world – be provided as effectively or as successfully by parents and family in the home. This seems to me to get over whatever difficulty might otherwise arise in reconciling the present claim with the view expressed by Kenny J. in *Ryan v. A.G.* that "education" as used in Article 42 of the Constitution was intended to mean "education of a kind which could be provided by parents in their homes, or alternatively in schools established or recognised by the State" and therefore "of a scholastic nature".[101]

The judge's ultimate conclusion on this point, therefore, was that the education claimed by the applicant could be described as "primary education" within the meaning of Article 42.4.

Given, however, that this education has to be specially designed to meet the needs of the applicant and others in similar circumstances, a question arises as to the precise extent of the State's obligations towards children with severe and profound learning difficulty under Article 42.4. Important guidance on this issue is offered by O'Hanlon J. in the context of his rebuttal of the State's third argument that, in the light of the facilities made available to the applicant after legal proceedings had been initiated, the entire claim was now moot. The judge rejected this submission on three grounds. First, the offer had been made as a matter of "grace and concession", without recognising the applicant's legal entitlement to primary education; second, it was far from clear that the actual offer made – a full time place at the Cope Foundation – could be regarded as meeting the specific obligation imposed on the State pursuant to Article 42.4; finally, the applicant was, in any event, entitled to damages for loss and damage occasioned by the State's failure in the past to discharge its constitutional obligations to him under Article 42.4. O'Hanlon J.'s comments on the second of these three grounds highlight four specific points in respect of which the State's obligations, under Article 42.4, towards children with severe and profound learning difficulty may be more extensive than its obligations towards children who are not so handicapped. To begin with, the judge clearly indicated that the existing ratio of 12 children to one teacher in the Cope Foundation was inadequate. Faced with that ratio, the Cope Foundation had had to divide the class of twelve into three groups, with four children being educated from 9.30 a.m. to 12 noon, two others from 12 noon to 12.45 p.m. and the remaining six from 1.50 p.m. to 3.30 p.m. Ratios in other jurisdictions were much better – in the UK the teacher-pupil ratio was two to five and in Denmark, two qualified teachers and one assistant had responsibility for seven pupils – and children received education for the entire school day. So while O'Hanlon J. did not actually prescribe a teacher-pupil ratio, he sent out a very strong message that a ratio of 1 to 12 would not discharge the obligations of the State under Article 42.4 towards children with this degree of handicap.[102] The judge also indicated that a new approach would be required in respect of the age of commencement, duration and continuity of primary education. In relation to the first of these, he expressed the belief that early intervention

---

[101] *Ibid.* at p. 67.
[102] It is worth noting that the *Report of the Special Education Review Committee,* published in 1993, called for the adoption of a teacher-pupil ratio of 1 to 6 in the case of children with severe and profound learning difficulty – p. 131.

and assessment was of vital importance if conditions of mental and physical handicap were not to become intractable. On duration of education, he said that the process of education should ideally continue as long as the ability for further development was discernible and that the age of 18 might not be unrealistic in this context.[103]

Finally with regard to continuity of education, the judge opined that the usual lengthy holiday breaks in primary education would cause serious loss of ground for children with severe or profound learning difficulty and that the teaching process should, so far as was practicable, be continuous throughout the year.[104]

O'Donoghue v. Minister for Health is clearly an important benchmark for determining the educational rights of children with severe or profound learning difficulty. It is clear now that the State's obligation to provide for free primary education covers all children in the State and that special measures have to be put in place for those children who, because of disability, are unable to benefit from conventional education.[105] Given O'Hanlon J.'s ruling that the State is obliged, under Article 42.4, to give "each child such advice, instruction and teaching as will enable him or her to make the best possible use of his or her inherent and potential capacities, physical, mental and moral, however limited these capacities may be", it is also clear that such measures include a modification of the primary school curriculum to accommodate children with disabilities who are not adequately catered for under current policy and the provision of special support services. Moreover, while this case is admittedly concerned only with primary education, O'Hanlon J.'s understanding of that concept suggests that, in appropriate cases, the State's constitutional obligation to provide for free primary education does not expire when a child reaches a prescribed chronological age.[106] Furthermore, while the judge was clearly referring to children with severe or profound learning difficulty, it may be that his remarks could also be

---

[103] In *Sinnott v. Ireland*, unreported, High Court, 4 October 2000, Barr J. subsequently ruled that the State's responsibility to provide for free primary education for autistic children does not end at age 18 – see below, pp. 205-210. But see now pp. 341-9.

[104] In addition to its implications for educational policy in relation to children with severe or profound learning difficulty, *O'Donoghue* had a wider implication in that it implicitly affirmed the constitutional legitimacy of the courts' involvement in issues of distributive justice and indeed it would appear to have been on this very point that an appeal against O'Hanlon J.'s decision was taken by the State to the Supreme Court. However because the State conceded on appeal that Paul was educable and that he had an entitlement to free primary education, some members of the Supreme Court appeared to view the appeal as raising a moot point in the context of the instant case. In any event, following an adjournment of the appeal hearing, a declaration was agreed between the parties that the applicant was entitled to free primary education pursuant to Article 42.4 and that the State was obliged under the Constitution to provide for such education – see [1996] 2 IR 20 at p. 72.

[105] Of course many children with disability wish to participate in conventional education and this goal of mainstreaming has been endorsed by the Commission on the Status of People with Disabilities – see *A Strategy for Equality: Report of the Commission on the Status of People with Disabilities*, ch. 11. However this was clearly not appropriate in the case of Paul O'Donoghue and so his case did not raise for consideration any right to participate in conventional education.

[106] A point subsequently developed by Barr J. in *Sinnott v. Minister for Education*, unreported, High Court, 4 October 2000 – see below, pp. 205-210. But see now pp. 341-9.

pressed in aid of children who were deprived of a primary education because of a failure on the part of the State to supply the place of their parents where, in those exceptional cases envisaged in Article 42.5, State intervention was called for.[107]

Following in the wake of this decision, hundreds of other cases were initiated by families seeking to compel the Department of Education to provide for an education for children with disability.[108] Many of these involved autistic children and some involved children with attention deficit disorder. It would appear that the Department responded to the claims on behalf of children with severe or profound learning difficulty on an *ad hoc* basis and that this eventually resulted in the State providing a teacher and two child care assistants for each of approximately 90 classes of six pupils each. In relation to children with other forms of handicap, including mild or moderate learning difficulty, a more pro-active policy was adopted and on 5 November 1998, the Minister for Education announced a package of measures, costing £4m p.a. and providing an extra 65 teaching posts and approximately 200 childcare jobs, designed to ensure that every child having a special educational need would have an automatic entitlement to special extra teaching or school-based childcare, or both, depending on the child's specific needs.[109] Children with autism were now recognised as having special needs and the State promised to provide such children with a pupil-teacher ratio in special schools of 6:1 plus the right to a childcare assistant. The State also undertook to provide a full-time resource teacher or a childcare assistant or both, where several special needs children attend an ordinary school, depending on their numbers and the severity of their disabilities. Where individual or small groups of children were involved, they would get part-time extra teaching or childcare or both and in special schools, classes of six children with severe or profound learning difficulty would be entitled to two childcare assistants for each class. While these measures applied only to primary level education, they were, nonetheless, warmly welcomed by the Down's Syndrome Association, the Disability Federation of Ireland and the Irish Society for Autism. In the next case to come before the High Court in this area, however, Barr J. held that the constitutional rights of autistic children to primary education could not be limited by reference to age and that the State had an ongoing constitutional obligation to provide for the educational needs of the plaintiff in the instant case, an autistic man in his early twenties.

---

[107] It is worth noting that O'Hanlon J.'s analysis of the constitutional duties of the State in relation to education was followed in two cases where such State intervention was warranted – *G.L. v. Minister for Justice*, unreported, High Court, 24 March 1995 and *Comerford v. Minister for Education* [1997] 2 ILRM 134 – though here the children were 13 and 11 years old and so still within the conventional age limits for primary schooling.

[108] See the comments of Barr J. in *Sinnott v. Ireland*, unreported, High Court, 4 October 2000, at p. 30. While most of these cases were settled out of court, in one case, the High Court granted an interlocutory order directing the State and the North Western Health Board to provide educational, therapeutic, psychological and support services for a two year old autistic child – see *The Irish Times*, 27 August 1999.

[109] The measures came into effect in April 1999 with the issuing, by the Department, of Circulars 8 and 9 of 1999.

Sinnott v. Minister for Education

Jamie Sinnott was born on 11 October 1977 and approximately four months later he began to develop symptoms of severe autism that rendered him severely or profoundly mentally handicapped. Despite heroic efforts on his behalf by his mother, Kathryn, the State failed dismally to provide him with any appropriate education or training and eventually legal proceedings were initiated in which both mother and son sought declarations as to their rights, a mandatory injunction directing the Minister to discharge the State's obligations towards Jamie and damages for negligence and breach of constitutional and statutory rights. After reviewing the evidence, Barr J. found as a fact that during the course of his life, Jamie had had not more than about two years of meaningful education or training provided by the State, despite incessant efforts by his mother to secure appropriate arrangements for him. According to the judge, Jamie suffered grievously as a result of this neglect.

> The end result is that he has lost many years which in all probability would have been of great value to him in the improvement of his physical and mental capacity and quality of life through education and training. Whatever happens to him in the future, that loss can never be fully restored because, as the experts point out, education is now arriving too late in his life to achieve optimum results. Progress is more difficult and potentially more stressful for him than would have been the case if he had been educated from an early age. At best he has suffered through lack of educational training a diminution in the quality of his life which has been substantial up to now but which will also continue significantly into the future – even if he derives major benefit from the education and training now proposed for him. It is probable that he will have a life-long need for on-going basic education and training consistent with his requirements as they emerge in the future.[110]

The judge attributed part of the blame for the State's failure properly to address Jamie's needs to the insufficient liaison between the Departments of Education and Health, both of whom had responsibilities towards Jamie. However he was also very critical of the Department of Finance, offering the view that Departmental officials

> appear to be insufficiently informed regarding the constitutional obligations of the State to the weak and deprived in society to enable them to assess realistically the degree of priority which should be attached to each such claim and the structure of priority which the State should devise in meeting its constitutional as distinct from other non-constitutional obligations.[111]

He continued:

> [T]he ultimate financial decision-makers and officials who devise annual revenue/exchequer budgets and administer State funds must have real awareness and appreciation of the constitutional obligations of the State to all sectors of the community and in particular to the rights of the grievously deprived in society, including those such

---

110 Unreported, High Court, 4 October 2000, at pp. 21-2. (For treatment of the Supreme Court decision in this case, see pp. 340-360 below.)

111 *Ibid.* at p. 26.

as Jamie Sinnott who suffer profound mental disablement. Those entitled to State aid by constitutional right should not have to depend on numerical strength and/or political clout to achieve their just desserts. Needs should be met as a matter of constitutional priority and savings, if necessary, should be made elsewhere. A citizen's constitutional right must be responded to by the State in full. A partial response has no justification in law, even in difficult financial circumstances which may entail the raising of new tax revenue to meet such claims – happily a situation which has not pertained for several years. Jamie Sinnott and those like him who are grievously handicapped have a profound need for on-going primary education, training and medical care and a constitutional right to such services from the State. Yet we find ... that [the Department of] Finance has persistently dragged its feet in recognising and implementing the obligations of the State as made abundantly clear by O'Hanlon J. in the O'Donoghue judgment. It seems that the reason for that unhappy state of affairs is a lack of understanding by finance providers of the status and implications of the constitutional obligations of the State and in consequence an inability on their part to prioritise in constitutional justice claims made on the resources of the State by those having such rights which the State has an obligation to vindicate in full and as a matter of urgency.[112]

Characterising the difficulties encountered by the Sinnotts as symptomatic of a widespread malaise, he said that the court, as guardian of the constitutional rights of the citizen, would be failing in its responsibility if it did not allude to these problem areas which contributed to the State's failure to honour its constitutional obligations to the plaintiffs.

After reviewing extensively the reasoning of O'Hanlon J. in *O'Donoghue v. Minister for Health*,[113] he adopted that judge's definition of education and his findings relating to the right of children with severe and profound learning difficulty to State-funded primary education, and the appropriate pupil/teacher and pupil/care assistant ratios.

In its defence, the State argued, *inter alia*, that its duty to provide for primary education for the plaintiff ceased when he reached eighteen years of age and that he could not claim relief in respect of the period prior to O'Hanlon J.'s decision in *O'Donoghue v. Minister for Health* on 27th May 1993.[114] In relation to the first of these, Barr J. noted that neither Ó Dalaigh C.J. in *Ryan v. Attorney General*[115] nor O'Hanlon J. in *O'Donoghue* had had occasion to decide this point when discussing the meaning of education for the purposes of Article 42.4. He also rejected the argument

---

112 *Ibid.*, pp. 26-7.
113 [1996] 2 IR 20. At p. 45 of his unreported judgment, Barr J. also expressed surprise at the fact that the State had pursued an appeal against O'Hanlon J.'s decision in *O'Donoghue* that Paul O'Donoghue was educable, offering the view that "such grounds of appeal were persisted in against an overwhelming tide of national and international expert opinion without any hope of success on the appeal but with the intention of delaying the implementation of the *O'Donoghue* judgment for as long as possible".
114 The State also argued that the plaintff was not autistic but rather was suffering from severe or profound learning difficulty with an overlay of autistic tendencies but Barr J. rejected this argument on the basis of the expert evidence adduced at the hearing.
115 [1965] IR 294.

that the recognition of an open-ended right to primary education amounted to the declaration of an unspecified personal right under Article 40.3 that was not warranted by the facts, holding instead that such a right derived from Article 42.4. He then held that there was nothing in the latter provision to support the argument that the citizen's right to on-going primary education was limited by reference to age, saying

> It is evident that the right to primary education would be fundamentally flawed if narrowly interpreted as ending at an arbitrary age – eighteen years. It has been conceded on behalf of the Minister for Education that Jamie Sinnott at twenty-three years of age requires on-going primary education and training and that he will probably continue to do so indefinitely. However it is submitted that his entitlement in that regard is not derived from Article 42, s.4 but, it seems, is an undefined "right" which is likely to be granted to him only by way of ministerial grace and favour. If the Oireachtas reduces the arbitrary threshold into adulthood as it has done in the past (from 21 to 18 years) does that entail also an arbitrary contraction of the citizen's constitutional right to free primary education? That cannot be so. The Oireachtas has no power to interfere with such rights – only the People by referendum may amend the Constitution.
>
> Jamie Sinnott's history graphically underlines the importance of on-going education and training from early childhood as advocated by the experts on both sides which should continue for as long as it is required. It follows, therefore, that in his case, and others like him, there is a fundamental need for continuous education and training which is not age related. In my opinion, in the absence of a specific provision in terms, it would be wrong to imply any age limitation on the constitutional obligation of the State to provide for the primary education of those who suffer severe or profound mental handicap. In the light of the foregoing I am satisfied that the constitutional obligation of the State under Article 42, s.4 to provide and continue to provide for primary education and related ancillary services for Jamie Sinnott is open-ended and will continue as long as such education and services are reasonably required by him.
>
> In the final analysis the defendants' contention that Jamie Sinnott, and others who suffer from severe or profound mental handicap, have no constitutional entitlement to primary education and ancillary services after the age of eighteen years has no reality. In my opinion the ultimate criteria in interpreting the State's constitutional obligation to provide for primary education of the grievously disabled is "need" and not "age". If a child's disability is such that he/she requires on-going specialist primary education and training for life, then the obligation of the State to provide for that service will continue into adulthood for the lifetime of the child. To cut off a crucial educational life-line because a child has reached his/her majority and to thereby condemn the sufferer to the risk of regression in hard earned gains which have enhanced his/her life would amount to an appalling loss, the effect of which might be to negative the advantages of the constitutional right to education (if provided) enjoyed by the sufferer for many years during infancy.[116]

In the instant case, Barr J. held that the form of ongoing education provided for him in consequence of this litigation did not discharge the State's constitutional

---

[116] Unreported, High Court, 4 October 2000, at pp. 49-50.

obligations because of its inadequacies and he indicated that, for the moment, the State should provide sufficient funds for an alternative system of primary education, therapy and training which is suitable to his needs.

The State's second argument was that the plaintiff's claim was tortious in nature, that this tort did not exist until established by the decision in *O'Donoghue* and that, consequently, the claim could not be applied retrospectively to any period prior to the date of that decision. However Barr J. rejected the argument that the plaintiff's right to primary education was created by O'Hanlon J.'s decision in *O'Donoghue*.

> In *O'Donoghue*, O'Hanlon J. did not create a new right but declared that the obligation of the State to provide for primary education under Article 42, s.4 of the Constitution applies to all citizens and that those who suffer from severe or profound mental handicap are not excluded from the constitutional benefit of appropriate education. That right has existed from the enactment of the Constitution in 1937 and failure to honour it has sounded in damages at least from the early 1970s when expert opinion widely accepted that those who suffer grievous mental disablement are capable of and would derive benefit from appropriate primary education.[117]

He went on to hold that though the Statute of Limitations 1957 applies to a claim for damages for breach of constitutional rights, Jamie Sinnott's action had been commenced within the appropriate period. Turning to the claim advanced by Kathryn Sinnott, the judge held that she was the head of a family which, by virtue of Article 41.2, the State was obliged to protect; that she and her family were entitled, by virtue of Article 40.1, to equality of treatment by the State and that they ought not to be deprived, without just cause, of basic advantages provided by the State for others; that the right to free primary education was for the benefit of the family as well as for individual members thereof; that the burden of caring for Jamie was greatly aggravated by the failure of the State to provide adequately for his education and that she was entitled to damages as a result. Characterising the wrong done to Kathryn Sinnott as a continuing wrong, Barr J. held that she was entitled to damages in respect of the period commencing three years prior to the initiation of her action, a claim in respect of any earlier period being barred by the Statute of Limitations 1957.

After summarising his findings of the essential facts of the case,[118] Barr J. held that both plaintiffs were entitled to the declarations they sought and to damages totalling

---

[117] *Ibid.* at p. 52.

[118] In particular, he held, at pp. 62-3, that the State was in breach of its duty inasmuch as it failed to provide Jamie with adequate primary education; continuity of educational and other services; necessary ancillary services such as speech therapy, occupational therapy, physiotherapy and music therapy; sufficient psychological and medical assessment and treatment and an appropriate curriculum for education and care. The State also failed to devise and review a viable programme for his education and care; failed to keep adequate records of his education, training and treatment; failed to keep Kathryn Sinnott adequately informed of her son's progress and of intended plans for his education and training; failed to collaborate with her in this regard; failed to recognise and respond adequately to Jamie's needs; failed to give him adequate training in personal care, hygiene and mobility; failed to treat his drooling problem; failed to provide him with occupational training; failed to provide him with a teacher and other ancillary experts familiar

£255,000 arising out of breach of their constitutional rights, negligence and breach of duty by the State. He held open the possibility that future damages might be awarded to Jamie Sinnott on review of his sitution in three years time and indicated that the mandatory injunctions sought by the plaintiffs should be considered by the Court as part of that review, though the plaintiffs had liberty to make earlier application in that regard. Then, in a telling postscript to his judgment, he said:

> The conscious, deliberate failure of Finance administrators to pay due regard to and take effective steps to honour the obligations of the State to Jamie Sinnott on foot of the *O'Donoghue* judgment opens up an issue as to whether punitive damages should be awarded against the defendants. As that point was not argued, I do not propose to pursue it in this judgment. However, it is proper to lay down a marker that the issue of punitive damages will arise if it transpires in future litigation that this warning is not heeded and decision-makers persist in failing to meet the constitutional obligations of the State to the grievously afflicted and deprived in our society with the urgency which is their right.[119]

The decision in *Sinnott v. Minister for Education* is very significant in a number of different respects. Its primary significance lies in the fact that it obliges the State to provide life-long education for people with severe and profound learning difficulty.[120] Clearly this has considerable financial implications for the Exchequer but once one accepts O'Hanlon J.'s definition of "education" in *O'Donoghue*, namely, providing

> each child [with] such advice, instruction and teaching as will enable him or her to make the best possible use of his or her inherent and potential capacities, physical, mental and moral, however limited these capacities may be,[121]

the introduction of an age-restriction on such education does appear to deprive people with severe or profound learning difficulty of the full benefit of the constitutional right to primary education.

---

with autism; failed to supervise adequately the services provided by the Cope Foundation on behalf of the State and failed to provide the Foundation with the resources necessary to meet the State's constitutional obligation to educate Jamie. Finally, the State had breached its duty to Jamie by placing him in an institution that was unsuitable for his needs, as a result of which he regressed in his behaviour.

[119] *Ibid.* at p. 69. Less than one week after this decision was handed down, McKechnie J. granted leave for the bringing of judicial review proceedings on behalf of four autistic children seeking State funding for a school providing specialised education for autistic children – see *Fulham and ors. v. Minister for Education, The Irish Times*, 10 October 2000. The following month the State agreed to provide interim funding of £1,300 per week to the school pending the outcome of this action – see *The Irish Times*, 3 November 2000. Three weeks later, the State agreed, as part of the settlement of two test cases, to fund the education of two autistic children in accordance with the method of Applied Behavioural Analysis which entails a one-to-one pupil/teacher ratio – see *The Irish Times*, 23 November 2000.

[120] At a High Court hearing concerning a disturbed 17 year old girl, counsel for the girl raised the possibility that, in the light of *Sinnott*, the State's constitutional obligation to provide for the needs of troubled children might not cease at the age of 18 – see *The Irish Times*, 28 November 2000.

[121] [1996] 2 IR 20 at p. 65.

Barr J.'s decision that Article 40.1 of the Constitution required that the Sinnott family should not have been deprived of basic advantages provided by the State to others also raises the interesting prospect of the guarantee of equality being prayed in aid in order to extend State social services, though one should always be alert to the possibility that where a case of unlawful discrimination is made out, it is usually open to the State to resolve the matter from its perspective by levelling down, *i.e.* by withdrawing the privileged treatment in question.[122]

Finally, his decision is further evidence of the willingness of some Irish judges to attempt to remedy systemic defects in the operation of State agencies by providing for ongoing judicial review of developments after judgment has been delivered and by threatening recalcitrant administrators with punitive sanctions, in this case, punitive damages.[123]

Evaluating impact of litigation

Reviewing generally the impact of litigation strategy taken in support of children's rights, one would have to say that it has produced beneficial, tangible results, particularly in relation to meeting the educational needs of children with learning difficulty. Placed in the context of persistent and egregious State neglect of the needs of these two distinct categories of children, the litigation, at a minimum, compelled the authorities to begin to address the problems encountered by the plaintiffs.[124] In relation to the litigation taken on behalf of autistic children and children with learning difficulty, one can go further and credit litigation strategy with having brought about a worthwhile and much needed change in educational policy. The precedent set by *O'Donoghue* was successfully used by a significant number of other parents to obtain improvements in the educational facilities provided for their children and the Department eventually responded with a more comprehensive approach covering the entire population of children with disability, including children with learning difficulty.[125] Two factors possibly account for the success of litigation strategy in this

---

122   See the legislative reaction to *Hyland v. Minister for Social Welfare* [1989] IR 624; [1990] ILRM 213, discussed at p. 162.

123   For treatment of the Supreme Court appeal against this decision, see below, pp. 340-60.

124   In an interview with *The Sunday Business Post* on 9 April 2000, the Minister with Special Responsibility for Children, Mary Hanafin, TD, said that on the morning the Taoiseach asked her to take responsibility for this portfolio, he specifically mentioned those children whose cases were coming before the courts. One week after the High Court decision in *Sinnott v. Minister for Education*, High Court, unreported, 4 October 2000, the Minister for Education, Dr Michael Woods, TD, announced a series of measures designed to help autistic children and also promised to set up an inter-departmental team of high-level officials to co-ordinate the State's response to the needs of autistic children – see *The Irish Times*, 13 October 2000. The political response to the decision in *O'Donoghue v. Minister for Health* [1996] 2 IR 20 is detailed above, p. 204.

125   In November 2001, the government announced that it would introduce a Children's Disability (Education) Bill designed to copperfasten the rights of special needs children to education – see *The Irish Times*, 23 November 2001.

context. First, the existence of an express constitutional duty on the State to provide for free primary education highlighted the extent of the State's dereliction of duty here and made it virtually impossible for it to argue that it was unaware of any legal responsibility towards these children. Second, the number of people benefiting from O'Hanlon J.'s ruling was relatively limited, to the point where implementing the reforms sought would hardly be any more expensive than contesting a series of actions taken on foot of *O'Donoghue*. *Sinnott* clearly builds on the success in *O'Donoghue* by extending the State's constitutional duties in this area to cover adults suffering from severe and profound learning difficulty but at the time of writing, it remains to be seen whether this development, with its significant financial implications, will be endorsed by the Supreme Court.[126]

The cases taken on behalf of homeless children and children at risk has also produced tangible results in the shape of an increase in the number of secure places for such children[127] and a more focussed approach to the provision of secure accommodation.[128] A leading campaigner on behalf of homeless children, Fr Peter McVerry SJ, has been quoted as saying,

> [Judge] Peter Kelly has been the best thing that has ever happened. He has got things done when nobody in the government has.[129]

Writing in January 2001, Fr McVerry predicted,

> Over the next twelve months, we can expect to see a significant expansion in services for homeless children. After twenty years of political apathy, when it was almost impossible to interest the government or Health Boards in the problem of homeless young people, we have moved into a phase of political panic. Getting the problem away from Justice Peter Kelly in the High Court, who has described the inertia of the Government as a "scandal", and off the front pages of the national newspapers has become an urgent priority. With no shortage of resources any longer, a significant increase in the level of services can be expected.[130]

---

126 Note, however, that in the immediate aftermath of *Sinnott*, the Department of Education made arrangements for a number of autistic children on whose behalf legal proceedings had been initiated – see n.119 above.

127 The Government also increased the powers of a new independent board, the Special Residential Services Board, to co-ordinate the provision of places for children at risk – see Part 11 of the Children Act 2001.

128 Thus towards the end of 1998, a group consisting of representatives of all of the health boards was set up to review the need for special residential child care provision – see Kenny, *Responding to the Needs of Troubled Children: A Critique of High Support and Secure Special Care Provision in Ireland* (Barnados, 2000) at p. 5.

129 See *The Sunday Business Post*, 9 April 2000. A similar opinion was attributed to an unnamed residential childcare worker in a report in *The Irish Times*, 18 October 2000. An indication of the steps now being taken to attend to the needs of some children at risk can be seen in the media report of court proceedings in which the High Court approved of proposals to move a 17-year old teenager with high functioning autism from a psychiatric unit to a two-bedroomed flat staffed by two nurses – see *The Irish Times*, 10 November 2000.

130 See McVerry, "Homelessness" in (2001) 52 *The Furrow* 12 at pp. 14-5.

Considering that child care activists having been campaigning for better facilities for deprived children and children at risk for the best part of the last thirty years, this is significant praise indeed.[131]

At the same time, litigation strategy in relation to children's rights has not been without its drawbacks. For a start, it did not succeed in producing a speedy, comprehensive, response in either context. *O'Donoghue* was decided in 1993 but litigation about the constitutional rights of children with learning difficulty to elementary education is still coming before the courts at the time of writing.[132] This delay in responding to the needs of such children is especially worrying given that early intervention is vital in order to maximise their potential. Similarly, the courts have highlighted the statutory and constitutional duties of the State towards children at risk since 1994 but progress in this area has also been slow. That said, there is evidence of growing judicial impatience with the delay in implementing change and in October 2000, Kelly and Barr JJ. threatened the authorities with, respectively, contempt of court and punitive damages if they did not effectively respond to court orders.

Another concern is that litigation strategy may focus attention on one particular group of children to the detriment of the needs of other children. In the context of children with learning disability, there is a concern that the State responds more effectively in the case of those families that initiate litigation, to the detriment of other families. Similarly, in relation to children at risk, by emphasising the provision of secure accommodation, litigation strategy may divert resources from other support mechanisms for families in difficulty. Thus Durcan observed that the history of these cases

> shows both the benefits and disadvantages of such litigation. The benefits are obvious in that the litigation is bringing about the provision of greater facilities for the care of children, the need for which has been clear. The disadvantages of acquiring facilities by reason of litigation are that the nature of the particular litigation tends to govern the nature of the facilities that are provided ... .
>
> This brings about a situation in which the facilities being provided are, to some degree, being decided on a case by case basis. Policy is determined by the need to respond to judgments in individual cases.[133]

Highlighting the danger of using litigation strategy in this context because of its focus on the provision of high support accommodation and its failure to promote a

---

131   Though Fr McVerry does express some concern about the appropriateness of the services to be provided, given what he considers to be the inadequacy of the planning preceding the formulation of policy.

132   In February 2001, it was estimated that there were almost 200 actions pending against the State on this issue – see *The Irish Times' Education and Living Supplement*, 6 February 2001.

133   Durcan, at p. 10. See also the comment of O'Sullivan in his concluding paragraph of "Dimensions of Campaigning for Homeless Children in the Republic of Ireland", a paper presented to the Third International FEANTSA Congress in Madrid, 1995, that this strategy, "while generating many positive developments, [has] also brought about some developments that have resulted in unease in some quarters. There can be unforeseen consequences to legal action and there are substantial limits to what legal action alone can achieve."

more multi-faceted approach to the needs of vulnerable children, O'Sullivan argues that

> if secure places exist they will be filled and the existence of more, and hence easier, secure placements may demotivate health board authorities in their efforts to produce creative alternatives to secure accommodation or improve the quality of their open establishments.
>
> The provision of secure accommodation is a regressive step in Irish child care evolution and represents an easy way out for those charged with the immensely difficult task of providing services for children which meet their needs, further their interests and protect their rights.[134]

Writing in similar vein, Kenny states:

> Barnados has long held the view that we need to develop an integrated approach to the delivery of our child care services, where a "continuum of care" is offered both to different age groups and to children with different needs. However, if such an approach is to work, the different pieces of the service "jigsaw" all need to be in place – from early childhood services to family support programmes to foster care and then to residential and specialist care. The danger with these proposed developments [resulting from High Court litigation] is that all the other pieces of the service continuum are not yet in place and, therefore, the new units may be used inappropriately.[135]

There is cogent evidence to suggest that the provision of high support accommodation without appropriate after care services for children who have left such accommodation is not very effective in promoting the welfare of such children. Thus recent research dealing with the fate of children placed in different residential units by court order showed that within six months of release, just over half had been back in detention at some point[136] and that within two years of release, this figure rises to

---

[134] "The Case Against Secure Accommodation" in *Secure Accommodation in Child Care* (Children's Legal Centre, 1997) at p. 18. See also the comments of Sr. Stanislaus Kennedy, RSC, in *The Irish Times*, 17 April 2000.

[135] Kenny, p. 7. Writing in the introduction to this report, Keenan states, at p.ii:

> It is … surprising that more rigour has not been brought to the challenge of providing for the young people coming before the High Court. However this would seem to be not unconnected to the fact that policy and provision in this area is now being driven by the Court, rather than by Executive action which would be more appropriate. Of course, this situation has arisen in the first place because of the inadequacy of planning and provision for children in need generally. It was out of frustration at the failure of the conventional system that resort was made to the courts. Nobody doubts the concern or conviction of the judges of the High Court who have heard these cases and have been scathing in their criticism of the failure to make adequate provision. But the effect of this now is that policy makers have seen their room to manoeuvre disappear and their hands tied with regard to the type of provision they can make. In other words, both the conventional policy making process and the conventional care system are currently being bypassed in a way which, though understandable, may not be in the interests of children and young people.

[136] Focus Ireland, *Out on Their Own: Young People Leaving Care in Ireland* (Dublin, 1998), at p. 45.

65%.[137] Moreover the focus on the provision of high support accommodation clearly does not protect the interests of those children whose needs lie elsewhere. A further criticism of the litigation strategy here is that even if one accepts the need for high support accommodation, such places should be provided in smaller units of not more than six or seven children rather than in the larger units proposed by the authorities.

Now of course the reason why the litigation strategy here led to a policy emphasising the provision of secure accommodation is that most of the cases featured children in need of such accommodation and, as Durcan points out:

> A court has to decide on the basis of the evidence and facts in particular cases what facilities are, or are not, necessary for the particular applicant in the particular case before it.[138]

This inbuilt limitation of litigation strategy means that it is unrealistic to expect the courts to formulate a comprehensive policy catering for all of the diverse needs of vulnerable children when confronted with the particular needs of one section of such children. If one hopes to develop other elements of child care policy through litigation, then the cases selected will have to identify the need for such elements. In the present context, one could argue that the litigation strategy here was successful insofar as it compelled the authorities to attend to the needs of those children in need of secure accommodation.[139] Insofar as the different needs of other children were not addressed, one might argue that this was because those needs were generally not put before the courts by the facts of the cases taken.

Thus the experience with litigation strategy in this context illustrates the fact that such a strategy often presents the courts with only a partial perspective on the underlying problem.[140] In such circumstances, one needs to consider carefully whether half a cake is better than no loaf or whether, in fact, a partial response may exacerbate the problem being addressed. That said, against a backdrop of shameful neglect by the State of the needs of children at risk and children with severe and profound learning disability, litigation strategy has succeeded in generating some progress and has arguably justified itself in the present context.

---

[137] Kelleher, Kelleher and Corbett, *Left Out on Their Own: Young People Leaving Care in Ireland* (Oak Tree Press/Focus Ireland, 2000) at pp. 81-2. According to *Magill*, (n. 3 above), the Laxton Report into the necessity for special residential child care provision in Ireland (commissioned by the Department of Health and Children and submitted to it in 1998 but not yet published), argued that, given the state of childcare services, short-term high support units for dysfunctional children will not work in the absence of adequate after-care. See also O'Sullivan, "Adolescents leaving care or leaving home and child care provision in Ireland and the UK – A critical view" in Hill and Aldgate (eds.), *Child Welfare Services – Developments in Law, Policy, Practice and Research* (Jessica Kingley Publishers, 1996).

[138] Durcan, p. 10.

[139] Though of course the criticism remains that such accommodation should be provided in smaller units rather than in the larger, campus-style institutions envisaged by the authorities.

[140] The experience of pursuing claims for civil legal aid through the courts arguably offers another example of this limitation to litigation strategy.

Chapter 6

Litigation and Travellers' Rights

Irish Travellers are arguably the most marginalised group in Irish society and consequently litigation concerning their rights is very relevant to any discussion about the role of the courts in promoting social inclusion.[1] Such litigation[2] has focussed on two areas, accommodation and discrimination, both of which are examined below. I begin, however, with some contextual material on the situation of Travellers in Ireland.

Traveller ethnicity

The origins of the Traveller community are lost in the mists of time. Popular belief sees them as descendants of misfits who were unable to function in normal society or of families who were dispossessed of their lands during the plantations following the collapse of the old Gaelic society in the seventeenth century or as a result of the Famine of the mid-nineteenth century.[3] MacNeill contends that Travellers may be descended from a pre-Celtic group that was marginalised by Celtic invaders from the

---

[1] Traveller organisations have also demonstrated an awareness of the possibility of using the courts to effect social change – see *Traveller Accommodation and the Law: Action for Change through the Courts* (Irish Traveller Movement, 1992).

[2] A certain proportion of litigation affecting Travellers does not get reported, such as the granting of interim *ex parte* injunctions restraining Travellers from trespassing on property or District or Circuit Court decisions dealing with objections to the renewal of pub licenses on grounds of anti-Traveller discrimination. Of necessity, the judicial decisions considered in this chapter are, for the most part, restricted to those in respect of which there is an approved judgment or note of a judgment and which establish precedents for subsequent cases.

[3] For refutation of this explanation of the origins of Travellers, see Ní Shúinéar, "Irish Travellers, Ethnicity and the Origins Question" in McCann, Ó Síocháin and Ruane (eds.), *Irish Travellers, Culture and Ethnicity* (Belfast, 1994) 54, at pp. 66-70 and McDonagh, "Origins of the Travelling People" in Sheehan (ed.), *Travellers: Citizens of Ireland*, (Parish of the Travelling People, 2000) at p. 21.

fifth century B.C. onwards.[4] A third hypothesis is that they may be the descendants of nomadic craftsmen in Celtic society.[5]

Whatever the truth of these various theories, this debate is of significance to the related debate about whether Travellers are a distinct ethnic group within Irish society as opposed to a sub-culture of poverty within an homogenous society. The policy implications of this classification are very significant. Defining Travellers as an economically deprived group, as a sub-culture of poverty, ineluctably leads to policies of assimilation and integration with the settled community. Viewing Travellers as a distinct ethnic group, on the other hand, calls for policies that make special provision for Travellers and that respect their cultural traditions and values, in particular, their nomadic lifestyle.

A very strong case can be made for Traveller ethnicity.[6] Certainly Travellers have a distinct culture, characterised by nomadism, a distinct spoken language, called Cant or Gammon, and a distinct written language called "patrin", involving the use of rags, sticks and embers.

Arguing for the view that Travellers are a distinct ethnic group, Crowley states:

> [Travellers] identify themselves as a distinct community and are seen by others as such. They share common cultural characteristics, traditions and values which are evident in their organization of family, social and economic life. Nomadism, in a range of forms, has been central to the development and expression of these characteristics, traditions and values. Travellers have a long shared history which, though undocumented, can be traced back before the twelfth century through mention of Travellers in the law and through analysis of their language, the Cant. They have a distinct oral tradition and largely marry within their own community. These elements have all been identified as defining an ethnic group.[7]

In recent times, arguments such as these have succeeded in moving policy formation relating to Travellers from an assimilationist approach to one predicated on the distinct ethnic status of Travellers. This process can be traced through the publication of the three major reports on Travellers published during the past forty years.

Thus, in 1963, the Commission on Itinerancy stated that

> Itinerants (or Travellers, as they prefer themselves to be known) do not constitute a single homogenous group, tribe or community within the nation. Neither do they constitute an ethnic group.[8]

---

4 *Phases of Irish History,* (Dublin, 1919).
5 Ní Shúinéar, at pp. 71-2.
6 See generally, Barnes, "Irish Travelling People" in Rehfisch (ed.), *Gypsies, Tinkers and other Travellers* (Academic Press, 1975) at p. 231; McCann, Ó Síocháin and Ruane (eds.), *Irish Travellers, Culture and Ethnicity* (Belfast, 1994); MacLaughlin, *Travellers and Ireland: Whose Country, Whose History?* (Cork University Press, 1995).
7 "Travellers and Social Policy" in *Contemporary Irish Social Policy,* Quin, Kennedy, O'Donnell and Kiely (eds.), (University College Dublin Press, 1999) at p. 244.
8 *Report of the Commission on Itinerancy* (pr.7272, 1963) at p. 37.

This led the Commission to advocate assimilation as the ultimate solution for the problems faced by Travellers:

> [I]t is not considered that there is any alternative to a positive drive for housing itinerants if a permanent solution to the problem of itinerancy, based on absorption and integration, is to be achieved.[9]

The *Report of the Travelling People Review Body,*[10] published in 1983, represented somewhat of an advance of this type of thinking – the term "Traveller" was used instead of "itinerant", a term used by settled people; it defined Travellers in a way which suggested that they were a distinct ethnic group[11] and it attempted to address the needs of Travellers who wished to continue to pursue a nomadic way of life. At the same time, however, this Report still focused on an assimilationist approach to alleviating the plight of Travellers, advocating policies designed to support Travellers adapting to the norms of the settled community.[12]

In 1995, however, the *Report of the Task Force on the Travelling Community,*[13] heralded a new approach to policy making in relation to Travellers which, according to Crowley, "involves making special provision, targeting the distinct needs and aspirations of Travellers as well as adapting standard provision to ensure that it is accessible and relevant to Travellers".[14] Thus in a wide range of areas, covering discrimination, accommodation, health, education, the Traveller economy, Traveller women, Travellers with disability, sport, culture and the arts, the Report advanced recommendations that took account of the distinct culture and identity of Travellers.

This new approach is also reflected in recent legislation concerning Travellers. The first explicit statutory reference to Travellers in modern legislation occurs in the marginal note to s.13 of the Housing Act 1988, entitled "Provision of sites for

---

[9] *Ibid.* at p. 62. Joyce argues that whatever about the theory underlying the 1963 Report, the policies actually pursued by local authorities in its aftermath can only be described as isolationist as halting sites provided by such authorities were invariably very remote from the settled community – "Accommodation: A new response or the same old story" in Sheehan (ed.), at p. 95.

[10] Pl.1552.

[11] "[Travellers] are an identifiable group of people, identified both by themselves and by other members of the community (referred to for convenience as the 'settled community') as people with their own distinctive lifestyle, traditionally of a nomadic nature but not now habitual wanderers. They have needs, wants and values which are different in some ways to those of the settled community" – *Ibid.* at p. 6. This definition was adopted by Costello J. for the purpose of his decision in *O'Reilly v. Limerick Corporation* [1989] ILRM 181.

[12] See criticisms of the 1983 Report by McDonagh, "Nomadism in Irish Travellers' Identity" in McCann, Ó Síocháin and Ruane (eds.), p. 95 at pp. 102-4; Crowley, pp. 247-8, and Binchy, "Traveller Culture and Ethnicity: Implications for Social Policy", paper presented to conference at Trinity College Dublin on Travellers, Society and the Law, 18 July 1997, at pp. 8-9.

[13] Pn.1726, July 1995.

[14] Crowley, p. 249. However Crowley also ruefully concludes that "While policy making is currently informed by the Task Force Report (1995), evidence would suggest that policy implementation continues to be informed by the thinking encapsulated by the Travelling People Review Body Report (1983), and even by the Report of the Commission on Itinerancy (Commission on Itinerancy, 1963)." – *Ibid.*

travellers". Sub-section 1 provides that "This section applies to persons belonging to the class of persons who traditionally pursue or have pursued a nomadic way of life". Significantly, Travellers are described here in cultural, rather than economic, terms. In 1989 and 1993, references were made to the Travelling community (though again, without definition) as a protected group under the Prohibition of Incitement to Hatred Act 1989[15] and the Unfair Dismissals (Amendment) Act 1993[16] while the first piece of legislation to concern itself exclusively with the situation of Travellers, the Housing (Traveller Accommodation) Act 1998, defined "Traveller" by reference to the description in s.13(1) of the Housing Act 1988. This process has culminated in the definition of "Traveller community" in s.2 of the Equal Status Act 2000 for the purpose of the Act as

> the community of people who are commonly called Travellers and who are identified (both by themselves and others) as people with a shared history, culture and traditions including, historically, a nomadic way of life on the island of Ireland.

This definition thus represents the successful culmination of a campaign by Travellers to be recognised as a distinct ethnic, as opposed to economically deprived, group in Irish society.[17]

Plight of Travellers

In 1999, there were 4,790 Traveller families in Ireland. An additional four to five thousand Traveller families live in the UK and a further community of approximately 10,000 Travellers live in the US states of Georgia, South Carolina, Mississippi, Louisiana, Texas and Tennessee, descendants of Travellers fleeing from the Famine.

While some of the Irish Traveller families are wealthy, most endure conditions of great deprivation. In 1999, 1,207 families lived on the roadside and Traveller infant and adult mortality rates are over twice those of the settled community.[18] Travellers also have a shorter life expectancy than settled people, with census information released in March 1998 indicating that only 1% of Travellers live to be 65. Traveller children do not remain in education for as long as their settled counterparts, though this situation is gradually improving. Thus the *Report of the Task Force on the Travelling Community* cited figures from two different sources (that admittedly do not co-relate) indicating that 80% of 12-15 year old Travellers did not attend school during the 1989-90 school year and that in the early 1990s, only 5% of all eligible

---

[15] See s.1 thereof.
[16] See s.5 thereof.
[17] It is perhaps worth noting that in August 2000, the Central London County Court decided that Irish Travellers constituted an ethnic group for the purposes of the UK Race Relations Act 1976 – see *The Irish Times*, 30 August 2000.
[18] The most recent figures here date from 1987. At that time, the infant mortality rate for Travellers was 18.1 per 1000 live births compared to a national figure of 7.4, while male Travellers had over twice the risk of dying, and female Travellers more than three times the risk of dying, of their settled counterparts – see Barry et al, *The Travellers Health Status Study* (1989).

Traveller children were attending mainstream second-level schools.[19] By the turn of the century, however, most Traveller children received some second-level education, though relatively few stay on after reaching the age of 15.[20] With the mechanisation of farm work and the advent of plastic, Travellers lost their economic role in rural society. This led to an increasing exodus to the towns and cities, where Travellers suffer from high levels of unemployment and as a result are very dependent on social welfare payments. Finally Travellers also suffer from pervasive forms of both direct and indirect discrimination.[21]

In tackling the social problems confronting them, Travellers' organisations have shown an awareness of the possibility of using the courts to effect change.[22] Such reliance has arisen primarily in relation to the provision of Traveller accommodation, though more recently, complaints of discrimination by publicans have been brought before the lower courts and with the enactment of the Equal Status Act 2000, it is likely that the courts will find themselves more heavily involved in this area in the future. Both of these areas will be examined in what follows.

Litigation and the accommodation needs of Travellers

Litigation pertaining to the accommodation needs of Travellers can be classified under five headings – a) Prosecutions of Travellers under the Local Government (Sanitary Services) Act 1948 arising out of the unlawful use of temporary dwellings; b) cases concerning the rights and duties of Travellers under the Housing Act 1966 as amended; c) cases challenging local authority decisions to provide accommodation for Travellers and taken pursuant to the Local Government (Planning and Development) Act 1963 as amended; d) cases seeking to hold local authorities liable in tort arising out of the behaviour of Travellers on land owned by such authorities; and e) cases taken by Travellers under the Constitution.

Local Government (Sanitary Services) Act 1948

Pursuant to Part IV of the Local Government (Sanitary Services) Act 1948, local authorities are empowered to make bye-laws regulating the erection and use of temporary dwellings in their area. Two prosecutions of Traveller families taken pursuant to such bye-laws are to be found in the law reports, with mixed results for the families concerned.

In *Limerick Corporation v. Sheridan*[23] the plaintiff corporation purported to make a bye-law prohibiting the use, without its consent, of any temporary dwelling on any street or roadway in its area or on any land within three hundred yards from the centre

---

[19] *Report of the Task Force on the Travelling Community,* p. 184.

[20] See *The Irish Times,* 2 March 2001.

[21] See *Travellers in Ireland: An Examination of Discrimination and Racism* (Report from the Irish National Co-Ordinating Committee for the European Year Against Racism, 1997).

[22] See fn.1 above.

[23] (1956) 90 ILTR 59.

of any such street or roadway. The defendant lived in a caravan on the side of the road and so contravened the bye-law. However when she was charged with an offence before the District Court, the court took the view that the bye-law was *ultra vires* the corporation and stated a case for the High Court on this issue.

Davitt P., in the High Court, agreed with the lower court. In his opinion, while the Act, in s.31(2), defined the land subject to the authority's control by reference to, *inter alia*, its distance from the centre line of a road, it was never intended that the local authority could regulate the use of temporary dwellings on virtually all land in its entire area through the simple expedient of specifying a distance extending to hundreds of yards. Moreover, s.31(2) required the authority to reach an opinion on whether a temporary dwelling would be prejudicial to public health or to the amenities of the locality or would constitute an unreasonable interference with traffic before the authority could prohibit its erection or retention and this precondition had not been satisfied in the instant case. Davitt P. also held that the bye-law, if valid, would constitute an oppressive and gratuitous interference with common law rights.

In the second reported prosecution under this legislation, Travellers fared less well. In *Listowel UDC v. McDonagh*[24] the defendant argued that a bye-law prohibiting the erection of temporary dwellings on a number of named streets in the town, and pursuant to which he had been convicted in the District Court, was made in bad faith and therefore *ultra vires*. The Supreme Court having held that the defendant was entitled to raise this argument in the course of the criminal prosecution,[25] it fell to Ó Briain P. in the Circuit Court, hearing the appeal against conviction in the District Court, to decide this issue.

While demonstrating some sympathy for the plight of the defendants,[26] Ó Briain P. rejected the defendant's contention that the UDC was motivated by an anti-Traveller bias when it made the bye-law in question. He held that the Council had ample evidence on which to come to an informed opinion that the temporary dwellings in the area covered by the bye-law were unsanitary. Moreover as certain members of the Council had assisted Travellers in the past, there was no justification for the allegation of bad faith on its part. Accordingly, the convictions were upheld.

While the litigation here produced mixed results for Travellers, *Limerick Corporation v. Sheridan* shows how Travellers can use the courts as a shield in the face of oppressive action by the State. The case is also a useful illustration of the fact that the pursuit of litigation strategy is not necessarily confined to plaintiffs and that

---

[24] (1971) 105 ILTR 99.

[25] See *Listowel UDC v. McDonagh* [1968] IR 312. (The prosecution had argued that such an argument could only be heard in judicial review proceedings.)

[26] In the opening paragraph of his judgment, Ó Briain P. commented that "The appellants are itinerant folk – a class amongst the least privileged in our society – and it is persons such as they who are particularly dependant on the Courts of Justice for the securing to them of their fundamental rights to life, person and property. Indeed, I think the Court has judicial knowledge of the fact that in recent times in this professedly Christian country, these people have been hunted almost like vermin, their flimsy houses attacked and in some cases destroyed." – (1971) 105 ILTR 99 at p. 100.

someone who is brought into court as a defendant can sometimes turn the litigation to his or her advantage. This is also a feature of two of the cases[27] in which the courts were asked to consider the position of Travellers under the housing code, though most of the cases in this category, to which we now turn, were initiated by Travellers.

Housing code

Prior to 1988, the housing code failed to differentiate between Travellers and non-Travellers in relation to accommodation. Thereafter, however, legislation sought to address the specific needs of Travellers, initially in s.13 of the Housing Act 1988 and then more extensively in the Housing (Traveller Accommodation) Act 1998.[28]

The courts have addressed a number of issues relating to the rights and obligations of Travellers under the housing code. Taken in chronological order, these are a) the right to protection against eviction; b) the right to halting sites; c) the standard of accommodation in halting sites; and d) the right to public housing of one's choice.

a) Protection against eviction – Judicial engagement with the position of Travellers under the Housing Act 1966 led to some limited improvement in the protection afforded to Travellers facing eviction by local authorities from unlawful halting sites. The principal, and earliest, authority here is *McDonald v. Feely and ors.*[29] in which the Supreme Court clarified the statutory obligations of housing authorities towards Travellers living on unlawful halting sites. In 1980, Rosella McDonald was living with her husband and ten children in a caravan on the Tallaght by-pass, which was then under construction. On 12 May, the defendant county council passed a resolution directing the county manager to move Mrs McDonald and other Traveller families off the site and on 14 May, she was given three days' notice by officials of the defendant county council to leave the area. Despite the fact that she told the officials that she had nowhere to move to, no offer of an alternative site or accommodation was made or suggested by the officials. In legal proceedings commenced two days later, Mrs McDonald challenged the validity of the council's resolution and sought an injunction to prevent the defendants implementing it. The High Court granted an interlocutory injunction and this decision was appealed by the defendants to the Supreme Court. In

---

[27] Both *University of Limerick v. Ryan*, unreported, High Court, 21 February 1991, and *Co. Meath VEC v. Joyce* [1994] 2 ILRM 210 started off as applications by the plaintiffs under s.27 of the Local Government (Planning and Development) (Amendment) Act 1976 to restrain Travellers from remaining on unauthorised halting sites. However in both cases, the Travellers were given liberty to join the relevant local authority as a third party and to assert claims based on the Housing Act 1988.

[28] This important piece of legislation, *inter alia*, obliges housing authorities to assess the need for halting sites in their functional area, to adopt an accommodation programme specifying the accommodation needs of Travellers and indicating how those needs will be met over a five year period, and to take any necessary reasonable steps to implement such programme. The provisions of the 1998 Act appear to have been considered for the first time by the courts on 1 March 2001 when it appears that Ó Caoimh J. required Donegal Co. Co. to provide two halting sites within three months – see *The Irish Times*, 2 March 2001.

[29] Unreported, Supreme Court, 23 July 1980.

the meantime, however, the council offered Mrs McDonald a three-roomed chalet in Rathfarnham but she decided not to take up the offer because of the presence on the same site of a rival Traveller family.

O'Higgins C.J., delivering the judgment of the Supreme Court, referred to, *inter alia*, s.60 of the Housing Act 1966 under which the council was under a duty to draw up a scheme determining the priorities to be accorded to categories of persons specified in the scheme in the letting of dwellings provided. He concluded that the council had a corresponding duty to operate this scheme of priorities and to have regard to the housing needs of all those in the council's area living in unsuitable or overcrowded conditions or in need of housing and unable to provide for themselves.

> It does not seem to me to matter whether in fact the Plaintiff's husband had been born in the County of Dublin and thereby qualified his family for housing by the County Council or whether the family had been over four years resident somewhere in the County or whether in fact they were not qualified – at least their housing needs deserved consideration and attention if a scheme of priorities paying due regard to the primary objectives laid down in Section 60(3) were effectively to be operated.[30]

While the plaintiff's housing needs had not been considered at all by the council when it initially moved to evict her family from the unauthorised site, this situation had changed by the time the case reached the Supreme Court. An offer of accommodation had been made to the plaintiff and this was not vitiated by the possibility of intimidation by the other Traveller family on the site. Accordingly, the Court refused to continue the injunction. However, though the injunction was discontinued in this case, *McDonald* did establish that before a local authority could evict Travellers from an unauthorised site, it had to give consideration to their accommodation needs.

McDonald v. Feely was subsequently distinguished on the facts in the case of *Wall v. Feeley*,[31] which also involved a Traveller family living on the Tallaght by-pass. Here Keane J. is reported to have held that the defendant council was attempting to meet the housing needs of the plaintiffs and that it had not taken any active steps to remove them from the by-pass. Accordingly, he held that the plaintiffs were not entitled to an injunction to restrain the defendants from taking any action to remove the plaintiffs from their unauthorised halting site. On the other hand, he knew of no authority for the proposition that where a local authority had failed in its duty, the persons so affected were entitled to occupy the authority's property and so he granted the

---

[30] *Ibid.*, at pp. 8-9. In the subsequent case of *McNamee v. Buncrana UDC* [1983] IR 213; [1984] ILRM 77, the Supreme Court, *per* O'Higgins C.J., held that this passage did not mean that a housing authority was precluded from giving priority to those people in their functional area who had been resident or domiciled there for a particular period of time.

[31] Unreported, High Court, 26 January 1984. At an earlier stage in these proceedings, Costello J. had granted the plaintiffs an interlocutory injunction preventing their removal, holding that they had established a fair and *bona fide* question as to whether, in the particular circumstances of their case, a breach of statutory duty under the Housing Act 1966 had occurred. Moreover, on the balance of convenience, very great hardship would be caused to the plaintiffs if they were ejected from the bye-pass and so he would not order their eviction – *Wall v. Feeley*, High Court, 26 October 1983.

defendants a mandatory injunction directing the plaintiffs to leave the by-pass, though he also put a stay of two weeks on this order to allow for a humane solution to the problem.

More recently, in *Harty v. Limerick County Council*[32] Smyth J. held that the defendant council was not in breach of their obligations under the Housing Acts when it exercised its powers under the Roads Act 1993 to extinguish the public right of way over the road where the plaintiffs were camped on the ground, *inter alia*, that an offer of accommodation, subsequently refused, had been made to the plaintiffs.

McDonald v. Feely represents some improvement in the legal position of Travellers inasmuch as it requires housing authorities to offer reasonable alternative accommodation to Travellers before taking steps to evict them from unauthorised sites. However it is only of relevance to Travellers facing eviction by housing authorities, providing them with a limited form of protection, and does not address the accommodation needs of Travellers generally. Even where *McDonald* does apply, it does not require housing authorities to take account of Traveller culture, specifically, the existence of rivalry between different Traveller families, in determining what constitutes reasonable alternative accommodation. Moreover, based as it is on the interpretation of legislation, the principle in this case is also susceptible to statutory modification, as appears to have happened in 1998 when s.32 of the Housing (Traveller Accommodation) Act 1998 amended s.10 of the Housing (Miscellaneous Provisions) Act 1992 to empower local authorities, *inter alia*, to require Travellers camped within a one mile radius of an official halting site or other Traveller accommodation provided pursuant to the Housing Acts to relocate to at least a distance of one mile from the site. The amended provision – s.10(1)(c) – places no obligation on the local authority to identify a suitable site for relocation and therefore, on the basis of the principle of statutory interpretation, *generalia non specialibus derogant*, would appear to modify the principle in *McDonald*.

b) Right to halting sites – Towards the end of the 1980s, Travellers began to pursue a right to halting sites through the courts. Initially unsuccessful, this approach eventually bore fruit when the courts were called upon to interpret s.13 of the Housing Act 1988.

The first case in which a right to a halting site was asserted was *O'Reilly v. Limerick Corporation*,[33] a case which vividly demonstrated the limits of the legal protection afforded to Travellers under the Housing Act 1966. We have already encountered this case in the context of our discussion of the constitutional legitimacy of public interest litigation[34] but to recap briefly, the plaintiffs were members of the Travelling community living in conditions of great poverty and deprivation and they took legal proceedings against the defendant corporation seeking a mandatory injunction directing the

---

[32] Unreported, High Court, *ex tempore*, 23 March 1999.
[33] [1989] ILRM 181. See Elder, "Travellers, Serviced Sites and the Law" (1988) 6 ILT 171 and a note by the present author in (1988) 10 *DULJ (n.s)* 189.
[34] See ch. 1.

corporation to provide serviced halting sites under the Housing Act 1966 and damages for breach of constitutional rights. The decision of Costello J. (as he then was) on the constitutional claim, which was dismissed, is examined in detail in ch. 1 and in the present context we need only consider the statutory claim advanced by the plaintiffs.

The claim here was for a serviced halting site, not housing, as the plaintiffs wished to continue with their nomadic lifestyle. In fact, the corporation had approved in principle the establishment of serviced halting sites in the city and had formally nominated three sites for such use. However only two of these sites belonged to the corporation and, in any event, the needs of less than half of the plaintiffs would be met by all three sites. The plaintiffs relied primarily on s.55 of the Housing Act 1966 which, *inter alia*, obliged housing authorities periodically to prepare a building programme setting out the works which they proposed to undertake having regard to the housing needs of their functional area and listed the factors to be taken into account by the authority. However Costello J.'s examination of this provision, and of the remainder of Part III of the 1966 Act, led him to conclude that s.55 did not impose a duty to provide halting sites on housing authorities. He said:

> [Section 55] imposes a duty to *prepare* and *adopt* a "programme" but does not contain any power to carry it out. It is … an important part of the machinery for the achievement of the overall objectives of Part III of the Act but it would be quite inconsistent with the general statutory scheme to suggest that each housing authority was obliged by law to give effect to every proposal contained in the programme they had adopted.[35]

The power to give effect to a building programme was contained in s.56(2) which provides in relevant part:

> A housing authority may … provide and, if they think fit, maintain in good order and repair roads, shops, playgrounds, places of recreation, parks, allotments, open spaces, sites for places of worship, factories, schools, offices and other buildings or land and such other works or services, as will, in the opinion of the authority, serve a beneficial purpose either in connection with the requirements of the persons for whom the dwellings are provided or in connection with the requirements of those persons and of other persons.

However Costello J. ruled that, because this provision was permissive only,

> it cannot be relied on by the plaintiffs to support a claim for an order to the housing authority to supply serviced halting sites if no provision for them is contained in their building programme.[36]

Section 60 of the 1966 Act did impose a duty on housing authorities to make a scheme of priorities for letting housing accommodation but that, according to the judge, did not encompass a duty to provide serviced halting sites as s.60 referred exclusively to the letting of *dwellings*. Nor did such a duty arise from the provisions of s.111 of the Act which empowered the Minister, whenever he was of opinion that a local authority

---

[35] [1989] ILRM 181 at pp. 188-9.
[36] *Ibid.* at p. 189.

had failed to perform any of its functions under the 1966 Act, to require the authority to perform the function. According to Costello J., this was merely an enabling section, which did not impose any duty on the Minister that the Court could enforce him to perform.

But though it appeared that a local authority could not be compelled to implement proposals in a building programme, it could be compelled to *include* certain proposals in such programmes. In particular, Costello J. held that circumstances could exist in which a local authority would be obliged to include in its building programme proposals for halting sites. He said:

> A housing authority is under a duty to have regard to the provision of suitable housing accommodation for persons who are in need of it and who are unable to provide it from their own resources. If therefore it is established that there are a group of persons whose need is for housing accommodation in caravans which are situated on serviced sites because their needs cannot be met by the provision of ordinary dwelling houses, then the housing authority must have regard to the needs of those persons. This does not mean that having considered them they may then ignore them. Bearing in mind the overall objectives of the statute it seems to me that once the existence of the special needs to which I have referred is established, then the housing authority is under a duty to include proposals to meet those needs in its building programme if the following conditions exist:
> i) that financial resources would permit the work involved in the proposals to be carried out;
> ii) that sites are available, that is that they are either in the possession of the Corporation or are capable of being acquired by them;
> iii) that the sites are suitable bearing in mind the reasonable needs of the travellers and the reasonable needs of the settled community, as well as the responsibilities and duties of the Corporation as planning authority in the area;
> iv) that the provision of serviced sites would not conflict with the achievement of other statutory objectives laid down in the Act or other statutory duties of the Corporation which in their opinion should reasonably take precedence.[37]

Furthermore housing authorities also had a duty to review an existing building programme which made no provision for halting sites so as to include proposals for such sites if, after the programme had been adopted, it was established that there was a need for such sites within the authority's functional area. In the instant case, Costello J. held that the defendant corporation had a duty to carry out such a review. It was now clear that there was a need for such sites; financial considerations permitted such a review as the Minister was prepared to fund the entire cost of the proposal; there were suitable sites available within the functional area; and finally it was not suggested that the provision of sites would in any way conflict with any other duties that the Corporation might have. Accordingly, the judge granted the plaintiffs a declaration that the defendants were obliged to review their building programme so as include proposals for halting sites. The judge did not make any mandatory order as it could not be

---

[37] *Ibid.* at pp. 189-90.

assumed that the corporation would neglect to perform this statutory duty or that if it did so fail, that the Minister would not exercise his power under s.111 of the Act to require it to discharge the duty in a prescribed manner and within a prescribed time. Rather than dismissing this application outright, however, he adjourned it, giving liberty to the plaintiffs to apply, thereby keeping some pressure on the defendants.

Finally, the plaintiffs had also argued that, pending the development of serviced sites, the corporation had a duty to service the existing unofficial halting sites through the provision of water supplies, refuse collection, provision of animal enclosures, etc. Costello J. dismissed this claim but did remark that if the corporation wished to exercise its undoubted powers to service such sites, it could do so without prejudicing in any way its entitlement to recover possession of the sites.

Costello J.'s rulings on the responsibilities of housing authorities under the Housing Act 1966 represented very limited gains for the Travelling community. A decision that such authorities could be obliged to make provision for halting sites in a building programme but could not be obliged to implement such provision was of very little help to Travellers living by the side of the road. Even the duty to make provision for such sites in a building programme had to be read subject to the planning code, as was illustrated by a decision of O'Hanlon J. less than two weeks later in which he held that a halting site contemplated in a high amenity area in Co. Dublin contravened the development plan for the county.[38] *O'Reilly* did give housing authorities the green light to service unofficial halting sites but this gain cannot disguise the fact that the plaintiffs had failed to establish a right to a serviced halting site.

Thus the absence of a duty on housing authorities to provide halting sites continued to be a major gap in the statutory regime governing the provision of accommodation for Travellers. Nor did this gap appear to have been filled when, for the first time, the Oireachtas specifically addressed the accommodation needs of Travellers in s.13 of the Housing Act 1988 which provides in relevant part:

(1) This section applies to persons belonging to the class of persons who traditionally pursue or have pursued a nomadic way of life.

(2) A housing authority may provide, improve, manage and control sites for caravans used by persons to whom this section applies, and may carry out any works incidental to such provision, improvement, management or control, including the provision of services for such sites.[39]

The use of the word "may" in sub-section 2 suggested that this was a permissive provision only and that housing authorities were still not *obliged* to provide halting sites. Judicial intervention, however, soon changed that perception.

---

[38] *O'Leary v. Dublin Co. Co.* [1988] IR 150.

[39] Section 13 cannot be considered in isolation, as controlling provisions dealing with unlawful halting sites were also enacted a few years later. Thus s.10 of the Housing (Miscellaneous Provisions) Act 1992 empowered housing authorities to move people living on unauthorised public sites within a five mile radius of an authorised halting site to that halting site, while s.69 of the Roads Act 1993 made it an offence to have a temporary dwelling by the roadside without lawful authority.

The breakthrough came in *University of Limerick v. Ryan.*[40] Here the plaintiff university had applied for an order, pursuant to s.27 of the Local Government (Planning and Development) (Amendment) Act 1976, that named Traveller families be restrained from remaining on land immediately outside the main gate of the campus and belonging to Limerick County Council. The Travellers, who were given liberty to join the council as third parties, sought, *inter alia,* an order requiring the council to assess their needs and to provide a halting site for them within a reasonable distance of a particular national school.

After detailing the harassment and intimidation experienced by the Travellers in the instant case, Barron J. held that the following were the essential relevant facts:

1) The Travellers had no right to be on the site outside the campus.
2) They had nowhere else in the area where they could go.
3) The Council was unable to provide them with anywhere to go.
4) The Circuit Court had already refused to move them because they had nowhere else to go.

After reviewing the various unsuccessful attempts made by the council to obtain a halting site for the Travellers in this case, Barron J. turned to consider the council's legal obligations as a housing authority. He began by pointing out that the council had a duty to rehouse those in need and that under the Housing Act 1966 the performance of that duty was dependent upon the building programme and scheme of priorities drawn up by the housing authority pursuant to ss.55 and 60 of the Act. These provisions had been replaced by provisions of the Housing Act 1988, specifically ss.9 and 11, but these latter provisions were not significantly different from their predecessors in the 1966 Act, applying only to houses and not to halting sites. Section 13 of the 1988 Act was, however, completely new and the Court had to consider whether its enactment imposed a duty on the council to provide halting sites or merely empowered it to do so.

Barron J. held that, in appropriate circumstances, s.13 gave rise to a duty to provide halting sites. After ruling that there was no distinction in principle between the manner in which powers to provide dwellings under s.56(1) of the 1966 Act were framed and that under which the power to provide halting sites under s.13 was framed, in that the powers in both cases had to be exercised in appropriate circumstances, he continued:

> The position of a traveller family which becomes entitled to be provided with a dwelling must be considered. It is uncontested that such family must be offered a dwelling. If this is refused because the family belongs to the class of persons who traditionally pursue or have pursued a nomadic way of life, does this mean that the Council now has a discretion whether or not to provide that family with a caravan site? The answer to the question is no. It would not be a proper construction to be placed upon the relevant provisions of the Act. Section 13 must be taken to intend that the obligation of the Council to provide for

[40] Unreported, High Court, 21 February 1991.

housing needs extends in the case of those to whom Section 13 applies to the provision
not of dwellings but of caravan sites.

It is, I think, significant that section 56(2) of the 1966 Act is to apply to serviced halting
sites as it does to dwellings. In my view, section 13 imposes on the local authority an
obligation to provide serviced halting sites to those who require them instead of
conventional dwellings in the same way as section 56(1) requires them to provide the
latter. Such obligation is, of course, subject to all the provisions which limit the
obligations of the housing authority under section 56 of the 1966 Act. The section does,
however, mean that the housing authority cannot meet its statutory obligations by offering
only a conventional dwelling to travellers ... .In the case of those persons to whom section
13 applies and who do not wish to be provided with dwellings, the obligation must be
fulfilled by the provision of caravan sites.

As a matter of construction of section 13, it seems to me that the statutory obligation to
provide a caravan site for travellers is identical to the statutory obligation to provide
dwellings for those of the settled community. The only difference in the obligation lies in
the nature of the housing to be provided.[41]

The judge added that he was referring only to the position of Travellers living
permanently in a particular area whose need for a caravan site was as a permanent
home and that the provision of temporary halting sites did not arise for consideration.

In the instant case, therefore, Barron J. held that the council had failed in its duty
towards the Travellers to provide halting sites.[42]

In 1994, the statutory obligation of housing authorities to provide halting sites
pursuant to s.13 of the 1988 Act was re-affirmed by both Flood and Costello JJ. in *Co.
Meath VEC v. Joyce*[43] and *O'Brien v. Wicklow UDC*[44] respectively. In the former case,
the plaintiffs had made a similar application to that made by the University of
Limerick in *Ryan* and, again, the Travellers had joined the local authority as a third
party.[45] After citing the views of O'Higgins C.J. on the Housing Act 1966, as
expressed in *McNamee v. Buncrana UDC,*[46] and reviewing the provisions of the 1988
Act, Flood J. concluded that one of the functions of a housing authority was to
eliminate, "in a realistic manner over a period of time",[47] the lack of accommodation
for persons in accordance with a scheme of priorities adopted pursuant to s.11 of the
1988 Act. In the instant case, the judge considered that progress on the provision of
halting sites was very slow:

---

[41] *Ibid.* at pp. 28-9.
[42] Barron J. adjourned the making of an order against the council for two weeks in order to see what
steps might be taken by the council in the meantime, an approach similar to that adopted by a
number of High Court judges when dealing with the issue of the State's responsibilities towards
children at risk – see ch. 5.
[43] [1994] 2 ILRM 210.
[44] Unreported, High Court, *ex tempore* judgment, 10 June 1994.
[45] The Travellers in the instant case were using a roadside adjacent to a community school as a
halting site.
[46] [1983] IR 213.
[47] [1994] 2 ILRM 210 at p. 218.

The situation would appear to be that sites for travellers, which are likely to be frequented by them, when located by members of the technical staff of the County Council do not find favour with the elected representatives essentially because they are not prepared to vote for sites for reasons which appear to be unrelated to the suitability of the sites and to be solely related to the geographical and social and future electoral implications.

This failure by the elected representatives on the County Council to follow the advice of the County Manager and his staff when taken in conjunction with the squalor, the health hazard and the misery of the unauthorised camp site in question, seems to me to be a far cry from a *bona fide* performance by the Council of its functions under the Housing Acts.[48]

He went on to hold that the council had a duty to perform their functions under the Housing Acts in a rational and reasonable manner and to provide accommodation for persons defined as homeless under the 1988 Act which clearly included the Travellers in the instant case. He ordered the council to update their assessment of the accommodation needs of Travellers in their area and to provide sufficient halting sites to meet these needs within a period of 12 months from the date of the court's order, subject to any extension the court might allow.[49] For their part, the Travellers were injuncted from trespassing on the VEC's property, committing any act of public nuisance within 100 yards of that property or harassing or intimidating anyone using the road on which they were camped.[50]

In his *ex tempore* judgment in *O'Brien v. Wicklow UDC*, Costello J. followed *University of Limerick v. Ryan* in inferring a duty to provide halting sites from s.13 of the 1988 Act once a need for halting sites had been established and there was no valid reason why they should not be provided. He ordered the local authorities to provide at least three serviced halting sites, two within a twelve month period. In the meantime, he ordered that a hardcore surface, electricity, drainage and sanitary facilities be provided at two of the sites where the Travellers were then located, though he accepted that it was for the housing authority to determine the priorities in the allocation of accommodation at the sites.

Two years later, in *Ward v. South Dublin County Council*,[51] Laffoy J. considered that the defendant's contention that it had no duty to provide halting sites pursuant to s.13 of the Housing Act 1988 was "wholly incomprehensible and unsustainable"[52] in the light of the decisions in *University of Limerick v. Ryan*,[53] *O'Brien v. Wicklow*

---

48 *Ibid.* at pp. 218-9.
49 The order made did not require the defendants to provide halting sites to named individuals as such an order would have disregarded the rights of other people on the housing list.
50 In a subsequent judgement dated 29 April 1994, Flood J. granted the VEC an order directing the Travellers to vacate the site within a week but, in a thinly veiled warning, noted, at pp. 4-5, that the council's failure to take any steps whatsoever to address the needs of the Travellers "has overtones, as yet inchoate, of contempt [of court]" which could become germane if steps were taken to initiate further proceedings at a later time.
51 Unreported, High Court, 31 July 1996.
52 *Ibid*, at p. 4.
53 Unreported, High Court, 21 February 1991.

UDC,[54] *Co. Meath VEC v. Joyce*[55] and *Mongan v. South Dublin County Council.*[56] She went on to state, however, that the court could not direct a local authority as to how it should deploy its resources or as to how it should prioritise the performance of its statutory functions, holding that a mandatory injunction directing a housing authority to provide halting sites would only be granted where inactivity on the part of the authority constituted a breach of s.13. The judge did indicate, however, that in the light of *McNamee v. Buncrana UDC,*[57] a housing authority would have to consider the needs of Travellers who had recently arrived in its functional area, even though they might have little prospect of qualifying for accommodation under the authority's priority scheme for allocation accommodation.

c) Standard of facilities at halting sites – The right to a halting site now firmly established,[58] attention then turned to the standard of facilities to be provided at such sites. In *Mongan v. South Dublin County Council*[59] the plaintiffs had been served with notices under s.10(1) of the Housing (Miscellaneous Provisions) Act 1992 directing them to move their caravans to an authorised halting site. By virtue of s.10(1) of the 1992 Act, housing authorities may direct people living on unauthorised sites within a five mile radius of an authorised site to move to that authorised site. The plaintiffs instituted proceedings challenging the order to move in which they sought a declaration that the Council had a statutory duty to provide accommodation for travellers in their functional area and that a temporary halting site is not sufficient performance of the duty. They also argued that facilties at the site in question were inadequate and that the site was also unsuitable because they would be required to share it with rival Traveller families.

   Barron J. reaffirmed that housing authorities had an obligation under s.13 of the 1988 Act to provide halting sites for travellers assessed under s.9(1) of the Act as being homeless. He said that there was nothing in the statutory provisions which suggested that the level of services to be provided with halting sites should be any less than the level of services provided with homes. Thus, Travellers were to receive permanent sites for their caravans in the same way as others receive homes and the quality of the services available at these sites had to be the same as the quality of the services provided for public housing.

   Turning to the two basic complaints made by the Travellers about the quality of the accommodation offered to them, Barron J. accepted that the services at one particular site, Lynch's Lane, were totally inadequate and that the Travellers were accordingly entitled to refuse to move there. However he rejected the argument that Travellers

---

[54] Unreported, High Court, *ex tempore*, 10 June 1994.
[55] [1994] 2 ILRM 210.
[56] Unreported, High Court, 31 July 1995. Discussed immediately below in the following section.
[57] [1983] IR 213.
[58] *University of Limerick v. Ryan* was subsequently followed by Laffoy J. in *Ward v. South Dublin County Council*, unreported, High Court, 31 July 1996 and by Kinlen J. in *Mongan v. South Dublin County Council*, unreported, High Court, 17 December 1999.
[59] Unreported, High Court, 31 July 1995.

could refuse otherwise suitable accommodation because it failed to take into account Traveller culture or identity and because the Travellers would be required to share it with rival families.[60]

As far as the size of sites was concerned, that, according to the judge, was a question of planning law and it was not a question of which complaint could be made by anybody placed or offered a place on the site. With regard to temporary sites, Barron J. held that facilities could not be any less than on permanent sites, though they could be provided on the understanding that they would not be permanent.

Finally, the judge considered whether the housing authority had an obligation to provide accommodation for every Traveller coming within its functional area, concluding that the answer here depended on whether or not there was a sufficient supply of accommodation. If there was not a sufficient supply, then the authority had an obligation within its resources to ensure that provision was made for the future to deal with the problem.

In conclusion, Barron J. held that the Travellers were entitled to refuse the accommodation offered at Lynch's Lane because of the inadequate facilities provided but that they had to accept the accommodation offered at a second site. From the perspective of Travellers, this decision was seen as very significant[61] because the High Court was asserting a jurisdiction to review the standard of facilities provided at halting sites and setting that standard by reference to the standard of facilities provided with public housing.[62]

The significance of the court's power to review the standard of facilities provided is also apparent in *Ward v. South Dublin County Council.*[63] Here the applicants, on whom s.10 notices had been served, sought a judicial declaration of the duty of the

---

[60] In similar fashion, the European Court of Human Rights has also taken the view that the failure of the UK planning code to make special arrangements for gypsies does not violate Article 14 of the European Convention on Human Rights – see *Chapman v. U.K.*, Application No.27238/95, *Beard v. U.K.*, Application No.24882/94, *Lee v. U.K.*, Application No.25289/94, *Smith v. U.K.*, Application 25254/94 and *Coster v. U.K.*, Application No.24876/94, all decided on 18 January 2001. The Court also decided, *inter alia*, that the refusal of the planning authorities to permit gypsy families to place mobile homes on land owned by such families was justified by the need to protect the rights of others through preservation of the environment and that, accordingly, there was no violation of Arts.8 of the Convention or of Article 1 of Protocol No.1 to the Convention. In the earlier case of *Buckley v. U.K.* (1997) 23 EHRR 101, the Court held, *inter alia*, that a refusal to allow a gypsy family to live in caravans on land that the family owned was justified in the interests of public safety, the economic well-being of the country, the protection of health and the protection of the rights of others.

[61] A report in *The Irish Times* on 9 August 1995 described Travellers and their support groups as being "elated" by the judgment.

[62] In a subsequent case decided more than four years later, also called *Mongan v. South Dublin County Council*, unreported, High Court, 17 December 1999, Kinlen J. held that the accommodation at Lynch's Lane was now of a sufficient standard as to entitle the council, acting pursuant to s.10 of the 1992 Act, to require the plaintiffs to move onto the site. This is a classic illustration of one drawback to litigation strategy in that an adverse result in the courts can copperfasten the policy or situation that the plaintiff is seeking to change.

[63] Unreported, High Court, 31 July 1996.

defendant housing authority towards them. Laffoy J.'s comments on the extent of the defendant's duty under s.13 of the Housing Act 1988 and on the role of the courts in enforcing this duty are summarised above.[64] In relation to the s.10 notices, the judge held that a precondition to the service of a valid notice is that there must be, within a distance of five miles from the location of the unauthorised site, a halting site provided by the housing authority that is capable of accommodating the person on whom the notice is served. In the instant case, Laffoy J. took the view that by reason of the physical condition of, and the inadequacy of services at, the halting site referred to in the notices, the notices were not validly served and the council was not entitled to take any action on foot of them. She also held, however, that service of a s.10 notice is not an implicit acknowledgement by a housing authority that it owes a duty to the person concerned under s.13 of the 1988 Act. Moreover, in directing a Traveller to move to a halting site under s.10, a housing authority does not have to take account of Traveller culture and, in particular, does not have to ensure compatibility with existing occupiers of the site. Nor was the fact that a halting site had been designated as a temporary halting site a factor which, on its own, would render that site unsuitable for the purposes of s.10.

> In short, in my view, if there is accommodation in the halting site to which a person is directed by a Section 10 notice, which is located in hygienic environs and is in proper physical condition and adequately serviced, the person on whom it is served disobeys the notice on pain of incurring the sanctions provided for in Section 10.[65]

In the instant case, Laffoy J. ordered the council to ascertain the accommodation needs of the applicants and restrained it from taking any action on foot of the notices served pursuant to s.10 of the 1992 Act.

d) Right to public housing of one's choice – In *McDonagh v. Cork County Council*[66] a Traveller family unsuccessfully sought to assert a right to be provided with the house of their choice by the housing authority. The plaintiffs had applied for permanent housing accommodation from the defendants and had been asked by the defendants to look out for a suitable house. Eventually such a house was identified and the defendants proceeded to purchase it, the Travellers believing that it was being purchased for them. When the other residents heard that a Traveller family was going to move in, in the words of Kinlen J., "all hell was let loose"[67] and a 24 hour vigil was mounted on the property to prevent anybody taking up occupation.[68] Under these

---

[64] See pp. 229-230.
[65] Unreported, High Court, 31 July 1996, at p. 15.
[66] Unreported, High Court, 12 January 1998.
[67] *Ibid.* at p. 2.
[68] Referring to the hostile reaction from the settled community, Kinlen J. commented, at p. 6:
    Unfortunately, probably everyone in the country of the settled community belong to the organisation known as NIMBY (Not in My Back Yard). Everyone agrees that people should not in this day and age be left in caravans or old fashioned tents on the edge of the roadside. Everyone agrees and it is the law that they must be housed... However in all the cases there

circumstances, the council decided not to offer the plaintiffs a tenancy in the house. Declining to order the council to provide them with the premises in question, Kinlen J. nonetheless directed that the plaintiffs be housed within twelve months. He said:

> [I]t is quite clear in that case that while there was possibly an expectation that [the plaintiffs] would get the house they had chosen themselves, there is nothing in writing or anything sealed by the County Manager which would entitle them to specific performance. This Court cannot order the local authority how to exercise its respective powers and direct for a certain person to be allocated a certain house in the absence of a specific contract...The County Council must not take into consideration threats of violence or any form of intimidation. They had a statutory duty to provide for the housing needs of all those qualified. In this case there is no doubt that Mr and Mrs McDonagh qualify. It is therefore the duty of the local authority to provide housing for this unfortunate family.[69]

Concluding this section, it is clear that, by taking cases to court, Travellers have made certain advances in promoting their rights under the housing code. Litigation has established defensive rights for Travellers facing eviction by a housing authority from unlawful halting sites in that the authority must generally give consideration to the Travellers' accommodation needs before taking any such action.[70] Moreover, if it is proposed to move the Travellers to an authorised halting site, the facilities on that site must be of an acceptable standard. Litigation has also established the more pro-active right to be provided with a halting site in appropriate circumstances.

However establishing rights in court is one thing – securing the implementation of those rights in practice is an entirely different matter and there is no evidence to date that judicial recognition of a right to a halting site has led to any dramatic improvement in the number of such sites being provided throughout the country. Indeed, even some of the families who took legal proceedings against local authorities have failed to benefit from judicial rulings in their favour, partly because enforcement is a lengthy process and the families have a tendency to move on, rather than remain in one location for the purpose of bringing enforcement proceedings. Moreover, the refusal of the courts to take account of Traveller culture allows housing authorities to

---

have been local complaints. These are perfectly understandable. They feel that settled itinerants beside them will create dirt, may increase the crime in the area and will probably diminish the value of the house which they may have devoted a lifetime to buying for themselves and their heirs. There have in fact been cases where halting sites have been imposed against the will of the local community and in one case at least a County Manager was picketed and retired prematurely. The reaction of the public is understandable. However, these people are Irish people also. We treasure all our people equally. They must get the same but no more than their fellow citizens.

[69] The judgment concludes by noting that while the case was at hearing, suitable alternative accommodation had been found for the plaintiffs and that they were well settled.

[70] Except where the Travellers are camped within one mile of an official halting site, in which case the authorities are empowered by s.10(1)(c) of the Housing (Miscellaneous Provisions) Act 1992, as amended by s.32 of the Housing (Traveller Accommodation) Act 1998, to direct the Travellers to relocate to a distance not less than one mile from the site.

provide large-scale sites that ghettoise Travellers and that arouse particularly strong opposition from settled people. Finally, Travellers have, on occasion, suffered defeat in the pursuit of litigation strategy as in *Mongan v. South Dublin County Council*[71] when an attempt to challenge the standard of facilities provided at a halting site backfired when the court held that the facilities were of an acceptable standard.

Litigation under the Planning Code[72]

In considering the impact of litigation on the issue of Traveller accommodation, one also has to take account of those cases taken pursuant to the Local Government (Planning and Development) Acts 1963-1999 by settled people opposed to the provision of halting sites for Travellers in their area. The litigation reveals three different grounds of objection. The most common argument advanced by the objectors is that the particular proposal for a halting site is contrary to the zoning objectives of the local authority's development plan. Less frequently, the substantive merits of a proposal to provide a halting site are challenged on the ground that the proposal is not consistent with the proper planning and development of the area. Finally, the legal authority of a county manager to direct that a halting site be provided in a particular area has been challenged in two cases.

a) Halting site contrary to zoning objectives in development plan – By virtue of s.19 of the 1963 Act, local authorities are obliged, *inter alia*, to indicate their development objectives for their area in a development plan and s.39 of that Act provides, *inter alia*, that local authorities shall not effect any development that materially contravenes such plan. Before a local authority can adopt a development plan or effect any material alteration to an existing development plan, it must comply with the statutory process for public consultation set out in ss.21 and 21A of the 1963 Act.[73] Since the mid-1980s, these provisions relating to development plans have been relied upon by residents opposed to the provision of halting sites in their area.

In a number of cases, the courts held that proposed halting sites were contrary to the zoning objectives in existing development plans. The earliest instance of this in the High Court[74] would appear to be *O'Leary v. Dublin County Council*[75] in which the

---

[71] Unreported, High Court, 17 December 1999.

[72] In preparing this section, I have derived considerable assistance from Scannell, *Environmental and Planning Law in Ireland* (Round Hall Press, 1995), especially pp. 82 to 109 and the following articles by Simons, "Travellers: Planning Issues" (1997) *IPELJ* 8, "Unauthorised Travellers' Halting Sites" (1997) *IPELJ* 53 and "Travellers' Halting Sites: A Special Issue in Town Planning", a paper delivered to a conference organised by Trinity Law School on "Travellers, Society and the Law" on 18 July 1997. I am also grateful to Professor Scannell for the very helpful comments she made on this section of the book.

[73] *Finn v. Bray UDC* [1969] IR 169. S.21A was inserted by s.37 of the Local Government (Planning and Development) Act 1976.

[74] In *Lally v. Mayo Co. Co.*, Circuit Court, 8 February 1985, a Circuit Court judge granted a declaration that the provision of a halting site beside a national primary road would constitute a material contravention of the defendant council's development plan.

[75] [1988] IR 150.

plaintiffs objected to the provision of halting sites for Travellers in Templeogue, Co. Dublin. The council had adopted a plan for the settlement of Travellers that envisaged the provision of two sites for Travellers within each electoral area in the county. A number of electoral areas had very little undeveloped land available and in one particular area, the sites were located on the only two stretches of land owned by the council. One of these sites was designated as a high amenity area in the County Development Plan and local residents challenged the decision to provide a halting site there on the ground that the use of the site for this purpose would amount to a material contravention of the Development Plan. After reviewing the provisions of the Development Plan, O'Hanlon J. agreed with this analysis and granted an injunction to prevent the council proceeding with the proposed development. Dismissing the council's argument that the small size of the development relative to the extent of the high amenity area meant that this was not a material contravention of the development plan, the judge said:

> I do not think a private developer would be allowed to argue that the area involved in his project was small in relation to the area comprised in a particular High Amenity Area, and that therefore the contravention, if any, was not "material". I think the requirements of the planning law have to be applied with the same stringency against the local authority in this case as would be the case if the proposal came from a private developer. The very praiseworthy motives of the County Council in endeavouring to make provision for deprived classes and to do it in a manner which seeks to involve all electoral areas within their territory, are not sufficient to absolve them from compliance with the planning law.[76]

In a subsequent case, *Tom Chawke Caravans Ltd. v. Limerick County Council*,[77] Flood J. quashed a decision of the defendant council to locate a halting site in an area zoned for commercial and business use in the existing development plan and in *Keogh v. Galway Corporation*,[78] Carney J. similarly quashed a decision of the defendant corporation to develop a halting site in an area which had not been identified in the development plan as a possible location for such a site. In this case, the judge also stressed the importance of residents being put on notice of a local authority's proposals in relation to the provision of halting sites in their area, saying:

> It is central to the scheme of the [Local Government (Planning and Development) Act 1963] that a citizen is to be given notice of a development which might affect him in a substantial way and have the opportunity of stating his case in relation to what is projected. The provision of halting sites is a matter of clear interest to adjoining householders and is also frequently a matter of great concern and controversy.[79]

---

[76] *Ibid.* at p. 154.
[77] Unreported, High Court, February 1991. See O'Sullivan and Shepherd, *Irish Planning Law and Practice* (Butterworths, 2000), para.1.646.
[78] [1995] 1 ILRM 141. See also the companion case of *McCann v. Galway Corporation*, unreported, High Court, 15 November 1994.
[79] *Ibid.* at p. 146.

A similar approach was taken in *Roughan v. Clare County Council*,[80] in which Barron J. held that a proposed temporary halting site contravened a general prohibition in the county development plan on development outside settlements and areas designated as special development zones. He also held that it was necessary for a local authority to include *all* of its development objectives in the development plan and noted that the absence of any provisions on Traveller accommodation in the Clare development plan "clearly imposes a severe burden on the planning authority in that no preparation has been made by way of the required consultation process and *ad hoc* decisions will be likely to be less well received than those made following such process."[81]

According to one commentator,[82] this imposition of a duty to include the proposed location of halting sites in a development plan was a judge-made requirement[83] that treated halting sites differently from most other forms of development.[84]

In a number of these cases, the local authority responded to its initial defeat in the courts by attempting to amend the zoning objectives in the development plan to include the particular proposal for halting sites. This tactic in turn provoked further litigation focussing on the statutory consultation procedure for the adoption of such amendments. Thus in the aftermath of O'Hanlon J.'s decision in *O'Leary v. Dublin County Council*,[85] the defendant council subsequently proposed a variation of the development plan to allow for the proposed halting sites. Over 5,000 objectors requested oral hearings of their objections to this variation in what one commentator described as "an obvious attempt to frustrate the process for varying the plan".[86] The residents then sought an injunction to prevent the variation, alleging that the statutory consultation procedure had not been followed by the Council. However this was refused by O'Hanlon J., who also discharged his injunction in the first case.[87]

Residents had more success in *Keogh v. Galway Corporation*.[88] Following Carney J.'s earlier decisions in *Keogh v. Galway Corporation*[89] and *McCann v. Galway*

---

[80] Unreported, High Court, 18 December 1996.

[81] *Ibid.* at p. 7 of his unreported judgment. In one further case, *Birmingham v. Birr UDC*, [1998] 2 ILRM 136, Morris P. granted an interlocutory injunction restraining the defendant council from proceeding with the development of a proposed halting site, holding that the applicants had established a fair question as to whether the proposal was a material contravention of the development plan and that the balance of convenience favoured the residents.

[82] Simons, "Travellers' Halting Sites: A Special Issue in Town Planning", paper delivered to a conference organised by Trinity Law School on "Travellers, Society and the Law" on 18 July 1997, at p. 3.

[83] Note, however, that s.10(2)(i) of the Planning and Development Act 2000 now requires local authorities to list proposals for the provision of Traveller accommodation in their development plans.

[84] A similar requirement has been imposed by the European Communities (Waste) Regulations 1979 [S.I. No.390 of 1979] in relation to waste disposal sites – see Scannell, p. 455.

[85] [1988] IR 150.

[86] Scannell, at p. 94.

[87] Unreported, *ex tempore* judgment, 20 November 1989. According to Scannell, the halting site was completed in June 1991 – Scannell, p. 94.

[88] [1995] 3 IR 457; [1995] 2 ILRM 312.

[89] [1995] 1 ILRM 141.

Corporation,[90] the corporation proposed to amend the development plan to include the objective of providing halting sites but without specifying any particular locations.[91] The corporation duly entered into the public consultation process required by s.21A of the 1963 Act in relation to this variation of the development plan but at the meeting of the corporation held to consider this change, the corporation agreed a further modification of the variation which purported to exclude three particular zones from the areas in which halting sites might be provided. The public was not consulted about this further modification, leading to a challenge to its validity in the courts.

In response to the corporation's initial argument that it had given full consideration to objections submitted by the applicants, Morris P. held that these objections related only to the original variation of the development plan and that the applicants had not been given any opportunity to respond to the subsequent change thereto. The corporation also argued that this subsequent change was not a "material alteration" of the development plan and that consequently no consultation process was required. On this argument, the President initially held, as an issue of fact, that the corporation had never decided that the amendment was not a material alteration and that in such circumstances, it was open to the court to decide this issue *de novo.*[92] He held, further, that the amendment did constitute a material alteration to the original proposed variation so that s.21A did apply. Consequently, the defendants' failure to comply with that provision rendered its decision to adopt this amendment invalid.

The net effect of these cases, therefore, is to ensure that the general public have the opportunity to voice their objections, pursuant to ss.21 and 21A of the 1963 Act, to any proposal to locate halting sites in their area. However the public only have a right to be consulted, not a right of veto, and once objections have been duly considered, a local authority may, if it wishes, proceed to adopt the particular proposal.

b) Inconsistency with proper planning and development – In a number of other cases, the substantive merits of proposals to establish halting sites were challenged on the ground that the proposals were inconsistent with the proper planning and development of the area.

Thus in *Lally v. Mayo County Council*[93] a Circuit Court judge granted a declaration effectively preventing the defendant council from providing a halting site beside a

---

[90] Unreported, High Court, 15 November 1994.
[91] The original version of the plan provided for the development of halting sites in four specific locations, leading the courts to restrain the provision of a halting site other than in any of these four areas – see above, p. 235.
[92] Other cases take a more robust view of the court's jurisdiction to determine whether a particular development constitutes a material contravention of a development plan, holding that this is in any event properly a matter for the courts and not for planning authorities – see *Tennyson v. Dun Laoghaire Corporation* [1991] 2 IR 527; *McGarry v. Sligo County Council* [1991] 1 IR 99, [1989] ILRM 768; *Roughan v. Clare Co. Co.*, unreported, High Court, 18 December 1996; *Wicklow Heritage Trust Ltd. v. Wicklow Co. Co.*, unreported, High Court, 5 February 1998 and *Duffy v. Waterford Corporation*, unreported, High Court, 21 July 1999.
[93] Circuit Court, 8 February 1985, cited in Scannell, pp. 93-94.

national primary road on the ground that this would constitute a material contravention of their development plan.

At issue in *Wilkinson v. Dublin County Council*[94] was a proposal to develop a site for 85 caravans in Tyrnellstown, Co. Dublin.[95] Costello J. held that the proposal did not infringe the zoning provisions of the defendant's development plan as that plan permitted the construction of residential caravan parks in areas like Tyrnellstown. However he went on to hold that the scale of the proposed halting site was such that it was not consistent with the proper planning and development of the area and, therefore, constituted a material contravention of the development plan.[96]

This ground of objection has arguably greater impact on a policy to establish halting sites than that discussed in the preceding section inasmuch as it cannot be overcome simply by amending the development plan to permit the development. Instead the proposal to establish halting sites has to be modified to bring it into line with the proper planning and development of the area. Thus in *Wilkinson*, Costello J. suggested that a development on a smaller scale might be acceptable.

In a sequel to this case, however, the Supreme Court set limits to judicial interference with planning decisions on this ground. Following Costello J.'s judgment, the County Manager made a further order, on this occasion providing facilities for thirty Traveller families for a maximum period of five years. This order was successfully challenged by residents in the High Court in *Ferris v. Dublin County Council*[97] but on appeal, a unanimous Supreme Court upheld the County Manager's order, relying on its earlier decision in *The State (Keegan) v. Stardust Compensation Tribunal*[98] that a judge should only intervene with a decision of a planning authority if the decision "plainly and unambiguously flies in the face of fundamental reason and common sense."[99] Such an approach offers a significant degree of protection to decisions of planning authorities and, correspondingly, reduces the prospects of successfully challenging a decision to establish a halting site on the ground that this is contrary to the proper planning and development of the

---

[94] [1991] ILRM 605.

[95] This had previously been the subject of High Court proceedings in which the residents had obtained an order restraining the defendant council from developing the site until a further managerial order was made specifying exactly the work to be done – *Reid v. Dublin Co. Co.*, unreported, High Court, 20 August 1990.

[96] Costello J. also held that the proposed halting site did not infringe the council's policy, as expressed in the development plan, to facilitate the growth of agricultural and horticultural industries in the county or to avoid abrupt transitions in the scale and use of land in transitional zonal areas. Finally, he also rejected the argument that as the decision to build the halting site would reduce the value of the applicant's land, the county manager should have consulted the applicant beforehand and that this failure to consult amounted to a disregard of the applicant's constitutionally protected property rights. According to the judge, the council was not required to hear representations from adjoining occupiers before developing its own property.

[97] *The Irish Times*, 13 October 1990.

[98] [1986] IR 642.

[99] Unreported, Supreme Court, 7 November 1990, *per* Finlay C.J. at pp. 8-9 of his unreported judgment.

area.[100] At the same time, in exercising even this restricted jurisdiction, the courts were precluded, prior to the enactment of the Planning and Development Act 2000,[101] from taking account of a local authority's obligations under the Housing Acts in determining the reasonableness of a decision to provide a halting site.[102]

c) Challenges to legal authority of county manager – Finally, note should be taken of two cases in which challenges were taken to the legal authority of a county manager to direct that a halting site be provided for Travellers. In *Wilkinson v. Dublin County Council*,[103] Costello J. rejected the applicant's contention that the provision of halting sites was a "reserved function" exercisable only by the elected members of the local authority and not falling within the competence of the county manager. According to the judge,

> S.13 of the Housing Act 1988 empowers a housing authority to provide sites for travellers' caravans but this is not expressed to be a reserved function and so the manager can exercise the statutory power thus conferred.[104]

The applicants in *O'Reilly v. O'Sullivan*[105] had more success in challenging the validity of a county manager's decision to authorise the establishment of a halting site in their area, though on a very narrow ground peculiar to the circumstances of that particular case. Pursuant to s.2(9) of the City and County Management (Amendment) Act 1955, a manager can deal forthwith with any situation which he considers to be an emergency situation calling for immediate action and s.27 of the Housing Act 1988 provides that an emergency situation for the purposes of s.2(9) of the 1955 Act shall be deemed to exist where, in the opinion of the manager, the works concerned are urgent and necessary in order to provide a reasonable standard of accommodation for any person. In the instant case, the manager made his order providing for a halting site for certain Traveller families on the understanding that the families in question were homeless within the meaning of s.2 of the Housing Act 1988. Section 2 provides that a person

---

100 In the subsequent case of *O'Keeffe v. An Bord Pleanála* [1993] 1 IR 39, Finlay C.J. said, at p. 71, that "the circumstances under which the court can intervene on the basis of irrationality with the decisionmaker involved in an administrative function are limited and rare". In *O'Reilly v. O'Sullivan*, unreported, Supreme Court, 26 February 1997, *O'Keeffe* was relied upon by the Supreme Court in holding that the applicants had not discharged the burden of proof of showing that the defendant's order providing for a halting site in their neighbourhood was unreasonable. The applicants did successfully challenge the order on another ground, however – see next section.
101 S.10(2)(i) of that Act now requires local authorities to include proposals for Travelling accommodation in their development plans.
102 Simons, "Travellers' Halting Sites: A Special Issue in Town Planning", paper delivered to a conference organised by Trinity Law School on "Travellers, Society and the Law" on 18 July 1997 at pp. 5-6.
103 [1991] ILRM 605.
104 *Ibid.* at p. 611. A reserved function must be expressly described as such in legislation or ministerial order for it to be exercisable only by elected members of a local authority – see Hogan and Morgan, *Administrative Law in Ireland* (3rd ed.) (Roundhall Sweet and Maxwell, 1998) at pp. 187-8.
105 Unreported, Supreme Court, 26 February 1997.

shall be regarded as being homeless for the purposes of this Act if, *inter alia*, there is no accommodation available which the person can reasonably occupy or remain in occupation of. In the instant case, however, the Traveller families had refused offers of housing from the council and so could not be regarded as homeless for the purposes of s.2. The Supreme Court held, accordingly, that in treating the families as homeless for the purpose of s.2, the manager erred in law and so his order was invalid.

Notwithstanding the fact that the Supreme Court invalidated the order to provide a halting site, *O'Reilly v. O'Sullivan* does not have any long term adverse implications for the powers of managers to direct that halting sites be provided for Travellers as the Court accepted that the manager would be entitled to provide a halting site at the same location for members of the Traveller community coming within the scope of s.13 of the Housing Act 1988, *i.e.*, living in unacceptable conditions but who wished to continue to pursue their nomadic way of life.

Summarising this litigation under the planning code, therefore, it is clear that in discharging its duty to provide halting sites for Travellers, a local authority must also comply with the planning code. There is some evidence, however, that in certain respects litigation in this context favoured the interests of residents. In particular, the courts imposed a duty on local authorities to include in their development plans specific details about the proposed location of halting sites. Second, while the jurisdiction of the courts to review the substantive merits of a proposal to establish a halting site was very limited, the courts tended to exercise that jurisdiction by reference only to town planning criteria and without taking account of the statutory duties of local authorities under the housing code. However s.10(2)(i) of the Planning and Development Act 2000 now requires local authorities to include proposals about Traveller accommodation in their development plans and this may broaden the criteria to be taken into account by the courts in the future exercise of this jurisdiction.

Tortious liability of local authorities arising out of behaviour of Travellers on local authority property.

On a number of occasions, the courts have held local authorities liable in tort arising out of the behaviour of Travellers on the authority's property. In *Lind v. Tipperary (North Riding) County Council*,[106] Carroll J. granted damages against the defendant council arising out of the nuisance created by Travellers on a halting site provided by the council. She also granted a permanent injunction restraining the council and others from causing or permitting a nuisance on the site, restricting the number of Traveller families and caravans on the site and excluding animals from the site.

In *Vitalograph (Ireland) Ltd. v. Ennis UDC and Clare County Council*,[107] Kelly J. granted an interlocutory injunction restraining the county council from permitting an actionable nuisance caused by the behaviour of Traveller families camped unlawfully on lands owned by the council. Acknowledging that the council had experienced great

---

[106] Unreported, High Court, 9 November 1990.
[107] Unreported, High Court, 23 April 1997.

difficulty in discharging its statutory duty to provide halting sites because of, *inter alia*, resistance from the local community, he held, nonetheless, that the council

> cannot seek to solve its difficulties by permitting an unlawful use to be made of land which it owns so as to give rise to an intolerable situation of nuisance which exists in the present case.[108]

Finally in this context, one should note the decision in *Treston v. Mayo County Council*[109] in which Moriarty J. held the defendant council liable in damages to the plaintiff for negligent misrepresentation. Prior to purchasing a house on a local authority estate, the plaintiff had received assurances from an employee of the council that the council had a policy of upgrading the estate and selling off houses to tenants already in occupation. Within a year of her moving in, however, the council allocated an adjoining house to a disruptive Traveller family whose behaviour significantly diminished the plaintiff's quality of life for a period of two and a half years. In these circumstances, the judge awarded her damages of £6,500.

The Constitution and Travellers' accommodation needs

I turn now to consider briefly the two attempts by Travellers to invoke the Constitution in support of their rights to accommodation.

The High Court has been asked to consider the constitutional rights of Travellers on two occasions and both cases, by coincidence, came before Costello J. (as he then was), though with dramatically different outcomes.

In *O'Reilly v. Limerick Corporation*,[110] the plaintiffs, who were living in appalling conditions on unofficial halting sites in Limerick, argued, *inter alia*, that the State's failure to provide them with appropriate accommodation amounted to a breach of their constitutional rights. As we have already seen in ch. 1, Costello J. held that he could not entertain this claim as this would involve the court adjudicating on issues of distributive justice which he held were reserved to the Government under the doctrine of separation of powers.

However in his subsequent *ex tempore* judgment in *O'Brien v. Wicklow UDC*,[111] he resiled from this position and held that the plaintiffs' constitutional right to bodily integrity was infringed by the appalling conditions under which they had to live. Reading s.13 of the Housing Act 1988 in the light of this constitutional right, he said:

> If statutory powers are given to assist in the realisation of constitutionally protected rights by a local authority and if the powers are given to relieve from the effects of deprivation of such constitutionally protected rights and if there are no reasons why such statutory powers should not be exercised then I must interpret such powers as being mandatory.[112]

---

108 *Ibid.*, at p. 6 of his unreported judgment.
109 Unreported, High Court, 6 July 1998.
110 [1989] ILRM 181.
111 Unreported, High Court, 10 June 1994.
112 *Ibid.* at p. 4 of his unreported judgment.

In the instant case, therefore, the judge ordered the defendants to provide at least three serviced halting sites, though he accepted that the court could not be involved in the allocation of these sites to particular individuals and that this exercise was a matter for the housing authority.

In the short term, this decision provides constitutional support for Barron J.'s earlier decision in *University of Limerick v. Ryan*[113] that in appropriate circumstances, s.13 of the Housing Act 1988 imposes a duty on housing authorities to provide halting sites for Travellers. However *O'Brien* potentially has implications for other areas of social policy such as education, health and social welfare for if it can be shown that a failure to exercise statutory powers in any of these areas affects the constitutional rights of Travellers, legal remedies may issue from the courts.

Litigation and discrimination against Travellers

Difficulty in obtaining accommodation is only one facet of the pervasive discrimination suffered by Travellers in our society.[114] In recent years, legislation has begun to address explicitly the problem of anti-Traveller discrimination. The earliest instance of this is s.5 of the Unfair Dismissals (Amendment) Act 1993 which deems dismissal because of membership of the Traveller community to be unfair. More recently, the Equal Status Act 2000 prohibits, *inter alia*, discrimination against Travellers in relation to the provision of goods and services, accommodation, education and the operation of clubs and it is very likely that, in the future, there will be an increasing amount of litigation addressing various aspects of this discrimination. At the time of writing, however, no complaints of discrimination under this Act have yet come before the courts.

However Travellers who suffer discrimination at the hands of publicans currently have some legal remedies open to them under the Licensing Acts and, according to the media,[115] a number of cases have been taken in the District Court by Travellers objecting to the renewal of a publican's licence because of a refusal to serve Travellers, at least two of which were initially successful.[116] It is probable that these cases were decided pursuant to sub-ss. 4(5) and 4(7) of the Courts (No.2) Act 1986 which provide that, where a notice of objection to renewal of a publican's licence has been lodged, the licence may only be renewed upon the production to an officer of the Revenue

---

113   Unreported, High Court, 21 February 1991.
114   See *Anti-Racist Law and the Travellers* (DTEDG/ICCL/ITM, 1993); *Report of the Task Force on the Travelling Community* (Pn.1726, 1995) at pp. 78-94; MacLaughlin; *Travellers in Ireland: An Examination of Discrimination and Racism* (Report from the Irish National Co-Ordinating Committee for the European Year Against Racism, 1997).
115   Licensing applications are heard initially in the District Court, with an appeal to the Circuit. However District Court cases are never reported in the published law reports and Circuit Court decisions hardly ever.
116   In a number of cases, however, the District judge held that allegations of discriminatory treatment had not been established and so dismissed objections to the renewal of the licence – see, *e.g.*, *The Irish Times*, 17 February 2000.

Commissioners of a certificate of the court as to, *inter alia*, the good character of the applicant. A leading commentator on the licensing laws has suggested that

> A 'capricious refusal' to serve customers might be made a cause of objection to the renewal of his licence at the annual licensing session: the refusal, for example, of some publicans to serve females in parts of their licensed premises may constitute a ground of objection to the renewal of the licence.[117]

The criminal law also offers Travellers protection against discriminatory behaviour that constitutes a criminal offence,[118] though in this context, Travellers depend on the Gardai or the Director of Public Prosecutions to pursue the wrongdoers through the courts. One particular offence is worth mentioning in this context. Section 2 of the Prohibition of Incitement to Hatred Act 1989 makes it an offence, *inter alia*, to use words which are "threatening, abusive or insulting and are intended or, having regard to all the circumstances, are likely to stir up hatred." To date, only two prosecutions have been taken under this legislation, both of which were unsuccessful. In 1999, a Co. Mayo councillor who had compared Travellers to "pedigree dogs"[119] was acquitted of an offence under s.2 on the ground that his comments were unlikely to incite hatred.[120] In September 2000, a Dublin Bus driver was initially convicted in the District Court of an offence under s.2 and fined a total of £900 after calling a Gambian national a "nig-nog" and telling him that he should go back to his own country. However that decision was subsequently quashed on appeal before the Circuit Court, again on the ground that the language used was not intended or likely to stir up hatred.[121] These decisions have led to calls from Traveller and other organisations for a strengthening of the Act[122] but it is difficult to see how this can be done without infringing constitutional and international guarantees of free speech.

Finally in this context of discrimination, it is worth noting briefly the Supreme Court decision in *In re F O'D, an infant; Southern Health Board v. An Bord Uchtála*[123] in which a Traveller family opposed the adoption of their son by a settled family pursuant to s.3(1) of the Adoption Act 1988. That section empowers the High Court to authorise the adoption of a child born to a married couple by another couple in circumstances where, *inter alia*, the original parents have failed in their duty towards the child. In the instant case, Costello P. held that the parents of a Traveller child had been guilty of substantial cruelty to and neglect of their son and so authorised his

---

[117] Cassidy, *The Licensing Acts 1833-1995* (Round Hall/Sweet and Maxwell, 1996) at pp. 467-8.
[118] On 11 September 1995, *The Irish Times* reported that four settled people had been jailed for maliciously damaging Travellers' caravans.
[119] The councillor was reported to have made the following comment at a meeting of the Western Health Board: "Travellers expect to have everything done for them and do nothing themselves. They are able-bodied men who should be made go out and do FÁS courses like everybody else but instead are lying out in the sun like pedigree dogs."
[120] *The Irish Times*, 2 March 1999.
[121] *The Irish Times*, 14 March 2001.
[122] See *The Sunday Tribune*, 14 March 1995; *The Irish Times*, 14 March 2001.
[123] [2000] 1 IR 165.

adoption by a couple from the settled community. On appeal to the Supreme Court, one of the grounds relied upon by the Traveller parents in opposing the adoption was that it failed to give due regard to the placing of a child in a different culture. Delivering the leading judgment in the Supreme Court, Denham J. accepted the validity of this concern, saying,

> There is no doubt that it is a matter of great importance to take care in placing a child in a family of different cultural or ethnic background – to ensure that the child's interests are served. These interests may include knowledge of his social, cultural and ethnic background.[124]

However she dismissed the argument in the instant case on the ground that there was no evidence that this matter had not been properly considered by the Adoption Board in the instant case. Nonetheless her remarks display judicial awareness of the particular problems inherent in the adoption of a child from a different ethnic group such as Travellers.

Conclusion

Reviewing the involvement of the courts with Travellers' concerns, it seems clear that, on balance, this involvement has produced some limited gains for Travellers. Granted, judicial decisions under the planning code affecting Traveller accommodation tend to focus on the rights of the settled community but the emphasis here is on the procedural right of settled people to be notified of proposals for the location of halting sites and once this is respected, the caselaw does not pose any insurmountable obstacle to the provision of halting sites by local authorities.

On the other hand, Travellers have achieved some successes through the use of litigation strategy in defence of their interests. In *Limerick Corporation v. Sheridan*,[125] judicial intervention neutralised oppressive action by a local authority; the Supreme Court in *McDonald v. Feely*[126] provided Travellers with some limited protection against eviction from unlawful sites by local authorities (albeit that this protection has been modified slightly by subsequent legislation[127]) and recent District Court cases have penalised anti-Traveller discrimination, albeit in the limited context of the licensing trade.

Judicial decisions over the past ten years or so have also recognised a right to a halting site in appropriate circumstances and to a certain standard of facilities on such sites, and have raised the possibility of the Constitution being successfully used to challenge other omissions in State provision for Travellers.

Unfortunately, however, victory in the courts has not led to significant tangible improvements on the ground and Travellers still await the provision of an adequate

---

124 [2000] 1 IR 165, at p. 179.
125 (1956) 90 ILTR 59.
126 Supreme Court, 23 July 1980.
127 See s.32 of the Housing (Traveller Accommodation) Act 1998, discussed above at p. 223.

number of halting sites to meet their needs, judicial rulings in their favour notwithstanding.[128] Moreover, litigation strategy has not been without its setbacks for Travellers – thus some complaints of discrimination by publicans have been rejected by the courts; a challenge to the standard of facilities provided at one halting site was dismissed by the High Court in 1999, thereby strengthening the hand of the authorities in this regard, and the courts have resolutely refused to require housing authorities to take account of Traveller culture when making provision for halting sites.

In conclusion, therefore, while litigation strategy has succeeded in generating some gains for Travellers, it has not yet produced the type of substantial reform needed to make any significant inroad into the myriad problems faced by this minority in our society.

---

[128] Thus as recently as January 2001, the Irish Traveller Movement expressed extreme concern at the lack of progress in the provision of halting sites around the country – see *The Irish Times*, 11 January 2001.

Chapter 7

Litigation and Access to Legal Services

The use of litigation to tackle social exclusion presupposes that the beneficiaries of such litigation would have ready access to the services of lawyers. However, as I discuss in ch. 9, a variety of factors can prevent marginalised individuals and communities from availing of legal services. In this chapter, I consider to what extent, if at all, litigation has succeeded in tackling these factors by tracing the impact of judicial decisions on the civil legal aid, the criminal legal aid scheme and the Attorney General's scheme of legal aid.

Civil legal aid

A striking feature of the development of civil legal aid in this jurisdiction has been the reluctance of the State to take on its responsibilities in this regard. Despite the publication of the Pringle Report in 1977 which recommended that the State should fund a "mixed-delivery" model of legal aid, embracing elements of both service and strategic models,[1] there was no evidence at that time that the State intended to provide any type of civil legal aid in the near future.[2] In such circumstances, it was understandable, and perhaps even inevitable, that recourse would be made to the courts in order to secure some improvement in the situation.[3] The litigation here falls

---

[1] On the "mixed-delivery", "service" and "strategic" model of legal aid, see ch. 9, at pp. 284-6.

[2] See pp. 288-9.

[3] Also inevitable, given the subject-matter involved, was the fact that some of these cases were taken by personal litigants and that consequently, the argumentation was not always as well developed as one might have wished. In *Application of J.C.*, unreported, High Court, 25 July 1985, the plaintiff's claim that he was denied access to the courts because of his poverty was not sufficiently well developed to allow Barrington J. rule authoritatively on the point, while in *MacGairbhith v. Attorney General* [1991] 2 IR 412, O'Hanlon J. dismissed the rather hopeful claim that personal litigants had a constitutional right to be provided with a law library by the State, a decision subsequently upheld on appeal by the Supreme Court in an unreported judgment

into two categories. Cases in the first category attempt to establish a general right to civil legal aid, based either on the Constitution or on the European Convention on Human Rights, seeking thereby to compel the State to make effective provision for such a right. Cases in the second category clarify the meaning of various provisions of the State scheme of civil legal aid and advice, first introduced in 1980 and put on a statutory footing in 1995.

a) Establishing a right to civil legal aid

The first attempt to secure State-funded civil legal aid through the courts occurred in *O'Shaughnessy v. Attorney General.*[4] In a judgment anticipating the more sophisticated reasoning of Costello J. in *O'Reilly v. Limerick Corporation*[5] almost twenty years later, O'Keeffe P. dismissed a constitutional challenge to the Criminal Justice (Legal Aid) Act 1962 arising out of its failure to make any provision for legal aid in civil cases on the ground that it was for the Oireachtas, rather than the courts, to determine how to vindicate the personal rights of the citizen. According to the judge, legislation affording assistance to one class of persons – those charged with criminal offences could not be held to be unconstitutional on the ground either that the Court considered that the priorities should be different or that in providing such assistance, the State had elected not to assist civil litigants. This decision is open to the same criticism that I have levelled against Costello J.'s judgment in *O'Reilly*, namely that far from being precluded by the Constitution from adjudicating upon claims of distributive, it is arguable that the courts are constitutionally obliged to vindicate socio-economic rights promoting social inclusion. The Irish courts have themselves accepted, in other contexts, that citizens have a right of access to the courts[6] but refusing to require the State to provide for civil legal aid makes this right illusory for some citizens at least. In the event, some of the arguments raised in *O'Shaughnessy* subsequently proved to be more fruitful in a different judicial forum.

In June 1973, a Cork woman, Mrs Josie Airey, wrote to the European Commission on Human Rights complaining about Ireland's failure to provide her with civil legal aid in her attempt to obtain a judicial separation from her husband. The Commission passed the letter back to a firm of Irish solicitors who then brought an action under the European Convention on Human Rights on behalf of Mrs Airey, alleging that Ireland was in breach of its obligations under Articles 6(1), 8, 13 and 14 of the

---

dated 29 March 1995. In *Coughlan v. Ireland*, unreported, High Court, 12 July 1995, a challenge to the constitutionality of s.65 of the Courts of Justice Act 1936, requiring the payment of £40 in order to lodge an appeal with the Supreme Court, was dismissed on the grounds that the plaintiff, by not applying for civil legal aid, had not availed of the means provided by the State for ensuring his access to the courts. (In this context, note that in *Murphy v. Minister for Justice, Equality and Law Reform* [2001] 1 IR 95; [2001] 2 ILRM 144, the Supreme Court dismissed the argument that the imposition of reasonable charges in respect of court services was an unconstitutional interference with the plaintiff's right of access to the courts.)

4 Unreported, High Court, 16 February 1971.

5 [1989] ILRM 181.

6 See *e.g. Macauley v. Minister for Posts and Telegraphs* [1966] IR 345.

Convention. In the present context, we need only concern ourselves with the arguments based on Article 6(1). This provides:

> In the determination of his civil rights and obligations or any criminal charge against him, everyone is entitled to a fair and public hearing within a reasonable time by an independent and impartial tribunal established by law.

Relying on *Golder v. U.K.,*[7] lawyers for Mrs Airey successfully argued before the European Court of Human Rights that Article 6(1) guaranteed her a right of access to the courts and that, given the prohibitive costs of obtaining a judicial separation in Ireland, this right had been infringed.[8] Having rejected the State's preliminary objection that Article 6(1) did not apply to proceedings for judicial separation, and having ruled that it was for the individual to select which legal remedy to pursue, the Court dismissed the State's central argument that Airey enjoyed access to the High Court since she was free to appear there as a personal litigant on the ground that "the Convention is intended to guarantee not rights that are theoretical or illusory but rights that are practical and effective".[9] Given the complexity of judicial separation proceedings, coupled with the fact that parties to matrimonial proceedings can hardly be expected to remain completely detached and objective in their presentation of their case before a court, the Court concluded that it was most improbable that someone like Airey could effectively present her own case.

The State then argued that the alleged lack of access to the courts arose not because of any deliberate attempt by the State to impede access, but solely because of the claimant's personal circumstances for which it could not be held responsible. The Court also dismissed this argument, pointing out that "hindrance in fact can contravene the Convention just like a legal impediment"[10] and that the duty to secure effective access to the courts may necessitate some positive action on the part of the State.

The State finally argued that the consequence of the Commission's earlier ruling in favour of Airey would be that, in all cases concerning the determination of a civil right, the State would be obliged to provide free legal aid, a consequence which was not warranted by the Convention, having regard to the Commission's case-law and the terms of Article 6(3)(c). The Court disagreed. According to the Court, the duty to secure an effective right of access to the courts did not involve the provision of civil

---

[7] (1979-80) 1 EHRR 524.

[8] (1979-80) 2 EHRR 305. See Thornberry, "Poverty, Litigation and Fundamental Rights – A European Perspective" (1980) 29 *ICLQ* 250. See also Cousins, "Access to the Courts: The European Convention on Human Rights and European Community Law" (1992) 14 *DULJ (n.s.)* 51. The European Commission on Human Rights had also ruled in Airey's favour at an earlier stage in the proceedings, stating, at para.77 of its Report, adopted on 9 March 1977, that

> a right of access to the courts cannot be understood as a merely general right which could be made ineffective by economic and other obstacles ... The Commission is of opinion that Article 6 must be understood to impose an obligation on the State to secure proper access by removing such obstacles.

[9] (1979-80) 2 EHRR 305 at p. 316.

[10] *Ibid.*

legal aid in all cases.[11] In some situations, the right of the individual to appear in person before the courts would satisfy Article 6(1); simplification of procedure could also ensure an effective access to the courts. In certain situations, however, the State might have to provide for legal assistance, particularly, according to the Court,

> when such assistance proves indispensable for an effective access to court either because legal representation is rendered compulsory, as is done by the domestic law of certain States for various types of litigation, or by reason of the complexity of the procedure or of the case.[12]

In the instant case, the Court concluded, *inter alia*, that Airey did not enjoy an effective right of access to the courts and that Ireland was, accordingly, in breach of its obligations under Article 6 of the Convention.

In her authorised biography, Mary Robinson, who had acted as senior counsel for Mrs Airey, described this case as "the most ground-breaking case I took as a legal practitioner".[13] The judgment of the European Court was certainly a major factor leading to the introduction, in 1980, of the first State funded and administered civil legal aid scheme.[14] However in one important respect, the judgment is inevitably limited, given the facts of the case. At issue in *Airey* was how the State should respond to the plight of an individual who was precluded from pursuing a case through the courts solely through lack of money. This is the issue addressed by "service" models of legal aid, in contrast to the broader objectives of strategic models of legal aid that focus on the social problems of groups or communities, that seek to address additional obstacles to access to legal services apart from simply lack of money and that do not confine themselves to litigation as a means of securing change.[15] Consequently, while the *Airey* judgment was a significant factor leading to the provision of a service model of civil legal aid, it focussed debate on this particular model, to the detriment of the case for State funding of a strategic model of legal aid.[16]

---

[11] The Commission had pointed out, at para.80 of its Report, that its finding in favour of Airey does not amount to a requirement of free legal aid to be granted automatically in this or other civil cases ... This complaint could be removed in several ways. It could, for example, be removed by introducing a system of legal aid dependent on a means test ... the complaint could also be met by the introduction of simplified and cheaper proceedings or the appointment of an official to help in the presentation of the case to the court.

[12] (1979-80) 2 EHRR 305 at p. 317.

[13] O'Leary and Burke, *Mary Robinson: The Authorised Biography* (Hodder and Stoughton, 1998) at p. 113.

[14] See pp. 288-9.

[15] See pp. 284-5.

[16] Commenting on the difficulties inherent in trying to establish a right to legal aid using litigation strategy, Cousins observes that "the main problem [with such an approach] is arguably that it sees access to the courts from a legal point of view only and thus it can only seek to respond to recognized legal difficulties, e.g., the lack of legal representation, long delays in proceedings, unfair procedures, etc. It ignores the sociological barriers, such as the disinclination of many persons to make use of the courts, and the fact that people need basic advice and information if they are going to have adequate access. Thus, even if the practical difficulties outlined above could be overcome, the existing concept of access to the courts as a human right does not enable many

While *Airey* did eventually result in the introduction of a State civil legal aid scheme, that scheme was very limited indeed[17] and further cases asserting a right to civil legal aid continued to come before the Irish courts.

In *E. v. E.*[18] a husband involved in matrimonial proceedings was refused civil legal aid under the State scheme and he claimed that the State should indemnify him against any legal costs incurred in vindicating his personal and family rights. Reliance was placed on *Airey v. Ireland*[19] but O'Hanlon J. held, following the Supreme Court decision in *In re Ó Laighléis*,[20] that as the European Convention on Human Rights was not part of domestic Irish law, any dispute about whether the State fully complied with *Airey* should be determined by the procedure provided for under the Convention and that the husband had not established that the State had infringed any existing right he enjoyed under domestic law. The husband had also argued that the failure of the State to provide him with legal aid amounted to a breach of his constitutional right of access to the High Court to defend and vindicate his personal rights. This argument was dismissed on the ground that, not having exhausted the procedures under the State scheme for obtaining legal aid, the husband lacked *locus standi* to make this claim. More ominously for future challenges to the adequacy of the State scheme, O'Hanlon J. concluded his judgment by remarking that, had the husband overcome these various obstacles,

> I should have great difficulty in holding with him that the provisions made under the Scheme of Civil Legal Aid and Advice were inadequate, in relation to the particular fields of civil litigation to which it relates, to satisfy – for the time being at least – any obligation cast on the State either by the Constitution or under the decision of the European Court in the *Airey* case to provide effective access for litigants to the High Court. The provisions of the Scheme governing financial eligibility appear to me to have been framed in a liberal manner.[21]

The applicant in *M.C. v. The Legal Aid Board*[22] fared little better in her attempt to establish a right to civil legal aid. She had applied to the Legal Aid Board for legal aid in respect of nullity proceedings to which she was a party but because of the build up of arrears of applications, caused by inadequate staffing levels, the Legal Aid Board had to defer consideration of her application. She then instituted legal proceedings against the Board, arguing, *inter alia*, that the Scheme of Civil Legal Aid and Advice was a purported compliance by the State with its constitutional duty of affording the applicant access to the courts and that the continuing unreasonable delay in processing her application for legal aid amounted to a deprivation of her right of access to the courts. Dismissing these arguments, Gannon J. said:

---

of the most important barriers to access to be removed." See "Access to the Courts – The Limitations of a Human Rights Approach" in Heffernan (ed.), *Human Rights: A European Perspective* (Round Hall Press/Irish Centre for European Law, 1994) p. 142 at p. 151.

17 See pp. 289-293.
18 [1982] ILRM 497.
19 (1979-80) 2 EHRR 305.
20 [1960] IR 93.
21 [1982] ILRM 497 at p. 500.
22 [1991] 2 IR 43.

The existence of [the nullity proceedings] does not confer any duty on the State nor on any of the Respondents to either of the parties thereto either under the Constitution or at law. The duty of administering justice and adjudicating by due process does not create any obligation on the State to intervene in any private civil litigation so as to ensure that one party is as well equipped for their dispute as is the other. The fact that the existence of fundamental personal rights is expressly recognised by the Constitution does not impose on the State any duty to intervene in aid of a party involved in any private civil dispute in relation to any such personal rights ...

...I am not convinced that there is any provision in the Constitution which imposes a duty on the State to provide any form of support for civil litigation among citizens. In the absence of such duty I can find no express or implied right in any citizen to require the State to provide financial support for, or to afford free facilities for, civil litigation of a dispute with another citizen.[23]

However in 1993, a limited version of a right to civil legal aid, grounded on the courts' obligation to administer justice under Article 34.1 was recognised by Lardner J. in two different cases.[24] In *Stevenson v. Landy and others*,[25] which concerned wardship proceedings taken by the Eastern Health Board, the Legal Aid Board had refused to grant legal aid to the mother of the child involved to contest the proceedings because she had failed to show that she was reasonably likely to be successful in the proceedings, as required by paragraph 3.2.3.4 of the Scheme of Civil Legal Aid and Advice. Lardner J. quoted from the judgment of O'Higgins C.J. in *The State (Healy) v. Donoghue*[26] wherein the Chief Justice had said:

The requirements of fairness and justice must be considered in relation to the seriousness of the charge brought against the person and the consequences involved for him. Where a man's liberty is at stake, or where he faces a very severe penalty which may affect his welfare or his livelihood, justice may require more than the application of normal and fair procedures in relation to his trial. Facing, as he does, the power of the State which is his accuser, the person charged may be unable to defend himself adequately because of ignorance, lack of education, youth or other incapacity. In such circumstances his plight may require, if justice is to be done, that he should have legal assistance. In such circumstances, if he cannot provide such assistance by reason of lack of means, does justice under the Constitution also require that he be aided in his defence? In my view it does.[27]

Lardner J. then continued:

---

[23] [1991] 2 IR 43 at p. 55. In *Corcoran v. Minister for Social Welfare,* [1992] ILRM 133, Murphy J. similarly held that there was no constitutional right to legal aid for persons appearing before administrative tribunals.

[24] Though note that in *The State (Haverty) v An Bord Pleanála* [1987] IR 485, [1988] ILRM 545, Murphy J. stated, *obiter*, that the principles of natural justice might, in appropriate circumstances, require the provision of legal aid.

[25] Unreported, High Court, 10 February 1993.

[26] [1976] IR 325.

[27] [1976] IR 325 at p. 350.

That statement was made in relation to a criminal prosecution. The present case is of a different nature. Having considered the circumstances of the applicant and in which the application for legal aid to be represented in the wardship proceedings is made, I have come to the conclusion that the dicta which I have quoted are applicable, *mutatis mutandis*, to the wardship proceedings.[28]

He then went on to construe paragraph 3.2.3.4 of the Scheme of Civil Legal Aid and Advice as being satisfied wherever an applicant for legal aid has a "worthwhile contribution" to make to the hearing of the case, commenting that "this approach is more in accordance with the requirements of the Constitution in regard to the administration of justice".

In the second case, *Kirwan v. Minister for Justice*,[29] the applicant complained about the absence of legal aid for persons seeking executive review of their detention pursuant to special verdicts of guilty but insane. The applicant had been found guilty but insane in relation to a charge of murder and, as a consequence, had been detained for a number of years in the Central Mental Hospital. He subsequently applied, through his lawyers, to the Minister for Justice to have his detention reviewed and was advised by the Department that his application would be considered by an advisory committee established by the Minister to consider such cases. The Department also requested a detailed statement from his solicitors outlining the grounds on which they were applying for his release but indicated that there was no provision for legal aid to enable the applicant to obtain legal assistance in presenting his application. Lardner J. held that the constitutional requirement of fair procedures applied to applications for review of detention in this type of case and that this obliged the executive to provide legal aid to any applicant who was "without the requisite means to procure the collection of the relevant information and to formulate and present the appropriate submissions".[30]

In the most recent case in this area, *Byrne v. Scally*,[31] however, the applicant failed in her attempt to establish that eviction proceedings taken against her by Dublin Corporation pursuant to s.62(3) of the Housing Act 1966 could only proceed when she had the benefit of legal representation. Following the decision of Geoghegan J. in *Dublin Corporation v. Hamilton*,[32] Ó Caoimh J. held that in the light of the restricted jurisdiction of the District Court under s.62 of the 1966 Act, proceedings for eviction taken by public authorities are straightforward and relatively simple, involving the establishment of certain straightforward proofs. That being so, the case did not come

---

[28] Unreported, High Court, 10 February 1993, at pp. 9-10.
[29] [1994] 1 ILRM 444.
[30] [1994] 1 ILRM 444 at p. 450. Lardner J. distinguished this case from *The State (O) v. Daly* [1977] IR 312 on the facts. In the earlier case, the Supreme Court held that the right to legal aid in criminal cases recognised in *The State (Healy) v. Donoghue* [1976] IR 325 did not apply to earlier or ancillary stages of criminal proceedings, such as, in *Daly*, proceedings to determine fitness to plead.
[31] Unreported, High Court, 12 October 2000.
[32] Unreported, High Court, 19 June 1998.

within the scope of the principle in *Stevenson v. Landy*[33] so as to give rise to a constitutional right to civil legal aid.

It is clear, therefore, that, in general, the Irish courts are reluctant to develop a right to civil legal aid. In one sense, this is surprising, given that the *Airey* case offers a promising line of argument for any judge interested in going down this road. In that case, the European Court of Human Rights held that the right of access to the courts guaranteed by Article 6(1) of the European Convention on Human Rights could oblige the State, in certain circumstances, to provide impecunious litigants with the assistance of a lawyer. On the face of it, this right would appear to be the same in substance as that protected by Article 40.3 of the Constitution,[34] and so one could argue that the reasoning in *Airey* is very persuasive for a judge construing the latter provision. However the fact remains that, to date, recourse to litigation to establish a right to civil legal aid has only had very limited success before the Irish courts.

While recourse to the European Court of Human Rights has been relatively more successful, even here the gains were limited to the introduction of a very basic service model of legal aid, the provision of which constituted the final nail in the coffin of the more comprehensive proposals contained in the Pringle Report on Civil Legal Aid and Advice.[35]

b) Improving the Scheme of Civil Legal Aid and Advice

Litigation in two cases[36] has succeeded in effecting some improvements to the Scheme of Civil Legal Aid and Advice introduced by the Government in the aftermath

---

[33] Unreported, High Court, 10 February 1993.

[34] As to which, see Kelly, *The Irish Constitution*, Hogan and Whyte (eds.), (3rd ed., 1994) at pp. 770-773.

[35] As to which, see p. 288.

[36] The operation of this Scheme was also considered by the courts in two further cases, though no improvement to the Scheme resulted therefrom. In *D.I. v. F.T.*, unreported, High Court, 16 February 1996, an attempt by a District Judge to direct the Legal Aid Board to pay the costs of a private practitioner who, at the Judge's request, agreed to assist an unaided litigant, failed when Murphy J. held that no judge had power or authority to appoint or nominate a solicitor on behalf of any of the parties appearing before the court on the basis that the costs of such solicitor would ultimately be borne by the Legal Aid Board. In *T.M. v. An Bord Uchtála*, unreported, Supreme Court, *ex tempore*, 17 November 1997, the Supreme Court reluctantly overruled an attempt by Budd J. in the High Court to enable the Legal Aid Board to pay the costs of a natural mother who had unsuccessfully challenged proceedings taken pursuant to s.3 of the Adoption Act 1974 to dispense with her consent to the adoption of her child. Because of the lengthy waiting list at her local centre, she had been unable to obtain legal aid from the Board and so had retained the services of a private firm of solicitors. By virtue of para.8(3) of the Scheme, the Board had a discretion to make an *ex gratia* payment towards the costs of a successful unaided litigant involved in proceedings against an unsuccessful person in receipt of legal aid. In order to come within the scope of this provision, Budd J. relied on *M.F. v. Legal Aid Board* [1993] ILRM 797 and *Stevenson v. Landy*, High Court, 10 February 1993 in classifying the natural mother as having been successful in the proceedings. He then dismissed the description in para.8(3) of the legally aided person as "unsuccessful" as "artificial and somewhat inappropriate" (at p. 13 of his judgment, delivered on 1 February 1996). On appeal, however, the Supreme Court, *per* Hamilton C.J., characterised this as a subterfuge and reluctantly allowed an appeal against Budd J.'s order.

of the *Airey* case. Thus in *M.C. v Legal Aid Board*[37] while the applicant failed to establish that she had a constitutional right to civil legal aid, she did obtain a declaration from Gannon J. that the Legal Aid Board was obliged to consider her application for legal aid within a reasonable time in order to determine if the application deserved priority. Accordingly the Board's policy of deferring the consideration of applications because of a build up of arrears of applications was an unlawful fettering of its discretion to decide whether legal aid should be granted.[38]

In *M.F. v. Legal Aid Board,*[39] the Supreme Court's interpretation of para.3.2.3(4) of the extra-statutory Scheme of Civil Legal Aid and Advice arguably diluted somewhat the impact of the ground for refusing legal aid stated therein. That provision imposed, as a pre-condition for the granting of legal aid, the requirement that the applicant establish that he is "reasonably likely to be successful in the proceedings, assuming that the facts put forward by him in relation to the proceedings are proved before the court". The applicant wished to defend matrimonial proceedings taken by her husband in which he sought, *inter alia*, a custody order in respect of their child. However she was refused a legal aid certificate initially on the ground that it was not reasonable to grant a certificate in the circumstances of the case – para.3.2.3(6) of the Scheme – but subsequently on the ground that she was not likely to be successful in the proceedings. In the High Court, O'Hanlon J.'s decision amounted to a virtual repeal of paras.3.2.3(2), 3.2.3(4) and 3.2.3(6) of the Scheme in relation to matrimonial cases involving the welfare of children, as he indicated that it could only be in "wholly exceptional circumstances" that any of those paragraphs could be used to deny legal aid in such a case.[40] While the Legal Aid Board retrieved the situation somewhat from their perspective on appeal, the Supreme Court decision still reduces the discretion of the Board to refuse legal aid pursuant to para.3.2.3(4). Delivering the unanimous decision of the Court, Finlay C.J. held that in cases taken pursuant to the Judicial Separation and Family Law Reform Act 1989 which involve questions as to the custody, guardianship and welfare of a child of the marriage,

> the provisions of paragraph 3.2.3(4) of the scheme should be interpreted and implemented by the board on the basis that for a person to be 'reasonably likely to be successful in the proceedings', it is only necessary that the board should conclude that there is a reasonable likelihood that the point of view and submissions of the person concerned, with regard to the welfare, custody and upbringing of the child concerned, should be amongst the material which would be relied upon by the judge in determining the issues concerning the child.[41]

---

[37] [1991] 2 IR 43.

[38] This decision enabled the Board to lobby successfully for an expansion in its staffing numbers. In 1993, in the first phase in an expansion of the Scheme, additional funding was provided by the Minister for Equality and Law Reform, Mr Mervyn Taylor, TD, for the recruitment of twelve additional solicitors and twenty seven support staff – see *Legal Aid Board Report 1992*, p. 12.

[39] [1993] ILRM 797.

[40] According to the *Legal Aid Board Annual Report 1992*, (at p. 9), the High Court took a similar approach in another case, cited as *R.S.*, heard around that time.

[41] [1993] ILRM 797 at pp. 804-5.

The Court also held that in applying para. 3.2.3(6) in such cases, the Board should, in taking into account the benefit to the applicant of taking the proceedings for the purpose of deciding whether or not it is reasonable to grant legal aid, equate that benefit with the interest of the applicant in the welfare of the child. This effective relaxation of the requirements of paras. 3.2.3(4) and (6) of the Scheme to matrimonial cases involving the welfare of children was subsequently reflected in the Civil Legal Aid Act 1995, which exempts such cases entirely from the corresponding statutory requirements.[42]

Having considered the relatively modest impact of the Irish courts on the development of a right to civil legal aid, I turn now to examine the contrasting judicial treatment of the right to criminal legal aid.

Criminal legal aid

The provision of criminal legal aid in this jurisdiction differs from its civil counterpart in a number of respects. For a start, it has an older pedigree and, unlike the Scheme of Civil Legal Aid and Advice, was not wrung from a reluctant State by virtue of a judicial decision. As early as 1924, the new State provided for legal aid in the case of defendants appealing against a death penalty to the Court of Criminal Appeal[43] and in 1928, s.5(1)(b) of the Courts of Justice Act of that year empowered both the Supreme Court and the Court of Criminal Appeal to direct that the costs of a re-trial ordered by the court following on a successful appeal against a criminal conviction, together with the costs of the appeal itself, be paid by the State.[44] The present, more extensive scheme was introduced in 1962 when the Criminal Justice (Legal Aid) Act of that year gave the courts a discretion to grant needy defendants legal aid in certain categories of case.[45] That Act provided that in the case of murder or in an appeal from the Court of Criminal Appeal to the Supreme Court, an applicant for criminal legal aid had to satisfy the relevant court that s/he was a person of insufficient means. In all other cases, an applicant additionally had to show that the provision of legal aid was

---

[42] See ss.28(2) and (3) of the 1995 Act.

[43] See Rule 43 of the Court of Criminal Appeal Rules, 1924.

[44] For an account of the development of criminal legal aid in the State following Independence, see Carney, "The Growth of Legal Aid in the Republic of Ireland" (1979) XIV *Ir. Jur. (n.s.)* 61 and 211, especially pp. 72-82 and pp. 211-221.

[45] In April 1998, the Department of Justice, Equality and Law Reform introduced the *Ad-Hoc Legal Aid Scheme (CAB)* which makes legal aid available to respondents or defendants in court proceedings taken by the Criminal Assets Bureau (CAB) and in tax and social welfare appeals to the Circuit Court in which the CAB is the respondent or defendant. The Department intends to extend the Criminal Legal Aid Scheme to these types of case but to date, the appropriate legislation has not yet been introduced. In addition to the Criminal Legal Aid scheme, it is also worth noting that by virtue of O.99, r.1(1) of the Rules of the Superior Courts 1986, the High Court may also award costs in criminal trials on indictment – see *The People (A.G.) v. Bell* [1969] IR 24 dealing with the interpretation of an identical provision in the Rules of the Superior Courts 1962.

essential in the interests of justice by reason either of the gravity of the charge or of the exceptional circumstances of the case.[46]

The factors impeding access to the law are also more straightforward in criminal cases than in civil matters. Essentially, it all boils down to lack of money on the part of the defendant and the coercive nature of the criminal process means that a criminal legal aid scheme does not have to concern itself with difficulties stemming from the defendant's ignorance of his or her rights or from his or her sense of alienation from the legal world, factors which can impede access to the law in civil matters.[47]

Penultimately, the Irish criminal legal aid scheme is a judicare model, whereby private practitioners who place their names on the legal aid panel are assigned by the courts to defend needy defendants and subsequently reimbursed by the State. The civil legal aid and advice scheme, in contrast, is primarily a salaried model whereby solicitors are employed on a full-time basis by the State to provide legal services to indigent litigants.

Finally, and most pertinent to this chapter, judicial intervention has had a greater impact on the criminal legal aid scheme than on its civil counterpart. As we shall see presently, that impact has been most significant in upgrading the right to criminal legal aid from a statutory to a constitutional norm. In addition, the courts have also provided some protection for the defendant's right to have the solicitor of his or her choice assigned to the case and they have also delineated the scope of the scheme.

a) Right to criminal legal aid

While it is quite clear from the wording of the Criminal Justice (Legal Aid) Act 1962 that defendants have, in appropriate circumstances, a statutory entitlement to free legal aid, this right was given a constitutional dimension in the leading case of *The State (Healy) v. Donoghue*,[48] with consequent significant implications for the Exchequer.

In two separate proceedings, two applicants had pleaded guilty to certain offences before the District Court and had been sentenced to terms of imprisonment. Neither applicant was legally represented before the court; in one case, the applicant had not been notified of his right to apply for legal aid under the 1962 Act, while in the second case, no legal aid was available because of a dispute between solicitors on the legal

---

[46] In *The People (A.G.) v. Tyrrell* [1970] IR 294; 1 *Frewen* 539, the Court of Criminal Appeal held, *inter alia,* that the 1962 Act did not apply to an appeal which was simply against severity of sentence and not against conviction. This *lacuna* was subsequently remedied by s.3 of the Criminal Procedure (Amendment) Act 1973.

[47] See ch. 9.

[48] [1976] IR 325. In *Gilligan v. Criminal Assets Bureau* [1998] 3 IR 185, McGuinness J. held, *inter alia*, that this decision did not mean that every accused was automatically entitled to legal aid and, accordingly, she upheld s.6 of the Proceeds of Crime Act 1996 which gives the court a discretion to allow assets otherwise frozen pursuant to that Act to be used for the purposes of legal expenses in proceedings under the Act. (Counsel for the applicant had argued that the fact that the courts had a discretion to refuse to allow assets to be used in that way amounted to an infringement of the applicant's right of access to the courts and his right to legal representation pursuant to *The State (Healy) v. Donoghue* [1976] IR 325.)

aid panel and the Department of Justice. The applicants then consulted the Free Legal Advice Centres Ltd., following which legal proceedings were instituted to quash the convictions because of the State's failure to provide the applicants with legal aid. Quashing the convictions, the Supreme Court held that the guarantee in Article 38 of the Constitution that no person should be tried on any criminal charge save in due course of law required the State to provide criminal legal aid in appropriate cases. According to O'Higgins C.J., Article 38 made it mandatory that every criminal trial should be conducted in accordance with the concept of justice, that the procedures applied should be fair and that the accused should be afforded every opportunity to defend himself. He then went on to describe the circumstances in which this guarantee obliged the State to provide criminal legal aid.

> Where a man's liberty is at stake, or where he faces a very severe penalty which may affect his welfare or his livelihood, justice may require more than the application of normal and fair procedures in relation to his trial. Facing, as he does, the power of the State which is his accuser, the person charged may be unable to defend himself adequately because of ignorance, lack of education, youth or other incapacity. In such circumstances his plight may require, if justice is to be done, that he should have legal assistance. In such circumstances If he cannot provide such assistance by reason of lack of means, does justice under the Constitution also require that he be aided in his defence? In my view, it does ...
>
> ... If the right to be represented is now an acknowledged right of an accused person, justice requires something more when, because of a lack of means, a person facing a serious criminal charge cannot provide a lawyer for his own defence. In my view the concept of justice under the Constitution ...requires that in such circumstances the person charged must be afforded the opportunity of being represented.
>
> This opportunity must be provided by the State. Only in this way can justice be done, and only by recognising and discharging this duty can the State be said to vindicate the personal rights of the person charged. To hold otherwise would be to tolerate a situation in which the nature and extent of a man's ability to defend himself, when accused, could depend on the nature and extent of his means; that would be to tolerate injustice.[49]

According to the Chief Justice, the 1962 Act constituted legislative recognition of the fundamental right of an indigent defendant to be legally represented. However that Act laid down as a precondition for the grant of legal aid that the defendant must apply for it to the court and this, according to the judge, did not adequately vindicate the defendant's constitutional rights for, "if a person who is ignorant of his right fails to apply and on that account is not given legal aid then, in my view, his constitutional right is violated".[50] He continued:

> For this reason it seems to me that when a person faces a possible prison sentence and has no lawyer, and cannot provide for one, he ought to be informed of his right to legal aid.

---

[49] [1976] IR 325 at pp. 350-1.
[50] *Ibid.* at p. 352.

If the person charged does not know of his right, he cannot exercise it: if he cannot exercise it, his right is violated.[51]

The Court's insistence on this procedural change had quite a dramatic effect, increasing State expenditure on the criminal legal aid scheme by 500%. In the year ending 31 December 1975,[52] the scheme cost the State approximately £54,200. In the year ending 31 December 1977, that figure had risen to approximately £252,000.[53]

Healy has had other implications for the criminal legal aid scheme. Thus in *O'Neill v. Butler*,[54] McMahon J. held that, in the light of that judgment, where a judge might consider a sentence of imprisonment on the basis of facts alleged by the prosecution,[55] it would not be open to that judge to treat the offence as a minor offence not requiring the provision of legal aid for the defendant. He also held that, in applying s.2 of the 1962 Act which requires a District Judge to have regard to any exceptional circumstances in deciding whether or not to grant legal aid, it would not be proper to leave the onus of establishing such circumstances upon a defendant who might be ignorant or inarticulate and that the judge should enquire into the matter himself. On the determination of means, McMahon J. held that where a defendant appeared to have adequate means to pay for his own representation, he should nonetheless be informed of the existence of the scheme and given an opportunity to explain any circumstance with regard to his means which might otherwise disqualify him from receipt of legal aid.

[51] *Ibid.* In his concurring judgment, Henchy J. said, at p. 355, that it was implicit in the 1962 Act that the court should inform an accused of his or her right to legal aid, commenting, "The Act would be but a hollow and specious expression of the constitutional guarantee if it is not given at least that degree of judicial implementation". An accused person may, of course, waive his right to legal aid – see *The State (Sharkey) v. McArdle*, unreported, Supreme Court, 4 June 1981 – and in *Rock v. Governor of St Patrick's Institution*, unreported, Supreme Court, 22 March 1993, the Supreme Court held that where an accused failed to turn up for his trial, he could not challenge a custodial sentence on the ground that he had not been afforded an opportunity to avail of legal aid. In *The State (Glover) v. McCarthy* [1981] ILRM 47, the accused had declined legal aid on the assumption, which subsequently transpired to be incorrect, that a custodial sentence would not be imposed. An application for *certiorari* to quash the trial judge's decision was refused on the ground that the accused was entitled to have a full hearing of her case, with the benefit of legal aid, on appeal in the Circuit Court.

[52] The Supreme Court decision in *The State (Healy) v. Donoghue* was handed down on 22 July 1976 so a comparison between the figures for 1975 and 1977 provides the clearest illustration of the impact of the judgment.

[53] By 1980, that figure had risen to £773,000, though at least part of this increase was due to the fact that the fees and expenses of lawyers under the scheme had been substantially increased since 1976 – see *Report of the Criminal Legal Aid Review Committee* (Prl. 9986) at para.2.3.1. According to the Committee, "It is impossible to estimate the precise effect of [*Healy*] as regards the increase in the number of persons being granted legal aid, but it seems clear that it has had a major impact". – *Ibid.*, at para.2.3.3.

[54] Unreported, High Court, 26 November 1979.

[55] In passing, it is worth noting that in *The State (O'Connor) v. Clifford*, unreported, High Court, 30 January 1987, a decision to refuse legal aid was quashed because it was based on an inaccurate statement of the facts by a Garda inspector which led the respondent to believe that the case was not of a serious nature.

In *Cahill v. Reilly*,[56] Denham J. appeared to restrict somewhat the scope of the duty imposed on a judge to notify an accused of his or her right to legal aid when she held that a prison sentence must be probable, rather than possible, before such a duty arose. Thus in the course of her judgment she said:

> I am not deciding that in all cases where there is a statutory sentence of imprisonment possible that the accused has to be told of his right to be legally represented or to apply for legal aid. But I do hold that when a custodial sentence becomes probable, or likely, after conviction or on a plea of guilty in a situation where it may not have been likely before, then at that stage at the sentencing, the District Court Judge should inform the accused, if he has not before, of his right to be legally represented or his right to apply for legal aid in relation to the sentence.[57]

It is submitted, with respect, that this is a more restrictive test than that postulated by the Supreme Court in *Healy* and Denham J.'s approach has not been followed in subsequent cases. Thus in *Byrne v. McDonnell*[58] Keane J. held that a defendant facing a possible custodial sentence is entitled to legal assistance in his defence while in *Clarke v. Kirby*[59] Shanley J. rejected any distinction between circumstances where a judge is actually considering the imposition of a custodial sentence and those where such a sentence may be imposed, stating

> In all cases where a judge is empowered to impose a custodial sentence and there is a possibility that such a sentence may in fact be imposed, he should advise the person before him of his right to legal aid and legal representation.[60]

b) Choice of solicitor

After upgrading the right to criminal legal aid to constitutional status, subsequent judicial intervention also enhanced the right of the accused to select the solicitor of his choice from the criminal legal aid panel, though initially the courts had refused to recognise such a right at all.

In *The State (Royle) v. Kelly*[61] the accused had been assigned a solicitor under the criminal legal aid scheme but the latter withdrew when his application for an

---

[56] [1994] 3 IR 547.
[57] At p. 552. Thus, in the instant case, where the accused had pleaded guilty to an offence and then faced the probability of a prison sentence because of the adducing, at sentencing stage, of evidence of prior convictions, the judge should have informed the accused of his right to apply for legal aid in relation to the sentence.
[58] [1996] 1 ILRM 543. This judgment was cited with approval by Murphy J. in *McSorley v. Governor of Mountjoy Prison* [1996] 2 ILRM 331 in which he granted writs of habeas corpus to two convicted prisoners because of the failure of the trial judge to advise them about their constitutional right to legal aid. (An appeal against Murphy J.'s decision was subsequently allowed by the Supreme Court on 24 April 1997 though on grounds not pertinent to the present discussion.)
[59] [1998] 2 ILRM 30.
[60] *Ibid.* at p. 35. The headnote to this report would appear to misrepresent Shanley J.'s conclusion on this point.
[61] [1974] IR 259.

adjournment of the case was not granted by the Special Criminal Court. The registrar of the Special Criminal Court subsequently wrote to the defendant asking him to nominate another solicitor from the legal aid panel but he insisted on having the services of his original solicitor. The Special Criminal Court refused to re-assign this solicitor to the case and the accused was tried and convicted without legal representation.

He subsequently applied for a writ of *habeas corpus* on the grounds that his detention was unlawful because, *inter alia*, he had been denied the right to choose his own solicitor under the criminal legal aid scheme. The Supreme Court dismissed this claim, holding that the Special Criminal Court was not bound to assign a solicitor nominated by the applicant. According to Walsh J.,

> the Special Criminal Court was acting within the powers granted to it under the statutory free legal aid provisions ... in refusing to assign Mr Concannon[62] and .. the court had a discretion as to whom it would assign. What the limits of that discretion are it is not here necessary to decide; but in view of the fact that Mr Concannon had expressly withdrawn from the case the court was entitled to hold him to that withdrawal.[63]

A broadly similar view was taken by O'Higgins C.J. in *The State (Healy) v. Donoghue*[64] in which he said:

> The Act of 1962 provides for a choice of both solicitors and counsel from amongst those in both branches of the legal profession who have agreed to operate the Act ... The only limitation on this choice has been that the practitioner concerned must have declared himself willing to provide legal aid by going on the panel. While I regard the Act as a recognition by the State of what is the constitutional right of a poor person facing a serious criminal charge, I do not say that the provisions of the Act match exactly what the Constitution requires. In particular, I would be slow to hold that the Constitution requires the choice which the statute gives. I can imagine circumstances in which, for one reason or another, the State cannot provide a choice of lawyer; in such circumstances the provision of a designated lawyer or lawyers, trained and experienced for the task, is an adequate discharge of the State's duty to provide legal assistance for the person without means.[65]

However in two subsequent cases, the courts have placed clear limits on the judge's discretion to refuse to assign a solicitor nominated by the accused. In *The State (Freeman) v. Connellan*,[66] the accused had requested a particular solicitor from the legal aid panel but the District Justice refused this request, following instead the practice at the time among District Justices in the Dublin area of nominating solicitors in alphabetical order from the panel.[67] Granting an absolute order of prohibition to the

---

[62] The solicitor requested by the accused.

[63] *Ibid.* at p. 265.

[64] [1976] IR 325.

[65] *Ibid.* at p. 352.

[66] [1986] IR 433; [1987] ILRM 470.

[67] This practice was designed to deal with the difficulties caused by the fact that criminal legal aid work in the city was dominated by six solicitors who were perceived to be unable to cope with the demand for their services.

accused, Barr J. in the High Court held that where an accused's choice of solicitor was duly qualified, a court should only refuse to nominate that solicitor for good and sufficient reason.

> It seems to me that a meaningful operation of [article 7(1) of the Criminal Justice (Legal Aid) Regulations 1965[68]] within the spirit and intention of the 1962 Act and in the light of the applicant's constitutional rights requires that in circumstances where the court has any reservation about the assignment to the applicant of a solicitor nominated by him, the judge should ask the defendant why he wishes to have the services of that particular solicitor. The court should then consider the reasons (if any) put forward by the applicant before assigning a solicitor to represent him. I am also of opinion that the court should be very slow indeed to refuse to nominate the applicant's choice of solicitor if the person nominated is duly qualified for assignment and should do so only if in the view of the judge there is good and sufficient reason why the applicant should be deprived of the services of the solicitor nominated by him. Where in any particular case the court, having considered and given due weight to the representations of the applicant, is satisfied, nonetheless, that there is a strong, compelling reason for refusing to assign the solicitor of the applicant's choice, the judge should state that reason and enquire whether the defendant wishes to nominate any other particular solicitor. If he does nominate a second solicitor then that application should be considered in the same way. The court should choose a solicitor for the applicant only where he has not nominated one himself or where any nominated by him are unable to accept assignment or are not acceptable to the court for good and sufficient reason.[69]

In *Mulhall v. O'Donnell*[70] a District Justice refused to assign the solicitor nominated by the accused because his three co-accused had been assigned another solicitor. Following the *Freeman* case, Murphy J. quashed this decision. He also inferred from the passage in Barr J.'s judgment quoted above that reason for refusing to assign a nominated solicitor must relate to the nominated solicitor and not the surrounding circumstances of the case.

c) Scope of scheme

Finally the courts have been asked to clarify the scope of the criminal legal aid scheme on two occasions. In *The State (O) v. Daly*,[71] the Supreme Court held that the principle in *The State (Healy) v. Donoghue*[72] did not apply to proceedings taken pursuant to s.207 of the Mental Treatment Act 1945 for the purposes of determining whether an accused is unfit to plead and which, in the instant case, resulted in the detention of the accused in the Central Mental Hospital. According to O'Higgins C.J., "the decision in [*Healy*] applies only to the trial of persons charged with criminal

---

[68] Which deals with the assignment of solicitors under the criminal legal aid scheme.
[69] [1986] IR 433 at pp. 439-40; [1987] ILRM 470 at p. 475.
[70] [1989] ILRM 367.
[71] [1977] IR 312.
[72] [1976] IR 325.

offences and not to the earlier or ancillary stages of criminal proceedings."[73]

In *Director of Public Prosecutions v. Felloni*,[74] Shanley J. formed a preliminary view that criminal proceedings do not conclude until, where applicable, proceedings for the confiscation of the assets of the accused under s.4 of the Criminal Justice Act 1994 are concluded. Accordingly, he held that an order granting legal aid under the 1962 Act in respect of such proceedings was *prima facie* valid and so refused to grant an order pursuant to s.24 of the 1994 Act allowing the defendants access to their frozen funds for the purpose of paying their legal expenses.

Attorney General's scheme

For the sake of completeness, I turn now to consider a recent judicial decision on the Attorney General's scheme for free legal representation

The origins of the Attorney General's scheme for free legal representation lies in a habeas corpus application, *Application of Woods*.[75] During the course of this case, the Attorney General gave an assurance to the Supreme Court that his office would, at the request of either the High or Supreme Court, pay the legal costs of an applicant for habeas corpus who was not, for personal reasons, in a position to retain the services of a legal team. This undertaking was subsequently reduced to writing and notified to the relevant court personnel and to the authorities in both branches of the legal profession. The scheme applies to habeas corpus applications, bail motions, judicial reviews involving *certiorari, mandamus* or prohibition and applications under s.50 of the Extradition Act 1965 challenging extradition.[76]

The nature and scope of the scheme would appear to have been considered by the courts on only one occasion. In *Byrne v. Governor of Mountjoy Prison*,[77] the applicant challenged the validity of his detention pursuant to an extradition warrant on the ground that the State did not make any effective provision for the payment of legal representation for indigent litigants involved in extradition proceedings before the District Court. The State countered by arguing that this situation was covered by the Attorney General's scheme.

Upholding the validity of the detention, Kelly J. noted that a booklet issued under the provisions of the Freedom of Information Act 1997 referred to the scheme as applying to, *inter alia*, extradition proceedings in the District Court and that this described the situation which had obtained for up to 15 years. According to the judge, the scheme had no statutory or contractual basis but rather constituted a voluntary assurance by the Attorney General that in certain types of litigation, indigent litigants

---

[73] [1977] IR 312 at p. 315.
[74] Unreported, High Court, 18 December 1997.
[75] [1970] IR 154.
[76] Prior to the introduction of the Scheme of Civil Legal Aid and Advice, the Attorney General's scheme also applied to applications to dispense with the consent of the natural mother in adoption cases, taken pursuant to the Adoption Act 1974 – see *In re M, an infant, J.M. and G.M. v. An Bord Uchtála* [1987] IR 522 and *In re J.H., an infant* [1985] IR 375; [1985] ILRM 302.
[77] [1999] 1 ILRM 386.

would have their legal representation paid for from funds at his disposal. As this administrative scheme had been created and operated by the Attorney General, it was open to him to expand or curtail it as he saw fit. Kelly J. subsequently held that, given the nature of the scheme, it did not require to be proven in court and that the Attorney General could dispense with the requirement that the court recommend the payment of legal fees.

In addition to the foregoing, in the instant case, an assurance had been given by counsel acting for the Attorney General that the scheme would apply to the applicant and Kelly J. held that such an assurance ought to have been accepted by the District Court without question except in truly exceptional cases of which this was not one. Accordingly, he held that the applicant was lawfully detained pursuant to the extradition warrant.

Conclusion

Reviewing the impact of judicial decisions on the right to legal aid, one is immediately struck by the contrasting fortunes of the right to civil legal aid and the right to criminal legal aid. The Irish courts have generally been very reluctant to compel the State to provide civil legal aid and advice to individuals unable to afford the services of private practitioners, the only exceptions being in relation to persons detained under mental health legislation and parties to wardship proceedings. In contrast, the right to criminal legal aid enjoys constitutional status by virtue of a Supreme Court decision. The difference in treatment between these two rights may possibly be explained by the argument that the right to criminal legal aid is necessary to protect the right to personal liberty, which is at the heart of liberal democracy, whereas the rights protected by a right to civil legal aid might not be perceived by the judiciary as so central to the liberal democratic project. Offering a more critical explanation of the judicial promotion of the right to criminal legal aid, Cousins argues that it was motivated by a desire to legitimate the criminal justice system at a time, during the 1970s, when there was a sharp increase in crime levels, repressive measures had been introduced to deal with the political situation in Northern Ireland and there was public disquiet about the treatment of persons in police custody.[78] Be that as it may, the effect of judicial intervention here was to make criminal legal aid significantly more accessible to impoverished defendants.

It can, of course, be argued that the decision of the European Court of Human Rights in *Airey v. Ireland*[79] had a significant impact on the provision of civil legal aid[80] and at one level this is quite true. However as I argue above,[81] the facts presented by

---

[78] "At the Heart of the Legal: The Role of Legal Aid in Legitimating Criminal Justice" in Young and Wall (eds.), *Access to Criminal Justice: Legal Aid, Lawyers and the Defence of Liberty* (Blackstone Press Ltd., 1996) at p. 98.

[79] (1979-80) 2 EHRR 305.

[80] And that *M.C. v. Legal Aid Board* [1991] 2 IR 43 and *Stevenson v. Landy*, unreported, High Court, 10 February 1993, succeeded in improving the extent of this provision.

[81] At p. 249.

the *Airey* case focussed judicial attention on the need for a "service" model of legal aid directed towards needy individuals seeking recourse to the courts. The case for a State-funded strategic model of legal aid thus went by default.

In conclusion, therefore, the pursuit of a litigation strategy to enhance access to legal services has had mixed results. It certainly resulted in a significant expansion of the criminal legal aid scheme and was arguably an important factor leading to the introduction of the Scheme of Civil Legal Aid and Advice but equally it ensured that the latter scheme would be bereft of any strategic element for tackling collective social exclusion.

Chapter 8

Public Interest Litigation – An Evaluation

Legitimacy of public interest litigation

To the extent to which there has been any debate about the use of litigation to secure social reform, the focus of attention has been on the constitutional and political legitimacy of relying on the courts in this manner. Thus in *O'Reilly v. Limerick Corporation*[1] Costello J. rejected the claims of Travellers seeking the provision by the State of halting sites on the ground that, under the Constitution, such claims should have been addressed to the Oireachtas, rather than to the courts, while a majority of the Constitution Review Group opposed the insertion of justiciable socio-economic rights into the Constitution on the grounds that the involvement of the courts in such matters would result in a "distortion of democracy".[2] It is my contention, however, that these objections to the use of public interest litigation promoting social inclusion are misplaced. The Irish Constitution does not unequivocally preclude reliance on such litigation and Costello J.'s position in *O'Reilly* rests on contentious preinterpretive principles that value a restrictive role for the courts in our constitutional order and that oppose their involvement with issues of social justice. Indeed, given the Preamble's commitment to the dignity of the individual and the attainment of true social order and also given the various socio-economic rights expressly protected by the Constitution, in particular, the right to free primary education and the right of children abandoned by their parents to be cared for by the State, a compelling case can be made for a position that is diametrically opposed to that adopted in *O'Reilly*, namely that a commitment to social justice and social inclusion is an important preinterpretive principle informing the Constitution, the policing of which is appropriately entrusted to the courts when the political system has patently failed to discharge its constitutional obligations.[3]

[1] [1989] ILRM 181.
[2] *Report of the Constitution Review Group* (Pn.2632) at p. 235.
[3] A position implicitly endorsed by Costello J. in his *ex tempore* decision in *O'Brien v. Wicklow UDC*, unreported, High Court, 10 June 1994, in which he acknowledged that his views on the role of the courts had changed since his earlier decision in *O'Reilly*.

Nor is judicial involvement with such matters a "distortion of democracy". Many constitutional norms are indeterminate and so a certain amount of judicial activism is inevitable in deciding what the norm requires in the context of a particular case. In any event, under our constitutional order, the People have, on a number of occasions in the past, modified or even nullified judicial decisions with which they did not agree so that, ultimately, the courts cannot usurp the will of the electorate.

Efficacy of public interest litigation

The real issue, therefore, concerning public interest litigation seeking to promote social inclusion is not the legitimacy of such litigation, but rather its efficacy. This immediately raises the question, how does one define efficacy or success in this context?

If what is sought to be achieved is a radical transformation of society, then it has to be conceded that public interest litigation is not up to the task. Even if we were to assume a judiciary willing to engage in this endeavour, the simple reality is that litigation, focused as it is on the situation of a particular litigant or group of litigants, is incapable of encapsulating the larger issues inherent in the process of altering the grundnorm of society. As Bellow observed, commenting on the utility or otherwise of litigation strategy in tackling injustice:

> This approach is a dead end … [because] it misconstrues the problem. The problem of unjust laws is almost invariably a problem of distribution of political and economic power; the rules merely reflect a series of choices made in response to these distributions. If a major goal of the unorganized poor is to redistribute power, it is debatable whether judicial process is a very effective means towards that end. This is particularly true of problems arising out of disparities of wealth and income. There is generally not much doctrinal judicial basis for adequately dealing with such problems, and lawyers find themselves developing cases whose outcomes are peripheral to the basic issues that these problems raise.[4]

In the light of this critique of the legal system, is there a case to be made in defence of public interest litigation targeting social exclusion? I believe there is. While in the last analysis the manner in which we structure our society is ultimately a matter of

---

[4] Quoted in R. Borosage and others, "The New Public Interest Lawyers" (1970) 79 *Yale Law Journal* 1070 at 1078. See also Duncanson, "Legal Need in England and Wales in the Sixties and Seventies: A Retrospect" (1981) 4 *University of New South Wales Law Journal* 113, in which he argues that structural social problems are not solved simply by making technical improvements in the delivery of legal services. In an empirical work based on the activities of the US Supreme Court in the areas of civil rights, women's rights, the environment, reapportionment of legislatures and the criminal law, Gerald Rosenberg argues that the courts are generally very limited in their ability to effect significant social reform – see *The Hollow Hope: Can Courts Bring About Social Change?* (Chicago, 1991). However Rosenberg's methodology is strongly criticised by Devins who argues, in (1992) 92 *California Law Review* 1027 at p. 1069, that, as a consequence, Rosenberg "underestimates the sweep of the judiciary's contribution to social reform."

politics rather than law, so that it is futile to expect judges to be able to alter the fundamental political premises of society, nonetheless it is arguable that public interest litigation can achieve results that, though reformist rather than radical in nature, are still of some significance to those who benefit from them.[5]

However it is important to note that litigation, in isolation, is rarely sufficient in achieving such results and that public interest litigants, even when successful in court, usually have to engage with the politico/bureaucratic system in order to make a reality of the rights assured to them by the judicial system. Often that system is not very accommodating of change emanating from judicial decisions. In some cases, subsequent amending legislation restores the *status quo ante*,[6] while in others, bureaucratic delay or obstruction, what Handler refers to as the "bureaucratic contingency",[7] frustrates change.[8] In yet other cases, political considerations impede change, as would seem to be the case in relation to the provision of halting sites for Travellers where, more than ten years after the courts first recognised a right to a halting site in appropriate circumstances, very little progress has been made in providing an adequate network of such sites.

---

5 In the Irish context, this is probably most true of litigation taken on behalf of children. In contrast, the gains secured by Travellers and social welfare claimants through litigation have, generally speaking, been rather limited.
6 As occurred with *Hyland v. Minister for Social Welfare* [1989] IR 624; [1990] ILRM 213 concerning the entitlement of married claimants to unemployment payments, reversed within four weeks of the Supreme Court decision by the Social Welfare (No.2) Act 1989; *The State (McLoughlin) v. Eastern Health Board* [1986] IR 416 establishing an entitlement to weekly additions under the supplementary welfare allowance scheme and eventually neutralised on this point by s.47 of the Social Welfare Act 1992; *Harvey v. Minister for Social Welfare* [1990] 2 IR 232; [1990] ILRM 185 concerning the operation of the overlapping benefits regulations, circumvented by s.43 of the Social Welfare Act 1991; *Louth v. Minister for Social Welfare* [1993] 1 IR 339; [1992] ILRM 586 concerning the welfare entitlements of dockers, neutralised by s.30 of the Social Welfare Act 1997; *Lundy v. Minister for Social Welfare* [1993] 3 IR 406 and *O'Sullivan v. Minister for Social Welfare*, unreported, High Court, 9 May 1995, both dealing with aspects of the adjudicative system and reversed respectively by s.31 of the Social Welfare Act 1993 and s.34 of the Social Welfare Act 1996; and, finally, *McDonald v. Feely*, unreported, Supreme Court, 23 July 1980, partially modified by s.32 of the Housing (Traveller Accommodation) Act 1998.
7 *Social Movements and the Legal System: A Theory of Law Reform and Social Change* (Academic Press, New York, 1978) at pp. 18-22. According to Handler, the most successful type of litigation strategy is one in which this bureaucratic contingency does not come into play because the problem is solved on the basis of a rule change – Handler, p. 209.
8 Thus, in *Sinnott v. Minister for Education*, unreported, High Court, 4 October 2000, Barr J. berated the Department of Finance for its failure to take on board the implications of O'Hanlon J.'s earlier decision in *O'Donoghue v. Minister for Health* [1996] 2 IR 20 in relation to the provision of educational facilities for children with severe or profound mental handicap while on a number of occasions, Kelly J. expressed his annoyance at the tardy response of administrators to the plight of children in need of secure accommodation – see, *e.g., D.B. v. Minister for Justice* [1999] 1 IR 29; [1999] 1 ILRM 93 and *T.D. v. Minister for Education* [2000] 3 IR 62; [2000] 2 ILRM 321. For a further description of this phenomenon in the context of attempts by the Ombudsman to ensure proper implementation of legislative policy on nursing home subventions, see *Nursing Home Subventions: an Investigation by the Ombudsman of Complaints Regarding Payment of Nursing Home Subventions by Health Boards* (Office of the Ombudsman, January 2001).

And yet in some cases, public interest litigation does bring about change, either as a direct and immediate response to a judicial order in a particular case or indirectly as a result of the less immediate and more intangible impact of the litigation on the politico/bureaucratic system. Where judicial decisions result *directly* in a change in policy, it is usually because the politicians and administrators do not object to the change proposed and occasionally because they have no real choice in the matter. Examples of the former include cases that have succeeded in improving access to unmarried mother's allowance for foreign divorcees,[9] broadening entitlement to fuel vouchers to claimants of long-term unemployment assistance,[10] improving the entitlements of unmarried mothers to disability benefit[11] and of married claimants to disabled person's maintenance allowance[12] and disability allowance[13] and improving, somewhat, the legal protection available to Travellers when confronted by a local authority seeking to move them from an unlawful site.[14] Examples of the latter include judicial decisions on procedural issues that set standards derived from the concept of constitutional justice which simply cannot be ignored or diluted by administrators;[15] the Supreme Court decision in *The State (Healy) v. Donoghue,*[16] which led directly to a significant expansion in the criminal legal aid scheme and the ruling of the European Court of Human Rights in *Airey v. Ireland*[17] which resulted in the introduction of the State Scheme of Civil Legal Aid and Advice. Insofar as *Healy* was grounded on the Constitution, the politico-bureaucratic system had little choice but to accept the Supreme Court's decision that indigent defendants had a constitutional right to criminal legal aid, given that it would require a constitutional referendum to modify that outcome. Similarly, the international status of the ruling in *Airey* meant that the political system here could not ignore it. In the Traveller and social welfare cases, however, one must assume that the politicians and bureaucrats had no objection to the changes required by the litigation. Certainly, a common factor in the social welfare cases listed above is that the class of beneficiaries in each case was relatively small, so that the changes effected had very little impact on the overall social welfare budget.[18]

---

[9] *The State (Kenny) v. Minister for Social Welfare* [1986] IR 693.

[10] *The State (Kershaw) v. Eastern Health Board* [1985] ILRM 235; *The State (McLoughlin) v. Eastern Health Board* [1986] IR 693.

[11] *McHugh v. A.B. (Deciding Officer)* [1994] IR 139.

[12] *J.H. v. Eastern Health Board* [1988] IR 847.

[13] *O'Connell v. Ireland* [1996] 2 IR 522; [1996] 1 ILRM 187.

[14] See *Limerick Corporation v. Sheridan* (1956) 90 ILTR 59 and *McDonald v. Feely*, unreported, Supreme Court, 23 July 1980.

[15] The experience of the Department of Social, Community and Family Affairs (formerly the Department of Social Welfare) suggests that eventually these standards may be internalised by the administrators and then reflected in formal rules. Thus in my experience in representing welfare claimants at welfare appeals, the appeals officers invariably began the hearing by summarising the impact of judicial rulings such as *McLoughlin v. Minister for Social Welfare* [1958] IR 1 on the independence of the appeals officer and ss.19 and 20 of the Social Welfare Act 1990 represent an attempt by the Department to enhance that independence in the social welfare code.

[16] [1976] IR 325.

[17] (1979-80) 2 EHRR 305.

[18] Indeed, in the case of the fuel vouchers, the cost of extending the scheme to claimants of long-term unemployment assistance was met by reducing the amount paid to existing claimants.

Of equal significance, however, is the manner in which public interest litigation sometimes leads *indirectly* to change by helping to convert a hostile or indifferent political system to the cause for reform. Perhaps the most dramatic example of this can be seen in relation to Directive 79/7/EEC on the progressive implementation of the principle of equal treatment for men and women in matters of social security. As I detail elsewhere,[19] full implementation of this Directive was stoutly resisted by various Irish administrations between 1984 and 1995. However a series of legal actions by married women kept up the pressure on the Irish authorities until eventually the State conceded, paying out in excess of IR£265 to more than 70,000 welfare claimants. The litigants here did, admittedly, benefit from the fact that, due to a change in government in 1994, the political climate changed with the appointment as Minister for Social Welfare of a left-wing politician, Proinsias de Rossa, TD, who was more sympathetic to their cause. Nonetheless, the litigation played a key role in ensuring that the Directive was properly implemented by clarifying the rights of the claimants, by keeping up the pressure on the Irish authorities over a ten-year period until the political climate changed and also by making other women aware of their entitlements through the media attention given to the cases.

It is arguable that something similar is also happening in relation to the protection of the rights of children with learning difficulty and children in need of secure accommodation. Both groups of children have suffered from egregious neglect of their interests over the years and in both cases, litigation would appear to have been the spur to recent executive action though, at the time of writing, it remains to be seen how successful that action is in meeting the needs of the children in question.

So in evaluating litigation strategy one has to take account not only of its ability to deliver a judicial order supporting the litigant's case but also of its ability to generate a number of highly desirable indirect effects.[20] Chief of these is the manner in which litigation highlights the predicament of the plaintiffs, thereby putting their plight on the political agenda. Thus media coverage of the decisions of Kelly J. in relation to children at risk contributed to the general political discussion about child care policy in this regard, eventually provoking the political establishment into beginning to address the plight of such children.[21] Even cases that are unsuccessful in court can

---

[19] See pp. 141 *et seq.*

[20] Indeed Prosser concludes that "the indirect effect of test cases [are] more important than the direct effect ... " – *Test Cases for the Poor,* (C.P.A.G., 1983), at p. 86.

[21] As a demonstration of this effect of Kelly J.'s decisions, see the interview with the Minister with Special Responsibility for Children, Mary Hanafin, TD in *The Sunday Business Post* on 9 April 2000, in which she said that on the morning the Taoiseach asked her to take responsibility for this portfolio, he specifically mentioned those children whose cases were coming before the courts. Writing in January 2001, a prominent activist on behalf of homeless children has also predicted that
> Over the next twelve months, we can expect to see a significant expansion in services for homeless children. After twenty years of political apathy, when it was almost impossible to interest the government or Health Boards in the problem of homeless young people, we have moved into a phase of political panic. Getting the problem away from Justice Peter Kelly in the High Court, who has described the inertia of the Government as a 'scandal', and off the front

have this effect insofar as they highlight the need to change the law to address a particular problem.[22] The publicity attendant on litigation can also help to organise an otherwise disparate group by making the various members of the group aware of their common cause.

Another desirable indirect effect of litigation strategy is that the threat of litigation can be used to increase bargaining power in the context of a political campaign for change. Thus Rosenberg comments:

> [R]ather than expend money, time and energy defending against a lawsuit and countering the publicity it generates, parties may find it more palatable to negotiate.[23]

A good example of this in the Irish context is the reaction of the Department of Education, facing a large number of High Court actions in the wake of *O'Donoghue v. Minister for Health*[24] where rather than contest those cases, the Department eventually began to improve educational facilities for children with special needs.[25]

Penultimately, litigation can, on occasion, be used as a means of gaining access to official documentation and of compelling officialdom to disclose their policy on the subject matter of the litigation. Presumably this could be done most effectively by seeking the discovery of the relevant documentation,[26] but it can also be achieved in some cases by relying on the constitutional obligation on an administrative authority to furnish a litigant with the pertinent details of a decision affecting his or her

---

pages of the national newspapers has become an urgent priority. With no shortage of resources any longer, a significant increase in the level of services can be expected.

See Fr Peter McVerry SJ, "Homelessness" (2001) 52 *The Furrow* 12 at pp. 14-5. He goes on to caution, however, that the problem of homeless children is not just a shortage of resources and that the adequacy of planning preceding this increase in resources is dubious, leaving some questions about the appropriateness of the services to be provided.

[22] See *e.g. Kearns v. Minister for Social Welfare*, unreported, High Court, 10 February 1982, concerning the welfare entitlements of workers affected by industrial action and *Kingham v. Minister for Social Welfare*, unreported, High Court, 25 November 1985, concerning the welfare entitlements of workers who entered insurance during the 1950s. See also the remarks of Henry Hodge in "A Test Case Strategy" in Partington, M. and Jowell, J. (eds.), *Welfare Law and Policy* (Frances Pinter, 1979) in relation to UK cases on the cohabitation rule, wherein he said, at p. 256, "Cases [on the cohabitation rule] were ... argued before tribunals, publicised and researched in an attempt to discredit the rule. The cases were also used in lobbying to illustrate the problems that the rule gave rise to, the concentration on peoples' sexual activities, the invasion of privacy by DHSS special investigators, the personal nature of the enquiries, the dependence on anonymous informers and the failure to concentrate on the financial support and position of the claimant."

[23] Rosenberg, p. 26.

[24] [1996] 2 IR 20.

[25] See *The Irish Times*, 6 November 1998. At the time of writing, the Department is again contesting litigation in this area, having appealed against the decision in *Sinnott v. Minister for Education*, unreported, High Court, 4 October 2000, but this is presumably because that decision could significantly expand the constitutional obligations of the Department by removing any age restriction on the right to free elementary education, at least in the context of children with special needs.

[26] Though I must confess that I am not aware of any case taken as part of a litigation strategy before the Irish courts in which the remedy of discovery was put to this use.

entitlements.[27] Moreover the existence of hitherto unpublished internal circulars will occasionally be disclosed as part of the defence to a claim taken by the plaintiff.[28]

Finally, one should note one further important, if intangible, effect of litigation generally and of public interest litigation in particular, namely the non-coercive manner in which judicial pronouncements can contribute to the content of political discourse by conferring legitimacy on certain claims and by broadly relating these claims to society's system of values. Writing in the context of US society, Mary Ann Glendon refers to the "radiating pedagogical effects of [the activities of judges and legislators] in a law-saturated society" and she comments further:

> Willing or no, judges and legislators can no longer afford to ignore the way in which law, especially criminal, family, and constitutional law, is aspirational and educational, expressing something about what kind of people we are and what kind of society we are in the process of creating.[29]

In this sense, an important function of a judicial decision is that, quite apart from any remedy that results therefrom, it articulates certain social values, values that hitherto may have been ignored by the political process.

Disadvantages of public interest litigation

Of course, even for those who support the idea of using the courts to effect social change, public interest litigation is not without its disadvantages. Chief among these is the risk that failure in court very often simply confirms the policy under attack. Thus, for example, the High Court decision in *Foley v. Moulton*[30] bolstered the welfare authorities in their interpretation of the cohabitation rule, which rule restricts entitlement to welfare,[31] while the decision in *Healy v. Minister for Social, Community and Family Affairs*[32] upheld the exclusion of participants in the Social Employment Scheme from family income supplement. By the same token, litigation taken by Travellers confirmed, against the interests of Travellers, that the authorities do not have to take account of Traveller culture in the provision of halting sites[33] and, in one particular case, that the standard of facilities provided at a halting site adequately

---

[27] See *Kiely v. Minister for Social Welfare* [1971] IR 21. This constitutional obligation is now supplemented by a statutory one provided for in the Freedom of Information Act 1997.

[28] As happened in *The State (Kershaw) v. Eastern Health Board* [1985] ILRM 235 when the defendant sought, unsuccessfully, to rely on the terms of an internal circular on the operation of the Fuel Voucher Scheme as a defence to the plaintiff's claim.

[29] *Rights Talk: The Impoverishment of Political Discourse* (New York, 1991) at pp. 104-5.

[30] [1989] ILRM 169.

[31] For further discussion of this case, see above, pp. 155-7. A corresponding case in the UK, in terms of its effect in confirming the policy being challenged, is *R. v. SBC ex parte Donlon* (1977) SB 93, discussed by Prosser, at pp. 54-5.

[32] [1999] 1 ILRM 72.

[33] See *Mongan v. South Dublin County Council*, unreported, High Court, 31 July 1995; *Ward v. South Dublin County Council*, unreported, High Court, 31 July 1996.

discharged the authorities' statutory obligations.[34] In this context, it is important to bear in mind that the judiciary are generally sensitive about being seen to interfere with fiscal policy so that the greater the demand on the public purse posed by a claim, the greater the difficulty in persuading the courts of the merits of the case and the greater the likelihood of defeat.[35] Put more formally in the context of judicial review of legislation, legislation dealing with social and economic matters enjoys a particularly strong presumption of constitutionality.[36] And, of course, if litigation is unsuccessful, the litigant will generally have to face the additional burden of paying the legal costs of his/her successful opponent.[37]

Gains secured through litigation are also susceptible to reversal by the enactment of subsequent legislation. Thus a victory for welfare claimants in *Hyland v. Minister for Social Welfare*[38] was reversed within weeks by the Social Welfare (No.2) Act 1989.[39] An important qualification here is that if the judicial decision is rooted in EU law or in the Constitution (other than in relation to guarantees of equal treatment[40]), its effect cannot be nullified by ordinary legislation.

Moreover, the cost of victory may simply be shifted onto the shoulders of other disadvantaged groups so that one person's gain becomes another person's burden. For example, the cost of giving claimants of short-term welfare payments access to the fuel voucher scheme, following the decisions in *The State (Kershaw) v. Eastern Health Board*[41] and *The State (McLoughlin) v. Minister for Social Welfare,*[42] was met

---

[34] *Mongan v. South Dublin County Council*, unreported, High Court, 17 December 1999.

[35] Which is not to say that such cases never succeed. The decisions of O'Hanlon J. in *O'Donoghue v. Minister for Health* [1996] 2 IR 20, Carroll J. in *Tate v. Minister for Social Welfare* [1995] ILRM 507, Kelly J. in *D.B. v. Minister for Justice* [1999] 1 IR 29; [1999] 1 ILRM 93 and *T.D. v. Minister for Education* [2000] 3 IR 62; [2000] 2 ILRM 321 and Barr J. in *Sinnott v. Minister for Education*, unreported, High Court, 4 October 2000 all placed significant financial burdens on the Exchequer. *Cp.* the U.K. experience in *Metzger v. DHSS* [1978] 1 WLR 1046, referred to by Hodge, p. 258.

[36] See *Kelly The Irish Constitution,* Hogan and Whyte (eds.), (3rd ed. 1994) at p. 452 and cases cited therein. See also *Lowth v. Minister for Social Welfare* [1998] 4 IR 321; [1999] 1 ILRM 5 and *In re Article 26 and the Planning and Development Bill 1999* [2000] 2 IR 321 ; [2001] 1 ILRM 81.

[37] Though the decision of Laffoy J. in *Village Residents' Association Ltd. v. An Bord Pleanála (No. 2)* [2000] 4 IR 321 suggests that in certain cases, public interest litigants who are acting solely in the public interest and who have no private interests at stake may be able to avoid liability for costs incurred by a successful opponent by obtaining a pre-emptive costs order directing that no costs be awarded against them irrespective of the ultimate outcome of the substantive proceedings.

[38] [1989] IR 624. Indeed, not only did the beneficiaries of this decision, married claimants, fail to retain the benefits of the decision, the case also led to a disimprovement in the legal position of cohabiting claimants. See further above, p. 162.

[39] For other examples of this phenomenon in the context of litigation taken by welfare claimants, see pp. 161-5.

[40] The reason for this exception is that, as *Hyland* demonstrates, the effect of decisions based on such guarantees can often be legitimately nullified by legislative amendment that "levels down", *i.e.* secures equal treatment by *removing* the privilege that the litigant sought to obtain.

[41] [1985] ILRM 235.

[42] [1986] IR 416.

by reducing the entitlements of existing categories of claimants covered by the scheme. In similar fashion, concern has been expressed that the focus on the provision of secure accommodation for children at risk, as a result of litigation, may divert resources from other support mechanisms for families in difficulty.

Public interest litigation also arguably reinforces the dependency of marginalised people on middle-class professionals and, indeed, has the potential to be more responsive to the agenda of the professionals than to that of their clients. Writing in the US context, Edgar and Jean Cahn observed:

> There are several contributing causes which induce lawyers for the poor to cease to be accountable to clients and to aggrandize their role as 'social engineers' and self-styled reformers. It is not clear whether they feel free to do so because the clients are poor or members of minority groups or because legal service programs have a monopoly which makes it impossible for the client not to concur in any decision by the attorney. All contribute: the arrogance of youth, the monopoly powers of attorneys, and condescension based on race and class. None are consistent with the traditional lawyer-client relationship. All are especially pernicious when the client is poor and when legal advocacy serves as a quasi-political form of enfranchisement, for then client manipulation perverts not only the legal system but also the democratic process itself.[43]

Penultimately, a victory in the courts may be frustrated by bureaucratic delay. In *D.B. v. Minister for Justice*[44] Kelly J. noted that, within one week of Geoghegan J.'s decision in *F.N. v. Minister for Education*[45] on the obligations of the State towards children at risk, that judge was made aware of developments proposed by the Minister for Health concerning the provision of residential places for both young offenders and children in need of special care. However, more than two years later, Kelly J. discovered, in the context of another hearing concerning a child at risk, that those proposals had been substantially departed from without that fact ever being made known to the Court, a development which he considered to be "unsatisfactory". Similarly in *Sinnott v. Minister for Education*,[46] Barr J. was very critical of the failure of the Department of Finance to respond in an appropriate manner to the decision of O'Hanlon J. in *O'Donoghue v. Ireland*[47] handed down some seven years earlier. Thus obtaining a judicial decision in one's favour is clearly no guarantee of a speedy response from the authorities, though perhaps significantly, both Kelly and Barr JJ. have shown a willingness to tackle this bureaucratic contingency, the former by threatening to hold

---

[43] See Cahn and Cahn, "Power to the People or the Profession? – The Public Interest in Public Interest Law" (1970) 79 *Yale Law Journal* 1005 at 1034. "The hallmark of an effective poor people's practice is that the lawyer does not do anything for his clients that they can do or be taught to do for themselves." Wexler, p. 1055. For further discussion of this problem, see Leat, "The Rise and Role of the Poor Man's Lawyer" (1975) 2 *Br. J. of Law and Soc.* 166 at pp. 176-181.

[44] [1999] 1 IR 29; [1999] 1 ILRM 93.

[45] [1995] 1 IR 409; [1995] 2 ILRM 297.

[46] Unreported, High Court, 4 October 2000.

[47] [1996] 2 IR 20.

the responsible Ministers in contempt of court[48] and the latter by hinting at the possibility that such behaviour might attract an award of punitive damages.[49]

Finally, the conventional conception of litigation, *viz.* that it involves a contest between two diametrically opposed interests who control the identification of the facts and issues involved, does not adequately accommodate public interest litigation[50] and can present difficulties in three different areas. First, the practice of restricting the evidence upon which the court may make its decision to that presented by the litigants means that the court may not be made aware of all of the interests relevant to the issue in hand[51] and that it may not be able to take into account the long term implications of its decisions. Thus the gains secured may be limited in nature. The decision of the European Court of Human Rights in *Airey v. Ireland*[52] is arguably a very good example of this particular problem in as much as the facts of that case only presented one aspect of the difficulties facing needy persons who do not have access to the law.[53] Consequently the decision cannot be regarded as a completely satisfactory resolution of the question of securing effective access to the law for all.[54] Second, the limited nature of judicial remedies reduces the potential for achieving

---

[48] See *The Irish Times*, 19 October 2000 and above, pp. 195-6.

[49] See p. 69 of his judgment in *Sinnott v. Minister for Education*, unreported, High Court, 4 October 2000.

[50] This matter is discussed in greater detail in ch. 2.

[51] Though I argue above that there is nothing currently preventing the Irish courts from developing the concept of the *amicus curiae* brief along the lines adopted in the U.S. – see pp. 99-101.

[52] (1979-80) 2 EHRR 305.

[53] Mrs Airey was unable to secure legal representation in proceedings for judicial separation solely because of lack of finance. However the *Report to the Minister for Justice of the Committee on Civil Legal Aid and Advice* (Dec. 1977, prl.6862), identifies as additional obstacles to effective access to legal services the facts that many disadvantaged people are unaware of their legal rights and that such clients often experience a sense of alienation from the legal system.

[54] Horowitz argues that such are the limitations on the courts' ability to deal with "social facts" – which he defines (p. 45) as "the recurrent patterns of behavior on which policy must be based" – and to resolve policy issues that "there will be some policy problems that are beyond the capabilities of even the most able judges to handle well". – D. Horowitz, *The Courts and Social Policy* (Washington, 1977), p. 298. He goes on to caution that seeking to enhance judicial capacity in this field may undermine the courts' ability to deal with individual dispute resolution. However, as Fiss points out – "The Supreme Court 1978 Term – Foreword: The Forms of Justice" (1979) 93 *Harv. L. Rev* 1, at p. 29 – this raises the question of whether such individual dispute resolution should have a prior or exclusive claim on the concept of adjudication. Fiss takes issue with Horowitz's assumption that non-judicial bodies would necessarily do a better job of assessing "social facts" and he also argues that even a partially successful example of social reform may be more valuable than all of the successes of individual dispute resolution – pp. 32-4. His fundamental objection to Horowitz's position, however, is that it misunderstands why the courts get involved in social reform litigation in the first place which is to give meaning to constitutional values in practical reality, a function which only the courts can discharge – pp. 34-5. For criticism of Horowitz's conclusions about the judicial capacity to make decisions on issues of social policy, see Youngblood and Folse, "Can Courts Govern? An Inquiry into Capacity and Purpose" in *Governing Through Courts* (California/London, 1981), Gambitta R., May M., and Foster J. (eds.), p. 23. See also, in similar vein, the review by Wasby in (1978) 31 *Vanderbilt Law Review* 727.

structural reform through litigation,[55] though as we noted earlier there is some evidence of Irish judges being more innovative in developing judicial remedies to counter bureaucratic inaction, following the example of the US judiciary.[56] Finally, litigation strategy sometimes throws up a tension between the interests of the litigant and those of the group that s/he represents which has to be resolved in favour of the litigant. The best example of this would be where the opposing side offers to settle the individual's case on condition, *inter alia*, that the settlement is not publicised. Under Irish law at present, it is generally not possible to litigate a case that is moot in order to obtain an authoritative judicial ruling on the point of law at issue.[57] Yet lawyers acting for the litigant could not advise him or her to forego the settlement in order to allow the courts to rule on the case.[58]

Conclusion

It is clear from the foregoing that litigation strategy cannot be regarded as a universal panacea for the social problems in our country. Some of those problems are simply not susceptible to judicial resolution. Even where litigation strategy is an option, careful consideration needs to be given to the risks attendant on such strategy and an evaluation made as to whether the possible benefits of involving the courts outweigh those risks. Certain procedural reforms, such as permitting *amicus curiae* briefs, modifying the doctrine of mootness and devising more effective methods of extending the benefits of judicial decisions to those not directly party to the litigation, would certainly enhance the advantages of litigation strategy but they cannot obviate all of the inherent risks, in particular, the risk that gains secured in court will simply be reversed by subsequent legislation. In the last analysis, therefore, one cannot avoid engaging with the politico-bureaucratic system in order to ensure that gains secured through litigation are properly "bedded-down". Contrary to the views of some commentators, litigation strategy does not pre-empt a political response to an issue; it generally provokes such a response. Thus litigation strategy should be seen as one element in an overall campaign for change in which the campaigners also work on shaping an appropriate political response to their demands.

It follows that lawyers working with those seeking social change should not restrict their efforts to the use of litigation only but should also be prepared to help organise their clients as a political force and to engage in political lobbying for change. Of course, conventional lawyers in private practice generally do not see this type of work

---

[55] See, in relation to the UK, the comments of Dhavan and Partington in "Co-optation or Independent Strategy? The Role of Social Action Groups" in Cooper and Dhavan, at p. 255.

[56] Where the courts began to issue positive orders directing public agencies as to how to discharge their functions. See Handler, pp. 23-5; Prosser, p. 12.

[57] See above, ch. 2.

[58] Thus one case taken by FLAC which sought to challenge restrictions on the payment of what was then called prescribed relatives allowance was settled in favour of the claimant on the night before the case was due to be heard in the High Court and on condition that the settlement was not to be made public. For a comparable experience in the UK, see Hodge, p. 258.

as falling within their remit. In any event, the world inhabited by such lawyers is very far removed from that of those experiencing social exclusion. Consideration needs to be given, therefore, to the manner in which the marginalised in our society can be provided with access to legal services and also to the type of services that should be provided. I turn now to consider these issues in the final part of this book.

PART 3

ACCESS TO LEGAL SERVICES

Chapter 9

Access to Legal Services

Section I: Prologue

Introduction

A necessary pre-requisite for the success of litigation strategy is that the potential client must have effective access to legal services and for individuals on the margins of our society, this can present a problem, given the extent to which the provision of legal services is market driven.

Even where the services of a lawyer are readily available, we also need to consider what *type* of legal service is most effective in tackling social exclusion. On the basis of my examination of litigation strategy in the previous parts of this book, I conclude that it is a worthwhile, if limited, mechanism for promoting social inclusion.[1] Clearly, however, it cannot be considered as a panacea for all ills – some issues are simply not susceptible to resolution through the courts and here recourse to the political system is inevitable if one is to secure change. Moreover, even where a social problem can be brought before the courts, experience indicates that it is naïve to believe that judicial decisions, in isolation, will resolve the issue. Judicial decisions in such matters tend to provoke, rather than to pre-empt, a political response to the problem. Therefore reliance on litigation strategy to solve issues of social exclusion must, in my opinion, be complemented by a readiness to seek to influence the political reaction to the decision of the court.

Thus for lawyers to be most effective in combating social exclusion, they need to look beyond litigation and the individual client; they need to be able to engage with the political process and to represent the needs of the group of which the individual client is a representative; in short, they need to embrace the approach encapsulated in what are referred to as "strategic" models of legal aid.

---

[1] See ch. 8.

Strategic models of legal aid are to be distinguished from "service" models of legal aid. In their purest form, service models are concerned exclusively with assisting individual clients who seek access to the courts in order to resolve their own difficulties while strategic models seek to tackle the social problems confronting the client-communities.[2] This difference is reflected not only in contrasting objectives but also in different methodologies. In particular, the strategic model does not confine itself to the conventional methods of lawyers in private practice as a means of advancing the interests of marginalised clients but also embraces such tactics as political lobbying, public education and community action. While the present book is concerned primarily with the role of the Irish courts in relation to issues of social disadvantage, it is important to remember that lawyers seeking to promote social inclusion are not confined to litigation as the sole means of obtaining progress. Consequently one important function of the description of the activities of the voluntary legal aid sector in Ireland in the present chapter is to offer a counter-balance to the emphasis on litigation which otherwise forms the focus of this book.

The chapter begins by outlining the factors that deny access to legal services for socially excluded individuals and groups before proceeding to examine the different models of legal aid adopted in the western world. Turning then to the position in Ireland, I consider, first, the role of the State in providing for civil legal aid and, second, the activities of the voluntary legal aid sector before concluding with a justification for the provision of civil legal aid and a defence of the strategic model of legal aid as the most effective means by which the legal system can seek to promote social inclusion.

Barriers to access

In the absence of any empirical research into unmet legal need in Ireland, one can only speculate as to the reasons why poor people do not avail of legal services where it would appear to be to their advantage to do so. In 1977, the Committee on Civil Legal Aid and Advice[3] concluded that there were four factors which appeared to deter poor people from availing of legal services:

(a) the belief that the cost will be beyond their reach,

(b) lack of knowledge of the types of service and doubt about the relevance to their problems of the services of solicitors – it is suggested, for example, that solicitors are trained only to handle legal difficulties which are of concern to the better off (property rights as distinct from social welfare rights, expertise in handling court proceedings but not tribunal proceedings),

(c) social underprivileged persons are reluctant to approach solicitors because they often find the atmosphere of a solicitor's office "intimidating" – there is what the

---

[2] In practice, however, legal aid schemes often share characteristics of both models. On the distinction between "service" and "strategic" models of legal aid, see Zemans, "Recent Trends in the Organization of Legal Services" (1985) *Anglo-American Law Review* 283, especially at pp. 291-3, and see below, pp. 284-5.

[3] Prl.6862. (Hereafter the "Pringle Committee"). See Zander, "The Pringle Committee's Report on Civil Legal Aid and Advice: An Outsider's View" (1978) *DULJ (n.s.)* 21.

Incorporated Law Society describe as a "psychological barrier" between socially deprived clients and solicitors which presents both with immediate communications difficulties, and

(d) difficulty in reaching solicitors' offices, particularly in Dublin where they are generally situated in the central business area.[4]

The cost of obtaining legal services is the most obvious likely factor impeding access to such services for poor people and the smaller the claim, the greater this impediment is.[5] However as the Pringle Committee point out, this is not the only barrier to access. Ignorance on the part of the potential client of the existence of a right, or of the means of enforcing such a right, and ignorance on the part of lawyers of the law relevant to problems of the poor are likely to be other important factors in this situation[6] as is the sense of alienation from the legal world experienced by many disadvantaged people.[7] The delay in obtaining a judicial remedy is also relevant as "[this] increases the parties' costs and puts great pressure on the economically weak to abandon their claims or settle for much less than that to which they are entitled".[8]

Empirical research in the UK raises the possibility that the nature of the problem experienced may also be a relevant factor in determining whether or not the services of a lawyer are sought. Thus Zander, referring to such research, observes:

[O]nce property matters are excluded, the use of lawyers is relatively uniform as between different social classes and income categories, and, ... the non-use of lawyers is very high even amongst the relatively affluent. Also, the use or non-use of lawyers is affected much more by the nature of the problem than by individual personal characteristics. So, in house purchase virtually everyone uses a lawyer regardless of social class or income; in consumer matters, on the other hand, virtually no-one uses a lawyer regardless of social class or income. In matrimonial matters or personal injury cases many do and many do not use lawyers, but again personal characteristics seem to have little or nothing to do

---

[4] *Ibid.*, pp. 38-9. It should be noted, however, that this conclusion was based on evidence submitted to the Committee by various bodies and individuals. The Committee did not commission any empirical research into this issue and indeed a dissenting report filed by Mr C.K. McGrath from the Department of Finance argued that a significant need for a legal aid scheme had not been established and that "little or no hard evidence is available that people who wish to do so are unable to gain access to the Courts solely through lack of means" – *ibid.*, p. 171.

[5] See Cappelletti and Garth, *Access to Justice,* vol. 1, book 1, (Sijthoff/Giuffre, 1978) at pp. 10-13.

[6] Grimes and Martin see this as "the major problem" to be tackled – see "Legal Aid in Great Britain and the Republic of Ireland – Some lessons to be Learnt" (1981) *Journal of Social Welfare Law* 282 at p. 294. A similar view was taken in the Report of the Royal Commission on Legal Services in Scotland, Cmnd.7846 (1980) – see Paterson, "Legal Services for All?" (1980) *Journal of Social Welfare Law* 321.

[7] Cousins argues that a lack of a consumer-orientated approach on the part of the courts contributes to this alienation but also leads to other practical barriers to access to the courts such as excessive legalism, courts in poor conditions, in awkward locations and at the wrong times – "Access to the Courts – The Limitations of a Human Rights Approach" in Heffernan (ed.), *Human Rights: A European Perspective* (Round Hall Press, 1994), at p. 145.

[8] Cappelletti and Garth, p. 14.

with it. In other words, there are areas of work in which the legal profession functions effectively and on a considerable scale but, even so, substantial numbers of those affected by the problem do not seek the help of lawyers, whilst in other areas there is not effective pattern of contacts between lawyers and potential clients.[9]

In particular, cases involving "diffuse" interests, *i.e.* collective or fragmented interests in areas such as environmental or consumer protection, raise special difficulties. According to Cappelletti and Garth,

> The basic problem they present ... is that either no one has a right to remedy the infringement of a collective interest or the stake of any one individual in remedying the infringement is too small to induce him or her to seek enforcement action.[10]

Even where access to legal services is obtained, certain types of party can make more effective use of such access than others.[11] Thus litigants with considerable financial resources can engage more readily in litigation than other parties and may be able to present their arguments more effectively. Conversely, marginalised individuals may have literacy problems and/or be inarticulate and therefore may find it very difficult to present their case.[12] Moreover, certain litigants, usually organisations, may have greater experience of going to court than other litigants, usually individuals, and this gives them certain advantages.[13] They can plan better for litigation and be more strategic in the use of the cases in which they are involved. Moreover, they have more opportunities to develop informal relations with the decision-maker than the individual litigant.

Summarising many of these points, Cappelletti and Garth conclude,

> [T]he obstacles [to access to legal services] created by our legal systems are most pronounced for small claims and for isolated individuals, especially the poor; at the same time, the advantages belong to the "haves", especially to organizational litigants adept at using the legal system to advance their own interests.
>
> Reflecting to this situation, we would expect that individuals would have most trouble asserting their rights when the vindication of those rights entails legal actions for relatively

---

[9] *A Matter of Justice: the Legal System in Ferment* (Oxford University Press, 1989) at p. 48. The same research also revealed that a high proportion of the population in the UK use lawyers, and that such differences as exist between young and old, men and women, and social classes in this matter are, to a considerable extent, explained by differences in life cycle – *ibid.* at p. 46. Of course the UK judicare system, whereby legal aid and advice is provided exclusively by solicitors in private practice, is not replicated in this country and so it remains to be seen whether similar research here would produce comparable results in terms both of the overall use of lawyers and of the pattern of use as between social classes.

[10] *Cappelletti and Garth*, p. 18.

[11] *Ibid.*, pp. 14-18.

[12] This problem is exacerbated in the common law world by virtue of the fact that, in most cases, the courts do not have independent powers of investigation but rather are wholly dependent on the litigants' evidence in the making of findings of fact.

[13] See Galanter, "Why the 'Haves' Come Out Ahead: Speculations on the Limits of Legal Change" (1974) 9 *Law and Society Rev* 95.

small amounts of damages against powerful organizations. The new substantive rights which are characteristic of the modern welfare state, however, have precisely those features: on the one hand, they involve efforts to bolster the power of citizens against governments, consumers against merchants, people against polluters, tenants against landlords, and employees against employers (and unions), and, on the other hand, the monetary interest of any one individual ... is likely to be small. To turn these new and ... very important rights into concrete advantages for ordinary people is evidently no easy task.[14]

Models of legal aid[15]

While the most significant developments in tackling these difficulties have occurred during the past fifty years or so, the legal system has a long history of making formal, if largely ineffectual, provision for individual needy litigants unable to afford legal services.[16] Thus the Scots Parliament Act of 1424 provided that where a person could not pursue an action because of lack of resources, the King "shall ordain to purvey and get a leal and wise advocate to follow such poor creature's causes; and if such causes be obtained, the wronger shall indemnify both the party injured and the advocate's costs and travail." In England, the *in forma pauperis* procedure, under which the poor did not have to pay for writs and could be assigned a lawyer free of charge in the common law courts, was established in 1494.[17] A comparable provision for this jurisdiction, dating from 1659, survived on the statute books in modified

---

[14] Cappelletti and Garth, p. 20.

[15] In their seminal work on access to justice, Cappelletti and Garth identified three phases, or "waves", in the attempts to make justice more accessible generally – *ibid.* pp. 21-54. The first wave focussed on the fact that, for economic reasons, poor people have no or limited access either to information or legal representation. The response to this obstacle was to develop legal aid and advice schemes and schemes of legal expenses insurance and this is the focus of this section of this book. The second wave addressed what the authors call the "organisational obstacle" to access to justice, namely the difficulty in protecting collective or class rights (including, but not limited to, the collective or class rights of the poor) within the legal system. Remedies advocated here include such devices as class actions, citizen actions ("actio popularis") and extending the right to sue to specialised government agencies, such as the Ombudsman, and to private associations representing distinct interests, such as consumer or environmental groups. Many of these issues are addressed in more detail in chapter 2. The third wave of reform focussed on the full range of institutions, devices and procedures used to resolve disputes in modern societies. This wave "includes, but goes *beyond advocacy*, whether inside or outside of the courts, and whether through governmental or private advocates ... [I]ts method is not to abandon the techniques of the first two waves of reform, but rather to treat those reforms as but several of a number of possibilities for improving access." – *Ibid.*, p. 49. I consider this last development briefly below in n. 210.

[16] See Cranston, *Legal Foundations of the Welfare State*, (Weidenfeld and Nicholson, 1985), pp. 84-90. In canon law, an obligation to provide legal aid for the poor was identified as early as 451 by the Council of Chalcedon. For an account of the influence of canon law on the development of legal aid for the poor, see Brundage, "Legal Aid for the Poor and the Professionalization of Law in the Middle Ages" (1988) 9 *Journal of Legal History* 169.

[17] See Egerton, *Legal Aid* (Kegan Paul, Trench, Trubner and Co. Ltd., 1945) (reprinted by Routledge, 1998), pp. 6-9. See also Molony, "Legal Aid for Poor Persons" (1930-31) 17 *Journal of the Statistical and Social Inquiry Society of Ireland* 16.

form into the early 1960s, although it seems to have fallen into disuse during the 1890s.[18]

The different models used for delivering legal services to the marginalised over the last hundred years or so can be classified broadly into four categories over a spectrum of models ranging from those concerned solely with the servicing of individual cases to those "strategic" models which attempt to tackle the social problems confronting their client-communities.[19] Describing the differences between these two poles of the spectrum, Zemans comments:

> The service model is the traditional and the most common form of legal services. An outgrowth of the juridical and charitable approach, service models confine their attention to discrete claims and problems brought to a programme by an individual with a readily categorized legal problem. This approach grows directly out of the traditional approach to protecting rights which [is essentially legalistic and individual] ...
>
> ... Inevitably over-loaded, service models can expend little time or energy in educating the community or on outreach programmes. Since service models accept the norms of the legal system and provide a service for poor people which, in the opinion of the administrators (inevitably lawyers), is the same for the poor as for the rich, poor people using service schemes face many of the same obstacles that they would encounter within the traditional setting. Such service models offer little recognition of the uniqueness of the poor person's lifestyle. They neither make the service psychologically more accessible, nor do they attempt to handle problems which have not been on the traditional agenda of legal services (e.g. eviction). The service model reinforces the distance between the "recipient" and the "deliverer" of the service by encouraging clients to assume passive and dependent roles in their relations with the legal-aid scheme. Lawyers write briefs; interview witnesses; negotiate settlements and go to court. The client's perspective is generally of an over-worked, under-paid lawyer who is dealing with the immediate problem and ignoring the fundamental cancer of poverty and poverty-related problems that continue to affect the client.[20]

Strategic models, in contrast, are

> orientated to identifying the significant social problems facing the community it is serving. While dealing with the inevitable daily problems, a strategic legal-services programme attempts to develop a long-term approach of research, reform and education to deal with the more fundamental issues. Rather than handling cases which are relevant to the lawyer's experience, a strategic programme sets priorities in one or several areas of concern to a particular community such as the environment, housing, land-ownership,

---

[18] See Carney, "The Growth of Legal Aid in the Republic of Ireland" (1979) XIV *Ir. Jur. (n.s.)* 61, 211, at pp. 70-72; Greer, "Legal Services and the Poor in Ireland" (1969) IV *Ir. Jur. (n.s.)* 270 at p. 273; Carr Lett, "Legal Assistance for the Poor" in *Public Administration in Ireland, Vol. II*, F. King (ed.), (Dublin, 1949) at pp. 217-8. (I am grateful to Dr Eoin O'Sullivan of the Department of Social Studies, TCD, for bringing the last article to my attention.)

[19] See Zemans; Paterson, "Legal Aid at the Crossroads" (1991) *Civil Justice Quarterly* 124.

[20] Zemans, pp. 291-2.

occupational health, or immigration. In concert with the geographic community or the community of interest, the professional will consider collective issues or the complaints of a class of individuals ... A significant distinction between the service and strategic models is in methodology. While the service model perceives itself as bound to the court and to litigation, the strategic model views advocacy as only one potential strategy. Other strategies might include tenant-organizing, lobbying the legislature, television and media coverage, or community picketing of a particularly abhorrent landlord.[21]

The earliest of these models, and one firmly located at the "service model" end of the spectrum, is the charitable model which appeared in England, the US, Germany, France and Italy towards the end of the 19th century. Charitable legal aid schemes were controlled by the profession and did not challenge in any fundamental way the biases of the legal system. Moreover assistance tended to be provided only to "the deserving poor"[22] and the schemes reinforced prevailing beliefs that poverty was primarily attributable to the perceived character defects of the poor.[23]

The latter half of the last century witnessed a move from voluntarism to State provision of legal aid with the growth of what is called the "Judicare Model" of legal aid in many western countries and which, again, is to be found closer to the "service model" end of our spectrum of models.[24] Under this model the state pays the legal profession to provide legal services to needy individuals. The first example of this type of model occurred in the UK immediately after the Second World War, a development which was brought about partly as a result of the number of people seeking divorces from partners they had married during the war, though the scheme also fitted in well with the Labour Government's aim of establishing a Welfare State. One of the strengths of this model is that it sees legal aid as an entitlement, however limited, of the needy client, rather than as a matter of charity. Moreover it provides greater coverage than the charitable model and a very wide choice of lawyer for the client. As against that, this type of model relies on the client taking the initiative to seek help and even then, private practitioners tend not to be conversant with those areas of the law of

---

[21] *Ibid.*, pp. 292-3.

[22] This characteristic is arguably still present in more recent models of legal aid. Thus Zemans observes that "Legal services continue to be allocated frequently on the basis of moral merit, rather than legal right, and controversies continue, particularly within judicare schemes, as to the type of service that should be provided. Legal services remain discretionary with respect to most minor criminal offences and with respect to civil and domestic disputes involving lesser amounts of money. Similarly, it is not universal in service-orientated schemes that private lawyers will be paid to represent low-income persons before administrative tribunals determining eligibility for social welfare, unemployment insurance and workers' compensation." – Zemans, p. 288.

[23] An important exception to this trend was the nineteenth century Settlement movement in the UK which operated, *inter alia*, a Poor Man's Lawyer scheme. One of the leading figures in this movement, Canon Samuel Barnett, argued that social conditions were very important in the development of individual responsibility and that such conditions could not be ignored in any attempt to solve the problem of poverty. For an account of this movement and for an examination of its relationship with the contemporary law centre movement, see Leat, "The Rise and Role of the Poor Man's Lawyer" (1975) 2 *Br. J. of Law and Soc.* 166.

[24] On the judicare model, see Paterson (1991) at pp. 128-131.

most relevance to poor people, such as welfare law, housing law and consumer law. Certainly during the 1960s there was a certain amount of dissatisfaction with the UK scheme insofar as it failed to protect the needs of those who were unaware of their legal rights or those who were unwilling to use the services of private practitioners.[25]

The third model of legal aid is the "salaried model" whereby lawyers are employed on a full-time basis either by the State or by NGOs to provide legal services to the marginalised. This model is available in both "service" and "strategic" versions. According to Paterson, both versions normally share certain characteristics.[26] They are publicly funded; independent, (in that the management of the schemes is intended to be independent of the legal profession and of the State); limited in scope; means-tested; free; and the services are provided by a closed panel of full-time salaried lawyers (as opposed to private practitioners). The strategic version of the model has four additional characteristics. It is proactive (*i.e.* it pursues "a proactive strategy of targetting the local problems which [it wishes] to focus on, collecting data and making submissions to relevant bodies and attempting to reach potential clients by advertising, circulars and public meetings"[27]); controlled (it only takes on certain types of case and in limited numbers); community orientated (its focus is on the problems faced by the community and on community organisation) and, finally, committed to law reform through litigation strategy or lobbying. In practice, however, very few salaried models are wholeheartedly committed to a strategic approach to legal aid and the "service" version is much more common. According to Paterson, the "service" version is essentially

(1) reactive in that the programmes wait to see which clients come through the doors;

(2) demand-led in the sense that the programmes encourages take-up by its location, publicity and work-style and places no limits on meeting the resultant demand except the capacities of the staff;

(3) individual orientated in the sense that the problems of individuals rather than those of groups or of the community are the primary focus; and

(4) routinised in the sense that staff time is spent mainly on highly routine, non-researched legal work with little impact in the law or the legal system.[28]

The fourth and final model is the "mixed-delivery" model which combines elements of the judicare and salaried models, particularly the strategic version of the latter model. In some jurisdictions, such as Sweden, the Netherlands and some Canadian provinces such as Quebec and Ontario, this integration was planned but in other jurisdictions this development came about in an *ad hoc* fashion with the two models existing side by side but operating independently of each other.

Where does the Irish experience fit into this categorisation of legal aid schemes? In fact there are elements of the first three models present in the Irish legal landscape,

---

[25] See Zander, "The Legal Profession and the Poor" (1969) 20 *N.I.L.Q.* 109, esp. pp. 112-4.

[26] Paterson, (1991), pp. 132-4. See also below, pp. 324-6.

[27] *Ibid.*, p. 133.

[28] *Ibid.*, p. 134.

though in relation to civil law it is the service version of the salaried model which predominates. The charitable model is represented by the tradition, within the legal profession, of doing *pro bono* work, though this is not at all as systematically organised as in the US where law firms allocate a designated proportion of their time to *pro bono* work. In the Irish context, personal injuries claims are often taken by lawyers on a "no foal, no fee" basis.[29] However more speculative claims involving worthy causes are sometimes taken on this basis as well and at a time during the 1980s when the Free Legal Advice Centres Ltd. could not afford to employ a solicitor, it had little difficulty arranging for its clients to be represented in court by sympathetic solicitors and barristers.

The only example of the judicare model in the Irish legal system is the statutory criminal legal aid scheme provided for in the Criminal Justice (Legal Aid) Act 1962.[30] Pursuant to this scheme, a court may, in certain circumstances, assign a solicitor and, where appropriate, counsel to represent a defendant with insufficient means in criminal proceedings. A committee established in 1975 to review the operation of the criminal legal aid scheme did consider the possibility of providing criminal legal aid through the offices of a Public Defender, a salaried lawyer employed at public expense to represent defendants in criminal proceedings.[31] However the committee was unable to agree on the principle of introducing such a scheme and criminal legal aid continues to be provided using the judicare model.[32]

In contrast to the criminal legal aid scheme, the state civil legal aid scheme run by the Legal Aid Board relies predominantly on full-time salaried staff, though there is some limited involvement of private practitioners. Introduced in August 1980 as an extra-statutory arrangement partly in response to the decision of the European Court of Human Rights in *Airey v. Ireland*,[33] the scheme is primarily concerned with the

---

[29] Though it should be noted that this practice may lead to certain difficulties with regard to the recovery of costs – see pp. 115-118.

[30] As amended by the Criminal Procedure (Amendment) Act 1973. See generally, Carney, pp. 76-82 and pp. 211-3; see also Cousins, "At the Heart of the Legal: The Role of Legal Aid in Legitimating Criminal Justice" in Young and Wall (eds.), *Access to Criminal Justice: Legal Aid, Lawyers and the Defence of Liberty* (Blackstone Press, 1996) at p. 98.

[31] See *Report of the Criminal Legal Aid Review Committee* (Prl.9986) at pp. 53-9.

[32] While the criminal legal aid scheme is clearly of importance to marginalised individuals – see Bacik, Kelly, O'Connell and Sinclair, "Crime and Poverty in Dublin: an analysis of the association between community deprivation, District Court appearance and sentence severity", published in Bacik and O'Connell, (eds), *Crime and Poverty in Ireland,* 1-30, (Dublin: Round Hall Press/Sweet & Maxwell, 1998) and also in (1997) 7 *Irish Criminal Law Journal*, 104-133, a study examining links between economic deprivation and crime and which found that defendants appearing before the Dublin District Courts are overwhelmingly young, male and from areas with high levels of community deprivation – the primary function of the criminal law is to identify and punish individuals who have engaged in proscribed behaviour. As such, it has no role to play in directly promoting social inclusion and for that reason, I do not propose to examine the criminal legal aid scheme in any further detail in this chapter, though I do consider the impact of judicial decisions on the development of the scheme in ch. 7.

[33] (1979-80) 2 EHRR 305.

servicing of individual cases. It was recently put on a statutory footing by the Civil Legal Aid Act 1995 and is examined in more detail in the next Part.[34]

Finally, two small non-governmental organisations each provide a strategic version of the salaried model of legal aid. These are the Free Legal Advice Centres Ltd., established in 1969, and the Coolock Community Law Centre Ltd., established in 1975.[35] The work of these NGOs is examined in more detail in Part III.[36]

Section II – State Provision of Civil Legal Aid and Advice

Background to introduction of Scheme of Civil Legal Aid and Advice

While the statutory criminal legal aid scheme was introduced in 1962, it was eighteen years later before the State assumed any responsibility for the provision of civil legal aid and advice[37] and a further fifteen elapsed before this responsibility was placed on a statutory footing. During the 1970s, the student run Free Legal Advice Centres Ltd. mounted a campaign for the introduction of a comprehensive statutory scheme of civil legal aid and advice. Official reaction to this campaign was slow in coming and it was only when the students threatened to close their own voluntary law centres that, in 1974, the government of the day established a committee to examine the question of access to law for the underprivileged and to make recommendations as to the type of scheme most appropriate for tackling this issue. A further three years elapsed before this committee, chaired by the late Mr Justice Denis Pringle, published its report.[38] In brief, the majority advocated the implementation of a comprehensive scheme of civil legal aid and advice administered by an independent Legal Aid Board appointed by the Government. In addition to administering the scheme, the Board would also have responsibility for educating the public as to their legal rights and for evaluating the results of its own work. This means-tested service was to be provided both by lawyers in private practice and by lawyers employed in community law centres.

In the event, the recommendations of this majority report were never adopted. Eleven months after publication of the report, however, the State found itself before the European Court of Human Rights defending the contention of Mrs Josie Airey, an Irish woman seeking a judicial separation, that Ireland's failure to provide her with legal aid amounted to a violation of her rights under, *inter alia*, Article 6(1) of the European Convention on Human Rights. The Court ultimately ruled in favour of Mrs

---

[34] See pp. 288-302.

[35] For other NGOs, such as the Children's Legal Centre, the Irish Traveller Movement and the environmental protection group, Lancefort Ltd., access to the courts is important so that they can pursue litigation strategy on behalf of their respective constituencies. However they are not concerned with the issue of access to legal services *per se* and as such fall outside the scope of this chapter.

[36] See p. 302 *et seq.*

[37] Apart from habeas corpus applications and state-side orders, in respect of which informal undertakings had been given in 1967 and 1976 by the Attorney General that legal aid would be provided in appropriate cases. This scheme is described in more detail in ch. 7 at pp. 262-3.

[38] *Report to the Minister for Justice of the Committee on Civil Legal Aid and Advice* (Prl.6862).

Airey[39] but not before the State gave a commitment to introduce legal aid in the area of family law. In December 1979, in discharge of this obligation, the then Minister for Justice, Mr Gerard Collins, TD, introduced an extra-statutory[40] legal aid scheme by laying a document entitled "Scheme of Civil Legal Aid and Advice"[41] before both Houses of the Oireachtas. In the same month, the first Legal Aid Board was appointed and in August 1980, the first State-controlled law centres opened their doors to the general public.

Salient features of the Scheme of Civil Legal Aid and Advice[42]

Despite the recommendations of the Pringle Committee that the Legal Aid Board should be empowered to organise programmes of education on legal rights and that it should engage in research and experimentation in the provision of legal aid and advice services,[43] the Scheme of Civil Legal Aid and Advice was geared solely towards providing legal advice and, where appropriate, legal representation in individual cases and eschewed any commitment to strategic work on behalf of the Board's clientele.[44] Thus the purpose of the Scheme was stated to be

> [T]o enable any person whose means are within the limits specified in the Scheme to obtain legal services in a situation where -
> (1) a reasonably prudent person whose means are outside those limits would be likely to seek such services at his own expense, if his means were such that the cost involved, while representing a financial obstacle to him, would not be such as to impose undue financial hardship, and
> (2) a competent lawyer would be likely to advise him to obtain such services.[45]

---

[39] See *Airey v. Ireland* (1979-80) 2 EHRR 305. For a more detailed account of this case, see above, pp. 247-9.

[40] For a consideration of the difficulties stemming from the fact that the scheme was not placed on a statutory basis, see Cousins, "Neither Flesh nor Fowl – The Status of the Scheme of Civil Legal Aid and Advice." (1992) 10 *I.L.T.* 41.

[41] Prl. 8543.

[42] For a more detailed description of this Scheme than that provided here, see, by the present writer, "And Justice for Some" (1984) 6 *DULJ (n.s.)* 88. See also Cousins and O'Hara, *Access to the Courts in Four European Countries* (FLAC, 1993) at pp. 56-62. For a recent account of the development of civil legal aid in Ireland, see Cousins, "Legal Aid Reform in France and the Republic of Ireland in the 1990s" in Regan, Paterson, Goriely and Fleming, *The Transformation of Legal Aid: Comparative and Historical Studies* (Oxford University Press, 1999) p. 159. In this comparative study, Cousins suggests that the development of legal aid may be linked to the type of legal system in a country and also that the state and legal profession are key players in such development.

[43] See paras. 4.7.4 and 5.5.5 respectively.

[44] However it should be noted that since the early 1990s, the Board has participated in the Co-operative Education Programme run by the University of Limerick whereby undergraduates are taken on by the Board to undertake project based research activities as part of their degree programme – see *Legal Aid Board Annual Report 1990/91,* p. 12 – though more recently the students are engaged more in practical work experience than in project based research. It would also appear that during the mid-1980s, the Board made certain suggestions to the Government about family law reform – see *Legal Aid Board Annual Report 1985*, para.11.1.

[45] See para. 1.2.1.

The government also rejected the Pringle Committee's proposal that the Board's services be provided through a mix of law centres and private practitioners,[46] initially opting instead, in the interests of public finance,[47] to rely solely on full-time salaried staff operating through law centres and part-time clinics.[48] This failure to use private practitioners, coupled with the limited number of law centres operating under the Scheme,[49] meant that, certainly until the early 1990s, large sections of the population were effectively denied access to the Board's services for simple geographical reasons and notwithstanding a significant increase in the number of law centres during the mid-1990s, the pressure on the Board's centres is such that many of them have waiting lists for appointments, in some cases of up to ten months.[50]

The Pringle Committee had also recommended that each law centre should have a consultative committee, a majority of whose members would be representatives of the local community, which would consult with the centre's director in relation to the running of the centre. While the Scheme did give the Board a discretion to establish such consultative committees,[51] it would appear that no such committees were ever established. This lack of community involvement in the running of individual centres was mirrored by a failure to make any provision for community representation on the Board itself. The Board consisted of a chairperson and twelve ordinary members, all part-timers appointed by the Minister for Justice. The Scheme stipulated that four of the ordinary members had to be practising lawyers[52] and the convention developed of appointing a fifth practising lawyer as chairperson and four representatives from

[46] See para. 4.2.1 of the Report.

[47] Thus, speaking at the Dáil Debate on the Scheme, the then Minister for Justice, Mr Collins TD said, with regard to the use of salaried solicitors, "The Government's decision in this regard was aimed principally at keeping the financial effects of the Scheme under control. We were concerned with the possibility that, without this feature, the Scheme might take off, as it were." 319 *Dáil Debates*, 22 April 1980, col.1781.

[48] In 1993, the then Minister for Equality and Law Reform introduced a pilot scheme allowing the Board to retain the services of private practitioners in certain limited type of District Court applications. Six months after its inception, this pilot scheme was restricted to the Dublin area and between 1994 and 1999, on average 1,100 cases each year were dealt with in this way. While the Civil Legal Aid Act 1995 empowers the Board to operate a permanent scheme involving private practitioners on a nationwide basis, industrial relations difficulties frustrated the Board's desire to extend the private practitioner scheme nationwide until May 2000 – see *Legal Aid Board Annual Report 1997*, at p. 8 and *Legal Aid Board Annual Report 1999,* at p. 10. The Board hopes to extend this scheme in the near future to cover certain family law proceedings in the Circuit Court. Private practitioners are also used by the Refugee Legal Service, as to which, see n. 82 below.

[49] Between 1980 and 1992, the number of law centres increased from 7 to 17. However, beginning in 1992, the resources of the Board were significantly increased so that by 1999, the Board had 30 law centres throughout the country and a centre for the Refugee Legal Service employing a total of 85 solicitors – *Legal Aid Board Annual Report 1999* at p. 18. This falls narrowly short of the Board's own objective of 33 centres, which it sees as the minimum necessary to provide a nationwide service (excluding the Refugee Legal Service) – see *Legal Aid Board Annual Report 1980,* para. 14.2.

[50] Figures for November 2000 supplied to the author by the Legal Aid Board.

[51] See para. 6.3.2.

[52] Para. 2.1.1.

relevant governmental departments as ordinary members of the Board. No discernible trend emerged with regard to the qualifications or experience of the remaining Board members, other than that no one was ever appointed specifically to represent the interests of the users of the service, Board employees or pressure groups such as the Free Legal Advice Centres Ltd. or Coolock Community Law Centre Ltd. who were actively involved in providing legal services for marginalised groups.

Legal services under the Scheme were restricted to certain types of case. In the case of legal advice,[53] four different categories of case were excluded from the scheme.[54] First, all criminal matters were excluded unless they arose out of the same set of circumstances as gave rise to the grant of civil legal aid or advice. Second, all matters listed in Schedule A to the Scheme, other than civil bills for sums below £150 and debt collection, were excluded.[55] Third, legal advice was not provided where the Board was of the opinion that it was possible for the applicant, without hardship, to obtain such advice without relying on the Scheme. Finally, legal advice was not provided where the sum involved was less than £20.

Turning to legal aid,[56] there were no fewer than sixteen different restrictions on the type of civil case which could be taken by the Board. These restrictions can be listed under five different headings. First, all matters in Schedule A, including debt collection and civil bills for sums below £150, were excluded.[57] Second, matters coming before tribunals were implicitly excluded by the terms of para. 3.2.2 which stated that a legal aid certificate would only be granted in respect of proceedings conducted in either the District, Circuit, High or Supreme Courts. Third, an application for a legal aid certificate would be refused if the application failed to satisfy any one of the six requirements[58] in para.3.2.3, namely, the application had to be in conformity with the purpose and terms of the Scheme; the applicant had to have,

---

[53] Defined in para. 3.1.1 as "any oral or written advice given by a solicitor or ... by counsel – (1) on the application of Irish law to any particular circumstances which have arisen in relation to the person seeking the advice, and (2) as to any steps which that person may appropriately take (whether by way of settling any claim, bringing or defending any proceedings, making an agreement, will, or other instrument or transaction, obtaining further legal or other advice or otherwise) having regard to the application of Irish law to those circumstances, [including] any assistance given by a solicitor or..by counsel, to any person in taking such steps as are mentioned in sub-Paragraph (2) above, whether the assistance is given by taking any such steps on his behalf or by assisting him in taking them on his own behalf."

[54] Para.3.1.3, as amended in 1981.

[55] The excluded areas were, subject to minor qualifications, defamation; disputes concerning rights and interests in or over land; cases of arbitration under the Landlord and Tenant Acts; licensing applications; conveyancing and election petitions.

[56] Defined as "representation by a solicitor and, (in so far as may be considered necessary by the Board), by counsel, in civil proceedings other than proceedings concerned with any of the matters referred to in Schedule A to this Scheme..[including] all such assistance as is normally given by a solicitor or counsel in the steps preliminary to or incidental to any proceedings or in arriving or giving effect to any compromise to avoid or bring to an end any proceedings." – Para. 3.2.1.

[57] Para. 3.2.1.

[58] Though neither the means test nor the merits test applied where the applicant sought relief under the Child Abduction and Enforcement of Custody Orders Act 1991.

as a matter of law, reasonable grounds for taking, defending or being a party to proceedings; the applicant had to satisfy the means test; the applicant had to show that he or she was reasonably likely to be successful in the proceedings; there had to be no satisfactory alternative to court proceedings for achieving the result which the applicant sought; and, finally, having regard to the circumstances of the case, it had to be reasonable for the Board to grant the certificate. Penultimately, para.3.2.4 excluded from the scope of the Scheme (a) applications made in a representative, fiduciary or official capacity in respect of a property or estate; (b) representative actions taken on behalf of numerous persons having the same interest; and (c) test cases. Finally, para. 3.2.5 directed the Board to refuse a legal aid certificate in five further situations, namely, where the applicant could obtain adequate financial support for the proceedings from any body or association of which he or she was a member; where the cost of the proceedings could be met by an insurance company or other source;[59] where the applicant had obtained legal services from the Board on a previous occasion but, without reasonable explanation, had failed to abide by the terms on which the previous services had been granted; where the cost of proceeding without a certificate is less than the maximum contribution payable by the applicant under the Scheme; and where such information as is required to enable any person, certifying committee, appeal committee or the Board to discharge a function under the Scheme has not been provided.

No one factor, other than perhaps a desire to save public money, can account for all of these restrictions on the services provided by the Legal Aid Board. However some of the restrictions do offer some illuminating insights into the priorities afforded by the State to the interests of different social groups and into the model of legal aid service provided under the Scheme. For example, the interests of the legal profession were clearly served by the exclusion of conveyancing, probate and cases involving insurance companies from the scope of the Scheme. On the other hand, the exclusion of tribunal work left people pursuing welfare appeals and employees appearing before the Employment Appeals Tribunal without any legal representation. As for the model of legal aid service provided, the exclusion of representative actions and test cases supports the view that the Scheme was concerned primarily with the servicing of individual cases and that it shunned any notion of strategic work aimed at provoking social or legal reform.[60]

As already intimated, the services provided by the Board were means-tested.[61] Applicants could not have more than £200,000 disposable capital or a prescribed

---

[59] It is worth noting that the Pringle Committee considered whether insurance-covered cases generally should be excluded from the scope of a legal aid scheme and concluded that "there are no clear grounds of principle which would justify the exclusion of insurance-covered cases from a full comprehensive scheme of legal aid" – para. 2.6.4. The Committee did concede, however, that if it were necessary to establish priorities as between various case categories, insurance-covered cases should be low on the list.

[60] Though see note 44 above.

[61] See Sections 5.1-2 of the Scheme and Schedule B thereto. The Board's Annual Reports from 1981 until 1986 indicate that a failure to satisfy the means test accounted for between one-third and a half

amount of disposable income. This latter figure was originally set at £3,500 *per annum* in 1980 but was raised at irregular intervals over succeeding years to £7,350 *per annum* by 1995. However the failure to review annually both this income limit and the allowances taken into account in calculating disposable income meant that, at various stages during the Board's history, inflation had the effect of reducing the pool of persons eligible for the Board's services.[62]

Applicants for legal services were also expected to contribute towards the Board's expenses, paying either the amount which the Board expected to spend on the case or a contribution calculated in accordance with formulae set out in the Scheme, whichever was the less.[63] These formulae were quite complex, distinguishing between income and capital and, in the case of capital, between farm stock or machinery, farm land and other capital resources. However, though presumably costly to administer, they did not generate much income for the Board.[64]

The Scheme of Civil Legal Aid and Advice was, therefore, very restrictive. Even in terms of providing a service model of legal aid, it was not comprehensive as significant areas of unmet legal need, such as representation before tribunals, were excluded from its remit and its strict financial provisions restricted the category of persons eligible for the services provided. To make matters worse, for much of its existence, the Scheme was hopelessly underfunded, to such an extent that much of the country did not have easy access to the scheme's law centres and even where centres did exist, there were invariably lengthy waiting lists for appointments to see solicitors.[65]

After assuming responsibility for civil legal aid in 1993, the then Minister for Equality and Law Reform, Mr Mervyn Taylor, TD, made a number of significant changes to the non-statutory scheme. Chief of these was unquestionably the major increase in funding which, through the provision of extra staff, law centres and part-time clinics, made the scheme much more accessible.[66] In addition, he also made provision for the limited involvement of private practitioners in meeting the need for

---

of all applications for legal services declared ineligible by the Board. Thereafter this figure declined to between one-fifth and one-eighth of all such applications, though a breakdown of the number of applications declared ineligible is not provided in the Board's Annual Reports after 1992.

[62] See *Legal Aid Board Annual Report 1981,* at para.3.1; *Legal Aid Board Annual Report 1982,* at paras.4.1 and 4.4; and *Legal Aid Board Annual Report 1983/4,* at para.6.3.

[63] Para.5.3.3.

[64] The Board's Annual Reports reveal that, as a percentage of the total annual income received by the Board, contributions from legally assisted applicants ranged from a low of 1.3% (in 1988) to a maximum of 2.8% (in 1997). Moreover the number of applicants paying the minimum contribution never dropped below 79% of the annual number of assisted persons.

[65] This lack of adequate funding eventually led, first, to the resignation, in January 1990, of the then Chairperson, Nial Fennelly, and three other member of the Board, Ernest Margetson, Denis McCullough and Fidelma Macken because of their dissatisfaction with the capacity of the Board to perform its functions adequately – see *Legal Aid Board Annual Report 1987, 1988 and 1989,* para. 1.4 – and, second, to the taking of a number of High Court cases against the Legal Aid Board, beginning in 1990, arising out of its inability to provide legal aid to the particular applicants. These cases are discussed further above, see pp. 253-5.

[66] See note 49 above.

civil legal aid[67] and for the employment of law clerks and solicitors' apprentices in law centres. However he remained wedded to the view that legal aid should be concerned exclusively with the servicing of individual cases, rather than with social and legal reform and so, when it came to placing legal aid on a statutory basis, relatively few changes were made to the non-statutory scheme by the Civil Legal Aid Act 1995.

The Civil Legal Aid Act 1995[68]

Confirmation that no radical change was effected by the Act can be seen in s.5(1) which provides that

> The principal function of the Board shall be to provide, within the Board's resources and subject to the other provisions of this Act, legal aid and advice in civil cases to persons who satisfy the requirements of this Act.

During the parliamentary debates on the Bill, the Minister stoutly defended this commitment to a service, as opposed to strategic, model of legal aid. The opposition parties had attempted, both in the Seanad and in the Dáil, to expand s.5 to include the functions of public education and research. However the Minister opposed these moves, arguing that there were insufficient resources available and also arguing that the National Social Services Board, which was established in 1984, was now providing the type of education as to rights envisaged in the Pringle Report. In support of this last argument, he cited the views of the UK Legal Aid Efficiency Unit that the dissemination of information about legal rights should be entrusted to Citizens' Advice Bureaux. However this argument fails to take account of relevant differences between the two countries. In the UK, unlike in Ireland, private practitioners were paid by the State to provide legal advice to indigent clients and the principal motive behind the recommendation of the Efficiency Unit was arguably to reduce costs, rather than to improve the legal aid scheme. In the event, that recommendation was rejected both by the National Association of Citizens' Advice Bureaux and by a Government White Paper published in 1987 on the grounds of the limited resources of the advice agencies, the difficulty of defining what should be done by solicitors and what by advice agencies and possible conflicts of interests if both sides were represented by the one agency.[69] In response to opposition pressure on this point, the Minister did introduce s.5(2) as an amendment at the Report Stage of the Bill in the Seanad. However this merely allows the Board to publicise its services and does not cover the provision of information about legal entitlements.[70]

---

[67] See note 48 above.

[68] The Act came into force by virtue of the Civil Legal Aid Act, 1995 (Commencement) Order, 1996 [S.I.No.272 of 1996] on 11 October 1996. The Act is annotated by the present author in (1995) *Irish Current Law Statutes Annotated* 32.

[69] See Zander, (1989) at pp. 63-9.

[70] Section 6 of the Act does empower the Minister, acting with the consent of the Minister for Finance, to confer additional functions on the Board as the Minister considers to be incidental to or consequential on the Board's statutory functions and at one point – see *Seanad Debates,*

In keeping with the ethos of its predecessor, the statutory scheme made no provision for community involvement in the delivery of the Board's services. Indeed, if anything, the Act represented a disimprovement on the extra-statutory scheme for at least that scheme had allowed for the possibility of the establishment of consultative committees representing local interests to consult with the managers of individual centres[71] whereas no such provision is to be found in the statutory scheme.[72] Of the thirteen places on the Board provided for in s.4, six were reserved by the Act to practising lawyers and representatives of the staff of the Board. Attempts by various Senators to have two of the remaining six ordinary places reserved for representatives of the users of the services, such as the Combat Poverty Agency and the Free Legal Advice Centres Ltd, were successfully opposed by the Minister on the ground that he did not wish to extend the size of the Board nor "to provide sinecures for any particular organisation".[73]

Executive control over the Board's activities (other than in relation to any particular case with which the Board was concerned) was maintained through ministerial control over its finances (s.18), its range of functions (s.6), its property dealings (s.3(2)), the size of its staff (s.11(1)), the terms under which the Board could retain independent contractors, including solicitors and barristers (ss.11(7) and 30(3)) and the location and establishment of law centres (s.30(1)). Moreover, in addition to the power to make such regulations as are necessary for giving effect to the Act, the Minister also retained, from the extra-statutory scheme,[74] the power to issue to the Board general directives as to policy in relation to legal aid and advice – s.7.[75]

---

vol. 142, 6 April 1995, col. 1922 – the Minister suggested that, if necessary, an order could be made under this provision to authorise the Board to disseminate information to the public. To date, however, no such order has been made. Yet notwithstanding this absence of statutory authority, the *Legal Aid Board Annual Report 1997* indicates, at p. 2, that Board solicitors are regularly asked to give talks on legal aid and family law by, *inter alia*, local community groups and during 2000, the Board produced a series of leaflets on family law matters. Moreover, there is also some evidence that the Board has, in the past, made suggestions to Government about law reform – see note 44 above.

71 See para. 6.3.2.
72 Notwithstanding the absence of such a provision, a Monitoring Committee comprising representatives of groups active in relation to asylum-seekers has been established to ensure that a quality service is provided by the Refugee Legal Service – see *Legal Aid Board Annual Report 1999* at p. 12.
73 *Seanad Debates*, vol. 142, 6 April 1995, col. 1889. Section 4 did represent an improvement on the extra-statutory scheme in two respects. Apart from providing now for the representation of staff interests on the Board, it also introduced gender-balancing into the composition of the Board by providing that not less than five members shall be men and not less than five members shall be women.
74 See para. 2.2.6.
75 An interesting constitutional issue arises in relation to this section. By virtue of Article 15.2 of the Constitution, as interpreted by the Supreme Court in *Cityview Press Ltd. v. An Chomhairle Oiliúna* [1980] IR 381, the Oireachtas cannot delegate a parliamentary power which is "more than a mere giving effect to principles and policies which are contained in the statute itself". It is certainly arguable that s.7, insofar as it appears to empower the Minister to determine policy in relation to legal aid and advice (and this was certainly how the Minister's power under the non-statutory scheme was used) appears to infringe this principle. One further point is worth making in this

In what represented a theoretical improvement on the non-statutory scheme as that scheme was originally drafted, s.30 allowed for the provision of legal services by the Board through a panel of solicitors in private practice, as well as through the law centres established by the Board throughout the country. A pilot scheme dealing with certain types of District Court cases operated countrywide between October 1993 and March 1994. Thereafter it was restricted to the Dublin area until May 2000, when it was relaunched on a nationwide basis. Private practitioners are also used in the recently introduced Refugee Legal Service.[76]

The restrictions on the type of service provided by the Board were broadly similar to those in the extra-statutory scheme, though some interesting changes were also introduced. Thus s.24, detailing the general criteria for the grant of legal aid and advice, effectively reproduced para.1.2.1 of the non-statutory scheme[77] while ss.25 and 27, defining legal advice and legal aid, respectively, for the purposes of the Act, largely followed paras. 3.1.1-2 and paras. 3.2.1-2 respectively.[78]

Three of the four restrictions on the provision of legal advice under the old scheme are carried over into the 1995 Act.[79] Thus s.26(2) excludes a criminal law matter unless the applicant is seeking advice as to how to obtain criminal legal aid.[80] Nor will legal advice be provided in respect of a matter where the Board considers that it would be possible for the applicant, without hardship, to obtain legal advice other than pursuant to the Act. Finally, advice will not be provided in respect of any matter listed in s.28(9)(a). This adds to the list of excluded matters in respect of legal advice

---

context. Section 7 requires that policy directives must be made by ministerial order. In *The Separation of Powers in the Irish Constitution* (Round Hall/Sweet and Maxwell, 1997), Professor Gwynn Morgan argues that a ministerial order is not capable of infringing Article 15.2 on the ground that it is not a "law". This in turn depends on the classification of an order, in contradistinction to other forms of delegated legislation, as an instrument referring to a single exercise of an administrative power in relation to a particular person or situation. Conceding that there is merit in relation to Professor Gwynn Morgan's view on orders and Article 15.2, the point then arises as to whether an instrument containing a directive envisaged by s.7 could properly be regarded as an order, giving that it will not be restricted to a particular person or situation. The difficulty with Article 15.2 remains, therefore.

[76] See n. 48 above. Section 30(6) generated some controversy insofar as it enabled a law centre to represent both parties to a dispute, provided separate solicitors and, where appropriate, barristers act for each side. While the motivation behind the provision is laudable – the provision is an attempt to improve the accessibility of the Board's services – concerns were expressed that, particularly in family cases, a party in need of legal services might be deterred from going to a law centre if he or she knew that their opponent was also availing of the Board's services through the same centre. An amendment to the sub-section requiring legal services in such cases to be provided through a combination of the Board's salaried solicitors and solicitors in private practice was withdrawn in the Seanad in the face of the Minister's opposition – *Seanad Debates*, vol. 143, 11 May 1995, cols. 592-606.

[77] As to which, see above, p. 289.

[78] Though in relation to legal aid for tribunal work, see below, n.82.

[79] The exception being cases where the sum involved was less than £20, which restriction is not contained in the 1995 Act.

[80] However a complainant in the prosecution of certain sexual offences prescribed in s.26(3)(b) is entitled to legal advice free of any contribution, presumably in respect of such prosecution.

contained in Schedule A to the extra-statutory scheme: (i) a matter in respect of which an application for legal aid is made in a representative, fiduciary or offical capacity where the Board, having regard to any source from which the applicant might be indemnified in respect of the costs of the proceedings and any resources of the persons who would be likely to benefit from the applicant succeeding in the proceedings, is of opinion that legal aid should not be granted; (ii) a matter in respect of which proceedings are to be brought by the applicant as a member of and by arrangement with a group of persons for the purpose of establishing a precedent in the determination of any question in which the members of the group have an interest – "test cases" in common parlance; and (iii) any matter in respect of which an application for legal aid is made by or on behalf of a person acting on behalf of a group of persons having the same interest in the proceedings concerned. On the positive side, legal advice may now be given in respect of cases of arbitration under the Landlord and Tenant Acts and in conveyancing matters connected to a matter in which legal aid or advice has already been given.

With regard to legal aid, virtually all of the sixteen conditions in the old scheme, together with one additional condition, were provided for in the 1995 Act, though five were downgraded, as it were, to the status of factors which give the Board a discretion to refuse legal aid.[81] Tribunal work, with the exception of appeals from decisions on applications for asylum,[82] continues to be excluded from the scope of the Legal Aid Board's services.[83] Section 28(2) mirrors para.3.2.3 in prescribing, in addition to compliance with ss.24, a set of five conditions, each of which has to be satisfied before legal aid may be granted to an applicant. First, the applicant must satisfy the means test prescribed in s.29. Second, the applicant must, has a matter of law, have reasonable grounds for taking, defending or being a party to proceedings. Third, the applicant must show that he or she is reasonably likely to be successful in the proceedings, assuming that the facts put forward by him or her are proved in court. One modification on the former provisions stems from the Supreme Court decision in

[81] However these restrictions are overridden where an application falls within the terms of s.28(5) of the Act (as amended by s.13 of the Children Act 1997), *i.e.* where the State has an obligation in international law to provide legal aid to a person, where an application comes within the terms of the Child Abduction and Enforcement of Custody Orders Act 1991 or the Maintenance Act 1994, or, lastly, where a court has ordered that a guardian *ad litem* appointed under s.28 of the Guardianship of Infants Act 1964 should be legally represented in proceedings under s.28(4) and any of the parties to those proceedings is in receipt of civil legal aid.

[82] By virtue of S.I. Nos. 74 and 262 of 1999, made pursuant to s. 27(2) of the Act, tribunals dealing with appeals from decisions on applications for asylum now come within the scope of the Civil Legal Aid Act and in February 1999, the Board established the Refugee Legal Service as a separate office to provide legal assistance to asylum-seekers.

[83] In a rare defeat for any government in the Seanad, an amendment to the Bill to allow the Board to provide legal aid in respect of cases going before the Employment Appeals Tribunal and social welfare tribunals was passed, notwithstanding the Minister's opposition on the ground of lack of resources, in the Upper House – see *Seanad Debates,* vol. 143, 11 May 1995, cols. 527-550. However this was subsequently rescinded at Report Stage – see *Seanad Debates*, vol. 143, 15 June 1995, cols. 2006-2039.

M.F. v. Legal Aid Board[84] wherein that Court held that under the corresponding condition in the non-statutory scheme (para.3.2.3(4)), it was only necessary to show, in cases involving the welfare of children, a reasonable likelihood that the point of view of the applicant should be among the material relied upon by the judge. Significantly, s.28(3) now provides that this particular condition shall not apply to such cases. The fourth condition imposed by s.28(2) is that legal proceedings must be the most satisfactory means by which to achieve the result sought by the applicant. Finally, the Board has to be satisfied that, having regard to all the circumstances of the case, it is reasonable to grant legal aid, though again this condition does not apply to cases involving the welfare of children.

Even where an applicant satisfies all five requirements in sub-section 2, the Board now has a discretion to refuse legal aid if the applicant comes within any one of the five different situations prescribed in s.28(4).[85] The first situation prescribed is where the applicant may obtain the cost of the proceedings from, or be provided with legal representation by, a body or association of which he or she is a member or any other source. The second situation is where the applicant has on a previous occasion obtained legal aid or advice from the Board in respect of another matter and has, without reasonable explanation, failed to comply with the terms on which such aid or advice was granted. The third situation is where the cost to the applicant of retaining the services of private practitioners would be less than the contribution payable by him or her under the Act for legal services from the Board.[86] Penultimately, legal aid may be refused where the applicant fails to furnish such information as is reasonably required by the Board to enable it to process the application for legal aid. Finally, legal aid may be refused if, due to the act, omission or neglect of the applicant, any regulations under s.37 cannot be complied with in respect of the application.

Section 28(9) excludes nine different "designated matters" from the scope of the legal aid scheme,[87] in the process providing some insights into the thinking behind the 1995 Act. The first seven of these excluded areas are defamation,[88] (except insofar as the

---

[84] [1993] ILRM 797.

[85] The corresponding provision in the non-statutory scheme – para. 3.2.5 – *obliged* the Board to refuse legal aid if the applicant fell within the scope of the provision.

[86] The type of case envisaged here is where a solicitor agrees to act on a "no foal, no fee" basis or where market forces compel members of the profession to undercut the Board. In fact, however, no such case had ever arisen under the corresponding provision of the non-statutory scheme – see *Seanad Debates*, vol. 143, 11 May 1995, col.563.

[87] Though it is worth noting that by virtue of s.28(10), the Minister may, by order and with the consent of the Minister for Finance, extend the legal aid scheme to cover any of the designated matters listed in the subsection. To date, no such orders have been made.

[88] Justifying this exclusion, the Minister offered the spectre of law centres being overworked with defamation cases which are "easily brought" – *Seanad Debates*, vol. 143, 11 May 1995, col. 572. In fact, the experience of the Free Legal Advice Centres Ltd., which has been operating since 1969, does not bear out this prediction and, significantly, the Pringle Committee came out against excluding defamation from their proposed legal aid scheme – para. 2.6.5. The exclusion of defamation also raises a constitutional point inasmuch as the State is constitutionally obliged, by virtue of Article 40.3.2, to defend and vindicate, *inter alia*, the individual's right to his

applicant is defending a counterclaim for defamation in proceedings for which he or she has already been granted legal aid – s.28(9)(b)), disputes concerning rights and interests in or over land (subject to some significant qualifications provided for in s.28(9)(c)(i)-(iv)[89]), civil matters within the jurisdiction of the District Court (Small Claims Procedure) Rules 1993; licensing matters (except where the granting of a licence might cause hardship to the applicant – sub.s.9(c)(v)), conveyancing matters (unless connected to a matter in which legal aid or advice has already been granted – sub.s.9(c)(vi)), election petitions and cases in which the applicant is acting in a representative, fiduciary or official capacity where the Board, having regard to any source from which the applicant might be indemnified in respect of the costs of the proceedings and any resources of the persons who would be likely to benefit from the applicant succeeding in the proceedings, is of opinion that legal aid should not be granted.

Section 28(9)(a) also excludes, *inter alia,* proceedings which are brought by the applicant as a member of and by arrangement with a group of persons for the purpose of establishing a precedent in the determination of any question in which the members of the group have an interest – "test cases" in common parlance – and representative actions. These exclusions mirror the provisions of para.3.2.4.(2) and (3) of the extra-statutory scheme and again underline the State's understanding of legal aid as being primarily about the servicing of individual cases rather than about achieving social reform.[90]

The financial provisions of the statutory scheme are also very similar to those of its predecessor. Thus services provided by the Board are means-tested[91] and applicants are required to contribute towards the cost incurred by the Board in providing them

---

or her good name. In the case of an indigent litigant who might wish to take an action for defamation, can it be said that the State has complied fully with its constitutional obligations if it will not grant legal aid for defamation cases?

[89] Thus legal aid may be granted in respect of proceedings under the Landlord and Tenant Acts, 1967-1994, in so far as they relate to residential property, the Married Women's Status Act, 1957, the Rent Restrictions Acts, 1960 and 1967, the Family Home Protection Act, 1976, the Family Law Act, 1981 or arising out of a dispute between spouses or engaged or cohabiting couples as to the title to or possession of any property. Legal aid may also be granted where (a) the subject matter of the dispute is the applicant's home, the Board considers that the applicant suffers from an infirmity of mind or body or may have been subjected to duress, undue influence or fraud, and a refusal to grant legal aid may cause hardship to the applicant or (b) in connection with the preparation of an assent where the assent relates to the applicant's home, a grant of representation has been taken out on behalf of the applicant (or s/he has taken out a personal grant of representation) and a refusal to grant legal aid would cause hardship to the applicant.

[90] Though it should be noted that the description of "test cases" in sub-para.(viii) allows the Board to provide legal aid to an individual who is pursuing a case, the outcome of which may affect many others in a similar situation – see also s. 28(9)(d). The Board has been involved in a number of such cases – see the *Legal Aid Board Annual Report 1995,* pp. 12-3 and 15, and the *Legal Aid Board Annual Report 1998,* pp. 15-18.

[91] S.29(1)(a). While the maximum limit of disposable capital remains at £200,000, the disposable income limit for eligibility has been raised to £7,350 – see article 13(3) of the Civil Legal Aid Regulations 1996 [S.I. No. 273 of 1996]. By virtue of s.29(2), it is open to the Board, *inter alia,* to waive the means test in accordance with regulations made pursuant to the Act. However the 1996 Regulations are silent on this issue and so it would appear that this power is not currently operative.

with legal services.[92] As we noted above, in the past, a failure to review periodically the income limits for eligiblity and the amounts of the allowances used in calculating disposable income meant that inflation reduced, over time, the number of people eligible for assistance. Notwithstanding this, a proposal to provide for an annual review of the means test was defeated in the Seanad.[93]

Evaluation of State provision of civil legal aid

> While I accept that the board has a role to play in the area of education and information and that in the normal course of its operation it must be required to undertake research as appropriate, the principal function of the board must, as the Bill provides, be the provision of legal aid and advice in civil matters to persons of insufficient means. To accord any other matter an equal or greater priority would result in limited resources being diverted from what must be the principal function of the board, namely, that of providing legal aid and advice.[94]

Ignoring the recommendations of the Pringle Report, public civil legal aid in Ireland is firmly based on the service model of legal aid, with its emphasis on the provision of conventional legal services to needy individuals.[95] A number of factors possibly account for this. Scarcity of resources is sometimes cited as a reason for focussing on the servicing of individual cases and eschewing more longer-term strategies.[96] However one might also suspect the innate conservatism of the Department of Justice, the department responsible for introducing the Scheme of Civil Legal Aid and Advice in 1980. Moreover, it was no doubt fortuitous, from that department's perspective, that the decision of the European Court of Human Rights in *Airey v. Ireland*[97] posed no challenge to the State's commitment to a service model of legal aid.

Since its inception in 1979, and under very difficult circumstances until the mid-1990s, the Legal Aid Board has provided legal advice to approximately 96,000 people and legal aid to more than 47,000, the majority of whom, in both categories, are female.[98] Family law cases constitute the vast majority of cases in both

---

[92] S.29(1)(b). See arts.17 and 20 of the Civil Legal Aid Regulations 1996 [S.I. No. 273 of 1996]. S.29(2) empowers the Board, *inter alia*, to waive contributions in accordance with regulations made pursuant to the Act and article 21(9) of the 1996 Regulations restricts this power to cases where the maximum income contribution assessed against the applicant is £23 or £46 where both an income and capital contribution are payable. It should also be noted that s.33(7), which replicates the thrust of para.8.4.1 of the non-statutory scheme, allows the Board to recover its costs from any general damages or money or property, (subject to certain exclusions prescribed in sub-section 8), recovered by a legally aid litigant.

[93] See *Seanad Debates*, vol. 143, 11 May 1995, cols.577-592.

[94] Mervyn Taylor, TD, then Minister for Equality and Law Reform, *Seanad Debates*, vol. 142, 6 April 1995, col.1920.

[95] Though see n.70 above.

[96] See, e.g., the comments of Minister Taylor at the Committee Stage in the Seanad of the Civil Legal Aid Bill 1995, *Seanad Debates*, vol. 142, 6 April 1995, cols. 1934-6.

[97] (1979-80) 2 EHRR 305.

[98] The most recent figures available, for 1987-89, indicate that during that time, almost 80% of all persons granted legal aid certificates were women and approximately 75% of all applicants for legal services – see *Legal Aid Board Annual Report 1987, 1988 and 1989*, p. 3 and para. 15.6(d).

categories,[99] with legal aid also being provided in a small number of landlord and tenant, tort, contract, employment and other miscellaneous cases.

Notwithstanding this achievement, and even within the terms of reference set by *Airey*, the State's efforts to provide civil legal aid are open to criticism. To begin with, the statutory scheme is not comprehensive – cases going before social welfare appeals officers and the Employment Appeals Tribunal are excluded, as are representative actions (such as those pursued during the 1980s by married women seeking social welfare equality arrears) and test cases.[100] Moreover, the failure to provide for periodic review of the financial limits on eligibility leaves open the possibility that inflation will restrict the category of eligible applicants.[101] And while the Board did receive a significant increase in funding in 1993, there are growing signs that, once again, demand is outstripping supply, with waiting lists for first interview with Legal Aid Board solicitors now extending up to ten months in some cases.[102] It is clear, therefore, that the present scheme is still quite restrictive. This raises the question of whether Ireland has complied fully with its obligations under Article 6 of the European Convention on Human Rights. In *Airey*, the Court of Human Rights held that the State had to provide for legal assistance "when such assistance proves indispensable for an effective access to court ... [because of] the complexity of the procedure or of the case".[103] It is certainly arguable that at least some indigent litigants involved in complex litigation will be unable to obtain legal aid from the State because of the restrictive nature of the statutory scheme and that consequently Ireland may still be in dereliction of its international obligations.

Of course, even full compliance with *Airey* does not mean that Ireland would have the most effective legal aid scheme possible. At this point, it is worth recalling Zemans' observations about service models of legal aid.

> ... Inevitably over-loaded, service models can expend little time or energy in educating the community or on outreach programmes. Since service models accept the norms of the legal system and provide a service for poor people which, in the opinion of the administrators (inevitably lawyers), is the same for the poor as for the rich, poor people using service schemes face many of the same obstacles that they would encounter within the traditional setting. Such service models offer little recognition of the uniqueness of the poor person's lifestyle. They neither make the service psychologically more accessible, nor do they attempt to handle problems which have not been on the traditional agenda of

---

[99] Thus, for example, the *Legal Aid Board Annual Report 1999* indicates, at p. 9, that family law constituted approximately 97% of all cases of legal aid and 90% of legal advice cases in that year.

[100] In its *Report on Civil Legal Aid in Ireland* (Law Society of Ireland, 2000), the Family Law and Civil Legal Aid Committee of the Law Society of Ireland recommended, *inter alia*, that the remit of the Legal Aid Board be extended to include tribunal work, test cases and representative actions subject only to the merits test in the particular case – see p. 8.

[101] The Family Law and Civil Legal Aid Committee of the Law Society of Ireland recommended, *inter alia*, that eligibility criteria should be regularly reviewed in accordance with increases in the Consumer Price Index – *ibid.*, at p. 16.

[102] See text accompanying note 50 above.

[103] (1979-80) 2 EHRR 305 at p. 317.

legal services (e.g. eviction). The service model reinforces the distance between the "recipient" and the "deliverer" of the service by encouraging clients to assume passive and dependent roles in their relations with the legal-aid scheme. Lawyers write briefs; interview witnesses; negotiate settlements and go to court. The client's perspective is generally of an over-worked, under-paid lawyer who is dealing with the immediate problem and ignoring the fundamental cancer of poverty and poverty-related problems that continue to affect the client.[104]

Conscious of the limitations attaching to service models of legal aid, the two organisations active in Ireland's voluntary legal aid sector, namely, the Free Legal Advice Centres Ltd. (hereafter "FLAC") and the Coolock Community Law Centre Ltd. (hereafter "CCLC"),[105] have repeatedly called for the State provision of a strategic model of legal aid and attempt to provide such a model themselves.[106] I turn now to consider their contribution to the debate on civil legal aid.

Section III – Civil Legal Aid and the NGO Sector

While there has been a long tradition of individual members of the legal profession providing free legal assistance, including legal aid, in needy cases, the first attempts to put this on an organisational footing occurred during the 1930s and involved charitable organisations such as the Poor Man's Lawyer Centres, the Labour Defence League, the Pearse Street Council of Action and the St Anne's Secretariat of the Society of St Vincent de Paul.[107] In more recent times, evidence to the Pringle Committee indicated that sixteen trade unions arranged legal aid and advice services for fully-paid up members, albeit usually only in respect of matters relating to employment.[108] However unquestionably the most important development in the provision of free legal services by the private sector occurred with the establishment, in 1969, of the Free Legal Advice Centres Ltd, a student-run organisation which successfully highlighted the extent of unmet legal need in Ireland and which, since its inception, has campaigned for the introduction of appropriate public services in this area.

a) Free Legal Advice Centres Ltd

The 1960s was an optimistic time in Irish history; the economy was growing and there was a sense that a better day for all was just around the corner. In the legal world, this was the decade of the Ó Dálaigh Supreme Court, a period of judicial activism which

---

104 Zemans, pp. 291-2.
105 The reader should note that I have worked with FLAC on various projects since the early 1980s and have been on the management committee of CCLC since 1994.
106 The Family Law and Civil Legal Aid Committee of the Law Society of Ireland has also recommended in its recent report that civil legal aid should be administered through a combination of service and strategic model law centres, supplemented by a nation-wide panel of private solicitors – *Report on Civil Legal Aid in Ireland* at p. 12.
107 See Carney, p. 72; Greer, pp. 274-5; Carr Lett, p. 219.
108 *Report of Committee on Civil Legal Aid and Advice,* p. 32.

witnessed an increasing role for the courts in the protection of fundamental rights. Against this background, the immediate catalyst for the establishment of FLAC was a law students' conference on legal education held in Trinity College Dublin in December 1968. One of the students attending this conference was a UCD undergraduate called David Byrne. According to Byrne:

> [t]he main themes at this Congress were, firstly, the role of the lawyer in society, and secondly the practical education of lawyers. It was generally agreed that the lawyer, including the student, could benefit his community by using his specialised knowledge to help the underprivileged members of that community. Also it was emphasised by many speakers, including Mr Justice Megarry,[109] that the law student should gain practical experience of the law as a social reality rather than as a theoretical abstraction.[110]

During the following Christmas vacations, Byrne discussed these ideas further with three friends, Denis McCullough, Vivian Lavan and Ian Candy and together they decided to establish a free legal advice service run by students.

While the late 1960s was an era of radical student politics in Ireland, as elsewhere, these founding members of FLAC were decidedly mainstream and pragmatic in outlook. This had an immediate advantage in that they were able to enlist the support of influential members of the legal profession. Thus the Dublin Solicitors' Bar Association, for example, organised a panel of solicitors who were available at the centres for consultation by the student volunteers about the more difficult cases appearing at the centres and who, if necessary, would act in those cases on a *pro bono* basis. Moreover the Executive Committee of the organisation also included an advisor from each of the four institutions of legal education in Dublin – the law schools at UCD and TCD, the Honorable Society of the King's Inns and the Incorporated Law Society of Ireland. However while this approach of working with the profession enabled the organisation to get off the ground, it also meant that the organisation was always controlled by law students (and latterly lawyers).

The new organisation had three objectives. The ultimate objective was to push the State into establishing a public legal aid scheme by demonstrating the extent of unmet legal need. The more immediate objectives were to provide free advice to those unable to afford the services of private practitioners and to give law students an opportunity to be involved in this type of work.[111] Three months of deliberation and planning eventually culminated in the establishment, in April 1969, of FLAC.

1969 to 1974 – Proving the need for civil legal aid

The first months of the new organisation were taken up with establishing centres in Dublin and publicising their existence. FLAC had no resources and so was dependant

---

[109] Of the English High Court.

[110] Byrne, "Equality before the Law" in (1970) 2 *DULR* 40 at 42.

[111] While it was originally intended that FLAC would provide legal advice only, such was the demand for legal representation that, shortly after its inception, the organisation began to provide legal aid through its panel of solicitors and barristers – see *FLAC Report 1972* at p. 2.

on other voluntary organisations to provide accommodation for the advice centres. Thus the first such centre opened in the premises of the Society of St Vincent de Paul in Mountjoy Square, soon to be followed by a centre in the offices of the Irish Society for the Prevention of Cruelty to Children in Molesworth St. Other centres followed in Crumlin, Rialto and Ballymun. These centres were only open on one night each week but even so, they quickly attracted a number of cases[112] and the energies of the volunteers were almost exclusively focussed on handling this workload. Indeed, with hindsight, it would appear that the proper relationship between the objective of securing a comprehensive legal aid scheme and the means adopted to achieve that aim, *viz.*, the provision of free legal advice, may not have been very clear to many members of the organisation for whom the means became an end in itself. Thus one chairperson of the organisation complained that

> It had always appeared to the members of FLAC that providing a service was more immediate and essential and consequently the political aim of pressurising the Government into introducing legal aid suffered and suffered badly.[113]

At the same time, one should not decry the importance of this casework, much of which related to family law, and FLAC's experience in this area was a very important factor in bringing the reform and modernisation of Irish family law to the top of the political agenda during the 1970s.

In the light of its early experience, FLAC redefined its objectives to include research and the making of recommendations in relation to law reform generally, and the provision of legal aid in particular. The organisation also sought to promote public interest in legal and social affairs generally. In 1972, FLAC published its first Annual Report which drew attention to the problems caused by the absence of legal aid and which highlighted the need for law reform in relation to family law and the law relating to children.[114] The fact that FLAC already had nearly three years experience of casework under its belt before this report was published no doubt helped to establish the credibility of the organisation, and enhance its reputation, in the eyes of the general public. Certainly publication of the report led to a large increase in the number of cases coming to FLAC and in its second Annual Report, 1974, it was able to show that, since its inception, it had dealt with more than 8,000 cases in its eight Dublin centres. By 1973, FLAC had established itself to such an extent that a threat to withdraw its services led to the announcement of the setting up of a Government working party on legal aid and the provision of some funding for FLAC, which included a grant towards the establishment of a full-time law centre. At this point, it could fairly be said that the organisation had succeeded in its initial objective of

---

[112] Writing less than 9 months after the establishment of FLAC, Byrne estimated that the three centres then up and running had already handled a total of 150 cases. By July 1972, the organisation had dealt with 2,437 cases – see *FLAC Report 1972* at p. 3.

[113] Mary Griffin, writing in the *Report to the Members of FLAC* for 1978 at p. 9. This tendency for casework to dominate FLAC's activities to the detriment of its strategic work is a recurring feature of its history, at least until recent times – see below, pp. 318-9.

[114] *FLAC Report 1972*, pp. 13-43.

demonstrating the need for a comprehensive legal aid scheme. All that remained was to persuade the Government to introduce such a scheme.

By mid-1974, therefore, FLAC was providing an emergency legal aid service in the Dublin area which was intended to be a stop-gap measure until the State faced up to its responsibilities. However the organisation was experiencing a number of problems. In the first place, it was finding it very difficult to cope with the demand placed on its services by the general public, a problem exacerbated by the fact that student volunteers were not available during exam time and the vacations. Second, FLAC had very little in the way of resources, the centres being located in the premises of other statutory and voluntary agencies, and locating ongoing funding was always a constant pressure. Third, FLAC was rather loosely organised at this time and was essentially a Dublin-based phenomenon.

1974 to 1978 – The years of the Pringle Committee

In July 1974, a committee chaired by Mr Justice Denis Pringle was established[115] and asked to inquire into the provision of free legal aid and advice in civil matters. In its submission to the Pringle Committee,[116] FLAC pointed out that, in its experience, the greatest single obstacle facing poor people in need of legal services was not lack of finance but rather the fact that, for a variety of social and psychological reasons, poor people were hesitant about approaching lawyers and were intimidated by the legal world. In addition, solicitors' offices were often geographically inaccessible and only open during normal office hours, rather than in the evenings or at weekends. The submission also contended that many people were unaware of their legal rights, that lawyers were, in turn, ignorant of the law most relevant to the problems of the poor and that many of the problems faced by poor clients could only be solved through effective community organisation and development, rather than on an individual case by case basis.

To tackle these problems, FLAC called for the introduction of a mixed-delivery system of legal aid, with a statutory Legal Services Board responsible for establishing and administering a panel system of free legal aid and advice, establishing and supervising law centres and conducting legal research into the need for legal services. The panel system of legal aid was to be a judicare model with four different panels – a Family Law Panel, a Criminal Law Panel, a Tribunal Panel and a Panel covering all other work normally within the scope of a solicitor's practice.[117] Clients would be means-tested[118] and would be liable to make contributions towards the cost of the service. Finally the scheme was to be comprehensive in that, considerations of

---

115 The Committee included a FLAC nominee, Mr Brian Gallagher.
116 The submission is set out in full in FLAC's 1974 Annual Report, pp. 14-37.
117 FLAC argued that the first three panels covered work outside the scope of a solicitor's normal practice and that therefore it was essential that clients would know what solicitors were prepared to do this type of work and that the Legal Services Board would know whether a sufficient number of solicitors were providing a service in these areas of the law – *ibid.*, p. 22
118 Though in order to minimise delay, FLAC argued that as much use as possible was to be made of previous means tests by public authorities – *ibid.*, p. 24.

financial eligibility apart, legal aid would only be refused where a claim was frivolous or vexatious or had no chance of success.[119]

Because of the limitations of the panel system,[120] this judicare model of legal aid was to be supplemented by a network of neighbourhood law centres which would service both individuals and groups and would also contribute to the development of the community in which they were located through programmes of legal education and by advising and assisting community groups and conducting research into the legal and social needs of the community. The centres would also seek to maximise the use of the law as a means of protecting and furthering the interests of the local community and would involve community representatives in their management.[121]

The third and final element in FLAC's proposal was that research should be conducted by personnel employed by the Legal Services Board into the nature and extent of unmet legal needs, particularly in rural and small-town communities.

The establishment of the Pringle Committee inevitably meant that FLAC's campaign for the introduction of a scheme of legal aid was put on the slow burner, as the organisation adopted a wait and see attitude to the committee's eventual report. FLAC continued to provide free legal services to the public and, indeed, 1974/75 witnessed a very significant growth in the number of cases taken on, more than 3,800 cases in that period alone, compared with a little over 8,200 for the previous five and a half years. 1977 witnessed another startling growth in the organisation, with the establishment of six new centres. By now, FLAC had twelve entres in the Dublin area, with additional centres in Galway, Limerick and Bray. Furthermore, it was during this period that FLAC first engaged in litigation strategy as two cases which it had initiated ended up in the Supreme Court, namely *The State (Healy) v. Donoghue*,[122] *The State (Gleeson) v. Minister for Defence*[123] and a third, *C. v. C.*,[124] was decided by the High Court.

FLAC also expanded its activities in a number of other areas during this period. It began to provide in-house training for its own members and also embarked on a series of public lectures and meetings designed to raise the public consciousness about the need for legal aid.[125] Considerable work was also done in relation to law reform and,

---

119   In relation to criminal cases, FLAC proposed that the means of the applicant should be the sole criterion for granting or refusing legal aid – *ibid*, p. 23.

120   According to FLAC, the panel system could not deal effectively with the geographical, social and psychological barriers to legal services experienced by poor people, deal properly with collective claims, facilitate community education and development nor produce a body of legal expertise in those areas of the law most relevant to the poor – *ibid.*, pp. 25-6.

121   *Ibid.*, p. 36.

122   [1976] IR 325; (1976) 110 ILTR 29. This concerned the defendant's right to criminal legal aid and is discussed further at pp. 256-8.

123   [1976] IR 280. This case concerned the application of the principles of constitutional justice to the dismissal procedures used by the Defence Forces.

124   [1976] IR 254. This case dealt with various family law remedies, including a wife's right to a beneficial share in the matrimonial home, the award of custody and the granting of barring orders.

125   Thus, in December 1974, FLAC held a seminar on the UK legal aid scheme and its lessons for Ireland and by the end of 1977, it was able to boast of having organised a series of one-day workshops evaluating the role of FLAC; a course of specialisation seminars in appointed areas of the law for FLAC members; and a further seminar on "Access to Justice" held in May, 1977.

apart from making the inevitable submission to the Pringle Committee, FLAC also made submissions to various public bodies on different aspects of criminal and family law.[126] It is interesting to note that the development of family law reform, in particular, in which FLAC had no small role to play, significantly increased the organisation's workload. This was not so much due to an increase in the number of persons seeking assistance but rather to the fact that now clients invariably had to be represented in court, whereas prior to these reforms, litigation was not a viable option for a spouse seeking maintenance or protection of his or her interest in the family home.

FLAC's financial position had also improved quite considerably, at least in a relative sense, and in 1977, it received a government grant of £15,000. FLAC also set about tackling its organisational problems. As early as 1970, it had been decided to incorporate FLAC as a limited company in order to protect members from liability for professional negligence, provide continuity and become eligible for official grants. This decision was finally implemented in 1974, when, on 17 October, FLAC was incorporated as a company limited by guarantee. By the end of 1978, it had acquired a central office in North Earl St and a full-time administrator.

But perhaps the most important development of this period was the establishment of the Coolock Community Law Centre Ltd.[127] The decision to set up a community based law centre, which would act as a practical illustration of the type of strategic legal aid scheme sought by FLAC, was made in May 1974; Coolock was selected as the location for this centre in November 1974 and the centre itself was opened on 1 April, 1975 with one solicitor and one secretary.[128]

1978-1980 – The Advent of Civil Legal Aid

FLAC's finest hour was arguably the publication of the Pringle Report in 1977.[129] The Report recommended that the State should provide eligible applicants with legal advice and assistance in relation to any type of legal problem and legal representation before any court and, where the legal issues justified the grant of legal aid, before tribunals.[130] The Scheme would be administered by an independent Legal Aid Board and legal services would be provided both by lawyers in private practice who were

---

126 These included submissions to the Government Task Force on children and child care; to the Criminal Legal Aid Committee; to the Law Reform Commission on the issue of the domicile of married women; to the Minister for Justice on the report of the Committee on Court Practice and Procedure on Desertion and Maintenance; to the Attorney General on his White Paper on the law of nullity, and to the Houses of the Oireachtas on the Family Law (Maintenance of Spouses and Children) Bill, the Family Home Protection Bill and the Consumer Information Bill.

127 See below, p. 326 *et seq.*

128 In December 1976, the National Committee to Combat Poverty gave a grant of £4,000 to FLAC to employ a Community Legal Officer in Coolock and the following April, Dave Ellis was appointed to the position, a position he was to hold for almost 22 years.

129 Prl.6862. See Zander, "The Pringle Committee's Report on Civil Legal Aid and Advice: an Outsider's View" (1978) *DULJ (n.s.)* 21.

130 The Report also recommended that a more limited scheme be brought into operation pending the introduction of the comprehensive scheme. An outline of this limited scheme is provided on pp. 13-15 of the report.

willing to have their names placed on legal aid panels and by salaried lawyers working at Community Law Centres and Legal Advice Centres. The work of the Board was not to be confined to the servicing of individual cases; instead the Report recommended that the Board should, working through its law centres, seek to make the public more aware of their rights and that it should evaluate its work in order to identify any need for law reform.[131] These proposals represented the essence of what FLAC had proposed to the Pringle Committee in 1974. However, as we saw above,[132] very little came of the Pringle Report.

During this period, casework continued to dominate the activities of FLAC. In the 1978 Annual Report, the administrator complained that "As an organisation we tend to lurch forward without any much direction, just about managing to cope with the problems which are presented on the doorsteps of our centres every week".[133] However the heavy caseload did not preclude other activities. A legislative committee had been established and was, at the time of the 1978 Annual Report, reviewing various Law Reform Commission reports on family law and also the report of the Committee on Court Practice and Procedure on the jurisdiction of the courts. A campaign committee had also been set up to organise the campaign for legal aid and December 1978 saw the beginning of a period of intense campaigning which lasted until early 1981, during which time there were at least two public marches and pickets were placed on the Department of Justice and at a Fianna Fáil Árd Fhéis. Meanwhile FLAC continued to be in receipt of public funding, receiving £27,000 in 1978.

Then, on October 9, 1979, the European Court of Human Rights ruled that Ireland was in breach of Article 6 of the European Convention on Human Rights because of its failure to provide legal assistance to Mrs Josie Airey who was seeking a judicial separation.[134] This decision increased the pressure on the Government to take action on the issue of legal aid[135] and in May, 1979, details of the Government's proposed scheme were made public by the Minister for Justice, Mr Gerard Collins, TD. Six months later, he laid a document entitled "Scheme for Civil Legal Aid and Advice" before the Oireachtas. As already mentioned,[136] this essentially provided for the establishment of State funded solicitors' offices, operating under the auspices of the Legal Aid Board, to provide a subsidised legal service to individual needy litigants in relation to specified areas of the law. In contrast to the Pringle Report, the Scheme implicitly rejected the idea that legal aid should have a strategic dimension and so the Board was given no responsibility for educating the general public as to their legal rights nor was it empowered to conduct any research into the legal needs of its clientele.

FLAC's response to the Scheme was, therefore, understandably hostile. In August 1979, it published a critical review of the Government's proposals for legal aid,

---

[131] *Ibid.,* pp. 12, 92-4.

[132] See p. 288.

[133] *Annual Report, 1978,* at p. 7.

[134] See above, pp. 247-9.

[135] During the course of the hearing of the *Airey* case, counsel for the State had already given an undertaking to the Court that legal aid would be provided in family law cases.

[136] See above, pp. 289-294.

following that up with the publication, in May 1980, of a detailed critique of the provisions of the Scheme which had been laid before the Houses of the Oireachtas, a critique which was subseqently updated in February 1981 after five months' experience of the Scheme in action.[137] FLAC was particularly critical of the State's implicit rejection of the strategic model of legal aid which had been endorsed by the Pringle Report in its recommendations on law centres. But even within the paradigm of the service model established by the State, FLAC found cause for serious concern. In particular, FLAC criticised the restrictions on the type of case in respect of which legal aid and advice could be provided, the severity of the means test, the highly bureaucratic application process and the fact that services would be provided solely through a limited number of law centres. While over time there have been limited improvements in relation to some of these aspects of the scheme, the fundamental nature of state funded civil legal aid as a service model only has remained unaltered since such legal aid was first introduced.

1980-82: Reacting to the Scheme of Civil Legal Aid and Advice

The introduction of albeit a very limited form of civil legal aid wrought very great changes in FLAC during the early 1980s. One immediate consequence was that State funding for FLAC was discontinued. This led to the resignation of the administrator and also posed great difficulties for the organisation during much of the 1980s in keeping its head office functioning. Thus FLAC's work was co-ordinated by part-time adminstrators until 1985, when two people were employed under a Teamwork Scheme. With the advent of the Scheme of Civil Legal Aid and Advice, FLAC decided, after what appears to have been a heated debate, to stand down its own centres. This process was completed by October 31, 1980. For a few brief months, therefore, FLAC continued in existence without the benefit of its principal tactic – the processing of individual casework. At its A.G.M. in February 1981, however, it was decided to open two emergency centres as a short term measure to assist people who had been unable to get legal aid under the State scheme. These two centres would appear to have ceased operations by the end of 1982. From this point on, it was FLAC policy that the organisation would not take on any cases which fell within the scope of the State scheme, the intention here being to put as much pressure as possible on that scheme in the hope that it would have to be expanded.

The closing down of its centres led to a complete re-organisation of FLAC's operations. Five new sections were established:

1. Publications and research – The period between October 1980 and July 1982 might well be described as the "Golden Age of FLAC Publications" as the publications and research group struggled to bring out a bi-monthly

---

[137] See *Free Legal Aid: A Review of the Government's Plans for Legal Aid* (August 1979); *It's Rough Justice without Legal Aid* (May 1980) and *It's Rough Justice with Legal Aid* (February 1981) respectively.

magazine, initially called "FLAC File", later renamed "New Deal". Eventually, however, this operation proved to be too arduous and after publishing ten issues, this section of FLAC ceased operations.[139]

2. Legal Advice Bureaux – This section was intended to provide a legal advice service for the clients of various social service organisations throughout Ireland. The Bureaux differed from FLAC's previous centres in that they were to provide advice only, and not legal aid.

3. Citizens' Rights Courses – This section was designed to increase public awareness of legal rights by means of lectures on topics of everyday importance and it did organise a course of such lectures in Finglas towards the end of 1980. However for much of the 1980s, FLAC did not actively pursue this objective, only returning to this task in any systematic way towards the end of the decade with the provision of lectures and seminars on different aspects of social welfare law, by which time the original section had itself ceased to exist.

4. Campaign – The campaign section had the task of continuing and intensifying the pressure on the State to introduce a comprehensive scheme of legal aid and advice. In fact FLAC had been engaged in a relatively intense campaign of protest marches, pickets, etc., since December 1978 but this petered out in 1981, taking with it the campaign section.

5. Staffing and Finance – This section, whose objectives were to ensure that adequate funds and personnel were available for all projects as they arose, also fell into desuetude during the early 1980s.

After an initial burst of enthusiasm, four of the above sections ceased to function. Why this is so is not immediately evident, though it may have had something to do with the fact that FLAC underwent one of its periodical changes in personnel around this time. One would also have to recognise that the introduction of the State Scheme of Civil Legal Aid and Advice took the issue of access to the law off the public agenda. In addition, FLAC's financial situation was very precarious during the first half of the decade and a lot of energy was expended in preventing closure of the organisation. The lure of casework proved irresistible, however, and the Legal Advice Bureaux continued to operate.[140]

---

[138] "FLAC File" did, in fact, pre-date the establishment of this section as three issues had been published between February and June 1980. However the formation of the publications and research section gave added impetus to this venture, resulting in the launch of a glossier and more professional publication in October 1980.

[139] In September 1990, FLAC resumed its publishing activities with the launch of a quarterly newsletter, "FLAC NEWS".

[140] The relationship between these bureaux, or clinics as they are now called, and the central organisation ebbed and flowed somewhat over the years. During the 1980s, the clinics became effectively autonomous units within the organisation, a situation which gave rise to some difficulties and concerns about the liability of the organisation, given the virtual absence of any communications between central office and the various clinics who, for example, repeatedly ignored requests for completion of statistical returns. This problem gave rise to a debate in the mid-1980s on a further rationalisation of FLAC's structures, in which it was suggested that the clinics be replaced by two or three centralised outlets. In the event, this proposal does not appear

The 1980s: Shift to welfare and employment law

During the early 1980s, a significant change in the nature of the casework handled by FLAC occurred. In July 1981, FLAC began to consider a new initiative – the establishment of a Tribunal Unit to specialise in tribunal work which was not covered by the State scheme of civil legal aid. That Scheme had largely taken on the burden of providing representation in family cases, which had previously formed a significant part of FLAC's caseload. Moreover the growth in the jurisdiction of the Employment Appeals Tribunal during the 1970s, coupled with the development of expertise in employment and social welfare law, (assisted indirectly by the introduction of social welfare law as an optional subject in Dublin's two University Law Schools) provided a favourable climate within which to attempt to meet this gap in the provision of legal aid. Thus FLAC resolved to provide legal aid and advice for employment and welfare cases through a number of Welfare Rights Centres.[141]

The new Welfare Rights Centres marked a radical departure in the type of casework handled by FLAC. In the 1970s, family law had dominated the organisation's caseload[142] while social welfare issues barely featured at all. But with the opening of the Welfare Rights Centres, social welfare and employment cases began to dominate the cases in which FLAC provided or otherwise organised legal representation These cases, in turn, tended to marginalise the organisation's other activities and for a time during the 1980s, FLAC engaged in relatively little educational or campaigning work.[143]

---

to have been acted upon and during the 1990s, FLAC's central office re-established links with fourteen clinics in the Dublin area. These clinics continue to provide legal advice only, though they do refer social welfare and employment cases back to the central office. FLAC, for its part, services the clinics through the provision of information packs and regular updating on legal developments.

[141] The first of these centres was established in early 1982 in St John's Lane, off Thomas St. It was soon followed by five others in Westland Row, East Wall, Prussia St, Tallaght and Rialto.

[142] Queries about family law continue to account for approximately 20-25% of all enquiries received by FLAC's central office to the present time.

[143] Though FLAC did make a submission to the Commission on Social Welfare. A further notable exception to the tendency of casework to dominate FLAC's activities at this time was the campaign for the establishment of a law centre in Tallaght. The Welfare Rights Centre in Tallaght had particularly good links with the community and it quickly became clear to both FLAC and the local community that the Rights Centre could not meet the demand for legal services coming from the community. Detailed discussions took place between FLAC and representatives of the local community as to the type of legal service needed in the area. After a public meeting, those representatives resolved to campaign for a Community Law Centre in Tallaght. Plans were drawn up and a premises was found. The Tallaght community, together with FLAC, vigorously campaigned for the proposed Law Centre to be funded from the Suitors' Fund, which consists of unclaimed monies held by the courts. The result of this campaign was that public attention was once more focused on the inadequacies of the State scheme and this led to an amendment act of the Fund of Suitors Bill 1984 then going through the Oireachtas to provide for the spending of some of this money on legal services. However this money was not used to fund a Community Law Centre in Tallaght. Instead, four more centres of the type already operating under the State scheme were established, one of which was based in Tallaght. This was the biggest expansion of the State scheme in the 1980s and came about as a direct result of the Tallaght campaign. However the opening of these new law centres again took the heat out of the debate on access to legal services and made it very difficult to sustain an ongoing campaign on legal aid.

Arising out of this casework, the organisation pursued a litigation strategy, bringing a number of issues in welfare and employment law before the courts.[144] This strategy had rather mixed success. While the cases were always successful in court, some of the victories were neutralised by subsequent legislative or administrative action. At the same time, some of these cases did lead to an improvement in the position of some disadvantaged groups, most notably the cases taken on behalf of married women pursuant to Directive 79/7/EEC on the progressive implementation of the principle of equal treatment for men and women in matters of social security.[145] From FLAC's perspective, the strategy had the additional advantage of raising its profile as an organisation with social welfare expertise. On the other hand, one further consequence of this strategy was that three of the cases taken, *McDermott v. Minister for Social Welfare*,[146] *Hyland v. Minister for Social Welfare*[147] and *McHugh v. A.B. and the Minister for Social Welfare*[148] gave rise to large representative actions in which other claimants sought to avail of the benefits of the original court rulings and organising these "follow-up" cases placed a great strain on FLAC's limited resources, impeding its ability to engage in other activities.

The change in the nature of the casework handled by FLAC also arguably affected the organisation's perception of its role. Having been formed initially to campaign specifically on the issue of legal aid, FLAC's work with social welfare cases in particular led to its involvement in a broader range of anti-poverty issues, detailed below.[149]

Late 1980s to the present: Focus on campaigning and educational work

Towards the end of the 1980s, FLAC's activities underwent another significant seachange, with campaigning and educational work coming more to the forefront and

---

[144] The following cases were initiated by FLAC during this period (though as the organisation could not employ a solicitor at that time, it had to rely on a network of sympathetic solicitors to take the cases) – *The State (Kershaw) v. Eastern Health Board* [1985] ILRM 235, *The State (McLoughlin) v. Eastern Health Board* [1986] IR 416, (both concerned with the operation of the National Fuel Scheme); *The State (Kenny) v. Minister for Social Welfare* [1986] IR 693 (concerning the operation of the former Unmarried Mother's Allowance); *McDermott and Cotter v. Minister for Social Welfare* [1987] ILRM 324, [1987] ECR 1453, *Hyland v. Minister for Social Welfare* [1989] IR 624, *Carberry v. Minister for Social Welfare*, unreported, High Court, 28 April 1989, *H. v. Eastern Health Board* [1988] IR 747 (all concerning gender or marital discrimination within the welfare code); *Duffy v. Eastern Health Board*, unreported, High Court, 14 March 1988, *Boland v. Eastern Health Board*, unreported, High Court, 10 May 1989 (two *ex tempore* judgments applying principles of natural justice to Health Board procedures); *M.C. v. Legal Aid Board* [1991] 2 IR 43 (on access to legal aid); *McHugh v. A.B. and the Minister for Social Welfare*, [1994] 2 IR 139 (on the operation of the Social Welfare (Overlapping Benefits) Regulations); and *Mythen v. Employment Appeals Tribunal* [1990] ELR 1 (on EC Directive 77/187 on the Transfer of Undertakings).

[145] For an evaluation of the impact of litigation strategy generally on social exclusion in Ireland, see ch. 8 above.

[146] [1987] ILRM 324; [987] ECT 1453.

[147] [1989] IR 624.

[148] [1994] 2 IR 139.

[149] See pp 316-8.

eventually beginning to dominate the organisation's workload. A number of factors accounted for this. First, there was a keen awareness within the organisation of the limitations of casework. Pursuing such cases required the commitment of relatively significant resources, in terms of time and energy, for very limited ends and it was felt that other policies, such as educational and law reform campaigns, might maximise the impact of the organisation's limited resources. Second, around this time a process of centralisation took place within the organisation, though this was not consciously planned. By the end of 1985, most of the Welfare Rights Centres ceased to discharge their original function of providing a specialised service in tribunal work, perhaps because of a lack of expertise on the part of the volunteers and instead ended up fulfilling the traditional role of providing legal advice on all areas of the law.[150] Most welfare cases were now referred into FLAC's central office, where, since 1987, there was again a full-time administrator, and indeed, a number of local groups tended to address their queries directly to head office. This process of centralisation gave staff at head office an overview of the important issues confronting FLAC's clientele and helped to form an agenda of topics around which campaigns for reform could be based. Third, the limited success of the litigation strategy highlighted the need to work in conjunction with other interested groups in order to create a political climate more sympathetic to the gains secured through the courts. During this time, FLAC worked closely with organisations such as Irish National Organisation of the Unemployed, the National Campaign for the Homeless and the National Campaign for Welfare Reform, and helped to establish the Dublin Welfare Rights Group, an alliance of organisations campaigning on welfare issues. Finally, and perhaps most significantly of all, for a period of two to three years towards the end of the 1980s, FLAC's financial position improved considerably, at least in a relative sense, allowing the organisation to increase the number of full-time staff to three, including a solicitor.[151] In addition, FLAC also employed four workers under the former Social Employment Scheme (now Community Employment Scheme). This influx of additional resources allowed the organisation to diversify the type of activity in which it was engaged and, in particular, to engage in more campaigning work.

---

[150] Westland Row continued to operate until 1989.

[151] Voluntary donations from legal practitioners organised by the Bar Council and the Law Society in the late 1980s meant that for the first time since 1980 FLAC enjoyed some measure of continuous funding. Funding from the People in Need Trust and the Ireland Fund allowed the organisation to run an Education and Training Project in Dublin while the community and anti-poverty aspects of the organisation's work enabled FLAC to obtain funding for several projects from the Combat Poverty Agency. The running of head office was also partly financed during the 1980s by funding from the Inner City Development Fund. However financial difficulties continued to beset FLAC and in 1992, closure was only narrowly averted when, on 5 February 1992, the then Minister for Justice, Mr Ray Burke TD announced that he was making provision in the State's Annual Estimates for the payment of £40,000 p.a. to the organisation, thus restoring the public funding which had been discontinued in 1980. In 1996, FLAC received a further significant boost to its finances from costs received for taking the largest representative action in the history of the State on behalf of approximately 1,800 married women seeking arrears of welfare pursuant to Directive 79/7/EEC.

In terms of campaigning work, FLAC's main objective remained the establishment of a State-funded strategic and community based legal aid scheme and a considerable amount of effort was invested in pursuit of this objective, though with very poor returns.[152] During this period, FLAC also revised its own thinking on legal

152   Thus throughout this period, the organisation monitored the length of the waiting lists at the Legal Aid Board's various law centres in an attempt to highlight the failure of the State scheme to deal adequately with the demand for legal aid. In 1987 FLAC, together with CCLC, published a report, *The Closed Door: A Report on Civil Legal Aid Services in Ireland,* to mark the tenth anniversary of the publication of the Pringle Report and to illustrate how little had been done to implement the main recommendations of that Report. As part of that report, the two organisations published a joint Legal Services Policy Document in which they re-iterated their call for implementation of the recommendations of the Pringle Report. In 1989, FLAC commenced the practice of making pre-budget submissions to the Government on legal aid and other issues. The following year, FLAC and CCLC organised two public seminars, one on the specific issue of legal aid and the other on the more general theme of the role of the legal system in tackling poverty. Both organisations also held a series of meetings on legal aid with representatives of the Department of Justice, the Irish Congress of Trade Unions, the Incorporated Law Society of Ireland and the various political parties. This last initiative led to the establishment, in 1990, of an *ad hoc* parliamentary committee on legal aid which held a total of three meetings attended by the various opposition party spokespersons on Justice and representatives from FLAC, CCLC, the Law Society, the Bar Council and the Legal Aid Board. In 1990, FLAC filed complaints with the Council of Europe and both the Commission of the European Communities and the European Parliament's Petition Committee alleging that Ireland was in breach of its obligations under the European Convention on Human Rights and EC law respectively because of its failure to provide an effective legal aid scheme. This approach proved, ultimately, to be fruitless, as did FLAC's attempt, in *M.C. v. Legal Aid Board* [1991] 2 IR 43, to persuade the High Court to recognise a constitutional right to civil legal aid. Also in 1990, FLAC campaigned for the setting up of a community law centre in Clondalkin, though once again, as had happened in Tallaght in 1984, the establishment by the Legal Aid Board of a centre in the area in 1993 led ultimately to the demise of this campaign. In September 1992, FLAC and the Catholic Social Service Conference jointly undertook a national review of the state of legal aid services in Ireland and that same year, FLAC was also instrumental in establishing a network of eleven organisations called the Legal Aid Alliance to campaign for improved services, though this campaign ultimately ran into the sands. In 1993, FLAC published a study on the right of access to the courts in France, the Netherlands, Northern Ireland and Ireland Cousins and O'Hara, *Access to the Courts in Four European Countries* (FLAC 1993), (see also Cousins, "Civil Legal Aid in France, Ireland, the Netherlands and the United Kingdom – A Comparative Study" (1993) *C.J.Q.* 154) – which showed that in many areas, the national systems examined did not ensure adequate access to the courts. In 1994, the organisation made a submission to the Joint Oireachtas Committee on Women's Rights, highlighting the fact that the absence of legal aid impacts to a disproportionate extent on women. In 1995, it worked jointly with CCLC in making a submission to the Government on its National Anti-Poverty Strategy, in which both organisations highlighted the need for effective legal services to tackle poverty, and in lobbying for amendments to the Civil Legal Aid Bill as that Bill went through the Oireachtas. That same year it also assisted the Irish Traveller Movement in formulating proposals for the establishment of a dedicated law centre designed to meet the needs of Travellers. More recently, in 1997, FLAC, together with CCLC, the Irish Refugee Council and Amnesty International (Ireland) called for the introduction of a legal aid scheme designed to meet the specific needs of refugees. The organisation is currently campaigning with others for the establishment of a law centre in Ballymun – see FLAC *Annual Report 1998,* p. 3 and *The Irish Times,* 9 November 2000.

aid to take account of the various developments which had occurred since 1974, in particular, the existence of the State Civil Legal Aid and Advice Scheme but also the evolution of public debate in other jurisdictions on access to legal services. In 1991, FLAC called for the establishment of a small claims court to process claims by consumers and outlined a 10-point plan for an informal procedure to cover claims valued at less than £1,000.[153] That same year, FLAC also called for local authorities to take a leading role in the development of local advice services, particularly in relation to social welfare and housing matters.[154] In 1992, a more comprehensive report looked at the issue of community involvement in legal services.[155] That research repeated FLAC's earlier analysis of the barriers to access to legal services, emphasising lack of information as the greatest barrier to access.[156] The report noted that the limitations of legal representation as a sole solution to the problem of access to legal services highlighted the need for a more strategic approach to legal aid services and that community based and community controlled law centres initially sought to fill this gap but that more recently it was felt necessary to supplement the work of these local centres with a national legal service which was not community based. Accordingly, the report recommended, *inter alia*, that a National Advice and Legal Services Council be established with the aim of achieving an adequate level of advice and legal services at both the local and national levels and the removal of procedural and substantive barriers to access to justice. The local, community based service would consist of a complementary mix of local advice services, providing advice, practical assistance (such as letter writing) and mediation services, and a specialised, community controlled, legal service providing representation for individuals and groups, legal services for voluntary and community groups, debt/money advice and training/ information. In addition to these local services, a national "law centre" would provide a national advice and strategic legal service. This service would encompass, *inter alia*, the running of programmes of public education about the law; the preparation of information guides for the local advice and specialist services; the provision of training for advice workers; campaigning for the improvement of public decision-making; the provision of a specialised casework service, with a commitment to a litigation strategy; the provision of other strategic legal skills such as the preparation of submissions, lobbying and assistance in the formation and support of groups; and the carrying out of research into the effect and impact of legislation and on ways of improving the responsiveness of the legal system to the demand for access to justice. This national law centre would be established and managed by the National Advice and Legal Services Council which, in turn, would be representative of, and accountable to, advice givers and

---

[153] *A small claims procedure in Ireland* (FLAC, June 1991).

[154] *Local government in Ireland, 1991: advice and information services* (FLAC, May 1991).

[155] *Models of Community Involvement in Legal Services* (FLAC, 1992).

[156] Borrowing from the seminal work of Cappelletti and Garth – see above, n.5 – the research also noted the role played by the nature of the problem in determining whether or not access to legal services was sought.

users.[157] More recently, FLAC campaigned successfully for the provision of legal aid and advice to asylum seekers[158] and also made a submission on legal aid to the Family Law and Civil Legal Aid Committee of the Law Society. FLAC is currently engaged in a year-long research project mapping the future for the development of civil legal aid in Ireland.

While clearly a lot of energy and time was devoted to the issue of access to legal services, this was not the exclusive focus of FLAC's campaigning work. In particular, its experience with social welfare matters led it to call for a number of changes to the social welfare code.[159] FLAC also carried on its campaigning work in family law matters, focussing particularly on the areas of domestic violence and divorce, and during 1995/96 in particular, the organisation was actively involved in campaigning for the removal of the constitutional ban on divorce.[160] The organisation also made submissions

---

[157] In a subsequent submission to the Department of Equality and Law Reform, FLAC summarised the key elements of its 1992 report by calling for the introduction of a three tiered scheme of civil legal aid. "At the first level would be a general non-means tested advice service, provided through Citizens' Information Centres. At the next stage would be Community Law Centres, supplemented by local private practitioners. Finally, a National Law Centre would oversee the delivery of legal aid and provide a more specialised service to complement the community law centres." – *Submission to the Department of Equality and Law Reform on Civil Legal Aid Services in Ireland*, (FLAC, October 1994), p. 9.

[158] See *FLAC Annual Report 1998*, at p. 20.

[159] Thus FLAC campaigned for reform of the social welfare appeals system, supporting a private member's bill introduced on the topic by Senator Brendan Ryan and engaging in discussion with officials of the Department of Social Welfare (as it was then called) on the matter. Some changes in this area were introduced by the Social Welfare Act 1990, though they did not go quite as far as FLAC would have wished, and the organisation followed up its work in this area with a study of the appeals system for the Supplementary Welfare Allowance scheme in 1994. FLAC also campaigned for the introduction of a Guaranteed Maintenance Allowance to be payable to all one-parent families, making a detailed submission on the issue to the Department of Social Welfare after consultation with Cherish, AIM, Gingerbread and the Federation of Services for Unmarried Parents and their Children. Eventually provision was made for such a payment in the Social Welfare Act 1990 and virtually all outstanding anomalies in the provision of social welfare income to one-parent families were abolished by the Social Welfare Act 1997. FLAC was also very active in campaigning for full implementation of Directive 79/7/EEC on the progressive implementation of the principle of equal treatment for men and women in matters of social security, using a combination of litigation strategy, political action – specifically, in February 1991, FLAC lodged a complaint with the European Commission about Ireland's failure to implement the Directive – and public information campaigns to highlight the State's default on its EC obligations in this area. It also made representations to the Department in relation to the Review Group on the Treatment of Households in the Social Welfare Code, the operation of the National Fuel Voucher scheme and the extension of social insurance to part-time workers and was involved in the carrying out of two welfare take-up campaigns, one in Clondalkin in 1990/91 and the other in Dublin inner city in 1995/96. In 1998, it campaigned, unsuccessfully, against the replacement of cash welfare payments to asylum seekers with benefit in kind.

[160] FLAC had earlier made a submission, in 1993, to the Department of Equality and Law Reform on the Government White Paper on Marital Breakdown. On the issue of domestic violence, FLAC participated in a seminar organised by the Department of Justice on the issue in 1992 and made submissions to both the Joint Oireachtas Committee on Women's Rights and the Dáil Committee on Legislation and Security in 1996.

to Government on a range of legislative measures in the area of employment law[161] and campaigned for reform of aspects of consumer law.[162] Penultimately, FLAC has become increasingly involved in human rights work, in particular on behalf of racial and ethnic minorities.[163] Finally, to complete the picture of FLAC's campaigning work during this time, in July 1995, the organisation made a submission to the Constitutional Review Group on the need to incorporate a range of socio-economic rights into the Constitution; in 1996, it made a submission to the Working Party on a Courts Commission calling for the establishment of a Courts Commission, seeking changes in the rules of court in order to facilitate group actions and outlining how the court service might be more responsive to the needs of litigants; and in 1998, it made one submission to the Working Group on Company Law, Compliance and Enforcement on the difficulties experienced by employees seeking to enforce EAT determinations against companies that have ceased to trade, and two submissions to the Law Reform Commission on the legal anomalies relating to cohabitation and on public interest cases, covering *locus standi*, costs, class actions and *amicus curiae* briefs.

---

[161] Including measures that were eventually enacted as the Unfair Dismissals (Amendment) Act 1993, the Adoptive Leave Act 1995, the Organisation of Working Time Act 1997, the Parental Leave Act 1998 and the Employment Equality Act 1998. FLAC also made submissions on the ill-fated Employment Equality Bill 1996. In 1995/6, FLAC assisted the Scheme Workers' Alliance in formulating a strategy for improving the employment and welfare rights of workers on Community Employment schemes.

[162] In particular, FLAC called for the establishment of small claims courts in 1991, did research on the topic of consumer credit in Ireland in 1993 and 1994 and made submissions to the European Commission and to the Government on the Commission's Green Paper on Access to Justice for Consumers and the Consumer Credit Bill 1994 (which subsequently became law the following year) respectively. As the Irish representative on the European Anti-Poverty Network, a coalition of NGOs concerned with poverty and social exclusion in the European Union, FLAC helped to organise an EAPN (Ireland) seminar on the Consumer Credit Bill in March 1994. FLAC was also one of the founding members of the Credit and Debt Policy Group which was established in 1995 to research and campaign on issues of credit and debt from the perspective of people on low incomes and in 1998/9, it carried out research into the use of attachment of earnings as a method of enforcing judgments for non-payment of civil debt.

[163] Thus in 1998, FLAC made a submission to the Government on the general scheme of the then Human Rights Commission Bill 1998 and, acting in conjunction with the University of Washington in Seattle, it also initiated an internship programme on human rights and public interest law for Irish and US law students. Specifically in relation to racism, in 1991/2, FLAC carried out a survey for the European Commission on legal measures designed to combat racism and xenophobia, subsequently updated in 1994. It also participated in the drafting of a model European code designed to combat racial discrimination in employment and has acted as the Irish rapporteur on an anti-racism network which reports to the Commission on developments in the law against racism. In 1993, FLAC, together with the Immigration Law Practitioners' Association, organised a seminar on the legal remedies available in relation to racial discrimination and racial attack and more recently the organisation has worked closely with the Irish Traveller Movement in making submissions to the former Department of Equality and Law Reform on the Equal Status Bills of 1997 and 1999 (the latter now the Equal Status Act 2000). During 1998-9, FLAC campaigned for improved procedures for processing requests for asylum, including the provision of legal aid for asylum seekers, and against Government plans to replace cash welfare payments to asylumseekers with benefit in kind.

FLAC also engaged in a considerable amount of educational work during the 1990s, organising seminars on various aspects of social welfare, employment, family and consumer law. The organisation launched FLAC NEWS, a quarterly newsletter, in September 1990 and also published a series of seven booklets on different aspects of social welfare rights, a guide to moneylending and the law, a leaflet on access to legal aid and, together with CCLC, a guide to maternity rights. It worked with the NSSB in providing training for community workers in relation to employment and social welfare law and also legal services and also co-operated with CCLC and the Irish National Organisation of the Unemployed in a pilot project on welfare rights training. During 1995/96, FLAC began to provide skills training for new information services and also sought to facilitate the development of a lay advocacy sector which could handle social welfare appeals and cases going to Rights Commissioners. During this time, FLAC and CCLC were also asked by the NSSB to update and expand the employment rights section of the NSSB's information files. In 1998, the organisation, acting in conjunction with the Office of the Director of Consumer Affairs, conducted four two-day training sessions on the Consumer Credit Act 1995 for money advisors in Dublin, Cork and Galway. That same year FLAC was part of a steering group that organised an international conference on debt and a FLAC representative also presented a paper at another conference on consumer law organised by the European Consumer Information Centre. FLAC also participates in two domestic networks working in the area of debt and credit – the Credit and Debt Policy Group, which is a collection of representatives from the voluntary, community and statutory sectors that examine credit and debt issues from a low income perspective, and the Complementarity Sub Committee on Money Advice, whose brief is to suggest how Government departments might best complement the work of the Money Advice and Budgeting Service – and in one European network, the Consumer Debt Net, which is a collection of credit and debt experts that attempt to influence policy at European level.

From approximately 1992 onwards, there was a reduction in the number of cases in which FLAC provided legal representation[164] and the organisation's activities were dominated, arguably for the first time in its history, by its campaigning and educational work.[165] This development would appear to be due to two factors. First,

---

[164] Thus, as late as 1991, FLAC provided legal representation in 82 employment cases and in 36 social welfare appeals. However in the calendar year 1996, FLAC brought only 11 employment cases and 5 social welfare appeals to completion, though it had 15 welfare cases ongoing into 1997. See *Equality before the law – the 1992 annual report of the Free Legal Advice Centres (FLAC)* at p. 5 and *Promoting Comprehensive Legal Services – the 1995/96 annual report of the Free Legal Advice Centres (FLAC)* at p. 6. FLAC continues to provide legal advice to members of the general public through a network of sixteen centres in Dublin and one each in Cork, Mullingar and Athlone.

[165] This development does have a potential pitfall, however, because, apart from its obvious value to the individuals who directly benefit from it, FLAC's work in providing legal representation enables the organisation to monitor the emergence of legal and social problems in the community and also provides it with the raw material for a litigation strategy. Moreover, this practical experience gives added weight to FLAC's submissions on legal and social reform. Consequently, any excessive decline in FLAC's casework could affect its strategic work and its effectiveness as a campaigning organisation.

long conscious of the manner in which its activities tended to be dominated by casework, the organisation made a deliberate effort to reduce its involvement in the servicing of individual cases and to enhance its strategic work by taking selective test cases only[166] and by working closely with statutory agencies and other NGOs, both as a referral agency[167] and through its second-tier training and educational work.[168] Second, the organisation's casework activity between 1992 and 1996 was dominated by its representative action on behalf of approximately 1,800 married women who were claiming arrears of social welfare payments pursuant to Directive 79/7/EEC. This case, the largest representative action ever taken in the history of the State, took up a huge amount of the solicitor's time, in particular, inevitably affecting the organisation's ability to provide representation in other cases.

FLAC: An evaluation

A comprehensive evaluation of FLAC's activities would require a detailed process of discussion and reflection involving the many key people who have been involved in the organisation down through the years and those others, clients, civil servants, legal colleagues, politicans, etc., who have dealt with it during that time. Accordingly, in this section, it is not possible to do more than sketch the picture in broad strokes.

In attempting even this cursory evaluation, it is important, at the outset, to highlight the very difficult financial situation that formed the backdrop to FLAC's activities for most of its history. Indeed, one might even count the organisation's very survival as a significant achievement, given how close it came to closure on a number of occasions because of lack of funds. It is also worth emphasising that the nature of FLAC's activities presents difficulties for any evaluation exercise. Writing about CCLC, which has a similar mission to FLAC, Dillon comments:

> Success or failure are not terms that can readily be applied where the principal activities are aimed at increasing awareness, campaigning for change or making the law understandable.[169]

---

[166] One interesting High Court action taken by FLAC concerns a claim by a transsexual to have her gender change recognised by the State – see *The Irish Times*, 17 October 2000. It remains to be seen whether this presages a further significant shift in the nature of FLAC's casework into the area of civil liberties litigation.

[167] Around this time, FLAC introduced a telephone helpline service which seeks to refer callers to appropriate services for further assistance (though in the case of employment or social welfare matters, FLAC specialists deal with the matter directly on the phone.) In 2000, this service handled 4,918 calls – figure supplied to the author by FLAC.

[168] First-tier work refers to work directly with members of the general public, while second-tier work describes assistance provided to other organisations who, in turn, work directly with members of the general public. For a listing of the type of second-tier work currently engaged in by FLAC, see the FLAC *Annual Report for 1998* which details, at p. 19, a range of information talks and training courses provided by FLAC in the areas of employment, social welfare, consumer and family law.

[169] *A Review and Recent History of the Coolock Community Law Centre* (Combat Poverty Agency, 1989), at p. 53.

FLAC can claim credit for a number of very worthwhile achievements. It was certainly very successful in proving the need for legal aid services and in getting this issue into the political arena and its role in establishing CCLC also made a very valuable contribution to the work of securing effective access to legal services, both directly, for those people able to avail of the services of CCLC, and indirectly, by demonstrating the effectiveness of this strategic model of delivering legal aid. Down through the years, FLAC also provided an essential service for tens of thousands of people who would otherwise not have been able to avail of legal representation. Moreover, FLAC's use of a litigation strategy secured some worthwhile gains for disadvantaged people, notably in relation to improvements in the criminal legal aid scheme and in relation to implementation of Directive 79/7/EEC on the progressive implementation of the principle of equal treatment for men and women in matters of social security. FLAC's campaigning work has also contributed to reform in the areas of family law, employment law, social welfare law and consumer law, while it has also done very important work in disseminating information about legal entitlements both to individuals and to other organisations. More recently, during the 1990s, FLAC augmented this very valuable role as a legal resource to other organisations through its provision of specialised training for community and advice workers. Finally, in its current pursuit of pioneering work in this jurisdiction in the area of public interest law, FLAC continues to challenge the conventional understanding of the role of lawyers in society.

On the debit side, it has to be acknowledged that, apart from its initial success with the Pringle Committee, FLAC has failed to persuade the State to adopt a strategic model for the delivery of legal services, despite investing considerable energy in this issue over the years. Perhaps the most significant reason for this failure lies in the fact that it is virtually impossible to organise a constituency around the issue of access to legal services which will have political impact. Those most directly affected by the absence of effective access to legal services, *i.e.* people in need of legal representation, are a transitory group whose composition changes daily and who, consequently, are impossible to mobilise for political action. Moreover, they understandably tend to focus more on their own immediate case than on the ancillary issue (for them) of access to legal services. This is also true of others for whom the existence in their community of a strategic legal aid scheme could bring tangible benefits through dissemination of information or campaigning around community issues. In the absence of an organised constituency of people directly affected by the absence of a strategic model of legal aid, FLAC, together with CCLC, had to rely on the weight of argument rather than of numbers in making the case for such a model of legal aid. Unfortunately those arguments did not prevail, arguably for a number of different reasons. Inevitably, given the radical nature of what FLAC and CCLC advocated, it was always going to be very difficult to persuade the political establishment, particularly the Department of Justice, to adopt a strategic model of legal aid as part of its agenda for reform and arguably this difficulty, in itself, was sufficient to defeat the efforts of FLAC and CCLC. However this difficulty was added to by virtue of the fact that the State began its direct involvement in the provision of civil legal aid during a period of severe economic difficulty which required stringent control of public expenditure. Consequently the State restricted itself to the provision of an extremely limited form of a salaried, service model of legal aid. While recognising the extent of the task confronting FLAC and CCLC, it also has to be said, with the benefit of hindsight, that both organisations made certain mistakes in the manner in which they put across their case. In particular, they failed to deal effectively with the argument that the judicare element in the scheme they advocated would lead to costly State involvement in the private legal sector which would be of more benefit to members of the legal profession than to the poor.[170] In addition, they did not succeed in developing the Legal Aid Alliance[171] into a strong and enduring network of allies to campaign on the issue. These failures were arguably compounded by the failure of the two organisations, until relatively recently, to examine alternatives to legal aid schemes as a means of ensuring effective access to justice.[172]

Another problem which has dogged FLAC's activities since its establishment is the difficulty in securing a proper balance between individual casework and strategic work. For most of its history, FLAC's casework overshadowed its strategic work. A number of factors arguably account for the lure of casework – casework plays to the strength of FLAC personnel who are, for the most part, lawyers; moreover casework has more immediate results than strategic work, with clearer parameters. The problem with overindulgence in casework, of course, is that it may not be the most effective use of scarce resources. Recognising this, in recent times FLAC has made a conscious effort to focus more on its strategic work. That said, one should not underestimate the importance of the organisation's casework for this enables FLAC to monitor social and legal developments in the community; it also gives the organisation a credibility with other community and voluntary groups and with public bodies; and, finally, it is an important element in any litigation strategy.

Finally, FLAC has always been controlled by lawyers, albeit by more radical members of the profession. This may have implications for the ability of the organisation to respond imaginatively to the needs of its clients, as there may be a tendency to analyse problems using legal frames of reference, and it also perpetuates the dependency of those clients on middle-class professionals. In contrast, (it is argued[173]), an organisation that is community controlled can develop the political as well as legal competence of clients, avoids total reliance on narrow legal remedies

---

170 See the dissenting report of Mr C.K. McGrath in the Pringle Report, pp. 171 *et seq.* where he argued against the introduction of a State-funded judicare system, calling instead for the provision of a reasonable measure of public financial support for voluntary local law centres.

171 A network of eleven organisations set up by FLAC and CCLC to campaign for improved legal aid – see n.152 above.

172 Using Cappelletti and Garth's terminology, one could argue that during the 1970s and 1980s, both FLAC and CCLC never moved beyond the "first wave" of attempts to make justice more accessible – see n.15 above.

173 See the following articles by Stephens, "The Law Centre Movement: Professionalism and Community Control" in Bankowski and Mungham (eds.), *Essays in Law and Society* (Routledge and Kegan Paul, 1980) at p. 127 and "Law Centres and Citizenship: The Way Forward" in Thomas (ed.), *Law in the Balance: Legal Services in the 1980s* (Martin Robertson, 1982), at p. 107.

and strategies and therefore has greater potential for securing meaningful change. Such was the philosophy inspiring the law centre movement and I turn now to outline and evaluate the impact of this movement in the Republic.

b) Law Centre Movement

Origins of Law Centre movement[174]

As we have noted, the salaried model of legal aid, whereby lawyers are employed on a full-time basis either by the State or by NGOs to provide legal services to the poor, was the third model of legal aid to emerge in modern times.[175] This model originated in the US during the 1960s as part of President Johnson's War on Poverty, pursuant to which the Federal Office of Economic Opportunity established a Legal Services Program.[176] Debate over whether the Legal Services Program should focus on law and social reform or instead concentrate on servicing individual cases was initially resolved in favour of the former, strategic approach and as a result, a number of law centres were established in various disadvantaged neighbourhoods throughout the country. These centres were designed to redress substantive inequalities through the use of test cases and class actions; by organising clients around common poverty issues and educating them as to their legal rights; and through political lobbying. Furthermore the centres sought to achieve meaningful representation of community interests on their management committees.[177] Using these tactics, the Law Centre movement hoped to assist marginalised communities in tackling structural causes of poverty and exclusion.[178]

---

[174] On the law centre movement generally, see Cooper, *Public Legal Services: A Comparative Study of Policy, Politics and Practice* (Sweet and Maxwell, 1983); Cranston, pp. 93-7.

[175] See above, p. 286.

[176] For a brief account of this development, see Zander, *Legal Services for the Community* (Temple Smith, 1978) at pp. 60-4.

[177] For a useful account of the development of the concept of "citizen participation" in legal aid in North America, see Larsen, "Seven Years with Legal Aid (1972-79): A Personal View of some Events and Background Literature" (1981) 11 *Manitoba Law Journal* 237, pp. 241-262. I am grateful to Sheena Walsh McMahon for bringing this article to my attention.

[178] Inevitably, however, the activities of neighbourhood law centres provoked a hostile reaction from the right and the Legal Services Corporation Act 1974 prohibited law centres from carrying out general law reform activities or assisting local people in forming community groups. Worse was to come in the guise of PL 104-134, the Omnibus Continuing Resolution that resolved the battle over the Federal budget between the Republican-controlled Congress and President Clinton in 1996. One small part of this law dealt with funding for the Legal Services Corporation and it prohibited recipient programmes from, *inter alia*, attempting to affect policy impacting on the marginalised and using class actions – see Kilwein, "The Decline of the Legal Services Corporation: 'It's ideological, stupid!'" in Regan, Paterson, Goriely and Fleming (eds.), p. 41 and, in the same volume, at p. 9, Johnson, "Justice and Reform: A Quarter Century Later".

Classification of law centres

Following on the US example, neighbourhood law centres were also established in Australia,[179] Canada,[180] Finland, New Zealand, The Netherlands and the UK[181] However they did not necessarily imitate the US model in all respects and, in particular, many law centres tended to concentrate on the servicing of individual cases, to the detriment of strategic work. Thus Stephens comments, *a propos* the law centre movement in the UK, that

> The idea of law centres [in the UK] was taken from [the US] experience, but their proposed operation did not incorporate the radical methods and goals espoused by some of the more notable agencies, such as California Rural Legal Assistance. The style of operation proposed for British law centres owed much more to the traditional, one-to-one, solicitors' service than to the group-based, proactive strategies of some American centres.[182]

So law centres range from purely service models to exclusively strategic models, with many centres trying to combine elements from both models. Law centres which veer towards the service model end of the spectrum are reactive in that they have to devote most if not all of their energies coping with the flood of individual cases coming through the door. In support of this approach, it can be argued that it meets a need for legal services; that it can enhance a centre's reputation in the community and also that, in ideal circumstances, it can usefully inform the centre's strategic work. However this approach to legal aid work does carry with it a number of disadvantages, of which the greatest is that the pressure of work it creates can seriously impair the centre's ability to engage in strategic action, thereby minimising the centre's impact on the problems facing the community. There is also some evidence that the quality of service devoted to individual cases can decline as, under the pressure of a heavy caseload, law centre employees tend to deal with those cases

---

[179] For an account of the development of the law centre movement in Australia during the 1970s, see Basten, Graycar and Neal, "Legal Centres in Australia" (1983) 6 *UNSW Law Journal* 163. See also Basten, "Legal Aid and Community Law Centres" (1987) 61 *Aust. L. J.* 714. See also Zemans and Thomas, "Can Community Clinics Survive? A Comparative Study of Law Centres in Australia, Ontario and England" in Regan, Paterson, Goriely and Fleming, 65, esp. pp. 65-71.

[180] For an account of the development of law centres in Ontario, see Zemans and Thomas, pp. 71-9.

[181] For an account of the development of the law centre movement in the UK, see Stephens, *Community Law Centres: A Critical Appraisal* (Avebury, 1990), ch. 3, Zemans and Thomas, pp. 79-84 and specifically in relation to N. Ireland, O'Neill, "Belfast Law Centre and the Law Centre Movement" in FLAC/CCLC, *The Closed Door: A Report on Civil Legal Aid Services in Ireland* (1987), p. 5. See also Leat, for an examination of the relationship between contemporary UK law centres and the Settlement movement of the nineteenth century.

[182] Stephens (1990) pp. 33-4. For an earlier piece in which Stephens classified UK law centres into four different categories, *viz.*, open (reactive) centres, CAB-linked centres, specialist (largely closed door) centres and resource centres, see Stephens (1980).

in a routine manner.[183] Moreover, the pressure of casework can often lead to a high level of staff turnover. Finally, reliance on the service model tends to blind law centres to the potential of non-legal tactics, such as lobbying, picketing, etc., for resolving community problems.

Law centres committed to both the servicing of individual cases and the pursuit of more long term strategies frequently impose limitations on the cases which they take on in order to create room for strategic action.[184] Thus a centre may restrict itself to representing people living within a defined catchment area and may also refuse to take on certain types of case. In very difficult circumstances, such a centre may also close its doors temporarily to new cases in order to enable it to clear a backlog of work.[185]

Characteristics of law centres

Notwithstanding variations in structure and functions, law centres tend to have certain shared characteristics.[186] In particular, law centres invariably provide their services free of charge, reflecting, according to Merricks, an implicit rejection of both means-related and cost-related charges.[187] The staff providing the service are salaried and therefore not hidebound by considerations of profitability in deciding what type of work to pursue. Moreover, recognising the limitations of conventional legal practice in meeting the needs of their clients, law centres often employ lay advisers, community workers and social workers alongside legal practitioners.

A commitment on the part of some law centres to empowering their clients, their staff and the local community results in some of the more striking features of the law centre movement. This commitment reflects the view that one of the more insidious consequences of poverty is the powerlessness of its victims and that the abolition of poverty entails giving marginalised individuals and communities control over their

---

[183] See Stephens, (1990), pp. 62-3.

[184] Cooper cites evidence of an experiment in the US which indicated that, without some restrictions on the type of cases taken on by a law centre, it was impossible to prevent all of the centre's resources being devoted to the servicing of individual casework – see "A Legal Services Policy for the Future: New Bottles for Old Wine" in Cooper and Dhavan (eds.), *Public Interest Law* (Basil Blackwell, 1986), p. 212 at p. 225.

[185] According to Stephens, restrictions used by some UK law centres involved "the reduction of catchment areas and the imposition of stricter eligibility criteria for clients; some categories of problems were no longer handled; increasing numbers of clients received advice only and/or were referred to other specialist agencies and to private solicitors; hours of opening were reduced; volunteer involvement in evening and weekend advice-giving sessions was increased; referral agencies were briefed to refer only cases falling within certain priority areas; do-it-yourself kits were instituted in order to encourage self-help activities by clients; in-service training became a feature within law centres as part of an attempt to make their services more efficient; internal reorganisation into units dealing with major problem areas occurred in several law centres; [and] solicitors were encouraged to become self-servicing ... " – see Stephens (1980), p. 131.

[186] See Merricks, "The Aims and Goals of the Law Centre Movement" in Partington and Jowell (eds.), *Welfare Law and Policy* (London, 1979) at p. 232; Campbell, "The Inner Cities: Law Centres and Legal Services" (1992) 19 *Journal of Law and Society* 101.

[187] Merricks, p. 233.

own destinies. More prosaically, community involvement in determining the policy of law centres arguably results in the most effective deployment of scarce resources as community representatives are best placed to identify the community's greatest needs. Related to this is the argument that public interest advocacy has the greatest chance of securing change if it is grounded in a popular mood[188] and that community involvement in the running of a law centre greatly facilitates the centre in tapping into such a mood.

Returning to the visible signs of this commitment, in relation to clients, the concept of "informed consent" seeks to involve the client in the process of deciding how to handle the case and is described by Rosenthal as follows:

> The lawyer draws upon his or her expertise to set out for the client the possible ways to proceed. The estimated costs and anticipated benefits of the available choices are carefully reviewed. Where the lawyer deems it appropriate, he or she counsels the client as to the choices the lawyer thinks to be preferable, explaining why. Proper counselling, therefore, does not mean presenting the client with the one approach the lawyer prefers, but is a mutual process of joint exploration of options, in which the lawyer tries to be responsive to the concerns of the client and feels free to express his or her concerns as well. If it works, the client weighs what has been discussed, chooses, and agrees to cooperate with the lawyer in pursuing the preferred strategy, or waives his right to choose by explicitly delegating the choice to the lawyer.[189]

With regard to staff, the concept of "collective working" eschews the conventional hierarchical structure of a solicitor's office, favouring instead salary parity, a system of day-to-day management in which all members of staff have an equal say and a system of work in which advisers are required to do their own typing, filing of documents, etc. While recognising that these work methods are not easy to implement, Grace and Levefre argue that

> The value and importance of working through these problems is obvious if one thinks of the alternative in terms of a transplant of a conventional lawyer in a conventional lawyer's office into a powerless community, in terms of dress, outlook, salary, internal office relationships, etc. This conjures up a grotesque vision of legal services, totally removed from its community and with limited capacity to do work that would be likely to achieve enduring gains.[190]

---

[188] See Grace and Lefevre, "Legal Services, Law Centres and the Public Interest" in Cooper and Dhavan (eds.), *Public Interest Law* (Basil Blackwell, 1986) p. 193, at p. 195.

[189] "Evaluating the Competence of Lawyers" *Law and Society Review*, (1976) Vol. 11, No.2, p. 257 at pp. 271-2.

[190] Grace and Lefevre, p. 204. However, as Campbell points out, "No large-scale analysis has been undertaken of the effects of this method of working on the quality of law centres' work, nor its impact on the number of clients seen or projects undertaken, nor on the effect of stemming the employment in law centres of skilled clerical and support workers with experience and expertise in the preparation of legal documents and materials. Nor has there been a sustained examination within the [law centre] movement of the ideological assumption underlying and justifying the abolition of separate support staff, namely that the nature of such work lends itself to exploitative relations between lawyer/adviser and support worker." Campbell, p. 103.

The goal of empowering the local community can be pursued in a number of different ways. One can vest control of the law centre itself in a management committee containing a built-in majority of community representatives, in that way seeking to ensure that the centre remains responsive to local wishes. However, as Stephens observes:

> [This] is not an easy concept to operationalize for it depends both on the willingness of local people to come forward for election to a management committee and on their abilities to function within that structure and not to be intimidated by any professional members of the committee.[191]

Another strategy here is to support and encourage (and sometimes initiate) local community groups who will campaign directly on behalf of their own members and who may also instruct the law centre to take legal action on its behalf.[192] Thus law centres may assist a local group with the process of incorporation or with drafting a constitution. Law centres may also help to organise clients with a common grievance into mutual self-support groups.

Having provided this outline introduction to the law centre movement generally, I turn now to consider the role of this movement in the Republic, beginning with an examination of the first such law centre established in this jurisdiction, the Coolock Community Law Centre Ltd.

Coolock Community Law Centre Ltd

Establishment – One of FLAC's major achievements, as noted above, was the establishment, in 1975, of the Coolock Community Law Centre Ltd. which remains the only neighbourhood law centre operating in the Republic. The background to this

---

[191] Stephens (1980), at p. 128. In a similar vein, Prior comments that "[t]he members of management committees are generally not lawyers and are therefore at a grave disadvantage in determining whether the members of the Law Centre staff are effectively and properly supplying legal services to the community. There is often a high turnover of members of management committees, and the attendance of the membership at their meetings is erratic and often then only a silent audience to the discussions of the members of staff." See *Law Centres: A Movement at a Halt* (1984, Conservative Political Centre for the Society of Conservative Lawyers) at p. 7.

[192] Commenting on this aspect of law centre work, Grace and Lefevre write, "Part of [the work of community workers] is to help community groups achieve sufficient organization and stability so that they are capable of formulating instructions which are stable enough for the centre to act on with confidence, and which have been developed in as clear as possible an understanding of the alternative approaches to a problem and the implications of any particular strategy. This may seem a somewhat dry and abstract sort of function, but anyone who has worked with residents in situations of proposed area redevelopment will appreciate the need for an effective and thoughtful local organization of those affected as a prerequisite for useful legal work. Community workers are an essential resource in legal work in disadvantaged communities. They are sometimes seen as a law centre's 'campaigners', but grasping the relationship of law centre work to community interests helps to emphasize that it is not a law centre's job to campaign, but to support the campaigns of community bodies. It is not the law centre's voice which needs to be heard, but that of the disaffected and of the local representative bodies who have the most legitimate claim to speak on the issues which affect the community." – Grace and Lefevre, pp. 196-7.

development was that in May 1974 FLAC decided, as part of its campaign to persuade the government to introduce a strategic model of legal aid similar to that operating in the US, to establish a community based law centre which would serve as a blue-print for the government model. Following consultations with comunity groups in the area, Coolock was selected as the location for the centre in November 1974 and the centre itself was opened in April 1975 with one solicitor and one administrator.[193] Two years later, a grant obtained from the National Committee to Combat Poverty enabled the centre to employ a community law officer to engage in strategic work such as educational programmes and research.[194]

During the first three years of its existence, the centre was managed by FLAC. However, mindful of the fact that one of the more insidious aspects of poverty is the manner in which it deprives its victims of any control over their lives, it was always FLAC's intention that the centre would be community controlled. Accordingly, one of the first tasks given to the community law officer was to re-establish links with community organisations with a view to setting up a community-based management committee. This committee was established in June 1978 and in May 1979, when the centre was registered as a company limited by guarantee, the management committee took over full responsibility for the running of the centre from FLAC.[195]

Over the years, the catchment area of the centre was amended until it was finally settled in October 1987 as the two Dáil constituencies of Dublin North Central and Dublin North East.

Prior to 1997,[196] a recurring theme in the history of CCLC was the precarious nature of its funding, arguably reflecting the centre's relatively weak political situation – no politican wished to be seen closing down the centre, but equally no politican ever felt under sufficient political pressure to provide adequate funding.[197] Thus, apart from the period between 1986 and 1991, when two three-year packages of funding were put in place, funding had to be re-negotiated each year with various reluctant Government departments. Consequently the task of securing adequate funding dominated the work of the management committee through much of the 1980s and again in the early 1990s and closure loomed on a number of occasions. In 1981, it was only averted

---

[193] For a number of years after the centre's establishment in 1975, volunteer staff also operated two advice clinics a week at the centre. Volunteer staff have also been involved in the operation of a weekly advice clinic since 1998.

[194] The initial grant only covered one year but the National Committee agreed to extend the grant to cover 1978 and in 1979, funding for the CLO's position was obtained from the Eastern Health Board. Thereafter the cost of this post was subsumed in the general budget of the centre.

[195] Though it was not until the following year that government funding for the centre was paid directly to this management committee rather than through FLAC.

[196] In 1997, responsibility for the funding of the centre was transferred to the NSSB (now Comhairle) which is, in turn, dependent for its funding on the Department of Social, Community and Family Affairs. This new arrangement has provided a much needed element of stability in the centre's funding.

[197] The alternative of private fund-raising was generally rejected by CCLC on grounds of principle – legal aid is seen as the State's responsibility – though pragmatic considerations may also have played a role here.

when the State agreed to pay the centre to represent the next-of-kin of the victims of the Stardust Fire tragedy at the hearings of the Stardust Victims' Compensation Tribunal[198] and in December 1991 the centre came to within thirty minutes of closing before State funding for the following year was announced. The only positive by-product of this situation was that it facilitated the bonding of the management committee established in 1978 by giving the members an urgent issue around which they had to campaign. However this positive result was more than offset by the fact that, prior to 1997, insecurity of funding diverted the energies of the staff and committee members away from strategic work on behalf of the community into campaigns for funding, thus impeding long-term planning for the centre.

Services provided – Over the years, CCLC has attempted to combine the servicing of individual cases and queries with strategic work.

Five features of the centre's work with individuals are worth noting. The first is that, notwithstanding certain restrictions on the type of case taken by the centre,[199] its activities were dominated by casework for the first ten years or so of its existence, with an average of 390 new cases being taken on each year. Given the absence of a State-funded legal aid scheme for the first five years of CCLC's existence, this emphasis on the servicing of individual cases was very understandable. However the number of cases taken on affected the centre's capacity to pursue strategic work and also gave rise to concerns about the centre's ability adequately to service these cases. As a result, in 1987, the geographical catchment area of the centre was restricted to the two Dáil constituencies of Dublin North Central and Dublin North East and it was decided that the centre would no longer prepare wills or take personal injuries cases, as both of these categories of case were adequately serviced by private practitioners. A temporary embargo on all new cases (other than emergencies) was imposed for a number of months in 1988 and again during 1989 and 1990. The enactment of the Judicial Separation Act 1989 prompted many former clients to return to the centre seeking judicial separations and this had quite an impact on the centre's workload at this time. However because of the significant number of this type of case, which was long-term, non-urgent work, the centre found that it could not adequately respond to emergency family cases, especially cases of domestic violence. In response to this, it was decided, in 1992, to confine CCLC's family law services to emergency cases where there was a threat of physical violence or the risk of a child being taken out of the jurisdiction and to refer all other family cases to the Legal Aid Board.[200] For the remainder of most of that decade, new cases averaged approximately 183 a year but even that level of casework has necessitated the imposition of embargoes on new work from time to time in order to enable the staff to deal adequately with the

---

[198] While the centre's solicitor was engaged in this work, a solicitor from the Legal Aid Board was seconded to the centre to deal with the other cases on the centre's books.

[199] From a relatively early stage, CCLC decided not to handle criminal cases, neighbour disputes and property disputes (other than family or landlord/tenant) and not to act for businesses.

[200] A weekly evening drop-in clinic was set up by CCLC at this time to provide information to those people whose cases would not otherwise be handled by the centre.

workload.[201] Following an extensive evaluation process during 1998-9, the organisation decided to discontinue its work in the family law area and to concentrate instead on employment law, social welfare law, debt collection, housing and anti-discrimination law, areas of the law not covered by the statutory civil legal aid scheme given that, with the exception of the Refugee Legal Service, it does not deal with tribunal work.

CCLC's experience with casework mirrors that of law centres in other jurisdictions[202] and supports the view that law centres who wish to pursue strategic work cannot afford to operate an open door policy in relation to casework.

The second interesting feature of CCLC's work with individuals arises directly from the changes in operations just noted and that is that between 1979 and 1997, family law cases declined as a percentage of the yearly intake of new cases in which representation was provided.[203] Thus from constituting approximately half of all cases taken by the centre in 1979, family law cases only exceeded 30% of the new yearly intake on two occasions between 1990 and 1997.[204] This contrasts with the growth in social welfare and employment cases which constituted approximately 7% and 3% respectively of new cases in 1979 but which ranged between 14%-35% and 11%-22% respectively during the 1990s. The other mainstay of CCLC's caseload, debt and consumer cases, usually accounted for between 15 and 20% of the new cases.[205] This profile differs significantly from that of the Legal Aid Board, where family law cases constitute over 95% of all court cases taken by the Board and 90% of all cases in which legal advice is provided. The difference is partly due to the fact that the Legal Aid Board has always been precluded from providing representation before tribunals,[206] raising the inference that this prevents the Board from satisfying a significant unmet legal need.

The third interesting feature of CCLC's work with individuals was the more than fivefold increase in the number of queries going to the centre between 1979 and 1997.[207] Given the improvement in the amount and quality of information available to the public from other sources since the 1970s, this is somewhat surprising but may perhaps have reflected a growing awareness on the part of the community, over the

---

[201] The imposition of such an embargo at various times between 1998 and 1999 saw the yearly number of cases taken on by the centre drop to 78 and 125 respectively.

[202] See pp. 323-4.

[203] It should be noted, however, that these statistics do not reflect the amount of time spent on the different categories of work and it is likely that one family law case would take up more time than a case from any of the other categories.

[204] Though family cases accounted for 35 of the 78 cases handled by CCLC in 1998 and 59 of the 125 cases dealt with in 1999, during which years, the centre operated an embargo on new cases at various stages.

[205] Though the manner in which debt cases are handled has changed over time and clients are now provided with money advice as well as legal advice.

[206] With the exception, since 1999, of tribunals dealing with appeals from decisions on applications for asylum – see n.82 above.

[207] The number of queries per year received by the centre rose steadily from 442 in 1979 to 2,472 in 1997.

years, of the work of the law centre. Following on the opening of the state-funded Northside Community Information Centre in April 1999, CCLC decided to discontinue its own information work and to pursue closer links with Northside CIC with a view to doing second-tier work with that organisation. This decision was not taken lightly, given that first-tier work of this nature provides a very useful mechanism for monitoring the social and legal needs of the community and also given the risk of lost referrals from one organisation to another.[208] However the provision of an information service did place a significant burden on CCLC personnel and it was reluctantly decided that the discontinuance of the service would enable the centre to target its limited resources more effectively.[209]

Penultimately, it is worth noting the centre's promotion of alternative methods of dispute resolution for individuals.[210] Thus CCLC staff regularly represented clients

---

[208] Thus, in the UK, Baldwin found low level of referrals from CABx to solicitors – see "The Role of Citizens' Advice Bureaux and Law Centres in the Provision of Legal Advice and Assistance" (1989) 8 C.J.Q. 24.

[209] The establishment of the Community Liaison Council around the same time also eased concerns about CCLC's ability to keep in touch with the needs of the community.

[210] ADR is an important element in what Cappelletti and Garth call "the third wave of reform" in securing access to justice. This wave focuses on the full range of institutions, devices and procedures used to resolve disputes in modern societies and "includes, but goes *beyond advocacy*, whether inside or outside of the courts, and whether through governmental or private advocates ... [I]ts method is not to abandon the techniques of the first two waves of reform, but rather to treat those reforms as but several of a number of possibilities for improving access." – Coppelletti and Garth, p. 49. See further Cappelletti, "Alternative Dispute Resolution Processes within the Framework of the World-Wide Access-to-Justice Movement" (1993) 56 *M.L.R.* 282. As this book is concerned primarily with the role of the courts in tackling social exclusion, I do not intend to examine this phenonomenon in any great detail. At the same time, one should strike a cautionary note about the use of ADR by those who are economically and socially disadvantaged. Aron argues that ADR is only effective where a number of conditions are satisfied:
  a) the controversy involves negotiable issues, as opposed to non-negotiable issues of principle;
  b) the number of people involved is relatively small;
  c) the interests of the principals have been defined and accepted as legitimate;
  d) the critical facts are known or knowable within reasonable cost and time constraints;
  e) there is rough parity of power among parties;
  f) there is some pressure, such as a statutory deadline, on everyone to reach agreement in a timely fashion.
  See *Liberty and Justice for All: Public Interest Law in the 1980s and Beyond* (Westview Press, 1989), p. 111. Aron's precondition of parity of power between participants may often be lacking in the case of disputes involving disadvantaged individuals and commentators such as Abel, *The Politics of Informal Justice* (New York, 1982), Auerbach, *Justice without Law?* (New York, 1983) and Fiss "Against Settlement" (1984) 93 *Yale Law Journal* 1073, at pp. 1076-8, argue that such individuals fare better under systems of formal adjudication. If ADR is pursued, a very strong case can still be made for the retention of skilled representation for participants, as recent research indicates that such representation significantly increases the prospects of success – see Genn, "Tribunals and Informal Justice" (1993) 56 *M.L.R.* 393 which presents empirical research on procedures, decions-making processes and outcomes in four different types of informal tribunals in the UK dealing with welfare benefits, immigration disputes, employment disputes and detention under mental health legislation.

before Rights Commissioners and in 1997, the organisation was involved in establishing, with the Medical Social Work Department in Beaumont Hospital, a pilot project to assist unmarried families in resolving disagreements regarding their children through mediation. The following year, the centre and the Department of Social, Community and Family Affairs began operating a pilot scheme for the resolution of disputes between the Department and welfare claimants before the matter went on appeal.

Finally, it is also worth noting that a majority of the centre's clients were women in family situations, less than one in ten were in employment and, as might be expected, a majority came from working class areas.[211]

CCLC's strategic work has tended to involve reliance on both the Fabian and community politics models of achieving social change.[212] According to Cranston:

> The Fabian model assumes that government responds when need is uncovered and the case for change is presented through reasoned argument, lobbying and publicity ... [while the] community politics model is based on the belief that feasible proposals must be supported by developing the political strength of a community, mainly through organizing, to force change.[213]

Thus over the years, CCLC has published reports and made submissions to various bodies on a range of issues affecting its clientele[214] and it has organised, or affiliated

---

[211] Dillon, p. 51.

[212] In addition, the centre had recourse to litigation strategy on at least three occasions. Thus in *McConnell v. Eastern Health Board*, unreported, High Court, 1 June 1983 and *The State (Hoolahan) v. Minister for Social Welfare*, unreported, High Court, 23 July 1986, the centre successfully challenged the procedures employed by the Eastern Health Board and the Department of Social Welfare respectively in dealing with two welfare cases. An attempt to challenge the fairness of a dismissal where the employee had failed to comply fully with the stringent requirements for notifying the employer of the intention to return to work was, however, less successful – see *Ski-line Ltd. v. Ivory* [1989] ILRM 433.

[213] Cranston, pp. 277-8.

[214] These include a report on the operation of barring orders (1978); a report on the operation of social welfare appeals and a report on the work of the centre to the Combat Poverty Committee (both in 1980); submissions to the Inter-Party Committee on Marital Breakdown, the Commission on Social Welfare and the Inter-Departmental Committee on Women's Affairs (all in 1983); a submission to the Department of Labour on reform of the statutory redundancy scheme (1984); a submission to the Garda Committee on Training (1986); a report, together with FLAC, on civil legal aid (1987); a joint submission with Gingerbread to the Department of Social Welfare on the welfare rights of lone fathers (1988); a presentation to the Joint Oireachtas Committee on Women's Affairs (1990); a submission to the Review Group on the Treatment of Households in the Social Welfare Code and a submission to the Department of Social Welfare on the Report of that Group (both in 1991); a submission to the Department of Social Welfare on the Social Welfare Bill 1992 (in 1992); a joint submission, together with FLAC, to the Government on its National Anti-Poverty Strategy, a submission to the Dáil Select Committee on Legislation and Security on the Domestic Violence Bill and a submission to the Department of Enterprise, Trade and Employment on the Consumer Credit Bill (all in 1995); a submission to the Working Group on a Courts Commission, a submission to the Commission on the Family, a submission to the All-Party Committee on the Constitution, a submission to the Working Party

to, a number of campaigns for law and social reform. Campaigning for improved access to legal services naturally features prominently in this latter context[215] but CCLC also worked to secure other reforms, especially in the areas of family law,[216] social welfare law,[217] consumer credit and debt[218] and the general issue of poverty.[219]

---

on the Legal and Judicial Process for Victims of Sexual and other Crimes of Violence against Women and Children and a submission to the Department of Social Welfare on the fuel schemes (all in 1996); a further submission to the Working Group on a Courts Commission and a submission to the Task Force on Violence Against Women (both in 1997); and, most recently, a submission to the Group Examining the Probation and Welfare Service (1998).

[215] Thus CCLC was instrumental in establishing the Law for All Group in 1980 and, together with FLAC, the ad hoc Parliamentary Committee on Legal Aid in 1990 and the Alliance for Civil Legal Aid in 1992. It organised a public seminar on legal aid in 1982 and two further seminars on the same topic, on both occasions jointly with FLAC, in 1987 and 1989. As already mentioned, in 1995 it made a joint submission with FLAC to the Government on its National Anti-Poverty Strategy, in which both organisations highlighted the need for effective legal services to tackle poverty, and it also campaigned with FLAC for amendments to the Civil Legal Aid Bill. In 1997, CCLC, together with FLAC, the Irish Refugee Council and Amnesty International (Ireland) called for the introduction of a legal aid scheme designed to meet the specific needs of refugees. More recently, it has been involved in a campaign to establish a community law centre in Ballymun.

[216] Thus CCLC was perhaps the first organisation in the country to call for repeal of the constitutional ban on divorce. A public meeting which it organised on this issue in 1979 led directly to the establishment of the Divorce Action Group and CCLC was active on the pro-divorce side in the constitutional referenda of both 1986 and 1995. CCLC had campaigned for improvements to the law on domestic violence since the early 1980s and in 1995 it published a report on this topic which resulted in the organisation being invited to make oral submissions to the Dáil Select Committee on Legislation and Security on the provisions of the Domestic Violence Bill 1995, the first occasion on which oral submissions from persons other than members of the Oireachtas were ever taken during the legislative process. In 1995, the centre also published a report calling for separate representation of children in certain types of court case concerning their welfare. The centre is currently represented on the Steering Group of the Inter Agency Initiative on Domestic Violence.

[217] In 1980, CCLC produced a report on the working of the appeals system and it organised a conference on various aspects of welfare reform in 1984. The following year, CCLC was instrumental in establishing an alliance of groups concerned with welfare reform, the Dublin Welfare Rights Group, and it was also active in the National Campaign for Social Welfare Reform, established in 1986. In 1991, CCLC carried out a study into the operation of the social welfare medical appeals system and in 1992 it campaigned actively to reverse social welfare cuts introduced by the government.

[218] Towards the end of the 1980s, CCLC began to take an interest in the area of debt and money management and in 1995, it made submissions to the Department of Enterprise, Trade and Employment on the Consumer Credit Bill and also helped to establish the Credit and Debt Policy Group, a network of organisations concerned with issues of credit and debt from a low income perspective.

[219] Thus CCLC was affiliated to the National Campaign for the Homeless, jointly organising with the NCH a conference on local authority rent arrears in 1994. CCLC was also affiliated to Action on Poverty, a network of groups which existed during the mid-1980s as an anti-poverty lobby, and in 1987, CCLC, FLAC and the present author jointly organised a conference in Trinity College on the role of lawyers in tackling poverty.

Empowering the community – In addition to pursuing this Fabian approach to social change, CCLC has also been committed to working to empower the local community, seeking this as an essential element in any anti-poverty strategy. The centre has pursued this objective in three different ways. First, since the appointment of the first community law officer in 1977, CCLC has been involved in programmes of legal education for the community in its catchment area and beyond. Prior to the mid-1980s, this consisted primarily of what is called "first-tier" work, *i.e.* working directly with the general public. Thus CCLC regularly ran Citizens' Rights Courses through the 1980s and published leaflets and guides to different aspects of the law,[220] together with a quarterly newsletter providing up-to-date information on legal developments of interest to the centre's clientele. It also devised and implemented a Schools' Project whereby talks were given to pre-employment year students in the local schools on such issues as employment rights, taxation, welfare rights, etc. However CCLC also carried out "second-tier" educational work, *i.e.* working with local and national groups who, in turn, deal directly with the general public, and with the improvement in the quality and range of information provided to the general public since the 1970s, this type of work has come more to the fore in the centre's activities in recent times. Thus in 1987, CCLC, together with FLAC, initiated a programme of training seminars for community workers involved in social welfare appeals; in 1989, it participated in a pilot project on welfare rights training with the Dublin Welfare Rights Group, the Irish National Organisation of the Unemployed and the Catholic Social Services Conference; in 1991, it participated in a similar programme with the National Social Services Board, FLAC, the Combat Poverty Agency and the Irish National Organisation of the Unemployed; in 1992, it ran a debt management course with Threshold; in 1993, it organised a training programme for debt advisers; in 1996, it ran a training course on the law on unfair dismissals and in 1997, it produced an Advisors' Manual on Social Welfare Appeals, also running a training seminar on appeals for community activists. More recently, CCLC worked with the National Social Services Board[221] in updating the latter's employment rights files.

Apart from trying to empower the local community through the provision of information, the centre has also campaigned on a number of local issues and has helped to form local community groups. Thus it has been a member of the Joint Care Group, a network of groups working in the Coolock area, since 1977. In 1980, the centre, together with others, successfully campaigned for the return of a post office to a local shopping centre and met with the ESB to discuss that board's policy on cutting off subscribers in arrears. In the same year, the Centre was instrumental in

---

[220] These included guides to employment rights, rights of persons with disabilities, rights of lone parents (with the Parents Alone Resource Centre), social welfare appeals (with the Dublin Welfare Rights Group), debt management and maternity rights and leaflets on the supplementary welfare allowance scheme, the criminal legal aid scheme, the criminal injuries compensation scheme, the operation of barring orders, the Family Home Protection Act 1976, the welfare and maintenance rights of deserted wives, the medical card scheme, pay-related benefit, unemployment payments, local authority differential rent scheme and judicial separation.

[221] Now Comhairle.

establishing a claimants' union in the area, though the union only remained in existence for approximately a year or so. An earlier initiative in 1977 setting up a women's group to provide mutual support for women involved in matrimonial disputes was relatively more successful and this group continued to function until the mid-1980s. In 1983, the centre campaigned against the imposition of water charges. More recently, it has been involved with other information providers in a project to set up a Civic Centre in the Northside area and in the establishment of the Dublin North East Money Advice Bureau. It is also represented on the Northside Partnership and is also actively involved in the Family Welfare Sub-Group, a body set up under the auspices of the Partnership to examine services available locally to families in need. CCLC has also occasionally set up companies for community groups and provided advice on issues such as public liability and employers' liability.

CCLC's commitment to empowering the local community is also manifested in the composition of its controlling body which contains an in-built majority of community representatives. Thus, since 1978, when the former management committee took over responsibility for the centre from FLAC, CCLC has been the only community-controlled law centre in this jurisdiction. In addition to reflecting an understanding of poverty as being about the powerlessness of its victims, this concept of a community-based controlling authority can also be defended as a mechanism for securing the most effective use of scarce resources, community representatives being best placed to identify the community's priority needs. While CCLC has benefited greatly from the very committed contribution of community representatives on the controlling body,[222] it is also fair to say that its experience shows that recruiting community representatives on to this body is not without its difficulties. A number of factors may account for this. To begin with, many community activists already have commitments to their own nominating group and understandably find it difficult to make the extra commitment to the law centre. This problem is exacerbated by the fact that, in recent years, there has been a general decline in the number of people in Irish society willing to work in the voluntary sector. The fact that the law is unfamiliar and intimidating to most people also presents difficulties here. New recruits to CCLC's management committee sometimes felt unable to make a useful contribution to the centre's activities and quickly lost interest in attending meetings. Even more experienced members still tended to look to the professional staff for guidance as to what the centre should do and, as a general proposition, it would appear that most initiatives for the centre's strategic work came from the professional staff rather than from community representatives. The other side of this coin is that there was arguably a tendency for the management committee to become involved in the routine, day-to-day administration of the centre, matters with which the members might have felt more familiar, as a result of which it may have lost perspective on the more long-term

---

[222] It is probably worth noting, in passing, the change, over time, in the nature of the community groups supplying representatives to the management committee. Whereas residents' associations constituted the majority of such groups in the early years of the committee, by the late 1980s other types of community organisations, such as women's groups or claimants' groups, had come to the fore.

development of the organisation. These problems highlight the need for a proper induction process for new members of the management committee in which the objectives of the centre and the role of the committee are fully explained. Over the years, CCLC has, in fact, periodically re-examined the role and operation of the management committee.[223] As a result of a very thorough evaluation of the centre's operations in 1998, the organisation decided to replace the management committee structure with a board of directors, of which a majority would again be drawn from the community. The motivation behind this change was to ensure that the new controlling body would be more distanced from the day-to-day administration of the centre and better able to focus its energies on the policies and long-term development of the organisation. In addition, CCLC sought to strengthen the contribution of the community to the policy-formation of the centre by establishing, in September 1999, a Community Liaison Council, comprising representatives of various local organisations, which meets once or twice a year to advise on the overall policy and direction of CCLC and also to discuss issues of common concern.

Evaluation – As with the examination of FLAC, I attempt here a rather cursory evaluation of CCLC and again, as with FLAC, it is important to remind the reader both of the insecurity of funding experienced by CCLC during much of its history,[224] resulting in the expenditure of an enormous amount of time and energy to ensure survival, and of the difficulties in evaluating activities aimed at increasing awareness of the law and securing change. It is also important to bear in mind that for the greater part of its history, CCLC has operated with the equivalent of only three full-time staff.[225] This meant, in practice, that the two professional staff members had to deal with a significant amount of administrative work which inevitably detracted from the time available for working with clients and the local community.[226]

At a very basic level, CCLC has provided effective legal representation for more than 6,000 people and has advised more than 20,000 others since 1975, in the process

---

[223] Thus in 1981, a sub-committee of the management committee prepared a report on the role of the management committee; in September 1985, a half-day seminar on the future of the centre led to the establishment of four different sub-committees of the management committee, (though this particular re-structuring did not take root); one-day seminars for management committee members were held in both 1987 and 1988; and in 1990, an executive committee was established.

[224] Though, again, I would acknowledge that since 1997, the funding of the centre by the Department of Social, Community and Family Affairs through Comhairle (formerly the NSSB) has introduced a much-needed element of stability into the situation.

[225] Since 1998, CCLC was able to avail of the services of a receptionist under the State-funded Community Employment Scheme and towards the end of 2000, the Department of Social, Community and Family Affairs agreed to fund this position on a permanent basis. Volunteers also operated advice clinics for a number of years after the centre's establishment in 1975 and more recently, since 1998.

[226] In December 2000, the Department of Social, Community and Family Affairs agreed to fund a full-time development manager for the centre for two years and it is hoped that this will result in improved organisational structures in the centre.

establishing considerable credibility for itself in the community and among both the statutory and NGO sector. It has also played a prominent role in providing legal information to the general public in its catchment area and, more recently, has become involved in the provision of legal training for community workers in its catchment area and beyond. In addition, CCLC has also made important contributions to debate on the reform of such areas as social welfare appeals, remedies for domestic violence, legal rights of deserted wives, legal representation of children, medical welfare appeals, garda training, debt management and court organisation. Evaluation surveys carried out by the centre in 1985 and 1997 and by Dillon in 1989 all confirm that, as a result of these different activities, CCLC has a high, positive profile in the local community. Thus it would seem that CCLC has succeeded very well in articulating the needs of its clientele. Moreover one could fairly argue that CCLC has also succeeded in demonstrating the advantages of a legal aid system combining service and strategic elements over a system which focuses exclusively on servicing individual cases.

However there are also a number of items on the debit side. Most obvious of all is CCLC's failure to persuade successive administrations to adopt its blueprint for law centres as part of the State civil legal aid scheme. While one should not underestimate the enormity of this task,[227] at the same time it could be argued that CCLC made certain mistakes in pursuit of this objective. In particular, the organisation failed to address the argument that the judicare element in the scheme it advocated would prove to be very costly. Moreover it also failed to mould an effective network of allies to campaign on legal aid.[228]

For much of its history, CCLC also arguably failed to strike a proper balance between casework and strategic work. Certainly, until the late 1980s, the organisation appeared to have been swamped with casework, leading to a lack of strategic planning. However the use of embargoes in more recent times has led to an improvement in this situation which hopefully will be maintained into the future. CCLC's experience certainly bears out the lesson that a law centre committed to pursuing strategic work cannot afford to operate an open-door policy on casework.

Finally, despite its commitment to the concept, it has to be said that CCLC has experienced difficulty in enduring community control of its activities. This is partly due to the difficulty of attracting community activists with existing commitments into this type of work, a difficulty exacerbated by the contraction in social capital in contemporary Ireland, and partly to the intimidating nature of the legal environment for lay people. While not wishing to underestimate the extent of these problems, at the same time, CCLC needs to consider ways of tackling them by, for example, putting on induction courses about the centre, its objectives and methods for new members of the management committee.

---

[227] On the difficulties here, see above, pp. 320-1.
[228] One such network, the Legal Aid Alliance, went out of existence after a number of years – see n.152 above.

Section IV – Conclusion

> [L]egal aid is a social reform that begins with a solution – lawyers – and then looks for problems it might solve, rather than beginning with the problem – poverty, or oppression, or discrimination, or capitalism – and exploring solutions.[229]

Justifying this depiction of legal aid, Abel argues that legal aid is inspired by the misleading presupposition that because legal rights were instrumental in the rise of capitalism, they would be equally important in subsequent class struggles. According to Abel, the rights of the primary beneficiaries of legal aid, women and children, do not have the same strength or durability as property rights or rights secured by workers through collective action, given that they are not backed up by capital or labour power. These "welfare" rights essentially exist at the whim of the State and all the law can offer is a guarantee that certain procedures will be followed in determining whether a particular individual is entitled to a particular benefit.

Abel contends, further, that legal aid is supportive of capitalism inasmuch as it tackles grievances from the perspective of the individual, thereby undermining the possibility of organising collective action around issues of social injustice. Legal aid clients, moreover, tend to be reluctant and reactive and, family law litigants aside, are generally "one-shot" players in competition with more experienced "repeat" players such as government departments, financial institutions and landlords.[230]

While it is arguable that specific aspects of Abel's argument may not be wholly applicable in this jurisdiction – for example, socio-economic rights enjoying constitutional protection are clearly not quite as vulnerable to hostile State action as welfare rights in the UK – nonetheless, it has to be conceded that there is nothing in the Irish experience to suggest that legal aid is capable of effecting a fundamental change in the nature of our society. The State provides a service model of legal aid that focuses exclusively on individual cases and contributes little to the elimination of social inequality between classes, given its preoccupation with family law. While the voluntary sector has demonstrated the advantages of a strategic model of civil legal aid, that model still operates within the paradigm of a capitalist social order. A defence of legal aid, therefore, must be based on the extent to which it is capable of promoting reform within capitalist society rather than on any claim that it is capable of changing the essential nature of that society.

Viewing the matter from that perspective, it is arguable that the strategic model of legal aid provided by the voluntary sector has promoted interstices of reform in Irish society, despite being severely hampered by a scarcity of resources. This is most apparent in relation to family law where the activities of FLAC and CCLC during the 1970s made a very significant contribution to the modernisation of Irish family law and, in particular, to the promotion of the rights of women within

---

[229] Abel, "The Paradoxes of Legal Aid" in Cooper and Dhavan, (eds.), 379 at p. 386.
[230] See Galanter, "Why the 'Haves' come out ahead: speculations on the limits of legal change" (1974) 9 *Law and Society Review* 95.

marriage.[231] The voluntary sector has also contributed to community politics through its establishment of, or support for, various community groups and it is increasingly operating as a valuable second-tier resource for community and national groups working in the areas of welfare, consumer and employment rights and equality issues. In addition, it has also contributed a low-income perspective to debate on the formulation of policy at national level in these and other areas. Finally, through its use of litigation strategy, FLAC, in particular, secured a significant extension of the criminal legal aid scheme, an improvement in the position of married women on social welfare through the full implementation of Directive 79/7/EEC and an increased awareness on the part of the administration of the procedural rights enjoyed by welfare claimants.

In emphasising the achievements of the voluntary sector, I do not wish to denigrate the importance of the services provided to tens of thousands of individuals by the Legal Aid Board. At the same time, the fact remains that the Civil Legal Aid Act 1995 does not envisage any significant role for the Board in relation to the pursuit of social reform. In any event, a service model of legal aid is, by definition, restricted in what it can achieve. Focused mainly on individual cases, it is limited to the provision of legal advice and legal representation. However my review of litigation strategy has led me to the conclusion that this strategy is a limited mechanism for achieving social change and that engagement with the political process is usually necessary to defend gains secured through the courts. A model of legal aid that strives to bring about social reform but yet does not provide for such engagement is, therefore, really operating with one hand tied behind its back.

In conclusion, therefore, the case for a strategic model of legal aid and for legal involvement with issues of social exclusion rests on the view that such involvement is capable of achieving worthwhile, if limited, gains for people living on the margins of our society. To the extent to which those gains are limited, reliance on the law is open to the criticism that it bolsters a system that is fundamentally unequal. However the significance of that support is highly questionable. It is hardly the case that the existence of legal aid and the activities of public interest lawyers are the sole, or even primary, barriers holding back the mobilisation of marginalised groups around issues of social injustice and the achievement of far-reaching social reform.

On the other hand, gains, even if limited, are still gains. No less a radical critic of capitalism than the Marxist historian E.P. Thompson has accepted that the law is capable of being used to advantage by those on the margins.

> If the law is evidently partial and unjust, then it will mask nothing, legitimize nothing, contribute nothing to any class's hegemony. The essential precondition for the effectiveness of law, in its function as ideology, is that it shall display an independence

---

[231] One person who was very active in FLAC during the 1970s and later in national politics, Alan Shatter, TD, expressed the view, in conversation with the author, that the reforms contained in the Judicial Separation and Family Law Reform Act 1989 and the Family Law (Divorce) Act 1996 represented the culmination of campaigns initiated by FLAC some twenty years earlier.

from gross manipulation and shall seem to be just. It cannot seem to be so without upholding its own logic and criteria of equity; indeed, on occasion by actually being just.[232]

In the perennial struggle to realise social justice, it seems unwise to forego any legitimate method of achieving change, however limited. As Abel himself concludes in relation to legal aid:

Legal aid cannot eliminate patriarchy within the family before or after divorce, but it can alter the balance of power between men and women. It cannot transform capitalist relations of production, but it can regulate the market and discipline the welfare state. It cannot eradicate the pain inflicted by the criminal process, but surely it mitigates that pain. It deserves our critical support.[233]

[232] *Whigs and Hunters: The Origin of the Black Act* (Peregrine Books, 1977) at p. 263.
[233] Abel, at p. 391.

Addendum

This book attempts to state relevant Irish law as of 1 March 2001. However after the main text had been sent to the printers, the Supreme Court handed down decisions in *Sinnott v. Minister for Education*[1] and *T.D. v. Minister for Education*[2] which bear centrally on the theme of this book.

Sinnott v. Minister for Education

Following the delivery of Barr J.'s decision in *Sinnott v. Minister for Education*,[3] High Court orders were issued on 31 October 2000 awarding Jamie and Kathryn Sinnott damages of £222,500 and £55,000 respectively, directing the Minister to provide free primary education for Jamie appropriate to his needs for as long as he was capable of benefiting from same and also providing, *inter alia*, that the plaintiff be provided with the necessary funding for the applied behavioural analysis home based programme for sufferers from autism for two and a half years and for other home based ancillary services.[4] Provision was also made for a review in April 2003 of the mandatory injunction and damages granted to the plaintiff.

An appeal was taken by the defendants against the finding that Jamie Sinnott was entitled to free primary education appropriate to his needs from the age of eighteen onwards for as long as he was capable of benefiting from such education and against the granting of the mandatory injunction enforcing this entitlement. The defendants also appealed against the award of damages to Mrs. Sinnott, other than the award of

---

[1] Unreported, Supreme Court, 12 July 2001.
[2] Unreported, Supreme Court, 17 December 2001. It is a measure of the significance of this case that, for the first time ever, a panel of seven Supreme Court judges – Keane C.J., Denham, Murphy, Murray, Hardiman, Geoghegan and Fennelly J.J. – sat to hear the appeal.
[3] Unreported, High Court, 4 October 2000. See pp. 205-210 above.
[4] Though in his judgment, Keane C.J. commented, at pp. 23-4, that it was "not clear that the trial judge envisaged the granting of an immediate mandatory injunction as set out in paragraph (2) [of the order in the proceedings involving Jamie Sinnott]: he appears to have taken the view that it might arise on the review which was to be carried out in April 2003." Geoghegan J. also noted, at p. 4 of his judgment, that the order as drawn up did not correspond, in certain respects, to the written judgment.

special damages of £15,000 and the order for costs.[5] No issue arose as to the facts of the case.

The issues for consideration on appeal essentially fell into three categories. First, the Supreme Court had to determine the extent of the right to free primary education under Article 42.4 of the Constitution. Did this right apply to adults in certain circumstances and could it amount to a right to education for life? Second, the Court had to decide whether Kathryn Sinnott had a derivative claim in law based on the infringement of her son's right to free primary education. The third and final issue raised the extent of the judicial power in cases such as this. This issue had two aspects. The State challenged the right of the High Court, having regard to the doctrine of separation of powers, to grant a mandatory injunction formulating and directing the application of future policy in relation to educational needs. In addition, it asked the Supreme Court to rule on whether Barr J. was entitled to provide for the review, in April 2003, of the award of damages and the mandatory injunction.

Extent of right to free primary education

Three different approaches were taken by the various members of the Supreme Court to the question of the extent of the right to free primary education. The majority[6] took the view that the State's duty to provide for free primary education, contained in the opening words of Article 42.4,[7] did not require the State to provide such education to adults and that the duty ceased to apply even in the case of a person with learning difficulties such as the plaintiff once such a person reached the age of eighteen.[8]

---

[5] In what presumably was an attempt to minimise any political fallout from being seen to oppose the claim advanced in the instant case, the defendants did not appeal the order for costs in the proceedings involving Jamie Sinnott and further undertook to pay the costs incurred by the Sinnotts in defending the Supreme Court appeal.

[6] Denham, Murray, Hardiman, Geoghegan and Fennelly JJ.

[7] Which provide: "The State shall provide for free primary education". At p. 9 of his judgment, Geoghegan J. appears to hint that the courts might entertain an argument that the State was constitutionally obliged to provide educational facilities for the plaintiff having regard to the State's duty, in the remaining part of Art. 42.4, to "endeavour to supplement and give reasonable aid to private and corporate educational initiative, and, when the public good requires it, provide other educational facilities or institutions with due regard, however, for the rights of parents, especially in the matter of religious and moral formation." This particular argument was not pursued, however, by the plaintiffs in the instant case.

[8] According to four of the five members of the majority, the issue of whether the education Jamie Sinnott received fell within the concept of primary education did not arise in this case, given the State's concession of this point, though Denham J. did observe, at p. 18 of her judgment, that much of the education that Jamie Sinnott was currently receiving did not fall within the scope of Art. 42.4, while Hardiman J. speculated, at p. 21 of his judgment, that educational facilities for children with severe learning difficulties might be covered by the phrase "other educational facilities or institutions" (as distinct from primary education) in Art. 42.4. As against that, Murray J.'s *obiter* comment at p. 10 of his judgment that "where children are capable of benefiting from primary education (however its content is defined) the State have (sic) an obligation to ensure that it is provided free to children who can benefit from it including those who suffer from severe mental

Denham J. reasoned that Article 42 located education in the context of the family and that the words "child" or "children" were very clear in this context - they referred to young people and were age related. Consequently she was satisfied that the right to free primary education in Article 42.4 did not apply to adults. While most children would finish primary education by the age of fourteen, in order to ensure that all children, including those with learning difficulties, enjoyed the benefits of this right, it was reasonable to treat the right as continuing to subsist until the beneficiary reached the age of eighteen, the age at which society treats a young person as an adult. A similar conclusion was reached by Murray J. who said that the ordinary and natural meaning of primary education related to the teaching of children only and that in fixing eighteen as the age at which the right to free primary education expired, the State was acting within an acceptable margin of appreciation for determining such matters. Hardiman J., like Denham J., emphasised the linkage between Article 42 on education and Article 41 dealing with the family, commenting,

> It is thus manifest that, whether one reads the Constitution in its Irish or English text, the primary provider of education is seen as the parent, and the recipient as a child of such parent. This appears to me plainly to involve the consequence that the recipient of primary education would be a person who is not an adult and in respect of whom the primary educator, according to the natural order, is his family.[9]

He also rejected the contention that the opening words of Article 42.4 imposed an unqualified duty on the State, pointing out that the duty to provide for free primary education was a complex one, involving enormous annual expense and requiring both the legislature and executive to formulate and review policy decisions. Furthermore, having regard to Article 17.2, the public financing of educational provision had to be effected by way of legislation, following a recommendation to Dáil Éireann from the Government. He continued,

> It seems to me that the constitutional requirements for the conduct of public business, and in particular the expenditure of public monies, as exemplified in [Article 17] and other provisions to be considered later, emphasise that the duty imposed by Article 42 must be discharged in a manner approved by the legislature on the recommendation of the executive. It is true that neither of these organs of Government are in a position to disregard a constitutional duty and that the Courts have powers and duties in the unlikely event of such disregard. But, excepting that extreme situation, the duty imposed by Article 42 is a duty to be discharged in the manner endorsed by the legislature and executive who must necessarily have a wide measure of discretion having regard to available resources and having regard to policy considerations of which they must be the judges.
>
>   This, in my view, is inconsistent with a concept of the duty imposed by the first eight words of Article 42.4 as a simple one, or as one different in kind from all other obligations

---

or physical handicap" appears to imply that the concept of primary education can embrace education suitable for children with learning difficulties. The remaining member of the majority, Geoghegan J., did accept that the expression "primary education" in Art. 42.4 included suitable education for children with learning difficulties – see p. 14 of his judgment.

[9]   At p. 14 of his judgment.

imposed on the State or its organs. Nor can the duty be regarded as existing ... on a higher plane than any other such duty. The right to education is undoubtedly a central and important one but it cannot logically be regarded as in some way outranking the right to life, or to bodily integrity, without which a right to education may be redundant.[10]

The judge therefore rejected the contention that the State's duty to provide for free primary education was qualitatively different to any other duty and that this duty was open ended, stating,

> Any terminal point would be to some extent arbitrary, but the age of eighteen as advanced by the State has the merit of being the latest at which a person could, with any element of reality, be regarded as a child.
>
> That is not to say that a person, such as the Plaintiff, with profound and obvious needs, is not entitled to have them appropriately met after this age, but simply that they cannot be compulsorily met thereafter (whatever about before) on the basis of the single part of the single constitutional Article on which this appeal was based.[11]

In his judgment, Geoghegan J. accepted that the concept of primary education, read in the light of modern knowledge of the educational requirements of children with disabilities, included suitable education for children with learning difficulties. According to the judge, the duty to provide for free primary education was owed to children and not to adults, having regard to the context in which Article 42.4 was placed, and he suggested, *obiter*, that in the vast majority of cases, this duty was discharged simply by ensuring that there were schools providing, free of charge, the necessary minimum education available for every child.[12] In the case of children with learning difficulties, however, the scope of the constitutional duty on the State was different.

> If I am right in my view that Article 42.4 relates only to children and not adults then I think that in the case of mentally handicapped children the duty is owed to them as children only and not as adults. I cannot accept that there is no such thing as a mentally handicapped adult. Merely because some mental or physical abilities do not surpass those of a young child if they have even reached that stage, does not mean that in ordinary parlance these children do not become adults. Adulthood is as much to do with physical development as anything else.
>
> If I am right in my view so far, then the practical effect is that whereas primary education might be regarded as education up to the age of twelve in the case of a normal child, because

---

[10] *Ibid.*, pp. 25-6.

[11] *Ibid.*, pp. 26-7. Hardiman J. went on to suggest that the plaintiff might be able to put his claim in other ways by relying on the provisions of the Education Act 1998, the Equal Status Act 2000 and the Education (Welfare) Act 2000 which imposed duties on public authorities that might be relevant to people in his position. A similar view was expressed by Geoghegan J. at p. 24 of his judgment.

[12] He also expressed the view that, "apart from possibly exceptional circumstances", a child who failed to acquire reading and writing skills because of learning difficulties combined with poor teaching would not be entitled to bring an action based on an alleged breach of Art. 42.4 – see p. 15 of his judgment.

of slow learning or learning incapacity, the period to be covered by the expression "primary education" may obviously have to be extended in the case of handicapped children. In that sense, the arbitrary choice by the State of the age eighteen is not necessarily illogical. In the perception of most people a child becomes an adult at eighteen.[13]

Thus the right to free primary education ceased to exist once the beneficiary reached eighteen years of age. This was the case even where, as with Jamie Sinnott, there was a danger that a person with learning difficulty would unlearn everything he had learned if he was not provided with continuous basic training and education, the judge reluctantly coming to that conclusion on the ground that to hold to the contrary "would amount to an excessive straining of the wording of Article 42.4 when read in context".[14]

The remaining member of the majority, Fennelly J., agreed with Hardiman and Geoghegan JJ. that primary education was owed to children and not to adults. He expressly reserved consideration of whether the plaintiff was in a position to enjoy primary education, the State's decision to admit that his constitutional rights were infringed having rendered that issue moot.

It is clear from the foregoing that the majority decision on this point ultimately turned on the view that a distinction between adults and children was of crucial relevance to the interpretation of the State's constitutional duty to provide for free primary education and yet the relevance of such a distinction to plaintiffs like Jamie Sinnott is very questionable. In reality, people in Jamie Sinnott's position straddle both sides of this distinction. Chronologically, they are over the age of eighteen but in terms of dependency, they remain in the same position as children under that age. This point possibly comes out more vividly when one looks at the term "parents" which, unlike "child" or "children", does feature in Article 42.4 which refers to the "rights of parents ... in the matter of religious and moral formation." For most parents, their rights in respect of the religious and moral formation of their children expire when those children attain eighteen years of age. However for parents of children with moderate, severe or profound learning difficulties, can it be doubted that such rights continue to exist until the death of either parent or child, given the dependency of the latter on the former? Can it seriously be contended that the State could provide for the religious and moral formation of persons with learning difficulties over the age of eighteen against the express wishes of the parents

[13] *Ibid.* at p. 16.
[14] *Ibid.* at p. 17. As we have already noted, Geoghegan J. had earlier pointed out that, in relation to the right to education, the appeal was concerned only with the opening words of Art. 42.4, raising the possibility that a constitutional claim might be based on the remaining words of that particular provision – "Conceivably, the constitutional requirement [in Art. 42.4] that "when the public good requires it" the State must provide other educational facilities or institutions could have been invoked by the plaintiff/respondent but as it was not, I do not intend to express any view on its relevance. The point was made at the hearing of the appeal that normally under the separation of powers principles, the courts do not determine what might be required by the common good. *But I am not convinced that there would not be exceptions to that principle.*" *Ibid.*, at p. 9 (emphasis added).

involved? In this context, the attainment by the child of the age of eighteen is entirely irrelevant and while the majority in *Sinnott* are concerned with a different issue, namely the extent of the State's duty to provide for free primary education, the point being made illustrates the very arbitrary nature of the age limit of eighteen in determining the scope of this duty.

The majority's reasoning would also seem to have a disturbing implication for certain aspects of constitutional policy towards the family. If one can use the concept of "child" to limit the State's duty to provide for free primary education, under Article 42.4, to persons under the age of eighteen, can one use similar reasoning to restrict the explicit constitutional right and duty, referred to in Article 42.1, of parents of children with learning difficulties to provide for the education of such children? If such parents abandon their offspring once the latter reach the age of eighteen, is the State powerless to intervene, given that Article 42.5 only authorises State intervention in cases where parents fail in their duty towards their "children"? If this is not the case, then what is the basis for arguing that the State's duty towards such children under Article 42.5 continues to exist after they reach the age of eighteen while the State's duty to provide for free primary education expires at that point?

One final disappointing feature of the majority reasoning is that, notwithstanding various references to a purposive interpretation of the Constitution, there is no consideration of what the *purpose* or *objective* of the State's constitutional duty to provide for free primary education might be. Yet even for an originalist like Bork, this is an absolute prerequisite to a proper interpretation of the Constitution.[15] Is the purpose of the duty to provide for free primary education to ensure that as many children as possible are educated to a basic level of literacy and numeracy, in which case the duty would not arise in the case of Jamie Sinnott? Or is the duty designed, as O'Hanlon J. held in *O'Donoghue v. Minister for Health*,[16] to ensure that every child can make the best possible use of his or her inherent and potential capacities, no matter how limited, in which case how can one justify restricting the duty to people under the age of eighteen where, as in the instant case, the beneficiary will unlearn all that he has been taught without continuous education?

In sum, therefore, the majority rely on a distinction between adults and children the relevance of which is questionable in the instant case and which, if persisted in, might given rise to undesirable consequences in other contexts. In addition, their approach to the interpretation of the Constitution is overly literal and fails to identify the constitutional value served by Article 42.4.

In his judgment, Murphy J. construed the right to free primary education even more narrowly than the majority, rejecting O'Hanlon J.'s conclusion in *O'Donoghue* that

---

[15] Recall his statement, "In short, all that a judge committed to original understanding requires is that the text, structure, and history of the Constitution provide him not with a conclusion but with a major premise. That major premise is a principle or stated value that the ratifiers wanted to protect against hostile legislation or executive action. The judge must then see whether that principle or value is threatened by the statute or action challenged in the case before him. The answer to that question provides his minor premise, and the conclusion follows." Bork, p. 162.

[16] [1996] 2 IR 20.

"primary education" for the purposes of Article 42.4 entailed "giving each child such advice, instruction and teaching as will enable him or her to make the best possible use of his or inherent and potential capacities, physical, mental and moral, however limited these capacities may be".[17] He took a rather strong anti-Statist approach to this issue, citing the opening words of the Preamble[18] in conjunction with Article 42 in support of the view that "the Constitution is careful to restrain the State and any other organisation from usurping the functions of the individual in her or her right and duty to achieve his purpose and fulfill his destiny to the best of his ability".[19] Turning to the concept of primary education as used in Article 42.4, he rejected the argument that this concept covered the type of services required by Jamie Sinnott.

> Whilst I would have no difficulty in accepting that Mr. Sinnott is in need of what would fall within the general ambit of education and has a proven ability of responding, albeit at a modest level, to such education, I could not accept that the needs which Mr. Sinnott had, or has, for assistance from therapists, teaching staff, paediatricians, consultant psychiatrists, social workers, family therapists and psychotherapists could be equated with primary education as that term was used in the Constitution and understood by anybody familiar with the system which existed when the Constitution was adopted or indeed the philosophy lying behind the enactment of the particular constitutional rights in respect of education. The imposition of an express obligation on the State to provide for primary education might...seem surprising but it was not revolutionary. When the Constitution was adopted such an obligation was already in existence as Murnaghan J. explained in *McEneaney v. The Minister for Education* [1941] IR 430 at 438 as follows:
>
> "For now more than a century it has been recognised that the provision of primary education is a national obligation; and for very many years this duty was entrusted to a corporate body created by royal charter called the Commissioners of National Education in Ireland."
>
> The nature of that education and the children for whom it was provided is well understood by the people who adopted the Constitution. Its meaning is not to be found by reference to experts however distinguished. No doubt improvements have been made in the buildings in which such education is provided and hopefully the facilities are better now than they were sixty years ago but these are changes in detail and in style. In my view primary education as identified in the Constitution is education provided for children the age limits of which were determined historically by the Education (Ireland) Act 1892, which required parents to send their children between the ages of 6 and 14 years to receive certain schooling. Primary education is provided by teachers in classrooms. It was and is a basic scholastic education in the sense that it is a first stepping stone on a career which may lead to secondary level and ideally graduate to the third level. It is distinguishable from secondary level education on the one hand and nursery schools, or any other form of pre-primary education, on the other.

---

[17] *Ibid.*at p. 65.
[18] "In the name of the most holy Trinity, from whom is all authority and to whom, *as our final end*, all actions both of men and states must be referred ...". (Emphasis added by Murphy J.)
[19] At p. 7 of his judgment.

If such needs are toilet training fell within the ambit of "primary education" at all, it seems to me that they would also necessarily come within the scope of the "minimum education, moral, intellectual and social" which every child is bound to receive. Having regard to the structure of the Constitution it is extremely unlikely that those who framed it or the people by whom it was adopted would have authorised the State to intervene in such intimate matters.[20]

Accordingly, Murphy J. held that the entitlement to receive free primary education ceased when a person reached the age of twelve years and so he allowed the State's appeal on this issue, though without prejudice to the concessions made by the Minister in relation to the payment of damages and costs to Jamie Sinnott.

This narrow reading of Article 42.4 by reference to the state of affairs that existed in 1937 – sometimes referred to as the "historical approach" to constitutional interpretation – is a very conservative approach to constitutional interpretation that is not even advocated by such staunch defenders of judicial restraint as Robert Bork. As we have already noted, Bork's originalism requires the judge to rely on a major premise supplied by the text, structure and history of the Constitution – it does not require the judge to decide an issue in the manner in which the framers or ratifiers of the Constitution would have done in their day.[21] In the instant case, the Constitution explicitly provides the major premise that the State is obliged to provide for free primary education. Applying that premise in the light of the changed circumstances of people with learning difficulty, specifically, the dramatic development during the twentieth century of appropriate educational courses for such people, is perfectly consonant with an originalist approach to constitutional interpretation while Murphy J.'s approach has the effect of fossilising the Constitution in 1937 when the concept of education for people with learning difficulties simply did not exist. Moreover a meaningful application of this major premise to changing circumstances must require the State to take account of significant differences between different categories of child, given that an insistence on a uniform system of primary education appropriate to children without learning difficulties effectively denies children with significant learning difficulties any right to primary education. It follows that the provision of appropriate training for children with learning difficulties, such as toilet training, does not, *pace* Murphy J., have to be provided to every child.

A more expansive reading of Article 42.4 was adopted by Keane C.J. who, alone of all of the Supreme Court judges, held that the first plaintiff's right to free primary education did not expire on his attaining the age of eighteen. After outlining the reasoning of O'Hanlon J. in *O'Donoghue v. Minister for Health*,[22] in which, it will be recalled, that judge held open the possibility that the right to free primary education lasted up to the age of eighteen in the case of children with learning difficulty, Keane C.J. endorsed O'Hanlon J.'s statement of the law.[23] With regard to the claim in the

---

[20] *Ibid.*, pp. 10-11.
[21] See the quotation at n.15 above.
[22] [1996] 2 IR 20.
[23] At p. 43 of his judgment.

instant case that this right continued to exist past the age of eighteen, the Chief Justice highlighted certain difficulties in the State's strategic approach to this case whereby, in an attempt to minimise political fallout from having opposed the claims of the Sinnott family, the State did not appeal against the award of damages in favour of Jamie Sinnott. As Keane C.J. pointed out, this meant that the High Court decision to grant Jamie Sinnott damages because of the violation of his right to free primary education up to the date of judgment, at which point the plaintiff was 22, constituted the law of the land unless and until another High Court judge or the Supreme Court took a different view. Consequently the State's position on the award of damages to Jamie Sinnott was inconsistent with its argument that the right to free primary education expired when the plaintiff reached the age of eighteen.[24] He also took the view that the State's strategy rendered this important point moot, noting that the Supreme Court generally declined to grant advisory judgments in such circumstances.[25] While Keane C.J. based his decision on this aspect of the case on his view of the implications of the State's strategy in not appealing against the award of damages to Jamie Sinnott, he did go on to state, *obiter*, that he would have upheld the High Court decision had the award of damages been subject to an appeal. Explaining his reasoning on this point, he argued that the ordinary meaning of primary education was inapplicable in the instant case and he noted with approval O'Hanlon J.'s conclusion in *O'Donoghue* that primary education for the category of children with severe mental or physical disability required, in the legal context, a new approach, in particular with regard to the question of duration. Moreover it was for the courts to determine when the right to free primary education expired, in the absence of any specific age limit to be found in Article 42. He then briefly reviewed the legal significance of different ages and continued:

[24] Keane C.J. summarised this point as follows, at p. 60 of his judgment: "In the result, [the Minister for Education] invites this court to treat a finding by the High Court judge as wrong in law, which he has already accepted, by declining to appeal, as being right in law. To accept that contention as correct involves a feat of mental legerdemain of which I am incapable." The Chief Justice also hinted, at p. 59, that as a result of this approach by the State, future plaintiffs in the same position as Jamie Sinnott might be able to rely on the Supreme Court decision in *McMahon v. Leavy* [1984] IR 525 in order to assert an entitlement to free primary education after the age of eighteen.

[25] These arguments were rejected by Geoghegan J., Hardiman J. concurring, who said, at p. 20 of his judgment, "… I entirely subscribe to the view of the Chief Justice that an unappealed High Court decision … must be treated as being an authoritative statement of the law. But rightly or wrongly, I interpret the approach adopted on behalf of the Minister in this appeal rather differently. He is accepting liability for the award of damages to date and neither the amount of the award or liability for it is in issue on this appeal. But in considering the potential future liability of the Minister, his counsel are not precluded, in my view, from arguing as a reason why there can be no liability into the future, that the constitutional right came to an end at age eighteen. They are putting forward that proposition as a legitimate argument in an aspect of the appeal which is before this court." Murray J. also agreed with this view at p. 5 of his judgment but gave as an additional reason for determining the issue the fact that it was "one of fundamental importance to both parties and has important constitutional ramifications for the organs of State, including the extent to which the powers of the Oireachtas should be limited in the choices it makes in the spending of the public purse in the interests of the community as a whole. In these circumstances it is clearly a constitutional issue which merits, if not requires, in the public interest a final determination and clarification on appeal to this Court as the Court of final instance."

Where in this spectrum [of ages] can it be said with any semblance of truth that the plaintiff passed from childhood to adulthood? So far as the evidence in this case goes, virtually none of these stages is of any significance in his case. He is one of a relatively small category of people in our society who, because of their mental handicap, can never enjoy life in all its diversity and richness but to whom at least a measure of happiness may be available. The uncontested evidence in this case is that, to attain even that low plateau, the plaintiff requires continuing access to what, in his case, is education, as defined by Ó Dálaigh C.J., albeit often extremely basic in character. No principled basis exists either in law or in the evidence for the contention advanced by the defendants that a person in his position ceases to be in need of primary education at age 18, at age 22 or at any age in the future which can now be identified with any precision.[26]

Accordingly he held that the plaintiff was entitled to a declaration that the Minister was obliged by Article 42.4 to provide for free primary education for the plaintiff appropriate to his needs for as long as he was capable of benefiting from the same, though, having regard to the doctrine of separation of powers, he also took the view that a mandatory injunction was not an appropriate relief where the case involved the raising of taxes and the appropriation of public monies.

The position of Kathryn Sinnott

With only one exception, the members of the Supreme Court rejected the contention that Kathryn Sinnott was entitled to compensation because of the failure of the State to provide for free primary education for her son. According to the Chief Justice, with whom Murray, Hardiman and Fennelly JJ, agreed, family members were not entitled to compensation where the constitutional rights of another member of the family had been violated, nor did the failure of the State to act amount to a violation of Kathryn Sinnott's right to choose the form of education appropriate to her son. A similar approach was taken by Geoghegan J. who held that any contraventions of the Constitution that occurred were breaches of constitutional duty owed to Jamie Sinnott rather than to his mother. As Murphy J. held that the State had not been in breach of its constitutional duty under Article 42.4, it followed that Kathryn Sinnott had no cause of action either.

The sole dissentient on this matter was Denham J. who held that Kathryn Sinnott had been subject to invidious discrimination, contrary to Article 40.1, as between herself and another mother of a child with no learning difficulty and that her rights as a parent under Articles 41 and 42 had also been infringed.

---

[26] At p. 67 of his judgment. It is worth noting that at an earlier part of his judgment – at pp. 55-6 – he rejected, on the ground of the separation of powers, the argument that acceding to the plaintiff's case here necessarily meant that the State would incur legal obligations towards other adults who left the primary school system without having achieved the minimum level of education that system was designed to impart, either because of the inherent inability of such individuals to benefit from such education or because of defects in the system itself, such as overcrowded classrooms, inadequate buildings, etc.

Extent of judicial power

While the first two issues in this case are clearly of central importance to people with learning difficulties and their families, the question of the extent of judicial power is of even greater significance to public interest litigation generally. As already noted, there were two distinct aspects to this issue - first, whether, having regard to the doctrine of separation of powers, the High Court had the right to formulate and direct the application of future policy in relation to educational needs by issuing the mandatory injunction and, second, whether Barr J. was entitled to provide for a review of the award of damages and the mandatory injunction in April 2003. In the event, the Court's conclusion that the State no longer owed a constitutional duty to provide for free primary education to the plaintiff meant that it was not necessary to determine these matters. However four of the judges[27] did address the issue of the extent of judicial power and their comments give us the first insight into the attitudes of the present Supreme Court towards public interest litigation.

The most extensive analysis of the first aspect of this topic is to be found in the judgment of Hardiman J. Describing the mandatory injunction granted by Barr J. as a most unusual one for a court to make inasmuch as it purported to deal with issues normally within the discretion of the executive, namely, the matter of the services to be provided to the plaintiff, the recruitment of persons to provide services, the mode of assessing the result of the provision of these services and the costs of the services, Hardiman J. said,

> Decisions of this sort are normally a matter for the legislative and executive arms of government. This is not merely a matter of demarcation or administrative convenience. It is a reflection of the constitutionally mandated division of the general powers of government, set out in Article 6 of the Constitution. A system of separation of powers of this sort is a part of the constitutional arrangements of all free societies.[28]

He then cited extensively from that part of the judgment of Costello J. (as he then was) in *O'Reilly v. Limerick Corporation*[29] dealing with the doctrine of separation of powers, and in particular the distinction between distributive and commutative justice,[30] before commenting,

---

[27] Keane C.J., Denham, Hardiman and Geoghegan JJ. Fennelly J. took the view that this issue did not arise for consideration, given the concessions made by the State in relation to the award of damages. Murray J. took a similar view, though based on the finding of the Court against the plaintiff on the issue of the extent of the State's duty to provide for free primary education. (However he did agree, *obiter*, at pp. 4-5 of his judgment, that the State's constitutional obligation to commit a proportion of national resources to the provision of free primary education was elevated "to a plane above the vast range of decisions concerning the allocation of the national budget which are normally a matter of political choice", from which one might infer that he would contemplate some role for the courts in the event of the State failing to discharge this obligation). Murphy J. did not advert to this issue at all.

[28] At p. 33 of his judgment.

[29] [1989] ILRM 181.

[30] See above, pp. 9-12.

In my view all of the considerations mentioned by Costello J. are of prime importance in dealing with the present case. In particular, the constitutionally mandated separation of powers is a vital constituent of the sovereign independent republican and democratic State envisaged by the Constitution. It is not a mere administrative arrangement: it is itself a high constitutional value. It exists to prevent the accumulation of excessive power in any one of the organs of government or its members, and to allow each to check and balance the others. It is an essential part of the democratic procedures of the State, not inferior in importance to any article of the Constitution.[31]

In the instant case, Barr J. had relied primarily on *O'Donoghue v. Minister for Health*[32] in support of his decision. However in that case, O'Hanlon J. granted declaratory relief only, stating,

> In a case like the present one it should normally be sufficient to grant declaratory relief in the expectation that the institutions of the State would respond by taking whatever action was appropriate to vindicate the constitutional rights of the successful applicant. I therefore propose to make no further order at the present time, save in relation to the costs of the proceedings, but I reserve liberty to the Applicant to apply to the Court again in the future should it become necessary to do so for further relief by way of mandamus or otherwise as may come within the scope of the present proceedings. A general liberty to apply will also be given to all the parties to the proceedings.[33]

While Hardiman J. expressly reserved his position on certain aspects of the decision in *O'Donoghue*, he expressly agreed with O'Hanlon J.'s reasoning for confining the relief granted to declarations. The subsequent history of the *O'Donoghue* litigation[34] and the concessions made by the State in the instant case left some uncertainty as to whether the State accepted the main features of findings of O'Hanlon and Barr JJ. in relation to the type of services to be provided to persons in the position of the plaintiff but this, according to Hardiman J., reflected concern within the public service about the implications of these two cases for the relationship between the judicial and executive arms of government, a concern which the judge viewed as entirely appropriate.[35] After referring to the strong judicial affirmation of the independence of the judiciary in *Buckley v. Attorney General*,[36] he said,

---

[31] At p. 40 of his judgment. Hardiman J. also noted that *O'Reilly* was approved by the Supreme Court in *MhicMhathúna v. Ireland* [1995] 1 IR 484; [1995] 1 ILRM 69 and that principles similar to those expounded by Costello J. in *O'Reilly* were to be found in cases like *Boland v. An Taoiseach* [1974] IR 338 and *Riordan v. An Taoiseach*, unreported, Supreme Court, 21 July 2000. Neither Hardiman J. nor the other members of the Supreme Court appear to be aware of Costello J.'s *ex tempore* decision in *O'Brien v. Wicklow UDC*, unreported, High Court, 10 June 1994, in which that judge resiled from his position in *O'Reilly*.

[32] [1996] 2 IR 20.

[33] *Ibid.* at p. 71.

[34] As already noted – see p. 203, n.104 – a new form of declaration was substituted for the one granted by O'Hanlon J. by consent of the parties on appeal.

[35] In that context, he criticised public comment which, in its turn, had criticised the State for exercising its right of appeal.

[36] [1950] IR 67.

It appears to me that the Courts must be equally concerned not to infringe upon the proper prerogatives and area of operations of the other branches of government. The functions of these branches, like those of the Courts, are themselves of constitutional origin and constitutionally defined.

In my view, the foregoing principles underlie the essential distinction drawn by Mr. Justice Costello between issues which can be pursued in the Four Courts and issues which, to comply with the Constitution, must be pursued in Leinster House. It is easy to imagine a particular case in which a party might think, and might convince a judge, that a particular act or omission of the legislature or executive was clearly wrong and that another course of action … clearly right or at least preferable. That indeed was what happened in *O'Reilly's* case. But even if a court were quite satisfied that this situation existed, that fact alone would not justify it in purporting to take a decision properly within the remit of the legislature or the executive. I reiterate that it is an independent constitutional value, essential to the maintenance of parliamentary democracy, that the legislature and the executive retain their proper independence in their respective spheres of action. In these spheres, the executive is answerable to Dáil Éireann and the members of the legislature are answerable to the electorate.

Moreover, the independence of these organs of government within their spheres must be real and not merely nominal. This is imperatively required by the Constitution. *[He then quoted Articles 15.2.1, 28.2 and 28.4.1 in full and referred to Article 17.2.]*

The plaintiffs attempted to justify the granting of the mandatory injunction by reference to a number of judicial utterances, of which the strongest, according to Hardiman J., was that of Ó Dálaigh C.J. in *The State (Quinn) v. Ryan*[37] in which he said,

> It was not the intention of the Constitution in guaranteeing the fundamental rights of the citizen that these rights should be set at naught or circumvented. The intention was that rights of substance were being assured to the individual and the Courts were the custodians of these rights. As a necessary corollary it follows that no-one can with impunity set these rights at naught or circumvent them, and that the courts' powers in this regard are as ample as the defence of the Constitution requires.[38]

Hardiman J. cautioned that this passage had to be read in the context of the case in which the applicant, having obtained an absolute order of habeas corpus, was subsequently re-arrested and bundled out of the jurisdiction before he could obtain effective relief from the courts. In that context, the passage quoted above was, according to the judge,

> not an assertion of an unrestricted general power in the judicial arm of government but rather a strong and entirely appropriate statement that a petty fogging, legalistic response to an order in the terms of Article 40.4 of the Constitution will not be permitted to obscure the realities of the case, or to preclude appropriate action by the Courts.[39]

---

[37] [1965] IR 70.

[38] *Ibid.* at p. 122.

[39] At p. 54 of his judgment.

The plaintiffs also contended that the courts had a residual power to ensure that a person's constitutional rights were not circumvented or denied and they raised the spectre of a hypothetical legislature and government simply ceasing to make any provision for free primary education. In such circumstances, it was argued, the courts had to retain the jurisdiction to enforce Article 42.4. Hardiman J. questioned the logic or desirability of relying on such an extreme situation in support of the contention that the courts had powers to deal with an altogether different situation. Nonetheless, he did concede that the courts retained the necessary discretion to deal with such extreme circumstances, citing *MhicMhathúna v. Attorney General*[40] in support of this view. Then he continued,

> The fact that powers to deal with extreme circumstances must be retained cannot be a basis for the exercise of such powers in any other circumstances. Firstly, to do so would offend the constitutional separation of powers. Secondly, it would lead the Courts into the taking of decisions in areas in which they have no special qualification or experience. Thirdly, it would permit the Courts to take such decisions even though they are not, and cannot be, democratically responsible for them as the legislature and executive are. Fourthly, the evidence based adversarial procedures of the Court, which are excellently adapted for the administration of commutative justice, are too technical, too expensive, too focused on the individual issue to be an appropriate method for deciding on issues of policy.[41]

There then follows a revealing passage that is worth citing *in extenso* because of its insights into the preinterpretive values informing Hardiman J.'s reasoning.

> The view of the separation of powers summarised above was for many years implicitly accepted by lawyers and jurists. It can be found in most if not all of the great constitutional documents and in the writings of such commanding figures as Aristotle, Locke, Montesquieu and the founding fathers of the United States. Central to this view is a recognition that there is a proper sphere for both elected representatives of the people and the executive elected or endorsed by them in the taking of social and economic and legislative decisions, as well as another sphere where the judiciary is solely competent.
>
> In the last quarter century, there has arisen another point of view whose major manifestation in a quasi legal context is found in the works of the American academic John Rawls. It subordinates politics to a theory of justice, seeming to view political philosophy as a branch of jurisprudence. Theorists of this view consider that they can provide a body of principles which can be interpreted and applied by the courts, to the virtual exclusion or marginalisation of the political process. Preferably, but not essentially, the mechanism of this process is to enshrine the selected principles in some form of code or charter. Failing this, one can try to imply them into older texts. The political process thus avoided or marginalised is regarded as too diverse, clamorous, and populist in values to be worth preserving as more than an inferior organ of government.
>
> In my view, conflicts of priorities, values, modes of administration or sentiments cannot be avoided or ignored by adopting an agreed or exclusive theory of justice. And if judges

---

[40] [1995] 1 IR 484; [1995] 1 ILRM 69.
[41] At p. 56 of his judgment.

were to become involved in such an enterprise, designing the details of policy in individual cases or in general, and ranking some areas of policy in priority to others, they would step beyond their appointed role. The views of aspirants to judicial office on such social and economic questions are not canvassed for the good reason that they are thought to be irrelevant. They have no mandate in these areas. And the legislature and the executive, possessed of a democratic mandate, are liable to recall by the withdrawal of that mandate. That is the most fundamental, but by no means the only, basis of the absolute necessity for judicial restraint in these areas. To abandon this restraint would be unacceptably and I believe unconstitutionally to limit the proper freedom of action of the legislature and the executive branch of government.[42]

Hardiman J. concluded this part of his judgment by emphasising that this was not a case where the law had no remedy for the plaintiff but rather was one where the plaintiff was not entitled to succeed on the sole argument that was pursued on his behalf. He went on,

[R]ecent statutory provisions have effected a revolution in educational legislation which will undoubtedly be explored by some person with grievances about educational services, but this has not been done here. Similarly, the Court retains its wide jurisdiction to ascertain and enforce the rights of individuals, whatever their origin in law or in the Constitution. The rejection of the very specific and unique claim advanced by the Plaintiff in this Action does not alter the fact that the Courts will continue to develop the jurisprudence of individual rights and enforce such rights on all appropriate occasions.

It is hardly necessary to point out that a case based on a duty to provide services imposed by statute would avoid the difficulties of principle described in *O'Reilly v. Limerick Corporation* and elsewhere. It is clearly not possible to say, in the abstract, whether other difficulties might await a specific case, but the enforcement of duties imposed by the legislature is obviously an exercise of a different kind to the devising or inferring of such duties without legislative intervention. The cases on autism cited from the United Kingdom and the United States have proceeded on the basis of a statutory duty.[43]

In his judgment on this point, Keane C.J. noted that difficulties in executing judgment against any of the organs of State have never been regarded, since the Supreme Court decision in *Byrne v. Ireland*,[44] as a ground for refusing relief to a person whose constitutional or legal rights had been violated. However, while relief in the form of an order for mandamus could be granted against organs of State such as Ministers, different considerations would apply where the granting of the relief sought would trespass on the exclusive role of Dáil Éireann in the raising of taxation and the appropriation of public monies. In such cases, the courts had never gone beyond the granting of a declaration that the expenditure of monies by the Oireachtas on an

---

[42] *Ibid.* at pp. 56-58.
[43] *Ibid.* at pp. 58-9. On the issue of whether the High Court had the power to review its award of damages and the granting of the mandatory injunction in April 2003, Hardiman J. concurred with the Chief Justice that no such power existed.
[44] [1972] IR 241.

unlawful object was in violation of the Constitution and he took the view that the Supreme Court would never grant mandatory relief requiring the Oireachtas to provide funds for a particular purpose in order to uphold the constitutional or purely legal rights of members of the public, citing *Brady v. Cavan Co. Co.*[45] in support. Then he continued,

> That is not to say that where a plaintiff successfully claims that his constitutional rights have been violated by the State in the past and will continue to be so violated in the future unless the court intervenes, the courts are impotent when it comes to the protection of those rights. That is of particular relevance in a case such as the present where it is not suggested that it is beyond the financial resources of the Minister to provide the facilities which the first named plaintiff requires, the situation that arose in *Brady*. As Lord Browne-Wilkinson, speaking for the House of Lords, observed in *R. v. East Sussex County Council, ex p. Tandy* (1998) AC 714, where a local authority contended that it lacked the resources to maintain home tuition for a schoolgirl suffering from a particular condition:
>
> "My Lords, I believe your lordships should resist this approach to statutory duties. First, the County Council has as a matter of strict legality the resources necessary to perform its statutory duty under s.298. Very understandably it does not wish to bleed its other functions of resources so as to enable it to perform the statutory duty under s.298. But it can, if it wishes, divert monies from other educational or other applications that are merely discretionary, so as to apply such diverted monies to discharge the statutory duty laid down by s.298."
>
> *A fortiori* those observations apply to the allocation by a Minister of resources sufficient to meet a constitutional obligation owed to a particular person. In such cases, while in principle there is nothing to preclude the granting of mandatory relief directed to the Minister concerned, it is appropriate, in my view, for the courts to presume that where this court grants a declaration that he or she has failed to meet his or her constitutional obligations, the Minister will take the appropriate steps to comply with the law as laid down by the courts.[46]

As we have already noted, Keane C.J. was the only member of the Supreme Court to uphold Barr J.'s decision that the State was obliged to provide for free primary education for the plaintiff for as long as he was capable of benefiting from same. However the Chief Justice disagreed with the High Court on the question of what remedy to provide. He took the view that the appropriate relief to provide in the instant case was a declaration rather than a mandatory injunction, given that the raising of taxes and the appropriation of public monies were quintessentially matters for Dáil Éireann alone. He also ruled that the purported retention by the High Court of jurisdiction to review its award of damages and the granting of the mandatory injunction was an erroneous exercise of the court's jurisdiction, though he continued,

> I can fully understand the misgivings of the trial judge in the light of the previous conduct of the defendants in this case but, despite the strenuous submissions to the contrary on behalf of the plaintiff, I have no doubt that the case should have been approached on the

---

[45] [1999] 4 IR 99; [2000] 1 ILRM 81.
[46] At pp. 49-50 of his judgment.

basis that, if the first named defendant was at any stage in the future found by the High Court to have been in breach of his or her obligation, the powers of the court to ensure the upholding and vindication of the plaintiff's rights would, in the famous words of Ó Dálaigh C.J. in *The State (Quinn) v. Ryan* [1965] IR 70 be "as ample as the defence of the Constitution requires".[47]

One might infer from this that Keane C.J.'s objection to the approach taken by the High Court was based more on the view that Barr J. had acted prematurely in the instant case rather than on the view that the High Court did not possess the power to grant such remedies in cases of egregious neglect of constitutional rights by the State. Admittedly the Chief Justice then went on to concur with Hardiman J.'s analysis of the impact of the doctrine of separation of powers but even that analysis anticipated the courts having adequate powers to deal with a situation in which a government defied a court declaration on the government's constitutional obligations.

The remaining two judges who addressed this question of the extent of the judicial power also appear to take a similar stance. Denham J. took the view, having regard to the finding of the majority in relation to the extent of the State's duty to provide for free primary education and also to the State's concession agreeing to continue the plaintiff's education, that no question of a mandatory order arose for the future and that consequently there was no issue of separation of powers to be decided in the case. In a significant *obiter*, however, she continued,

> In general the matter of a mandatory order will not arise. It is a practice for the executive, when an issue is being litigated that could give rise to a mandatory order, to indicate that should the decision be against the State a declaratory order would be sufficient. Similarly, the courts assume that decisions will be implemented and that mandatory orders are not necessary. Thus a declaratory order, if any order is necessary, is usually appropriate. However, I would not exclude the rare and exceptional case, where, to protect constitutional rights, the court may have a jurisdiction and even a duty to make a mandatory order.[48]

Geoghegan J. also suggested, *obiter*, that in exceptional cases the courts could grant mandatory orders against the executive. After pointing out that he did not have to decide this issue, having regard to the finding that the State did not have an ongoing constitutional duty into the future to provide for free primary education for the plaintiff, he expressed support for the view of Costello J. in *O'Reilly v. Limerick Corporation*[49] that the courts were singularly unsuited for the task of determining whether there had been an unfair distribution of national resources. However he went to state, *obiter*, that

> in very exceptional circumstances it may be open to a court to order allocation of funds where a constitutional right has been flouted without justification or reasonable excuse of any kind.[50]

---

[47] *Ibid.*, p. 69.
[48] At p. 20 of her judgment.
[49] [1989] ILRM 181.
[50] At pp. 23-4 of his judgment. As we already noted – see n.14 above – Geoghegan J. had earlier responded to the argument that the courts could not enforce the State's obligation, under Art. 42.4,

As against that, he had "great doubts…that the courts should ever involve themselves in making the detailed kind of orders which were made in some of the American cases cited in relation to education."[51]

The Supreme Court decision in *Sinnott v. Minister for Education*[52] brought mixed results for people with learning difficulties. Clearly the refusal of a majority of the Supreme Court to read the duty to provide for free primary education as applying to such people over the age of eighteen was a major disappointment for the plaintiffs and for people with learning difficulties and their families generally. At the same time, there should be some comfort in the fact that the decision copperfastens the right to free primary education for people with learning difficulties up to the age of eighteen. Potentially of more significance, however, is the fact that the litigation provoked a political response that may yet bring more improvements, with the Minister for Education, Dr. Michael Woods, T.D., stating on the day the Supreme Court handed down its decision that Government had given him "practically a blank cheque" to improve services for children in the schools and an announcement coming the following day that he would meet with the Minister for Health to discuss how to improve services for adults with autism.[53] It remains to be seen what the outcome of this development will be but the history of the *Sinnott* litigation illustrates the potential of public interest litigation, identified above,[54] to convert a hostile or indifferent political system to the cause for reform.[55]

T.D. v. Minister for Education

At the same time, the strong endorsement of Costello J.'s reasoning in *O'Reilly v. Limerick Corporation*[56] by three members of the Supreme Court majority in *Sinnott* clearly signalled a reluctance on the part of senior members of the Irish judiciary to

---

to provide other educational facilities or institutions when the public good requires it because of the principle that, under the doctrine of separation of powers, the courts do not determine what might be required by the public good with the comment that, "I am not convinced that there would not be exceptions to that principle." *Ibid.*, at p. 9.

51 *Ibid.* On the matter of the court's power to review its award of damages and the granting of the mandatory injunction, Geoghegan J. held that it followed logically from his conclusion that the State's duty to provide for free primary education did not extend beyond the age of eighteen that provision for such a review in the instant case should be set aside. However he does not appear to offer any view as to whether, in different circumstances, the courts might be able to order such a review.

52 Unreported, Supreme Court, 12 July 2001.

53 *The Irish Times*, 13 and 14 July 2001. The following month, it was reported that the Cabinet had endorsed proposals to move responsibility for special education from the Department of Education to a new National Council for Special Education and there was some speculation that legislation might be introduced obliging the State to provide adequate special education for children who require it.

54 At pp.269-70

55 This also demonstrates the need for public interest litigation to be accompanied by a political campaign to try to influence the political response to the outcome of the litigation.

56 [1989] ILRM 181.

entertain public interest litigation affecting public expenditure and based exclusively on constitutional norms.[57] Admittedly, *Sinnott* did not seem to close the door completely on such litigation insofar as certain members of the court accepted that in exceptional cases, the courts could still grant mandatory injunctions against organs of State in order to vindicate constitutional rights.[58] However the judgments of the majority[59] in the subsequent case of *T.D. v. Minister for Education*[60] allowing the State's appeal against an order of Kelly J. directing various ministers to take all steps necessary to facilitate the building and opening of twelve specified secure and high support units for children,[61] provide a reading of the Constitution that is inimical to the type of public interest litigation discussed in this book in two key respects.[62]

First, the majority judgments indicate that mandatory injunctions (or affirmative decrees) vindicating constitutional rights can only be obtained against the executive in the rarest of circumstances and that in reviewing executive action that trenches on constitutional rights, the courts are essentially restricted to the remedies of prohibitory injunctions, damages and declarations. Murray J. said that it was not in issue that the superior courts may make orders affecting, restricting or setting aside actions of the executive which were not in accordance with law or the Constitution or that they may make declaratory orders as to the executive's obligations.[63] He did not rule out the possibility of the courts granting a mandatory order against an organ of State but held that this could only arise in exceptional circumstances.

> [A] mandatory Order directing the Executive fulfil a legal obligation (without specifying the means or policy to be used in fulfilling the obligation) in lieu of a declaratory Order as to the nature of its obligations could only be granted, if at all, in exceptional circumstances where an organ or agency of the State had disregarded its constitutional obligations in an exemplary fashion. In my view the phrase 'clear disregard' can only be understood to mean a conscious and deliberate decision by the organ of State to act in breach of its constitutional obligations to other parties accompanied by bad faith or recklessness. A Court would also have to be satisfied that the absence of good faith or the reckless disregard of rights would impinge on the observance by the State party concerned of any declaratory Order made by the Court.[64]

---

[57] One might infer from various references in the judgments to recent legislation in the area of education that some members of the Supreme Court will look more favourably on public interest litigation rooted in statutory norms - see, e.g., the comments of Hardiman J. at pp.5-6, 27-29 and 58-9 of his judgment in *Sinnott* and at pp.18-9 of his judgment in *T.D.*

[58] See the remarks of Denham J. at p.20 of her judgment, Hardiman J. at pp.54-6 of his judgment and Geoghegan J. at pp.23-4 of his judgment.

[59] Keane C.J., Murphy, Murray and Hardiman JJ. in the majority; Denham J. dissenting.

[60] Unreported, Supreme Court, 17 December 2001.

[61] For an account of the High Court decision in this case, see above, pp.192-4.

[62] On another issue, namely, whether the plantiffs had *locus standi* to bring this case, Murray and Hardiman JJ. held that they did not, while Keane C.J. and Denham J. took the contrary view, (Murphy J. not expressly addressing this point.)

[63] At p.16 of his judgment.

[64] At pp.23-4 of his judgment.

Concurring with Murray J. on this point, Hardiman J. said,

> Such an order ... could only be made as an absolutely final resort in circumstances of great crisis and for the protection of the constitutional order itself. I do not believe that any circumstances which would justify the granting of such an order have occurred since the enactment of the Constitution sixty-four years ago.[65]

While Keane C.J. and Murphy J. do not advert to the possibility of obtaining mandatory injunctions against the executive, one can readily infer from their robust rejection of Kelly J.'s power to grant such an injunction in the instant case that if they were prepared to contemplate such a possibility, it would only be in very extreme circumstances. So notwithstanding the fact that Denham J. dissented on this point in *T.D.*, and that she and Geoghegan J. appeared to take a more liberal line on this point in *Sinnott*, it seems very unlikely that future litigants will be able to obtain affirmative decrees against the organs of state, a serious setback for public interest litigation in this jurisdiction.

Second, a number of the judgments in *T.D* also signal opposition to the judicial recognition of implied socio-economic rights. Questioning the very existence of the constitutional rights upon which Kelly J. had based his order, Murphy J. said,

> With the exception of Article 42 of the Constitution, under the heading "Education", there are no express provisions therein cognisable by the courts which impose an express obligation on the State to provide accommodation, medical treatment, welfare or any other form of socio economic benefit for any of its citizens however needy or deserving. It is true that the exploration of unenumerated constitutional rights in *Ryan v. Attorney General* [1965] IR 294 has established the existence of a constitutional right of "bodily integrity". The examination of that right in *The State (C) v. Frawley* [1976] IR 365 and *The State (Richardson) v. Governor of Mountjoy Prison* [1980] ILRM 82 certainly establishes that the State has an obligation in respect of the health of persons detained in prisons. However these authorities do not suggest the existence of any general right in the citizen to receive, or an obligation on the State to provide, medical and social services as a constitutional obligation....
>
> With the exception of the provisions dealing with education, the personal rights identified in the Constitution all lie in the civil and political rather than the economic sphere...
>
> The absence of any express reference to accommodation, medical treatment or social welfare of any description as a constitutional right in the Constitution as enacted is a matter of significance. The failure to correct that omission in any of the twenty-four referenda which have taken place since then would suggest a conscious decision to withhold from rights which are now widely conferred by appropriate legislation the status of constitutionality in the sense of being rights conferred or recognised by the Constitution.[66]

In his judgment, Keane C.J. called into question certain aspects of the doctrine of implied rights generally as endorsed by the Supreme Court in *Ryan v. Attorney*

---

[65] At pp.74-5 of his judgment.
[66] At pp.3-5 of his judgment.

General.[67] First, he doubted whether the criteria used by Kenny J. in *Ryan* for the identification of such rights – the "Christian and democratic nature of the State" – were satisfactory for the task. Second, he pointed out that the Supreme Court in *Ryan* had not discussed whether the duty of identifying unenumerated rights should be the function of the courts rather than the Oireachtas and he expressed the view that judicial restraint was now called for in identifying new unenumerated rights. He continued,

> I would have the gravest doubts as to whether the courts at any stage should assume the function of declaring what are today frequently described as "socio-economic rights" to be unenumerated rights guaranteed by Article 40.[68]

Similar sentiments were expressed by Hardiman J.[69] and though she dissented on the question of the court's power to grant a mandatory injunction, Denham J. also accepted the view expressed by Costello J. in *O'Reilly* that the courts could not get involved in issues of distributive justice.[70]

Though these remarks are all *obiter*, they clearly indicate that the present Supreme Court is extremely unlikely to accede to claims seeking constitutional protection for socio-economic rights.

While the Supreme Court's stance on these two issues of the use of mandatory injunctions and the recognition of implied socio-economic rights was predictable, it was not inevitable, relying as it does on a number of contentious views. For a start, the Supreme Court's endorsement of Costello J.'s reasoning in *O'Reilly v. Limerick Corporation*[71] is open to the criticism levelled at that decision in chapter 1 above. Thus, the distinction between distributive and commutative justice may not be as clearcut as the Supreme Court assumes and judicial decisions on issues of commutative justice can directly affect public expenditure.[72] More fundamentally, the understanding of the doctrine of separation of powers advanced by the Supreme Court rests on certain pre-interpretative values that prize judicial restraint[73] and fails to take account of other elements in the Constitution which support a commitment to social inclusion as another important pre-interpretative value in our constitutional order, thereby affording

---

[67] [1965] IR 294.

[68] At p.42 of his judgment. In the instant case, however, he accepted that the issue of whether the courts could recognise socio-economic rights had not been fully argued and he proceeded on the basis that the applicants were entitled to be provided for by the State.

[69] See p.52 of his judgment.

[70] See p.26 of her judgment.

[71] [1989] ILRM 181.

[72] See, e.g., *The State (Healy) v. Donoghue* [1976] IR 325; *Murphy v. Attorney General* [1982] IR 241 and *Blake v. Attorney General* [1982] IR 117 where judicial decisions resulted in either increased public expenditure or reduced tax yields. Ironically, the Supreme Court appear to be unaware of the fact that Costello J. resiled from his position in *O'Reilly* in the subsequent case of *O'Brien v. Wicklow UDC*, unreported *ex tempore* judgment, High Court, 10 June 1994. See above, p.57.

[73] This is most explicit in the judgment of Hardiman J. in *Sinnott* where he invokes, at pp.56-8 of his judgment, the views of Aristotle, Locke, Montesquieu and the founding fathers of the United States in support of his understanding of the doctrine of separation of powers, rejecting a contrasting position exemplified in the work of John Rawls.

legitimacy to judicial action in defence of that value.[74] *Pace* the Supreme Court, it is simply not the case that the text of the Constitution provides us with an unequivocal and determinate understanding of the impact of the doctrine of separation of powers on our constitutional order. To put flesh on the very bare bones of Article 6, the reader of the Constitution, including judges, must necessarily supply certain background principles or pre-interpretative values. In identifying such principles or values, it is important to note that the Irish Constitution, unlike its US counterpart,[75] is not simply concerned with establishing a system of government – it also endorses, through the Preamble and Articles 40, 42 and 45, an ideological position that (I argue) commits the State, *inter alia*, to working for social inclusion. I further contend that in cases where ordinary politics has failed a marginalised individual or group, this ideological commitment justifies the courts in acting to protect such socio-economic rights as are necessary to enable the individual or group to participate in society. The interpretation of the doctrine of separation of powers adopted by various members of the Supreme Court in *Sinnott* and *T.D.* is also ideological, derived as it is from the liberal democratic tradition of the common law. My difficulty with this position, however, is that it completely ignores the fact that the Irish Constitution is not drawn exclusively from that liberal democratic tradition. Our Constitution derives its philosophical inspiration from two very different sources – liberal democracy and Christian democracy. The former prizes the autonomy of the individual and rejects the idea that any other conception of the common good can be objectively justified. The latter, however, argues that it is possible to discern the existence of an objective moral order and that a key element in such order is the recognition of the mutual interdependence of individual and social progress. In particular, Christian democracy promotes the value of social inclusion and recognises socio-economic rights as indispensable to the common good. Reliance on this aspect of the Constitution would, therefore, in my opinion, justify a robust approach on the part of the courts towards problems of social exclusion where it is apparent that such problems are being neglected by ordinary politics.[76]

In addition to these philosophical difficulties, the rejection of any role for the courts in the recognition of socio-economic rights involves the drawing of a distinction

---

[74] These elements include the language of the Preamble, which commits the Constitution to assuring the dignity and freedom of the individual and to attaining true social order and which, together with Art.45, alludes to the virtues of justice and charity, the fact that the drafters of the Constitution saw fit to provide explicit protection to two socio-economic rights, namely, the right to free primary education in Art.42.4 and the right of children abandoned by their parents to be provided for by the State pursuant to Art.42.5, and the commitment in Art.40.3 to the protection of implied rights which (I argue) includes certain socio-economic rights. See further pp.43-54.

[75] Recall Ely's comment that "What has distinguished [the US Constitution], and indeed the United States itself, has been a process of government, not a governing ideology." Ely, p.100. See also Ackerman, pp.10-16.

[76] It is important to emphasise that my defence of judicial activism is limited to cases where the political process has shown itself incapable of defending the right in question. As I accepted above, at p.54, there are good institutional reasons why we should look initially to the legislature and executive for policies to tackle social exclusion. Unfortunately, however, these policies are not always forthcoming in particular cases.

between civil and political rights, on the one hand, and socio-economic rights, on the other, that is difficult to defend. The people saw fit to provide expressly for instances of both categories of rights in the Constitution and the vindication of both types of right can require the State to take positive action, entailing public expenditure. Moreover, it is arguable that the effective vindication of basic socio-economic rights is necessary in order to ensure that citizens can participate effectively in our representative democracy and enjoy fully their civil and political rights.

Penultimately, the Supreme Court's fears that an activist role in promoting socio-economic rights would give paramountcy to the judicial branch over the other branches of government are, I respectfully suggest, misplaced. The constitutional provisions for amending the Constitution provide the People (and their elected representatives) with the means to respond to judicial interpretation of constitutional norms, a facility that accounts for no fewer than eight of the twenty-one amendments to the Constitution effected to date. Where judicial decisions are based on statutory norms, they are even easier to nullify or modify. Given the availability of this facility, a refusal to use it in response to a judicial decision must presumably be based on an acceptance of the decision or, in the case of a decision based on constitutional norms, on a view that that decision is likely to have popular support among the electorate. The existence of this facility, however, clearly means that the judiciary cannot have paramountcy over the other branches of government in relation to the interpretation of constitutional norms unless the People so decree. Moreover, my review of the impact of judicial decisions affecting various marginalised groups indicates that relatively few decisions resulted in a direct change in policy through the coercion of unwilling politicians and administrators.[77] Changes in policy more often occurred because the litigation helped to convert an indifferent or hostile political system to the cause for reform.[78] Thus litigation strategy, far from usurping the role of the political system, arguably functions as a very useful corrective mechanism, ensuring that issues which hitherto have been ignored by that system receive proper attention.[79]

Finally, as for the concern expressed by various members of the Court about the ability of the judiciary to deal with public interest ligitation, this is a pragmatic objection to this type of litigation that can be met by introducing the sort of changes that I consider in Chapter 2 above, though I do not underestimate the extent of this task.

Conclusion

In the aftermath of the *Sinnott* and *T.D.* cases, the portents for public interest litigation targeting social exclusion in this jurisdiction are not good. However there is more to be said in favour of such litigation, both in terms of its constitutional legitimacy and

---

[77] See p.268 above.

[78] See pp.268-271.

[79] In the context of this discussion, it is somewhat ironic that the public reaction to the Supreme Court's rejection of the plaintiff's claim in *Sinnott* was, in the main, hostile, suggesting that, among those members of the public who voice an opinion on such matters, there is little opposition to judicial activism.

its contribution to the proper functioning of democratic politics, than the Supreme Court allows. A commitment to social inclusion can readily be inferred from the text of the Constitution and where the political system is guilty of egregious failure to attend to the needs of a marginalised group, the judiciary is the most appropriate agency to police this constitutional norm. At the same time, it is not the case that judicial intervention in this context usurps the functions of the other branches of government and one should be careful not to overestimate the impact of judicial decisions on public policy. A more realistic appraisal of the value of this type of public interest litigation is that it functions as a corrective mechanism for the political system, requiring that system to address issues of social exclusion that would otherwise be ignored. Ultimately, however, it is the political system that will determine what that response should be. Inasmuch as the present Supreme Court appears to be setting its face against public interest litigation targeting social exclusion, it may unwittingly impede the development of a fully participatory system of politics in this country. It is certainly the case that we need to have a more informed debate about the role and impact of public interest litigation on the ordering of our society and I hope that this book may be regarded as making some contribution to such a debate.

Bibliography

Abel, R., "The Paradoxes of Legal Aid" in Cooper and Dhavan (eds.), *Public Interest Law* (Basil Blackwell, 1986).

Ackerman, B., *We The People: Foundations* (Cambridge, 1991).

Angell, E., "The *Amicus Curiae*: American Development of English Institutions" (1967) 16 *International and Comparative Law Quarterly* 1017.

Aron, N., *Liberty and Justice for All: Public Interest Law in the 1980s and Beyond* (Westview Press, 1989).

Avineri, S. and De-Shalit, A., *Communitarianism and Individualism* (Oxford, 1992)

Bacik, I., Kelly, A., O'Connell, M. and Sinclair, H., 'Crime and Poverty in Dublin: an analysis of the association between community deprivation, District Court appearance and sentence severity', published in Bacik and O'Connell, M. (eds), *Crime and Poverty in Ireland,* 1-30. Dublin: Round Hall Press/Sweet & Maxwell, 1998. (Also in (1997) 7 *Irish Criminal Law Journal* 104-133.)

Baldwin, J., "The Role of Citizens Advice Bureaux and Law Centres in the Provision of Legal Advice and Assistance" (1989) 4 *Civil Justice Quarterly* 24.

Bamburger, C., "Legal Aid" (1978) 2 *University of New South Wales Law Journal* 199.

Bandes, S., "The Negative Constitution: A Critique" (1990) 88 *Michigan Law Review* 2271.

Barnes, B., "Irish Travelling People" in Rehfisch (ed.), *Gypsies, Tinkers and other Travellers* (Academic Press, 1975).

Barrington, D., "The Constitution in the Courts" in Litton, F. (ed.), *The Constitution of Ireland 1937-1987* (IPA, 1988).

Basten, J., "Legal Aid and Community Law Centres" (1987) 61 *Australian Law Journal* 714.

Basten, J., Graycar, R. and Neal, D., "Legal Centres in Australia" (1983) 6 *University of New South Wales Law Journal* 163.

Baxi, U., "Taking Suffering Seriously: Social Action Litigation in the Supreme Court of India" in *Judges and the Judicial Power: Essays in Honour of Justice V.R. Krishna Iyer* (London and Bombay, 1985), (eds. R. Dhavan, R. Sudarshan and S. Kurshid).

Berry, S., "Ending Substance's Indenture to Procedure: The Imperative for Comprehensive Revision of the Class Damage Action" (1980) 80 *Columbia Law Review.* 299.

Bickel, A., *The Least Dangerous Branch: The Supreme Court at the Bar of Politics* (Yale, 1962).

Binchy, A., "Traveller Culture and Ethnicity: Implications for Social Policy", paper presented to conference at Trinity College Dublin on Travellers, Society and the Law, 18 July 1997.

Bork, R., *The Tempting of America: The Political Seduction of the Law* (New York, 1990).

Borosage, R. and others, "The New Public Interest Lawyers" (1970) 79 Yale Law Journal 1070.

Brady, J., "Legal Certainty: The Durable Myth" (1973) VIII *Irish Jurist (n.s.)* 18.

Brest, P., "Interpretation and Interest" (1982) 34 *Stanford Law Review* 765.

Brest, P., "The Misconceived Quest for the Original Understanding" (1980) 60 *Boston University Law Review* 204.

Brundage, J., "Legal Aid for the Poor and the Professionalization of Law in the Middle Ages" (1988) 9 *Journal of Legal History* 169.

Bryden, P., "Public Interest Intervention in the Courts" (1987) 66 *Canadian Bar Review* 490.

Butler, A. and O'Connell, R., "A Critical Analysis of Ireland's Constitutional Review Group Report" (1998) XXXIII *Irish Jurist (n.s.)* 237.

Byrne, D., "Equality before the Law" (1970) 2 *Dublin University Law Review* 40

Cahn, E. and Cahn, J., "Power to the People or the Profession? – The Public Interest in Public Interest Law" (1970) 79 *Yale Law Journal* 1005.

Campbell, R., "The Inner Cities: Law Centres and Legal Services" (1992) 19 *Journal of Law and Society* 101.

Cane, P., "Standing up for the Public" (1995) *Public Law* 276.

Cane, P., "The Function of Standing Rules in Administrative Law" (1980) *Public Law* 303.

Cappelletti, M , "Alternative Dispute Resolution Processes within the Framework of the World-Wide Access-to-Justice Movement" (1993) 56 *Modern Law Review* 282.

Cappelletti, M. and Garth, B., *Access to Justice: Vol. 1 – A World Survey* (Sijthoff, Giuffre, 1978).

Carney, C., "The Growth of Legal Aid in the Republic of Ireland" (1979) XIV *Irish Jurist (n.s.)* 61, 211.

Carr Lett, L.G., "Legal Assistance for the Poor" in *Public Administration in Ireland, Vol. II,* F. King (ed.), (Dublin, 1949).

Casey, J., *The Irish Law Officers: Roles and Responsibilities of the Attorney General and the Director of Public Prosecutions* (Round Hall/Sweet and Maxwell, 1996).

Cassels, J., "Judicial Activism and Public Interest Litigation in India: Attempting the Impossible?" (1989) 37 *American Journal of Comparative Law* 495.

Chayes, A., "The Role of the Judge in Public Law Litigation" (1976) 89 *Harvard Law Review* 1281.

Chayes, A., "The Supreme Court 1981 Term – Foreword: Public Law Litigation and the Burger Court" (1982) 96 *Harvard Law Review* 4.

Children's Legal Centre, *Annual Report 1995-6.*

Clark, R., "The Case of the Tenacious Widow" (1978) *Gazette of the Incorporated Law Society of Ireland* 79.

Clark, R., "Towards the 'Just' Strike" (1985) 48 *Modern Law Review* 659.

Clarke, D., "The Role of Natural Law in Irish Constitutional Law" (1982) XVII *Irish Jurist (n.s.)* 187.

Cohen, B. and Staunton, S., "In Pursuit of a Legal Strategy: The National Council for Civil Liberties" in Cooper and Dhavan, *Public Interest Law* (Basil Blackwell, 1986).

Cohn-Sherbok, D., "A New Agenda for Society" in *The Liberation Debate: Rights at Issue,* Leahy and Sherbok (eds.), (Routledge, 1996).

Cooper, J. and Dhavan, R., *Public Interest Law* (Basil Blackwell, 1986).

Cooper, J., "A Legal Services Policy for the Future: New Bottles for Old Wine" in Cooper and Dhavan (eds.), *Public Interest Law* (Basil Blackwell, 1986).

Cooper, J., *Public Legal Services: A Comparative Study of Policy, Politics and Practice* (Sweet and Maxwell,1983).

Costello D., "The Irish Judge as Law-maker" in Curtin and O'Keeffe (eds.), *Constitutional Adjudication in European Community and National Law* (Dublin, 1992).

Coughlan, A., "The Constitution and Social Policy" in Litton (ed.), *The Constitution of Ireland 1937-1987* (Dublin, 1987).

Cousins, M., "Access to the Courts – The Limitations of a Human Rights Approach" in Heffernan (ed.), *Human Rights: A European Perspective* (Round Hall Press, 1994).

Cousins, M., "Access to the Courts: The European Convention on Human Rights and European Community Law" (1992) 14 *Dublin University Law Journal (n.s.)* 51.

Cousins, M., "At the Heart of the Legal: The Role of Legal Aid in Legitimating Criminal Justice" in Young and Wall (eds.), *Access to Criminal Justice: Legal Aid, Lawyers and the Defence of Liberty* (Blackstone Press, 1996).

Cousins, M., "Civil Legal Aid in France, Ireland, the Netherlands and the United Kingdom – A Comparative Study" (1993) *Civil Justice Quarterly* 154.

Cousins, M., "Equal Treatment and Social Security" (1994) *European Law Review* 123.

Cousins, M., "Legal Aid Reform in France and the Republic of Ireland in the 1990s" in Regan, F., Paterson, A., Goriely, T. and Fleming, D., *The Transformation of Legal Aid: Comparative and Historical Studies* (Oxford University Press, 1999).

Cousins, M., "Neither Flesh nor Fowl – The Status of the Scheme of Civil Legal Aid and Advice" (1992) 10 *Irish Law Times* 41.

Cousins, M., "The Protection of Collective Rights Before the Irish Courts" (1996) *Irish Law Times* 110 and 134.

Cousins, M. and Charleton, B., *Benefit Take-Up: A Report of a Benefit Take-Up Project in Dublin* (FLAC, 1991).

Cousins, M., and O'Hara, G., *Access to the Courts in Four European Countries* (FLAC 1993).

Cousins, M., Note (1992) 14 *Dublin University Law Journal (n.s.)* 193.

Cousins, M., *The Irish Social Welfare System: Law and Social Policy* (Round Hall Press Ltd., 1995).

Craig, P.P. and Deshpande, S.L., "Rights, Autonomy and Process: Public Interest Litigation in India" (1989) 9 *Oxford Journal of Legal Studies* 356.

Cranston, R., *Legal Foundations of the Welfare State* (London, 1985).

Crowley, N., "Travellers and Social Policy" in *Contemporary Irish Social Policy*, Quin, S., Kennedy, P., O'Donnell, A. and Kiely, G. (eds.), (University College Dublin Press, 1999).

Dan-Cohen, M., "Bureaucratic Organizations and the Theory of Adjudication" (1985) 85 *Columbia Law Review* 1.

de Villiers, B., "Social and Economic Rights" in *Rights and Constitutionalism: The New South African Legal Order* (van Wyk, Dugard, de Villiers and Davis, eds.) (Clarendon Press, 1996)

Devins, N., book review of *The Hollow Hope: Can Courts Bring About Social Change?* (1992) 92 *California Law Review* 1027.

Dhavan, R., "Managing Legal Activism: Reflections on India's Legal Aid Programme" (1986) 15 *Anglo-American Law Review* 281.

Dhavan, R. and Partington, M., "Co-optation or Independent Strategy? The Role of Social Action Groups" in Cooper and Dhavan, *Public Interest Law* (Basil Blackwell, 1986).

Dignam, C., "Lancefort and *Locus Standi*" (1997) 3 *Bar Review* 65.

Dillon, B., *A Review and Recent History of the Coolock Community Law Centre* (Combat Poverty Agency, 1989).

Dorr, D., *The Social Justice Agenda: Justice, Ecology, Power and the Church* (Gill and Macmillan, 1991).

Duncanson, I., "Legal Need in England and Wales in the Sixties and Seventies: A Retrospect" (1981) 4 *University of New South Wales Law Journal* 113.

Dworkin, R., *Freedom's Law: The Moral Reading of the American Constitution* (Cambridge, 1996).

Dworkin, R., "Comment" in Scalia, *A Matter of Interpretation: Federal Courts and the Law* (Princeton University Press, 1997).

Elder, S., "Travellers, Serviced Sites and the Law" (1988) *Irish Law Times* 171.

Ely, J., *Democracy and Distrust: A Theory of Judicial Review* (Cambridge, 1980).

Ewing, K., *The Right to Strike* (Clarendon Press, 1991).

Feldman, D., "Public Interest Litigation and Constitutional Theory in Comparative Perspective" (1992) 55 *Modern Law Review* 44.

Feldman, D., *Civil Liberties and Human Rights in England and Wales* (Oxford, 1993.)

Festenstein, M., "Contemporary Liberalism" in *New Political Thought: An Introduction,* Lent, A., (ed.) (London, 1998).

Fisher, E. and Kirk, J., "Still Standing: An Argument for Open Standing in Australia and England" (1997) 71 *Australian Law Journal* 370.

Fiss, O., "The Supreme Court 1978 Term – Foreword: The Forms of Justice" (1979) 93 *Harvard Law Review* 1.

Fletcher, W., "The Discretionary Constitution: Institutional Remedies and Judicial Legitimacy" (1982) 91 *Yale Law Journal* 635.

Frazer, E., "Communitarianism" in *New Political Thought: An Introduction,* Lent, A. (ed.), (London, 1998).

Free Legal Advice Centres Ltd., *Access to Justice – the 1993/1994 annual report of the Free Legal Advice Centres (FLAC)* (Dublin, 1995).

Free Legal Advice Centres Ltd., *Report 1972* (Dublin, 1972).

Free Legal Advice Centres Ltd., *Annual Report 1974* (Dublin, 1975).

Free Legal Advice Centres Ltd., *Annual Report 1978* (Dublin, 1979).

Free Legal Advice Centres Ltd., *Annual Report 1998* (Dublin, 1999).

Free Legal Advice Centres Ltd., *Annual Report to the Members of FLAC for 1978* (Dublin, 1979).

Free Legal Advice Centres Ltd., *Equality before the law – the 1992 annual report of the Free Legal Advice Centres (FLAC)* (Dublin, 1993).

Free Legal Advice Centres Ltd., *Free Legal Aid: A Review of the Government's Plans for Legal Aid* (August, 1979).

Free Legal Advice Centres Ltd., *It's Rough Justice with Legal Aid* (February 1981)

Free Legal Advice Centres Ltd., *It's Rough Justice without Legal Aid* (May 1980).

Free Legal Advice Centres Ltd., *Poverty and the Law – FLAC 1991 Annual Report* (Dublin, 1992).

Free Legal Advice Centres Ltd., *Promoting Comprehensive Legal Services – the 1995/96 annual report of the Free Legal Advice Centres (FLAC)* (Dublin, 1997).

Free Legal Advice Centres Ltd./Coolock Community Law Centre Ltd., *The Closed Door: A Report on Civil Legal Aid Services in Ireland* (1987).

Friedenthal, J., Kane, M. and Miller, A., *Civil Procedure* (2nd ed., 1993).

Galanter, M., "Why the 'Haves' Come Out Ahead: Speculations on the Limits of Legal Change" (1974) 9 *Law and Society Review* 95.

Galanter, M., *Law and Society in Modern India* (Oxford University Press, 1989).

Galbraith, K., *The Culture of Contentment* (Penguin Books, 1993).

Galvin, T., "Democracy in Ireland: Collective Somnambulance and Public Policy" in (1991) 39 *Administration* 42.

Gambitta R., May M. and Foster J., (eds.) *Governing Through Courts* (California/London, 1981).

Genn, H., "Tribunals and Informal Justice" (1993) 56 *Modern Law Review* 393.

Grace, C. and Lefevre, P., "Legal Services, Law Centres and the Public Interest" in Cooper and Dhavan (eds.), *Public Interest Law* (Basil Blackwell, 1986).

Greer, D., "Legal Services and the Poor in Ireland" (1969) IV *Irish Jurist (n.s.)* 270.

Grimes, R. and Martin, R., "Legal Aid in Great Britain and the Republic of Ireland – Some lessons to be Learnt" (1981) *Journal of Social Welfare Law* 282.

Groenendijk, K., "Litigation, Politics and Publicity: Public Interest Law or How to Share the Burden of Change" (1985) 14 *Anglo-American Law Review* 337.

Gwynn Morgan, D., *The Separation of Powers in the Irish Constitution* (Round Hall/Sweet and Maxwell, 1997).

Handler, J., *Social Movements and the Legal System: A Theory of Law Reform and Social Change* (Academic Press, New York,1978).

Hardiman, N., "Inequality and the representation of interests" in Crotty, W. and Schmitt, D., (eds.), *Ireland and the Politics of Change* (Addison Wesley Longman Ltd., 1998)

Harlow, C. and Rawlings, R., *Pressure Through Law* (London, 1992).

Hodge, H., "A Test Case Strategy" in Partington, M. and Jowell, J. (eds.), *Welfare Law and Policy* (Frances Pinter, 1979).

Hogan, G., "Constitutional Interpretation" in Litton (ed.), *The Constitution of Ireland 1937-1987* (Dublin, 1987).

Hogan, G., "The Supreme Court and the Equality Clause" (1998) 4 *Bar Review* 116.

Hogan, G., "Unenumerated Personal Rights: *Ryan's* Case Re-Evaluated" (1990-1992) XXV-XXVII *Irish Jurist (n.s.)* 95.

Hogan, G. and Whyte, G., *Kelly's The Irish Constitution* (3rd ed.) (Dublin, 1994).

Hollenbach, D., "A Communitarian Reconstruction of Human Rights: Contributions from Catholic Tradition" in Douglas, R.B. and Hollenbach, D. (eds.), *Catholicism and Liberalism: Contributions to American Public Philosophy* (Cambridge University Press, 1994).

Honohan, I., "The Common Good and the Politics of Community" in Dunne, Ingram and Litton (eds.), *Questioning Ireland: Debates in Political Philosophy and Public Policy* (IPA, 2000).

Horowitz, D., *The Courts and Social Policy* (Washington, 1977).

Hoskyns, C., and Luckhaus, L., "The European Community Directive on Equal Treatment in Social Security" (1989) 17 *Policy and Politics* 321.

Hough, B., "'Standing' for Pressure Groups and the Representative Plaintiff" (1991) *Denning Law Journal* 77.

Humphreys, R., "Constitutional Interpretation" (1993) 15 *Dublin University Law Journal (n.s.)* 57.

Humphreys, R., "Interpreting Natural Rights" (1993-1995) XXVIII-XXX *Irish Jurist (n.s.)* 221.

Humphreys, R. and O'Dowd, T., "Locus Standi to Enforce the Constitution: Society for the Protection of Unborn Children (Ireland) Ltd. v. Coogan" (1990) *Irish Law Times* 14.

Irish Commission for Justice and Peace, *Re-Righting the Constitution – The Case for New Social And Economic Rights: Housing, Health, Nutrition, Adequate Standard of Living* (Dublin, 1998)

Irish Traveller Movement, *Traveller Accommodation and the Law: Action for Change through the Courts* (Irish Traveller Movement, 1991).

James, F., Hazard, G. and Leubsdorf, J., *Civil Procedure* (Little Brown and Co., 1992).

Joyce, D., "Accommodation: A new response or the same old story" in Sheehan (ed.), *Travellers: Citizens of Ireland*, (Parish of the Travelling People, 2000).

JUSTICE/Public Law Project, *A matter of public interest: Reforming the law and practice on interventions in public interest cases* (London, 1996).

Kavanagh, A., "The Quest for Legitimacy in Constitutional Interpretation" (1997) XXXII *Irish Jurist (n.s.)* 195.

Kenny, B., *Responding to the Needs of Troubled Children: A Critique of High Support and Secure Special Care Provision in Ireland* (Barnados, 2000).

Keogh, D., "The Irish Constitutional Revolution: An Analysis of the Making of the Constitution" in Litton (ed.), *The Constitution of Ireland 1937-1987*, (Dublin, 1987).

Kerr, A , and Whyte, G., *Irish Trade Union Law* (Abingdon, 1985).

Kilwein, J., "The Decline of the Legal Services Corporation: 'It's ideological, stupid!'" in Regan, F., Paterson, A., Goriely, T. and Fleming, D., *The Transformation of Legal Aid: Comparative and Historical Studies* (Oxford University Press, 1999).

Krislov, S., "The *Amicus Curiae* Brief: From Friendship to Advocacy" (1963) *72 Yale Law Journal* 694.

Kymlicka, W., *Contemporary Political Philosophy* (Oxford, 1990).

Kymlicka, W., *Liberalism, Community and Culture* (Oxford, 1989).

Langan, J., "Human Rights in Roman Catholicism" in Curran, C. and McCormick, R. (eds.), *Readings in Moral Theology No.5: Official Catholic Social Teaching* (Paulist Press, 1986).

Larsen, N., "Seven Years with Legal Aid (1972-79): A Personal View of some Events and Background Literature" (1981) 11 *Manitoba Law Journal* 237.

Leat, D., "The Rise and Role of the Poor Man's Lawyer" (1975) 2 *British Journal of Law and Society* 166.

Legal Aid Board Annual Report 1980 (Dublin, 1981).

Legal Aid Board Annual Report 1981 (Pl. 1159, Dublin, 1982).

Legal Aid Board Annual Report 1982 (Pl. 2771, Dublin, 1983).

Legal Aid Board Annual Report 1983/4 (Pl. 3794, Dublin, 1985).

Legal Aid Board Annual Report 1985 (Pl. 4549, Dublin, 1986).

Legal Aid Board Annual Report 1987/9 (Pl. 8277, Dublin, 1990).

Legal Aid Board Annual Report 1990/91 (Dublin, 1992).

Legal Aid Board Annual Report 1992 (Dublin, 1993).

Legal Aid Board Annual Report 1995 (Dublin, 1996).

Legal Aid Board Annual Report 1997 (Dublin, 1998).

Legal Aid Board Annual Report 1998 (Pn. 7535, Dublin, 1999).

Legal Aid Board Annual Report 1999 (Dublin, 2000).

Lewis, C., *Judicial Remedies in Public Law* (London, 1992).

Lister, R., "Supplementary Benefits Appeals Tribunals: An Urgent Case for Reform" in Adler and Bradley (eds.), *Justice, Discretion and Poverty: Supplementary Benefit Appeals Tribunal in Britain* (Professional Books Ltd., 1975).

MacLaughlin, J., *Travellers and Ireland: Whose Country, Whose History?* (Cork University Press, 1995).

Mair, P., "The Absence of Class Politics" in *The Development of Industrial Society in Ireland,* Goldthorpe and Whelan (eds.), (Oxford University Press, 1992).

McBrien, R., *Catholicism* (3rd ed.) (Geoffrey Chapman, 1994)

McCann, M., Ó Síocháin, S., and Ruane, J. (eds.), *Irish Travellers, Culture and Ethnicity* (Belfast, 1994).

McCarthy, N., "To do a great right, do a little wrong" (1987) 6 *Journal of the Irish Society for Labour Law* 1.

McCarthy, N., "Observations on the Protection of Fundamental Rights in the Irish Constitution" in Curtin, D. and O'Keeffe, D. (eds.), *Constitutional Adjudication in European Community and National Law* (London, 1992).

McDermott, P., "The Separation of Powers and the Doctrine of Non-Justiciability" (2000) XXXV *Irish Jurist (n.s.)* 280.

McDonagh, M., "Nomadism in Irish Travellers' Identity" in McCann, Ó Síocháin and Ruane (eds.), *Irish Travellers, Culture and Ethnicity* (Belfast, 1994).

McDonagh, M., "Origins of the Travelling People" in Sheehan (ed.), *Travellers: Citizens of Ireland,* (Parish of the Travelling People, 2000).

McVerry, P. S.J., "Homelessness" (2001) 52 *The Furrow* 12.

Merricks, W., "The Aims and Goals of the Law Centre Movement" in Partington and Jowell (eds.), *Welfare Law and Policy* (London, 1979).

Michelman, F., "Welfare Rights in a Constitutional Democracy" (1979) *Washington University Law Quarterly* 659.

Miller, A., "Of Frankenstein Monsters and Shining Knights: Myth, Reality and the 'Class Action Problem'" (1979) 92 *Harvard Law Review* 664.

Molony, T., "Legal Aid for Poor Persons" (1930-31) 17 *Journal of the Statistical and Social Inquiry Society of Ireland* 15.

Monaghan, H., "Our Perfect Constitution" (1981) 56 *New York University Law Review* 353.

Mossman, M.J., "The Baxter Case: De Facto Marriage and Social Welfare Policy" (1977) 2 *University of New South Wales Law Journal* 1.

Mulhall, S. and Swift, A., *Liberals and Communitarians* (2nd ed.) (Blackwell Publishers Ltd., 1996).

Mullally, S., "Searching for Foundations in Irish Constitutional Law" (1998) XXXIII *Irish Jurist (n.s.)* 333.

Murphy, T., "Economic Inequality and the Constitution" in Murphy and Twomey (eds.),

Ireland's Evolving Constitution 1937-1997: Collected Essays (Hart Publishing, 1998).

Ní Shúinéar, S., "Irish Travellers, Ethnicity and the Origins Question" in McCann, Ó Síocháin and Ruane (eds.), *Irish Travellers, Culture and Ethnicity* (Belfast, 1994).

Nino, C., *The Constitution of Deliberative Democracy* (Yale University Press, 1996).

Note "Implementation Problems in Institutional Reform Litigation" (1977) 91 *Harvard Law Review* 428.

Note in (1976) 89 *Harvard Law Review* 1318.

Note in (1982) 91 *Yale Law Journal* 590.

Nowak, J., and Rotunda, R., *Constitutional Law* (4th ed., 1991).

O'Neill, J., "Belfast Law Centre and the Law Centre Movement" in FLAC/CCLC, *The Closed Door: A Report on Civil Legal Aid Services in Ireland* (1987).

O'Sullivan, E., "Adolescents leaving care or leaving home and child care provision in Ireland and the UK – A critical view" in Hill and Aldgate (eds.), *Child Welfare Services – Developments in Law, Policy, Practice and Research* (Jessica Kingley Publishers, 1996).

O'Sullivan, E., "Dimensions of Campaigning for Homeless Children in the Republic of Ireland", paper delivered to the Third International FEANTSA Congress in Madrid, 1995.

O'Sullivan, E., "The Case Against Secure Accommodation" in *Secure Accommodation in Child Care* (Children's Legal Centre, 1997).

Parker, K. and Stone, R., "Standing and Public Law Remedies" (1978) 78 *Columbia Law Review* 771.

Partington, M. and Jowell, J., *Welfare Law and Policy* (Frances Pinter, 1979).

Paterson, A., "Legal Aid at the Crossroads" (1991) *Civil Justice Quarterly* 124.

Paterson, A., "Legal Services for All?" (1980) *Journal of Social Welfare Law* 321.

Peiris, G.L., "Public Interest Litigation in the Indian Subcontinent: Current Dimensions" (1991) 40 *International and Comparative Law Quarterly* 66

Perry, M., *Morality, Politics and Law* (Oxford University Press, 1988).

Perry, M., *Religion in Politics* (Oxford University Press, 1997).

Perry, M., *The Constitution in the Courts: Law or Politics?* (Oxford University Press, 1994).

Perry, M., *The Idea of Human Rights: Four Inquiries* (Oxford University Press, 1998).

Peters, C., "Adjudication as Representation" (1997) 97 *Columbia Law Review* 312.

Phelan, D., "The Concept of Social Rights" (1994) 16 *Dublin University Law Journal* 105.

Powell, F, "Citizenship and Social Exclusion" (1995) 43 *Administration* 22.

Powell, F. *The Politics of Irish Social Policy 1600-1990* (The Edwin Mellen Press, 1992).

Prior, R.B.L., *Law Centres: A Movement at a Halt* (Conservative Political Centre for the Society of Conservative Lawyers, 1984).

Prosser, T., *Test Cases for the Poor* (C.P.A.G., 1983).

Quinn, G. "Reflections on the legitimacy of judicial activism in the field of constitutional law" (Winter, 1991) *Dlí* 29.

Quinn, G., "Rethinking the Nature of Economic, Social and Cultural Rights in the Irish Legal Order" in Costello (ed.), *Fundamental Social Rights: Current European Legal Protection & the Challenge of the EU Charter of Fundamental Rights,* (Irish Centre for European Law, Dublin, 2001).

Quinn, G., "The Nature and Significance of Critical Legal Studies" (1989) 7 *Irish Law Times* 282.

Re, L. "The *Amicus Curiae* Brief: Access to the Courts for Public Interest Associations" (1984)

14 *Melbourne University Law Review* 522.

Report of Committee on Civil Legal Aid and Advice (Dublin, 1977) (Prl.6862)

Report of the Commission on Itinerancy (pr. 7272, 1963) .

Report of the Constitution Review Group (1996, Pn. 2632).

Report of the Criminal Legal Aid Review Committee (1981, Prl. 9986).

Report of the Task Force on the Travelling Community (Pn. 1726, July 1995).

Report of the Travelling People Review Body (Pl. 1552, 1983).

Report on Civil Legal Aid in Ireland (Law Society of Ireland, 2000).

Report to the Minister for Justice of the Committee on Civil Legal Aid and Advice (Dec. 1977, prl. 6862)

Reynolds, B. and Healy, S., *Power, Participation and Exclusion* (Conference of Major Religious Superiors, 1992).

Ring, M. E., "A Right to an Education" (1997) 2 *Bar Review* 219.

Rosenberg, G., *The Hollow Hope: Can Courts Bring About Social Change?* (Chicago, 1991).

Rosenthal, D., "Evaluating the Competence of Lawyers" (1976) Vol. 11 *Law and Society Review* 257.

Rupp-von Brunneck, W., (1972) 20 *American Journal of Comparative Law* 387.

Sackville, R., "Property, Rights and Social Security" (1978) 2 *University of New South Wales Law Journal* 246.

Sadurski, W., "Economic Rights and Basic Needs" in *Law, Rights and the Welfare State* (Sampford and Galligan, eds.) (Croom Helm, 1986).

Sandel, M., *Liberalism and Its Critics* (New York University Press, 1984).

Saphire, R., "Originalism and the Importance of Constitutional Aspirations" (1997) 24 *Hastings Constitutional Law Quarterly* 599.

Scalia, A., *A Matter of Interpretation: Federal Courts and the Law* (Princeton University Press, 1997).

Scannell, Y., *Environmental and Planning Law in Ireland* (Round Hall Press, 1995).

Scannell, Y., "The Taxation of Married Women: *Murphy v. Attorney General* (1982)" in O'Dell (ed.), *Leading Cases of the Twentieth Century* (Round Hall Ltd., 2000).

Schiemann L.J., "Interventions in public interest cases" (1996) *Public Law* 240.

Second Progress Report of the All-Party Oireachtas Committee on the Constitution (1997, pn. 3835).

Seymour, J., "Representative Procedures and the Future of Multi-Party Actions" (1999) 62 *Modern Law Review* 564.

Sherlock, A., "Constitutional Litigation in Ireland" (1991) 40 *International and Comparative Law Quarterly* 425.

Sherlock, A., "Self-executing Provisions in EC Law and under the Irish Constitution" (1996) *European Public Law* 103.

Sherlock, A., "Understanding Standing: *Locus Standi* in Irish Constitutional Law" (1987) *Public Law* 245.

Simon Community, *Practical Aspects of bringing a Right to Shelter Case to the Supreme Court* (Dublin, 1985).

Simons, G., "*Locus Standi* to Challenge Planning Decisions" (1998) 5 *Irish Planning and Environmental Law Journal* 96.

Simons, G., "Travellers' Halting Sites: A Special Issue in Town Planning", paper delivered to a conference organised by Trinity Law School on "Travellers, Society and the Law" on 18 July 1997.

Simons, G., "Travellers: Planning Issues" (1997) *Irish Planning and Environmental Law Journal* 8.

Simons, G., "Unauthorised Travellers' Halting Sites" (1997) *Irish Planning and Environmental Law Journal* 53.

Smith, R., "How Good are Test Cases?" in Cooper and Dhavan, *Public Interest Law* (Basil Blackwell, 1986).

Stephens, M., "Law Centres and Citizenship: The Way Forward" in Thomas (ed.), *Law in the Balance: Legal Services in the 1980s* (Martin Robertson, 1982).

Stephens, M., "The Law Centre Movement: Professionalism and Community Control" in Bankowski, Z. and Mungham, G. (eds.), *Essays in Law and Society* (Routledge and Kegan Paul, 1980).

Stephens, M., *Community Law Centres: A critical appraisal* (Avebury, 1990).

Sunstein, C., *The Partial Constitution* (Cambridge, 1993).

Thornberry, P., "Poverty, Litigation and Fundamental Rights – A European Perspective" (1980) 29 *International and Comparative Law Quarterly* 250.

Tobias, C., "Public Law Litigation and the Federal Rules of Civil Procedure" (1989) 74 *Cornell Law Review* 270.

Traveller Accommodation and the Law: Action for Change through the Courts (Irish Traveller Movement, 1992).

Travellers in Ireland: An Examination of Discrimination and Racism (Report from the Irish National Co-Ordinating Committee for the European Year Against Racism, 1997).

Tribe, L., *American Constitutional Law* (2nd ed., 1988).

Twomey, A., "Bork's Originalism: Reconciling Judicial Constitutional Interpretation with the Rule of Law" (1996) 14 *Irish Law Times* 278.

Walsh, B., "The Constitution and Constitutional Rights" in Litton, F. (ed.), *The Constitution of Ireland 1937-1987* (Dublin, 1987).

Walsh, W., "Redefining Radicalism: A Historical Perspective" (1991) 59 *George Washington Law Review* 636.

Ward, P., "Homeless Children and the Child Care Act 1991" (1995) *Irish Law Times* 19.

Wexler, S. "Practicing Law for Poor People" (1970) 79 *Yale Law Journal* 1049.

Whyte, G. (ed.), *Sex Equality, Community Rights and Irish Social Welfare Law* (ICEL, 1988).

Whyte, G. and O'Dell, E. "Welfare, Women and Unjust Enrichment" (1991) 20 *Industrial Law Journal* 304.

Whyte, G., "A Comment on the Constitution Review Group's Proposals on Equality" in Duncan, W. and Byrne, R. (eds.), *Developments in Discrimination Law in Ireland and Europe,* (I.C.E.L., 1997).

Whyte, G., "And Justice for Some" (1984) 6 *Dublin University Law Journal (n.s.)* 88.

Whyte, G., "Constitutional Adjudication, Ideology and Access to the Courts" in Whelan, A. (ed.), *Law and Liberty in Ireland* (Oak Tree Press, 1993).

Whyte, G., "Discerning the philosophical premises of the Report of the Constitution Review Group: an analysis of the recommendations on Fundamental Rights" (1998) *Contemporary Issues in Irish Law and Politics* 216.

Whyte, G., "Education and the Constitution: Convergence of Paradigm and Praxis" (1990-1992) XXV-XXVII *Irish Jurist (n.s.)* 69.

Whyte, G., "Gender and Equality in the Irish Social Welfare System" in Quinn (ed.), *Irish Human Rights Yearbook 1995.*

Whyte, G., "Natural Law and the Constitution" (1996) *Irish Law Times* 8.

Whyte, G., "Religion, Education and an Indeterminate Constitution" (1997) *Doctrine and Life* 274.

Whyte, G., "Report of the Review Group on the Treatment of Households in the Social Welfare Code: A legal perspective" (1992) 40 *Administration* 134.

Whyte, G., "The Role of Religion in the Constitutional Order" in Murphy and Twomey (eds.), *Ireland's Evolving Constitution 1937-1997: Collected Essays* (Hart Publishing, 1998).

Whyte, G., "Travellers and the Law" (1989) 11 *Dublin University Law Journal (n.s.)* 187.

Whyte, G. and Cousins, M., "Reforming the Social Welfare Appeals System" (1989) *Irish Law Times* 198.

Yeazell, S., *From Medieval Group Litigation to the Modern Class Action* (Yale University Press, 1987).

Youngblood and Folse, "Can Courts Govern? An Inquiry into Capacity and Purpose" in *Governing Through Courts* (California/London, 1981), Gambitta R., May M. and Foster J. (eds.).

Zander, M., "The Legal Profession and the Poor" (1969) 20 *Northern Ireland Legal Quarterly* 109.

Zander, M., "The Pringle Committee's Report on Civil Legal Aid and Advice: an Outsider's View" (1978) *Dublin University Law Journal (n.s.)* 21.

Zander, M., *A Matter of Justice: The Legal System in Ferment* (Oxford University Press, 1989).

Zander, M., *Legal Services for the Community* (Temple Smith, 1978).

Zemans, F. and Thomas, A., "Can Community Clinics Survive? A Comparative Study of Law Centres in Australia, Ontario and England" in Regan, F., Paterson, A., Goriely, T. and Fleming, D., *The Transformation of Legal Aid: Comparative and Historical Studies* (Oxford University Press, 1999).

Zemans, F., "Recent Trends in the Organization of Legal Services" (1985) *Anglo-American Law Review* 283.

Index